On Behalf of the Committee

A History of Northern Comedy

On Behalf of the Committee

A History of Northern Comedy

TONY HANNAN

Scratching Shed Publishing Ltd

Cover Illustration © John Ireland, 2009
www.john-ireland.co.uk

First published by Scratching Shed Publishing Ltd in 2009
Registered in England & Wales No. 6588772.
Registered office:
47 Street Lane, Leeds, West Yorkshire. LS8 1AP

www.scratchingshedpublishing.co.uk

ISBN 978-0956007568

A catalogue record for this book is available from the British Library.

Typeset in Georgia Bold and Goudy Old Style

Printed and bound in the United Kingdom by
L.P.P.S.Ltd, Wellingborough, Northants, NN8 3PJ

For Jacqui
- the wings beneath my wind

Contents

Acknowledgements

In the five or so years it has taken to research and compile this history, a number of people have offered useful advice, articles, links, suggestions and - most of all - patience. First in the latter category is my northern rose Jacqui - to whom the book is dedicated - and three fast-growing children Robyn, Lauren and Louis, whose smiles would brighten any day.

Thanks, too, to Chapel Allerton's finest double act Phil and Ros Caplan; uncle Charlie and the clan in South Shields; the Hannan posse in Bradford and Spain; Derek Proud and the team at Tyne Tees Television; and the illustrator John Ireland for his superb cover artwork.

On the photographic front, I am hugely indebted to Dr. C.P. Lee of the University of Salford - and his website *itsahotun.com* - for providing me with a splendid selection of images from the Mancunian Film Studio; and also Stephen Atkinson of Rex Features; Roy Baines; Mrs. Joan Moules; Nev Jopson; John Baucher (a.k.a. Moochin Photoman on *www.flickr.com*); Bernie Clifton; Bobby Ball; Freddie Davies; *Viz*; Jimmy Tarbuck; Phil Cool; Steve Delaney and dear Count Arthur Strong (!).

A big thank you, too, to all of the comedians who grace these pages - dead or alive, northern or otherwise - for the laughs, entertainment and social insight they have shared with us over this past century-and-a-half. The world would be a gloomier place without them.

And finally a big 'howay' to my beloved mother-in-law, Anne Marie. What would any book about northern comedy be without her?   TH

"To this house I came just ere dark on an evening marked by the characteristics of sad sky, cold gale, and continued small penetrating rain."
- *Jane Eyre, Charlotte Brontë (1847)*

"It's that fine rain that soaks you right through..."
- *Peter Kay, Mum Wants A Bungalow Tour (2002)*

Prologue

"We would like to apologise to viewers in the north.
It must be awful for them."
- *Television announcer, 'Victoria Wood on TV'*

Prior to his mid-nineteenth century trips to Manchester for a pint and a chinwag with Friedrich Engels, Karl Heinrich Marx, Prussia's best-known stand-up, quipped that religion was: '...the opium of the people'. As one-liners go, it was provocative rather than side-splitting. Yet if Marx could have hung around for just a little while longer, let us say another one hundred and fifty years or so, then the world's foremost proponent of class struggle might also have concluded that comedy is the people's best bitter or, perhaps, a fruit-based drink for the lady (chicken-in-a-basket optional). Ooh, as one spangly suit-wearing wannabe 'lefty' from Catford was later to put it. Little bit of politics.

As a perusal of the following six hundred or so pages will confirm, if there is one cliché that rings true about us British, it is that when times are at their toughest we really do cherish our famous sense of humour. And the grimmer those times were over the past century and a half, the more likely it is that our favourite comedians will have been products of the north of England.

At which suggestion, no doubt, a fair proportion of our potential readership is already bristling like Jeremy Hardy at a Jim Davidson concert. What's that you say in Birmingham, London and Glasgow? Sweeping generalisation? What about Sid Field, Ricky Gervais and Billy Connolly, you ask. And lo, down there in Brighton, Norwich and Weston-super-Mare, can someone *really* be reaching for the words 'chippy northerner' already? In which case, hey, calm down... calm down. We come to bury clichés, not to praise them. Or, at least, that was the original intention. For even in the north, where it is commonly supposed that men treat pigeons better than their wives, that doesn't necessarily mean we want to be holed up in the coop ourselves. Nobody enjoys being a stereotype. And is there really any such thing as specifically 'northern' English comedy anyway?

Let it be stated openly that the author's original expectations leant very heavily towards a debunking of the northern comedy myth. Without a doubt, there were quite obviously loads of comedians who, traditionally, had mined their northern roots for the bulk and shape of their material; George Formby, Gracie Fields, Hylda Baker, Les Dawson, Bernard Manning and so on, right up to Johnny Vegas and Peter Kay, spring most readily to mind. Ultimately, though, wasn't the term 'northern comedy' just one more example of regional and cultural apartheid, often self-inflicted? At best lazy, at worst designed to keep everyone north of Watford Gap very firmly in their place, out there among the simple folk in the sticks? Comedy is just comedy, isn't it? It either makes you splutter into your ale or it does not. The village, town or city in which a comedian told his or her first gag is surely irrelevant.

Well, happily for those who like their books to last longer than just a couple of pages, the evidence amassed in half a decade of enjoyable research would seem to suggest otherwise. There is indeed a recognisable strain of British humour that is transparently northern in style and outlook, even if, in more recent years, a once clear line has blurred, possibly to the point of extinction. Historically, it turns out that northern comedy has not at all resembled southern comedy (i.e. that which originated in and around London, but more of that anon). Nor, although there are similarities, has it entirely been the same as Brummie, Irish, Scottish or even Welsh comedy. No, the comedy of England's north has been a distinctive and homely beast indeed. More than that, far from being a mere off-shoot and single strand of British humour among many, it has consistently provided comedy in the United Kingdom with its very backbone and heart. Let us risk another generalisation: more often than not northern comedy is the self-deprecating yin to London's self-aggrandising yang.

Actually, we could - and do - go further. If we are looking to sum up much southern-derived comedy, we might employ terms like gag-driven, witty, flamboyant, cocky, competitive, aggressive and overtly political, characteristics which, rightly or wrongly, are traditionally felt to drip with testosterone and masculinity. Northern comedy, in contrast, has tended to be defined by a perhaps more feminine emphasis on character and the minutiae of everyday domestic life. Never mind the big issues, the comics of the north have seemed to say, it is the smaller personal things that matter. And although anyone who steps out onto a stage or in front of a television camera can hardly be said to be averse to showing off, the most successful northern comedians seem to have learned very early on that it is best to be one of the crowd. An everyman. Cleverness you might just get away with. Flaunting it, no chance.

Take, for example, the classic 'Hitler in the fish shop' monologue by the north east's very own Bobby Thompson, a.k.a. the Little Waster, as beautifully judged a comic masterpiece of downbeat surrealism as ever was told. 'On the Wednesday, I was talking to Hitler in the fish shop,' Thompson begins, in that reassuring County Durham twang, so familiar upwards of Middlesbrough and so alien all points south. 'Aww, he liked his batter. I was just standing there at the counter and I seen this man come in with a black 'tache on. He says to me: "Is that Bob?" I says: "...hello, Adolf." He says: "Bob, has tha seen 'owt of Chamberlain?" I says: '...no, what for, like?' He says: "...he promised me he'd meet us at eight o'clock and if he doesn't turn up there's gonna be war on".'

Elsewhere in Thompson's act, as in northern comedy and the society from which it springs in general, on stage or off, women - whether controlling or nurturing - are another constant presence, albeit as viewed through the eyes of men. In northern comedy, the usually, though not always, malign influence of girlfriends, wives and mothers-in-law is ubiquitous. Maybe, to spin the first of several half-baked/ingenious*

(*delete as preferred) theories to be found within these pages, that is one reason why northern comedians have traditionally been portrayed - or played - as hapless, weak and uneducated fools. After all, if centuries of conventional male wisdom have taught us anything, it is that a woman's featherlight brain is far less able to cope with intellectual rigour and complexity than that of a man. Consequently, a man's place is out there in the concrete jungle, isn't it? Arguing about party politics, fighting the good fight and bringing home whatever wages are left after he has finished blowing the rest of it on booze, fags and a surefire bet on the horses. A woman, meanwhile, is traditionally the 'dumb' one - in both senses of the word. Life for her is more about the 'smaller' picture. Her role is to keep the home fires burning, and feed and protect the family. In short, men are supposedly ruled by the head, women the emotions. And certainly, as has already been stated, in its greatest hours of need the British nation has invariably run like a child with a bloodied knee into the comforting embrace of its reassuring northern figureheads.

So, that's that then. If the north is traditionally the mother figure in British comedy; the south is its bossy and opinionated father. Full speed ahead into chapter one. Well, not quite. A bit more housekeeping first.

If it *had* turned out that there is no such a phenomenon as specifically northern English comedy, this book would have been written anyway.

For on the most basic level, who could deny the huge enjoyment that northern-born comics have given the nation down the years, whatever the actual composition of the humour itself? So, along with investigating just what makes the process tick, *On Behalf of the Committee* is also intended to celebrate the contributions of many of Britain's best-loved comedians. And that is an ambition supported by sheer weight of numbers. In just about every area of UK entertainment, front of cloth or behind, you can bet that there will be at least one very important northerner present and that he or she won't just be there to stir the tea. So why not recognise and give thanks for that?

That said, and here's where those potential bristlers referred to earlier will hopefully leap back on board, one pitfall resolutely to be avoided was that this book should be some sort of anti-everywhere-but-northern-England rant. Well, it isn't. Northern humour is frequently parochial but that's no reason for us to be so. With the possible exception of Marcus Brigstocke and those BBC Radio 4 commissioning editors who, for some strange reason, continue to view an Oxbridge education as a guaranteed short-cut to eye-watering satirical genius, the rest of the country's comedians are often very funny too, including those from London and the Home Counties like Marie Lloyd, Mark Steel, Jo Brand, Joe Pasquale and Boris Johnson. Nor, for that matter, will we indulge in pages of pseudo-scientific waffle, intended to establish just what it is that makes human beings laugh and why.

There is however one important matter that should be cleared up sooner rather than later. It surrounds the issue of geography. Where, exactly, does the north begin and the south end? Walsall? Wakefield? Warrington? Up one's own snicket (or ginnel), second shelf? Midlanders by birth, can Tony Hancock and Stewart Lee be classed as northern comedians? And, for that matter, just how far north should 'north' stretch? As far as York? Newcastle? Carlisle? Berwick-upon-Tweed? The Outer Hebrides?

For our purposes, to qualify as northern a comedian will usually have been born or spent his or her childhood gambolling merrily - or more likely not so merrily - in the nirvana that lies uppermost of Shropshire, Staffordshire, Derbyshire, Nottinghamshire and Lincolnshire, and a field or two below Hadrian's Wall. In other words, the north is that part of the country viewed as such by the inhabitants of Yorkshire and the county that was once known as Lancashire - i.e. people like me. It shall not begin on the outskirts of Enfield, nor will it reside in Solihull. Equally, by 'the south', unless we say otherwise, read England's south east - i.e. our capital city and those heavily populated connurbations within its most immediate gravitational pull. Cornwall, Devon and Somerset can rest at ease.

Even going by that narrow and unilateral definition, though, further problems arise. Why should the north west - in which Manchester and Liverpool are far and away Britain's largest providers of comic talent - share the spotlight with Cumbria, Geordieland and us dour buggers east of the Pennines? After all, apart from Ulverston's Stan Laurel, how many other famous funny folk have the areas formerly known as Furness, Westmorland and Cumberland produced in the past one hundred or so years? Newcastle, Sunderland and the rest of England's far north east have been slightly more prolific, but they too can't begin to compete. As for Yorkshire, while that county has produced a number of memorable double-act straight men, out-and-out comics are decidedly fewer. As that great Mancunian grumbler Les Dawson once put it, in explaining how Marriott Edgar's monologues capture the warmth of the north: '...well, Lancashire. After all, Yorkshire's only there to keep the wind out.'

Well, leaving aside geographical neatness, the main reason for the inclusion of each of those areas is an obvious degree of shared social experience, as shown in the bulk of their comedy. There is also a more subtle opportunity for contrast. For if the north can be contrasted with the south, then the east can surely also be contrasted with the west. In Yorkshire - by far England's largest county at six thousand square miles, some four times the size of Lancashire - no-nonsense miserablism, for example, is often worn like a rusty badge of honour. Lancastrian comics, on the other hand, have traditionally taken a more whimsical and optimistic view of life, whatever the depth of their troubles. If humour west of the Pennines is usually upbeat and chipper, in the east it can be pointedly blunt and drier than a Dales stone wall. In the north east, we tend to find a combination of the two. Again there is a theory. Just how much can all of this be laid at the feet of those regions' defining and now dwindling major industries? In Yorkshire, wouldn't farming in solitude on the wide open hills, with only a passing sheep for company, and the tyrannical claustrophobia of life down the pit promote an inward-looking disposition? Similarly, might the more communal trades of shipbuilding and mill-working not forge a stagier and more visual style of humour? I can't pretend that you will be given definitive answers to those questions here, but there will certainly be plenty of food for thought.

And how about the importance of dialect? These days, a distinctive regional accent will most definitely be to a comedian's advantage, from whichever part of the country he or she derives. Yet it was not ever thus. Northern-born comics like Arthur Askey, Ted Ray, Robb Wilton and Tommy Handley, for example, quickly discovered that a prerequisite for a career in early radio was a willingness to leave one's provincial tones at the stage and studio door. Despite the thick north west brogue of many of his fictional creations, when that wonderful Salford character comedian Al Read introduced his own radio show, he might have been mistaken for Professor Henry Higgins. As late as the 1960s, a person's manner of speech remained a hurdle to be overcome. As one bright young thing of that revolutionary era, Alan Bennett, later recalled in his book *Writing Home* (Faber and Faber, 1994): 'I tried to lose my northern accent at one period, then reacquired it, and now don't know where I am, sometimes saying my "a"s long, sometimes short, and "u"s a continuing threat, words like "butcher" and names like Cutbush always lying in ambush. Anyone who ventures south of the Trent is likely to contract an incurable disease of the vowels...'

At which point, let us return for a moment to Bobby Thompson, that true comedic legend in his own backyard and archetypal little man in a big flat cap. Virtually unknown south of the coalfields and shipyards from which he sprang in 1910, tab-end doubtless drooping from lip, 'Wor Bobby' was born into a mining family in Penshaw and first took to the stage as a musician aged eleven. By the time the curtain fell on his lengthy and turbulent career, despite a troubled personal life, the battle-worn septuagenarian had forged a reputation as the finest comic ever to emerge from the north east's notoriously tough working men's club scene, even if few people from outside the immediate area had even heard his name.

There was little wrong with his material. Heard today, Thompson's routines still have the power to surprise and delight, mainly through the force of their sheer inventiveness. Clad in that aforementioned cap and worn-out stripey woolly jumper (known colloquially as a 'gansey'), roll-up clasped idly between yellowing finger and thumb, here was a comedian who, it seemed, was every bit as familiar with hardship and debt as his audience. In the Little Waster's pantomimic depiction of married life, they saw their own situation reflected right back at them, albeit in a heightened and more cartoonish form. Bobby Thompson was one of them, or at least it felt that way, and the people of Newcastle, Gateshead and beyond indulged his every flight of fancy.

And what flights of fancy they were. Take the time when, amid rumours of war in 1939, Bobby - the secretary of his street - telephones Prime Minister Neville Chamberlain personally for the latest news. Alas, the great leader has just popped out (to get some coal), and it is Chamberlain's wife who answers the phone instead. 'Just a minute,

Bobby,' she tells her caller, in her finest Geordie falsetto. 'I've got a pan of chips on.'

Once again, thanks to Bobby Thompson, we have hit upon another of our recurring themes here: surrealism. But doesn't that just knock the theory that northern comedy might be said to originate from the heart rather than the head on its backside? Well, not really, no. For while it is true that so much of the humour within these pages is grounded very firmly in a daily and often unforgiving reality, when life is lived hand to mouth and all around is grime, struggle and toil, isn't escape to the farthest reaches of the imagination a perfectly natural response, not all that far removed from dreams? In Bobby Thompson's hands, such silliness might even border on the heroic but, in any case, we see it time and time again, whether in the celebrated 'Lion in the Box' routine of Jimmy James, or Bob Mortimer's 'Man with the Stick'.

In common with the vast majority of comedians in this book then, Bobby Thompson knew of that which he spoke. And he set it all, intelligibly or otherwise, against a backdrop of local community. Ah, community. Such a positive and binding phenomenon in so many ways, but cursed with a capacity to spin off into bigotry and small-mindedness if left unchecked.

In more recent years, that always inventive troupe of northern comedic actors and writers known as the League Of Gentlemen have captured the suffocating qualities of just such an overbearing communal environment to perfection: 'This is a local shop for local people; there's nothing for you here'. And one thing is for sure. Any northern comedian possessed of an urge to make a national reputation for him or herself has been required, at some point, to up sticks and head south. Until Peter Kay came along, those such as Bobby Thompson who resisted the call were destined to remain a big fish in a medium-sized provincial pond.

As the story of Dave Morris confirms, no matter how popular an act was in, let's say, the once-mighty seaside mecca of Blackpool, in which summer seasons were far from handed out willy-nilly, Variety's power-brokers and impresarios all made their homes and signed their contracts in London. Quite apart from his perplexing colloquial delivery, the Little Waster's unshakeable attachment to his roots was another big reason for his failure to take the rest of Britain by storm. Thompson's London Palladium debut, for example, came at the ripe old age of 74. It is worth noting too that, some one hundred years earlier, George Formby senior, who we might see as the very first typically 'northern' comedian, only rose to the heights he did after appearing alongside the likes of Marie Lloyd and Dan Leno in Victorian West End music hall.

Today, amidst a whizz-bang explosion of unfettered global travel and twenty-first century electronic communication, England's capital is still where it's at for ambitious comedians of every hue and denomination. As Dara Ó Briain, some time Ireland resident, explained to *Word* magazine in April 2006: 'You just have to come to London. This is the world centre for what I do. This is where everyone gathers...' For sure, a handful of regional satellites apart, Britain's major media companies are all based there, as close as ever to the BBC's beloved Oxford and Cambridge. The north of England may well be the engine that drives the country, but London is its shop window. And it pays to show off in a shop window. Even so, the times may just be a changing.

On one level, the reluctance of the aforementioned Peter Kay to spend as little time as possible away from his hometown of Bolton is an encouraging development for those modern-day comedians who quite enjoy living in the north of England and prefer to stay there. And his liking for home certainly doesn't appear to have done his popularity with the public any harm at all. In 2006, Kay became one of the fastest-selling non-fiction writers of all time when his autobiography, *The Sound Of Laughter* (Century), sold over 600,000 copies in its first eight weeks. The BBC itself is scheduled to relocate a number of key departments to Salford's so-called 'Media City' in the summer of 2011, as the area in and around Manchester continues to grow in confidence after its successful hosting of the Commonwealth Games in 2002. Should the London Olympics of 2012 fall flat, we can only guess at the levels of *schadenfreude* that will cough like soot into once-grimy northern skies.

You see, Manchester is no longer the forlorn industrial nightmare that at least partially inspired the Communist manifesto of Marx and Engels, nor the century or so of revolutionary social reformers who came along behind them (although it must be admitted that, on many a grey winter's day, the ghosts of a drearier past still hang heavy - in many ways,

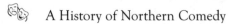

that is part of the city's charm). And the world's latest 'credit-crunch' turned economic recession notwithstanding, with one or two exceptions, this upbeat mood of cultural positivity can be seen in just about every other major city across the north of England too; Liverpool, Hull, Leeds, Sheffield, Newcastle ... take your pick.

But then again, however grim the prevailing social conditions, in the region's predilection for comedy, at least, we find a seemingly endless inclination to look on the bright side, particularly west of the Pennines. Compare the nation's favourite television soap operas, *Coronation Street* and *EastEnders*. Both regularly feature plots that are mired in the trials and tribulations of everyday life, yet only one routinely handles those issues with a smile on its face, and no prizes for guessing which. In fact, since its first appearance on British TV screens in 1960, *Coronation Street* has been an astonishingly prolific provider or utiliser of British comedy talent - wartime radio comic Bill Waddington, *Carry On* starlet Amanda Barrie, Les Dawson's oppo Roy Barraclough and a veritable northern avalanche of comedy names like Arthur Lowe, Jean Alexander, Shobna Gulati, Jack Rosenthal, Betty Driver, Kenneth Cope, Graham Fellows and our old friend Peter Kay among them. In fact, it would be quicker to list those members of the *Coronation Street* cast down the years who have *not* influenced British comedy in one way or another.

However you add it up, since the dawn of mass media popular culture, the north of England has rolled humourists into Britain's comedy industry like pennies into end-of-the-pier slot machines.

From music hall and Variety through to radio light entertainment; from the highly influential northern members of satirical 'sixties shows such as *Beyond The Fringe* and *Monty Python's Flying Circus* to the mother-in-law goading frilly shirts of the following decade; from the black and white stars of early film to three colourful pints of lager and a packet of crisps on satellite television; from do-it-yourself alternative punks to do-it-yourself internet You Tubers, the northern influence on what Ken Dodd would call our national chuckle muscles has been immense.

Yet we should beware of getting carried away with the notion that it is all about geography. Not so. For if location is important then class has historically been an even greater defining feature of British comedy. And more often than not it is the working class with whom we laugh loudest, while the middle and upper classes act as fall guys. There's nothing unusual about that. Comedy cannot help but be intrinsically subversive, wherever you happen to live in the world. Usually, it originates at the bottom of the pile and makes its way to the top. As working class London comedian Mark Steel once put it, in one of his reliably enjoyable and wise BBC radio lectures: 'Silliest of all are these people who go [adopts comedy northern accent], "oh, it's you posh, middle class southerners what's got all t' money", as though there is no working class in the south. In which case, what do we say when the drains are busted? [Adopts comedy posh middle class southerner accent] "Oh dear, what a pong. Better ring a northerner"...?'

And despite the non-confrontational nature of much of its comedy, it remains an inescapable fact that, socially, the north has been left wing and radical to its political bootstraps. The Independent Labour Party has its roots there and held its foundation conference in Bradford. Along with introducing Gracie Fields, Norman Evans and Cyril Smith to the world, Rochdale can boast the profit-sharing Co-operative movement. In Manchester, the Trades Union Congress - or TUC - held its first meeting in 1968. At various points in British history, the north's dockers, miners and other striking workers have brought the entire nation grinding to a halt, unable even to bury its dead. On any given election night, the BBC's increasingly hallucinogenic graphics department still paints the north of England red. Chances are that, unless your name is Betty and you run a teashop in Harrogate, or are maybe married to a millionaire footballer in Alderley Edge, anti-establishment sentiments will drift as readily from your northern lips as the air that you breathe (and, who knows, maybe Betty was once a Labour voter too). In 1936, two hundred weary Geordies marched from Jarrow to London in protest at mass unemployment and poverty. Vegetarians first declared that meat is murder in Salford. Women's suffrage radical, Emmeline Pankhurst, was born next door in Manchester, the same city where, let us not forget, a certain Karl Marx and Friedrich Engels cobbled together at least part of their Communist manifesto. In so many ways, the north seems perpetually determined to upset the national applecart.

So why then, in a culture marked by such a blatant predilection for stirring it up, should northern comedy seem almost completely to shy away from open politics? Go on, apart from Liverpool's Alexei Sayle (who spent his formative years at art school in London and, anyway, Liverpool is a case out on its own, as shall be discussed in greater detail), how many other northern political comedians can you name? Maybe it is simply the case that northern political comedians *are* out there, but that they just don't fit the regional stereotype and are therefore ignored by those in charge of Britain's London-based and Oxbridge-educated entertainment industry. Or maybe it is time for one final theory (for now).

Perhaps, across the majority of England's north, political discontent has historically been taken as read. In that sense, the battle for hearts and minds is already won. In other words, if the failure of those in authority is an everyday workaday reality, then why go on and on and on about it in your own precious time? Like beer, bingo and skittles, a hearty laugh was an opportunity to forget about all of that for a while. The class war, if class war it was, could be joined again in the morning.

Traditionally, expressions of political unrest in northern comedy, where they exist at all, are way more subtle and even stoical than spouting polemics in a students' union bar about the evils of 'Thatch' or George W. Bush. Their opening line of choice might well be: 'I wouldn't say we were poor, but...'. Such reticence can extend to matters of race, too, as in the case of the black comedian Charlie Williams who, before his death in 2006, claimed in his trademark Barnsley tones that he had been able to tackle racism far more effectively by undermining its prejudices from within, rather than by being openly antagonistic and getting nowhere. Whatever the truth of that position, it can't have been comfortable and he was most certainly not alone in believing it to be so.

In any case, wherever you look in northern comedy, self-deprecation rules. No one, especially a comedian, is allowed to be too flash and the performer him or herself is often their own best joke. Furthermore, there is an almost perverse delight in the levels of suffering endured, as so successfully sent up in *Monty Python*'s classic 'Four Yorkshiremen' skit, first aired courtesy of *At Last The 1948 Show* in 1967: 'We used to have to lick t' road clean wi' t' tongue...' etc. If a spirit of competition does exist in northern comedy, it will most likely be found in such material.

Prologue

Above all, and whatever the rhyme or reason, northern comedy has held huge appeal for an awful lot of people, wherever they originated. On the unduly pessimistic Channel 4 documentary *Who Killed The British Sitcom?* (2005), Granada Controller of Drama and Comedy, and executive producer of *The Royle Family*, Andy Harries, put it best. 'Culturally,' he said, 'comedy is what buoys and binds the nation. There's nothing greater than a hit comedy on a run.' During the Second World War, that honour fell to George Formby, Gracie Fields and Tommy Handley. In the strike-bound 1970s, Morecambe and Wise, Mike Yarwood and, to a lesser extent, Little and Large and Cannon and Ball fulfilled the brief. As the echoes of alternative comedy and Thatcherism faded, the country turned its attentions to Steve Coogan, Craig Cash and Caroline Aherne. Conversely, whenever the nation has begun to feel better about itself - the swinging 'sixties, 'Cool Britannia' and the like - the cocky southern smart-alecs of little Britain move back to the fore. These days, in the still-early stages of another recession which many financial 'experts' predict will reap the biggest economic whirlwind since the Great Depression of the 1920s, Saturday night is Ant and Dec night. Light entertainment is back and northerners are again at the forefront, although matters are by no means as clear cut as all that.

In October 2008, an almighty media storm broke over the antics of Jonathan Ross and Russell Brand on BBC Radio 2. Certainly, if the *Daily Mail* would have had its way, both men would now be languishing with the ravens in the Tower of London, no doubt abusing passing beefeaters with their saucy innuendo. Their crime was to make juvenile on-air prank calls to the former *Fawlty Towers* actor Andrew Sachs. For a while, it all got a little bit silly and hysterical.

Other than to point out how two more ostentatiously southern comedy popinjays than Ross and Brand never walked this earth, further detail of such a sorry episode for everyone is unnecessary here. But it is worth comparing *that* reaction with the response to the aforementioned Anthony McPartlin and Declan Donnelly, when their show, *Saturday Night Takeaway*, was implicated in a telephone vote-rigging scandal exactly one year before, from which the pair themselves were later exonerated from blame. 'We're extremely disappointed to discover irregularities occurred,' read a joint-statement. '*Takeaway* viewers are of the utmost

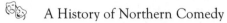

importance to us.' But even if that had not been the case, it is hard to imagine that Ant and Dec would have faced anything like the hostility that those southern show-offs Ross and Brand endured. We British love our northern comedians, you see, we really do.

Overlooked in the furore, of course, was the somewhat ironic fact that without its championing by Jonathan Ross and his production company Channel X in the late 1980s, the very same brand of Variety entertainment now filling the Saturday night schedules might never have made a comeback at all. Conveniently forgotten, too, is a similar BBC uproar sparked by Liverpool's Kenny Everett as long ago as 1970. How interwoven the geographical and cultural make-up of British comedy has since become.

As this book progresses, northern writers and performers will be found on every page. In much the same way as Jewish culture has, to a large extent, moulded American comedy, so has the voice and culture of northern England shaped the personality and style of British humour too. Both have their roots in struggle, often of the most terrible and potentially soul-destroying kind. Both can be thankful for the inherently funny qualities of their localised rhythm of speech. For America's Jewish community, the trauma of years spent carrying the weight of the world on its shoulders has found comical form in neuroses and an ongoing tilt at the cruelty of fate. In the harsh, filthy and downright dangerous mills, mines, shipyards, engine rooms, slums, hospital wards and workhouses of England's northern industrial revolution, a brutally oppressed people came to the conclusion that you had to laugh, or else you'd cry. Comedy as a survival mechanism, nonetheless.

One major difference, of course, is that in the so-called Land of the Free, the once-oppressed has since all-but taken control of the industry. In class-conscious Britain, where a London middle-class elite continues to pull the strings, proper acknowledgment of the north's true place in our comedy history has been notable only by its absence. Well, that story is told now. Let the comedy - and tragedy - begin.

1
Coughing Better Tonight

"History? It's just one fucking thing after another..."
- *Rudge, 'The History Boys', Alan Bennett.*

Northern comedy was born in 1709, in Coalbrookdale, Shropshire. Well, in a way. For it was on that date and in that place that Abraham Darby's growing dissatisfaction with charcoal finally led to his experimentation with a coke-fired ironworks, thereby setting in train the seismic cultural shift that came eventually to be known as Britain's Industrial Revolution. Pioneers beyond the West Midlands played their part too, but it is Darby's furnace that is best remembered.

If that seems rather a perverse geographical note on which to begin a history of northern English humour, it isn't really. For it was at that moment that the future complexion of modern British comedy was first nudged on course. And certainly, by the time James Watt began to power stationary engines with steam some seventy-odd years later, a period of intense social and technological transformation was taking on a more obviously northern appearance entirely. With the arrival of the 1800s, as the brutal and labour-intensive second phase of Revolution kicked in, the north of England - and in particular the grimy, soot-belched city of

Manchester - was most definitely where its grinding, degrading impact was keenest felt. Manchester. Cottonopolis. Britannia's black and beating heart and soul.

The rise to industrial prominence of England's 'Second City' had begun, in all together more innocent fashion, around half a millennium before. According to historians, among the initial groups of people to settle there was a community of Flemish weavers who, from around 1363, began an on-going association with the textile trade that first resulted in the building of actual mills at the end of the Middle Ages. Some three hundred and fifty years later, and with the Revolution now in full swing, Manchester then became home to Britain's original steam-driven cotton mill. Consequently, the exponential increase in factory production that followed rendered the place vital to national prosperity and prestige. It had water. It had land. It had natural resources. Most importantly, it had people. Lots and lots of vulnerable, hungry and uneducated people. A passport to heaven if you were a mighty Victorian industrialist. Or, if you belonged to a once-rural population now being squeezed into an often short and inhuman urban existence, a one-way ticket to hell.

With people mere fuel for the machine, the cost to humanity was seldom at issue as the importance of mechanised industry to the wider British economy grew apace. And as the levels of production rose, with the manufacture of textiles and iron crucial, so too did the national influence of Manchester and its major northern neighbours. Supporting industries like coal mining and transport also boomed, initially through the development of an intricate canal system and then, after George Stephenson completed work on his Stockton to Darlington route in 1825, the railways. The twenty-five mile track in question enabled coal dug in Darlington collieries to be transported for loading at the Stockton shipyards. For his next trick, the father of the railways came up with his famous Rocket locomotive in 1829 - complete with iconic tubular boiler - and the rate of acceleration went up a further notch. And when, in 1830, the world's first passenger service opened between Liverpool and Manchester, it was soon followed by others across the rest of the country. Distances and travel time really had begun to diminish. For the privileged few, times had never been so good.

Coughing Better Tonight

One year after Liverpool and Manchester became linked by rail, in 1831, Michael Farraday's electrical experiments upped the revolutionary ante still further. As the century progressed, advantage began increasingly to be taken of foreign inventions such as telephones, light bulbs and, later, petrol-driven motor vehicles too. And even as Manchester's trading fortunes began to wilt in comparison to its closest major neighbour in the second half of the nineteenth century, the city fathers stayed quick on their entrepreneurial feet. A long-held - and some argued crazy - ambition to build a thirty-six mile long ship canal from the heart of Manchester to the mouth of the river Mersey was at last brought to fruition in 1894 and opened by Queen Victoria herself. Again, that did not come without cost, be it human or financial. Yet against all odds, in-land Manchester had transformed itself into one of the largest sea ports in the country. It was an astonishing achievement and, in the face of such a gargantuan appetite for scientific innovation and rampant imperialistic showboating, who was going to worry about the tiny lives of the great unwashed? With the dawn of the twentieth century, fired by the furnaces of England's north, Britain could lay claim to being the leading industrial empire in the world.

Not that, to begin with at least, its victims were dragged onto this production line of extreme toil and misery without a degree of struggle. Back in the eighteenth century, when the invention of machines such as James Hargreave's 'Spinning Jenny' and Samuel Crompton's 'Mule' threatened the livelihoods of handloom weavers and manual cotton spinners, regular riots were the result. And in 1819, a growing mood of unrest culminated in the infamous Peterloo Massacre, when upwards of 60,000 people protesting for Parliamentary reform were charged first by the sabre-wielding local Manchester and Salford Yeomanry and then by a company of Hussars, at St. Peter's Field. In the resulting crush, eleven protesters were killed while hundreds more - many of them women and children - were severely injured.

In terms of everyday existence, however, aside from the occasional 'rabble-rousing' of Chartists (who emerged from the ranks of a reform movement outraged by the massacre, and engaged in frequent bouts of popular radicalism), the sporadic bursts of unrest in and after the Great Strike of 1926 and, much later, the miners strikes of the 1970s, open

27

displays of civil disobedience were the exception rather than the rule. Industrial working class lives were more commonly imbibed with a feeling of powerlessness. Day-to-day living was about drudgery and a debilitating struggle to get by. Along with enduring a squalid slum environment in which it was common for several families to occupy the same single cold, damp and unventilated room or cellar, the average Joe and his kin laboured for pitiful pay in the most appalling conditions. In a working life that could begin as early as four years of age, the average employee was effectively driven to an early grave, while the rest of society reaped the fruits of that suffering. In factories, mills, coal mines or shipyards, working class folk were treated as mere possessions, chattel, to be used or abused as appropriate. Those who stumbled were thrown, destitute, to the merciless cruelties of the poor house. How did such a downtrodden mass remain sane?

Wherever there is pain and humiliation, there is comedy. For whenever life is at its most fearful, laughter is paradoxically the cheapest and yet most precious of commodities. It feels almost banal to say it. As a result, therefore, the most popular and effective humour throughout history has mostly tended to spring from below, whether that be the belly, the sewer or the bottom of the social heap; i.e. the place where it is most needed.

Yet although comedy's professional practitioners - the comedians - have by and large colluded in that world view, they have simultaneously done so from a position of detachment. Up there on the stage, or maybe looking back at us through the television screen, holding a mirror to our quirks, sufferings and foibles, comedians have at once been part of the community and yet also outside it. From medieval jesters poking fun at the King, to hirsute Glaswegians urging murderous Iraqi hostage takers to get on with it, the comic's job has always been to say the unsayable, accentuate the absurd and poke a tickling stick in the eye of authority, whether political, religious or domestic. Our comedians acknowledge the rules and our comedians break the rules. They define the norm and they defy the norm.

In trying to identify what we mean by modern northern comedy, it would probably be a good idea to explore what came first, and the job of professional fool has been a feature of civilisation since time immemorial.

African pygmies danced in the sands of Egypt's mighty Pharoahs. Magical dwarves teased the warlords of ancient Ireland. Alas, poor Yorick! Shakespeare knew him, Horatio. And the first direct evidence of humour being used as mass entertainment comes from Greece, circa fifth century BC. It was there that pantomimes were first performed, albeit in a form far removed from the one with which we and Les Dennis have become so familiar today. To your average ancient Greek, a panto was a farcical mythological dance told through the medium of mime, and featuring characters from everyday life. Pantomime comedy was most popular with rowdy commoners, leaving tragedy to be fenced off as the proper theatrical preserve of the gods and upper classes.

Then, with the rise and fall of the Roman Empire, public entertainment received a widespread infusion of vice and vulgarity, courtesy of satyrists, naked ladies and mimis, a band of zany funnymen who are said to have enlivened many a Roman dinner party with their irreverent mimicry. Much later, the mimis would influence, in dress and style, the Harlequins of Italy's Commedia dell'Arte.

Having its roots in unruly knockabout carnivals deep in southern Italy, by the late 16th century, with a bit of help from the French, the Commedia dell'Arte (comedy of the artisan) had tightened into a solid theatrical form that, in the centuries ahead, would spread across much of western Europe. An average Commedia dell'Arte troupe was made up of dedicated professional actors in half-masks, who performed a variety of stock routines based upon recognisable characters. Of these, mischievous servants, greedy employers, cuckolded suitors, lecherous doctors, cowardly captains and boastful fathers were favourite, with no perceived failing left unridiculed.

Most often, the story was told from the perspective of a couple of servants, the smarty pants Harlequin and his beautiful and dutiful lover Columbine. As the Commedia dell'Arte grew in reach and popularity, new characters were added or old ones adapted, according to where it was being performed. In France, for example, by the late nineteenth century, the melancholic love-struck servant Pedrollini had evolved into the white-faced Pierrot, single tear drop and all. And even in England, when republican charmer Oliver Cromwell brought the curtain down on theatrical performances completely after 1642, the grotesque and yobbish

Punchinello held on, destined to become better known as Mr Punch. So much so that by the mid-eighteenth century, this stick-wielding wooden puppet, an anarchic wife-beating baby-basher, had become an unlikely working class hero. In London, anyway.

Sadly, it is in the nature of the study of British popular culture that, until relatively recently, the vast bulk of primary historical evidence will concern life in and around our capital cities, and then only be written by a certain class of people. The common experience of life in the provinces has all too often gone unrecorded, at least by the participants themselves. But in Punch's case, we do know that he went on to enjoy a superstardom of sorts in towns and seaside resorts up and down the land. To a far lesser extent, he still does. We can also say that if London street theatre is anything to go by, such as that found at the St. Bartholomew Fair from the twelfth century onwards, of which Punch and his wife Judy became such an integral part, then the ordinary British sense of humour pre-Industrial Revolution was an earthy and unsophisticated thing indeed.

Held at Smithfield, outside the then city walls, the St. Bartholomew Fair was, in the words of London's best-known modern biographer Peter Ackroyd, '...a place of riotous vulgarity and disorder' where 'the London crowd could indulge all of its appetites.' Seeking to earn a living amidst this apparent sea of gin, puppetry and prostitution there appeared a lowly class of entertainer, of which a little more anon. His origins too can be traced back to the Commedia dell'Arte and, in particular, its leading man Harlequin.

By the time London's Drury Lane staged its and England's first official pantomime in 1717, Harlequin's profile was such that he was still being called upon to take centre stage. Only a century or so later, however, and his star status was now rapidly beginning to wane. Taking his place as the audience's favourite was a formerly minor English stock character known as Clown. With Clown, slapstick tomfoolery was the key. He and his dimwit partner Pantaloon - the former wealthy employer of Harlequin, ironically - robbed shops, applied red hot pokers to unwary posteriors and generally went around upsetting better heeled members of society. And ruling the roost in that regard was one Joseph Grimaldi, the most famous British clown of all.

Born in London in 1778, Joseph Grimaldi is supposed to have made his stage debut at just five years of age, when he fell through a trap door while dressed as a cat. Happily, the durable tot somehow survived the forty-foot drop and, before his actual death in 1837, drew enormous admiration for his ability to move an audience to laughter or tears, seemingly at will and most often without words. By the second half of the nineteenth century then, and influenced in no small part by Grimaldi's more versatile and nuanced acting skills, British pantomimes were far removed from their Greek origins and surging towards the very height of their popularity.

However, even before Grimaldi's demise, panto had already begun to rely less heavily on mime. Soon some of them were evolving into full-blown entertainment spectaculars, with all the trimmings. As the century advanced, a major factor in their success was the presence on the bill of stars from the burgeoning world of music hall. Not only did these people bring talent, they brought glamour and fame too, perhaps the earliest example of what we would now describe as showbiz celebrity culture. Before long, that meant goodbye silent Clown and hello wise-cracking Widow Twankey although, by then, the traditional clown figure had found another and perhaps more suitable home away from traditional theatre: namely, the equestrian tent shows which originated in the 1770s and became better known to all as the circus.

In *Voices of Victorian London*, a 1996 edition of the BBC's television documentary strand *Timewatch*, presented by Jonathan Miller, street characters of the mid-1800s are brought brilliantly and vividly back to life by an assortment of actors, who read from contemporary interviews conducted by the journalist and founder of *Punch* magazine, Henry Mayhew. Some fifty years before the first mechanical recordings of the human voice, Mayhew's transcripts lay bare a desperate world of rat catchers, costermongers, rag and bone men and, amongst other trades, a breed of worker known as a pure finder, whose days are spent collecting dog shit for use in the purification of leather.

Thanks to Mayhew's diligence and sensitivity, the words of several thousand men and women who would otherwise have gone unheard were laid down on paper forever. And there, mired deep in a veritable cess pit of pointlessness and despair, we meet one of the most pathetic and miserable figures of the lot. This is a street clown, complete with hastily painted face and tatty jester's hat.

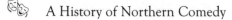

'My necessities forced me into a public line which I am far from liking,' he says, in a sad shambling voice haunted by the ridiculousness of its own mortality. 'Many times I have to play the clown and indulge in all kinds of buffoonery with a terrible heavy heart. I have three children, one now only eight weeks old. You can't imagine, sir, what a curse the street business can become with its insults and starvations. The day before, my wife was confined. I jumped and laboured doing Jim Crow for twelve hours, in the wet too, and earned one shilling and thru'pence. With this, I returned to home without a bit of coal and with only half a quarter of loaf in it.' The clown concludes: 'I dare say no persons think more of their dignity than such as are in my way of life. I'd rather starve than ask for parochial relief. Many a time I have gone to my labour without breaking my fast and played clown until I could raise dinner.'

For men such as these, peddling weak visual slapstick and even weaker verbal puns, redolent already of a bygone era, the show was over. Nowadays, if it has a few spare ha'pennies to rub together, the public craves a more sophisticated - although not *that much* more sophisticated - and professionally presented style of comedy. What's more, they know exactly where to find it.

London. The 1870s. There are around three hundred noisy and colourful venues in which the average working class pleasure seeker can indulge his or her rumbustious tendencies, sink copious amounts of grog and be thoroughly entertained by music and comedy; never a bad combination whatever your walk in life.

Meanwhile, across the rest of the nation, hundreds more such dens of amusement do good business, each building on the tradition set by the pleasure gardens of the previous century and the saloon bars that followed. A rather more genteel forerunner was the middle class song and supper room, wherein Variety and alcohol were also key ingredients until the Theatre Act of 1843 decreed that all such establishments would be licensed only if, first and foremost, they were being run as theatres. Cue the arrival in Britain of the first suburban music halls.

In London, especially, these music halls would also attract more aristocratic members of society from time to time, keen to get a buzz from slumming it and enjoy the unpretentious entertainment for themselves. The Victorian temperance movement, on the other hand, was quite driven to distraction by the idea that men and women of the lower orders might actually take some pleasure and even comfort from such alcohol-fuelled debauchery. This was, they felt, the road to ruin - a philosophy which, although driven by philanthropy, ignored the inconvenient truth that, more often than not, ruin was a destination long ago reached.

Wherever there's fun there's a puritan and, on its own terms, the temperance movement did have a point. For, as a general rule, those halls which sold nothing stronger than sarsaparilla sank faster than the Titanic a few decades hence. Furthermore, the influence of alcohol was indeed a major factor in the prevalence of working class criminality, albeit one thorny social issue amongst many. For the halls' customers, however, the apparent dregs of society, the combination of booze, music and comedy also provided a heady, if temporary, release from hardship and obligation. However rough at the edges, music halls were a short cut to a happier and more relaxed state of mind.

Still, Victorian paternalism never could be resisted for long, and although, in their infancy, the mood of the halls might best be described as unruly, they were never quite allowed to descend into absolute anarchy. In fact, the ways in which Victorian and Edwardian music halls were structured carries a beery whiff of the working men's clubs yet to come. Whether in the gloomy subterranean cellars and spit and sawdust taverns of the halls' earliest and wildest nineteenth century incarnations, or the grandly-designed theatres that increasingly began to dominate with the introduction of more changes to the licensing laws from 1878, music hall presentation ran along similarly recognisable lines. Principally, there would be a master of ceremonies - or chairman - whose chief function was to introduce acts ahead of their 'turn', hence the subsequent use of that word, on stage. At first, the stage in question was just a fenced-in ground-level performance area. Over time, it would develop into the raised proscenium arch with which theatre-goers are so familiar today.

Around a century or so later, the image of a music hall chairman would forever be immortalised by the loquacious, hyperbolic and lexicologically flamboyant ('oooooh!') Leonard Sachs, in the popular BBC TV series *The Good Old Days*. Produced by Barney Colehan and

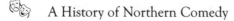

recorded at the City Varieties theatre, Leeds, *The Good Old Days* ran for thirty years between 1953-1983. However, while the programme was all good fun and performed before an enthusiastic audience of specially bussed-in amateur dramatic societies (each member clad in Victorian fancy dress whilst vigorously belting out 'Down At The Old Bull And Bush' and other such favourites), it was a long way indeed from early music hall reality. If anything, *The Good Old Days* bore closer resemblance to Variety theatre, which came to dominate popular live entertainment after the First World War. Not that historical accuracy mattered much. With a roster of regular performers which read like a northern Variety who's who, as its title suggested *The Good Old Days* was simply a harmless exercise in nostalgia for an era that never truly existed.

Certainly, England's capital city in the eighteenth and nineteenth centuries could be a wild and predatory place, a million miles removed from middle class amateur operatics. In his 2004 BBC TV series, *Peter Ackroyd's London*, for example, the eponymous writer and broadcaster describes how David Garrick's Drury Lane theatre was wrecked by rioters no less than six times. 'Rival gangs packed the theatres in order to support or shout down the latest productions,' Ackroyd recalls. 'Fights would break out which frequently developed into riots. It became so dangerous that a row of sharp iron spikes was set along the front of the stage in order to protect the actors from the London mob.' In fact, such explosions of public violence were a far more commonplace feature of life in London during this period, than they appear to have been in the north of the country, as further exemplified by the Gordon Riots of June 1780. That particular dust-up began when Lord George Gordon organised an anti-Catholic march to Parliament, and it was only settled by the military after six days of fires, looting and indiscriminate destruction, during which an estimated seven hundred people met their early and grisly deaths.

Throughout the eighteenth century and well into the next, to be a Londoner meant subscribing to a necessary philosophy of every man for himself. London was, quite simply, the biggest and most frightening city in the world. By the turn of the 1700s, its number of inhabitants had boomed to one million, with around ten per cent of the entire English population living there. At the close of the century after, that figure had risen to five million. Such phenomenal growth was almost exclusively down to migration; huge numbers of disparate peoples were lured to the place by its commercial possibilities. Although there were small pockets of community dotted here and there - in the docklands of the east for example - a mood of shared fellow feeling was far harder to achieve. In summing up the London of those days as 'a heartless vortex of humanity', Peter Ackroyd also drew on a quote from the Manchester-born essayist Thomas de Quincey, who had himself described living in London as being like: 'a poor shivering unit in the aggregate of human life'.

On the whole, then, the heroes of lower class Londoners tended to be individualistic survivors. Londoners idolised the sort of person who might regularly cock a snoop at established law and order in the pursuit of personal gain, thereby beginning a long-standing tradition that the city's inhabitants appear reluctant to shake off even today. Leaving aside our old friend Mr Punch, celebrity crooks down the years have included the highwayman Dick Turpin, six-times Newgate Prison escapee Jack Sheppard and, most recently - unless were are ready to count Phil and Grant Mitchell in *EastEnders* - the twin brothers Kray. Sheppard's case is particularly interesting. When he was finally tracked down and hung at the Tyburn gallows (now Marble Arch) in 1724, the day was declared a public holiday and the event attracted the largest crowd that London had ever seen. By then, of course, public executions had been a recognisable feature of London life for hundreds of years. Indeed, they had practically become a vicarious and cruel theatrical genre all of their own.

In contrast, for all its rabble rousing and vulgarity, a trip to the Victorian music hall must have been like a night at the opera. In their earliest incarnation, music hall audiences sat on Bavarian bierkeller style benches around enormous wooden tables. If the act was any cop, people would crane their necks to watch, cheer or sing along, while doubtless keeping a tight grip on the ale over their shoulder. If it left a bit to be desired, it would either be ignored completely or jeered from the stage. And if it was particularly atrocious, the performer might be assailed with a handy local object, an empty bottle say, or rotten fruit or, on one notable occasion, a dead cat. To think the Comedy Store alternative comedians of the 1980s thought that they had it tough. Little wonder that orchestras were frequently protected by metal grilles, or that waiters had to chain beer bottles to their trays.

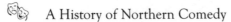

As for the flavour of the actual comedy itself, there seems to have been a considerable amount of shared empathy between audience and entertainer, particularly when it came to the most popular entertainers. Given the usually working class backgrounds of both, that is hardly surprising. And although, at this stage in comedy's development, these performers were far from being the stand-up acts that we would recognise today, your life is my life, they seemed to say. Aren't we all a bit daft?

In time, the increasing presence of higher class audience members in the boxes threw a further, more subtly intellectual, ingredient into the mix, allowing music hall to become the ideal breeding ground for often quite shrewd social satire and less subtle displays of fervent patriotism. On a superficial level, the very broadest music hall humour may appear simplistic and even chauvinistic to modern eyes and ears. But it could also be rather subversive and was able to convey veiled social messages, recognisable only to those with the wit or life experience - or both - to understand them. As ever, political and cultural oppression meant that artists, of whatever denomination, just had to work harder; a fact which at least partly explains how, in an age of supposedly strait-laced piety, sexual innuendo too began to flourish.

Despite their down to earth and largely uneducated existence then, everyday Londoners, scratching a living in the busiest and most impersonal city on earth, grew used to living off their wits. In doing so, they developed a simultaneous knack for rather clever wordplay. The average Londoner's liking for linguistics can most readily be heard in Cockney rhyming slang which, itself, appears to have its roots in the influence of the devoutly cerebral French, just across the water. And France is, after all, the nation that has more recently given us the decidedly eccentric author Georges Perec, among whose bizarre achievements are an entire novel written without use of the letter 'e' (*La Disparition*, published in 1969) and a 5,566-letter palindrome on the subject of palindromes.

Of course, the influence of the French language on the south of England, in particular, goes way back. To 1066, in fact, when William the Conqueror's Norman invasion resulted in French temporarily becoming the *lingua franca* of England's upper classes and was, presumably therefore, heard far more widely by southern serfs than their counterparts in the north. And, for sure, humble French Protestant tradesmen became a predominant part of London's cultural patchwork of a personality when thousands of Huguenot weavers and other workers fled to the city in 1685, in a bid to escape persecution by Louis XIV. Of those who settled there, the majority set up shop in places like Shoreditch, Spitalfields and Wandsworth where, even today, the echoes of their influence can clearly be detected in road signs and local street talk. To parlay, or chat, for example, is simply a derivation of the French verb *parler* - to talk, or speak. Less obviously, the phrase 'Sans Fairy Ann' (initially meaning 'don't mention it' and subsequently abbreviated to 'sweet FA'), is widely held to be an anglicisation of *ça ne fait rien* ('it's nothing').

London's story, then, is one of an exciting cosmopolitan melting pot, wherein different ideas, cultures and nationalities have simmered and bubbled for centuries, seasoned with a liberal sprinkling of humankind's basest instincts. Faced with the demands of a scavenger's life in the capital jungle, few but the fittest and smartest survived, never mind thrived. And in the land of Pearly Kings and Queens, and Chelsea Pensioners, there was no shame in being noticed either. In fact it paid dividends. The weak and unfortunate were trampled underfoot.

In England's north, meanwhile, amidst the looms and spewing mill chimneys, the coal pit wheels, steelworks and shipyards, and where the wind through the cultural barley spoke more of Celtic creativity, the Norse story telling tradition and brutal Viking invasion, harsh experience had taught that there was safety and reassurance in numbers. Keep your head down, light up the camp fire and gather around, everyone. Uncle Ernie is going to read us the play what he wrote.

North or south, however, wherever Victorians went to the music hall, the performers were pretty much without exception extensions of themselves, writ large. As with the Commedia dell'Arte, the imaginative settings were everyday too. Nagging wives, monstrous mothers-in-law, foolish drunken husbands, bent coppers, bailiffs and other contemporary types made up an all-too familiar cast list for the audience.

In the genre's earliest days, music hall comedy was a low craft indeed. At first, funny men and women were no more than novelty acts, falling over, singing songs or maybe reciting monologues, well down the

running order. So popular did many of them become, though, that over time a professional humourist's lot grew to be increasingly glamourous. And when that happened, comedy was on its way to becoming a valuable, if not all that highly respected, performing art.

The best known of these original music hall comic pioneers was the parasol-wielding Marie - 'I haven't had it up in ages' - Lloyd, who made a huge mark on British popular culture with mildly risqué comic ditties like 'The Boy I Love is Up in the Gallery', 'I Sits Among My Cabbages and Peas', 'A Little of What You Fancy Does You Good' and 'Oh, Mr Porter'. So renowned a performer was she that, by the end of her life, Marie Lloyd bore the epithet 'Queen of the Music Hall' - no mean achievement, given her humble upbringing and the relentless and unforgiving nature of the theatrical lost world she bestrode like a saucy colossus.

Born Matilda Victoria Wood - no relation - in 1870, just seven years before Thomas Alva Edison made his first tentative recital of 'Mary Had A Little Lamb' on phonograph, Lloyd's career trajectory coincided with the invention and rise in popularity of the gramophone record, a technological advance that went into mass production by the 1890s, but enjoyed its earliest commercial success courtesy of Italian operatic tenor Enrico Caruso, who cut his first record in 1902. The upshot for Lloyd was that, however the new invention's impacted on her career at the time, her voice and manner of performance would be captured for posterity.

Sadly, for us and them, those performers who came and went before the advent of the spinning shellac disc were not so fortunate. Second hand evidence can give little more than a flavour of their acts and the vibrant experience that the earliest days of music hall must have provided. That said, the recorded scraps which do survive - from Lloyd and her later contemporaries, in particular - reveal a jauntily irreverent phenomenon to which, by the turn of the century, character-driven comedy was crucial.

If Marie Lloyd was the best known female comedian of her day - and she was, by some distance - then the best known male comic was without doubt Dan Leno, a.k.a. the 'Funniest Man on Earth'. A world champion clog dancer as well as a comedian, Leno - real name George Galvin - began his showbusiness career in the 1860s, as four-year-old 'Little George, the Infant Wonder, Contortionist and Posturer', an indication of the novel and eclectic range of skills which music hall acts of the time were frequently forced to display. With the untimely demise of his father in 1864, Leno's widowed mother Louisa, a performer herself, married the Lancashire-based comedian William Grant - stage name 'Leno' - and moved from London to Liverpool, taking George and his older brother, Jack, with her. Henceforth, the boys toured the northern halls of England, Scotland and Ireland as 'The Brothers Leno - Champion Dancers'. Having moved back to London in his teenage years, and now an out-and-out solo comedian speaking directly to the crowd, the adult Leno developed a range of street-based Cockney characters drawn from normal life, in an age when some Londoners, at least, still liked to chat over the garden wall, pass the time of day with strangers in the street and lean out of open windows.

Famously, as a way of beginning his act, Leno would hurtle towards the front of the stage, thump his feet double quick time like some sort of manic rabbit, and then hold one leg in the air before bringing it down with a resounding clatter on the wooden boards. He also developed a reputation as a first class pantomime dame. Yet with Leno it wasn't all about visual zaniness and slapstick. Standing just 5 feet 3 inches tall, Dan Leno was the archetypal little man laughing in the face of adversity and a comedian who, like Joseph Grimaldi before him, could reduce an audience to tears with just one pathetic or humourous look. As his most famous admirer, Marie Lloyd, put it: 'Ever seen his eyes? The saddest eyes in the whole world. That's why we all laughed at Danny. If we hadn't laughed we should have cried ourselves sick. I believe that's what real comedy is. You know, it's almost like crying.'

And Marie Lloyd knew all about sadness. The oldest child in nine, she had been no stranger to adversity and deprivation herself, instilling in her an empathy for the underdog that was never lost. Despite her own future wealth and success, Lloyd remained a supporter of the homeless and destitute, among other good charitable causes, often at great personal expense. Most famously, it has been claimed that her support of a music hall strike cost her a spot in the first ever Royal Variety Performance in July 1912, intended to be a celebration of the genre at London's Palace Theatre. Her 'crime' had been committed some five years earlier, when she allowed the lesser-known music hall artists whose grievance it chiefly was to hold their first strike meeting at her Hampstead home.

Another feasible reason for Lloyd's absence at the Palace Theatre is the risqué nature of her act. Had she been born a half century later, for Marie Lloyd, a career in *Carry On* films would surely have been a given. But with the approach of World War One, music hall seemed intent on ditching its vulgar past and travelling in a more sophisticated direction. Certainly, the one hundred and forty-two other music hall stars who were invited to entertain King George V and Queen Mary were ordered to be on their very best behaviour. The uproarious old 'nudge, nudge, wink, wink' style, it seemed, was no longer in favour.

At least, that was the way the theatre owners and impresarios, with the whiff of money and social prestige in their nostrils, appeared to want it. For a performer like Marie Lloyd, however, such a feat of reinvention was beyond her. It would been like turning around a runaway train. As she had told the *New York Telegraph*, whilst on a tour of the USA some fifteen years earlier: 'They don't pay their sixpences and shillings at a music hall to hear the Salvation Army. If I was to try to sing highly moral songs they would fire ginger beer bottles and beer mugs at me.' Whether the establishment liked it or not, Marie Lloyd was old school and old school she would remain.

If Lloyd's on-stage behaviour was thought to be shocking, her antics off it frequently verged, to contemporary audiences, on the scandalous. With a private life that took in three disastrous marriages, deportation from the United States for 'moral turpitude' in 1913 (she travelled in the same ship's cabin as her lover, Bernard Dillon, an Irish jockey eighteen years her junior, while still married to her second husband) and several public accusations of obscenity, she was seldom out of the newspaper headlines. And, in the end, it was heavy drinking that finished her off. Marie Lloyd died in 1922, three days after falling over on stage, apparently the worse for wear, while singing, 'It's A Bit of a Ruin That Cromwell Knocked About a Bit'. The audience, unaware of her private anguish, roared with delight. She was 52.

Though nothing like as abundant as Marie Lloyd recordings, the few surviving examples of Dan Leno's act give a tantalising glimpse of an altogether more droll, endearing and ever so slightly barmy style. Mostly, Leno would spin apparently autobiographical monologues in which he was usually cast as an innocent abroad. One such routine, 'Going To The

Races' (recorded 1903), sees Leno's naïve punter robbed of his shillings and sixpences at every turn, on each occasion claiming to find the experience 'very funny'. Though Leno's humour is by any definition gentle, there is a frequent note of surrealism too, as in the 'Good Old Tower of London' routine - 'If you've never been there, go again' - wherein a beefeater gives visitors a tour, while paying particular attention to the refreshment room.

As with the working class existence from which much of its material was drawn, life on the music hall and, later, Variety circuit was a tough and unrelenting treadmill. No matter what their status, performers were expected to appear at as many as four different venues a night, frequently working six nights a week right across the country and travelling on the seventh. Dan Leno himself performed almost daily for thirty-six years solid until, in 1904, he suffered a mental breakdown - varying reports also point the finger at a brain tumour or even syphilis - and died at the wastefully young age of 43.

Another huge favourite with Victorian audiences was George Robey, the fabled 'Prime Minister of Mirth' who, rather unusually for the era, had a middle class background. Certainly, Robey was the first music hall entertainer to be knighted, although not before declining a previous offer as being 'too much for a comedian' and accepting instead a CBE. Where the northern storytelling influence can easily be detected in Dan Leno's work, Robey's comedy was a far more ostentatiously intellectual affair. For him, playfulness with language was the thing. In departing the stage, for example, Robey might puncture his world-weary character's pretentiousness with a flowery, over-poetic pay-of line: 'From his baronial mansion he bade me exit, and said I might expeditiously migrate. In other words, buzz off!'. And in his regular requests to audiences that they 'kindly temper [their] hilarity with a modicum of reserve,' a prophetic hint of Frankie Howerd ('Desist!'), Tony Hancock and, in his wordiest mood, Les Dawson, are unmistakeable.

Along with the likes of Hetty King and Ella Shields, the Worcester-born comedian Vesta Tilley was part of a comic tradition that, until French and Saunders and Catherine Tate came along, had all but vanished completely; that of the male impersonator. Perhaps Tilley's best known comedy tune was the story of Burlington Bertie, although there

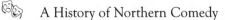

seems to be a degree of controversy among those who get worked up about such matters over just which version (either 'Burlington Bertie from Bow' or the earlier 'Burlington Bertie - The Boy With The Hyde Park Drawl', now forgotten), she actually performed. Whatevah! Vesta Tilley was certainly the most famous female cross-dresser to take on the appearance of a smart, middle class man about town.

On such a slim portfolio was many a music hall career based, and that was certainly the case with Charles Coborn who, around 1892, first introduced the world to 'The Man Who Broke The Bank at Monte Carlo'. With no television or radio to induce over-familiarity, music hall performers of every type could stick to doing the thing that they knew best, safe in the knowledge that no one would notice them trotting out the same tired routines, night after night. That was certainly the case for Coborn, whose only other hit of any note was 'Two Lovely Black Eyes'.

More prolific was the exuberant force of nature that was Harry Champion who, although possessing nothing like the repertoire of modern day entertainers, certainly had his share of catchy musical ditties that were easy to sing along to, destined to be music hall standards the lot of them. One more reliable feature of music hall comedy and a further reflection of its working class origins was an infatuation with the pleasures of food and drink, to which Champion subscribed with vigour. His own 'Boiled Beef and Carrots' was one such tune, and others ran the gamut from pickled onions, tripe, meat pies and pigs trotters to the more exotic charms of asparagus and chaffinches. Among the rest of Champion's still memorable 'hits' are 'What a Mouth', 'I'm Henery the Eighth I Am' and the immortal 'Any Old Iron'.

In fact wherever you looked in music hall, amidst all the offbeat acrobats, jugglers and other speciality acts, amusement and pathos ran like a thread. There was Vesta Victoria with her 'Daddy Wouldn't Buy Me a Bow-Wow' and 'Waiting at the Church'. There was the skirt twirling Lottie Collins and her trademark 'Tar-ra-ra-boom-der-ay'. El Nino Farini hung from a trapeze by his neck, while playing a drum. From Australia came Florrie Forde of 'Down At The Old Bull and Bush', 'Oh! Oh! Antonio' and 'Hold Your Hand Out, Naughty Boy' fame, along with her antipodean countrymen Albert 'The Whistling Boy' Whelan and the 'Man in the Blue Velvet Suit' Billy Williams. Then there was the eccentrically attired Mark 'I Do Like To Be Beside The Seaside' Sheridan, and what night out would be complete without the physical knockabout comedy of Little Tich - widely credited as the first named comedian to top a music hall bill - and his utterly bizarre 'Big Boot' dance?

Nor must we overlook the distinctive Cockney 'Coster' comedians, a perky breed of comic derived from London's costermonger trade, barrow boys, of which the brilliant Gus Elen, Albert - 'Kipling of The Music Hall' - Chevalier and Fred Earle were but three of the best known. To dig out a recording of Elen's 'If It Wasn't For The Houses In Between' is to be transported back in time to a place - and working class accent - now all but disappeared. Elen's wistful and satirical little take on overcrowding and simultaneous social aspiration - 'we're as countrified as can be, wiv a clothes prop for a tree' - is a passport to a 'wery pretty garden' that would soon be swept away forever.

As the music hall blossomed in London, a growing provincial population was proving equally hungry for distraction. In the north of England, for example, it was possible for a hard-working and half-decent comic to scratch a meagre income without ever moving very far from home. Yet if that same entertainer really wanted to establish a national reputation, then tackling the 'Big Smoke' at some point was crucial. And therein lay the genesis of many a cultural and geographical stereotype.

For sure, the need to head south was recognised by the great Scottish comedians Harry Lauder and Will Fyffe, both of whom initially served their apprenticeships at the notorious Glasgow Empire where, as Ken Dodd would later contest, if the locals liked you, they let you live. Audiences in London must have seemed like well-behaved choirboys in comparison. And certainly, it is the tartan kilted Lauder - complete with his crooked walking stick - who is often blamed for introducing the idea of the penny-pinching 'Jock' to English audiences. His rousing renditions of 'I Love A Lassie' and 'Roamin' in the Gloamin'' are still guaranteed to induce a cultural cringe in many folk north of the border.

Will Fyffe, too, made great play of his fellow countrymen's alleged chrematophobia. Fyffe's 'Scot's Lament', in which he tracks down his beloved runaway wife in London is a classic example. 'She gasped with

delight as I rose from ma seat,' he begins, after spotting his errant missus from his coach. 'But a harrowing thought made me wince, I could'na get off... for I'd paid ma fare, and I've never caught sight of her since.' According to Roy Hudd's *Cavalcade of Variety Acts* (Robson Books, 1997), by the 1930s, the stereotype had become so established that Fife-born acrobats 'The Three Aberdonians' could bill themselves as 'too mean to tell you what they do'. If that wasn't enough, Will Fyffe also introduced the drunken Glaswegian to the world in his most memorable song, 'I Belong To Glasgow', before falling from a window to his death after an attack of post-operation dizziness, rather than heavy drinking, in 1947.

Other music hall turns boosted by 'breaking' the capital include Liverpool's original comic export, Harry Weldon. Weldon, a former Fred Karno man whose understudy was, at one time, none other than Charlie Chaplin, made his London debut in 1900 and became known for his catchphrase '...s'no use!'. Later, Great Harwood-born comedian Tubby Turner - a bear of a chap who would throw a recalcitrant deckchair across the stage only to have it open perfectly upon landing - came down from Blackburn. Nevertheless, tours of the provinces were still a vital part of a comedian's life. And another talented member of that wandering tribe was Nottingham's own Billy Merson.

Southern audiences nevertheless thought of Merson as a northern entertainer, although that appears to be an image which the man did not cultivate himself. For sure, no trace of a recognisably northern twang can be heard on any of his existing recordings. And in his song 'The Spaniard That Blighted My Life', recorded in 1911, Merson is quite obviously at pains to avoid being seen as an outsider through the common music hall tactic of focussing on a real foreigner, in this case Alphonso Spagoni, the 'dirty dog' toreador who steals the unlucky Englishman's girlfriend at the bullfight, when he nips out for some nuts and a programme.

Less obviously nationalistic and a better example of Merson's drily surreal style is his 'A Life on the Prairie For Me': 'Miles and miles way in Indiana, in a little place called Parson's Green, there I met a sweet young Mexicana and said, "have a banana my dusky queen".' After persuading a member of the audience to dress up as a horse - '...you won't act the goat, will you?' - the comedian then proceeds to kick the poor volunteer (a stooge, but no less amusing for that) for his perceived misdemeanours.

When he thinks he is about to be shot, the victim hurriedly scrambles out of his costume. 'What have you taken the skin off for, in front of the audience?' asks Merson. 'You don't look a bit like a horse now. You look more like a kangaroo.'

While the new recording technology undoubtedly offered a potential career boost to the likes of Billy Merson and his contemporaries, the dawn of moving pictures hinted at even greater things to come, for those with the vision to realise it anyway. And fewer English comedians were swifter to embrace the possibilities of film than the lad from Nottingham. In 1915, Merson began to make two and three reel comedies for a company called Homeland Productions in Kew. When talkies came along, he quickly got to grips with those too, making full use of his trademark comic patter. In fact, *Billy Merson singing Desdemona*, made in 1926, is widely held to be one of Britain's first ever sound films in any genre - if not the very first.

Somewhat ironically, then, the blame for Billy Merson's downfall, when it came, can be laid at least partially at the door of this exciting new medium. And in particular on a legendary entertainer whose reputation was built almost exclusively on cinema's move to sound, the American 'blackface' minstrel Al Jolson. As the powerful star of the world's first full-length talking picture, *The Jazz Singer*, in 1927, Jolson was a long-standing and notoriously lax observer of copyright laws. If he liked a song, he would record it himself, simple as that. When Jolson performed 'The Spaniard That Blighted My Life' in a hit New York musical in 1913, its aggrieved writer began a long-running campaign for due credit that was never successfully resolved. Eventually, Merson's obsession with winning recompense for that blatant plagiarism drove him to financial ruin.

Another massively ambitious comedian who, like Billy Merson, had no qualms about ingratiating himself with the capital's music hall public was Wilkie Bard. Born in Chorlton Cum Hardy, Lancashire in 1874 and christened William August Smith, this high-foreheaded Shakespearean loon with a black spot on each eyebrow cut a strange and unique figure indeed. His showbusiness career began as a 21-year-old, singing and clowning around at venues in and around Manchester where, in 1893, he earned his first professional engagement as Will Gibbard - his mother's maiden name - for a fee of £4 a week. Two years later and keen for bigger

things, the young man moved south, where he made his London debut at Collins' Music Hall, Islington Green. Tellingly, Wilkie Bard's first attempt to make his mark on the capital public was as a Coster comic, singing 'My Little Nipper', a tune more usually associated with Albert Chevalier. He included other Coster songs in his repertoire too. A first serious taste of fame, however, came when he landed the part of Idle Jack in pantomime at Drury Lane in 1908. After which, his rich and fruity theatrical tones would become familiar right across the country.

In common with other performers, Wilkie Bard soon began to develop an array of keenly-observed yet highly exaggerated characters - a park keeper, a washerwoman, a railway guard and so on - who all featured in sketches which gently satirised workaday life. More inventive was his knack of wrapping the audience up in elaborate little tongue twisters. And then there was perhaps his greatest innovation of all, a breaking of theatrical conventions that was post-modern in its conception. Namely, it was the way in which Bard would interrupt other turns on the bill while they were already performing, at least half a century before rule-breakers such as Spike Milligan, Morecambe and Wise and the *Monty Python* team were praised for their own groundbreaking originality.

Whatever his enduring influence, from such humble northern roots and under a stage name apparently derived from a wrongly-addressed parcel, Wilkie Bard went on to rake it in. In his prime, he commanded around £250-300 per week and made a number of successful tours of the United States. Indeed, so entrenched did his name become in the theatrical establishment that it was used as cockney rhyming slang for the membership cards given out by Equity, the actors' union. Wilkie Bard himself died of a heart attack in 1944, aged 70. He is buried in Highgate Cemetery.

As Edward VII succeeded Victoria, and George V in turn followed him, any distinction between a northern and southern style of comedy was less than obvious. For a start, as a nineteenth or early twentieth century comedian, you didn't have to originate in the north to play it daft rather than clever. As we have seen, early music hall was a working class pastime, by and large and so intellectual expectations, rightly or wrongly, were low. Gradually, however, with the rising influence of the moneyed classes -

which itself influenced the transformation of music hall into fashionable Variety theatre - a more 'civilised' view of the world was likely to be paraded; in cosmopolitan and upwardly-mobile London society anyway. Out there on the provincial tour circuit, in coke-stained Barnsley or Bradford, rainy Manchester or wind-lashed Blackpool, where the slums, mills and miserable workhouses were a raw and festering wound still weeping, and where the urge to be seen as fashionable was not quite so acute, a deep-seated distrust of the ostentatiously cerebral held firm.

On top of which, for all their shared membership of the working class, if London's music hall audiences considered their north country counterparts at all, it was with a distance-fuelled feeling of superiority. After all, and despite its own squalor, London was an important city - the most important city in the world, no less. The very centre of the known universe. So, by definition, those Britons who made their homes in less busy and complex places must, by necessity, be less complex and therefore more simple-minded themselves. And into this mix came the man who could be justly described as Great Britain's first true nationally popular northern comedian.

To baby boomers reared on a diet of ABC cinema minors' matinees, Saturday morning 1970s children's television and holidays spent in an array of chilly boarding houses by the sea, the name George Formby will doubtless invoke nostalgic images of ukuleles, little sticks of Blackpool rock and those cheerful black and white films of the 1930s and '40s, in which our toothy hero gurned his way through such all-time classics as 'Leaning On A Lamp Post' and 'The Window Cleaner'. Yet that particular George Formby, by some distance the most popular male entertainer of his day, was actually preceded in the national affection by his father, George Formby senior.

The original George Formby was born James Booth in 1875, the illegitimate son of an illiterate and probably alcoholic working class mother in Ashton-Under-Lyne, Lancashire. Young James endured a truly miserable childhood. Amongst a multitude of horrors, he underwent regular physical abuse from a violent step-father and was often half-starved, a situation that led to him running away from home when aged just nine years old. In order to finance her drinking, his mother - who was herself convicted over one hundred times for drunk and disorderly

behaviour - sang in local ale houses and often ended the evening sleeping off her excesses in police cells. Her son, meanwhile, was left to fend for himself, frequently huddling for warmth in the outside lavatory or bedding down on the doorstep in the freezing cold.

The maternal influence did at least suggest a way out of all this suffering. At the age of 13, Formby began to sing soprano as one half of 'The Brothers Glenray', the self-styled 'Songbirds of the Music Halls' in the pubs of nearby Wigan. Up until then, he had been working in an iron foundry and that, coupled with those long nights under the stars, appears to have played a major role in developing the asthma and bronchitis that would plague him for the rest of his life.

The music act was moderately successful at first. But with the onset of puberty a new approach would clearly be needed if Formby - a stage name that is said to have occurred to him whilst standing on a railway platform and seeing a train roll in from that coastal town - was to continue to make a living in showbusiness. It was time for a stroke of inspiration. And it came as a result of the duo's breaking voices, which had inadvertently begun to reduce their audiences to tears of laughter. At this, it is said, Formby did a mental somersault. If people were going to laugh at him, then they might as well laugh with him too. Whichever dropped first, the penny or the balls, one of the most formidable careers in the history of British comedy was up and running.

Initially, though, for George Formby the solo comedian, professional bookings proved stubbornly tough to find. Still, he persevered and, over time, audiences did begin to warm to this droll, chatty and engaging little bloke who, between performing songs adapted from Methodist hymn sheets, would stand at the front of the stage and natter away as if he and the crowd were merely a gathering of friends out sharing a pint. Then, in 1899, Formby married a part-time dressmaker named Eliza Hoy.

Of all the images traditionally associated with northern comedy, it is perhaps the little man and his rolling-pin wielding missus that has, until recently at least, proved most enduring. The reasons for that may become apparent as our story progresses. It is sufficient for now to note that, in the case of this, our first 'official' northern comedian, a key ingredient in George Formby's subsequent ascent to music hall Valhalla was the unshakeable iron will of his wife. It was Eliza who held her husband's professional and personal lives together. It was she who encouraged George to take himself off to the great metropolis, after music hall giant George Robey spotted the young comedian on stage in Manchester and recommended him to the manager of the London Pavilion. And, over the years ahead, it was Eliza who picked her husband up when he was down and provided motivation when it was most needed. She also gave birth to no less than twelve children, seven of whom, including George junior, the oldest, survived.

After debuting in the capital in 1899, George Formby senior was an instant phenomenon. Audiences lapped up his self-deprecating portrayal of the innocent abroad - 'Hello, I'm Formby fra' Wigan, I've not been in England long' - a character organised by his wife in much the same way as a small boy might be pushed around town by his mother, despite all the while considering himself to be extremely grown-up. To audiences in the north, this brow-beaten man-child was simply one recognisable type among many, a downtrodden husband such as one might see being dragged around any Saturday afternoon market, and all the funnier for that. To southern crowds, though, Formby's act confirmed their every preconception. The northern male was indeed a half-witted, hen-pecked idiot, just as they had always suspected. For better or worse, it seems, 'Formby fra' Wigan' did for England's north what Harry Lauder and Will Fyffe achieved for the lasting reputation of the Scots. George Formby wasn't just a simpleton who came from the north. He was a simpleton *because* he came from the north.

At least that's how it looks in hindsight. Yet we ought not to forget that when Formby brought it to the stage, his act was the very opposite of cliché. Equally, few stereotypes become so without containing at least an ounce or two of truth. And outlandish though it was, leaving aside all issues of geography, Formby's gormless stage persona had very much touched a nerve in what would come to be known as the battle of the sexes. Who, in most working class families, really did wear the trousers?

George Formby's best-loved alter ego was undoubtedly John Willie, 'up' in London from Wigan for t' Cup, or on some other once-in-a-lifetime outing. This wide-eyed wanderer span charming tales of home, in which he would either subtly ridicule or reinforce his more sophisticated metropolitan audience's prejudices, depending upon your point of view.

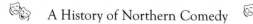

It was Formby, for example, who came up with the mock-grandeur notion of Wigan Pier, an old coal-loading staithe on the Leeds and Liverpool canal exaggerated for humourous effect, later seized upon by the writer George Orwell. Wigan, as described by John Willie, was a humble and homespun place, simultaneously blessed with a possibly ridiculous urge to fight above its own cultural weight. Much like John Willie himself. When viewed from this distance, Formby's portrayal of John Willie seems to imply that the natural position of the north in the social fabric of this country is one of subservience to its more refined southern patron. All else smacked of comic pretension.

Few folk, if any, judged Formby's act in such terms at the time, of course. And maybe we are in danger of taking the whole thing a little too seriously ourselves. Back then, after all, a trip to London could indeed be an expensive, unusual and eye-opening experience for many in the north, even though large groups of people were hardly an uncommon sight in Leeds or Liverpool, Newcastle or Manchester. George Formby Sr, however, took all that relative innocence one step further and he did so very well, thanks to a nicely judged acting style that still carries the power to amuse.

Led by his domineering wife, John Willie would wander through the capital streets staring at the sights and bright lights like some sort of bewildered imbecile: 'Did you see the crowd in Piccadilly', went one such musical reflection. And in another, 'John Willie, come on!', we get even closer to the rhythm of his act. 'Mind you don't get run o'wer,' his wife - voiced by Formby - warns him. The recording which survives of this routine was made in 1908, one year after the comedian launched the first of an eventual one hundred and eighty such gramophone records. 'She took me by the hand into a picture gallery,' John Willie continues, to the gentle accompaniment of a scarcely audible cuckoo. 'I saw a champion picture there. It fairly tickled me. It was a woman in the sea with long hair on her 'ead; I was getting interested when my wife turned round and said: "John Willie, come on..."!'

Along with just about every other comedian before or since, George Formby had a ready supply of catchphrases, of which this was but one. And again these verbal tics - born of a twin urge to both recognise and ward off the monotonous regularity of everyday life - will figure in greater detail as we go along. George Formby's best-known phrase, however, was more deeply grounded in reality than most. 'Coughing better tonight,' he would rasp and splutter, as his bronchial lungs did their utmost to choke him. 'Coughing summat champion.'

Such was the level of acclaim that came George Formby senior's way during his lifetime, that it wasn't long before he acquired the mantle of the comedian's comedian. Marie Lloyd herself admitted that there were only two music hall entertainers she would actually stand in the wings and watch - the great Dan Leno and Formby. And as if planting the seeds of modern-day northern comedy was not enough, Formby senior is also said to have influenced popular comedy in at least one other major and even international way. Among his earliest on-stage get-ups was a bowler hat, baggy black coat, concertina trousers and a pair of boots that more often than not appeared to be on the wrong feet. The possibly apocryphal story goes that an ambitious young Londoner named Charles Chaplin spotted the costume whilst working as a member of the famous Fred Karno troupe and asked to borrow it. Formby kindly agreed and when Chaplin then took off to America and a glittering future in Hollywood, the outfit went with him.

For George Formby, meanwhile, his future lay very much in England and, more specifically, Warrington, near to his Wigan birthplace. Despite having established a major national reputation in the capital, George and Eliza remained happiest at home and it was there that they were determined to stay. Improved travel links notwithstanding, it was a decision for which George would pay the ultimate price. In common with all music hall artists, he worked himself hard, moving from town to town, city to city and often performing several times a night. In doing so and driven, no doubt, by inner demons whispering reminders of his destitute past, he exacerbated the ill-health that had plagued him since childhood. A sadly prophetic variation on Formby's most famous catchphrase went: 'It's not the coughin' that carries you off, it's the coffin they carries you off in!'.

The first signs of serious trouble came during the Christmas of 1918, when Formby was forced to pull out of a pantomime with agonising chest pains. At first, supported by his wife's diligent home-nursing, he fought his way back to the stage, trademark coughs, splutters and all, but it wasn't long before his dodgy health again intervened. At the Newcastle Empire two years later, he coughed too hard, burst a blood vessel and hit the deck. This time, neither Eliza nor anyone else could help him. After succumbing to tuberculosis, George Formby senior departed this world on Shrove Tuesday, 1921.

Upon his death, it was reported that the one-time pauper had left an impressive £21,000 in his will, along with a diary fully booked for the following five years. An even more valuable legacy for his son, however, was the trail triumphantly blazed. For in time, and treading pretty much the same path, George Formby junior would meet with a still greater degree of mass adulation. Northern comedy was 'oop' and running.

2
Can You Hear Me, Mother?

"It's being so cheerful as keeps me going..."
- *Mona Lott, 'It's That Man Again'*

Just as the improved transport systems of the Industrial Revolution were effectively shrinking Great Britain by road and rail, so too did comedy born in the north of England begin to touch upon the lives of every Tom, Dick and Harriet, no matter where in the country they resided.

Mostly, that was down to the invention of a couple of ingenious new electronic mediums, commonly known as the wireless and moving pictures. Nevertheless, it would be a while yet before the irrepressible spirit of music hall was exorcised completely - if indeed it ever was at all. Throughout their early development, radio and film stayed inextricably tied to the stage; very definitely the place where both found the majority of their talent.

For all that the British public continued to enjoy a good night out, with the approach of World War One the original smaller music halls had begun rapidly to decline in numbers. Instead, much grander palaces of Variety, altogether less riotous venues often run by large families or management companies, began to dominate, attracting the best-known

acts and, therefore, the biggest box-office returns. Usually bearing pseudo-classical epithets like The Hippodrome or The Empire - later to be immortalised by Bradford-born writer JB Priestley in his masterpieces *The Good Companions* and *Lost Empires* - their rise was mirrored across the Atlantic by the equally successful, if marginally less eccentric, American Vaudeville.

Back in Britain, a number of Variety theatre's most entrepreneurial owners - men such as Sir Edward Moss and Tynesiders Dick Thornton and Tom Barrasford - were either born or educated in the north of England, ensuring that the region's influence extended beyond simply the performers on the stage. Barrasford, for example, after running music halls in Jarrow, Leeds, Edinburgh, Hull and Birmingham, built and opened his first hall in Liverpool, calling it the Royal Hippodrome, in 1902. It seated over one thousand people and boasted an ornate painted ceiling, featuring pastel cupids hovering above beds of clouds. Come the end of the Great War, this ongoing upgrade in middle-class friendly facilities ensured that the spit and sawdust of early music hall was well on its way to becoming an historical and cultural footnote, especially when it was combined with the audience's new-found taste for all things American and the loss of so many jugglers, acrobats and other speciality acts to the deadly battlefields of Europe. Nor had it helped when, in 1914, after a series of fires, London Council banned eating and drinking in theatre seats. The upshot being that the unmistakeable working class music hall of yore was all-but extinct by the start of World War Two.

Still, it wasn't all bad news. Alcohol could still be served outside the auditorium, helping to elevate everyone to an appropriate level of mass-sentimentality beforehand or during the interval. And with the public now tidily facing front in seated rows, the performers had even less space to hide. Whereas, in the old days, audience members could simply lean over and have a natter with their neighbours if they grew tired of hurling cabbages, Variety turns were now the absolute focus of attention. As a result, the best acts flourished, which was pretty good timing given the arrival of BBC radio in 1922, and the coming of the BBC's Home Service in the late 1930s.

From the outset, and notwithstanding a determination on the part of the national broadcaster to educate rather than merely entertain, radio and Variety theatre enjoyed a symbiotic relationship. For its part, the new medium could be used as a very effective promotional tool, enticing people out of their homes and into the halls. In return, Variety's array of familiar faces - and more importantly voices - were ideal for giving radio instant credibility with the public and filling up the airwaves. Less positively, radio's rapacious appetite for fresh material left many a comedian wary about throwing away gags on air that might sustain an act for months, or even years, on the road. Even so, as it became apparent which of the two was destined to dominate longer term, entertainers grew less apprehensive about committing themselves and the star-making axis of power inevitably began to shift. Increasingly, it was the wireless which made national reputations. Variety was at best bread and butter.

At this stage in British comedy history the quickfire rat-a-tat gag held sway over character-driven observational humour, which is not to say that the notion of character was completely unimportant. Without doubt, the best known proponent of the on-stage one-liner during the inter-war period was Max Miller, a supposed commercial traveller complete with lurid kipper ties, outrageous suits, two-tone shoes and deftly-cocked white trilby hat, just one size too small. In many eyes the first great truly modern stand-up, the Brighton-born Miller made his London debut at Shoreditch Music Hall in 1922. Prior to that, he had served in the First World War and performed as part of a concert party on the sea front of his south coast hometown.

As with Marie Lloyd, Max Miller became best known as a master of saucy innuendo, boasting a notoriously risqué style that earned him the epithet 'Cheeky Chappie': 'I like the girls who do. I like the girls who don't. I hate the girl who says she will and then she says she won't. But the girl that I like best of all, and I think you'll say I'm right, is the girl who says she never does but looks as though she...hey!'.

Famously, the depths of depravity to which Miller would descend were dictated by the response of his audience to a couple of joke books - one with a white cover, one coloured blue. If they chose white, his routine would be 'respectable'. Blue, and they got quips like this: 'I was walking along this narrow mountain pass, so narrow that nobody else could pass you, when I saw a beautiful blonde walking towards me. A beautiful blonde with not a stitch on, yes, not a stitch on, lady. Cor blimey, I didn't

know whether to toss myself off or block her passage.' No prizes for guessing which book won out most frequently.

Max Miller's technique of speaking directly and conspiratorially to the women in the auditorium, whilst looking nervously off to the wings, worked perfectly in the intimacy of live Variety theatre. However, it was less effective in the fourteen feature films he also made and starred in between 1933 and 1942. And the controversial nature of much of Miller's material meant that, unusually for so popular a figure, he never managed to forge much of a career in radio either. In fact, he was banned by the BBC for five years in the 1940s, allegedly for closing a show thus: 'When roses are red, they are ready for plucking. When girls are 16, they're ready for... goodnight, ladies and gentlemen!'. In Max Miller, then, we catch the first brazen whiff of a brash and flashy southern-based comedy culture of the future, together with the last hurrah of a more ribald yet somehow innocent time.

Radio or wireless telegraphy had been around in various forms since British physicist James Clerk-Maxwell first revealed his theory of electro-magnetic waves in 1873. And yet the first advertised broadcast for public consumption did not occur until 1920. The venue was a Chelmsford workshop belonging to one Guglielmo Marconi, from where a musical recital by the singer Dame Nellie Melba heralded the beginning of experimental twice-daily programmes. Marconi, it was, who had invented the first apparatus for transmitting radio waves in 1895.

The technology's commercial potential quickly became clear and, in October 1922, the six existing private radio companies - including Marconi's - were brought together to form the British Broadcasting Company, as the BBC was initially known, with daily broadcasts commencing from London on 14th November of that year. Indeed, a test broadcast made by the new company, featuring the wireless engineer Captain Peter P. Eckersley, could at a stretch be described as the inaugural example of improvisational radio comedy. Eckersley's impression of a rabid Italian tenor, plonking away at a grand piano while emitting a series of high-pitched silly noises, not only put his studio through its technical paces, it pre-dated the groundbreaking *Goon Show* by some thirty years.

Can You Hear Me, Mother?

A day after regular broadcasts began from London, the cities of Birmingham and Manchester followed suit. After which, the pace of growth continued rapidly, with transmitters popping up right across the United Kingdom. By 1925, BBC radio could be received just about everywhere, usually on home-made crystal or 'cat's whiskers' sets, which the listener would enjoy via headphones, although amplifiers did make group listening possible. As the technology developed further, battery-powered valve sets became the norm and, by the 1930s, a fair number of homes boasted mains-powered radio sets housed in nicely-polished wood or moulded Bakelite cabinets. In short, mass media home entertainment had arrived.

But what was actually being 'radiated'? Well, the man who can claim to be the first ever northern-style radio comedian for a start.

Somewhat appropriately, the laconic John Henry was a product of the music halls. His gloomy, long-suffering take on life proved immensely popular with those who could afford to tune in and hear his distinctive north country accent - not a large number of people by any means. In keeping with his stage background, existing audio records reveal that much of Henry's material was of what might euphemistically be called the traditional kind, complete with verbal sideswipes at his long-suffering wife, Blossom. And like much radio output at the time, the bulk of his material focussed on the exciting new medium itself: '...t' wireless is a very wonderful thing. Anything that will make a woman listen must be wonderful, mustn't it?'.

The exuberance of Captain Eckersley's early antics notwithstanding, when it became clear that original radio microphones were best suited to people being positioned directly in front of them and standing still, a preponderance of lectures and reflective monologues ensued. Under its first general manager, the fiercely moral and high-minded Scottish engineer John Reith, the BBC - now known since winning its Royal Charter in 1927 as the British Broadcasting Corporation - was keen on lectures anyway, and broadcast talks on all manner of improving subjects. John Henry, meanwhile, got stuck into the second genre with gusto.

Then again, perhaps gusto isn't quite the right word. His wondrously lugubrious tones were more redolent of a wet weekend in Wakefield. 'My wireless set has no loudspeaker,' he told what were back then known as

57

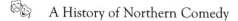

his 'listeners-in'. 'No married man wants two loudspeakers in the house, do they?'. Henry's plaintive and downbeat 'hello, everybody,' at the start of each programme may also be the earliest example of a radio comedy catchphrase.

As wireless broadened its horizons, so, to an extent, did John Henry. He graduated from monologues to dialogues, wherein wife Blossom was now liable to answer back. From a business point of view, he also became one of the first to use broadcasting celebrity as a means of promoting a parallel stage career. In that, he was followed by the otherwise full-time Sheffield schoolteacher Arthur Clifford Baines, better known as Stainless Stephen, whose own radio career began in 1923 with an amateur broadcast from Sheffield Relay Station.

The name of Stainless Stephen was destined to spread quickly - his was an act ready made for the ear. In many ways a forerunner of the style of comedy adopted by Victor Borge, 'Clown Prince of Denmark', this particular northern comic's patter was peppered with bizarre spoken-out-loud punctuation: 'This is Stainless Stephen comma comedian question mark.' On stage, he must have cut an even more eccentric sight. Clad in bowler hat, revolving bow tie and tailor-made stainless steel waistcoat, complete with illuminated buttons, Stainless Stephen's act was a classic music hall mix of visual comedy, dexterous wordplay and song that, in 1932, put him top of a newspaper vote for the nation's twelve most popular wireless turns. When Arthur Clifford Baines retired in 1952, he had a 1945 Royal Command Performance appearance, among much else, to look back upon. He lived to the ripe old age of 79, passing away in 1971. And yet by then, and despite the pioneering nature of their comedy careers, both he and John Henry were all but forgotten.

That obscurity can largely be explained by sheer weight of numbers. Stainless Stephen and John Henry are far from being the only comedians to see high-profile reputations swept away in the avalanche of performing talent that drove radio onward and upward. As the 1920s turned into the 1930s, the new medium was positively awash with Variety comics, most of them male but, and perhaps surprisingly given the social stigma attached to working women at the time, a sizeable number female. Of these, the popular Liverpudlian impressionist Beryl Orde was one of the best known and ahead of her time in every respect. And when it came to character comedy, for every male comedian like plum-voiced Gillie Potter, the self-styled sage of Hogsnorton, or Wireless Willie Rouse, the likes of Bertha Wilmot and Mabel 'Grandma Buggins' Constanduros were able to offer their own more affectionate take on a working class woman's lot. The most famous of these female comics was Helena Millais. Her cockney char lady, Our Lizzie, replete with her 'comedy fragments from life', was descended directly from the music hall costers: 'Handy things, string bags, ain't they? I lost two pound of beans last week. Been and dropped through the 'oles!' It's tempting to add: 'Am I bovvered?'.

By 1932, the BBC had grown to the extent that the organisation now required a purpose-built production centre. And so one was duly built at Portland Place, subsequently to become known as Broadcasting House. Henceforth, radio listenership was numbered in millions rather than thousands, especially when a single Home Service - introduced to replace the national and regional programmes in 1939 - set about lifting national morale with popular entertainment rather than paternalistic finger-wagging and 'improving' classical music, during World War Two.

The resignation of Director-General John Reith a year before had further allowed for a lightening of the mood and that process gathered still greater pace with the arrival of the Light Programme - a domestic replacement for the wartime BBC General Forces Programme - on 29 July 1945. But whatever the station, during the war or after it, with air-time to fill the BBC bosses continued to plunder Variety theatre, where there was plenty of ripe and juicy fruit just begging to be plucked, much of it imported from northern orchards.

Robert Wilton Smith - Robb Wilton to his fans - was one such artist. Born in Everton in 1881, as an older man, flowering late, Wilton utilised his finely tuned ear for the poetic vagaries of everyday speech to craft some of wartime radio's most memorable comedy moments, revealing a talent for rhythmic repetition and confusing double negatives as he did so. 'I went before the Magistrate, and he fined me 20 bob. I said: "Ow much?" He said: "A pound!" I said: "I'll have some job!" I said: "I can't pay it Guv'nor!" He said: "Who can't?" I said: "I can't!" He said: "You can't?" I said: "Yes I can, I can't!".'

Robb Wilton's stage career began in 1898 when he joined a stock melodramatic company and uncharacteristically played the villain in *Sweeney*

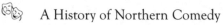

Todd - The Demon Barber of Fleet Street who, like many on the Pennines' western fringes, was partial to a nice pie. In 1903, Wilton turned solo performer, with a couple of one-man character comedy acts at Everton's Lyric Theatre and the New Brighton Pavilion. It was there that he was spotted by the famed music hall impresario, Sir Walter De Freece. Later that same year, on the opposite coast in Hull, Wilton met an actress who would go on to play a major role in both his private and public lives, his future wife and comedy foil Florence 'Florrie' Palmer, whom he married in 1907.

In tandem with Florence and with the continued patronage of Sir Walter, Robb Wilton built a devoted following on the music hall circuit, eventually finding his way into radio and, always a popular man, collected friends and admirers as he went. One particular character honed during this period and destined to be a major ingredient in Wilton's wartime radio success was the pompous Mr Muddlecombe JP, magistrate of Nether Backwash. Way into the future, the Derbyshire-born actor, Arthur Lowe, would admit that Muddlecombe had been a big influence on his own subsequent portrayal of everyone's favourite bank manager, the vainglorious Captain George Mainwaring, in Jimmy Perry and David Croft's classic television and radio situation comedy *Dad's Army*. Certainly, listen to the sketch in which Wilton's Private Muddlecombe goes into a sulk after discovering that, had it been peace time, his Home Guard sergeant would in fact be his social inferior and you might indeed be in the Walmington-on-Sea church hall.

The hugely gifted Robb Wilton had three main strings to his comedic bow. The first was his relatively straightforward stand-up joke telling, with which he usually introduced his shows. Then came one-on-one situational sketches, usually involving games of verbal tennis with his wife, in which both were able to show off their classy slow burning acting skills to good effect. Indeed, these routines could well be seen as some of the earliest examples of radio sitcom, a genre still to be invented when Mr and Mrs Wilton were busy perfecting their 'Fireman' and 'Policeman' sketches, a couple of particularly well-loved staples back in the music hall days of the 1920s. In the latter, Florence arrives at the local police station announcing that she has just poisoned her husband. 'Is your husband with you?' asks Wilton, playing a relentlessly polite, if bureaucratic desk sergeant. 'Oh no, of course, you've poisoned him. When did this happen?' 'Last night, we had some friends for supper.' 'I see, and did you poison them too?' 'No!' 'I see, just the one poison, then, just the one poison. At what time did this happen?' 'At midnight.' 'At midnight? At midnight. You poisoned your husband at midnight, that's the idea....' and so on, as though the woman is reporting a lost dog.

Like John Henry before him, Wilton's third and perhaps finest talent was for the delivery of comic conversational monologues, often played out against a backdrop of mournful instrumental music with heaps of lyrical invention, apparently borne of personal experience. In these, Wilton didn't tell jokes as such. Instead, his seemingly insignificant reflections were charged with the empathy that comes from recognition of character and circumstance. One such monologue, 'The Home Guard' or 'The Day War Broke Out', from 1939, and this time performed without music, has entered radio legend.

On the face of it, 'The Day War Broke Out' is little more than a stereotypical vision of an average 1930s northern working class marriage, complete with the nagged husband imagery that was so commonplace at the time. Yet looked at in another way, this little comic masterpiece is a refreshing insight into contemporary social attitudes, and not only in relation to the battle of the sexes. Here, there is a mood of honest realism afoot, which takes us behind closed doors and speaks of the mundane truth beyond conventional ideals of unbridled wartime patriotism and widespread self-sacrifice. 'The Day War Broke Out' shows that not everyone was interested in this war business at first and certainly didn't view the threat from that little German clown Adolf Hitler particularly seriously. To your average little man, blessedly ignorant of the horrors to come, a war with Germany was more likely to be seen as an adventure, even if he had to base himself in a little wooden hut in the back yard of the 'Dog and Pullet' in order to fight it. For the womenfolk, meanwhile, the real adventure was finding enough money to put food on the table, never mind all this bigger picture global political nonsense. However gentle comedy may seem on the surface, it is almost always, to some degree, engaged in a process of social subversion.

'The day war broke out, my missus said to me... she looked at me and she said: "What good are you?" I said: "Who?" She said: "You!" I said: "How do you mean, what good am I?" "Well..." she said, "you're too old for the army..." she said, "you couldn't get in the navy... and they wouldn't have you in the air force... so, what good are you?" I said: "I'll do something!...." She said: "What?" I said: "How do I know?... I'll have to think!" She said: "I don't see how that's going to help you... you've never done it before!...".' Wilton's character, of course, then joins the Home Guard, leading to the immortal enquiry: '"Do you know this Hitler? Have you ever..." I says: "Do I know...don't talk rubbish, Rita. I'm not even in the paint business.." "Well, how are you going to know which is him if they do land?" "I've got a tongue in my head, haven't I?".'

Sadly for the Wiltons, real family life took a tragic turn for the worst when, in 1942, the couple's only son Robert was killed, aged 36, after falling 25ft from a second-floor window while on a night out in London's West End. To compound the couple's misery, Florence then developed a drink problem from which she never recovered. She died in 1956, the same year that her husband made his final radio broadcast. One year later, Robb Wilton too passed away, aged 76, at Liverpool's Broadgreen hospital. Fittingly, in 1959, a plaque was unveiled in the foyer of the city's Empire Theatre which read: 'Laughter was his life and life was his laughter.'

Robb Wilton cheered up a nation during the cold, dark days of World War Two, but it was another Liverpudlian comedian who might fairly be described as the greatest radio star of the age.

From his earliest days as a choirboy at Toxteth Congregational Church, Thomas Reginald Handley, born in 1892, had long shown a talent for amusement. As a youngster, living with his widowed mother, he became fascinated with disguise, ventriloquism and magic, and spent what little pocket money he had on masks, false moustaches and makeup. The young Thomas learned how to throw his voice and, after leaving school at 14, took up amateur dramatics, before deciding to try his hand as a professional funnyman in 1917. It was a good move. By 1923, he had appeared in his first Royal Variety Performance. With the arrival of radio, Handley seized the opportunity and went on to star in such hits as *Radio Radiance*, *Tommy's Tours* and *Handley's Manoeuvres*. Then, in September 1939, the skies darkened considerably over Europe.

Can You Hear Me, Mother?

A couple of months earlier, in July, Tommy Handley had already embarked upon a four-show trial run of a new radio series called *It's That Man Again*, based in a pirate commercial station. The title was inspired by a phrase coined by a *Daily Express* headline writer, employed whenever Adolf Hitler made his latest territorial claim. Initially, after Handley and his friend, Ted Kavanagh, had devised the format over a few pints in the Langham Hotel, opposite Broadcasting House, audience reaction was less than ecstatic. Yet, when the programme made a return upon the outbreak of hostilities, with its name whittled down to an acronym as a result of a wartime propensity to abbreviate anything that moved, *ITMA* would grow to become one of the most popular wireless shows of all time. At its height, it boasted some 16 million listeners per week, heading a bill that at various times included such radio gems as *Band Waggon*, *Hi, Gang!* and Forces sweetheart Vera Lynn's *Sincerely Yours*.

Once *ITMA* got into its stride, Tommy Handley himself deposed Herr Hitler as the eponymous 'man' in the title. And with a pirate radio station considered an inappropriate setting during wartime, Handley was now cast as Minister of Aggravation and Mysteries at the Office of Twerps, with a supporting cast that would, over several incarnations and twelve full series in a ten-year run, include such notable character actors as Maurice Denham, Sam Costa, Deryck Guyler and Hattie Jacques. The brilliant Jack Train was on board too, as the perpetually pickled Colonel Humphrey Chinstrap, catchphrase: 'I don't mind if I do'. Train was also the voice behind Mark Time, a somewhat depraved, elderly chap, whose response to any request was: 'I'll 'ave to ask me dad.' Among *ITMA*'s post-war settings was the South Sea island of Tomtopia - in which supposedly exotic paradise Handley's fellow Liverpool-born comedian Fred Yule played the parts of the perpetually hungry George 'lovely grub' Gorge and native chief Bigga Banga, who spoke only in the fictional language of Utopi.

As is doubtless apparent by now, *ITMA* owed much of its success to the constant regurgitation of catchphrases, a broad comedic device that was especially valid during the turmoil caused by war, given that it offered a comforting dose of reassurance and predictability. Yes, the hundreds of such 'jokes' scattered across each show were weaker than tinned custard. But, quite clearly, that didn't matter much and anyway the comic acting

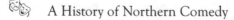

on display was reliably strong. In *ITMA*, one of several stock characters would knock on an imaginary radio door, exchange some banter with the cheerfully zany Handley, deliver his or her best-known line - such as Mrs Mopp's 'Can I do you now, sir?' - and exit to hearty and, to modern ears, astonishing levels of hilarity. Decades on, in the 1990s, Paul Whitehouse and Charlie Higson's *The Fast Show* would tread a similar path, albeit with far stronger material and in a less cataclysmic social landscape.

Rather poignantly given what was to follow, the milestone 300th episode of *ITMA*, broadcast on 28 October 1948, was set at the Madame Tussaud's waxworks in London where, passing through the 'Hall of *ITMA*'s Past', Tommy Handley was briefly reunited with many of the show's most loved characters, each played by a former cast member such as Horace Percival, Clarence Wright, Dino Galvani or Dorothy Summers. Around two months later, the man who gave the nation *ITMA* was dead, as a result of a brain haemorrhage suffered on 6 January 1949, three days after recording what turned out to be his final show.

With its ringmaster gone, the BBC duly cancelled the series. The British public were distraught and thousands of mourners lined a six-mile route from a private chapel to Golders Green Crematorium, London. Memorial services were held in Handley's native Liverpool and St Paul's Cathedral, where the Bishop of London paid a great entertainer the most moving of tributes, describing Handley as a man who had 'transmuted the copper of our common experience into the gold of exquisite foolery. From the highest to the lowest in the land, people had found in his programme an escape from their troubles and anxieties into a world of whimsical nonsense.'

Almost twenty years later, in 1967, Tommy Handley's lasting impact on British popular culture was confirmed when fellow Liverpudlians The Beatles, and the artist Peter Blake, included his image on the cover of the now iconic album *Sgt Pepper's Lonely Hearts Club Band*, alongside Marilyn Monroe, Shirley Temple, Albert Einstein, Lawrence of Arabia and, it's that other man again, Max Miller. Meanwhile, across the Atlantic, another *ITMA* catchphrase, 'TTFN' or 'ta-ta for now', would endure as the parting shot of the lunatic Tigger in Walt Disney's animated version of *Winnie The Pooh*.

Given the enormous impact of *ITMA*, it might be supposed that Tommy Handley and his team were responsible for inventing the compendium of comedy catchphrases genre. In which case, suppose again. For along with being a nod in the direction of the George Burns and Gracie Allen show already wowing the American public, those early episodes of *ITMA* were unashamedly modelled on another groundbreaking radio programme broadcast this side of the Atlantic.

Again it was built squarely on constant catchphrases and again its lead comic hailed from Liverpool. His name was Arthur Askey and the show was called *Band Waggon*. Compered by Askey's long-time colleague Richard 'Stinker' Murdoch, it aired for the first time in 1938.

Initially, the bespectacled Askey, five foot three in his high heels and a radio novice whose own career in Variety began as a member of an army concert party in 1924, was employed merely as resident comedian. And even then, legend has it, only on the toss of a coin. The show's producers, Gordon Crier and Harry H Pepper, couldn't decide whether Askey or South London comic Tommy Trinder would be best for the role, and so set about making their minds up in time honoured fashion. Heads for Tommy, tails for Arthur. As it turned out, they needn't have bothered. Trinder, the winner, was booked elsewhere anyway and Askey was duly given his big break by default, launching a showbusiness career that lasted for over fifty years.

In time, Askey and Murdoch's comedy sparring proved so popular that they began to dominate *Band Waggon*, originally intended, as its name suggests, to liven up the BBC's wartime output of big band shows. In a stroke of whimsical genius, the pair were said to reside in a flat on the top floor of Broadcasting House which, listeners were told, they shared with a quartet of pigeons, Basil, Ronald, Lucy and Sarah, and Lewis the goat. Extending an already impressive imaginary cast list, 'big-hearted' Arthur also had a girlfriend who went by the wonderful name of Nausea, the daughter of char lady Mrs Bagwash, although neither was ever heard. The 45-minute running time was spent awash in a sea of catchphrase lunacy, of which 'ah, happy days', 'you silly little man' and 'light the blue touch paper and retire' are but three examples. At the end of each programme, the silliness was usually topped off by some sort of violent incident; Arthur might come plummeting off a ladder for

example. Thus was born the famous *Band Waggon* crash, in which a large number of metal objects were pushed over at one corner of the stage by a sound man. The chap in question would then bow to the audience and enjoy a rapturous round of applause, much to Askey's feigned annoyance: 'Oi! I'm the comedian! I get the laughs.'

Although, as we have seen, catchphrases had been common currency for music hall and Variety theatre comedians for years, *Band Waggon* - and, soon after, *ITMA* - were the first shows broadcast on British radio to use them as a staple comedy diet with little else going on at all. Of no little assistance in establishing the format was the scheduling of the actual programmes themselves. The then innovative idea of giving a show a regular weekly slot - same day, same time, same place - helped to stamp Arthur's opening gambit, 'hello, playmates', onto the mind of a nation. The welcome itself, incidentally, had originally been 'hello, folks', but Askey agreed to change it when his friend Tommy Handley complained that it was his introduction. No matter. 'Hello, playmates' served Arthur Askey well. In the 1950s, it became the title of a show of its own and, along with Arthur's other signature line 'Ay Thang Yew' - mimicking the pronunciation of London bus conductors - both were soon as ubiquitous as ration books.

Unlike the long-running *ITMA*, *Band Waggon*'s stay at the top was relatively brief. By the time a film and third series came around in 1939, so great was Askey's workload that the programme had to be scrapped after fifty-five shows. The final episode, broadcast on 2 December, in which Askey and Murdoch moved out of their 'flat', is said to have left listeners in floods of tears. There was still enough of an impetus left for a short stage tour but, when Murdoch then volunteered for the RAF, that was it until November 1947, when *Band Waggon* made a one-off comeback as part of the BBC's Silver Jubilee celebrations.

While the rest of Arthur Askey's career was rather less revolutionary, it was nevertheless similarly hyperactive, spanning stage, radio, film, television and an often-overlooked area of showbusiness that would play a huge role in maintaining the spirit of Variety entertainment throughout the twentieth century, seaside summer seasons. Askey recorded a fair few playful comic ditties too, including 'The Bee Song' and 'The Worm', while proving himself an impressive ad-libber on the long-running panel show *Does The Team Think?*. He also appeared in films as diverse in content and quality as *Charlie's Aunt* and the risible 'seventies soft-core porn flick *Rosie Dixon, Night Nurse*. He was a judge on the ITV talent show *New Faces* and regularly hammed it up as a dame in pantomime.

Away from the stage, however, the bubbly Askey's personal life was a less happy affair, especially as the years advanced. His wife of many years, Elizabeth, developed Alzheimer's Disease and was unable to cope, in public anyway, with the consequences of his fame. When she died in 1974, Arthur, undaunted, battled on into his eighties, making his last TV appearance in the 1980 Royal Variety Show. Distressingly, problems with blood circulation led to him having both legs amputated soon afterwards. For such a jaunty soul, never one to stand still when he could buzz around like the honey bees of his song, it was a terrible and traumatic fate indeed. As the old trouper himself put it, shortly before death mercifully claimed him on 16 November 1982: 'What a lousy exit'.

You didn't have to be made on the Mersey to work in early radio, although the evidence does seem to suggest that it helped. Sandy Powell, for example, another northern-born comedian who became a huge household name, had the temerity to hail from Yorkshire.

Once again, Powell's astonishing levels of popularity owed much to a catchphrase, in his case the bizzarely flustered 'Can you hear me, mother?'. With it, he caught the attention of the British public and never let it go. Like Arthur Askey, Powell entered this world in 1900 and, again like Askey, he worked on into his eighties, before passing away in 1982.

A child of Rotherham, Albert Arthur Powell also shared a middle name with the star of *Band Waggon*, although both forenames were dispensed with shortly after his father, noticing that his son had red hair, renamed him Sandy. In fact, that was to be just about the only useful thing that Powell senior ever did do for the boy. When Sandy was just four years old, his father, a stagehand at a local theatre, promptly scarpered, leaving Powell's mother Lily to bring up her son and younger daughter alone. Predictably, a hand-to-mouth childhood of poverty and struggle ensued, although Lily did at least have a background as a music hall artist. To make ends meet, she found work waitressing and singing in pubs, on which occasions young Sandy would hide under the piano.

A year after his father's unscheduled departure, Powell began to earn extra money for the act by sitting in the audience and belting out the choruses to songs, thereby encouraging everyone else to sing along. Then, in 1907, came his stage debut as a boy soprano, an occupation to which he was evidently suited until his voice broke and he was forced to turn to comedy, most often clad in a kilt and claiming to be Scottish. In so doing, he proved to be particularly adept at impersonations and, as one half of 'Lily and Sandy', went on to develop an eventually well-known double act with his mum. Now then, little boys in kilts, quite literally hiding beneath a mother's skirts - does anyone else hear the words 'armchair Freudian psychoanalysis'..? Hmmm. Suffice to say that during a childhood spent drifting from town to town, constantly making and losing new friends along the way, the urge to please Mrs Powell must have been strong in young Sandy. Theirs was the closest-knit of relationships. And, in later life, he would go on to marry three times.

Whatever the psychological impact of Sandy Powell's upbringing, the lure of the halls, with their promise of instant popularity and affection, proved irresistible. With the advent of World War One, Powell had already developed a promising reputation as a solo performer and, by the time it ended, he had topped his first bill as an eighteen-year-old. Ten years later, at the end of a decade spent sparkling on the Variety and pantomime stage, it was radio's turn to come calling. Disarmingly batty, Powell was an immediate hit and, in 1929, he made the first of over eighty hugely popular and highly profitable gramophone recordings of his radio and music hall sketches, *The Lost Policeman*.

Amiable confusion was Sandy Powell's calling card, as symbolically illustrated in the origins of his best-known catchphrase. According to most accounts, 'Can you hear me, mother?' first came about when Powell dropped his script during one radio recording and began to *ad lib* whilst frantically putting the pages back together. Elsewhere, it is reported that Lily was genuinely hard of hearing and that the phrase had simply come about in response to a request, made in 1930, that her son should speak up as she looked on from the audience. Either way, from this distance it seems likely that both kerfuffles would have been part of the act. After all, another speciality for the disorganised Powell was deliberately bad ventriloquism, wherein his magnificently unconvincing puppet would fall regularly to pieces, a gag that must have gone down especially well on radio. And alongside his third wife, Kay White - herself fifty per cent of a wartime double act with Liverpudlian comic Cyril Dowler - Powell spent a large part of the 1950s playing a hopeless magician.

However he happened upon his famous catchphrase, once it had taken hold Sandy Powell milked it to the full. Driven by his burgeoning fame, along with stage shows and gramophone recordings he appeared in numerous films, radio and, later, television shows, year after year. And, along with many of his contemporaries, Powell regularly entertained the British troops when Europe once again went to war in the 1930s. In 1935, *Can You Hear Me Mother?* actually became the name of a film, followed four years later by an acclaimed West End stage production at the London Coliseum. So much for heroic ineptitude.

Meanwhile, back in Rotherham, and some thirty-one years later, Sandy Powell was given the mother of all accolades for a northern comedian - he had a pub named in his honour. Thus did he pull the first-ever pint at 'The Comedian', nowadays sadly derelict. Rather more genteely, in 1977, he was also awarded an MBE. Yet no matter how high up the social ladder Powell climbed, the lad from South Yorkshire never forgot his humble roots and would often give unpaid concerts for the unemployed, amongst other charitable works. As the curtain came down, the now-elderly comic could often be found entertaining free of charge in the old folks homes dotted around Eastbourne, the English south coast resort where he saw out the remainder of his days.

3
In't It Grand When You're Daft?

"There's eight of them in every bottle."
- Frank Randle, taking a swig of ale and belching loudly

Reared on a diet of music hall and Variety entertainment, the war-weary British public did not turn to radio alone during their darkest hour. Another more glamourous, communal and visual electronic medium also cut brightly through the gloom.

As the 20th century progressed, the attraction of moving pictures had grown steadily until, with the outbreak of World War Two, every cinema in the land was forced to shut down as a safety precaution. The clampdown didn't last long. Almost immediately, the authorities realised that 'going to the pictures' carried the potential to improve the national mood and a number of cinemas reopened within a week. In the event of an air raid, a warning would flash up on screen, allowing audiences to gather under the balcony for protection. Where heavy bombing was common, film-going was understandably disrupted. Elsewhere, it thrived and cinema underwent a massive boom in popularity from 1941 onwards.

As with radio, many of the stars responsible for that surge in public interest had either cut their teeth in Variety theatre or were on the verge of making it big there. And where Robb Wilton, Sandy Powell, Arthur Askey and Tommy Handley had all been central to the wireless war effort, the biggest film stars of the era bar none were also northerners to their toecaps.

In George Formby (junior) and Rochdale's finest, Gracie Fields, Britain would know its first true cinema superstars. For a time, the appeal of the pair was absolute. It crossed all class and geographical boundaries and ensured that clichés such as 'warming the hearts of a nation' became a simple statement of fact. As with all such phenomena, such heady levels of fame could not be sustained forever. Yet, for the first time, the nation had supped deep at the well of mass media celebrity culture. From a purely pragmatic point of view, it could not have been any better timed.

Not that George and 'Our Gracie' were *entirely* without competition. In the case of Formby, a couple of fellow north west comics - namely the loveable Albert 'in't it grand when yer daft?' Modley and the magisterially unpredictable Frank Randle, a childhood friend of Formby's from Wigan - gave him the occasional run for his money.

Born in 1901, Albert Modley was another product of Liverpool, not that he stayed there long. Soon after his birth, the Modley family moved east and set up home across the Pennines in Yorkshire, allowing young Albert to develop the broad Tyke tones that, along with overt self-deprecation and a keen ear for the absurd, would become a chief tool of his trade: 'I'm a fool of a man. I'm not fit to be in the place'. Modley dealt in stories rather than out-and-out jokes, each told in an authentic white rose dialect that was nevertheless careful never to need subtitles. 'I heard two old farmers arguing o'wer who could grow t' biggest veg-it-ubble,' he says, in one such tale. 'One says: "ah'll grow a bigger veg-it-ubble than thee." T' other says: "gerraway". He says: "..ah will. For a pint." "Right." So a few weeks went by when Old Giles says to his lad: "...ey, come 'ere. Now, ah want thee to go to old Earnshaw. Ask Mr Earnshaw to lend his cross-cut saw. He'll want to know what you want it for. Tell 'im your father wants to cut a turnip in two. D'you understand what ah'm saying?" "Yes, dad. A turnip in two. Saw." Alreet. He goes across to old Earnshaw, knocks at t' door. Earnshaw asks him what he wants. He says: "me father wants to know if you'll lend him your cross-cut saw?" Earnshaw says: "what's he want it for?" "He says he wants to cut a turnip in two." Earnshaw says: "...thee go back and tell thee dad ah've gorrit jammed in a 'tatie...".'

So amusing did folk find Modley's persona that, before long, he was given the epithet 'Lancashire's favourite Yorkshireman', a compliment which, when you come to think about it, must be right up there with a postman's favourite paper cut. And, for sure, his popularity in Lancashire can't have been hindered by the fact that he spent such a sizeable lump of his adulthood living there. As a devoted resident of 'Bradford-by-the-sea', a.k.a. the north west seaside town of Morecambe, Modley became something of a fixture and fitting in a resort where, it was often joked, an evening at the illuminations meant sitting on a windswept bench waiting for the traffic lights to change. In fact, Modley had the honour of switching on the annual lights there himself in 1960.

Albert Modley's stage career first took flight during the Great Strike of 1926. Thereafter, he was a regular presence in radio, pantomime and film, his best-known efforts in the latter genre including *Bob's Your Uncle* (1942), *Up For T' Cup* (1950) and *Take Me to Paris* (1951). So instantly recognisable did his face become that Modley's caricature was the last ever to be featured on the cover of *Comic Cuts*, when that popular publication folded after over three thousand issues in 1953. With the arrival of television, Modley's star began to wane although, as late as 1971, he remained well enough known to be a regular on *The Leslie Crowther Show*, alongside the eponymous host, Arthur English and Chic Murray. Then, in 1974, he had a cameo role in the Leeds-born playwright Alan Bennett's moving BBC comedy drama, *Sunset Across The Bay*, albeit not without incident. Bennett - for whom Modley was a boyhood hero - recalls the circumstances of their meeting in his 2005 tome, *Untold Stories*.

'Included in the script,' writes Bennett, 'was a scene in which two old men chat outside the hut on the Leeds allotment which one of them is having to abandon before retiring to the seaside. When it came to the shot Albert turned out to be none too sure of the words, covering up his uncertainty just as he'd done all those years ago on the stage of the Theatre Royal with a good deal of laughing and stock phrases like, "By! It's a beggar is this" or "By shots, this is a funny do. Hee hee...".'

If that made life difficult, at least Bennett and his director, Stephen Frears, could console themselves with Modley's undoubted authenticity, dressed in flat cap and old battered raincoat. Until, that is, a hovering and formidable Mrs Modley suddenly wandered up with an oversized hatbox, prior to shooting. The writer continues: '..."He's never wearing that old cap," said Mrs Modley. "Folks won't recognise him in that fiddling thing," and she opened the hatbox to reveal a cap of truly epic proportions. It was the cap he had worn on the halls.' An awkward situation is only averted when the cameraman suggests that Albert should save 'The Cap' for the actual shot, and that his wife should look after it while her husband rehearses 'with headgear of normal dimensions'. Of course, after several takes, when the hat is finally placed on Albert's head, neither he nor his better half realises that there is no longer any film left in the camera. '..."By shots, that feels better. This is more like it, hee hee..".'

There were clearly no hard feelings on either side because, in 1979, Modley also took a bit-part in another Alan Bennett television play, *All Day on the Sands*, starring Alun Armstrong and Marjorie Yates and again set in the comedian's hometown of Morecambe. Sadly, shortly after filming his contribution, Albert Modley suffered a fatal heart attack and died. Whether or not 'The Cap' was buried with him has, alas, gone unrecorded.

When recalling the music hall tradition, there is an unfortunate tendency amongst modern comedy critics, performers and audiences to denigrate the innocent amusement that it provided. Silly outfits, singsongs and catchphrases? We fancy ourselves far more sophisticated than that.

And, for sure, comedy is very much a beast of its time. With very few exceptions, much of it has not survived the electronic age unscathed, even where the sweet deceit of nostalgia insists otherwise. Yet within an appropriate historical context, it is surely possible to enjoy the creakiest of material on its own terms, even if sitting through an entire show or episode may be pushing it. Comedy gives us a snapshot of a parallel world or universe; a place simultaneously dissimilar and similar to our own.

Offbeat though it undeniably was, Albert Modley's humour might best be filed under 'gentle'. Frank Randle, on the other hand, was edgier than a threepenny bit. The archetypal enfant terrible who never grew up, by today's standards Randle was about as offensive as a kiss-me-quick hat in Harrogate. Yet for contemporary audiences, either thrilling to his

nerve or appalled by his vulgarity, he frequently stretched the limits of what was socially acceptable to breaking point.

Facially, Mr Punch personified, the outrageous Frank Randle took to the stage without a tooth in his head, though whether or not he had them pulled deliberately for professional purposes is open to debate. Either way, being dentally-challenged was certainly of use in the face-pulling department. And when he did open that mouth of his, Randle, as earthy as he was disarming, got away with much that would have seen lesser comics lynched. Once, when his act fell foul of the authorities in his hometown Blackpool, he is said to have gone up in an aeroplane and bombed the seafront with toilet rolls. At the start of each performance, he would stagger on stage clutching a beer bottle, apparently half-cut, while also carrying a lamp or some other municipal utility lifted from the street outside. 'Look what some damn fool left in t' road,' he would tell his appreciative and noisy crowd.

Born illegitimately as Arthur Hughes, later McEvoy, in Standish, Wigan, but raised in Blackpool, Randle's theatre debut came as a 15-year-old acrobat in 1916, under the lovely stagename Arthur Twist. In his jobbing early years, Randle also played the part of a strongman in a comic double act. It was as a solo comedian, however, that his notoriety really began to spread, although he had to wait a while yet for more widespread attention. In December 1934, his originality was noticed by the well-known local producer Jack Taylor, who belatedly pounced on a comedian he confidently predicted would become a major star. Taylor was right. By 1950, Frank Randle could claim to be Britain's highest-paid comedian and he was certainly the first to command regular earnings of £1,000 per week.

A sizeable lump of Randle's earning power came courtesy of his regular film appearances, of which more in a while. Then there was *Randle's Scandals*, his very own entrepreneurial touring company which played to huge audiences everywhere from the 1930s onwards. Indeed the very name of that show indicates that Randle was only too aware of the value of his controversial reputation. And behind the scenes he could be equally as fiery as an employer. Despite or maybe because of his own humble background, the law was laid down with gusto. Midway through the 1953-54 pantomime season, for example, he went so far as to sack twenty cast members after they had walked out in a pay dispute. They were lucky. Another to fall foul of Randle's capricious nature was the well-known drag comedian Gus Aubrey.

Born Edward Brown in Salford, 1909, the conspicuously gay Aubrey had, like Sandy Powell, originally been a boy soprano, before going on to join the *Randle's Scandals* troupe. Henceforth, he became a constant presence at Randle's side, whatever the medium. Unfortunately, Aubrey's flagrant homosexuality also marked him as a frequent target of the older man's withering humour, whether in public or private. In fact, Randle appears to have run poor Gus Aubrey ragged, often firing him several times in the same week and once, the story goes, persuading the hapless comic to extract his own teeth for the sake of his art, only to sack him again shortly afterwards.

The myths surrounding Frank Randle are many and varied, but there is no doubting his accomplishments as a comedian. And if any northern comic was a master of boisterous character-driven observational humour, rather than a ten-a-penny gagsmith, it was he. At his height, Randle had three favourite characters: the seaside boatman trying to attract customers; the knobbly-kneed old hiker; the incorrigible grandad. And to the particular dismay of Blackpool's puritanical chief of police, he got away with some quite blatantly outrageous innuendo because, much of the time, whatever his accompanying physical antics, he stuck to an, on the face of it, innocent and Lord Chamberlain-approved script. As Marie Lloyd had discovered all those years before, it wasn't so much the jokes that you told as the way that you told them.

Appropriately enough for such a mythological comedy figure, reports of Frank Randle's off-stage personality vary. Some describe him as a quiet and unassuming man, shy even, whose darker side manifested itself in the way he was almost driven mad with jealousy over the activities, real and imagined, of his loyal wife of thirty years, Queenie, whom he had trailed by private detectives every time she left the house. Others tell of loutish behaviour, with Randle often vanishing on drinking binges for days at a time with his equally enigmatic pal, the Irish tenor Josef Locke, leaving an understudy to pick up the pieces in the shows he left behind. On such occasions, drunken bouts of rage were the norm, and Randle smashed up many a dressing room. In short, he indulged a rock 'n' roll lifestyle before

anyone knew what rock 'n' roll was. And despite his possessiveness over Queenie, he is known to have had at least one extra-marital girlfriend, while also becoming infatuated with fast cars.

Maybe both versions are true and Randle's was the ultimate in spilt personalities. Certainly, a man who could set fire to pantomime scenery after a row with a theatre manager is clearly not a man marked by mental stability. A fact, of course, that did his wild and unpredictable public persona no harm at all.

Perhaps the roots of Randle's contrariness with theatre authorities lie in two episodes from the late 1930s. Despite their aforementioned childhood friendship, Randle's relationship with George Formby took on a distinctly frosty hue after both appeared in *King Fun*, a spectacular revue at the Blackpool Opera House in 1936; the crux of the problem being that the upstart second comic Randle had proved more popular with the public than his old mate, who was then soaring high on stage and screen. Career-wise, it had been the breakthrough of which Randle had dreamed. The price, though, was a relationship with Formby that would be strained for years to come. And the affair of Randle's next scheduled spot at the Opera House in 1940, two years after topping his first Blackpool bill at the North Pier Pavilion, was unhappier still.

In that instance, Randle was initially booked by Jack Taylor as his headline act; no mean achievement given that the show was also set to feature *Band Waggon* star Arthur Askey, as part of that programme's final stage tour. However, it seems that no one had thought to tell Askey about the risqué Randle's high-profile involvement. And once he did find out, advised by the great Lancastrian band leader and impresario Jack Hylton (who owned the *Band Waggon* stage rights), Askey threatened to pull the plug, worried that his wholesome reputation might be damaged by the vulgarity in his presence. Or maybe it was just fear that, like Formby before him, the man in the baggy khaki shorts, with a beer bottle in his hand and a bugle around his neck, might actually prove funnier than he was. Who knows? In any event, given the radio show's popularity, a simple business compromise was soon reached whereby Randle was paid £150 per week for staying out of the way. He never played a summer season at the Opera House again.

To say that both incidents left Frank Randle outraged would be an understatement. At times, the rebellious chip on his shoulder threatened to tip him over the edge completely. Certainly his attitude towards theatre managements deteriorated from that moment onward and he did little to enamour the legendary theatre owners Moss and Stoll, who kicked him off a tour when he swore at the audience at London's Shepherds Bush Empire. Randle also became a regular at Blackpool Magistrates Court, where he was prosecuted more than once for breaking the Sunday Observance Laws and using material that had not been anywhere near the Lord Chamberlain's seal of approval.

Nor can an increasing dependence on alcohol have helped. Yet while the effects of alcoholism derailed many another Variety comedian's career - who nowadays recalls the lanky Stafford-born eccentric Claude Lester, for example - the constant brushes with authority that it brought him had the opposite effect on Randle's standing. If anything, they reinforced the vicarious thrill of being in his company, especially for the working class northern audiences who continued to pour in by the thousands. 'By... I've supped some ale ter'neet,' he would proudly inform the menfolk in his audience. Women, meanwhile, seem by and large to have considered him a lovable rogue, no doubt making their own bedraggled husbands look like Douglas Fairbanks Jr. in comparison.

And for the public, Frank Randle was as entertaining away from the theatre as he was in it. He was seldom out of the headlines. There was the time, for instance, when the comedian, several pints the worse for wear after an all-night drinking session in his Central Pier dressing room, drove his car along the Blackpool tramline. Unfortunately, in doing so he collided with the tram that tootled up and down in the early hours of the morning, sweeping the tracks. When the police arrived, the paralytic prankster entertained his rescuers with a series of balletic pirouettes. On another occasion, the brave - or foolhardy, take your pick - management of Manchester's Hulme Hippodrome booked both Randle and Locke to appear together in Christmas pantomime, a task completed a mere four times in the entire run. The only thing Frank Randle didn't do, it seems, was eat someone's hamster. Lord knows what today's tabloid newspapers would have made of him.

Even the brightest sparks burn out eventually and, when Randle's health failed in the early 1950s, the fire in the belly of a man who, for

many of that era, remains as the funniest northern comedian ever, went with it. Most damagingly, despite one or two relatively subdued later Blackpool appearances - one of which, in 1955, bore the hopeful title *I'm A Good Boy Now* - Randle's worsening alcoholism had left him virtually unemployable and, with the shadows lengthening on a remarkable career, his remaining days took on a distinct air of repentance. He converted to Catholicism, the religion of his wife, Queenie, and after one period of recuperation in a sanatorium wrote a piece for the local paper detailing how the experience of collapsing after a show had made him 'a changed man'. He even embarked upon a final farewell tour that featured his last Blackpool appearance in February 1957. In the end, though, the effects of those hard-living years were not to be denied and a few months later, on 17 July, the inimitable Frank Randle died courtesy of a combination of TB, cirrhosis of the liver, pneumonia and acute gastritis.

By now bankrupt, Randle's pockets contained little in the way of cash; the Inland Revenue and years of missed income tax payments had seen to that. There was, however, a scrap of paper on which was written a poem. 'I got nothing that I asked for,' it began, 'but everything I had hoped for. Despite myself, my prayers were answered. I was among all men richly blessed.'

One of Blackpool's most colourful lights was extinguished but, with or without Frank Randle, the seaside resort to end all seaside resorts would illuminate Variety entertainment for quite a while yet. Indeed, far off in the future, Blackpool would be largely responsible for keeping the lungs of the genre pumping, long after it had seemed to flat-line elsewhere.

In his pomp, Frank Randle had been almost as integral to the town's good fortunes as the famous Blackpool tower itself which, along with the circus underneath, had first opened to the pubic in 1894. The new landmark, inspired by the Eiffel Tower built five years earlier for the International Exposition in Paris, was an instant phenomenon. On its opening day, over three thousand people paid 6d each to ascend the wondrous steel structure in order to take a vertiginous look at the ants below. Goodness knows how many millions of visitors have done so since. Trips to the summit were stopped for the duration of the Second

World War but resumed in 1946, by which time the Blackpool summer season, boasting twenty weeks of twice-nightly spectaculars featuring rafts of big name stars and showgirls, had become a working class institution.

Along with the chips, ice cream, candyfloss and amusement arcades of Blackpool's legendary Golden Mile, not to mention the bracing Irish Sea winds which rattled the timbers of the town's three piers, the brash and bubbly resort's lifeblood was comedy and, in particular, northern comedy. In fact, the traditional harshness of holiday weather was an important factor in Variety's success there, ensuring that enough folk would tire of frostbite and donkeys on the resort's endless stretch of sands and head indoors. As a result, Blackpool was home to a golden era for seaside entertainment right up to the 1960s.

It would not be going too far to suggest that, during this period, the place evolved into something of a mini-London when it came to making or breaking showbusiness reputations, particularly among northerners. On top of that, Blackpool developed a sub-culture and stage hierarchy all of its own, based in and around the town's myriad Variety venues, some of which are still with us, while a number - such as the Palace and Queens Theatres - have subsequently made way for department stores. Unlike success in the capital, though, making it big in Blackpool was not always a guarantee of national fame and fortune.

Compile a top fifty of Britain's best loved comedians over the past century and a half, and it is unlikely that either Dave Morris or Harry Korris will feature in it. Yet both were massively popular in their day, as evidenced by Morris's nickname, 'The Bard of Blackpool'. Where smut, sin and Frank Randle went together like buckets, spades and sandcastles, Dave Morris built his act on altogether more wholesome fare. And it was a philosophy that earned him an unsurpassed thirteen successive summer seasons.

That Morris scaled the heights he did was all the more remarkable given that he suffered badly with his health, a victim of chest difficulties and having been half-blinded in a World War One German gas attack while serving on the Western Front. In fact, he turned those handicaps to his advantage, and created a distinctive comedic presence in which he wore thick horn-rimmed spectacles, a smart suit and cheerful straw boater hat, all the while puffing on an enormous cigar. If the latter can't have done his breathing any good, it nevertheless left him with a deliciously rusty voice, later described by the Lancashire comedy historian Barry Band as sounding like 'gravel tumbling down a chute'.

Despite his celebrity, Morris - who was actually of working class Jewish stock in Middlesbrough - was very much a man of the people. He was frequently to be found in his favourite haunt, the promenade bar of the Clifton Hotel, where he sank his customary 'glass of wallop' and chatted amiably to friends and admirers alike. His journey to the stage had begun as an 11-year-old in 1906, when he won a talent contest and joined a juvenile troupe, 'The Stable Boys'. On the outbreak of the First World War he joined the Green Howards and was sent to France, where the gas attack already referred to led to several months in St. Dunstan's hospital for the blind. In later years, Morris would quietly become a patron of that organisation.

Upon his discharge from the Army in 1916, and with his eyesight only partially restored, Morris set off for Blackpool, where he was soon regularly engaged at Fred Waller's Palace of Varieties. Given that the town was home to the Royal Army Medical Corps at the time, Morris decided to put his own recent experience to good use and he began to perform a soldiering comedy act that was an immediate hit. Afterwards, he toured nationally for several years and met his wife Lil, a Lyons Corner House tea waitress, while appearing in Manchester in 1919.

The couple married in 1922 and embarked upon a decade that began as a financial struggle - Lil is said to have pawned her wedding ring to pay for Sunday dinner - but which ended with the purchase their first home, just up the railway line from Blackpool in Lytham St. Annes. Morris was to remain a Fylde Coast resident for the next quarter-century. Throughout the 1930s he became known - along with stooges Harry Vardon and brother-in-law Billy Smith - as a crowd-pulling turn who could be relied upon to bring the house down with his gently satirical yet good-natured verbal assassinations of local personalities including, most popularly, the town's notorious landladies. So much so that by 1939 Morris had reached the heady heights of joint-top of the bill in a touring revue at the Palace, *Too Funny For Words*.

In December of that year, an opportunity arose that cemented the reputation of Dave Morris as Blackpool's favourite 'local' comic. It came when Morris was visited in his dressing room by the celebrated impresario and music publisher Lawrence Wright, who offered Morris top billing in his summer season production of the following year, *On With The Show*, to be staged on the North Pier, a venue that, over the past two seasons, Frank Randle had made his own. Now, though, Randle had been lured away by Jack Taylor to star in what turned out to be his ill-fated revue alongside Arthur Askey at the Opera House. One man's loss is another man's fortune. Wright, quite rightly, saw Morris as the ideal man to fill the gap.

The comedian did not let him down. Despite a visual disability that meant the stage manager would occasionally have to rap on the floor three times with a stick if Morris strayed too close to the edge of the stage, six more consecutive seasons with Lawrence Wright followed. During which time, Morris also appeared in pantomime, winter Variety shows and broadcast locally on the BBC, completing a residential upgrade from St. Annes to Blackpool's affluent North Shore area in the process.

Although Dave Morris knew more than his fair share of tragedy in his private life - 20-year-old daughter Rene, one of four children, was killed in a car crash just one month after leaving for America as a GI bride in 1946 - his comedy star continued to climb. So much so that by 1947, shortly after sharing top billing with the loose-limbed Nat Jackley in Tom Arnold's Opera House revue *Ev'ry Time You Laugh*, he was self-assured enough to assume management of his own affairs. As the 1950s loomed, thus did *The Dave Morris Show* begin, a touring revue organised by the man himself and his family, who read to him from newspapers so that his gags might be as topical as possible. Being virtually blind, Morris never used scripts and preferred to memorise everything.

A further chance to increase his profile came via the opportunities offered by radio. Morris had already recorded comedy spots for the bandleader Geraldo's *Open House* at the BBC studios in Manchester, before reports surfaced of a weekly spot on the Light Programme's *Variety Fanfare*. His big chance for wireless fame, however, came after a beer-fuelled conversation in the bar of the Palace Theatre. It was with the man who would eventually become the controller of the BBC's north region, Robert Stead. The outcome was *Club Night*, an enormously popular show set in a northern working men's club that featured a range of clubland

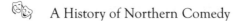

stereotypes from wise guy (Morris) to officious steward (Smith), from cadging Liverpudlian Wacker (played by Liverpool comedian Fred Ferris) to mournful henpecked husband Cedric (Joe Gladwin), best known for his 'only them as knows their own knows' catchphrase. In contrasting 'showbiz glamour' with ordinary working class northernness, Morris had hit upon a comic formula of formidable resonance and, as it now turns out, longevity.

Ever the shrewd and resourceful businessman, Morris soon realised that if *Club Night* took off as he hoped, then the Bolton-born impresario Jack Hylton would, true to form, seek to buy the stage rights from the BBC, just as he had with *Band Waggon* amongst others. So in a move typical of Morris's stubborn refusal to be a pawn in the big agents' game, he retained the rights to his own show, cutting Hylton off at the pass and anyone else who may have come sniffing around. In the short term at least, that spirit of independence paid off. When *Club Night* was staged on the South Pier in 1951, its profits duly went to Morris and his family bank account. Longer-term, this unwillingness to toe the usual showbiz line had more negative repercussions.

Not that the immediate radio residency of *Club Night* ran entirely without hitches either. For a start, Morris was unhappy with the BBC's insistence that, due to the so-called parochial nature of the show, it would only be understood in the north, an attitude which resulted in a refusal to repeat it on the Light Programme. This lack of a national audience upset Morris so much that, in January 1952, he scrapped *Club Night* entirely. A grand northern gesture indeed were it not for the fact that, later the same year, he returned to the radio airwaves at the helm of *Pull Up At Dave's*, a show set in a transport café on the Great North Road. This time, Morris put pragmatism ahead of northern non-conformity. Despite *Pull Up At Dave's* being to all intents and purposes pretty much the same show as *Club Night*, a wider array of accents were included and the 'new' Dave Morris vehicle duly took its place in the BBC Light Programme's starting line-up as intended. The nation at large could now appreciate this apparently common man with the common touch.

Meanwhile, back on the Variety stage and, in 1952, Morris decided to put his famous Blackpool summer season run on hold. After thirteen consecutive campaigns, he opted instead to take a new show on the road across the north, while also staging *Pull Up At Dave's* as a one-week-in-every-month stage production from June to September at the Palace of Varieties. Over the next two years, the live version of *Club Night* also rose like a phoenix from the ashes, resulting in the show finally winning the national Light Programme repeat that Morris had always fought for.

But, in April 1955, the true cost of going his own way in showbiz became painfully apparent. It came with the exciting news that, due to its pivotal position in the theatrical firmament, that year's Royal Variety Performance was to be staged at Blackpool's Opera House rather than in London. Astonishingly, however, the name of Dave Morris was nowhere to be seen on the bill. Given his local popularity, the decision to ignore one of Blackpool's favourite sons seemed perverse, especially given that the show was supposed to showcase and celebrate great northern stars like Albert Modley, George Formby, Arthur Askey, the legendary Tower Circus clown Charlie Cairoli and a radio comic who we shall meet anon, the incomparable Al Read. To appear in a Royal Variety Performance was, for a comedian, like being selected to play in a Cup Final; it was a prestigious reward for all your earlier hard work and confirmed your reputation as a giant of the game. Yet to the bewilderment of all, Morris had been rebuffed. As the Queen and Duke of Edinburgh looked down from the Royal Box, the underlying message was clear. Dave Morris had surrendered his place in the Establishment.

In truth, no one has ever been able to explain Morris's absence that evening, although the fact that the bill was put together by a certain Jack Hylton - rather than the Blackpool Tower Company itself - just may provide a clue. Royal protocol dictated that the matter could never be discussed in public and, patriotic to the end, Morris himself seldom if ever made reference to it. According to one later account by *News of the World* showbusiness reporter, Weston Taylor, however, Hylton offered Morris a three-minute walk- on with the Crazy Gang, a sextet of southern comedians comprised of three double acts including the well-known duo Flanagan and Allen, with the words: 'take it or leave it'. Insulted, Morris left it. A determination to fly solo had cost him his one and, as it turned out, only chance of a Royal Variety Performance.

Come July 1957, Morris was able to put the incident behind him when the BBC commissioned *Club Night* for its increasingly influential

television service. The programme's star was by now 62 years of age and the show, produced in Manchester, ran nationally for seven weeks before returning for a second series the following year. In fact, it proved so popular that Morris was invited to turn it into the Palace Theatre's summer season show of 1958, which he did to great acclaim. Alas, in as appalling a display of cultural vandalism as has ever been wreaked, all radio and television tapes of *Club Night* have long since wiped - a not uncommon fate, as we shall see.

More immediately, another Blackpool summer season - Morris's fourteenth - followed the *Club Night* revival, entitled, appropriately enough, *Dave's Back*. Again it was a huge hit, with the local *Gazette* declaring Morris to be: '...as much a part of the Blackpool holiday season as peppermint rock.' During its run, Morris and local scriptwriter Frank Roscoe were busy collaborating on yet another six-part television series, set to be called *The Artful Dodger*, in which Morris would play the work-shy central character. It took to the airwaves after the *Six O'Clock News* in September 1959, again to great critical acclaim.

Sadly, before his TV career could get properly underway, Morris suffered a massive stroke. After weeks spent in a Blackpool nursing home, he died one month short of his 65th birthday on 8 June 1960. As the BBC scriptwriter and producer Ronnie Taylor remarked in tribute, when it came to exaggerating the ordinary, '...Dave Morris was in a category all by himself'. Not until Brian Potter wheeled into view at the turn of the century would British comedy see anyone like him.

Dave Morris is a classic example of a comedian whose overt northernness and determination to play the game his own way led in some measure at least to historical obscurity, but he was by no means alone in his fate. Another name now all but lost to posterity is Harry Korris, albeit, in his case, for rather different reasons.

Korris, born on the Isle of Man in 1892, was 49 years old before finally being recognised as a nationally known figure. The key to that success was once again a radio show, *Happidrome*, which at the height of its run from 1941 to 1947 attracted some 12 million regular listeners. The 'Happidrome' in question was a small fictional theatre owned and managed by Mr. Sheridan Lovejoy, as played by Korris (born Corris) himself. Much of the comedy came from Lovejoy's ongoing battle of wits with his employees, namely the call-boy Enoch (Robbie Vincent - later replaced by the Bradford-born Elva Sheridan and renamed 'She-noch') and stage manager Ramsbottom (played by Cecil Frederick).

By the time radio fame called, Korris was already well established on the Blackpool circuit, primarily as a fixture of its *Arcadian Follies*, one of the pierrot shows that were so prevalent on many a seaside promenade and pier in the first half of the 20th century. Although, on the whole, such concert parties did not encourage star billing, from his first appearance on Blackpool's South Pier in 1931, Korris's bluff and jocund persona transcended the pierrot's quaint ruffled costume and silk skullcaps to confirm him as an engaging personality in his own right. Upon leaving the show in 1939, his place was taken by Albert Modley who, incidentally, had appeared in the original live *Happidrome* sketch in 1933. Having played with the concept once, *Happidrome* was an idea that would ferment in Korris's mind for years to come, while he headlined countless more Variety bills, wrote and performed in over a hundred regional radio broadcasts and even caught the attention of film companies keen to utilise the talents of the 'Falstaff of the South Pier' or, as the BBC's northern region promotional publicity had it, 'Blackpool's other Tower'.

When it came to live entertainment, not even the arrival of the Second World War could knock Harry Korris off his stride. Although a projected 1940 season in his hometown Douglas on the Isle of Man was now firmly out of bounds, the intended 'spectacular' was simply relocated to Blackpool's Grand Theatre, where he proved a smash hit. At first, the revue was to be called *Blackpool One*, a pun on the theatre's telephone number. But the wartime censor fretted that the title might contravene Government security guidelines and help any passing invader to gain his geographical bearings, so the name was changed to *It's A Funny Thing*, a favourite Harry Korris catchphrase. Less amusingly, the outbreak of War also meant that a lifelong ambition to see his name in lights was thwarted due to theatre frontage black-outs.

There was also a movie breakthrough to get excited about. It came when Korris appeared alongside Frank Randle in *Somewhere in England*,

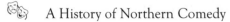

suitably premiered at Blackpool's Palace Pictures in August 1940. Yet if that was a thrill, it was as nothing when compared with what was to follow. At last, Korris's discussions with the BBC over his *Happidrome* project were about to firm into an actual programme. Nothing, though, could have prepared him for the impact his show would have on the British public once it finally aired in February 1941. Originally planned as a six-episode series, so popular did *Happidrome* prove that it remained in the Light Programme schedules for a full twelve months.

The show's theme tune, 'We Three in Happidrome', grew wildly popular, as did its characters and their ready supply of catchphrases. These included Enoch's 'let me tell you...' and 'take him away, Ramsbottom', along with Mr. Lovejoy's own tragi-comic lament, '...if ever a man suffered...'. And running through the knockabout fun was a detectable vein of showbusiness satire. Korris played Sheridan Lovejoy as a high and mighty former music hall act himself who, while puffing away on giant cigars, tried in vain to disguise his northern accent. One innovation that proved a major triumph was the decision to record the show in a genuine theatre before a live audience, allowing well-known guest stars to pop up as support acts on the 'Happidrome' bill.

The enthusiastic reaction to *Happidrome* was the cue for Korris and Company to take the show on the road, leading to inevitable runs in Blackpool and a 1942 season at the Prince of Wales Theatre in London's West End. More radio series followed too, the third of which ran from October 1945 to Boxing Day 1947. Harry Korris's future status as a British comedy institution was surely secure.

Then, in 1950, at the height of his powers and upon the closure of *Mr Lovejoy Goes to Paris*, a spin-off revue, the financially comfortable Harry Korris did the unthinkable - in showbusiness anyway - and retired. Just as suddenly as that.

Coming as it did on the brink of the television era, the decision to take it easy would cost the comedian hugely in terms of his subsequent impact on popular culture. Out of sight, he slipped quietly out of mind and, eventually, memory, never to return. Retirement did not, however, do his chances of personal survival any harm at all. With all professional pressures behind him, Harry Korris lived on into his late seventies. Before his death in 1971, his days were largely spent helping out local charities.

He also assisted his wife, Connie, in her six years spent working on Blackpool Council. Very occasionally, he was persuaded to deputise, reluctantly, for absent stars in their summer season shows. Otherwise, in the autumn of his life, showbiz to Harry Korris meant organising daytime family shows in smaller venues such as Fleetwood Pier, up the coast.

Along with a 1943 film version of *Happidrome* and that movie debut in 1940, Harry Korris also co-starred in a couple more Army-based films with Frank Randle, in which he played a kindly sergeant major. Yet if, for a brief while at least, Randle's pulling power matched that of his great rival George Formby, there is no doubt whatsoever about who would enjoy most prominent pride of place in any subsequent hall of fame.

So popular was George Formby over a forty-year career that took in twenty-one massively successful films, over 230 top-selling records, two Royal Command Performances, trips with ENSA (Entertainment's National Service Association) to entertain as many as three million servicemen and women during the Second World War in Europe and the Middle East, performances in Australia, New Zealand, South Africa and Canada and goodness knows how many stage shows in the UK, the words 'northern' and 'icon' barely do him justice. Yet, if his famous father had got his way, young George could have been riding the favourite in the 2.30 at Haydock.

It was nothing personal. Knowing showbusiness to be a cruel master, George Formby senior did not desire that fate for any of his seven children. The oldest to survive childbirth, George Hoy Booth, born 26 May 1904, was duly apprenticed as a jockey aged just seven years old. His first professional race came three years later, at which point the boy weighed in at a mighty 3st 13lbs. Unfortunately for his father's equine ambitions, but fortunately for him, Formby Jr. began to put on weight and soon grew too heavy for the saddle. And anyway, after his dad's sudden death in 1921, there was no longer any barrier to the stage. Encouraged by his mother, Eliza, George Formby Mark II set about following in the old man's illustrious footsteps.

In time, he would be helped considerably in that aim by the tireless energy of his formidable and infamous wife, Beryl, whom he met while performing in Castleford. Just as Eliza had been the rock upon which his

father's career was built, so did history repeat itself in this one-time clog dancer, who cut an elegant and formidable figure at George's side, with her insistence on running a tight financial ship and constant antagonism towards potential female competitors. Indeed, when George debuted in his first proper film, *Boots! Boots!* in 1934, Beryl insisted that his intended co-star in the production, a glamourous young actress named Betty Driver, should be replaced by herself - a stipulation adhered to, despite Betty's name still being included in the closing credits. These days, that same Betty Driver is a dab hand at Lancashire hot pot in the Rovers Return, a long-running star of the television soap opera *Coronation Street*. Beryl, meanwhile, handled all her husband's live Variety theatre bookings too, and even accompanied him on his trips abroad to entertain the troops.

As we have seen, gormless men and dominant women have been integral to both the style and content of northern comedy right from the start, a phenomenon for which Beryl was perhaps the latest and most obvious high-profile embodiment. And if it isn't wives, it is mothers-in-law, those fearsome wife figures times ten. That said, although these days they are most often associated with northern humour of a particular era, such jokes have never really been geographically or time specific at all. In fact, digs at the mother-in-law have been around since the first century AD at least, when the Roman satirist Juvenal is said to have rocked his audiences with the following: 'Give up all hope of peace while your mother-in-law is alive'. It can be no coincidence, though, that when this particular facet of British humour was given its most frequent expression in the 20th century, it was in the clubs, cobbled streets and naughty seaside postcards of England's north.

Whether in the work of Formby (senior or junior), Albert Modley, Les Dawson, Bobby - the Little Waster - Thompson, or many another funnyman across several generations, northern comedians have reliably portrayed women as 'the boss'. It is a stereotype, of course, but one which is nevertheless grounded in reality. For decades, your average working class male's prime responsibility was either to find work or do it, ahead of bringing home the money, via the pub, club or bookies if he could get away with it. His wife, meanwhile, was expected to run the family home, usually on the most meagre of financial resources, all the while keeping superfluous spending to a minimum. And even when it was necessary for a woman to go out and work herself - a not uncommon fate - it was usually in some poorly-paid factory or mill job, with domestic duties still waiting on her return.

So, given a simultaneous tendency towards self-deprecation on the part of northern and almost inevitably male comedians, perhaps it should come as no surprise that when such a scenario was pushed to its logical comedic extreme, men were left looking like juvenile or even infantile selfish fools, while women took on the role of domineering and often physically larger control freaks. Whether we are talking about Flo, Andy Capp's newspaper cartoon missus, waiting, arms folded, with the rolling pin in *The Daily Mirror*, or Bobby Thompson's wife feeding him his tea with a baby's bottle, the theme of strong woman and weak feckless man became a comedy staple not quite shaken from the popular imagination to this day (particularly, it seems, in television advertising). Even within the parameters of a relatively more modern and realistic sitcom like *The Likely Lads*, Rodney Bewes's Bob spent much of his homelife constantly being nagged by Brigit Forsyth's Thelma, while James Bolam's single man Terry provided a perfect symbol of what men might get up to if left to their own devices. A couple of decades later, Victoria Wood would offer a subtly different take on the marital power struggle with her very witty song, 'Let's Do It', in which wife Freda, trapped and bored, longs for thrills and excitement while her brow-beaten other half Barry yearns only for a quiet life.

Back in George Formby's day, at least, northern working class women were strong because they had to be. And while, again, that was hardly a phenomenon restricted to the north, the fact remains that women were more obviously central to the region's social structure. Down in London, impersonal national capital and bubbling financial melting pot that it was, the rules of social interaction were being dictated by blokes in suits, or so it seemed on the surface. The establishment world was a man's world - maybe that is why such supposedly 'male' characteristics as aggression, political activism, open intellectualism and flamboyant self-promotion became such defining features of southern comedy. Or maybe not. Either way, up north, in communities that were more blatantly matriarchal, more complex 'feminine' notions of strength and importance - albeit as seen and expressed largely through male eyes and voices - held sway.

But what about George? Well, operating under his mother's maiden

name on the advice of Scottish music hall legend Harry Lauder, the young master Hoy's first tentative steps into showbusiness gave no hint of the phenomenal fame to follow. Using his father's material and stage clothes, but losing the trademark cough, he was by all accounts awful and frequently spent long periods 'resting'. Until his marriage to Beryl in 1924, that is. At that point, and with the nuptials barely completed, there came both a change of stage name and one of those little twists of fate upon which many a fable is constructed. After working with a performer who passed his time between shows playing a banjo ukulele, Formby fell in love with the instrument and bought it for the princely sum of £2. 10s. It was a wise investment. He swiftly learned to play his new toy and, for a bet, included it in his act at Barnsley. From that moment on, George Formby and his rudely symbolic little ukulele - or banjulele to be strictly accurate - were inseparable.

Ah, the ukulele. As a metaphor for the inadequacies of its owner, has any comedic accessory ever been more inspired? Blithe ineptitude; an over-eagerness to please; childlike innocence edging towards irritating childishness; a stunted libido; all of it there in every pluck. With his instrument in his hand, the grinner from Wigan went on to perform around three hundred songs, a good number of which were co-written by himself. Mostly, they were notable for a brand of sexually dubious innuendo that passed largely unnoticed, springing as it did from such an unthreatening source. One such was 'Oh, Dear Mother': 'I called round last night, my best girl to see. Felt in such a plight when she sat on my knee. Oh, dear Mother, well I didn't know what to do. Oh, dear Mother, we shared the same chair too. She clung to me both hard and fast. And thought her chance had come at last. But oh, dear Mother, well I didn't know what to do.'

George Formby's first big hit record, 'Do De O Do', was made with the Jack Hylton Band in 1932, although the title track was widely ignored in favour of its 'B' side, 'Chinese Blues'. George - or maybe it was Beryl - took the hint and renamed the song 'Chinese Laundry Blues', complete with a certain Mr. Wu, whereafter it soon became known as the Formby signature tune: 'He's got a naughty eye that flickers. You ought to see it wobble when he's ironing ladies... blouses.'

Most significantly career-wise, four years later, Formby released *No Limit*, his fifth film by then and the first of eleven made for the producer

In't It Grand When You're Daft?

Basil Dean, whose Associated Talking Pictures company would later be transformed into Ealing Studios. The upshot being that by the time war broke out, George Formby was Britain's highest paid entertainer, with estimated earnings of over £100,000 a year. Nor was that the end of it. In 1942, a seven-film contract with Columbia netted him the astronomical figure at the time of £500,000. Despite his wealth, when Formby wasn't shooting pictures or away on tour, he pitched in as a corporal dispatch rider in the Blackpool Home Guard.

Formby's bankability as a wartime movie star owed much to his wide-mouthed, toothy charisma, of course. Equally important, though, was the warm reassurance that his films provided in a cynical world growing ever more cold and violent beyond the cinema doors. The plots were as predictable as fairy tales. George falls for girl. George hits trouble with bad guys. George vanquishes bad guys and somehow muddles through. George gets girl, grins to camera and chuckles: 'turned out nice again!'. Throw in a few cheeky songs and there you had it. In the 1940 offering, *Let George Do It*, for example, widely considered to be Formby's best, our hero takes the wrong boat and finds himself in Norway, ahead of a Nazi invasion. Cue slapstick and mayhem. At one point, George even manages to grapple *mit der fuehrer* himself, all the while cracking his daft little jokes about Wigan. Given the brutal reality of what was actually going on out there in the real world, you don't have to be a paid-up member of the George Formby Appreciation Society to note a degree of spiritual bravery in that, even if it is in inverse proportion to the subtlety of the humour employed. In the event of future occupation, it is certainly reasonable to suppose that this latest Formby fra' Wigan would have been straight up against the wall.

The determinedly upbeat mood was even more explicit in the title of one of the best-loved songs in *Let George Do It*, 'Count Your Blessings and Smile'. Having appeared in a George Formby film, such tunes would go on to sell in their tens of millions, whether as shellac 78s - in the days before LP records - or as sheet, I said 'sheet', music. Indeed, many are still popular with those of a certain generation - 'Leaning On A Lamp Post', 'The Window Cleaner' and the downright pornographic 'My Little Stick of Blackpool Rock' ('...it may be sticky but I never complain, it's nice to have a nibble at it now and again...') to name but three.

That lucrative move to Columbia Pictures notwithstanding, George

Formby's film career took a sharp nosedive when global hostilities ended. The nation, it seemed, no longer needed quite so much cheering up. He even had a run-in with Clement Atlee's new Labour Government who, George claimed, were taking away nearly all his savings in exorbitantly high income tax, a state of affairs that saw him temporarily go 'on strike' in terms of performing in the UK. 'Why should I work for tanners?' he asked, before later allowing one theatre to pay him with a new lounge carpet rather than his usual fee.

Elsewhere, the Formby star glittered as brightly as ever. There were tours to Australia, Canada, Japan and Denmark amongst other exotic places and, in 1951, he won a starring role in Emile Littler's massively successful West End musical, *Zip Goes A Million*, based on the play *Brewster's Millions*. Unfortunately, six months after it opened, Formby suffered a heart attack, bringing his involvement with the enterprise to a close. Displaying the resilience of his father and with Beryl nursing him around the clock, he battled back to fitness and, two years later, returned with a much lighter schedule of one-nighters, pantomimes, occasional television appearances and those ubiquitous seaside summer shows.

But as the 1950s progressed it was Beryl's health that now began to fail with what would, in time, be diagnosed as leukaemia. George, for his part, struggled on alone, making what would turn out to be his last record, 'Happy Go Lucky Me', as the decade came to a close. That was followed, in December 1960, by a final appearance on television - a medium that he wasn't really around long enough to milk to its full potential - on the BBC's *The Friday Show*. The programme in question took the form of a one-man confessional, in which George recognised Beryl's profound influence on his career and admitted that, despite his huge personal fortune, he was basically illiterate and couldn't read music. The comedian also revealed how he deeply regretted never having had any children. Beryl, looking on from her sickbed at home on the Fylde coast, died soon afterwards, on Christmas Eve.

It was the end of a rock-solid if occasionally turbulent partnership that, to outsiders at least, had seemed more like a business arrangement than a marriage at times. Yet if anyone assumed that, without Beryl, George Formby would fall apart, they were soon to be surprised. In fact, he did nothing of the sort. Just weeks after Beryl's sad demise, George instead announced his engagement to a 36-year-old schoolteacher named Pat Howson. To a fair proportion of his astonished public, the timing seemed scandalously insensitive. Not unreasonably, however, the man himself insisted that he was merely looking for a companion, someone to 'give me a bit of happiness in what years I have left'.

In normal circumstances, seeing as how he was only 56 at the time, the end to which Formby referred should still have been some way off. Yet, sadly, the statement proved worse than sadly prophetic as the couple's planned spring wedding never materialised. While eating a roast duck dinner at his fiancée's Preston home, Formby received a second visit from what he always referred to as 'Mr. CT' - Coronary Thrombosis - and was rushed into hospital. At first, he again appeared to make progress. But then, ten days later, on 6 March 1961, he suffered a relapse and died. After his funeral in a tiny church near Liverpool, George Formby was buried in the family grave at Warrington's Catholic cemetery. An estimated 100,000 mourners turned out to say goodbye.

Forget her supposed Roman origins, the fabled goddess Britannia was quite obviously of northern stock. How so? Look on in shock and awe as Gracie Fields marches imperiously through the pre-war streets of Lancashire, trailing mill workers and a passing brass band in her wake, as she belts out the title song of *Sing As We Go*, a film which defines her contribution to British popular culture absolutely. All that is missing is a trident and a rather dopey lion. 'Hey! Who are you shovin'…?'.

Co-scripted by the Bradford-born novelist JB Priestley and one of the first British films ever to be shot on location, *Sing As We Go* is more than just a charming snapshot of life in 1934. It allows us to grasp immediately the appeal of a classic working class battler, a woman who epitomised every indefatigable quality that the British liked to imagine in themselves. Playing a redundant Lancashire mill girl who heads west to Blackpool in search of work, Fields's performance is rich in spontaneity and humour. It is the final scene, though, in which 'Our Gracie' leads her fellow workers back to the re-opened Greybeck mill, while warbling her rousing refrain, that best illustrates the effect she had on a public desperate for hope and confidence in a period of darkest depression. In a life that

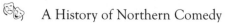

began in the back streets of Rochdale and finished on the sunshine isle of Capri, she made the country laugh and, along with Vera Lynne and Anne Shelton, sing too. As she moved from music hall to Hollywood and back again, the nation could not take its eyes off her.

The enormous popularity enjoyed by Gracie Fields could hardly be put down to conventional glamour. For in comparison with other female movie stars of the day, this one time cotton mill girl was, physically, rather plain. Nor was she the proud possessor of a sexy and alluring voice. True, Gracie could deliver a perfectly-pitched operatic soprano when called for, but it was for her singalong choruses and quirky comic ditties that she was most cherished. Blessed with a vocal range that began somewhere down near croaky bullfrog in squeaking clog and veered giddily towards a top note that could make a whippet wince, she didn't so much sing songs as purge herself of them, like some cheerfully demented foghorn. Certainly, no pane of glass within a five-mile radius was secure until she had been safely moved along. And to complete a formidable musical repertoire, she had a whistle on her like an industrial-strength kettle.

Gracie's chief attribute, however, was her warm and simultaneously down-to-earth personality. Audiences were on her side the second she opened her mouth. In a fantasy celluloid world where just about every other actress came complete with a Mayfair accent, Our Gracie was, if not a breath of fresh air exactly, then certainly a smokey gust of authenticity. Like George Formby, the transparently working-class Fields wouldn't have known pomposity if it had hit her in the gob. And also like Formby, her amiable and plucky brand of north country 'Englishness' transcended all boundaries of class, gender and geography entirely.

Born above a Rochdale chip shop in 1898, as a child, Gracie Stansfield - alas, no relation to latterday Rochdalian chanteuse Lisa - took her first theatrical steps at the instigation of a stage-struck mother. By her teenage years, she was already touring the music halls, in between working shifts at the local mill. Such openly ambitious behaviour caused quite a stir, it is said, leading to accusations from neighbours that young Gracie was 'getting above her station'. Unperturbed by such petty smallmindedness, Mrs Stansfield simply chopped her daughter's surname back to more manageable proportions and supported her talented offspring well into young adulthood.

In't It Grand When You're Daft?

Maternal influence, though, can only push a person so far. The major upturn in Gracie's fortunes came via her relationship with the Cockney comedian Archie Pitt, whom she met in 1915 and married in 1923. Though he was, by all accounts, no great shakes in the rib-tickling department, Pitt did have a habit of staging very popular touring revues. It was whilst headlining in one such, *Mr Tower of London*, which reached London's West End in the early-to-mid-1920s and wherein she first played a lass called Sally Perkins, that Gracie Fields really began to catch the eye of the right people. Also part of that production, incidentally, was Gracie's younger brother Thomas. Born in 1908, Tommy Fields too was destined to become well known as a comedian and pantomime dame, although with nothing like the impact of his sister. But then again, Formby apart, who did? It was in a Pitt revue that Gracie and Tommy's sister, Edie, met her own future husband, the zany Douglas 'Duggie' Wakefield. Before his death in 1951, Wakefield - actually born in Hull in 1901 - was best known as the leader of a slapstick gang named Four Boys From Manchester (hilarious catchphrase alert: 'We're acrobats - I'm acro, they're bats').

For all that it helped to make her an immediate stage sensation, for Gracie, emotionally, the marriage to Archie Pitt seems quickly to have become a joyless and barren one. Instead, over the next decade, she threw her efforts into further establishing herself as a major entertainer, on stage and in the recording studio. She made the first of an eventual ten Royal Variety Show appearances in 1925 and sold out venues up and down the land. Upon turning to cinema, her popularity hit new heights with the release in 1931 of *Sally In Our Alley*, her debut film made by Basil Dean's Associated Talking Pictures.

Movies and Gracie Fields were a perfect match, even if a measure of audience rapport and her trademark spontaneity were diminished in the process. As with George Formby, her subsequent success owed much to ATP's liking for easily recognisable signature tunes. Songs such as 'Sally', 'Wish Me Luck As You Wave me Goodbye', 'Singing in the Bath Tub' and 'The Biggest Aspidistra in the World' became as widely recognisable as air-raid sirens.

On screen, then, no problem. Off it, life was not quite so smooth. Where gormless George had slotted into movie acting with apparent ease, Fields was a far more reluctant participant - film-making's emphasis on

hard work and strict timekeeping reminded her far too much of the Rochdale cotton mills of her youth, thank you very much. Nor were she and her Croydon-born producer/director Basil Dean the best of pals. No doubt, that was at least partially down to Gracie's reluctance to play the celluloid game, a fact which handily ensured that the price of her services remained high. Not that the paying public noticed any of this. Between 1931 and 1939, Gracie Fields appeared in eleven hugely popular British-made films in total, including the aforementioned *Sing As We Go*, *Look Up and Laugh* - in which Duggie Wakefield also took one of several bit-parts - and *Keep Smiling*.

With the approach of World War Two, few could match Gracie's ability to captivate an audience and she was duly given the freedom of Rochdale in 1937. Away from the public glare, however, her marriage to Archie Pitt was tilting badly. During the making of the film *Queen of Hearts* in 1936, she met and fell in love with an Italian director named Monty Banks, a development that, while bringing her great happiness, would also herald a period of great turmoil and controversy.

Ironically, things started to go wrong for Gracie at the very height of her popularity. In 1939, she developed cancer of the cervix and was only given a fifty per cent chance of survival. The extent to which she had by now captured the public affection was clearly shown in the half-a-million-plus get well soon cards sent to her hospital bed. National newspapers, pandering to the public mood, circled. Feature writers penned heartfelt and melancholy columns assessing the implications of her imminent demise; photographers were dispatched to wait on the pavement outside; political cartoonists sketched symbolic representations of her desperate plight. Britons everywhere, on the verge of another fearful war and already low on optimism, held their breath.

Yet in her own hour of need, Gracie still had that legendary fighting spirit to call upon. Its origins, perhaps, laid in a traumatic episode during her childhood when, as a 12-year-old performing in music hall under the name 'Miss Gracie Stansfield - Rochdale's Talented Child Singer', her first professional tour had ended in sexual assault, after which she was hospitalised for six weeks. Whether at her own instigation or that of her mother, once physically recovered, the young Gracie was soon back up on stage, displaying the same defiantly determined grit that was to become such a distinctive feature of her work ever after. Behind all the superficial bluster, however, the incident had left the deepest of psychological scars. As an adult, Gracie Fields paid for the upkeep and running of a Sussex orphanage for around thirty years.

Meanwhile, back in 1939, and Britain's reaction to Gracie's brave victory over cervical cancer might best be described as euphoric. It wasn't long, however, before the mood, like the skies over Europe, began to darken. A diagnosis of full recovery was on condition that the entertainer should take a two-year rest from her previously workaholic schedule. The place for that recuperation, it turned out, would be Capri, the Italian island in the Bay of Naples upon which Gracie and loveable rogue Banks - whom, upon divorcing Archie Pitt, she wed in 1940 - made their home. It is a geographical association that still attracts tourists to this day.

Upon the outbreak of hostilities, Gracie cut her initial stay on Capri short. In doing so, she also packed her mother and other family members off to America - ostensibly for health reasons - and headed straight back to the UK. Whilst there, she embarked on a morale-boosting if gruelling tour. It coincided, though, with a major new complication. With the imminent entry of Italy into the war, her husband - an Italian resident - ran the serious risk of being interned if he remained on British soil. The couple opted to avoid that possibility by leaving for Canada, on the rather flimsy excuse that they were off to raise funds for war charities.

Whatever the motivation, the move damaged Gracie's reputation enormously. Overnight, she went from pinny-clad, public-spirited patriot to pariah as the press, already whipping itself into a state of indignant frenzy over stars supposedly fleeing the country, attacked her without mercy. Stopping just short of branding their former sweetheart a deserter, her true motives, they claimed, were finance and fear. True to form, although stung by the accusations, Gracie took the criticism as a direct challenge. Henceforth, no entertainer would be more blatantly patriotic than she. As a result, many of the world's most treacherous war zones - in both hemispheres - were soon echoing to her unmistakeable tones. Not that the British newspapers took notice. They carried on in much the same malign way, obliging no less a figure than Prime Minister Winston Churchill to stand up in the House of Commons and insist that: 'the press must stop this vilification of Miss Fields'. Giving more than a hint

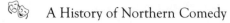

that the British public weren't completely taken in by the media hysteria, while residing in Canada, Fields made a further four films in Hollywood that enjoyed modest success despite her supposed infamy.

As the War moved towards its conclusion, so did Gracie Fields brave the home reaction and return to her roots. She toured factories and armed forces bases, and found broadcasting work in radio. Initially, the still-affronted media stayed on her case, but her audiences proved more forgiving, especially after a show-stealing return to the London Palladium in 1948. Telling no one of the opening song she intended to perform, Gracie walked on stage to a polite ripple of applause. Yet by the time she had concluded her immaculate version of 'La Vie en Rose' - a paean to the healing powers of forgiveness with its famous opening line: 'Take me to your heart again...' - the most hard-hearted of her critics were said to have had tears rolling down their cheeks. If anyone knew how to work an audience, it was Gracie Fields.

Nevertheless, the times and public taste were moving on. And with the Second World War finally over, a battle-weary and more cynical population needed to look forward, not back. Never again would Gracie or any other entertainer bask in such unquestioning, cross-generational mass adoration. By the time Monty Banks died in 1950, in appropriately dramatic fashion of a heart attack on the Orient Express, Gracie's film career had already hit the buffers. More happily, she soon met and married a third husband, Boris Alperovici, a fellow resident of Capri.

In later years, though her public appearances became much less frequent, Gracie Fields made a number of one-off forays into television, occasionally appearing on ITV's popular religious entertainment show *Stars on Sunday* in the 1970s. She also made what turned out to be her last Royal Variety appearance, aged 80. Mainly, though, Our Gracie chose to stay at home in the Bay of Naples. And it was there that this earthy Lancashire lass who, at one point in her life, had been one of the three highest-earning entertainers in the world, died of a heart attack in 1979, shortly after being made a Dame of the British Empire.

Her death also came one year after the lady herself formally opened the Gracie Fields Theatre in Rochdale, an event also attended by, amongst others, Sandy Powell.

4
Of Jollywood and Hollywood

"Let a fellow try to outsmart his audience and he misses..."
- *Stan Laurel*

When Basil Dean lured George Formby south, along with an early turn as a ten-year-old jockey in a 1915 silent called *By The Shortest of Heads*, everyone's favourite window cleaner had made two low-budget films, *Boots! Boots!* (1934) and *Off The Dole!* (1935). The producer in both cases had been John E. Blakeley, head of an organisation called the Mancunian Film Corporation which, in its day, enabled many a northern music hall or Variety comedian to take the leap from stage to screen, Frank Randle and Harry Korris among them.

George Formby first encountered Blakeley in Warrington in 1933, when the Lancashire-born entrepreneur knocked on his theatre dressing room door. Shortly afterwards, *Boots! Boots!* went into production. In it, Formby reprised his father's John Willie character, albeit with a few twists of his own. The film was based around a script that George and Beryl had written in tandem with a fellow performer, Arthur Mertz. And if the phrase 'went into production' sounds in any way glamourous, the reality was otherwise. The film cost peanuts to make and was shot in a room above a garage in Camden Town, London. No matter. Such was Formby's profile that the public flocked to see it anyway, smashing many a box office record as they did so. When its follow-up, *Off The Dole!*, directed by Mertz, performed equally well, George was duly whisked off to bigger and better things by Dean in Ealing. John E. Blakeley, meanwhile, knew that there were plenty more where Formby had come from.

Born in the Manchester suburb of Ardwick in 1888, Blakeley was the son of a man who had also dabbled in cinema ownership and film rental when the lights dimmed and the reels took their first blurred and jumpy turns in the late-nineteenth century. At which point, and before we continue along Blakeley's particular strand in our tale, we are probably overdue a broadsweep look at the history of film so far. Once again, it seems, it is a story in which the northern England's role has most often been unsung.

Conventional wisdom has it that, after the first public display of a cinematographe by France's Lumiere brothers in 1895, the first major motion picture, *The Great Train Robbery*, arrived in 1903, for which audiences were kept pinned to their seats for a buttock-numbing eight minutes. Henceforth, sex, excitement and laughter were the primary popularisers of the new invention and the first internationally recognised 'stars' in the latter genre were the Keystone Kops, a slapstick comedy troupe produced by the Canadian film-maker Mack Sennett. And when, in 1911, the first studio was opened in the sleepy Los Angeles district of Hollywood, California, the USA was very firmly in the box seat. Which is all well and good, but what about Blackburn and Holmfirth?

For, as revealed in a couple of BBC TV documentary series, *The Lost World Of Mitchell And Kenyon* and *Holmfirth Hollywood*, originally shown in 2005 and 2006 respectively, a fair number of the world's earliest box office smashes, on both sides of the Atlantic, were in fact filmed there.

Take *The Lost World Of Mitchell And Kenyon*, in which it was revealed that over eight hundred rolls of early nitrate negatives, made by photographic pioneers Sagar Mitchell and James Kenyon, had lain undiscovered for at least seventy years in sealed churns in an uninhabited Blackburn basement. When building work again brought them to light in 1994, the negatives were rescued by an astonished local historian named Peter Worden. In 2000, Worden handed over his find to the British Film

Institute in order to enable safer preservation. Here was evidence of a thriving commercial film industry long before Los Angeles got in on the act. And thanks to the business acumen of messrs Mitchell and Kenyon, its original epicentre was 22 Clayton Street, Blackburn, followed by the partnership's later premises at 40 Northgate, the derelict shop at which the nitrates reappeared. Mulholland Drive it wasn't, but what the heck.

Mitchell and Kenyon seem to have realised quite quickly that there was money to be made in moving images. Moving, for modern audiences, in both senses of the word. Once carefully restored, those forgotten rolls of negatives revealed stunningly clear 'documentary' scenes of mill workers pouring through factory gates, assorted religious parades and excitable early sports crowds. In terms of narrative stories, the partners were also responsible for some of the genre's first attempts at comedy. Operating under the trade name Norden, their subsequent one-reelers mostly continued the already age-old music hall tradition of cocking a snoop at authority. Policemen were often the butt of its necessarily visual humour. In *Diving Lucy* (1903), for example, the local bobby is lured into a park pond ducking by a pair of protruding cardboard legs in the water.

Meanwhile, over the hills in Yorkshire, Steve Webb's *Holmfirth Hollywood* told of how a family called the Bamforths - destined to win greater notoriety for saucy seaside postcards - had also been international comedy pioneers, and from a still earlier date: 1890. Yes, some five years before the Lumieres first set up shop in the basement of the Grand Café on the Boulevard des Capucines, local businessman James Bamforth (until then a painter and decorator) was already establishing himself as one of the world's most prolific producers of magic lantern slide shows. In essence, these were a succession of still photos shown on a large screen to musical accompaniment. With the development of the Cinematograph camera, followed by the first movie projector soon after, the Bamforth's big screen ambitions gathered pace.

As with Mitchell and Kenyon, the Bamforths' very earliest moving pictures amounted to reportage; brief snatches of everyday social activity, shown in music halls, theatres and fairgrounds, intended to make money from the public's curiosity at seeing itself in action. The first, *Men Leaving The Factory*, lasted one minute and nine seconds. Soon, Bamforth realised that the new medium might also be used to tell morality tales, already the

staple ingredient of his magic lantern shows. And, in due course, the
world's first recognisably northern silent comedy shimmered into view,
albeit at just over a minute in length. Its title is *Weary Willie* (1898) and it
tells the story of a tramp who uses his own pungency and the snobbery of
a group of well-dressed park-goers to grab their bench for himself. With its
broad humour, gurning faces and distinct lack of reverence for 'the Man',
the story of this particular little tramp preceded Charlie Chaplin's by
some fifteen years.

That said, there was nothing particularly revolutionary in having a
tramp as the star in either case. The downtrodden hobo was something
of a stock character by the turn of the nineteenth century. For sure,
Bamforth's Weary Willie was based upon a tramp of that name created
by the cartoon illustrator Tom Browne. From 1896, Browne's Weary
Willie had appeared in comic strip form in *Illustrated Chips* and hung
around in one form or another until 1953. The character became
particularly popular in America where, from the 1920s, he was both
drawn and played on stage and screen by the circus clown Emmett Kelly.

But back to Holmfirth, and one of the most fascinating aspects of
his early films was the extent to which the racy storylines contrasted with
Bamforth's temperance-led Victorian lantern shows. Back then, good
little girls praying to Jesus were a running motif. Now, the distinctive
whiff of low music hall was apparent. Why? Pure economic pragmatism.
The canny Bamforth had long since learned that, unless they were in
church, northern audiences would not be preached at.

It was not just about the north, however. For Bamforth and
innovators like him, the absence of language meant that silent movies
held the promise of a more universal appeal. Consequently, they were
thought of as a potential goldmine, a fact much later borne out by the
cross-cultural successes of, say, Jacques Tati's Monsieur Hulot and Rowan
Atkinson's Mr Bean. And just to help Bamforth's films a little further
down the populist road, they included some of the earliest displays of
what might now be seen as northern comedy's unreconstructed political
incorrectness. In *Women's Rights* (1899), for example, the 'trouble causers'
of the suffragette movement are ridiculed mercilessly when two gossiping
housewives have their skirts nailed to a fence.

Alas for Bamforth, if not social progress, the financial windfall that he had anticipated remained stubbornly unforthcoming. So, in 1902, he brought his moving picture concern to a halt and concentrated instead on those aforementioned postcards, an already proven money maker. The Bamforth family's film history, though, was far from over. As movies grew in length and popularity over the next decade and audiences became more sophisticated in their tastes, so the emphasis switched to America where, by 1915, a burgeoning star system saw Mary Pickford become the highest paid female actor in the world and Chaplin the best paid man. In Britain, Hollywood's glamourising influence drove the introduction, in 1909, of the nation's first dedicated cinemas, each of them hungry for suitable films to project. And once again, that did not pass unnoticed in Holmfirth. Despite initially having agreed with his father's decision to knock film-making on the head, since James Bamforth's death in 1911 his son, Edwin, had grown increasingly keen to revive that part of the family business. And comedies, it seemed, were particularly popular. So, in 1914, the Bamforths again set about producing a few of their own.

The star of the show this time was a tousle-haired chap named Winky - so named because of his trademark cheeky wink to camera. As broadcast on *Holmfirth Hollywood*, the earliest surviving example of his work is *Winky Causes A Panic*. In it, our man, real name Reggie Schwitz, finds a bear suit which he uses to wreak havoc and steal some free booze. Winky, or 'The New King of Picture Comedians', as he is officially billed, looks suitably northern and gormless, and is yet another tramp figure blessed with an infectious grin. Although still silent, by now moving pictures were punctuated with title cards, on which was written occasional snippets of dialogue, such as the following from *Winky's Ruse*: 'Will you spare a poor chap a sup of cold tea, lady?'. In the same year as Charlie Chaplin began to appear as the Little Tramp across the Atlantic, *Winky's Ruse* was already Winky's seventh known film. As a forerunner to another childlike figure destined to grace the cobbled streets of Holmfirth sixty-odd years hence - Compo from Britain's longest-running situation comedy *Last Of The Summer Wine* - Reggie Schwitz's Winky eventually appeared in over fifty films in all. There's obviously something in them there hills.

Nor did Winky have the screen to himself back then. In what was still a fledgling medium, the Bamforth's took the financially cautious and

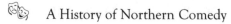

geographically sensible decision to develop its own repertory troupe of actors. And from that merry band there emerged a rival for the Winky crown. His name was Alf Foy and he was primarily known for waddling around in a pigeon-toed stoop with his arse sticking out. The talking heads on *Hollywood Holmfirth* seemed to favour Foy's antics over those of Winky, but it must be a close-run thing. True, Foy was surreal and zany in a more recognisably modern way. But how can anyone not love a man who, when ordered to sweep the chimney by his wife, simply nicks a load of chickens and throws them up it?

Come World War One, the Bamforth's movie-making business was really in its stride. And the film that turned out to be Winky's last, *Sharps And Flats*, was marked by the same use of double entendre that would later characterise the films of George Formby junior and Old Mother Riley, among many others. Here, Winky played a draft dodger, ironically enough, given that in real life the actor playing him was also about to go missing, albeit in rather more enigmatic fashion. In attempting to explain Schwitz's subsequent disappearance, *Holmfirth Hollywood* posits a couple of plausible theories. The first was that the actor's Germanic surname had rendered him box office poison, causing the Bamforths to drop him like stale tripe, whereafter the man himself simply vanished into wartime obscurity. A second, more romantic suggestion is that Schwitz eloped to Australia with a Bamforth leading lady named Lily Ward, who was already married to another of Winky's fellow comics. Given the cockiness of those saucy winks to camera at the close of every picture, it would be nice to believe the latter.

Whatever Winky's fate, for Bamforths and many another pioneering British film production company, international hostilities soon brought their growing confidence and business promise crashing to a halt. When male actors began to depart for the Front and money ran low, Hollywood increasingly began to look too big and powerful a competitor for these relatively little firms. As before, Edwin Bamforth took his family back to the safe haven of postcards - only this time for keeps. Nor, in Blackburn, could Sagar Mitchell and James Kenyon compete with such financial American clout. The pair closed for business in 1913, before returning to their separate interests. Although Kenyon died in 1925, Mitchell lived on to the ripe old age of 85, before passing away in 1952.

Although the effects of World War One and a subsequent boom in the US movie industry were too much for many an independent British company to handle, for individual performers who could avoid Europe's battlefields it was a time of great opportunity.

Not that all of them would have necessarily realised that, of course. Like so many other music hall turns, when Charlie Chaplin set sail for the States in 1910, for example, with or without George Formby senior's stage props in his suitcase, he was no doubt hoping to do little more than try out an already successful British act in American Vaudeville. The fact is, however, that upon reaching New York City, those out-sized boots of his were planted firmly on the right side of the ocean.

As, when he finally realised it, would be Arthur Stanley Jefferson, a co-passenger of Chaplin's eventually to find fame as Stan Laurel. This red-haired comedy technician par excellence had lived and breathed the stage from his earliest years. Born in 1890 in the Lancashire town of Ulverston, now in the county of Cumbria on the northern edge of Morecambe Bay, his father was a well-known actor-manager and his mother a singer. Young Stan's dad was no slouch as a character comedian and scriptwriter, and he also built a reputation as a theatrical entrepreneur. Over time, Arthur Jefferson senior opened a string of theatres across the north of England and Scotland, a lifestyle that involved moving his family to North Shields, on England's north east coast, when Stan was aged just seven. It was, however, to be Jefferson's Glasgow venue - the Metropole Theatre - that proved most crucial to his stagestruck son's future. For it was there, when a teenager, that a nervous Stan presented his card to one of the most successful showbiz impresarios of the day, Fred Westcot, also known as the legendary Fred Karno. The showman was suitably impressed and Stan Laurel departed for London in 1909.

Karno, a former stage performer himself, was born in Exeter but raised in Nottingham. As a comedy guru of the highest order, he is widely credited with creating the custard pie in the face gag, among many other slapstick staples. His anarchic acrobatic gangshows not only made him a fortune, they brought world fame the phrase 'Fred Karno's Army', used to describe a shambolic group of people, into the English language. Less happily, in his private life Karno is said to have been a brutal, unfaithful

dictator of a husband, who practically burst the springs on his casting couch. Yet as Stan Laurel - understudy to Charlie Chaplin in the same troupe - discovered, a comedian could benefit hugely from his patronage. For one thing, it got him on the same trip as Chaplin and fourteen other members of Karno's company when, in 1910, they went to tour America.

For Chaplin at least, the journey would herald big things. After making an astonishing impression on the Vaudeville stage, in 1913 the Little Tramp answered a call from Mack Sennett and scuttled off to Tinseltown. By which point, an unhappy and possibly homesick Stan had gone back to England in the summer of 1911. The return was temporary. Realising that life for a struggling comedian in Britain was grimmer than he had recalled, the following year he rejoined Karno's troupe in the USA and this time, elected to stay; a timely decision given the ominous rumblings in Europe.

Success, though, did not come quickly. For the immediate future, working life for Stan meant a series of ill-fated double acts and Vaudeville bit parts that kept him in employment but hardly set the world alight. In 1917, however, all that began to change. For that was the year in which the jobbing comic appeared in *Nuts In May*, shot in Hollywood and, all the available surviving evidence suggests, his very first film. From there onward, Stan Laurel - and no one is quite sure exactly how the new *nom de plume* came about - was a regular if usually low key presence on movie screens. It wasn't until he and a certain Oliver Norvell Hardy signed separate contracts for the American director Hal Roach in 1925 that his cinematic fate was truly sealed.

Ironically, the pair - Stan thin, Ollie fat - had already appeared in one film together by then, in the same year that Fred Karno went bankrupt, 1921. The Vitagraph Pictures short was called *The Lucky Dog*. In it, a boater-hatted Stan - bearing an uncanny resemblance to Holmfirth's Alf Foy, funnily enough - befriends a troublesome stray canine with predictably comical results. No one at the time was thinking in terms of a permanent partnership and the amiable Georgia-born 'Babe', as Hardy was widely known, had only a small role as a villain who tries to separate Stan from his wallet. In fact, it was half a decade more before the Hal Roach Studios cast the boys together again, in *Forty Five Minutes From Hollywood*, made in 1926. That heralded a further spurt of comedies in which they appeared together separately, so to speak, before the duo was officially born as Laurel and Hardy in the 1927 silent film *Duck Soup* (not to be confused with the later Marx Brothers offering). The suggestion of a proper screen partnership is often credited to the film's supervisor, Leo McCarey, although Hal Roach was never slow to take praise for the idea himself. Either way, it was by any definition inspired.

A pair of small-time incompetent losers, with pompous tie-twiddling Ollie but a tiptoe up the food chain from his mewling sidekick Stan, Laurel and Hardy's enormous popularity was rooted squarely in the stock music hall theme of the embattled 'little' guy taking on the world. The same was true of Chaplin's tramp. However there, if the subsequent critical reaction is to be believed, the similarities end. As a rule, more high-minded metropolitan critics have detected something satisfyingly artistic and intellectual in the London-born Chaplin's comedy; even his knockabout slapstick is described as being akin to ballet. As the creative force behind Laurel and Hardy, the humour of Lancashire's Stan Laurel is for some reason felt to be lower brow, not so complex and therefore much less worthy of serious attention.

Although Chaplin's earliest films brim with a physicality and pathos born of his Victorian music hall roots (his first full-length feature *The Kid,* in 1920, cloys like bubblegum on a sun-scorched pavement), the response to his later work in particular is usually admiration for its pioneering qualities and overt intelligence rather than genuine hilarity. Belly laughs, for modern audiences at least, are few and far between. In his earliest two-reelers, Chaplin's iconic tramp was just a stock music hall figure, bringing chaos to an otherwise ordered world. Later, and certainly by the time of his silent movie swansong *Modern Times* in 1936, Chaplin had reversed that idea and his films became more blatantly satirical and political. With the coming of the talkies and his courageous 1940 masterpiece, *The Great Dictator,* a quite brilliant parody of Nazi Germany, in which Chaplin was inspirational as Adenoid Hynkel, this was no longer 'just comedy'.

Stan Laurel, meanwhile, seems merely to view the world as one big cosmic joke. Yes, life can be relentlessly unkind and is apt to dump on Laurel and Hardy from a very great height. But both he and his bumptious, exasperated pal have little choice but to accept it for what it is and struggle along anyhow, making the best of things. The prospect of

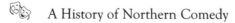

change is remote and if you can't change a situation, well, why not just laugh at it instead? In other words, Chaplin, of desperately poor South London stock, born to a mentally ill mother and the victim of an impoverished childhood characterised by spells in the dreaded workhouse, seems inclined to meet indignity head on. If there's a bully in the way, comedy will help him to flatten and publicly vanquish it. For the very northern Stan Laurel, all sense of social critique is buried at a deeper, more instinctive and subtle level, where it might even appear not to exist at all. When all is said and done, whatever horrors are thrown at you, the most important thing is to not to show you are hurt. If the audience wants to look for greater complexity then by all means let it but, as Laurel himself once put it: '...we were just two-reel comics. That wasn't art.'

He was wrong, of course. Art is precisely what it was. If comedy is first and foremost a psychological coping mechanism - and it is - then Laurel and Hardy films, whether the boys knew it or not, were as profound an insight into the human condition as anything by Ingmar Bergman or Jean-Luc Godard, while being a good deal more amusing too. How about the habitual ploy of deliberately pointing up a gag - usually involving physical and mental pain for Ollie - well before it actually occurs? Tack on the floor? Ollie, in his stockinged feet, will inevitably step on it, won't he? Of course he will. Now, keep watching and he will do exactly the same thing again. And again. It would have done Samuel Beckett proud.

In Laurel and Hardy's world, just as in our own, repetition is the natural order of things. They and we never learn. Physical pain, futile endeavours, social and sexual confusion and, yes, even nagging wives are borne like afflictions, yet hope will always triumph over experience. It has to be that way, otherwise we would have no option but to jump under the nearest passing train. In the appeal on Ollie's face as he looks direct to camera, struggling vainly to retain some last shred of dignity in the face of Stan's - it can't possibly be his own - stupidity, don't we see a reflection of our own bewilderment? And, in the films generally, how about the subversive notion that despite the surface appearance of class, etiquette and confidence of those in authority, everyone is just as clueless as everyone else when you really get down to it?

With the advent of Al Jolson's *Jazz Singer* in 1927 and cinematic sound, Laurel and Hardy suddenly had another, equally magnificent, string to their bow. Fortunately, and unlike Chaplin, their voices seemed perfectly suited to their image and a first talkie, *Unaccustomed As We Are*, was duly released two years later. Even allowing for an ongoing supply of visual gags bearing the influence of Fred Karno, Mack Sennett and, more often than not, Arthur Jefferson senior, the playful misuse of language would henceforth be another recurring feature of the pair's comedy. In 1932's *Towed in a Hole*, for example, in which the boys play a couple of fish salesmen, an uncharacteristically brilliant idea from Stan unravels completely once Ollie asks him to repeat it. 'You know Ollie, I've been thinking.' 'What about?' 'I know how we could make a lot more money.' 'How?' 'Well, if we caught our own fish we wouldn't have to pay for it. Then whoever we sold it to, it would be clear profit.' 'Tell me that again.' 'Well, if you caught a fish, and whoever you sold it to they wouldn't have to pay for it. Then the profits would... they'd go to the fish....'. Then, of course, there are the Hardy catchphrases - '...here's another nice mess you've gotten me into..' etc - usually accompanied by a cluster bomb prod of spread fingers, or the supremely pained: 'Why... don't... you... do... something... to... help... me?'.

In 1931, under the auspices of Metro Goldwyn Mayer, Laurel and Hardy made *Pardon Us*, their first feature-length movie. Directed by James Parrott, it began a series of MGM classics that would eventually assume all-time great status. These included *Pack Up Your Troubles* (1932), *Sons of the Desert* (1933), *Our Relations* (1936) and *Way Out West* (1937), more often than not preceded by the duo's legendary 'Cuckoo Song' signature tune. Yet by the time the latter film was released, newspaper reports suggested that the duo's personal relationship had grown strained. Certainly, workaholic Stan seems to have earned twice as much as Ollie who, once filming was over, would head off straight to the golf course or home to one of seven wives in eight marriages that the pair managed to accumulate between them. Given how, creatively, Stan was undoubtedly the driving force, such a financial arrangement was no doubt justified. Even so, it did run the risk of upsetting an otherwise happy apple cart, bearing in mind Ollie's crucially charismatic on-screen contribution.

In public, Oliver Hardy always reacted to such talk with a straight bat.

'If Stan says it's funny, I do it,' he said. And in the pair's latter years, they appear to have rubbed along well enough. In Bruce Crowther's book, *Laurel and Hardy - Clown Princes of Comedy*, the British ventriloquist Ray Alan recalls a gem of an exchange from 1954, when he met the duo backstage on the last of four rapturously received UK tours, a full twenty-two years after Laurel and Hardy's first trip back to Stan's northern English roots:

> '...."Was it true that at one time you and Stan didn't talk to each other?" [asks Alan]. Hardy chuckles and calls for Stan, who is in an adjoining dressing room with the doors open between the two. "Hey, Stan! Ray's just mentioned when we didn't talk. Do you remember when we read about that in the paper and you said to me, 'hey, look, we're not talking, it says so here in the paper?'.." "Yes, I remember that. Didn't we have a row over something? Wasn't it something to do with my second wife - weren't you going to run away with her?" "I don't know, something like that." "Or didn't I complain that you were on the golf course and never came to rehearse?" "Yeah, I think so. I know we didn't talk to each other. It said so in the paper."...'

Echoes there surely of the patter in *Sons of the Desert*, when Ollie asks: 'do you have to ask your wife everything?' To which Stan replies: '...well, if I didn't ask her, I wouldn't know what she wanted me to do.'

After leaving MGM in 1938, with the notable exception of *A Chump At Oxford* made for United Artists the following year, Stan and Ollie's film career hit a downward curve. Always one to bridle at Hal Roach's control-freakery, Stan did achieve greater creative independence by launching the pair's own production company but it came at a cost. Although he could now negotiate his own deals with studios, the development was not a success. A tired procession of mediocrity ensued until, in 1951, the big screen contribution of cinema's finest comedy double act fizzed to a desperately unworthy end with the distressingly poor *Atoll K*, or *Utopia* as it is occasionally and inappropriately known. In it, the now aged 'boys' appear older and wearier than the jokes. Stan looked particularly adrift, suffering with prostate problems and heat-induced dysentery throughout.

An otherwise exceptional film career was over but worse was still to come. Isn't it always? Five years later, with the pair still dreaming of an unlikely comeback, each suffered a stroke within months of the other. Thankfully, Stan's was relatively mild. His former partner, however, was far more seriously affected. Bed-ridden from that moment onward until, after a period of great suffering undeserved by a man who had spent so much of his life spreading such joy, the trials of Oliver Norvell Hardy mercifully reached their end in 1957. He was buried in north Hollywood. To widespread surprise, but on the orders of a doctor, Stan did not attend the funeral, insisting that: 'Babe would understand'. Despite his own brush with mortality, Stan recovered fully and lived on for another eight years in a modest Santa Monica apartment by the sea, wherein he spent his last few reels responding to letters from fans the world over and dreaming up routines that would never be performed. Until, in 1965, the 74-year-old Stan Laurel suffered a second and this time fatal heart attack. He too was buried beneath the Californian sunshine. Meanwhile, some five-and-a-half-thousand miles away in rainy Ulverston, a Laurel and Hardy Museum was opened which remains as popular today as it ever was.

It doesn't always rain in the north west of England. Sometimes it just feels that way. Which was good news for a British cinema industry that, despite Hollywood's burgeoning empire, could still produce homegrown stars of its own. And which brings us neatly back to John E. Blakeley.

Out of a total population of some 46 million, domestic cinema admissions hit an impressive 20 million per week in the 1930s. True, much of that hard-earned box-office cash filtered into the wallets of US film moguls. And true, the gangs of kids who rampaged like Visigoths to the local Odeon or Gaumont every Saturday morning did mainly hoop and holler their way through the adventures of such all-American heroes as the Lone Ranger and Flash Gordon, or were held spellbound by the transatlantic appeal of Shirley Temple, Mickey Mouse and the Little Rascals. Nevertheless, with war imminent, homelier talents like George Formby, Gracie Fields and the Crazy Gang were, as we have seen, also enormously popular. Thanks in no small part to the vision of Blakeley, so were a whole roster of other comics drawn largely from the backstreets of England's north.

Whenever the story of British cinema is told, Shepperton, Pinewood and Elstree are the studios that not unreasonably loom largest. Yet in pre-war, inter-war and post-war days, another thriving and often overlooked studio did its bit to keep the public entertained. Making up in vibrancy for what it lacked in polish, it found a regional and transient niche that, for a while anyway, meant the Mancunian Film Corporation was king.

For owner John E. Blakeley, those two early features with George Formby had proved to be huge moneyspinners; clear confirmation that here was a gap in the market waiting to be plugged. With Formby having departed to ATP and Blakeley increasingly in the director's chair, in a bid to repeat the formula he turned to the ukulele man's great rival, Frank Randle. The idea worked a treat. Randle, after all, was not just a technically gifted funnyman, he attracted more attention than a bag of aniseed balls in a kennel. Equally useful was his near-the-knuckle earthiness. Randle spoke directly to the very same northern working class audiences that the Homburg-wearing 'Pop' Blakeley had set so firmly in his sights.

More of a mixed blessing was the fact that, while much of Blakeley's output was conceived, filmed and edited up north (a few early efforts notwithstanding, including Formby's, which were shot in rented space at London's Albany Studios), Mancunian films were most often ignored by the southern-based critics and Establishment alike. The plus side of this, though, was that in contrast to the aesthetic and ideological restraints placed on more mainstream London-based productions, when it came to dealing with issues like sexuality, gender and class, Frank Randle and his comical co-stars could get away with murder.

Over time, John E. Blakeley's cinematic repertory company went on to feature a small army of northern music hall eccentrics; Sandy Powell, Gus Aubrey, Dan Young, 'Duggie' Wakefield, Harry Korris and, of course, Randle himself among them. Another regular was Dave Morris's 1947 Blackpool Opera House partner Nat Jackley, a surreal and loose-limbed Sunderland-born oddball who spent a fair proportion of his time on stage dressed as a snooker table.

Born Nathaniel Jackley-Hirsch into a family of entertainers in 1909, initially, the young Nat Jackley played straight man to the comedian Jack Clifford. Inevitably, given Jackley's unusual physicality, the roles were soon switched. Along with his beanpole frame, telescopic rubber neck and what became known as his 'educated' legs, Jackley also developed a bizarre (and entirely fake) speech impediment which sounded not unlike someone struggling with a lisp, whilst simultaneously attempting to flick a toffee from the roof of their mouth with their tongue. Although, eventually, Jackley left Clifford to go solo, he was soon performing with a wide variety of other stooges, including his second wife Marianne Lincoln and Norman Wisdom's future straight man, the Middlesbrough-born Jerry Desmonde, whose pompous know-all stage personality had been honed alongside the Brum-born 'comedian's comedian' Sid Field. Alas, the cruel vagaries of showbiz fashion. Owing mainly to the absence of recorded material, Field's public reputation is now all-but overlooked. And when Desmonde died, equally forgotten in 1967, he was working as a taxi driver. Somewhat ironically, that was the very same year in which rock and roll's own music hall comics, the Beatles, cast his former stage partner as 'Happy Nat the Rubber Man' in their self-consciously bizarre film, *Magical Mystery Tour*.

Though never quite reaching the realms of comedy superstardom, Nat Jackley nevertheless enjoyed a long and varied career in which he made an unusually wiry pantomime dame throughout no less than fifty pantos, not to mention a couple of BBC TV specials under the name *Nat's In The Belfry* with wife Marianne in 1956. Indeed, by September 1988, he had forged a second career as a television character actor.

That was a fate he shared with another star of the Mancunian Film Corporation, the magnificently irascible Jimmy Jewel, one half of the enormously popular and long-standing double act, Jewel and Warriss. The story goes that, as first cousins, Jimmy Jewel and Ben Warriss were not only born in the same Sheffield house, they were born in the very same bed, albeit three years apart in 1906 and 1909 respectively. Both were the sons of entertainers and, as a result, regularly performed together as sailor-suited toddlers in the family living room. Some forty years later, for John E. Blakeley, they and Frank Randle featured in *What A Carry On!* (1949), pre-dating an altogether different series of films under that title entirely.

After a couple of modestly successful solo careers of their own -

Jimmy's London debut came in 1925, whilst Ben's was made five years later - the pair first teamed up professionally in Newcastle in 1934. The launch of a bona fide double act proved a real turning point and by the early 1950s Jewel and Warriss were the highest-paid comedy duo in the country, going on to perform thirteen Blackpool summer seasons and seven Royal Variety Performances. Like Jackley and many other entertainers of their period, they also became regulars on the pantomime circuit, usually as a couple of robbers - one good, one bad - as in the 1949 production of *Babes in the Wood* at Manchester's Palace Theatre and the London Palladium a year later.

It was the wireless, though, that really turned Jewel and Warriss into household names. From 1947 to 1952, their series *Up The Pole* was a mainstay of radio's glory years, catapulting 'that crazy couple' into the national consciousness. Sounding not unlike an anglicised Abbott and Costello - an American double act with all the verbal dexterity of Laurel and Hardy and none of their heart - Jewell and Warriss were the classic smooth guy and childlike simpleton. The silver-tongued Warriss and his velvety tones provided an aural counterpoint to Jewel's zany and, to begin with, almost effeminate brand of vocal bufoonery. More often than not their material creaked like an old barn door - heard today it is marginally less hilarious than swine flu. But in the UK at least their crackpot style won a dedicated following. A bid to break America flopped horribly when the duo was introduced on the *Ed Sullivan Show* as 'Jewels and Walrus'.

As the appeal of radio Variety waned so did the pair's desire to work together. Even so, they continued to put on a united front in public and, in the 1950s, had a brief flirtation with television before deciding, maybe prematurely, that the new medium was not for them. After kicking their heels on the wireless for a few years, they eventually and acrimoniously split for good in 1966, whereupon Warriss ran a restaurant in Bath before being coaxed back on stage as a straight actor. Finally reconciled with his cousin, he died in 1993. Two years later, Jimmy Jewel too was gone, but not before he had further branded his hangdog looks on the rump of national popular culture through the medium of television after all. More on that later, along with the stories of how two more Blakeley Babes, Jimmy James and Norman Evans, made equally valuable contributions to the evolution of British comedy.

But for now let's return to our movie mogul Blakeley. So popular did his films prove, particularly with northern audiences, that by 1947 he felt confident enough to gamble an enormous sum for the times, £70,000, on turning an old Wesleyan church in Rusholme, a suburb of Manchester, into bona fide studios. To an extent, his hand was forced. The widespread boom in film production had led to a dramatic rise in London studio costs. Yet it was still an innovative development. Rather unimaginatively named Film Studios (Manchester) Ltd, the place was soon re-christened the 'Fun Factory' or 'Jollywood' by local residents.

Launched with a grand fanfare, the new facility opened on 12th May 1947 with a ceremony attended by a number of the stars associated with the company. Frank Randle, by now on the board of directors, was there, as was Sandy Powell who, along with George Formby, made a speech wishing the studios well. In the event, this brave new era lasted precisely six years and kicked off with *Cup Tie Honeymoon*, a musical burlesque timed to coincide with the opening of the 1948 football season, that starred Powell, Dan Young, Betty Jumel and a certain Pat Pilkington, later Phoenix, who, as Elsie Tanner, was destined to find future fame in *Coronation Street*. As indeed was another young actor named Bernard Youens who, after appearing in the company's second production, *The International Circus Revue*, went on to win great notoriety as Stan Ogden.

Of all the Mancunian Film stars, however, it was Randle who was by far the biggest. And although his screen persona was very much a toned-down version of the devil he took on stage, his cheeky edge still gave Blakeley his biggest pay days. Randle made ten Mancunian films in total, with *Somewhere In England*, *Holidays With Pay* and the pun-tastic *School For Randle* three of the best-known. If they noticed them at all, London's middle class film critics tended to sneer at the hackneyed, rambling plots. But, so what? The public lapped them up and artistic concerns were never much part of John E. Blakeley's philosophy. It was quite straightforward. Give the star comedian enough room to reproduce what he did on stage and the money would surely flow in. And so it did until *It's A Grand Life*, the last of twenty two Mancunian Film Corporation pictures in all, gave Randle his final movie appearance in 1953.

By then, with films increasingly feeling the pressure from the upstart

television, cinema audiences appeared to be on a rapid downward spiral into permanent decline. Blakeley was ready for retirement anyway, and his Manchester studios were sold to the BBC who, for a time, used them as a base for regional outside broadcasts. In 1958, after a short illness, John E. Blakeley died. His Rusholme studios were demolished in 1967.

Owing to its restricted geographical and cultural ambitions it was perhaps inevitable that the Mancunian Film Corporation would become a relic of its time. With a fair wind, Frank Randle at least may have had the ability and charisma to become an international star. The parochial horizons of Mancunian, however, ensured that this was never really likely to happen.

Nevertheless, Blakeley's productions did provide a platform for a number of other performers to go on and enjoy bigger and better things. These included Britain's answer to Marilyn Monroe, Diana Dors, who in 1953 had starred with Randle in his final feature. The incomparable 'Two Ton' Tessie O'Shea got her start there too, as did Jack 'Dixon of Dock Green' Warner and the diminutive 'schoolboy' comic, Jimmy Clitheroe.

Before appearing with Frank Randle in the Mancunian feature *Somewhere in Politics* (1949), Jimmy Clitheroe had also played stooge to another British comedic institution, the drag artist Arthur Lucan, whose first shot at the cinematic big time came in 1936. The name of that film was *Stars On Parade* and its cast also included Jimmy James, Albert Whelan and Robb Wilton. Lucan, for his part, took on the role of Mrs O'Flynn, an Irish washerwoman. Precisely one year later, in Lucan's second movie outing and at the insistence of a screenwriter called Con West, the name of the crone was changed to Old Mother Riley.

Born in Boston, Lincolnshire, in 1885, legend has it that Arthur Towle adopted the name Lucan after spotting a horse-drawn milk float bearing that moniker. To begin with, he had been just a run-of-the-mill provincial music hall turn but, after appearing in panto in Dublin as Jack Horner's mother, the penny dropped and in came similarly unglamorous women's clothing. As Old Mother Riley, the cantankerous single parent of headstrong daughter Kitty, a girl ahead of her time played by Lucan's own young wife Kitty McShane, he struck a socially astute chord with

116

adults and children alike. When spotted by Variety impresario Dennis J Clarke at the Argyle Theatre, Birkenhead, a place on the bill of the 1934 Royal Variety Performance followed, along with a fifteen-film series which ran from 1937 to 1952. Old Mother Riley was also a big hit on radio and even featured in a couple of comic strips in the *Radio Times* and *Film Fun* magazines.

Upon reflection, the old bird's popularity with children may not be so remarkable. On one level, the malapropistic Old Mother Riley was a silly old grandma figure, prone to comical outbursts when her supposed authority was crossed but ultimately well-meaning: 'I'll give you a party! I'll open a tin of sardines.' Her frightful appearance and an apparent urge to smash every piece of crockery in sight did not make her scary, it just emphasised her anarchic craziness. Essentially, Old Mother Riley's unruly grotesquery was simply harmless slapstick; the equivalent of a pantomime decorating sketch. And on top of that, in the films anyway, there was her penchant for purveying her services like some superannuated superhero - whether it be as a private eye, headmistress or circus owner - ever ready to put the big bad world to rights. Children, fearful and ignored in the shadow of overbearing adult brutality, like that sort of thing.

Yet peek beneath the surface of the slapstick and there is a darker, more covertly political side to Arthur Lucan's comedy too. For a start, many of Old Mother Riley's conversations with Kitty are the stuff of 'sixties kitchen sink comedy. 'Did he kiss you?', she asks, worried, after her daughter returns late from a date. 'Yes, I liked it and kissed him back.' 'Come over.... where did he kiss you?' 'Between the Post Office and the railway station.' And what is there in this perennial underdog's ongoing struggle with slum-living, poverty and domestic violence but admiration for the indefatigability of her class and a clarion call for greater social justice? As so often in northern comedy, in the midst of broadness we are in subtlety.

Perhaps the film that best sums up Old Mother Riley's contribution is the 1938 offering, *Old Mother Riley MP*, in which our eponymous hero runs for parliament in order to stop her former employer knocking down the neighbourhood. After some typically manic shenanigans, she duly takes a seat in the House of Commons where her impassioned speeches see her promoted to the Cabinet. Once there, she somehow secures the

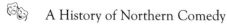

repayment of a foreign loan, thereby providing full employment for a grateful nation. In Arthur Lucan's final film, meanwhile, *Old Mother Riley meets the Vampire*, made in 1952 with the character now deeply in decline, she merely had to deal with a terminally bemused Bela Lugosi.

Away from the public glare, Lucan's partnership with Kitty McShane - whom he had met and married in Dublin while she was only 15-years-old - was every bit as tempestuous off-stage as the fictional relationship was on it. Still, if the fall-out from their arguments ever spilled over into the actual performance, it no doubt benefitted the act. Various reports describe Lucan as an alcoholic who the allegedly nymphomaniac Kitty taunted cruelly about his impotence. Others insist that Lucan was an incorrigible womaniser. Either way, after their marriage ended in 1951, Lucan is said to have given his ex-wife threequarters of his income when she lost a fortune investing in an ill-fated beauty salon.

Arthur Lucan made his last stage appearance as Old Mother Riley at Barnsley's Royal Theatre on 14th May 1954. By then, his life was riddled with loneliness, stress, bankruptcy and booze. The final curtain, when it came, dropped three days later. Minutes before a scheduled performance at the Tivoli Theatre, Hull, the comedian collapsed in the wings and died in his dressing room shortly afterwards. Undeterred, Lucan's understudy Frank Seton donned Old Mother Riley's famous little black hat, blond wig and shawl, and played a couple of repeat performances to audiences who were unaware of the real star's demise. The show must go on.

When telephoned with the tragic news by the theatre management, Kitty is said to have enquired where the tragedy had occurred. 'Hull,' she was told. To which the reply came: 'Typical!'. Arthur Lucan fell in Hull and in Hull he remains, buried in the city's cemetery. Around ten years later, when found dead at her London home, Kitty joined him in the same graveyard.

Another northern-born entertainer who made the most of the lucrative growth of talking pictures throughout the 1930s and 'forties was the bumbling, blustering and bespectacled Will Hay.

Born William Thomson Hay in Stockton-on-Tees, as a young man he appeared destined for a life in industry rather than showbusiness. During his formative years, Hay and his family relocated - via Lowestoft, Hemel

Hempstead and London - to Manchester, where his father established a successful engineering company. Upon leaving school, Hay, a bright and inquisitive pupil, declined the opportunity to work at his father's firm but did serve as an apprentice engineer elsewhere in the city. After tiring of that trade, he taught himself French, German and Italian and found employment as a translator for the Calico Printers Association. In 1908, at 19 years of age, he married his 16-year-old girlfriend, Gladys Perkins. It wasn't long before the couple had produced their first child, also called Gladys. A traditional life of steady work and happy families lay spread out before him.

Secretly, however, Hay had long harboured an ambition to perform on stage. And eventually, with the support of his wife, he plucked up enough courage to give music hall comedy a go. While hunting around for suitable material, he recalled the humourous classroom tales of his sister, Eppie, a teacher in the Manchester suburb of Cheetham Hill. Hay worked her stories of how unruly pupils were asked to come to the front and 'bend down' into a comical musical routine. The phenomenon of his inept and dotty schoolmaster was up and running.

Like many an artist who swaps the security of a regular pay packet for the uncertainty of following a vocation, for Hay, early married life was a hand-to-mouth existence. So when, in 1914, a successful audition at the Palace Theatre, Manchester, led to a year of paid acting work, it was a welcome development. Better, though, was to come. During the course of that year, Hay met and worked with the touring Fred Karno's Army. Karno was so impressed with Hay that he invited him to join his troupe, thereby beginning a four-year spell in which the young comedian grew in confidence and built an impressive reputation. Upon going his own way in 1920, Hay further developed his early classroom idea, this time as a fully-blown comedy sketch in which the roles were actually acted out by a troupe of fellow comics, rather than just made into the lyrics of a song. He called that sketch 'The Fourth Form at St Michael's' and had a first big hit on his hands.

Will Hay's Variety career, then, had finally begun to bloom. So much so that, in 1925, Hay and his 'Fourth Form' team, which by now included two real-life nephews, were invited to perform before King George V and Queen Mary at that year's Royal Variety Performance in Leicester Square,

London. He embarked on tours of Australia, America and South Africa, the latter enabling Hay, as bright as his best-known character was dumb, to add Afrikaans to his list of spoken languages. He formed an unlikely friendship with Edward the Prince of Wales too, frequently being called upon to entertain at private gatherings or parties at Windsor Castle. His son, Will Jr, was also brought into the act.

Successful as it was, Will Hay's growing stage profile was as nothing on the impact he would soon have on radio and, most especially, film. His first moving picture appearance had already taken place in 1922, when a short sequence from his Variety show, *Listening In*, was committed to celluloid. Over ten years later, he also appeared in a Pathé short, *Know Your Apples*. However, it was with his starring role in *Those Were The Days*, a 1934 adaptation of Sir Arthur Pinero's play *The Magistrate*, that the cinematic die was truly cast. At the grand old age of 46, Will Hay's box office smashes came thick and fast from that point onward.

As in the theatre, Hay's on-screen persona was grounded squarely in a lack of self-awareness, that grand old comic tradition in which authority figures are completely unable to grasp just what an ass they really are. That was certainly the case when Hay reprised his schoolmaster's role with the release of *Boys Will Be Boys* for Gainsborough Pictures in 1935, and it continued in further Gainsborough smash hits like *Where There's A Will* and *Good Morning, Boys* in the years ahead. Yet Will Hay had far more under his mortarboard than a simple classroom mentality. In his expert hands, any professional figure was rendered shifty, stupid and dissolute, whether it be a barrister, policeman, prison governor or, in what is widely regarded as his finest work, the 1937 classic *Oh, Mr Porter!*, untrustworthy railway stationmaster.

Co-written by Val Guest and the serial monologuist Marriot Edgar, upon its release *Oh, Mr Porter!* took an astonishing half a million pounds. In it, Hay was cast as the typically incompetent William Porter, the new man in charge at Buggleskelly, an Irish country railway station. His co-stars were a couple of actors with whom Hay had first appeared in *Windbag The Sailor* the year before, Graham Moffatt as the fat, cherubic Albert and Moore Marriott as the dentally-challenged old timer, Harbottle. As in his schoolteacher role, Hay's character faces a constant struggle to establish anything approaching control through traditional authoritarian means. Harbottle, for example, is admonished by his boss for kicking a dispensing machine in the hope of getting some free chocolate. 'What's the idea of kicking it?', asks William Porter. 'What do you think the slots are for?' 'To blow down if the kicks don't work,' is the reply. Seconds later, with Harbottle off the scene, Hay gives the machine a boot himself. The rest of the film is a somewhat convoluted story of gun runners, a local football team called Buggleskelly Wednesday, random acts of drink and violence and an all-round endearing display from a cast that is clearly enjoying itself immensely.

One of the many lessons learned by Hay during his time with Fred Karno was the usefulness to a comedian of a stooge. In Moffatt and Marriott, he had two of the best but upon making *Convict 99* in 1938, he ditched the pair in favour of a new partner in Edgar Kennedy - the king of the double-take - for his next project. An obvious attempt to promote Hay across the Atlantic, *Hey, Hey, USA* enjoyed nothing like the popularity of his earlier efforts. Moffatt and Moore were duly reinstated for the next feature, *Old Bones Of The River*.

Hay's own old bones were, by now, rattling around with Randi Kopstadt, a Norwegian girlfriend half his age. Separated from his wife of 27 years, Gladys, the comedian had developed a bit of a reputation as a ladies man; beautiful women were frequently pictured on his arm. Whilst his relationship with Randi never grew into marriage - as a staunch Roman Catholic, Gladys would never entertain the idea of divorce - it was a partnership that nevertheless lasted until the end of his days. It also let Hay indulge another of his life passions, sailing, courtesy of a boat on the fjords, and add yet one more language to his repertoire.

After releasing *Ask A Policeman* and *Where's The Fire* in 1939, his last two films with the Gainsborough production company and Moffatt and Marriott (both of whom went on to work with Arthur Askey), Will Hay switched sides. From 1941, he made films for Ealing Studios - *The Ghost of St Michael's* and *Blacksheep of Whitehall* being two of the most notable - and toured factories and Armed Forces camps to aid in the war effort. He also made a couple of propaganda shorts in which he explained how to defuse bombs and, as a Sub Lieutenant in the Royal Navy Volunteer Reserve, spoke to House of Commons Select Committees on the subject of navigation.

Sadly, at the height of his intellectual powers, a life that had always been full and varied went into all-too early decline. Firstly, while shooting the last of his nineteen films, an unusually dark 1943 crime caper called *My Learned Friend*, Hay was diagnosed with cancer. Once caught, the condition was treated and, after a lengthy period of recuperation, he returned to the stage and radio. Unfortunately, a movie career whose longevity was been beaten only by George Formby had come to a halt every bit as juddering as that of Gladstone the steam engine in *Oh, Mr Porter!*. The illness took a physical toll too. In 1946, whilst on holiday, Hay suffered a stroke that left him disabled down one side of his body and badly affected his speech.

Effectively, that meant the end of any public appearances, although Hay still did his bit for the Grand Order of Water Rats, the charitable showbusiness club of whom he had been elected King Rat in 1931 and 1940. It was after one such function in 1949, during which he had given a warmly-received speech and spoken optimistically of his plans for the future, that Hay suffered a second, and this time fatal, stroke. He died at home in Chelsea on Easter Monday, aged 60.

As his academic background and further reputation as an aeroplane pilot and notable amateur astronomer suggests, the real Will Hay was far removed from the scatter-brained crackpot that he portrayed in his films. In 1933, for example, Hay was credited with having discovered a white spot on the planet Saturn. He also became well-known for his regular appearances on BBC radio's *Brain Trust*. For all its surface silliness, his comedy too was blessed with a much harder, socially satirical edge. The grimaces, coughs and trademark sniffs, all honed in music hall and perfected on a big screen that exaggerated them to great effect, belied a subversive wit that was, in many ways, ahead of its time.

Do you know, he seemed to suggest, not everyone in authority is the well-informed expert that they would have us believe. And certainly no authoritarian figure was safe from his horn-rimmed gaze, even those who paid his wages. Once, when the insulted star had a public fall-out with the all-powerful BBC, he vowed never again to appear before one of their microphones. The Corporation's crime? To have prematurely faded one of his televised music hall sketches in favour of a General Election broadcast by Neville Chamberlain. And the result? A full public apology from the BBC's Director of Variety, Eric Maschwitz.

5
I Thought, Right Monkey...

"Are you putting it around that I'm barmy...?"
- *Hutton Conyers*
"Did you want to keep it a secret...?"
- *Jimmy James*

Against a background of black-outs, bombings and full-on austerity, the northern stars of British film had been a major boost to morale. And with hostilities over, to begin with at least, the pull of the medium remained strong. Yet as the decade advanced, cinema attendances went into steady decline. Wireless audience figures, in contrast, grew stronger. A weary public, it seemed, was enticed by radio's more domestic charms.

Mostly, they tuned into the BBC's Light Programme, which first crackled into life on 29th July 1945. Natural heir to the popular wartime Allied Expeditionary Forces Programme, the new service was a hit from the start. In its day, the Forces Programme had been characterised by a strong Vaudevillian presence, the better to appeal to legions of American servicemen based right across the UK. As a result, it had been brighter and less stuffy than the more formal Home Service. With the launch of the Light Programme, Variety's influence held firm, which was continued good news for many a northern comedian.

The Light Programme's dominance of the British airwaves would

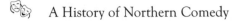

last some twenty-two years before, with the arrival of BBC Radio 1 and 2, it eventually fell silent on 30th September 1967. In between, it introduced or nurtured many an all-time wireless classic. The lowing of Ambridge cattle, in the long-running soap *The Archers*, was first heard on New Year's Day 1951. The equally popular trio *Music While You Work* (1940-67), *Desert Island Discs* (1942-present) and *Worker's Playtime* (1941-64) were brought successfully out of uniform and into civvies. Comedy shows were one other major ingredient in a golden radio age.

Although, to begin with, much Light Programme comedy was quite contentedly in the same vein as those Home Service favourites *ITMA* and *Band Waggon*, as the 'forties became the 'fifties, the comfortable status quo began to be challenged by a more ostentatiously intellectual brand of wit. True, the BBCs biggest immediate post-war hit was the RAF-based *Much-Binding-In-The-Marsh* (1944-54), as homely and undemanding a piece of hokum as there ever was, while old-style comedies like *The Navy Lark* (1959-77) continued to command tremendous audiences as the 'sixties swung into view. Radio revolution, however, was undoubtedly in the air. The first rumbles came with the decidedly left-field *The Goon Show* in 1951. Equally revolutionary, if rather more traditionally structured, was the cerebral existentialism of Tony Hancock's *Hancock's Half Hour* three years later. By 1960, both those innovative shows had run their course - on radio at least - at which point cocky young upstarts like *Round The Horne* (1965-69) took up the saucy baton of irreverence and pressed on.

Little did it know, but Britain was witnessing the birth and pre-pubescence of modern-day, mass media comedy. Whereas, in the past, British comedy had, on the face of it at least, been preoccupied with giving a beleaguered public a reassuring hug, tickle or both, as the last war faded into memory and a more forward-looking and self-confident society began to evolve, humour was more frequently and obviously aimed at the head. And where, in the old days, working class northerners had been very much to the fore, in these less stressful times well-educated and usually southern middle class comics moved into the spotlight. Although they would never disappear entirely, the traditionally 'feminine' qualities of northern comedy - i.e. a tendency towards self-deprecation, emotion and the minutiae of shared daily life - didn't seem so important anymore.

Not that the comedy of heart and head have ever been mutually exclusive, of course. One of the stars of *The Goon Show*, along with Spike Milligan, Harry Secombe and Michael Bentine, was the great Peter Sellers, a music hall product through and through. Sellers spent the war perfecting his silly voices in RAF concert parties before winning his first radio break in the Variety offering *Show Time*. With the advent of more openly political 'sixties satire, the concept of established Variety troupers popping up in more avant garde offerings was far from rare, as the long-standing tradition of theatrical revue continued to be a staple ingredient of such shows. It is interesting to note, too, how often among the gangs of bright young and scurrilous things to come, it was the northern or working class members of the troupe who gave sympathetic human ballast to perhaps more cynical, emotionally colder material.

Take the non-stop riot of risqué invention and eccentricity that was *Round The Horne*. Although cheerfully willing to draw on the traditions that had gone before, with an endless barrage of catchphrases and gallery of colourful characters, its twin qualities of outrageous daring and subtle iconoclasm attracted an equal measure of listeners and opprobrium from the morally-affronted. That they got away with it owed everything to the good-natured urbanity of the eponymous host, Kenneth Horne, whose very name was an irresistible excuse for double entendre. Pushing at the accepted boundaries of decency beneath him were Bill Pertwee, Hugh Paddick and the extraordinary Kenneth Williams, whose 'Julian and Sandy' routine with Paddick first introduced the delights of Polari, a form of homosexual slang that got to the parts other tongues dare not reach, to suburban Britain. Book-ending this taboo-busting lunacy was Horne's fellow totem of superficial respectability, the one and only Betty Marsden.

Born in Liverpool in 1919, most of Betty Marsden's childhood was spent on a Somerset council estate before, on the advice of a local music teacher, she embarked on a six-year scholarship at the Italia Conti stage school in London. As a professional actor, she performed with ENSA throughout the war years, before subsequently turning her attentions to Variety theatre and musical revue. As the only female member of the *Round The Horne* cast, her knack for character comedy and remarkable range of vocal caricatures proved priceless. She quickly proved that she could match it with the best of them.

A typical introduction to the show went thus: 'The story so far...

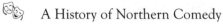

swaggering, gold-toothed buccaneer Betty Marsden, he of the barrel chest and eyes like bung holes, sat idly tying a granny knot in his granny, played by sweet, lavender smelling Bill Pertwee...'. A list of Marsden's characters, meanwhile, both in *Round The Horne* and *Beyond Our Ken*, an earlier show in which she also starred with Kenneth Horne, gives a further indication of her gifts of parodic invention; among them the conflicted Australian feminist Judy Coolibar, cookery expert Fanny Haddock and buttoned-up Noel Coward-esque Dame of the theatre, Celia Molestrangler. As with Horne himself, if respectable salt-of-the-earth Betty thought it okay to be secretly smutty, then why should anyone else be offended?

An example of *Round The Horne's* cleverness comes in the routine that featured Marsden and Paddick's painfully-repressed couple, Fiona (i.e. Celia) and Charles, played to polite perfection as a pair of lovestruck, stiff-upper-lip matinee idols, in the manner of *Brief Encounter*. Charles: 'I know.' Fiona: 'I know you know.' Charles: 'I know you know I know.' Fiona: 'I know you know I know you know.' Charles: 'I know.' And then, once they had pulled themselves together - Charles: 'Everything is the same...' Fiona: '...and yet, somehow, different.'

In her latter years, Betty Marsden lived on an 82ft-long converted coal barge on the river Thames, near Kew Bridge. She shared this unlikely residence with her two children, a collection of dogs and her husband, the consultant anaesthetist Dr James Wilson Muggoch, whom she had married in a bamboo hut in Nigeria. When she died of a heart attack in 1998, aged 79, it was with an unspilled glass of gin in her hand.

Back in the late 1940s, and the level of social change required to allow for *Round The Horne* was still a long way off indeed. Hungover by war, radio humour continued to be about Variety-style jokes and gentle character comedy rather than anything intended to engage the brain, seriously or otherwise. It was not until the turn of the decade and the arrival of the Goons that the creative types began to find the confidence to do both.

Not that anyone - audience, performers, producers or writers - cared much about any of that at the time. For who knew any better? And if much of the comedy of the period had an amiable and unthreatening grin on its face, then that was all the better for taking advantage of what was now a direct route into millions of homes. No longer were the music hall and Variety stars who became such a large part of the wireless firmament simply distant acts on stage or screen. Growing familiarity had quite literally turned them into household names. Family friends even.

One direct beneficiary of this surge in wireless popularity was the spectacularly-talented Al Read who, after making his first show in 1950, developed into one of the biggest radio stars this country has ever seen, regularly attracting audiences of several million.

Read's '...so I thought, right monkey,' drawled ahead of dealing with a troublesome person, was mimicked nationwide. As was his stuttering '...you'll be lucky, I say, you'll be lucky...' style of delivery, later used to similarly comic effect by the giant chicken Foghorn Leghorn and the actor John Savident as the butcher Fred Elliott in *Coronation Street*, which continues to coil around northern comedy history like some Newton and Ridley-addled python. Al Read was much more than a mere purveyor of catchphrases, however. He dealt only in the finest observational humour, particularly in the working class domestic arena. The bulk of it still rings true today.

Born in Broughton in 1909 and the son of a Salford sausage and potted meat manufacturer, Read drew superbly on his Lancashire roots to conjure a world of easily recognisable situations and characters such as the 'Johnny Know All' next door and the little boy who just won't shut up in public places. 'You've met 'em,' as he would regularly remind his listeners. Then there was his hapless hen-pecked husband, permanently at the mercy of a pathologically irritated other half. If some of Read's material might nowadays be considered a bit stereotypical, it did contain a balancing element of emotional truth. 'We all like to sink back into that armchair with a paper and solve the problems of the world. But do we? You've hardly time to work out where we are going to get the battleships and planes for defence let alone where we are going to get the thousands of millions to pay for them and what does the wife say? When are you going to get a latch on that gate?' It is the language of existentially disappointed marriage partners, each one struggling on in the knowledge that the alternative might well be worse.

Alfred Read's performing career had an uncharacteristic start. As a stage-struck young man he inherited the family firm and developed a nice

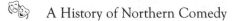

line in snorker sales patter and after-dinner speeches. He met his first wife, Joyce, at one such function at the Little Lever Golf Club, near Bolton, while parading his gallery of 'typical' characters from what he called his 'Pages From Life'. A decade later, in direct contrast to the local success of Joyce, who had her own concert party, he was still doing pretty much the same routine and, as far as the bright lights of showbusiness were concerned, getting nowhere fast.

At some stage during his young adulthood, Read is reported to have secretly entered and won a talent contest. Even then, though, his Variety career steadfastly refused to take off, as nerves and maybe embarrassment got the better of him. In fact, it took the approach of his 40th birthday to trigger Al Read into serious action. Probably as a result of mid-life crisis, it was then that he began to develop a professional sense of purpose about his act to the extent that he landed a first national Light Programme appearance in the BBC's *Variety Fanfare* the following year.

Like many an episode in Al Read's story, the exact details of how that big break came about are elusive. Contemporary newspaper reports indicate that the regional BBC producer, Bowker Andrews, had heard Read speaking at a tea dance in Fleetwood, just up the road from the comedian's home in nearby St Annes, during a programme broadcast only to the north. Impressed, the BBC man asked Read if he had anything else in his locker other than, presumably, tales about sausages. Al mentioned his 'Pages From Life' characters and, after Bowker agreed to give them a go, they went down a storm. Read's own version had Bowker seeing him perform his 'Decorator' monologue at the Queens Hotel, Manchester, after which he received his invitation to take part in the programme. Either way, on the back of that one *Variety Fanfare* appearance his profile rocketed and a series of his own, *The Al Read Show,* also known as *Such is Life,* followed later that same autumn. Al Read was the classic slow-burning overnight star.

After a blast of cheesy theme music - 'Such is life, life is what you make it, such is life...' - the show got underway with Read promising to 'introduce us to ourselves'. Had he wanted to, he could have introduced himself to himself too. For Read had the wonderful ability to hold a make-believe conversation, often featuring two or more characters, on his own. For obvious reasons, radio is not often seen as a visual medium. But in Al Read's hands, the most subtle rise or fall in vocal tone created aural pictures of which LS Lowry would have been proud. Read - who was a notoriously nervous performer to the end of his days - was rock solid confident when it came to juggling characters on air. Even to modern ears, stumbling across a vintage *Al Read Show* on BBC digital radio, it is easy to forget that you are listening to just one person.

One of Read's many specialities was his relentless moaner 'Cheerful Charlie', a downbeat dour character for whom life was but a perpetual parade of problems jostling to be complained about. Less a stereotype, more an archetype, as ubiquitous in the north as red bricked houses. The sort of man who, in 1955, shared with Read his wealth of knowledge on the subject of cafeteria food. '..."Ow do. Are you bothered with wind?" "No." "You soon will be."...' Or how about the pedestrian, unwisely asked by the motorist Read for directions? Salford accent essential: 'You're miles out, you'll have to turn round. Better still, to save you turning round, nip up here to the left, go straight up that road as far as you can go. When you get to the top, turn left, turn right, turn right again and turn that radio off. Can't hear myself speak....'.

If any comedian's material is better heard than read, it is Al Read's. You just have to be there. The sketch in which he is a rent man collecting money from a house while being watched by a very large dog - 'relax, he'll not hurt you..' - is, quite simply, one of the funniest things ever recorded. In it, Read not only plays the two lead characters, he plays the offending hound too. It is equally tricky to do written justice to a sketch in which another of his regular characters, the embarrassed man, is pulled over by the police. The abashed motorist proceeds to crack a desperate array of feeble 'jokes' while chuckling ingratiatingly like a nervous hyena.

Faring slightly better in that regard is the family picnic outing, before which the wife and mother sobs that she has 'been up since half past four this morning cutting sandwiches and I don't damn well want to go now'. And how about the magically observed request to their father from one of the kids in the back seat: 'Will you pull up? He wants to whisper something.' Cars, in fact, are a recurring motif in Read's comedy, possibly owing to his background in sales. And each show comes complete with its own middle-brow musical interlude, doubtless intended to inject a touch of impressive cultural 'class' into the proceedings.

That last point may or may not be significant, given that, among the

entertainment community along the Blackpool coast at least, Read had a reputation for getting 'above himself' once success came his way. In one of Barry Band's *Blackpool Comedy Greats* books, for example, we learn that: 'Part of Al's motivation was his conceit, which grew to laughable levels after he became a star.' Despite his nerves, as a stage-struck young man, Read certainly seems to have been ambitious. Along with his daily commute to the family sausage works in Salford, he played golf on the links of a St Annes club that was very popular with show folk, well before he, Joyce and the couple's three children actually moved into a house in the resort, in the mid-1940s. Yet whether for reasons of snobbery or self-preservation, the very people whom he longed to stand amongst often saw that as unforgivable social climbing.

Despite - or maybe because of - his future popularity with the British public, the theatrical seaside establishment remained lukewarm, at best, about this 'salesman' in their midst. In referencing that fact, Read is accused in Band's book of embellishing his autobiography, *It's All in the Book* (WH Allen, 1985), for the sake of posterity, but surely we can't just take the complaints of a notoriously envious profession at face value, can we? According to Read, for example, his debut on Blackpool's South Pier was on the bill of a Sunday concert in which he was asked to appear by the local producer, Jack Taylor. Barry Band, on the other hand, quotes the future *Carry On* star Jack Douglas as saying that Read actually offered to pay Taylor for the right to appear and the producer, amused by the proposition, agreed. Either way, as Read himself writes, he was hopeless. Are those really the words of someone out to airbrush history?

More likely, the ambitious Read had encountered a traditional obstacle that will be familiar to anyone who has had the temerity to break into a new career later in life, and done so with apparent ease. Often, those within an industry who have slogged their way through a more traditional apprenticeship do not take kindly to such 'good fortune'. The result, frequently disguised as affronted professionalism, is resentful envy.

The aforementioned Jack Douglas, for example, was born Jack Robertson in Newcastle-upon-Tyne in 1927, to a family whose theatrical routes could be traced back four generations. The Robertsons moved to

Blackpool when Jack was 11, in order to escape wartime bombing. On his 15th birthday, the boy was presented with a pantomime script by his producer father, along with the instruction: 'Go to Sunderland and direct the show yourself!' He did so, and the panto, *Cinderella*, ran for twenty-two weeks. His performing career, meanwhile, began when the original captain to Joe Baker's mate suffered a heart attack after a dress rehearsal for *Dick Whittington*, a panto Douglas was about to direct at the Kingston Empire, starring Lupino Lane. One man down on opening night, Jack took to the stage himself and to he and Baker's immense good luck, an influential agent was in the audience. In its way, it was a start every bit as fortuitous as Al Read's. Douglas and the rotund Joe Baker spent the next ten years travelling the world together as a popular double act.

Along with being in at the launch of the long-running children's TV series *Crackerjack* in 1955, the pair continued to work together on stage and screen before Baker's desire to make it big in the United States led to an eventual parting of the ways. Baker then embarked on a solo television career that, in 1964, was at its height with the zany Will Hay-inspired situation comedy *Fire Crackers* and ended with the innovative British-American impressionist collaboration *Kopykats* in 1972. As for Douglas, after a short spell as a Blackpool restaurateur, the 6ft 4' former straight man returned to performing with an eccentric alter-ego destined to become the stuff of British comedy legend. His name was Alf Ippititimus, the fidgeting fumbler in overalls, whose outrageous nervous twitch was accompanied by the catchphrase: 'phwaay!'.

In the years ahead, Douglas would go on to appear in no fewer than eight *Carry On* films - plus two *Carry On* Christmas specials and a TV series. Outside that brand, there were stage and television shows galore, all lovingly detailed in his autobiography, *A Twitch In Time*, published some six years before the comedian's death, aged 81, in December 2008. Back in the late 1940s, perhaps the showbiz-in-my-blood Douglas was not alone in feeling affronted by the sudden upward trajectory of a Salfordian upstart with sausage meat on his hands.

All supposition, of course. It could be that, owing to his ambitious nature, Al Read was indeed a right royal pain in the neck. And although his pathway into the industry was out of the ordinary, he was hardly *that* unusual in embarking upon a life on stage despite lacking any traditional

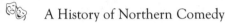

theatrical background. When, for example, the down-to-earth Keighley-born comic Cecil Emmott - stage name Joe King - turned pro' in 1937, he could boast previous jobs as a bus driver and full-time rabbit catcher. Yet given the number of lives brightened by Al Read's humour down the years, it seems only reasonable to give him the benefit of the doubt.

Whatever the personal allegations against Al Read, there is usually another potential explanation for his behaviour, should anyone wish to find it. Yes, his homegrown Lancashire accent was kept firmly in check until his gallery of characters had need of it, replaced by a posher and more pronounced BBC style of diction. But wouldn't polished patter have been equally useful as a salesman? One thing's for certain, his vocal clarity helped to ensure that Read became every bit as popular in the southern counties as he was in the north of England.

For many a comedian, a high-profile radio show invariably translated into greater popularity on stage and that is exactly how it turned out for Al Read. His longed-for first Blackpool summer season soon followed; a *Right Monkey* spectacular staged in 1951 at the Central Pier, the first of six such outings. And as with Dave Morris before him, already a successful businessman in his own right, the immaculately-tailored Read was never going to allow himself to be at the whim of showbusiness agents. A self-negotiated deal which left him not only with a large weekly pay packet, but also a decent percentage of the box office takings, was one more reason for the hackles of more established entertainers to rise. No matter. The Blackpool holidaymakers loved him and *Right Monkey* was the hit of the season. A second radio series further boosted his fame.

Through it all, Read continued to run his sausage factory, much to the amusement of many a journalist. Less comical was the fact that, as his performing activities increased, his marriage grew increasingly strained. Wife Joyce, it seems, had become disillusioned with the insincerity of showbiz parties and fed up with the procession of celebrity visitors who knocked endlessly at the family door. That, though, was everything for which Read himself had ever yearned. The outcome was separation and eventual divorce, bringing yet more criticism down on that Brylcreemed and unbeaten head from Joyce's own long-standing showbiz friends.

If any of this bothered him, he had a funny way of showing it. For if Read's upwardly mobile lifestyle was marked by anything, it was an uninhibited and ostentatious attitude towards personal expenditure. He owned racehorses, joined an upper class hunting set, bought homes in Cheshire, Jersey, Bermuda and Weybridge, drove a succession of expensive cars - including a baby blue Rolls Royce with matching luggage - and dressed in only the smartest clobber. In other words, the world in which he surrounded himself was as far removed from the fictional characters who serviced that fame and fortune as it was possible to get. Accusations of conceit and off-handed aloofness, particularly towards newspaper interviewers, duly followed.

Read's already sizeable wealth increased dramatically when he finally sold the family business in 1955. That was one year after he had made a massive impact at London's Adelphi Theatre in his long-running show *You'll Be Lucky*, another Read catchphrase, for Jack Hylton, followed by an appearance in the 1954 Royal Variety Performance. Subsequently, it was back to the Adelphi with *Such Is Life* - the show in which, incidentally, a Welsh chanteuse by the name of Shirley Bassey got her first big break - and a return to Blackpool for the same Royal Variety Performance at the Opera House from which Dave Morris was so remarkably excluded.

Professionally, all was set for the coming decade to be triumphant. And so it was. Yet by 1964, when Read was sharing the Central Pier bill with an up-and-coming group of Irish vocalists called The Bachelors, his act was undoubtedly the worse for over-familiarity. At some point, it is inevitable that every comedian will be viewed as old-fashioned. Equally inevitably, in the case of a still dapper Al Read, lots of people were eager to enjoy his fall from grace. Sadly, in these later years, he appears to have won more laughs for his off-stage demeanour, at least in Blackpool where they fancied they knew him better than most. Appearances at the stage door, where he would first feign reluctance and then flamboyantly sign autographs for screaming teenagers who, it was said, were actually waiting for the Bachelors, left him a sneered at figure of fun.

Even so, given how television was by now very much considered to be the medium of the future, Read might have been expected to make the leap there with more success than he managed. In the event, he did just three shows of any note: *Life And Al Read* for ITV in 1963, *Al Read Says What A Life* for the BBC in 1966 and, almost ten years after his first ITV appearance, *It's All In Life* in 1972. Maybe this is not so surprising. Read's

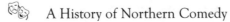

true talent lay in painting pictures for the imagination. His gift for voices and verbal mannerisms had a natural beauty to them on radio, where listeners could conjure their own images, unrestrained by anything so vulgar as the naked glare of a television camera. Just as prosaic was the fact that, in a reversal of the fate suffered by silent movie stars, Al Read, visually, was a bit of a disappointment. His own fate was to see out his performing days on stage, more often than not in the cabaret clubs that, by now, were the dying embers of what had once been Variety theatre. He also did a couple more Blackpool summer seasons in 1967 and 1970.

Al Read retired from showbusiness in the middle years of that latter decade when, with his second wife Elizabeth, he began to divide his time between Spain and the Yorkshire Dales. He did return to the microphone to re-record some of his original scripts, however, when it was discovered that much of his earliest work had been 'accidentally' wiped by the BBC. It is those tapes which are most often heard on radio today. This too-often overlooked, genuine comedy genius died in 1987.

Honestly, you wait ages for an overlooked, genuine comedy genius and then two come along at once. And while we are on about outstanding radio legacies, the gravel-voiced Jimmy James - born James Casey in South Bank, Teesside - didn't do too badly in that department either.

Admittedly, in James's case, that legacy isn't solely due to what this most surreal of comedians got up to himself, although his was an act indisputably splendid. It also owes a very great deal to the son who followed in his footsteps. In his own later years, Jim Casey junior would go on to recreate his father's routines as a way of keeping the memory of the great man alive. But by then, he had already made a name for himself as a respected radio comedy producer and scriptwriter, and had a spell as BBC Manchester's Head of Light Entertainment. None of which could have possibly been foreseen when Casey senior - later to take Jimmy James as a stage name - entered this world in 1892. Months after his birth, the family upped sticks for nearby Stockton.

The son of a steelmaker and amateur clog dancer, Jimmy James's showbusiness career began as a touring juvenile singer with the unlikely moniker, 'Terry - The Blue-eyed Irish Boy'. Accounts of how he went from singing to comedy differ. One version describes how, after he was gassed in the First World War, James discovered that his voice box could no longer carry a tune and so switched to the funny stuff instead. Another says that when the resident comic on one of those touring shows eloped with the leading lady, James strode gallantly into the breach. Most likely, there is at least a bit of truth in both. However it came about, when he did take to the stage, like many a music hall comic of the age it was initially in over-the-top garb. Gradually, though, he began to rely more upon his own highly original and idiosyncratic sense of humour, along with an equally unmatched talent for evoking the most bizarre images.

Like Sid Field, James became known throughout the entertainment industry as a 'comedian's comedian', largely as a result of his immaculate timing; 'the best timer of a joke that ever lived', according to his great pal Robb Wilton. His ability to ad-lib was way ahead of its time, often putting lesser comedians off their stride completely. In his book *Kindly Leave The Stage, The Story of Variety 1919-1960*, the author, Roger Wilmut, reveals that James once lost his script in the dark, seconds before going onstage at London's Garrick Theatre. Given that it was during the live recording of the radio show, *Star Bill*, that could have been a problem. Undaunted, James trotted on anyway. There to greet him was no less than a personage than the great Tony Hancock, who turned a whiter shade of pale as James proceeded to riff with a level of unpredictability that left the fictional resident of 23 Railway Cuttings, East Cheam, floundering. Apparently, some bloke he knew had been given two little blue bags of salt in his crisps by mistake: 'That means somebody will have to go without, doesn't it? He won't enjoy them anyway. They'll be too salty. It's not right.'

Mirroring the professional admiration of Marie Lloyd for George Formby senior, James's fellow comics - a competitive crowd as a rule - were frequently unable to resist watching his gloriously preposterous act from the wings. It is easy to see why. Take the celebrated 'chipster' routine, which grew out of an ad-libbing session in a failing London Hippodrome show, *Jenny Jones*, which he had rescued single-handedly. It concerned his uncle Joe's fish and chip shop. Informing his stooge that the correct way to hold the potato is between the forefinger and thumb, James continues: '....you put it on the block and it's on, pull, chop - on, pull, chop... only get your fingers out quick otherwise you'll be thinking you've got more

chips than you've chopped. Bad chipsters, you'll see them. Hundreds, walking about like that [holds up hand with two fingers missing]. You can always tell a bad chipster - he walks into a pub and says, "Four pints" [holding up index and little finger only]. He forgets you see...'

The most popular Jimmy James routines often featured his amiably inebriated drunk - quite ironic, really, seeing as how the man himself was a non-smoking tee-totaller. Alcoholic abstinence certainly didn't do the portrayal any harm. It was widely held to be the best and most technically accomplished of its kind. On the Variety stage, the idea of a music hall drunk was nothing unusual in itself - among the most notable was the dinner-suited Mancunian comedian Archie Glen, born in 1889, and the uncle of another north country comic, Tony Dalton. Glen's billing, 'Blotto as usual!', makes his approach abundantly clear. The comedy of Jimmy James was of an altogether more sophisticated hue.

So convincing was James's apparent inebriation that in his fierce concentration and determination not to topple over, as he meandered precariously across the stage, he is said to have left audiences feeling dizzy themselves. Nor, unlike other pseudo-drunks, was shouting his thing. He never did anything so obvious as to raise his voice. The closest he came to traditional slapstick was a perpetually thwarted attempt to find the cigarette perched precariously in his own mouth. His cheery demeanour was also a great way of getting out of trouble. 'Where's yours?' asks one increasingly convivial policeman, whom James has befriended by sharing his bottle of whisky. 'Under yours, if we can get to it.'

Stooges were another big part of Jimmy James's act; indeed son Jim took on such a role in his early career days. The two most famous were Bretton Woods - who later became 'Our Eli', as played by James's stuttering nephew Jack Casey - and Hutton Conyers, both named after actual locations. Bretton Woods was an international conference site and Hutton Conyers is a small village near Ripon, off the Great North Road. Certifiable idiots they may have been but, on stage, James went along with his stooges absolutely, possessed as they were by some sort of eccentric logic. Along with Jim Casey, a long list of other such co-stars included an up-and-coming young showman named Roy Castle.

The entry of Hutton Conyers, in his trademark long coat and silly hat, was guaranteed to produce uproar. 'Are you putting it around that

I'm barmy?' he would ask. Once the had laughter subsided, James denied ever having done any such thing before Conyers, nodding towards the tall, thin and magnificently ugly Eli, wearing a too-small jacket and cloth cap, demanded: 'Well, is it him, then?' Eli: 'I don't want any.' James [to Conyers]: 'He doesn't want any.' Conyers: 'Well, somebody's putting it around that I'm barmy.' James: 'Did you want to keep it a secret?'

This three-way dynamic continued in what is undoubtedly the most popular Jimmy James sketch of all, his legendary 'lion in the box' routine. In it, Conyers has just returned from a trip to South Africa where, it seems, the African people bequeathed him a 'sentimental gift'. James: 'What did they give you?' Conyers: 'Two man-eating lions.' James [startled, but not too much]: 'Did they give you a few yard's start as well?' It soon emerges, though, that Conyers has brought said creatures home with him. James: 'Where do you keep them, then?' Conyers [indicating the shoe box under his arm]: 'In the box.' James: 'Are they in there now?' Conyers: 'Yes.' James: 'I thought I heard a rustling.' It later turns out that there is a giraffe and caged elephant in there too.

Despite later forays by James into radio and television, there is little doubt that his natural and certainly most successful home was on the Variety stage. That TV output, for example, mainly consisted of three brief series and a one-off special made for the BBC throughout the 1950s. The first, *Don't Spare the Horses*, shown in 1952, consisted of three hour-long Variety-style sketch shows, shown live on Saturday night, in which *The Goons* trio Harry Secombe, Peter Sellers and Spike Milligan featured, among others. James then popped up in a 1955 show, *Christmas Box*, which travelled around the country in search of showbiz stars, supposedly enjoying themselves at Christmas parties. The following year he got what on paper should have been his biggest break yet; three hour-long shows with his name in the title, *Home James*, and a potential viewing audience of millions. And that was pretty much it until, in 1960, he co-starred as Bernard Bresslaw's unscrupulous manager J.J. in *Meet the Champ*, an ill-fated sitcom that only completed six of its intended nine-programme run. Five years later, he was dead of a heart attack.

Jimmy James was the last in a long line of high-profile music hall comedians for whom a live theatre audience was everything. Ultimately, television could not contain his personality, although his surreal brand of

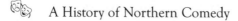

zaniness would later be detected in the small screen work of Eric Morecambe and, more recently, James's fellow offbeat Teessiders, Vic Reeves and Bob Mortimer. And while he never quite managed top-of-the-bill superstardom, James's stage career had highlights aplenty. Whilst supporting the Hollywood film star Mickey Rooney at the London Palladium in 1948, for example, James once again came to the rescue of a sinking show after Rooney had bombed and been replaced by the wise-cracking American comic Sidney Fields, a well-known co-star of Abbott and Costello. And, in 1953, he even made royalty chuckle, with a well-received 'chipster' performance at that year's Variety Performance.

In common with many comedians in our story, upon his demise such glories may well have faded from public memory, had Jim Casey junior not taken it upon himself to ensure otherwise. It was an all the more important act of family loyalty, since his father's preference for live theatre work had ensured that recorded remnants were rare. More often than not, these tribute performances were put on in tandem with cousin Eli, who developed a solo career of his own after James's death. It was a busy one, too, taking in Variety clubs, holiday camps and TV, film and radio work, alongside the likes of Paul Squires and Des O'Connor. Our Eli also appeared in *Mr H is Late*, a 1988 Eric Sykes production with a cast that reads like a comedy who's who: Sykes, Jimmy Edwards, Charlie Drake, Roy Kinnear and Mike Yarwood to name just five among many.

Throughout his own lengthy career Jim Casey wrote and produced radio shows for a vast number of comedians. On television, among other things, he contributed scripts to *The Good Old Days* and the diabolical Yorkshire TV-produced quiz series *3-2-1*. In 1981, Casey also popped up on the ratings-busting Saturday evening chat-show, *Parkinson*, as a result of host Michael Parkinson's recent description of Jimmy James in a book as 'the funniest comedian I have ever seen'.

With his memory jogged, Barnsley-born 'Parky' had invited Jim, Eli and a now fully adult Roy Castle to perform the 'lion in the box' sketch on his show. Once again it was a huge hit. So much so that the trio was asked to revive it at the 1982 Royal Variety Performance at the Theatre Royal, Drury Lane.

Some six years later, Jim and Eli revived another popular element of Jimmy James's act by appearing as 'First Drunk' and 'Second Drunk' in an episode of television's longest-running sitcom, *Last of the Summer Wine*. They obviously enjoyed themselves because, in the Christmas specials of 1993 and 1995 they were back, repeating their roles.

As a real life resident of *Last of the Summer Wine* country, Roy Castle may seem like a surprising inclusion in a history of northern comedy, especially to those who spent the best part of the 1970s, '80s and even '90s watching him play the trumpet - and as many as forty-seven other musical instruments - on the equally protracted children's BBC TV series *Record Breakers* (1972-2001). Yet he is very much included here on merit.

For one thing, when Castle was described by his old friend Bernard Cribbins as 'our Sammy Davis Jr' in a two-part BBC Radio documentary called *Leave 'em Laughing* in 2004, the description was a perfectly valid one. Although being born in the hills above Holmfirth and Huddersfield had not led to the same sustained heights of giddying international fame enjoyed by Davis, Castle had been an equally adept song and dance man in his way. He had also briefly headlined in Las Vegas and spent some of his most successful career moments in the company of Frank Sinatra.

And for another, along with Jimmy James, he had worked on stage and screen alongside some of the best known northern comics of all, right throughout his career.

The only child of an insurance man and hairdresser, Roy Castle was born in Scholes in 1932. The Castle clan were a musical lot, comprised of trumpeters, saxophonists and pianists. A grandfather, who didn't have a tooth in his head, made up for the lack of molars by leading a brass band and playing the cornet, while Castle's mother was a keen member of the Huddersfield Choral Society. That the young Roy should follow a musical path, therefore, was inevitable. At his mother's instigation he took tap-dancing lessons and, at just eight-years-old, gave concerts as a boy tenor, becoming known locally as 'the little boy with the big voice'.

Castle's professional career began equally early. As a 13-year-old, in fact, when he joined a troupe of touring boy performers in a music hall revue called *Happiness Ahead*. It was a prescient title for a relentlessly cheerful entertainer whose chief attribute, apart from musical ability, was an ever-ready and engaging smile. When the obligatory spell in National

Service arrived in 1950, he used the two-year break from the stage to teach himself the trumpet, an instrument that would serve him well to the end of his days.

On rejoining civilian life, Castle returned to the boards, initially in the role of Dick Whittington's cat, for which he earned £5 per week 'and all the milk I could drink'. Then, in 1956, Castle's father fell ill and the family decamped to Blackpool, doubtless hoping that the sea air would help with his recuperation. Career-wise, the move proved pivotal for Roy. Shortly after his arrival he landed a role in a Central Pier show starring our next great northern comic, Jimmy Clitheroe, a booking that soon led to a spell as Frank Randle's stooge in *Randle's Scandals*.

It is hard to think of two more contrasting personalities than Roy Castle and Randle. The former was sunny-natured and clean-living, the latter anything but. And to make matters more difficult, by the time Castle came on the scene Randle was very much on his downward spiral, either failing to turn up completely or coming over all grumpy with his rapidly diminishing audiences. More positively, moving in such circles allowed Castle to meet Jimmy James who had no hesitation in asking him to stay on as his second stooge, when Eli fell ill. Blessed with that trademark northern knack of gentle self-deprecation, together with a generosity of spirit which meant he was quite happy to let others grab the limelight, Roy Castle made the ideal comedy straight man.

It was around now, too, that Roy Castle met another entertainer who would have a profound influence on his life, the singer Dickie Valentine. In later years, Castle described Valentine as his great mentor. It was certainly he who brought the young entertainer to London's West End. And, in 1958, that was followed by a debut TV appearance, on the programme that had also helped to launch the television careers of Jack Douglas and Joe Baker, Val Parnell's *New Look* comedy talent show. So well did it go that Castle was asked to appear in that year's Royal Variety Performance too, after which he left the stage to a standing ovation.

Two years later, Roy Castle's international stock had risen to the extent that he was now considered an appropriate guest for prime-time American television. 'Our English friend,' as he was described, was such a hit that he went on to make forty-two appearances on *The Gary Moore Show* among many of the biggest names in world showbusiness of the day.

A three-week booking in the Nevada desert followed, during which time he was introduced to his all-time hero Sinatra, an enthralled member of his final-night Vegas audience. Sinatra, ostensibly there to watch his daughter Nancy, clearly liked the look and sound of Castle, because he later asked him for an impromptu personal display on the trumpet and gave Castle a recording deal on his own label, Reprise.

With friends in high places and now an American household name, a life as a big-time global entertainer was there for the taking. Yet through it all, Roy Castle stood tall and did it his way. Struggling to settle to the American way of life, at first he continued to commute over the Atlantic. And when he was given the starring role in a Broadway musical, he made a more concerted go of it by renting a New York apartment, before the project was scrapped after six months. Yet at that point, rather than staying stateside and waiting for the next big thing to come along, he chose instead to return to the working men's clubs of northern England.

It was probably for the best in the long run, certainly in terms of personal contentment. In 1963, Castle married Fiona, a dancer he had first met as a result of his friendship with Eric Morecambe. Another pal, Harry Secombe, was best man at the wedding. Two years later, he fronted his very own BBC programme, *The Roy Castle Show*, scripted by future *Morecambe and Wise* writers Sid Green and Dick Hills. And by then Castle had made a film too, *Doctor Who and the Daleks*, a cinematic outing for television's most eccentric timelord, played on this occasion by Peter Cushing. As the '60s progressed, more film roles ensued, most notably as one of the men on a doomed train in *Dr Terror's House of Horror* , a portmanteau horror film of the type spoofed so successfully in the 1990s by Steve Coogan and the League of Gentlemen. In 1968, Castle also proved to be an excellent stand-in for Jim Dale in the *Carry On* franchise's best picture by far, the superior *Carry On Up The Khyber*. By the close of the decade his reputation as an all-rounder was assured. 'Whenever Roy is in town,' colleagues joked, 'eight other entertainers are out of work.'

Along with regular guest slots on such mainstream TV favourites as the Royal Variety Show, *The Good Old Days* and *Morecambe and Wise*, on the radio Roy Castle also had his own long-running 1970s series, *Castles in the Air*, which featured one of the medium's best-loved catchphrases of the time: 'Roy! Are you coming out to play, Roy?' But it was for his move

into children's television that he would become best remembered by younger audiences at least. During his time at the helm of *Record Breakers*, he managed to break no less than nine records himself; including an incredible twenty-four taps in a single second while tap-dancing. Even more astounding was the million taps he somehow squeezed into twenty-three hours and forty-five minutes, at an average of eleven taps a second. As the theme tune said, dedication's what you need.

After having fronted the programme since its origin as a one-off pilot in 1970, Castle's reign on *Record Breakers* was only brought to a close when, tragically, he developed lung cancer in 1992. Such things are never expected, of course, but even less so in someone so physically fit and clean living. The man himself heaped the blame for his predicament in the ashtrays of the hundreds of tobacco-stained clubs in which he had sucked up smoke whilst blowing his trumpet. Yet rather than hiding away in despair, Castle, ever the committed Christian, decided instead to use his celebrity to campaign vociferously for change. He helped to fund a cancer research centre in Liverpool and his name remains attached to a charity devoted to warning against the dangers of passive smoking.

In 1994, and by now cruelly under the impression that he had conquered the disease, Roy Castle was told that the cancer had moved into his brain. Later that same year, he died early one morning while, according to *Leave 'Em Laughing*, smiling at an old Eric Morecambe joke. 'Sorry to hear that your dad has died,' it went. 'I hope so,' came the reply. 'We've buried him.'

Among Jim Casey's myriad scriptwriting and production credits can be found one particular radio series upon which he worked for fourteen years in all, as a co-writer and producer. It starred the vertically challenged Jimmy Clitheroe.

After landing his big break alongside Old Mother Riley in the 1939 pantomime *The Old Woman Who Lives In A Shoe*, and the subsequent launch of his film career in *Old Mother Riley In Society* one year later, Clitheroe's reputation as a nationally renowned Variety great was about the only aspect of his being which grew during the later 1940s and 'fifties. Well, not quite, but we'll come to that later. Previously, his earliest stage appearances had been as a diminutive stooge to the South Shields-born revue comic Albert Burdon - far from basketball material himself. Like Clitheroe, Burdon (1900-1981) was best known for his knockabout physicality and, at the time, he had developed a successful career on film and stage of his own. Come the 1950s, however, and his days in the limelight were dwindling. He could most frequently be found in panto alongside his son Bryan, with whom he formed an ugly sisters double act.

By then, Clitheroe was moving onward and upward. The 'fifties were very much his glory years, especially in his beloved Blackpool where, eventually, he would be able to boast a record sixteen Summer Season shows. Towards the end of that decade, in 1958, Clitheroe appeared with Al Read in Read's second Blackpool summer season. Prior to that, alongside Frank Randle, he had reprised a routine first performed with Burdon, in which he pretended to be a ventriloquist's dummy before leaping off his master's knee and heading for the wings under his own steam, a turn of events that, by all accounts, a sizeable proportion of the audience found creepy rather than amusing. On the big screen, after co-starring in George Formby's 1942 picture, *Much Too Shy*, Clitheroe also went on to star with Randle in a couple of Mancunian Films, *Somewhere In Politics* and *School For Randle*, in which Jewel and Warriss also appeared. But it was on stage and, later, radio where he really made a name for himself and, as it turned out, others. In 1955, for example, while treading the boards on Blackpool's Central Pier, his path crossed with three names of the future, a comedy double act named Morecambe and Wise, and a tatifilarious new kid on the block, Ken Dodd.

Radio, though, was the thing. And for Clitheroe, when it arrived, it must have felt like a natural and yet long overdue progression. As time went on, touring the halls with an act that, not notwithstanding his high-pitched voice, began increasingly to require a formidable suspension of disbelief, the opportunity to hide his amassing years in a wireless box on the mantelpiece can only have been a godsend.

As it turned out, 1954 gave Clitheroe his first ride on the airwaves, in *The Mayor's Parlour* with Jimmy James. So impressed was James's son, Jim Casey, that he wrote a seven-minute sketch for the schoolboy and his fictional mother, which was performed in the 1956 Variety show *Call Boy*. It proved to be a big hit and a full-length pilot, *The Clitheroe Kid*, followed.

So successful did that become with listeners and radio bosses, that fifteen full series followed between 1957 and 1972, making it the BBC's longest-running radio sitcom. At its height, *The Clitheroe Kid* was heard by a quarter of the entire population.

The philosophy of making the best of what you've got had no better exponent than James Robinson Clitheroe. In a life that coincidentally began in the Lancashire town of Clitheroe in 1922, 'Jimmy' never grew taller than four foot three or lost the looks of an 11-year-old boy, well, from a distance anyway. When he turned a social handicap to his showbusiness advantage by donning a schoolcap and blazer, whether on stage or during those radio broadcasts, the nation and studio audiences loved him for it.

Not that Jimmy Clitheroe was the first (or indeed last) Variety comic to turn a lack of height to his theatrical advantage. The 4ft 9ins Wee Georgie Wood, for example, beat him to it by several years. Born George Balmer on Wearside in 1897, Wood was also able to turn his diminished physical stature into a professional positive. Complete with monocle and miniature suit, his act made him one of the biggest names in music hall right across the world. Roy Hudd's book, *Cavalcade of Variety Acts*, gives an admiring account of the little comic's progress from his days as a pre-World War One star in the UK, America and South Africa to his demise in 1979, when a vociferous, out-spoken member of the British Music Hall Society. What he lacked in personal inches, he seems to have made up for in opinions. He wrote columns for *The Performer* and *The Stage*, which Hudd describes as 'a fascinating mixture of sharp insight, gossip and prickly comment'. When, in 1951, 'Wee Georgie Wood' was finally put to bed, Wood continued in a 'new' guise, Wee Macgreggor, alongside his long-time stage mother Dolly Harmer, before he retired for good in 1953. The Leeds-born Billy Kay, born a year later than Wood in 1898, was another comedian for whom height - or rather the lack of it - proved no barrier to widespread popularity.

There was, however, only one Jimmy Clitheroe. And his career had begun as a genuine kid in 1936. It was then that the 14-year-old 'Little Jimmie' Clitheroe, raised in the small mill town of Blacko, near Nelson, joined a troupe of juvenile entertainers, in which he was the only boy. By all accounts he enjoyed the experience, allegedly pinching the girls' hair clips and selling them back at a profit. At which point, for Jimmy, the hands of time appear to have stopped, at least in public. Henceforth, he would never grow up, an illusion of youth which was maintained by a steadfast refusal ever to reveal his actual age. Also contributing to the myth was the fact that, in real life, upon the death of his father, Clitheroe lived a quite literally semi-detached and romance-free existence with his over-protective mother, Emma, in Blackpool.

On radio, *The Clitheroe Kid* shows had a settled, comforting pattern. First, a burst of cheerful orchestral music. Next, a plummy BBC type who would announce the programme. And then the 'Kid Himself', Jimmy, squealing that week's title - *The Day The Fun Fair Hit Town, The Evils of Tomato Juice* or *Clitheroe and the Hound Dog*, say. After which the ball would begin rolling via the manufacture of some sort of comical scrape, in which Jimmy would contrive to embroil members of his supporting cast. Although the exact make-up of that troupe would vary down the years, among the best known were Peter Sinclair as Jimmy's Scottish grandad, Patricia Burke as his mam, Diana Day as his posh older sister Susan, the Oldham-born comedian Danny Ross as Alfie Hall and gravel-voiced Yorkshireman Tony Melody, who played Jimmy's sworn enemy, Mr Higginbottom. With the half-hour up and all scrapes sorted, the usually indefatigable Jimmy would deliver a neat little monologue and depart to appreciative applause. In her earliest incarnation, Jimmy's mum was played by no less a personage than Violet Carson who, complete with fearsome hair net, was destined to wreak terror in *Coronation Street*, as Weatherfield's sunniest pensioner Ena Sharples. Another famous television face, Judith Chalmers, later to turn orange, played Jimmy's sister at one point too. While Leonard Williams - to be better known as grandad Trotter in *Only Fools and Horses* - enjoyed a spell as the nemesis next door.

However else we might describe *The Clitheroe Kid*, his endless supply of inventive insults and schemes were hardly the stuff of ground-breaking social satire. For one thing, as with so much of the Variety-based comedy that was current and had gone before, the show owed much of its appeal to its largely undemanding supply of catchphrases. One such was 'I'm all there with my cough drops'; a simple affirmation of Jimmy's legendary cunning and intelligence on the one hand, a cheeky rebuttal of perceived inactivity in the gonad department on the other. In any case, it became hugely popular as did the rather less imaginative 'Ooh, flippin' 'eck', yelled at the first sign of bother. Most famous, though, was 'Don't some mothers 'ave 'em,' which is only a beret and raincoat away from the name of a certain 1970s television sitcom favourite. Ooh, Betty.

Homely rather than cutting edge, with his own penchant for having a bit of trouble *The Clitheroe Kid* made perfect family radio fodder. For an older generation struggling to come to terms with the rise of a growing and, to some, frightening American-imported phenomenon called the teenager, there was a reassuring note of harmlessness in his pranks. In Jimmy Clitheroe they heard a nostalgic echo of their own and apparently more innocent childhood, while also feeling relief that here was one kid whose mess they wouldn't have to clear up themselves. For the younger generation, meanwhile, there was the vicarious thrill of listening to a rebellious character who said everything you wanted to say but probably didn't dare. 'Do you put fertiliser on your rhubarb,' Jimmy grills his neighbour at one point. 'Yes, I do.' 'Well, each to their own taste. We put custard on ours.'

With its grotesque yet ultimately unthreatening lead character and accent on chuckles rather than gut-wrenching belly laughs, *The Clitheroe Kid* might in many ways be seen as a forerunner to the brand of modern-day 'gentle' Sunday tea-time humour that has come to be epitomised by Roy Clarke's television sitcoms of the 1970s onwards. The kid himself is surely detectable in the rascally Compo of *Last of the Summer Wine* fame, albeit now as a fully-fledged OAP. On Sundays more than any other day, it seems, traditional northern comedy is there to make you feel better.

And even when it does come over all contemporary and topical - 'Can we go to the pictures, Grandad? There's an animal film on. It's got a kitten in it.' 'That sounds nice.' 'Aye, Bridget Bardot.' - it simultaneously manages to undermine the very notion of fashionable savvy. No, this is a forgotten world of escaped white mice, kali dabs and, as in the *Hound Dog* episode, secret pet greyhounds - '...be quiet Lightning. You're a greyhound, you should know how to keep your trap shut.'

An equally important aspect of the comforting northern world invented or reflected - take your pick - by *The Clitheroe Kid* is the wide array of amusing regional accents on display, provided by a cast who seldom had anything other than impeccable comic timing, especially Clitheroe himself.

His voice, with its 'lukes' rather than 'looks' and disarming Lancastrian refusal to take a punctuating breath before happening upon the end of a particularly lengthy and unnecessarily tortuous sentence, was a delight then and is a delight now. Furthermore, as the creators of Bart Simpson would discover some half a century on, little boys are frequently blessed with a similar vocal timbre to middle-aged ladies, a fact that can also help them to sound much wiser than their years. That was certainly how it was with Clitheroe. If we close our eyes, can we hear his mother?

A career that eventually spanned five decades made a less successful transition from radio to television in the 1960s, with *That's My Boy* and *Just Jimmy*, shown on ITV between 1963 and 1968. On telly, the role of Jimmy's mother went to the Keighley-born Mollie Sugden, who had taken on the role in live stage-shows and also played it on radio for three years. The main difference, of course, was that the public were now able to see their favourite characters in the flesh and, as with Al Read but more so, the professional implications were hardly positive. Where, on radio, the now ageing Jimmy could get away easily with pretending to be an 11-year-old boy - and indeed might just about manage it in pantomime at a push, given enough make-up and distance between himself and the audience - television cameras were far less forgiving.

Just as damaging to Clitheroe's ambitions of developing a national television profile was the fact that the programmes were originally shown only in the Midlands and the north, admittedly a not particularly rare situation at that stage of independent television development, as we have seen with Dave Morris and Harry Korriss, among others. Nevertheless, for someone who had been such a huge hit on radio, it was hardly ideal. Equally, the shows went out at tea-time on weekends, bracketing him as a children's entertainer. The glory years, it seemed, were over although, as an historical aside, one of the writers on *Just Jimmy*, Alick Hayes, had earlier been responsible for *My Sister And I*, the first ever ITV sitcom made exclusively for the north, starring Dinah Lee and Jane Taylor.

Like the Variety trouper that he was, Jimmy Clitheroe nevertheless battled on and, in 1966, another big break appeared to have arrived, this time in cinema. A major colour adaptation of Jules Verne's *Rocket To The Moon* was to be made, in which the comedian was cast as General Tom Thumb. Alas the film flopped and was soon forgotten.

Sadly, the Clitheroe Kid's fall from grace continued on radio where, by the end of the fifteenth series, ratings had plummeted to just over a million (a figure that many radio comedies would nevertheless be ecstatic with today). As a result, the naughty schoolboy was permanently sent to his room on 13th August 1972. Dejected, Clitheroe blamed his demise on the modern-day audience's lack of an appetite for good clean family fun. At this distance, it seems more likely that the public was simply tired of an act that, to be honest, had already done remarkably well to achieve such longevity.

Although Jimmy Clitheroe's childhood had hardly been poverty-stricken, it wasn't exactly cash-rich either, leaving him with an instinct to work hard, invest wisely and watch the pennies. In fact, he had developed something of a reputation over the years as a tight-wad, a not uncommon accusation among comedians, it has to be said. The upshot was that when his showbiz career began to slow, there were plenty of outside business interests to boost his income, including the ownership of a number of betting shops and a racehorse. Even so, he never felt able to turn down work. With no broadcasting jobs on the horizon he resorted to working the clubs and making commercial appearances, which often entailed driving long distances and twice landed him in hospital suffering from exhaustion in the early 1970s.

Whatever his later hardships, throughout his life the devotion and goodwill that Jimmy Clitheroe engendered in the British public seems to have been equalled by the popularity he enjoyed among his friends and peers. Read any account of Clitheroe's career today and most, if not all, of his contemporaries will agree that his was a warm and mischievous personality, on stage and off. Yet, really, that can hardly be the full story, can it? We all have our inner demons and Jimmy Clitheroe, 4ft 3ins on his tiptoes, could be excused for having more than most. Despite an, on the face of it, cheerful acceptance of his condition, we can only really guess at his levels of personal sadness. In those less politically correct - or some might say sensitive - times, Clitheroe was a midget, simple as. He knew it, his audience knew it and, deep down, he may well have feared that potential life partners would know it too.

As a result, and with the exception of the company of his mother, he spent much of his life romantically unattached or, again, that was how it appeared to the outside world. Love affairs and Jimmy Clitheroe were clouded in mystery. The most sensational rumours surrounded an hotel he had bought and renovated at Preesal, near Blackpool. It was said that the comedian had purchased it at great personal cost so that it could act as a luxury rendezvous for meetings with a secret girlfriend, his personal assistant. But the relationship, if it existed at all, was destined to end in tragedy. The unlucky fiancée was killed in a car crash as she stormed off home after a row. That was the story, anyhow.

Ultimately, all speculation as to the truth of Jimmy Clitheroe's state of mind - whether peaceful or volatile - is futile. Did he consider himself to be a carnival freak? Or was he genuinely unfazed by a condition that had brought him great wealth and fame? It is impossible to know. What is certain, however, is that he was always hugely dependent on his mother's companionship. So much so that when she died in June 1973, her son too was found dead, on the very day of her funeral. An inquest blamed an accidental overdose of sleeping pills rather than suicide; 'accidental' given that the dose taken with a glass of whisky by the distraught 51-year-old would not have been enough to kill an adult of normal physical stature.

6
Over the Garden Wall

"Hello, I don't think you've had the pleasure of me yet..."
- *Hylda Baker*

The tragic fate of Jimmy Clitheroe echoed the demise of live Variety theatre itself. Even in his hometown Blackpool, where the likes of George Formby, Frank Randle and the rest had once bestridden that resort's star-struck Golden Mile like so many comedy colossi, a once proud genre looked shabby and past its sell-by-date by the early 1970s, as cash-strapped theatre managements sought to cut back on expenditure.

The rot, however, had set in long before that. Having acted as social cohesives through troublesome times, radio and cinema emerged from the Second World War stronger than ever and were seemingly on course to conquer the entertainment world. Indeed, radio was to make a particular success of peacetime, embarking on what is still described as the medium's Golden Age. In the short term, for live Variety, that might have been seen as beneficial. After all, the promotion of more well-known national names ought to translate into more bums on theatre seats. In the mid-to-long term, though, habits were being changed forever.

And especially so given that, along with radio and cinema, there was now a third competitor waiting in the wings. As long ago as 1922, early demonstrations of a mechanically scanned television system had been held by Scottish inventor John Logie Baird, in which objects were able to be transmitted in outline. By April 1927, the invention was developed to the extent that an Irish-American comedian named Dolan became the first Variety-style entertainer to use the new medium to deliver a 'short act of monologue and song', courtesy of the American Telephone and Telegraph (AT&T) Company in New Jersey.

In Britain, the first public high-definition service came courtesy of the BBC, at 3.00pm on 2nd November 1936, when Leslie Mitchell's now famous words, 'Good afternoon, ladies and gentlemen. It is with great pleasure that I introduce you to the magic of television,' were followed by a Movietone cinema newsreel and a Variety show 'with an international flavour'. The move into television was very much against the high-culture instincts of the fastidious Lord Reith, who refused to see the value of the invention and retreated - or was pushed - out of the BBC and into a career in business and politics as World War Two came into view.

Initially broadcasting from Alexandra Palace for just two hours every day (except Sundays), and notwithstanding its chairman's ambivalence, the BBC continued to develop its new television project over the following three years until, upon the outbreak of hostilities on 1st September 1939, transmissions ceased. Some seven years later, in June 1946, those same blank screens suddenly spluttered back into life, picking up exactly where they had left off before and destined to be flooded by many of the very same Variety performers so prevalent elsewhere.

Until rudely interrupted, the signs that television might develop into an unstoppable entertainment medium had been there almost from the start, at least in hindsight. The BBC's second outside broadcast, for example, the Coronation of King George VI on 12th May 1937, had been an enormous success. The first was an all together less complicated affair. Transmitted a year before, it had featured a comedian named Leonard Henry (no relation), pictured driving away from Alexandra Palace - or 'Ally Pally' as Gracie Fields had rechristened the nation's first major television production centre.

A first sporting outside broadcast from the Wimbledon Tennis Championships followed and, by 1939, the BBC was on air seven days a

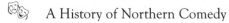

week with picture quality dramatically improved from its earliest output and 23,000 TV licences sold. To the BBC, Britain's unofficial war slogan, 'It'll all be over by Christmas', must have felt more like a prayer. It predicted that some 80,000 receivers - i.e. television sets - would be in use by the close of the year and came up with an advertising slogan of its own: 'You can't shut your eyes to it'. History, alas, dictated otherwise. The blackout came during a Mickey Mouse cartoon, in which the animated rodent mimicked Greta Garbo's immortal catchphrase: 'I vant to be alone'. Literally, there was now nothing on the telly.

While that must have been perplexing for viewers who waited in vain for an explanation of what had just happened to their pictures, it can have been as nothing to the bemusement they must have felt when BBC TV finally sparked back into action, at precisely the same point in the Disney cartoon at which Hitler had decided to butt in.

Post-war, the fledgling visual service continued to be broadcast with a similar degree of pre-war decorum. Over the next two years, on-air time was restricted to two hour-and-a-half sessions per day (from 3.00pm - 4.30pm and 8.30pm - 10.00pm), although the price of a licence rose to a hefty £2.00. Nevertheless, a landmark of 100,000 licences was soon passed and, when the BBC broadcast the 1948 Olympic Games live from London's Wembley Stadium, that figure shot up to 150,000.

Yet if such rapid progress was impressive, it was an event five years later that really signalled the arrival of television as a major mass media entertainment player. The Coronation of Queen Elizabeth II left no one in any doubt as to the medium's future prospects.

By then, the BBC had moved to larger premises in Shepherds Bush, West London. Then, in 1951, transmitters were erected in the north of England followed, a year later, by Wales and Scotland. Theoretically, it was now possible for 81 per cent of the British public to watch television, providing they had a receiver obviously. Once doubts over the morality of cameras being allowed inside Westminster Abbey had been allayed, the televising of the Queen's big day was duly announced. And to say that the sale of television sets boomed would be to suggest that Frank Randle had supped the odd pint. Not everyone had the money available, of course, but for those who did, it was a fast track to becoming the centre of neighbourhood attention. By the time the Archbishop of Canterbury, Dr

Geoffrey Fisher, solemnly placed the crown on the young sovereign's head, British streets were deserted while an estimated 20 million viewers looked on.

The idea, often expressed in highly-educated quarters, that television might just be a luxurious gimmick was shot clean out of the water. By 1955, the number of licences reached 4.5 million. With such popularity, however, came problems for the broadcaster. Most obviously, an increase in sales of TV sets was accompanied by a consequent rise in audience numbers, each of whom had paid to be entertained. If the public wasn't to be short-changed, longer broadcasting hours would be needed and, to fill those hours, a greater volume of original programming.

As with that other great domestic invention, radio, when television grew hungry for talent it was towards Variety that it turned. Inevitably, therefore, a fair amount of cross-pollination between the two was only to be expected. This especially became the case when a drop in employment opportunities offered by cinema was taken into account. After a burst of post-war popularity, the attraction of movie-going had begun to dwindle alarmingly in the early 1950s, with admissions more than halving by the end of the decade.

For television, meanwhile, the need for quality entertainment rose still more dramatically upon the arrival of something that the BBC had always fought most strenuously against: competition. In 1955, commercial television appeared, ostensibly as a result of concern that the Beeb would not be able to cope with the demand for public choice, although it seems likely that the many Conservative politicians whose business interests were linked to advertising will not have failed to notice the increased potential for personal profit.

Whatever the motives behind its existence, the first commercial television channel to be handed a franchise to broadcast by the newly-appointed Independent Television Authority was Associated Television (ATV), headed by former BBC Controller Norman Collins. ATV were just one of ninety-eight companies originally to apply for the privilege. The principal difference between the two networks, of course, would be in the manner of their funding; the BBC would continue to be paid for via its already-established licence fee and ATV by on-screen advertising, a method that left rather an unpleasant taste in the mouth of some.

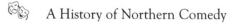

As Labour Party leader Hugh Gaitskell put it: 'It is utterly wrong that what we see in our homes should depend on the advertisers to make profits.' For the many independent channels which came and went over subsequent years, it was an attitude that they would continually have to face down. The BBC, a paid-for public service, was a wholesome force for establishment good, certainly as far as the educated ranks of the middle classes from whom it drew its own employees were concerned. Commercial television on the other hand, with its open pursuit of money, was unspeakably vulgar. Fingers were pointed towards America, where a reliance on advertising was felt to have had clear implications for programme quality. Would educational high culture and 'British standards' be replaced by frivolity here too? It is a debate that endures still with regard to contemporary pressures on the BBC's traditional licence fee system, in the face of an exponential increase in satellite, cable and internet television choices.

Despite all opposition, ATV duly became Britain's second television service on 22nd September 1955. Granada were next out of the blocks, winning the Independent Television (ITV) franchise for the north west the following year. The Associated British Picture Corporation (ABC) began to serve the Midlands and north shortly after. Scottish TV was up and running in 1957, but it was not until 1959 that ITV could be said to have fully broken out of its original London confines and made it to the rest of the United Kingdom.

The bulk of national 1950s broadcasting, then, still belonged to the BBC in any meaningful way. And the effect was to leave the organisation in a complacent frame of mind. Mainly, although the man himself was now long gone, the BBC continued to subscribe to Reith's paternalistic ethic of 'giving the people what they need, not what they want'. In short, it maintained its long-held remit to provide cultural enlightenment by way of information, education and entertainment. Whatever the rights and wrongs of that, a virtual single service monopoly did not encourage innovation when it came to programme making. And so, in thinking how best to fill its television schedules, the BBC simply repeated what it was already doing so successfully on radio. It called upon such proven shows as *The Billy Cotton Bandshow* and many of British comedy's biggest hitters.

For some of those comedians, like Al Read and Jimmy Clitheroe, who relied heavily on painting imaginative mental pictures, television proved to be little more than a not particularly useful detour. For others, it was nothing less than the key to immortality.

One indication of the BBC's sniffy suspicion of modernity lies in the way that, in attempting to build an audience for the new service, it came up with two of the most high-profile (and, it should be admitted, popular) bastardised historical throwbacks ever. One of these was *The Black and White Minstrel Show*, a then-innocently intended celebration of blacked-up Vaudeville 'Coon' singers which, when viewed today, is apt to leave the reception given to Mel Brooks's 'Springtime for Hitler' scene in his film *The Producers* looking like the audience reaction to a primary school play. The second was the less dubious if equally anachronistic *The Good Old Days*, a wallow in pure music hall nostalgia.

In these more socially enlightened times, the least said about the former show the better, even if it did prove popular enough to run for twenty years after first making its debut in 1958. In the case of the latter, however, a non-stop conveyor belt of northern comedy talent was unleashed, introducing British living rooms to one particular female performer who had already carved a formidable reputation for herself in Variety theatre throughout the 1940s. Ladies and gentlemen. Welcome into your homes that magnificent pocket battleship of malapropism, Hylda Baker. And we can say that without fear of contraception.

Hylda Baker is the classic example of an overnight success who had actually trodden the boards relatively unnoticed for years. Born in Farnworth, near Bolton in 1909, her background was showbiz from the start. Her father, Chucky Baker, was also a comedian and, by the age of 10, as the oldest of seven children, Hylda was soon following in the family footsteps.

Like many a Lancashire lass of the time, she went straight into the cotton mills upon leaving school - in order 'to learn a trade' as her parents put it. She didn't last long, around six months in fact, but it was enough time in which to learn to read lips, a not uncommon skill in that noisy line of work. Mill drudgery held no attraction for young Hylda. Equipped with a fierce sense of individuality, she had bigger dreams and they all revolved around the stage. The silent mouthing of words, though, would one day prove useful.

By the age of 14, Hylda was already showing great promise as a stage comedian of some ability in musical revue. That solid early reputation grew further throughout the 1920s leading, eventually, to a decision to try her hand as a solo act on the far less forgiving Variety stage. In a very real sense, this was a courageous break with convention. Unless their act was predominantly musical, female stand-ups were a rare sight indeed. And even if they did sing, dance or play the odd tune, funny women on stage were still far outnumbered by males - to a lesser extent, that remains the case today. Happily, for Hylda, her bravery did at least earn her a living. Although glory was not instantly forthcoming, by Easter 1933 she was making her first named Blackpool appearance at the town's Feldman's Theatre, billed as 'The Popular Lancashire Comedienne'.

The following twelve years, though, were a long and on the whole unglamorous haul, spent engaged in similar work that included another ten Blackpool appearances alongside such stars of the day as the deadpan Liverpudlian street comic Billy Bennett and 'dancers of distinction' Delfont and Toko, the former being the major agent of the future Bernard Delfont, and the latter his Japanese girl partner. Displaying that aforementioned independent streak, Baker formed a company of her own in 1939 and began to write and produce revues that were taken on tours of the lower-league Variety circuit. It was in one those revues, *Meet The Girls* in 1940, that she first unveiled a sketch in which a character called Cynthia appeared, at that point played by a girl.

Over the decade that followed, a steady stream of work rather than out-and-out fame continued to be the reward for what was nevertheless an innovative and popular act locally. In it, this tiny ball of attitude would stand clad in big woollen overcoat, knitted gloves and scruffy old feather boa, holding forth in her soon-to-be trademark Lancastrian tones. As the 'forties became the 'fifties, and with the popularity of live Variety theatre very much on the slide, Hylda Baker's career appeared to have gone as far as it could.

Then, in 1953, she returned to Feldman's Theatre - now refurbished and renamed The Queens by its new northern owner James Brennan - as second on the bill to the pianist Billy Thorburn. Among Brennan's drinking buddies was the influential local producer Jack Taylor. After the pair watched and were impressed with Baker on the opening night, Taylor booked her for a belated first summer season show at the Blackpool Hippodrome, alongside London comedian Max Bygraves and the hugely popular Trinidadian pianist Winifred Atwell. He also gave her the part of Widow Twankey in his Christmas production of *Aladdin*, in which she became that rare thing, a genuinely female pantomime dame.

Baker's impact in both productions was such that, finally, her profile had begun to rise to the levels for which she had so tirelessly worked. The newspapers took note of this 'newly-discovered' talent in their midst and regular radio appearances were also soon the norm. On stage, a return to the Queens Theatre was made in February 1955 in which she starred alongside the Blackpool ventriloquist Arthur Worsley, supplemented by a number of appearances on Brennan's *Lancashire Hotpot* Variety circuit.

That, though, was as nothing to what came next. When Baker lined up in *Pick Of The Pack*, her second summer season show for Brennan at The Queens in June 1955, her star had shot well and truly in orbit. It got there as a result of a notorious television appearance on *The Good Old Days*, in which the Cynthia sketch first created all those years ago was revised. Now, the 6ft tall and utterly silent Cynthia was played by a man in drag. For a watching audience of millions at home, the contrast with the short and pugnacious Hylda was hilarity itself.

Having at last been bathed in the national spotlight, the routine was immediately being talked about up and down the land. It went like this. Baker, after sharing a bit of friendly 'women's talk' with the audience, would confide that she was waiting for a friend, and a friend who was obviously late for the appointment, given the frequency of exasperated tugs at the boa and unnecessary adjustments of her hair. Upon her long-awaited arrival, Baker would then rebuke the deadpan Cynthia for her tardiness: 'Didn't I tell you to be soon? Be soon, I said. Be sooooon.' As the act progressed, the audience was also treated to a distinctive variety of Bakerisms such as, 'Hello, I don't think you've had the pleasure of me yet,' 'She's probably sat sitting somewhere having halcofrolic liquor' and 'What are you incinerating?'. Finally, at the close of a conversation that was as magnificently one-sided as any conversation could be, Hylda would assure her new friends that, actually, Cynthia was not as daft as she looked: 'She knows, y' know.'

If ever a line was destined to become a catchphrase, it was that one.

And sure enough, 'she knows, y' know' soon ranked alongside Al Read's 'right, monkey' in the national vocabulary. It also became the name of Baker's third Blackpool summer season and the first in which she topped the bill herself, breaking all South Pier records in 1956. Otherwise, where Read had struggled to adapt to television, Hylda had no such difficulties. Five more Blackpool summer seasons followed, as she set about building a symbiotic relationship between television, radio and stage work.

Less happily, after thirty-five years or so of unheralded struggle, this sudden explosion of fame and fortune was seen by many as having gone straight to her head. At the very least, an independent streak that had never been far from the surface found new form in upwardly-mobile eccentricity. Hylda bought a smart new home in the upmarket area of Cleveleys and proceeded to have it decorated in a style that might most charitably be described as flamboyant. Barry Band's *Blackpool Greats* reveals that the living room boasted: '...a cocktail bar designed like an opera box with a purple and gold canopy'. Nice. There were Fragonard murals, or 'murials' as Hylda herself referred to them, beating *Coronation Street*'s Hilda Ogden to the honour by a couple of decades. The bedroom ceiling was quilted, which must have been useful, and the new star reportedly told local newspaper reporter Bill Burgess: 'Don't be dazzled by the decor. It's contemporary.'

Pride of place, though, and just edging out a doorbell that chimed the first few bars of 'Come Back To Sorrento', was a flagpole on the front lawn which, when she was in residence, flew a blue and gold pennant bearing her most famous catchphrase. Barry Band declares such taste, or lack of it, to be 'vulgar', which it most likely was. It was also undeniably individual. No surprise, therefore, that her community-minded northern neighbours got a successful petition together to have it removed. Boo!

If the bricks and mortar of Hylda Baker's domestic arrangements were a couple of thousand miles west of extraordinary, her love life was even more so. Briefly, she had been married to her manager, Charles Martin, but never had any children. All mothering instinct was instead lavished on a couple of pet monkeys, Chico and Coco, whom she clad in little fur jackets and fed bananas and cream when they felt under the weather. This simian double act lived in a furnished cage at her Cleveleys home, although she often took them to her theatre dressing room where, by all accounts, they could be relied upon to disgrace themselves.

As, indeed, could Baker herself, especially where young men were concerned. The long list of males drafted in to play the part of Cynthia season after season became a standing joke, with a fair number objecting to the extra duties they were apparently asked to perform. Unfounded rumours of orgies swept the town and she found herself ostracised by many showbusiness folk who professed themselves disgusted by her real or imagined neurotic and erotic backstage behaviour.

At which point, and as with Al Read, the danger bells must surely begin ringing. All of the above may well be true but, equally, could it not simply be the case that Hylda and her reputation were the victims of straightforward professional jealousy and the cattiness of showbiz society - particularly, it seems, in Blackpool? Can an equal case not be made that the high turnover in Cynthias owed more to perfectionism than insatiable sexual appetite? One such foil was a certain Matthew Kelly, who would go to make a name for himself as host of the Saturday night family TV shows *Game For A Laugh* and *Stars In Their Eyes*. Kelly has subsequently said that Baker would accept nothing less than a cast-iron deadpan from each of her Cynthias. If the face cracked, out they went. It is also worth bearing in mind that here was a woman making a living in a man's world. She would have learned from a very early age that, in this business, there were plenty of people around who would try to take advantage of her size and sex. Clearly, someone who had the gumption to run her own touring revue, with all that entailed, was not a person who would allow herself to be walked over by anyone. Hylda Baker was not the first strong woman to be labelled negatively, nor would she be the last.

Undeniably, though, by the close of the 1950s Hylda had become deeply unhappy, and increasingly sought refuge in drink. Five years of national fame, it seems, were not all they were cracked up to be. And when *The New Hylda Baker Show* at the Blackpool Winter Gardens Pavilion failed to repeat the success of its predecessors, her spirits - in both senses of the word - took a hammering. Furthermore, thanks to over-exposure on TV and radio, the Cynthia routine had begun to pall too. Her most recent television reviews were lukewarm to say the least. A sudden bout of pneumonia, then, ought perhaps to have compounded her problems. In fact, the opposite was true. Enforced recuperation simply concentrated her mind on what she might do to bounce back.

The result was reinvention as a high quality character actor, both in film and television. Whether through luck or judgement, that entailed a move away from the claustrophobic Blackpool scene to London, where a new mood of cinematic kitchen sink realism was in the process of taking flight, much of it based back in England's north. As a seedy backstreet abortionist in the 1960 Albert Finney film, *Saturday Night And Sunday Morning,* Baker was a revelation, but she nevertheless remained unwilling or unable to give up the funny stuff completely. Her first TV situation comedy, *Our House,* was aired the following year. There were more straight parts in the landmark television dramas *Up The Junction* and *Seeing A Beauty Queen Home,* plus an appearance alongside *Carry On* star Charles Hawtrey in a 1963 sitcom that lasted just one series, *Best Of Friends,* together with a role in the Lionel Bart film musical, *Oliver!.* Theatre work at the time included a part as a trashy mother in the touring stage version of Shelagh Delaney's *A Taste Of Honey.* Suitably revitalised, in 1964 she returned to Blackpool for a first summer season in six years with *What A Joyride* at the Grand Theatre.

By any standards it had been an astonishing comeback, but the most popular contribution to an eventful career was still to come. In 1968, in tandem with Jimmy Jewel of earlier Jewel and Warriss fame, Hylda Baker first appeared a Granada sitcom set in a Colne pickle factory. Its name was *Nearest And Dearest* and there will be more about that show and the colourful off-screen relationship between its two central characters anon. Suffice for now to say that it ran for five series and even topped the traditionally huge ratings for *Coronation Street* at one point.

So successful was *Nearest And Dearest* that it also spawned spin-off stage shows. These included the 1971 Blackpool summer season Grand Theatre show, *Not On Your Nellie,* in which the pickles were replaced by black puddings and Jimmy Jewel's part was taken first by the comedian Ken Platt and then Joe Gladwin, who had form as a regular on the original TV show. The spin-off span full circle when Baker then starred in a sitcom of the same name, *Not On Your Nellie,* for London Weekend. In that show, Bolton-based Nellie Pickersgill (Baker) was summoned to Fulham to help her father run a pub, where a clash of regional accents seemed to be the main gag. *Not On Your Nellie* stuck around for three series, at the end of which Jack Douglas was installed as new landlord.

The Nellie Pickersgill character sternly disapproved of alcohol, but away from *Not On Your Nellie* Baker still drank heavily. Her need for the old-fashioned morphine had never truly gone away. Adding to her woes was the sad fact that she was also showing signs of senile dementia, or Alzheimer's as we would know it today, and struggling to remember her lines. Fear of failure, the effects of her illness and a dark reputation built up over the years all combined to alienate her still further from a showbiz society that increasingly didn't want to know. Privately, she seldom made new friends and the few she had drifted by the wayside. Publicly, work all but dried up.

Somewhat remarkably then, despite her growing personal problems, Hylda Baker once again fought her way back to national prominence, albeit briefly, when she teamed up with the bluff Cockney character actor Arthur 'Arfur' Mullard. The double act gave Hylda her final television appearance and a bizarre one at that. The occasion was an August 1978 episode of the BBC's musical chart show, *Top Of The Pops*. Mullard and Baker were there to promote 'You're The One That I Want', a novelty hit spoof of a song in the film version of the musical *Grease*, as performed by a couple of sex symbols, John Travolta and Olivia Newton John. In her version, it was the indefatigable 73-year-old Hylda who was clad in blonde wig and painted-on black leather jeans, crooning such immortal lines as: "If you're filled with infection, you're too shy to convey, medicate in my direction..." Despite boasting the worst display of lip-synching since Sergio Leone's spaghetti westerns and doubtless ruining many an evening meal, this mindbogglingly camp display led to a rush of bookings on the gay cabaret circuit.

As a last throw of the dice, it took some beating. But with her health continuing to deteriorate, for Hylda the work soon dried up as before. Once again she was largely left to fend for herself and in 1983 was hospitalised after a nervous breakdown. The remainder of her life was spent in a London nursing home provided by the Entertainment Artiste's Benevolent Fund. Alone and lonely, she passed away aged 81 in May 1986, in Horton Hospital, Sussex. The newspapers scarcely noticed and there were fewer than ten people at her funeral. It was a sad if somehow appropriate farewell for a comedian who had once demanded that a potential admirer should: 'stop dallying with my afflictions'.

Although the late 1940s and 'fifties were very much the Golden Age of radio - replete as it was with such staples as *Take It From Here*, *Hancock's Half Hour* and Peter Brough's *Educating Archie*, ventriloquism and all - as a greater proportion of the public began to invest in television sets, so did the popularity and influence of the visual medium rise accordingly.

Television's first ever comedy series was *How Do You View?*, a title which emphasised its novelty value, as had been the case on the wireless so many years before. Broadcast in 1949, the programme starred the gap-toothed cad-about-town Terry Thomas, who welcomed his viewers thus: 'Are you frightfully well? You are? Oh, good show.' Whether *How Do You View?* actually was a good show is now sadly lost to the mists of time, although the fact that it was broadcast live and had Jimmy Young as a regular vocalist might give us a clue. Another to star was the Liverpudlian comedian, Avril Angers who played a character called Rosie Lee.

Of firm music hall stock, Angers was the daughter of the comedian Harry Angers and Fol-de-Rols dancer Lilian Erroll. After debuting in a Brighton concert party aged 14, the young miss Angers embarked on a similar path to that trodden by her parents, which took in wartime tours with ENSA and Variety appearances in cabaret and on radio. Her success alongside Thomas eventually won her a sitcom of her own. Shown in 1954 and set in the offices of the fictitious women's magazine *Lady Fare*, it was called *Dear Dotty* and was the first such sitcom to be headlined by a solo female comedian. In it, Angers played wannabe journalist Dotty Binns whose attempts to win promotion to the fourth estate inevitably led to 'hilarious' consequences. Throughout a long and varied career on stage, screen and radio, Angers would continue to spring up in television sitcoms from that moment on.

Until *How Do You View?*, much early television output had consisted of spruced-up radio shows - such as *The Charlie Chester Show*, better known on the wireless as *Stand Easy* - or short sketches featuring the likes of the BBC's resident clown and children's entertainer, Mr Pastry. Played by the Norwich-born comedian-cum-acrobat Richard Hearne, *Mr Pastry* was a fixture of BBC television in its earliest days at the Alexandra Palace and remained so for over thirty years. Such talents as Joyce Grenfell and Bobby Howes also provided occasional comic turns and monologues. The shortest television career ever, meanwhile, was surely that of well-known child impersonator Harry Hemsley, whose unintelligible and imaginary little boy had already proved a major hit on radio (catchphrase: 'What did Horace say?'). When the BBC adapted the idea for television with *Mind Your Manners*, to be shown in the children's strand *Telescope*, Hemsley must have welcomed the development as a significant career opportunity. Tragically, though, on 8th April 1951, he suffered a heart attack two days before making the last in a seven-episode run and that was very much that.

Otherwise, for most entertainers, the 1950s were a great time to take a first fledgling step towards national fame and fortune. Among a whole raft of up-and-comers who made full use of the opportunities offered by television to lift their public profile and gain invaluable front-of-camera experience can be found Charlie Drake, Terry Scott, Bob Monkhouse, Max Wall, the prat-falling Norman Wisdom and the much-maligned Benny Hill, whose early sense of visual fun and invention mark him out as a true pioneer of groundbreaking television comedy whatever his later detractors may claim.

An act of equal, if not even greater originality was Tommy Cooper. Clad in his trademark fez and a purveyor of magic tricks that went hopelessly and hilariously wrong, Cooper was one of several comics whose TV debut came on the BBC talent show, *New To You*, in 1948. At first, it seems, the viewing public did not know quite what to make of the amiably incompetent giant, reacting to his disasters with pity rather than amusement. They caught on eventually and a show of his own, *It's Magic*, followed in 1952. Just like that. From there, it was onward and upward. Tommy Cooper is, in fact, one of the first examples of a comedian who owes his status as a 'British comedy legend' almost entirely to the new invention. Certainly, it is difficult to imagine him doing so well on the wireless. The common consensus is not wrong: he really was a comedian that you only had to look at to laugh. How would the nation ever have known that without the presence of a TV set in the corner?

Meanwhile, among the northern comics attracted by the pull of the small screen during this period was a 'northern comedian' who was not actually northern at all. His name was Reg Dixon and he was a man who offers a vivid illustration of the impact the switch from radio might have on a performer's public perception. Not to be confused with the Reginald

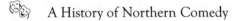

Dixon of Blackpool Tower organ playing fame, on the wireless, Dixon and his entirely manufactured softly-spoken northern tones - he was actually born in Coventry - were popular indeed. It must have come as some surprise, then, for TV viewers to discover that he was actually six feet tall and weighed 16 stone. His gentle catchphrase, 'I've been proper poorly,' can't have been quite the same after that.

By the time of his first TV appearance, a fifteen-minute stand-up set in 1953, Dixon was already a Variety theatre entertainer of some renown, notably taking over from George Formby in *Zip Goes A Million* at the Palace Theatre, when the bigger name star fell ill. To his great credit, *Zip* continued to play to packed houses without Formby for another eighteen months and was no doubt a deciding factor in him being asked to make that television debut.

Dixon - who also had a reputation as one of the great pantomime dames - had to wait over two years for his next small screen outing. But when it came it was suitably historic: a starring role in *Confidentially*, an ITV sketch show shown the day after the service launched in September 1955. A year later, he made eight episodes of another comedy sketch show for the same channel, *Let's Stay Home*, in which he starred alongside a man who would go on to become one of Benny Hill's trusty sidekicks, Henry McGee.

Dixon's third ITV series in 1957 proved to be his last. *People Like Us* was set in an unexceptional boarding house in a provincial town, with Dixon and the waif-like Mancunian Sally Barnes, who had starred alongside Frank Randle in the Mancunian films *Holidays With Pay* (1948) and *Somewhere In Politics* (1949), playing a librarian and a shop assistant. If that doesn't sound like a particularly intriguing premise for comedy, then that's because it wasn't. The show was pulled after three episodes with the critics circling like vultures. Sadly, the TV careers of both Dixon and Barnes never really recovered, although, years later, the former did at least get to make one last television appearance in *The Gang Show Gala*, a Christmas special to celebrate the 30th annual reunion of Ralph Reader's RAF *Gang Show*, in 1970. Reg Dixon's retirement from radio and stage eventually came about as a result of ill health and he died in 1984.

Among several comedians who were able to use television as a means of prolonging a simultaneously successful wireless career was Wigan-born funnyman Ted Ray. In an era that wasn't exactly starved of popular radio series, his long-running *Ray's A Laugh* show was a mainstay of the airwaves for twelve years, turning its eponymous hero into a genuine household name in the process.

By the time of its first broadcast in 1949, Ted Ray - or Charles Olden as he was born in November 1905, his family soon re-locating to Liverpool - had long been following in his comedian father's footsteps. Having launched a career on the music hall stage as Nedlo (Olden backwards, geddit?), the violin-playing gypsy, he made his professional stage debut at the Palace Theatre, Preston in 1927. It was in a show that was billed as a mixture of 'fiddling and fooling' and, in the space of just three years, he rose to become a regular on the London stage.

As his violin-playing appearance alongside Will Hay in the film *Radio Parade of 1935* confirms, Ray was quickly accepted as a bona fide member of the comedy establishment. And it is that group which Hay is blatantly championing in a typically subversive attack on the reluctance of the BBC to embrace the possibilities of popular entertainment during that pre-war era. Hay is cast in the film as a thinly-disguised Lord Reith, determinedly trying to keep his radio station (NBG - i.e. 'No Bloody Good') as dull and highbrow as possible.

No one knew it then, of course, but that was a situation which was never destined to last. Indeed, Reith himself was already well on his way to becoming a spent BBC force. Even so, at this early stage of his career, the canny Nedlo sniffed that very same wind of change. Influenced by the cool, wise-cracking urbanity of American comedians and ever a keen lover of golf, he adopted the moniker of 1920s golfer, Ted Ray, and kicked his violin into the long grass. Instead, he concentrated on quickfire comedy patter and quips. He also took the then highly unusual step of eschewing a visually amusing music hall style outfit and appeared on stage in a smart modern-day lounge suit, jostling with Sunderland's George Doonan for the honour of being the first ever British comedian to do so.

Doonan, born eight years earlier than Ray in 1897, was another to come from a theatrical family who ended up being a hit on the wireless. His signature tune, 'Make It A Party, Gay and Hearty,' gives a clue to his easy going style. Doonan's own debut had come as an eleven-year-old in a touring revue called *Casey's Court*, in which the likes of Jimmy James and Charlie

Chaplin also made very early appearances. According to Roy Hudd's *Cavalcade of Variety Acts*, on radio, Doonan used regularly to kick himself in the backside, to the accompaniment of a beat on a drum. 'I don't much care for that very much, old man,' he would admonish himself. 'You deserve a kick in the pants. Take that.' In later years largely forgotten, he died in 1973.

Ted Ray's confident persona was to win him much greater longevity. When *Ray's A Laugh* began in 1949, it was if its protagonist-in-chief had spent a lifetime preparing for the moment. Alongside the Australian actress Kitty Bluett, who played his wife, Ted's domestic capers quickly caught the national imagination and provided a radio springboard not only for Ray himself, but many another future talent too.

One such was an aspiring 23-year-old impressionist named Peter Sellers, who played Crystal Jollibottom, a woman with a bizarre penchant for howling 'Stop it! You saucebox!' in a crazed soprano. The character actor Patricia Hayes and *Carry On* star-in-waiting Kenneth Connor also appeared, the latter as the flamboyantly effeminate Sidney Mincing. A one time oppo of Tommy Handley, Fred Yule, played Ray's brother-in-law. Laidman Browne was his boss, Mr Trumble, Pat Coombs took on the role of the splendidly named Ursula Prune and there was even a part for the animal impersonator Percy Edwards, who played Gregory the chicken.

For his musical interludes, Ray and his producers turned to Bob and Alf Pearson - 'We bring you melodies from out of the sky, my brother and I' - a sibling singing duo who hailed from Sunderland, having been born in 1907 and 1910 respectively. Their gentle and pleasant harmonies complemented the style of the show perfectly and it was Bob who also provided the voice of a little girl, Jennifer, whose catchphrase was, wait for it, 'my name's Jennifer'. Another much-loved catchphrase was the uncannily accurate: 'If you haven't been to Manchester, you haven't lived.'

So successful was *Ray's A Laugh* that Ray subsequently made four Royal Variety Performance appearances, three of them consecutive. It also won him a role as MC on the BBC's radio Variety show *Calling All Forces* in 1950. That same year, Ted Ray embarked on a second consecutive term as King Rat of the Grand Order of Water Rats, a role that he returned to for a third go fourteen years later, in 1964.

If Ted Ray had revealed himself to be a radio natural, he looked equally at home in front of the telly cameras once a monthly comedy series, *The Ted Ray Show*, was launched in 1955, running parallel to a radio programme that had still six years left in it. The first series of *The Ted Ray Show* was Variety-driven and featured a wide array of well-known international guest stars. Subsequent series, however, went down the stand-up comedy route as its producers struggled to find an ideal format. By series four, in 1958, the domestic routines favoured by *Ray's A Laugh*, but this time starring Diane Hart as Ray's wife and Kenneth Connor as her interfering brother, were deemed the best way to go. It flopped horribly and so a whole new team of writers was drafted in for series five and six in which sketch comedy now became the mantra. In many ways, such chopping and changing was merely indicative of a medium still trying to find its feet and, amid this creative maelstrom, Ray also found time to record a 1956 show, *Hip Hip Who Ray*, for ATV. In it, he performed stand-up routines over six consecutive Saturday nights, penned by his BBC writers Sid Colin and George Wadmore.

A taste for diversity would be a feature of Ted Ray's television career from then onward. And while he never quite hit the same huge heights that he had managed in radio, as TV grew in popularity so too did Ray's friendly face become increasingly familiar. Perhaps most famously, he was a regular game show panelist alongside the likes of Arthur Askey, Jimmy Edwards and Cyril Fletcher on McDonald Hobley's *Does The Team Think?*. Along with a whole host of other such 'family' entertainers, he read stories on the BBC's long-running children's show *Jackanory*, tried his hand at acting in an ill-fated 1965 *Comedy Playhouse* pilot *Happy Family* and earlier that year popped up on an improvisational courtroom-style game show, *I Object*, in which Ray and Charlie Chester appeared as counsels for or against topical propositions put before a twelve-man jury, with the impressively mustachioed Edwards acting as judge.

In 1966, with Hobley and Chester, Ted Ray was also in on the first series of *It's A Knockout*, a rather more athletic and physically inventive game show in which town was pitted against town. At the height of its popularity in the 1970s, *It's A Knockout* went on to make enormous stars of the northern sporting trio Eddie Waring, Arthur Ellis and Stuart Hall. Sadly, owing to a car crash that led to a reduction in public appearances in the middle years of that decade, Ray was unable to join his original co-hosts in the programme's tenth anniversary special.

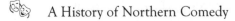

Nowadays, the notion of an entertainer flitting between radio and television has become so commonplace as to be beyond notice. As one of that concept's earliest success stories, however, Ted Ray was able to make good use of the profile gained in both mediums by winning a starring role in a third: cinema. A 1959 role as headmaster William Wakefield in *Carry On Teacher* was his one and only appearance in a series that, once it found double entendre, was up for much saucier things. Although Ted was one of the best things in it (damned faint praise, admittedly), the film's producers, Peter Rogers and Gerald Thomas, never called on his services again.

It hardly mattered. By the time of his death as a result of a heart attack a fortnight before his 72nd birthday in November 1977, and two years after the motor accident that had so badly shaken him up, Ted Ray had already enjoyed the fullest of lives. Not only had he straddled four entertainment mediums, he had written a couple of autobiographies too; *Raising The Laughs* (1952) and *My Turn Next* (1963). With the help of his wife, Dorothy, he also left two sons, both of whom went on to carve influential television careers of their own: the actor Andrew Ray and his BBC producer and *Face The Music* panelist brother, Robin.

The unusually sharp-dressed Ted Ray, then, was a born entertainer with an equally sharp eye on the future. But a more traditional northern comedian who also made the most of the career opportunities offered by early television, Norman Evans, had a far less conventional theatrical background. Nor was he able to enjoy the length of service on the medium that his talents deserved.

Like Al Read before him and a great northern comedian still to come whom he would influence enormously, Les Dawson, Evans first developed his comic patter as a salesman. Also like Read, he did not hit the professional showbiz trail until relatively late in life. In fact, he would probably never have done so at all had another northern comedy legend not given him the encouraging shove that he needed. Gracie Fields was the catalyst in question. After appearing with the former Castleton office boy in a charity show at the pair's hometown Rochdale Hippodrome in 1932, it was she who enthusiastically suggested that he should make a paid career of it. More importantly, 'Our Gracie' then backed up her initial encouragement by giving Evans his debut in professional theatre at the Chiswick Empire, in front of Sir Oswald Stoll, in 1934.

In the mid to longer-term, though, it was Evans's own talent and friendly nature that were the true engines of his success. Within three years he had made his Royal Variety Show debut, the first of three as it turned out. From there, his fame grew to the extent that, over a decade later, he made an unlikely guest appearance on America's long-running *The Ed Sullivan Show*, in those days known as *Toast of the Town*.

Why unlikely? Well, mainly because of the unashamedly northern English nature of Evans's act. Oh, to be a fly on an uptown New York apartment wall as this everyday bloke from Rochdale introduced the residents of that bustling metropolis to the immortal Fanny Fairbottom and her imaginary neighbour over the garden wall. What *can* they have made of his gossiping northern housewife, lacking in false teeth but blessed with a mammoth bosom, in the Bible belt down south or on the sun-drenched beaches of California? One thing is for sure, Fanny, all gurn and grimmace, was more working class Oldham than trailer trash Ohio.

Then again, Sullivan's Vaudeville show did have a reputation for diversity - later guests would include Noel Coward, Rocky Marciano, Nat King Cole, the Lone Ranger and, most famously, the Beatles and Elvis Presley - so there was usually something for everyone. And Evans himself wasn't daft. He went on to make three appearances on the show in total, mainly because he adapted his parochial routine accordingly, and threw his trumpet-playing glove puppet Eddie Panda more prominently into the mix. The Yanks were won over by chain-smoking Eddie and Evans was widely credited with 'putting the Vaudeville back on Broadway'.

Ultimately, however, the transatlantic conquests of Norman Evans and Eddie Panda are but a footnote in an important comedy career. His greatest legacy is the redoubtable Fanny Fairbottom. Readers who are too young to have enjoyed Fanny at first hand, so to speak, but who can recall the Cissie and Ada routines of Les Dawson and Roy Barraclough, will have a rough idea of the divine Mrs Fairbottom's *modus operandi*. Here, though, the discussions of medical ailments and scandalous goings on were performed as a monologue, as Fanny all the while adjusted her mop cap and glanced around as if on permanent watch for eavesdroppers. Anything unmentionable was mouthed silently, as per the cotton mill

manner also employed by Hylda Baker. Physically, Fanny had a face like a defecating bulldog munching on a colony of wasps. The true mark of her creator's humour, however, lay in the quality of observation. In more recent times, the playwright Alan Bennett has recognised Evans as an influence on his own love of the rhythms and cadences to be found in everyday northern speech.

Norman Evans was born on 11th June 1901, in Rochdale, where he attended Castlemere Council School. Early on, he was taken to be a quite unremarkable member of the community, and his days as a 25p per week office boy preceded later jobs in paper tube sales and as an insurance man. Yet the world of, albeit amateur, entertainment was never far from the surface. Work done, Norman played the organ at Castlemere Street Wesleyan Chapel, was a member of local amateur dramatic groups and, when prodded, could even manage a turn as an after dinner speaker. Otherwise, he liked nothing better than to disappear into the attic to play with his model railway, a hobby he maintained throughout his life.

With the dawn of World War One, Evans was excused military service as a result of a heart murmur. And it was now that he met his Yorkshire-born wife of 41 years, Annie, whom he married in 1921. Although she does not appear to have had any great influence on the development of Fanny - Evans always gave credit for that to his mother - Annie would later provide invaluable support in volatile days. It seems she wasn't too keen on the train set, mind.

Resolutely unambitious on the surface, down-to-earth Norman must nevertheless have harboured some sort of desire to display his performing skills more widely. Certainly, by the time he was spotted by Gracie Fields in 1932 he had already devised what were to become his two of his best known routines - Over The Garden Wall and At The Dentist's. His was a wicked sense of humour on the quiet and by the time Gracie's first husband, Archie Pitt, gave him his third big professional booking in 1935, Evans's days of knocking on Lancastrian doors were behind him. The booking in question was a revival of Mr Tower of London, made possible because Pitt was still in possession of all the props and scenery from a decade or so before. With Norman as its new leading man and a 14-year-old leading 'lady' in the future Corrie star Betty Driver - who would eventually headline a BBC Variety show of her own in 1952 - the updated revue ran for another two years.

For Norman, an equally successful transition from stage to radio and film followed and, in the years ahead, the *Over The Garden Wall* format was adapted for both. John E. Blakeley's Mancunian Films took it to cinema in 1950, with Fanny switching surnames from Fairbottom to the presumably more refined Lawton. Norman's co-star on that occasion was the great Jimmy James whose son, Jim Casey, provided the scripts. Evans continued to develop his garden wall gossiper on stage too, where the squawking Fanny was apt to appear one gigantic breast at a time. In the middle of the act, Evans would often pretend to slip, inducing a cringe in his female admirers. 'Ooh, that gave me a belt,' Fanny would say. 'That's the third time on the same brick this week.'

By now, Evans had already seen another couple of films off the Blakeley production line. Released in 1946, *Demobbed* and *Under New Management* put Evans alongside Nat Jackley and a diminutive female comedian who would go on to become his long-standing partner in pantomime, Betty Jumel. Born in Fairhaven in 1901, Jumel was highly respected as a versatile performer in her own right. And aside from those seasonal panto appearances, she was also regularly to be found alongside Evans in his tour revues and also on radio, whether in *Over The Garden Wall* or another of his wireless outings, *Good Evans!*. Betty Jumel lived a long and fruitful life before passing away in 1990.

In their own private life, Norman and wife Annie eventually moved to Blackpool where, due in large part to Norman's generous and amiable nature, he was met with universal affection from colleagues, locals and holidaymakers alike. Norman Evans, it seems, was something of a northern comedy cliché. He had a smile on his face no matter what his personal troubles. And his priceless sense of fun was catching. His act may have been verbally witty - 'You know that Ethel Higginbottom? She's had her face lifted. Not safe to leave anything lying about these days, is it?' - but his popularity was built firmly around warmth of personality.

Well, that and the fact that he dressed as a woman. Like Old Mother Riley before him and, in later years, Dame Edna Everage, whether Norman was being Fanny Fairbottom or another of his creations, Auntie Doleful the funereal sickbed doom-monger, while you were never really in doubt that 'she' was actually a man in woman's garb, so successful was the transition that it did tend to slip your mind. Anyhow, the sexuality on display was blurred to say the least. Evans wasn't so much a drag artist as a dealer in comedy grotesques, and easily recognisable ones at that.

And Evans did have male characters too. The hapless star of his dentist sketch, for example, was the pain-wracked, mustachioed Joe Ramsbottom, complete with giant flat cap and muffler, who would chat to an imaginary fellow patient whilst awaiting his fate. Evans also played the dentist himself, who would put his feet on his patient's chest as he tugged at the offending molars: 'Aaagh! It's come out t' back of me collar!'

Every entertainer endures spells when things are not running quite so smoothly as they once did and Norman Evans was no exception.

Evans's own relative dip in fortunes came in the early 1950s, but that did at least allow him to concentrate on his first love, pantomime, in which he was widely regarded as the best dame since Dan Leno. Here was an era in which this grand old theatrical form was studded with Variety stalwarts such as Dudley Dale (a dancing dame) and Billy Danvers, a Buttons par excellence, equipped with the splendid middle name Mikado. Those two were Liverpudlians, and from the less obvious comedy hotbed of Bridlington came 'old-man' Norman Caley.

Given the moniker 'The Mad Earl' while on a concert party tour in the Middle East, Caley, born in 1920, had an act that was every bit as wildly imaginative as the ones we see today, maybe more so. According to Roy Hudd's *Cavalcade of Variety Acts*, Caley was: 'an unpredictable, very off-beat comic whose patter and visual gags were always interspersed with a wild, maniacal infectious laugh.' Topping bills headed 'The Acme of Idiotic Entertainment', Caley's barmy old toff, described as 'still fighting against fate', was a distinct precursor of today's grand old gent of English theatre, Count Arthur Strong. Who knows, maybe the Caley and Count Arthur once worked together?

Just down the coast from Brid in Hull, local boy Bunny Doyle was another huge panto favourite. Described by that doyen of northern producers Francis Laidler as 'one of the finest pantomime comedians ever to tread the boards', Doyle's oddball persona as 'Minister for Idiotic Affairs' was perfect seasonal silliness. Clad in top hat and baggy checked suit, audiences loved him, particularly in his home city on the Humber. Already a veteran of seaside concert parties by the time he won a Croix de Guerre for Conspicuous Gallantry in the First World War, Doyle died in 1955, just as he was turning into an increasingly busy character actor.

Then there was the Sheffield-born Terry 'Toby Jug' Cantor, father of modern day comic Kenny Cantor and so named because he was shaped like a... well, you can guess the rest. Born in 1912, Cantor senior made great use of his short and chubby build, and beaming smile. Then, when his stage career was over, he produced Britain's longest-running pantomime ever at the City Varieties, Leeds, and died in 1979.

At the height of his popularity on stage, radio and in film, Norman Evans was reportedly commanding £1500 a week, a massive figure for the day. One 1947 production in which he appeared, *Red Riding Hood*, at the Theatre Royal, Leeds, proved such a hit that it continued its festive run until May the following year. Yet come the mid-fifties and - pantos apart - things were not running quite so smoothly. A car accident in 1955, in which Evans badly damaged his leg and, worse, lost an eye, could well have been a crushing blow.

A year later, though, and he was not just back in broadcasting favour, thanks to television he was apparently sitting pretty. A BBC keen to add sparkle to its small screen invited him to make the first of an eventual four shows, each named *The Norman Evans Show*. The programmes went out as part of the *Saturday Comedy Hour* and, as usual, drew heavily on the music hall tradition. Among a number of similarly surreal guests were the uniquely eccentric trio of sand-dancers, Wilson, Keppel and Betty.

Theirs was an act once seen, never forgotten. And, it has to be said, well, *seen*. The format never changed. Donned in fezs and nightshirts, all the better for displaying their scrawny legs, the male two-thirds would dance, deadpan, in what appeared to be a couple of cat litter trays. Accompanied by Luigini's 'Egyptian Ballet', the pair were supposedly performing for their seductress, the glamourous Betty Knox. That was the idea anyway. Mostly, it just looked like a couple of old men acting daft around a pretty young girl. And the older those old men became, the funnier that audiences seemed to find it. Age, however, was not allowed to wither poor 'Betty'. Over the years ahead, she was replaced more often than a fifty watt light bulb. In England's north east meanwhile, on the banks of the river Tyne, there is still an assumption that at least one of those sand-dancers must have originated in South Shields, since 'Sand-dancers' is how the residents of that fine town are collectively known, as opposed to Newcastle 'Geordies' or Sunderland 'Mackems'. Alas, it is not so. Jack Keppel was born in Liverpool, while Joe Wilson was an Irishman from Cork.

For Norman Evans, the popularity of his first BBC television outing led to *Evans Abode*, another four-show run in which he played a boarding house landlady. And, in 1958, he compered a trio of televised Variety concerts under the name *Make Yourself At Home*, one of which featured his own daughter, the singer Norma Evans. By now, though, her father was not in the best of health. Adding to his long-standing worries with regard to that First World War heart murmur, in 1945 he had also been diagnosed with cancer, a disease that he had subsequently fought off, albeit at some cost to his physical and most likely mental well-being. Nor did it help that the 1955 car accident which had put him back in a hospital bed was followed not only by a large amount of television work, but also a summer season in Llandudno and a three-month charity fund-raising tour of Canada. In 1957, he was readmitted to hospital with a strangulated hernia.

Still this most dignified and relentless of cheerful battlers fought on, entertaining the doctors and nurses as he did so. He continued to work professionally too. When, in November 1962, death finally did catch up with him, it was shortly after making his final television appearance on *Comedy Bandbox*. Years of almost continual illness were not going to stop Norman.

Gracie Fields never forgot her roots, and nor did Norman Evans. If any comedian had the 'common touch', it was he. At the peak of his fame he remained a frequent visitor to Lancashire, and hometown Rochdale in particular. And over the course of a career in which he shone as brightly as any northern star before or since, Evans raised money for a number of charitable causes and visited local schools and hospitals.

That loyalty was to be repaid after his death, albeit after a thirty-seven-year wait. On 8th August 1999, a plaque to Norman Evans was unveiled at Manchester's Opera House Theatre, on the very same day as Les Dawson was posthumously honoured in similar fashion at the nearby Palace Theatre. The headstone on Norman Evans's Blackpool cemetery grave sits snugly in an effigy of 'His Last Garden Wall'.

7
Bold as Brass

"I'd offer you a beer, but I've only got six cans."
- *Terry Collier, 'The Likely Lads'*

The dawn of television had broken too late for Norman Evans, in terms of his place in modern-day popular folk memory, if not his actual legacy. For other comedians, the medium's burgeoning popularity was mirrored by a rise in personal stature and increased career longevity.

The development of a national television service was particularly good news for wannabe professional wordsmiths, especially those of a younger vintage. On the wireless, your average comedy writer was treated, more often than not, like an uncredited ten-a-penny journeyman. Among those who were able to build a more lucrative profile on television were the southern-based duo, Frank Muir and Dennis Norden, who had already risen above the radio herd with *Take It From Here*. Another of Muir and Norden's shows, in which their dysfunctional family *The Glums* featured, accompanied their creators to the small screen, albeit not until twenty-five years later and on commercial television in 1978. Back in the 'fifties, along with offering a sharper-edged retort to the BBC's more usually winsome and nonconfrontational radio comedy fare, *The Glums* showed a new way forward and proved that well-observed character comedy with a socially satirical edge was not the exclusive preserve of England's north.

On radio, the show's star trio was Jimmy Edwards, Dick Bentley and June Whitfield who, respectively, played the cantankerous and boorish Pa Glum, his gormless son Ron and prospective daughter-in-law Eth. Mrs Glum, the mother, appeared only through the odd muffled yell and off-stage crash. Much later, on television, Bentley and Whitfield's parts went to Ian Lavender - of *Dad's Army* Private Pike fame - and Patricia Brake, although the gruff Jimmy Edwards - a clear antecedent, personality-wise, of Alf Garnett and Homer Simpson - continued in the role he was born to play.

Muir and Norden's first TV writing credit came in 1951 with *Here's Television*, a New Year review of the previous year's TV programmes. Their earliest runaway success, though, was *Whacko!*, in which Edwards, a Londoner, shone in another role for which his talents were made, that of the cane-wielding headmaster of Chiselbury public school, Professor James Edwards. Ah, a sitcom about a man who enjoys beating children... they don't make them like that anymore, do they? To be fair, *Whacko!* wasn't *just* about the humour to be derived from child abuse. The butt (ahem) of the comedy was usually the monstrous Edwards himself, a character influenced in no small way by Will Hay's schoolmaster persona, with a dash of added brutality. The show ran from 1956-1960 with a brief reprise in 1971-72 and a feature film spin-off - *Bottoms Up!* - was released in 1959. *Whacko!* then made a two-year trip to radio, where the BBC Light Programme broadcast forty-five episodes with adapted Muir and Norden scripts from 1961-1963.

By then, such a route was unusual. Normally, it worked in the opposite direction. Another hugely important reconstructed radio programme of the era was Anthony Aloysius St. John Hancock's *Hancock's Half Hour* (1956-1960), the first real example of TV situation comedy as we would know it today. Hancock's own comedic ability, honed on stage and radio, was a large part of the show's success. His portrayal of what was essentially an exaggerated version of himself - frustrated and laconic self-styled creative genius, engaged in a battle with delusion and depression, yearning to rise above his present dreary station - was sublime in its mundanity. Especially when those same ambitions were revealed as being founded on little more than angst-ridden hot air. 'Does Magna Carta mean nothing to you? Did she die in vain?'

Mainly, however, the men most responsible for this groundbreaking show were its writers, Ray Galton and Alan Simpson. Sadly, as time went on, and at the behest of various demons including his own tortured personality and worsening alcoholism, 'the lad himself' grew blind to that fact. Eventually, after firing Galton and Simpson and trying to make a solo go of it, he headed off to Australia on tour where, alone in a Sydney hotel room in 1968, Tony Hancock took his own life at the tragically wasteful age of 44. Back in England, Galton and Simpson were already moving onward and upward.

As we will see, much of Britain's best-remembered and certainly most often referenced 1950s and 'sixties television comedy series tend to be marked by intelligent writing and a more theatrical range of acting skills, as a greater taste for realism began to sweep society.

There remained, however, plenty of time for good old fashioned fun. And while Tony Hancock's deficiencies might best be described as pretentious and even philosophical, then no such accusations could be levelled at another comedy misfit who stumbled towards televisual fame as the 'fifties drew to a close. As usual, the amiably bumbling complainer in question was, of course, played by a northerner. His name was Harry Worth. I don't know why, but there it is.

At the end of a decade spent popping in and out of the medium - and often broadcasting on the northern networks alone - Harry Worth was given a first national televised vehicle of his own on New Year's Day, 1960. Its name was *The Trouble With Harry*, and in it our eponymous hero played an ineffectual wannabe author, perpetually kept in check by a domineering auntie. Over six thirty-minute episodes, it laid the platform for a remarkable surge in popularity.

So much so that when Worth's next show, *Here's Harry*, arrived, it grew into a mainstay of the schedules for the following five years, while offering a first venture into television sitcom for two writers who would become synonymous with the genre, Vince Powell and Harry Driver.

Here's Harry also gave British television one of its most iconic opening sequences ever. Who, in their time, has not tried to throw a star shape at the corner of a department store window, just like Harry Worth did? The actual window in question was located in Manchester, the city in which most of his TV shows were made. Worth himself was born and raised on the opposite side of the Pennines, in Tankersley, near Barnsley.

The fact that his father had been killed in a coal mining accident in 1918, only one year after his son's birth, did not at first appear to alter the destiny of young Harry Illingsworth. Like so many of his Barnsley contemporaries, he seemed fated to a life down the pit and duly went underground at the age of 14. If anything, he was saved by the arrival of the Second World War, during which he was stationed in Burma with the RAF. It was there that he discovered his talents as an entertainer. Upon being demobbed, Harry borrowed a book on ventriloquism from the local library. In 1946, he and two dummies, Fotheringay and Clarence, performed their first professional gig at Bradford Mechanics Institute.

Success was hardly instantaneous. In fact, Harry failed to get any more bookings at all for almost two years until, on the verge of giving up his showbusiness dreams and returning to the coal face, he finally landed a twelve-week contract in Southsea. If that was a stroke of good fortune, it was as nothing compared to his appearance on the same BBC talent showcase that had provided debut television appearances for Tommy Cooper and Peter Sellers, *New To You*, in 1948. Although, like them, he can have only been watched by the relatively small number of people who actually owned sets at that time, to have won such recognition from the respected national broadcaster instilled in Harry Worth the confidence and determination to persevere.

In 1952, ventriloquist Harry's career took another prestigious leap forward when he appeared on the same bill as Laurel and Hardy during their British tour of that year. He became so friendly with the legendary pair that when they came back to the UK to tour in 1953-54 the duo insisted that Harry should again be their supporting act. This time, however, they suggested that he should lose the ventriloquist dummies and try his hand as a stand-alone comedian instead.

Harry obliged and, despite a nervous solo debut in Newcastle, soon discovered that audiences warmed to his disarming and apologetic style, thinking it was part of the act. Harry's portrayal of a nervous wreck had been entirely genuine at first, but it was quickly obvious that it could be a useful comedy persona. By the time *Here's Harry* came along in 1960, he had honed it to perfection.

Clad in his trademark overcoat, trilby, grey suit and dark-rimmed glasses, 'Harry' was in many ways a prototype Victor Meldrew figure; only in his case good-natured and without the cantankerous attitude, but nevertheless constantly engaged in petty little brushes with authority and official bureaucracy. And where Meldrew was swiftly exasperated, the well-meaning Harry battled on cheerfully in a world that was clearly not tuned into his personal wavelength. To where did he want to travel on his return train ticket? 'Well, back here of course.' Here, in *Here's Harry*, meaning the fictional town of Woodbridge where, at 52 Acacia Avenue, Harry and his never-to-be-seen aunt, Amelia Prendergrast, lived with their pet cat, Tiddles.

So popular was *Here's Harry* that, in 1962, it won its star a Variety Club of Great Britain Award for BBC TV Personality of the Year. Displaying their usual liking for an underdog, the British public had warmed to a man for whom attempting to do the right thing, even if it was doomed to failure, meant everything. Against a background of great social change, such gentle humour was hardly fashionable and, as a result, its grace note of quiet subversion went all-but unnoticed by those with more obviously satirical works to compose and enjoy. No matter. Harry Worth soldiered on regardless. Further TV series followed, although none of them ever quite reached the heights of *Here's Harry*.

One such made for the BBC, this time called simply *Harry Worth* and running from 1966 until 1970, saw our hero leaving Woodbridge for the big wide world, where the old misunderstandings continued to ensue. Tacit recognition, perhaps, that even in mainstream Britain, once-parochial horizons were beginning to widen. In one episode, Harry was even stalked by a French femme fatale, Alexandro Bastedo, who, for reasons best known to herself, was desperate to drag him down the aisle. Nevertheless, on the surface at least, the comedy of *Harry Worth* remained defiantly unsophisticated and otherworldly.

In recent years, it has become relatively common for comedians who are normally associated with 'simple' humour, northern or otherwise, to

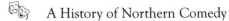

want to show off their hidden depths in more ostentatiously cerebral and theatrical productions. Harry Worth was a forerunner of this trend. In 1972, he played William Boot in Barry Took's serial adaptation of Evelyn Waugh's literary satire of war and journalism, *Scoop*. In adapting a book so rich with misunderstandings and disasters, it is easy to see why producer Michael Mills might have thought that Harry Worth was the ideal man for the part, even if just about no one else did. Sadly, the nay-sayers were proved correct. For one thing, Worth looked far too old in the role and this particular version of *Scoop* was a critical flop.

Before *Scoop* had even reached its final episode, however, Harry Worth was making the first of three series of *Thirty Minutes Worth* for Thames Television, squeezed into just thirteen months. ITV hyped the defection as a comedy coup, but the public weren't fooled. Mainly it was the same stuff that they had already seen over the past decade and a half on the BBC, only now in sketch show format. An unsuccessful follow up in 1974, *My Name Is Harry Worth*, took Harry back to a domestic setting. This time it was the boarding house of widowed landlady Mrs Maybury, played by the Oldham-born actress Lally Bowers.

After *Harry*, a one-off 1976 special back at the BBC that led to nothing, Harry Worth's television comedy career appeared to be over until, in 1979, he made an unexpected comeback as Harry Matthews, the widowed father of two teenage children in the ITV sitcom *How's Your Father?*. When questioned about that three-year screen absence, Worth insisted that he had simply been waiting for the right script to come along. Doubtless he also hoped that the more topical subject matter would be better in tune with younger, modern audiences. Teenage issues or not, however, Harry was essentially the same mildly exasperated bumbler and *How's Your Father?* was pulled after two series.

Just as unexpected was Harry Worth's final TV outing made the following year. In it, Worth again went back to the BBC for a starring role in an ill-fated Jeremy Lloyd and David Croft sitcom, *Oh, Happy Band!*, a story of brass bands and airport planning japes in which Harry played the band leader, also named Harry Worth, presumably to avoid confusion. Widely panned, it did well to complete six episodes and was an unworthy way to end a television career that had, in its day, been genuinely popular.

Afterwards, Harry Worth was shunted off to radio, a medium that was also, by common consent, on its last legs. He continued to work there relatively unnoticed before passing away in July 1989.

The belated intrusion of teenagers into Harry Worth's comedy was, in many ways, reminiscent of the BBC's own initial struggles to get to grips with a more socially and commercially fluid modern age.

For one thing, the teenage concept itself had caught the Corporation on the hop with its first appearance on these shores in the mid-1950s, via the hip-swinging antics of a young American rock 'n' roller named Elvis Aaron Presley. In Britain, to a cacophony of ear-splitting screams, four mop-topped Liverpudlians named The Beatles took up that youthful baton and ran off up Abbey Road with it. More and more, older children and younger adults no longer looked like cardboard cut-outs of mum and dad. Shockingly, for a generation who had clung on to the security blanket of 'knowing your place' throughout the austerity years of two World Wars, their offspring were developing minds of their own. The upshot: lots of new and exciting ways to challenge authority were soon being explored.

However, if it was to maintain its position as self-styled king of the broadcasting castle, the BBC had more immediate problems. Namely, competition. By 1959, the spread of ITV to the nation as a whole had brought obvious implications for its authority. As one decade ended and another began, 10.5 million licences were in circulation and around 72 per cent of the population could now access both channels. Prior to this point in British broadcasting history, the only things that swung were big bands. With the arrival of the so-called swinging 'sixties, society was well and truly embarked on a less fixed course, both morally and culturally, an upheaval for which a complacent BBC was simply not prepared.

During its first year of operations ITV had struggled financially. But by 1958 its more inventive and blatantly commercial programming had begun to reap impressive profits. Of those viewers who could receive both channels, ITV had 79 per cent of the audience share and it earned that through adopting a more populist approach. Riotous sitcoms like *The Army Game* and *The Larkins* were huge hits, as were American imports such as *I Love Lucy*. In comparison, the BBC seemed staid and out of

touch. Of those three big ITV favourites, *The Army Game* is most relevant here, starring as it did - from series three to five anyway - the goggle-eyed 'Lad from Lancashire' Ted Lune as the cowardly Private Leonard Bone.

Born Harold Garnett in Ainsworth, near Bolton, in 1922, Lune is neatly described in *Roy Hudd's Cavalcade of Variety Acts* as looking like: 'a stretched out Marty Feldman, without teeth and with a frame that made Twiggy look like Charles Atlas'. After leaving school aged 15 and starting out in life as an apprentice engineer who, in his spare time, chanced his arm delivering comic monologues at works socials, he eventually turned professional in 1947 and became hugely popular in the local working men's clubs of the early 1950s.

Lune's flat cap and gentle daftness soon earned him the nickname 'The Lad from Cocky Moor' and wider attention came when a Variety booking at the Hulme Hippodrome resulted in a call to work on radio's *Variety Fanfare*, the launching pad of many a northern comedy career, as we have seen. So well did Lune go that his own headline show, *Get Lune*, swiftly followed. Although wireless exposure unquestionably did Lune's career a huge amount of good - top-billing summer spots in Blackpool were soon a formality - an unlikely physical appearance like his was always going to prove priceless on television. As part of *The Army Game* team, Lune - named after the north Lancashire river - was right at home.

By the time Ted Lune arrived in the cast, the show - set in Hut 29 at the Surplus Ordnance Department, Nether Hopping, Staffordshire - was already a national institution, thanks in no small part to the effectiveness of its central idea. First broadcast in 1957, only twelve years after the end of World War Two, *The Army Game* was the story of a group of conscripts who were intent, one and all, upon seeing out their days in uniform by having as much fun as they could get away with and doing as little work as possible. In a country where National Service was still an obligation, that was a situation which struck a major chord. So popular did the show become that its stars were lauded with extraordinary levels of adoration; from Bernard Bresslaw, whose catchphrase as Private Popeye Popplewell, 'I only arsked!', was eventually made into a film of that name, to Dick Emery, whose turn as Private 'Chubby' Catchpole came in the fifth and final series in 1961. A madcap environment that, at various times, also included Charles Hawtrey as the knitting Private 'Professor' Hatchett,

Doctor Who-in-waiting William Hartnell as bullying Sergeant Major Percy Bullimore and Michael Medwin's Sergeant Bilko-esque cockney Corporal Springer, ratcheted up another manic notch with Lune's arrival.

To be fair to the BBC, it had actually dipped a tentative toe into the waters of American sitcom with *The Phil Silvers Show* - in which Sergeant Bilko himself appeared - a couple of years before *The Army Game* hit ITV screens. However, the inspiration for *Army Game* writer Sid Colin had not been that transatlantic smash, it was a rather less wonderful 1956 British film, *Private's Progress*, in which that archetypal upper class toff, Ian Carmichael, appeared. Also in *Private's Progress* was William Hartnell, who left *The Army Game* for a role in another British comedy film, *Carry on Sergeant*, two years later. Given that he was joined in that venture by fellow cast members Charles Hawtrey and Norman Rossington, who played Private 'Cupcake' Cook (so named after his penchant for food parcels from his Liverpudlian family), then the influence of *The Army Game* on the *Carry On* tradition that followed is clear.

If any British character comedian had the potential to be a major *Carry On* star it was surely Ted Lune. Sadly, it was not destined to happen. Despite troubles in his personal life that saw him swap his first wife Florence for a fellow entertainer named Valerie Joy, in public Lune appeared to be doing well. He made a cameo appearance as a dishwasher alongside Frankie Vaughan in the 1959 film, *The Lady is a Square*, and also had a slot in a short-lived BBC stand-up-cum-revue show, *Double Six*, hosted by Morecambe and Wise. The situation, though, was about to take a sharp turn for the worse.

Having made stars of many of its principals - not least Alfie Bass and Bill Fraser, who would continue their roles as Private Montague 'Excused Boots' Bisley and Sergeant Major Claude Snudge in a follow-up series of their own - *Bootsie and Snudge* (1961-63, with an up-dated reprisal in 1974) - *The Army Game* itself reached the end of its run. In 1962, a particularly nasty bout of bronchitis forced Lune, always dogged by ill health, to stand down from the cast of *Humpty Dumpty* at the Liverpool Empire. Apart from a cameo as a circus 'Skeleton Man' in the camp 1967 British slasher movie *Berserk!*, he never really worked again. Ted Lune died, aged just 46, in 1968.

Even today, there is a certain class of person for whom watching ITV would be akin to spooning their dinner from a discount-supermarket bean tin. Only considerably more vulgar.

In 1960, it was just such an attitude - dressed in a concern for standards - that encouraged the Government to set up the Pilkington Committee, a group of manual labourers and working class housewives from Manchester, Leeds, Liverpool and Newcastle, who were given a brief to report on the current state of British broadcasting. The scathing nature of that committee's findings left the BBC rubbing its hands in glee. Just joking about the labourers and housewives, by the way.

Almost since ITV's birth, the BBC had been on the back foot, audience-wise. On ITV, for example, teenagers were well catered for from the start, with exciting rock 'n' roll shows like *Cool for Cats* (1956-61) and *Oh Boy!* (1958-59). The BBC, in contrast, looked about as hip as Lord Reith's bushy eyebrows. And even when it did heed the warning signs, by ending its long-established 'Toddler's Truce' hour between 6.00-7.00pm, for example, to launch *Six-Five Special* in 1957, it was being - in modern-day marketing speak - *reactive* rather than *proactive*. When the BBC began to dabble in soap opera, it did so via the *Grove Family* (1954-57), a group of nice lower middle-class southerners. On ITV, the introduction of an avowedly northern working class *Coronation Street*, in 1960, showed that culture could have a more popular definition entirely. In fact, by the middle of 1961, there were more people watching *Coronation Street* than had gathered around those flickering TV sets for the Queen's Coronation eight or so years before. Cinema also developed an appetite for gritty northern kitchen sink realism, with films like *Room At The Top* (1959) and *Saturday Night And Sunday Morning* (1960), helping to re-popularise that medium too.

The most potent weapon in ITV's audience-attracting armoury, however, was its liking for gaudy old-style Variety, the very definition of 'low-brow' entertainment. Programmes such as *Sunday Night at the London Palladium*, which ran, initially, from 1955-67, attracted the viewers in their millions and that, in turn, attracted advertisers. Sensitive to accusations of what today would be called 'dumbing down', and aware of the need to fulfill its own lesser public service commitment, ITV did at least pay lip service to some of the old Reithian ideals, primarily through its Sunday night *Armchair Theatre* programme, which featured adaptations of the work of Oscar Wilde and F. Scott Fitzgerald among others. Later, there was the odd socially engaging new play by the likes of Harold Pinter but, really, it wasn't fooling anyone. Bums on seats were what mattered.

This, of course, upset everyone for whom broadcasting was held in a 'higher', and 'purer', regard. And when the voices of complaint grew loud enough, the Government finally felt compelled to act. The result was the aforementioned Pilkington Committee report, published in 1962, in which, to cut a very long story short, a commercial television company at the peak of its profitability was judged to have become too trivial.

The gist of the report ran thus: In the brazen pursuit of ratings, ITV had slid too far downmarket. It was producing too much mindless pap for the masses, and not enough intellectually improving material of a higher educational quality. The undiscerning working classes were in danger of being depraved by rampant commercialism.

In hindsight, the Pilkington Committee was clearly swimming against the tide of history. But for the publicly-funded BBC such findings were manna from heaven, especially as a third television channel would shortly be up for grabs. In April 1964, the same year in which Harold Wilson's Labour Government ended thirteen years of Conservative rule, BBC2 was launched on the technically superior 625-line UHF frequency, leaving the various regional ITV companies to fight among themselves for a bigger share of advertising revenue.

By then, a previously-stagnant BBC was fast making up lost ground in the ratings war. Under the leadership of new Director General, Hugh Carleton Greene, brother of novelist Graham and a man with a stated aim of dissipating the 'ivory tower stuffiness' which still clung to the Corporation, 'Auntie Beeb' was subtly changing her approach. Let the commercial channels chase money via the lowest-common denominator, the BBC was about quality rather than quantity. It would no longer, however, talk down to audiences, working class or otherwise. Instead it would assume that its viewers were as bright and intelligent as the programmes themselves ought to be. As Greene later reflected in his 1969 autobiography, *The Third Floor Front*, he chose: 'to encourage enterprise and the taking of risks. I wanted to make the BBC a place where talent of all sorts, however unconventional, was recognised and nurtured.'

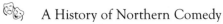

Whether elitism was indeed henceforth banished from the BBC, to be replaced thereafter by a shining torch of quality for its own sake, must be debatable. After all, the Corporation's modern-day schedules are as likely to include such 'reality' shows as *Snog Marry Avoid*, as they are Mendelssohn recitals from the Royal Academy of Music. And distinctions between 'elite', 'quality' and 'popular' entertainment cannot help but be riven with value judgements. Equally, the BBC continues to be accused of inhabiting a self-contained world of its own creation, oblivious to the realities of life in the north and all areas distant of London. Yet as the 1960s progressed, it *did* undergo a distinct and detectable shift in attitude.

In response to *Coronation Street*, for example, the Beeb came up with a twice-weekly soap opera of its own, *Compact*, which ran for three years. Longer running were *Dr Finlay's Casebook*, a medical drama that saw out the decade and, from 1962, a series that revolutionised the portrayal of policemen on our TV screens, *Z Cars*, set in the north west of England and performed almost exclusively in regional working class accents. Between 1964 and 1970, the BBC also produced *The Wednesday Play*, a strand which featured such naturalistic masterpieces of TV drama as *Up The Junction*, with Hylda Baker and all, *Stand Up, Nigel Barton* (also 1965) and *Cathy Come Home* (1966), giving a start to writers and directors like Dennis Potter and Ken Loach along the way.

And where the BBC went with drama, it also went with situation comedy. Its preference now was for a more naturalistic and authentic brand of humour, building on the trail already blazed by *Hancock's Half Hour*, in which single set theatricality became the norm.

At one, less well-populated end of the spectrum, that meant physical farce - a genre in which a chap from Yorkshire was soon to become king. In 1962, the BBC began to broadcast a series called *Dial RIX*, named after that show's star, Brian Rix, whose trousers were destined never to rise above his ankles. Born in 1927 in Cottingham, near Hull, Rix had served in the RAF and as a Bevin Boy before forming his own theatre company in 1947. Its speciality was farce, defined in the *Oxford English Dictionary* as: 'coarsely comic dramatic works based on ludicrously improbable events', a theatrical tradition stretching back to Aristophanes. In *Dial RIX*, each episode was topical in nature and nine episodes were made in all, some of which also starred Rix's wife, Elspet Gray. From that point onward, television farce and Brian Rix were inseparable bedfellows.

Although Rix was a northerner by birth, it is nevertheless a fact that densely-plotted farce, as a theatrical form, has hardly been a defining feature of northern English humour, where character and personality have tended to be more significant. The modern-day king of northern comedy, Peter Kay, probably put it best in his 2006 autobiography, *The Sound Of Laughter* (Century): 'All that running around half naked and tripping over next door's dog never did it for me.'

Brian Rix's comedy may not have been to everyone's taste, but he was undoubtedly a pioneer in one other important area. In the 1970s, a show presented by him called *Let's Go* was one of the first television programmes to be made specifically for people with learning difficulties. With *My Farce From My Elbow*, Rix must also surely be in the running for a prize in the best autobiography title stakes, although the names of his theatrical histories, *Tour de Farce* and *Life in the Farce Lane*, do pale significantly in comparison.

More in keeping with the northern comedy tradition were the BBC comedies that took a more down-to-earth approach, even when they were set in the south. One such early success was *The Rag Trade* (1961), set in the raucous workshop of Fenner Fashions, wherein Miriam Karlin played the shop steward Paddy - complete with catchphrase 'everybody out!' - and a young Sheila Hancock also appeared. Here, for the time, an almost exclusively female cast got all the funny lines. *The Rag Trade* ran for thirty-seven episodes and went on to become a stage show too, before making a bit of a limp comeback on London Weekend Television in 1977.

If *Dial RIX* could never be described as landmark television, another BBC sitcom to first see the light of day in 1962 certainly was. Its writers were Ray Galton and Alan Simpson, fresh from being unceremoniously dumped by Tony Hancock. The fourth in a strand of one-off comedies by that pair, under the name *Comedy Playhouse*, was called *The Offer* and it featured a couple of West London rag and bone men, played by respected stage actors Wilfrid Brambell and Harry H. Corbett. The BBC suggested that it might make rather a good series.

At first, Galton and Simpson weren't keen. After their Hancock shenanigans, they now had creative freedom and were reluctant to be tied down to a single series again so soon. Opting to keep their employers happy, however, and suspecting that Brambell and Corbett would be too busy to repeat their parts anyway, they said yes, only for the actors to do likewise. Thus was *Steptoe And Son* born, the first truly magnificent British situation comedy.

Of its two central protagonists, Brambell, born in Dublin in 1912, already had a reputation for playing wizened old men when the grasping, lazy widower Albert Steptoe came his way. Physically, therefore, he was ideally suited to the role. And although much of Albert's comedy was quite broad - disgusting personal habits provided one rich comic seam - Brambell's qualities as a serious actor ensured that his more subtle emotional insecurities were displayed equally well. The Steptoe of the title may have been a cunning, selfish and, you suspected, malodorous piece of work, but he was also mortally terrified of being left alone by the one person in his life upon whom he could depend. Step forward the equally terrific Harry H. Corbett, as Albert's unmarried son Harold.

Born in Rangoon, Burma in 1925, but raised by an aunt in the schools and mean streets of Manchester, Harry H. Corbett arrived in northern England at just three years of age, after the untimely death of his mother. His father had been an army officer and Corbett too ended up serving his country as a Royal Marines radiographer during World War Two. Drama, though, was his thing and with the war over, he returned to England's north west, where he became an understudy at the Chorlton Repertory Company. There he gained enough experience to win a place in Joan Littlewood's famously idealistic Theatre Workshop of the 1950s, where he soon gained a solid reputation in productions of Ibsen, Jonson and Shakespeare. As something of an earnest, tortured soul himself, Joan Littlewood's fierce and uncompromising attitude to theatrical 'reality' struck a chord with Corbett. 'Piss off to Shaftesbury Avenue,' she is said to have once told a young Michael Caine. 'You will only ever be a star.'

As Harold Steptoe, whose dreams of escape from his narrow and humdrum life are thwarted at every turn, Corbett juggled hilarity and poignancy to stunning effect. In this, he was helped both by the quality of the writing and the situation in which the characters were trapped. Steptoe's junkyard, with its echoes of decay and the unforgiving march of time, was a perfect, poetic, metaphor. It spoke brilliantly of the ultimate futility of existence and of how family responsibilities can become an emotional cage. In Harry H. Corbett, with his own back story of loss and displacement, the show's makers had the perfect embodiment of Harold's inner psychological battle. Like all great art, *Steptoe And Son* provided far more questions than answers.

To what great heights might Harold have climbed had he not been cursed by this accident of birth? Must love always be about possession? How far will human selfishness go? And was Harold actually his father's prisoner at all? Maybe he was just an ineffectual dreamer, who lacked the courage to change, and old Albert was merely a cash-strapped, genuinely worn-out pragmatist. After all, no matter how often Harold liked to play the sophisticated, literate man about town, he *was* just an unkempt rag and bone man, wasn't he? Aside from his father, Harold's closest true friend was his horse, Hercules, another creature who would doubtless have preferred to be running around in a field somewhere. Along with his heightened sense of self-preservation, perhaps Albert simply didn't want to see his son get hurt. For let us suppose that Harold *had* found the courage to get up and go, could he have ever *really* made a mark in the glamourous world of his imagination? And if not, then just who *was* mostly to blame for imprisoning poor Harold? Harold himself? Albert? The restrictive rules of a class-ridden society? Life itself? And when it all came down to it, did any of it really matter anyway? Wouldn't Harold Steptoe have just been better off whistling a happy tune and feeding his horse? All that philosophising and thinking never made anyone happy. Samuel Beckett, Jean-Paul Sartre and Bertolt Brecht never managed anything so existentially profound between them.

Deciding to go out on top, Galton, Simpson, Corbett, Brambell and the rest called it a day at the end of a fourth series in 1965, before twice bringing the characters back for brief appearances in a 1966 sketch on *The Ken Dodd Show* and a 1967 Christmas special. Yet the show never stopped being repeated and, eventually, *Steptoe And Son* moved to radio where it managed fifty-two episodes, in 1966-67 and from 1971 to 1976. Just before that latter run, in 1970, the BBC finally responded positively to calls for the show to be revived on television. If later biographical dramas are to be believed, Corbett at least had his doubts about being irredeemably typecast in the role, but by then it was probably too late

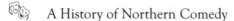

anyway. With the return of Harold and Albert, *Steptoe And Son* duly ran for a further four series, this time in colour. If anything, it was now an even bigger success and a couple of predictably average feature film spin-offs followed, *Steptoe And Son* (1972) and *Steptoe And Son Ride Again* (1974). The formula was also successfully exported to American television by the US producer Norman Lear, whose *Sandford And Son* (1972-75), wherein the lead characters were black, followed another major trans-Atlantic hit, *All In The Family*, which was also based on a landmark British 'sixties sitcom, *Till Death Us Do Part*.

So, all was good then? Well, not quite. For although the role of Harold Steptoe brought in regular work for Harry H. Corbett, it seems that he and the actually rather fastidious Wilfrid Brambell were as apt to fall out off the screen as they were on it. And then there were those ever-present typecasting worries. Perhaps displaying not a little of Harold's own longing for escape and spiritual fulfilment, Corbett's over-riding wish to be seen as a serious actor continued to torment him. The public, though, went blithely about their business. They wanted the catchphrase - 'you dirty old man' - and the funny voices. And yet ironically, in Harold Steptoe, Harry H. Corbett was playing one of the great dramatic figures of the twentieth century.

Certainly, when the original four series of *Steptoe And Son* came to a close, Corbett didn't exactly rush headlong off to *Hedda Gabler*. Instead, he continued to trade on his comedy reputation and made a one-off appearance with the *Carry On* team in *Carry On Screaming*, a superior 1966 spoof horror contribution to the series. In it, the artist still widely known as Harold played the hopeless Detective Sidney Bung, on the trail of nefarious duo Kenneth Williams and Fenella Fielding, busy turning maidens and a dragged-up Peter Butterworth into shop mannequins. Corbett was great in it, although it now appears that he suffered all manner of psychological torment over what he perceived, inwardly, to be a waste of his talent and training.

After a Christmas special in 1974, *Steptoe And Son* finally came to an end on British television, although repeats continue to be aired to this day. With the last radio series over, in 1977, Galton and Simpson wrote a cabaret show for the pair which was taken on a tour of Australia. It went reasonably well but, by now, the duo's real-life relationship had all but disintegrated completely.

Bold as Brass

Back in England, Corbett battled gamely on as a comedy actor, in now long-forgotten comedies like the Arthur Lowe vehicle *Potter*. His final role, *Grundy*, the eponymous puritan of the Thames TV series of the same name, constantly railing against falling standards and a permissive society, came in 1979, but was broadcast a year later after an ITV strike. In between those events, Harry H. Corbett suffered his first heart attack. A second and this time fatal one followed in 1982. In the aftermath of his former comedy partner's demise, a grief-stricken Brambell castigated the British public for never having appreciated the depths of Corbett's talent. Just three years later, Brambell himself passed away, aged 72.

As for Harold and Albert, in 1999 the pair made a one-off radio comeback as part of *The Galton And Simpson Radio Playhouse*, a BBC Radio 4 series honouring the fiftieth anniversary of that writing partnership. In a new version of the *Steptoe And Son* pilot, Freddie Jones played the dirty old man, with Mancunian comedy actor John Thomson as his son.

Steptoe and Son had shown that audiences could be attracted to intelligent comedy but, for much of the 1960s, television continued to reverberate with echoes of a less-obviously complex past. One such show starred Jimmy Edwards and the Hereford-born but Manchester-raised Beryl Reid.

Originally conceived as an hour-length comedy in 1963, *Bold As Brass* - or *Man O' Brass* as it was first known - featured Edwards as a northern brass band devotee. Reid played his wife, Bessie, for whom the attractions of brass bands and the people who played in them were a closed book. Although the programme proved popular enough to be turned into a six-episode series - in which rising comedy actor Ronnie Barker also had a bit-part - the best thing about *Bold As Brass* was Reid, already embarked upon a long and accomplished television career on the back of her dim-wit Brummie character, Marlene, first seen in the 1957 sitcom *The Most Likely Girl*.

Born in 1920, the stage-struck Beryl Reid had left her Manchester home as a 16-year-old, after which she worked as a shop assistant and won a part in a Bridlington summer season review. It is a bit of a leap from Brid to London's National Theatre, but young Beryl managed it in style. And after making the transition from stage to radio, this most versatile of comic actors spent much of the 1950s as a household name, mainly as a result of her regular appearances on *Educating Archie*.

Reid's first television break came alongside the madcap Norman Wisdom in *Vic's Grill*, a 1951 spin-off from radio's *Variety Bandbox* in which the ostentatiously Jewish comedian Vic Wise starred as café owner 'Wicky Wise'. Henceforth, like many wireless stars, she dipped in and out of the fledgling medium, although the impact of Marlene six years later, just as television was really beginning to hit its stride, could not have been better timed. *Bold As Brass*, then, was but a natural progression.

Although that particular situation comedy was around for no more than one short-lived series, Beryl Reid herself was in for the long haul. As a dyslexia sufferer she struggled to learn her lines, but it didn't get in her way. Over the decades to come, she would enjoy still greater popularity, whether in her own name or alongside the likes of Dick Emery, Marty Feldman and a man soon to be at the forefront of a new wave of British comedy, Peter Cook. Oblivious to changing tastes in comedy, Reid was as happy to be in an episode of *The Comic Strip Presents...* during the alternative comedy boom of the early 1980s, as she was alongside Archie Andrews some thirty-odd years before. In the 1985 television adaptation of Sue Townsend's comic novel *The Secret Diary of Adrian Mole, Aged 13 and 3/4s*, she won plaudits for her role as the grandma and was presented with an OBE the following year.

Away from the small screen, Reid also made a number of feature films. Perhaps the most notable was the 1968 offering, *The Killing Of Sister George*, a lurid and decidedly off-beat story of a heavy-drinking, vicious-tongued lesbian soap opera star, who fails to deal with the fact that her character is about to be killed off and relies ever-more desperately on her lover, the baby-doll Susannah York. Camper than a Butlins redcoat, *The Killing Of Sister George* was one of the first films to be given an over-18s only X certificate in British cinemas and is surely long overdue a spoof by *French and Saunders*.

In fact, Beryl Reid's straight-acting skills earned her a BAFTA in 1982, for her performance alongside Alec Guinness in the Cold War mini-series *Smiley's People*. Her final comedy role came exactly ten years later, in *Shall We Gather At The River*, an appropriately morbid Channel 4 sitcom pilot. In it, Beryl played the bed-ridden grandmother of the

Music hall maestros: George Formby senior, left, was the first recognisably modern 'simple' northern comedian. Right - Dan Leno was a champion clog dancer, raised in Lancashire

Like father, like son: George Formby junior - pictured here in John Willie mode with co-star Tonie Ford in 1934 film 'Boots! Boots!' - carried on where the old man left off. His amiable simpletons were a huge favourite with the British nation in its darkest hours. *Pics: www.itsahotun.com*

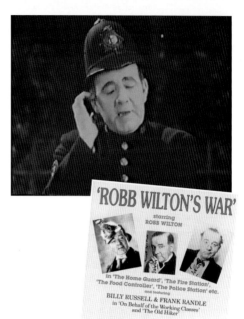

'ROBB WILTON'S WAR'
starring
ROBB WILTON

in 'The Home Guard', 'The Fire Station',
'The Food Controller', 'The Police Station' etc.
and featuring
BILLY RUSSELL & FRANK RANDLE
in 'On Behalf of the Working Classes'
and 'The Old Hiker'

Talking funny: Sandy Powell, left, son of
Rotherham and very bad ventriloquist.
Above - the great monologuist Robb
Wilton was a character comic supreme.
Pics: www.itsahotun.com

On the Band Waggon:
Arthur Askey
pioneered wireless
catchphrase comedy

Radio fun: Robb
Wilton and Askey's
fellow Liverpudlian
Tommy Handley -
star of 'It's That Man
Again' - goes over
scripts with writer
Ted Kavanagh and
BBC producer
Francis Worsley.

The boundary pusher: Frank Randle was the rogue prince of Blackpool. He is pictured below in his guise of the incorrigible old man and, along with drinking buddy Josef Locke (left) in the 1948 Mancunian film 'Somewhere In Politics'
Pics: www.itsahotun.com

Lancashire's favourite Yorkshireman: Albert Modley in uncharacteristic debonair pose. 'I'm a fool of a man, not fit to be in the place...'
Pic: www.itsahotun.com

Stars on parade: Mancunian Film Corporation entrepreneur John E. Blakeley directs
Frank Randle in the 1953 picture 'It's A Grand Life'.   *Pic: www.itsahotun.com*

Now listen, son: Frank Randle hands out a life lesson to Jimmy Clitheroe in the 1949 film
'School for Randle'. Clitheroe's Mancunian debut had come the year before.

Pic: www.itsahotun.com

Taking northern comedy to the world: A mature George Formby, left, in his Basil Dean days, complete with famous ukulele. Right - Stan Laurel and friend leaning on a lamp post.

Kicking up a stink: Coffee stall keeper Tommy Fields and his sister Gracie beg to differ regarding the freshness or otherwise of a sausage roll.   *Pic: Mrs Joan Moules*

STAR ♪ ARTISTS

HARRY KORRIS

A native of the Isle of Man, Harry Korris started in show business at 16. His material is always up-to-date and his supply of gags inexhaustible. An established favourite in the North, it was on the strength of a music hall broadcast that he was engaged, with his assistants, to star as the genial Mr. Lovejoy in "Happidrome," the popular weekly radio feature.

RECORDS FOR COLUMBIA

We three in Happidrome: Harry Korris illuminated Blackpool for many a year and delighted some 12 million listeners with his radio show 'Happidrome'.
Pics: www.itsahotun.com

Comedy originals: Norman Evans and Jimmy James go gardening.
Pic: www.itsahotun.com

Big on boaters: Dave Morris and Nat Jackley.
Pic: www.itsahotun.com

NORMAN EVANS • JIMMY JAMES • DAN YOUNG • SONYA O'SHEA
in
"OVER THE GARDEN WALL"
A FILM STUDIO (MANCHESTER) LTD. PRODUCTION
DISTRIBUTED BY MANCUNIAN FILM CORPORATION LTD., MANCHESTER

Surreal and zany: Jimmy James and Eli, above, are apprehended while out for an afternoon stroll.

Right - Jewel and Warriss were favourites on the wireless and at the pictures
Pics: www.itsahotun.com

Three aces: Jimmy Clitheroe, Norman Evans and Jimmy James.   *Pics: www.itsahotun.com*

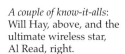

The people's champion: Arthur Lucan - a.k.a. Old Mother Riley - and Kitty McShane.

A couple of know-it-alls: Will Hay, above, and the ultimate wireless star, Al Read, right.

It'll never catch on: Jimmy Jewel and Ben Warriss introduce a new electronic friend

Pic: www.itsahotun.com

funeral-obsessed Herbert Alcock, played by Gwilym Cox. Beryl Reid died of pneumonia in 1996, her latter years spent living among a collection of stray cats in a Berkshire cottage on the banks of the River Thames.

Beryl Reid, Harry H. Corbett, Wilfrid Brambell... the thespians were on the rise. As sitcoms began to be crafted like stage plays, so were trained actors increasingly preferred to old-style Variety comics.

None of which met any opposition from the growing band of writers who were fuelling the televisual fire. The likes of Galton and Simpson, for example, had already experienced how, via Hancock and Steptoe, the BBC's unstuffy new approach might provide a creative environment in which to wrestle with the truths of contemporary British life. And as the old certainties were stretched to breaking point, so did writers dare to tread in areas that, previously, had been no-go.

The most obvious example of this was in a Johnny Speight sitcom alluded to earlier, *Till Death Us Do Part* (1965). Where the reality of *Steptoe And Son* had been tempered by at least a handful of sympathetic character traits, Speight gave his protagonist-in-chief, the loud-mouthed, right-wing, cockney bigot Alf Garnett, no such saving graces. Here was a true television monster; one of the most memorable of all-time. Played to imbecilic perfection by Warren Mitchell, another fine actor rather than traditional comedian, the splenetic misanthrope Garnett spewed forth a non-stop illiberal barrage of racist and misogynist outbursts, prompting floods of complaints from viewers outraged at the bad language and frequently oblivious to the programme's satirical intentions.

Set in a then run-down Wapping, still to be rebuilt after the Luftwaffe's fondest World War Two caresses, *Till Death Us Do Part* had little in common with traditional northern comedy. This was always a sitcom of the head rather than the heart. True, its characters were keenly-observed and family relationships were well to the fore. The Garnetts, though, were a family for whom affection was an alien concept, all publicly-expressed emotion was negative. The show's writer, Speight, was London born and bred, as were lead actor Mitchell and his long-suffering 'silly moo' of a wife, Else, played by the lugubrious Dandy Nichols. Daughter Rita, played by Una Stubbs, hailed from Leicester.

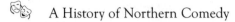

Interestingly, however, Speight found a son-in-law for his monarchist anti-hero in Liverpool, that most politically active of all northern cities. As the equally argumentative long-haired, republican lefty 'Scouse git' Mike, the actor Anthony Booth - a future father-in-law of former British Labour Prime Minister Tony Blair, funnily enough - was Alf's ideal political foil.

Given his polemical roots, Alf Garnett was always likely to be more of a two-dimensional caricature than a fully-rounded human being. That said, Mitchell's portrayal did on occasion introduce a touch more nuance, hinting at the humanity of a man crushed by a bitter sense of his own insignificance. One unfortunate drawback of this was that for some in the audience, who were perhaps themselves further down the evolutionary chain than they might care to admit, Alf's outrageous opinions reinforced their own twisted prejudices, much to the writer and cast's continued irritation. On the whole, though, *Till Death Us Do Part* was a funny and courageous attempt to lift the lid on an unpleasant aspect of British society that few, if any, sitcoms before or since have had the guts to face.

Equally revolutionary in its own way was *The Likely Lads*, a this time very definitely and defiantly northern take on modern British life. Its creators were Dick Clement and his Whitley Bay-born writing partner Ian La Frenais, who had first met in an Earls Court pub in 1961. After knocking out a sketch together for a BBC staff drama group, based upon the antics of a couple of mates, their careers were heading in different directions until Clement, a radio producer, took a trainee television director course. As part of it, Clement was required to make his own TV programme and given a budget of £100 and limited use of a studio with which to do so. Being very much a TV novice and in urgent need of a script - any script - he approached his old drinking pal La Frenais. The pair duly dug out their earlier effort, gave it a more naturalistic 'kitchen sink' feel in line with the cinematic times, and howay - Terry and Bob, the original Geordie likely lads, were born.

The BBC TV bosses were impressed and offered Clement a job right there and then. They also requested that he turn that one-off production into the fully-fledged series that first invaded the nation's living rooms - courtesy of the new BBC2 channel - in December 1964. In so doing, *The Likely Lads* was an early nod towards a process that has since become the established BBC television comedy norm. Back then, to appear on BBC2 was very much to dip a toe in the water - more so, even, than is the case with comedy shows first shown on BBC3 today. You would only be seen by a small percentage of those viewers who fell within the relevant footprints of the Midlands and London. It was only when *The Likely Lads* was repeated on BBC1 the following March that it soared in popularity.

As with *Steptoe And Son*, when the creators were looking for their principal leads, they went for a couple of bona fide actors, cast to provide as realistic a character portrayal as possible. This time James Bolam (Terry Collier) and Rodney Bewes (Bob Ferris) were the chosen two and, again, they proved inspired selections. Kitchen sink-wise, they already had a pedigree of sorts. Both Bolam and Bewes had played minor roles in two of the most successful films of the period, Willis Hall's adaptation of the Stan Barstow novel *A Kind Of Loving* (1962) and *Billy Liar* (1963), the latter with a screenplay by Hall and the writer of the original novel, Keith Waterhouse.

Given the more youthful nature of its chief protagonists - Terry and Bob were just 21-years-old, single and in their first jobs when the series began - *The Likely Lads* had an altogether more upbeat mood than *Steptoe And Son*. Yet in turning their gaze upon everyday life and finding fun in working class aspiration and class issues in general, Clement and La Frenais, and Bolam and Bewes, were just as effective as their predecessors.

If for no other reason than it was set in the north, *The Likely Lads* was indeed a groundbreaking sitcom, even if, in some ways, the depiction of life in the north east could be a tad stereotypical. On occasion, the activities of Terry and Bob drifted into territory not a million miles from that occupied by the newspaper cartoon strip *Andy Capp*, who had sprung from the pen of the Hartlepool-born cartoonist Reg Smythe, in regional editions of the *Daily Mirror*, in 1957. A quick-witted northern chancer with a love of beer and football and an unreconstructed view of women would pass as a viable description of either Andy Capp or Terry. All that was missing, in Terry's case, was a 'tab' behind the ear and a giant flat cap. Oh, and a wife waiting at home with a rolling pin. Bob had that.

No surprise, then, that it was James Bolam who got the call when *Andy Capp* went from newsprint to small screen in a disappointing Keith Waterhouse-scripted ITV adaptation in 1988. On telly, Andy lasted a

mere six episodes. In the papers, he is still going strong despite the death from cancer of his creator, Reg Smythe, in 1998. In fact, the *Andy Capp* cartoon strip has subsequently been syndicated to over fifty countries in fourteen different languages. In Denmark he is known as Kasket Karl. In Sweden, Tuffa Victor. German newspaper readers would recognise Andy as Willi Wakker and, in Italy, he is Angelo Capello. In France? What else? André Chapeau. As ever, the universal qualities in northern humour ensure that it continues to travel well.

Despite that degree of traditional northern stereotyping, then, that the *The Likely Lads* was also a genuine boundary-pusher owed much to the way in which the humdrum banality of its characters' lives contrasted so starkly with the so-called glamourous decade in which the show itself was set. Much fun was had in juxtaposing the grinding and often downright dull reality of daily existence with the aspirational expectations of a younger generation yearning for so much more than their parents had settled for. In the grey north east, the bright lights of 'swinging' 'sixties London weren't just several hundred miles away geographically, they were on another planet psychology, economically and sexually. Free love? In the north of England, there was no such thing. Take the *Likely Lads* episode 'A Romantic Evening', for example. In it, Terry appears to be in the bathroom getting ready for a night of cocktail-sipping passion with a lounging Welsh femme fatale, only for us to discover that he has actually been unblocking her sink ('Ooh, look at your tie.' 'Aye. I think I must have trailed it in the cat meat...').

The show's trump cards, however, were its eponymous fresh-faced young heroes. Terry, glum, cynical, northern and chippy with it; Bob, his more sensitive, thoughtful and easily-led social climber of a mate. On the face of it working class reactionary chalk and lower-middle class liberal cheese, Terry and Bob nevertheless shared one particular trait with the rest of their generation: a hunger for more. If Bob's ambitions in that regard were socially pretentious - nice home, nice wife, nice car - for Terry that just meant more money, more birds and more Newcastle Brown. As such, it was totally in tune with the times.

In the first ever episode of *The Likely Lads*, 'Entente Cordiale', the boys are shown returning from a Spanish holiday, thereby providing what is perhaps the first televisual indication that, for the nation's newly-aspirational working class, the days of queueing in the wind and the rain along Blackpool's Golden Mile to see Frank Randle, Dave Morris, Harry Korris and Co were already fast becoming a distant memory.

And in Terry's oft-stated antipathy to anything from outside the north east - 'I haven't got much time for the Irish or the Welsh, and the Scots are worse than the Koreans.' Bob: 'And you never could stand southerners.' Terry: 'To tell you the truth, I don't much like anyone outside this town and there aren't many families down our street that I can stand' - *The Likely Lads* also dealt with the long-standing northern comedy concern of community acting as comfort blanket and prison. It can be tricky to see the world as your multicultural oyster when the actual horizons of your life are pub, football match, bookies and five days a week bored out of your wits in an electrical components factory.

Born in Sunderland in 1938, Bolam, a one-time trainee chartered accountant, made his professional stage debut at the Royal Court in 1959, after training at the Central School of Speech and Drama. Thanks to the widespread move towards social realism, though, a north country accent actually began to come in useful and, as a result, his *The Likely Lads* break came one year after the actor made his television debut in an episode of Granada TV's detective series, *The Odd Man*.

A deeply private individual whose actual personality seems to be far removed from that of the character with whom he will most likely always be associated, James Bolam was ever the reluctant star. For him, the work itself was the thing. After impressing in classical roles on stage and screen, and a clutch of quality television drama series which have included James Mitchell's South Shields-based 1976 series *When The Boat Comes In*, in which Bolam played shipyard union official Jack Ford, and Alan Plater's *Beiderbecke* jazz-driven trilogy of the 1980s, he grew reluctant to so much as discuss *The Likely Lads* and its subsequent impact on his career.

Not that it stopped him from appearing in more television comedy. Among Bolam's other sitcoms are the aforementioned *Andy Capp* (1988), *Room At The Bottom* (1986-88), *Father Matthew's Daughter* (1987), *Second Thoughts* (1991-94) and *Pay And Display* (2000). None came close to *The Likely Lads*. Aside from Terry, Bolam's best known other comedy role is undoubtedly that of Roy Figgis in Eric Chappell's hospital sitcom, *Only When I Laugh*, a show which proved inexplicably popular through four

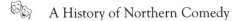

series from 1979-83, despite being about as funny as a slipped disc. And, in fact, Bolam's finest television role of recent years was another less than amusing medical one. In 2002, he played Manchester's mass-murdering GP, Harold Shipman. Most recently, he has appeared alongside Dennis Waterman, Amanda Redman and Alun Armstrong in the BBC's highly-acclaimed crime series, *New Tricks*.

Rodney Bewes, too, was classically trained, this time at Rada where he studied after winning his first professional role at the age of 14. Like Bolam, Bewes was also born in 1938 but, in his case, a hundred miles or so further south in Bingley, West Yorkshire. By all accounts a sickly child, he was confined to the family home with asthma until he was 12 years old. Maybe that experience at least partly influenced his *The Likely Lads* portrayal of Bob, for whom fragility and timidity were never far away.

After its initial BBC1 run in March and April 1965, a second series of *The Likely Lads* was again aired first on BBC2 later that year. Series three followed in October and November 1966 before the show, with scripts adapted by Bolam, made a sixteen-episode move to radio from 1967-68. Unfortunately for Bewes, although the Gods of TV and theatre continued to smile down on his long-time bar stool partner, once the curtain had fallen on those three series of *The Likely Lads* for him it was a different story. Regular work proved hard to come by until he found the answer in self-help.

The result, a new sitcom called *Dear Mother... Love Albert*, was starred in, produced and co-written by the actor, and Bewes sang and co-wrote the theme tune too. In it, Bewes cast himself as the naive 24-year-old northerner Albert Courtnay (an amalgam of original stage Billy Liars Albert Finney and Tom Courtenay, perhaps?), who found himself down in London and searching for streets paved with gold. The plot, based upon Bewes's own real-life letters home, revolved around Albert's highly exaggerated and romanticised accounts to his mother of the upward trajectory his new life was taking, despite the reality of his scraping to make a living in a confectionery factory. Though not as well-realised as *The Likely Lads*, it was an idea clever enough to result in three series and a sequel - *Albert!* - in 1971.

If Rodney Bewes was ever going to escape being typecast as Bob, then *Dear Mother... Love Albert* was his best chance. Yet when Dick Clement

198

and Ian La Frenais came calling with the temptation of a sequel, *Whatever Happened To The Likely Lads*, the urge to return was too great. Albert and his letter-reading mum were swiftly consigned to TV comedy oblivion.

Clement has since revealed that, owing to a lack of Geordie actors, he and La Frenais had initially considered that *The Likely Lads* should be set in Middlesbrough or even Liverpool. However, while the first three series were a little vague in terms of precise geography - and indeed the earliest episodes were actually filmed in Willesden Junction - when Terry and Bob did return in what became an even more impressive incarnation in 1973, there was no doubt at all that we were in Newcastle. That great city virtually became a character itself.

With its extra ingredient of wistful nostalgia, *Whatever Happened To The Likely Lads* built brilliantly on the themes of the 1960s episodes. All the old subjects of friendship, community, changing social landscapes and personal improvement took on even more potential for comedy and pathos with the passing of the years, and the show's writers and actors had lost none of their touch. With the advance in technology, the show was now broadcast in colour too, offering even more of a contrast with days that had appeared modern at the time but which, in the early 1970s, seemed quaint, monotone and alien indeed.

In 1966, the original series had ended with one of British television comedy's most oft-repeated moments. Keen to get his static life moving and experience everything that the wider world could offer, Terry decides to join the army. In keeping with the established device of Bob reluctantly and nervously agreeing to go along with Terry's bright-spark schemes - in which its originator usually came off worst - Bob finally succumbs and agrees to enlist himself. However, as Terry implores his friend to hurry up and jump aboard the army vehicle that is about to transport the pair to a brave new future, Bob reveals that he is no longer coming after all. The army won't let him. He has flat feet. The expression on Bolam's face, hang-dog at the best of times, is a picture as he realises the most important relationship in his life is finally about to be broken.

Seven years later, and preceded by the now classic theme tune co-written by La Frenais and Mike Hugg - 'Oh, what happened to you? Whatever happened to me? What became of the people we used to be? Tomorrow's almost over, today went by so fast. The only thing to look

forward to is the past?' - *Whatever Happened To The Likely Lads* began with a de-mobbed Terry returning to the north east, looking for work and keen to pick up loose threads. Unfortunately, although still in the area, his old friend Bob has otherwise moved on.

Despite Tyneside's ongoing and weary struggle with unemployment and industrial action, in Terry's absence bourgeois Bob has landed a very respectable white-collar job as a surveyor, along with a flash new Vauxhall Viva. Furthermore, old Labour Terry is appalled to discover that his pal is engaged to the boss's daughter, Thelma, played by the Edinburgh-born Brigit Forsyth, a prim, strong-minded librarian intent on dragging both herself and her future husband up the ladder of semi-detached respectability and for whom footloose and fancy free Terry is nothing short of a threat.

Bob's soft-hearted decency leaves him as piggy in the middle, as the duo's friendship struggles to cope with the changes in Bob's lifestyle and Terry's refusal to throw off his ingrained prejudices re. booze, birds and class politics. Despite Terry doing his best to sabotage the relationship, Bob and Thelma are married as planned at the end of the first series with Terry an unlikely best man. In the second series, however, Terry's increasingly malign influence does lead to Thelma going back to her mother before she and Bob again reunite. Aside from a one-off 45-minute Christmas special in 1974, and a further radio stint in 1975, that would have been that had not a feature film spin-off been made two years later.

It took as its premise that old British sitcom staple of placing regular characters in unusual surroundings, most often on holiday, albeit in this case on a wet and miserable British caravan site rather than the sun-kissed Spanish resorts so beloved elsewhere. As a result, the big screen *Likely Lads* could have been as alluring as a soggy beer mat, a best-forgotten blemish on an otherwise masterful piece of popular culture. Surprisingly, though, it wasn't so bad. For one thing, it gave Clement and La Frenais the chance to move their characters on again. Now, Terry was divorced and living in a high-rise flat, while the still-married but suffering Bob was undergoing something of a mid-life crisis himself. Symbolically, for the era, the street in which the pair used to live was now demolished in the rush to construct a bright new north east of England.

The film was also responsible for a couple of Terry and Bob's best-remembered lines; words, in fact, which sum up their characters perfectly. Terry: 'I'd offer you a beer but I've only got six cans.' And Bob: 'In the chocolate box of life, the top layer's already gone and someone's pinched the orange cream from the bottom.' Eat your heart out, Forrest Gump.

Sadly, with the end of *The Likely Lads*, and despite Bolam's growing reputation as a very fine actor indeed, Rodney Bewes again continued to struggle to match the levels of public acclaim that the role of Bob Ferris had brought him. In 1980, he made another sitcom comeback as a fussy travel agent in John Esmonde and Bob Larbey's *Just Liz*, in which Sandra Payne was the Liz in question. The show was intended to recreate the success of Esmonde and Larbey's classic opt-out comedy of manners, *The Good Life*, but it only managed one six-episode series. Much later, in 2004, there was also a guest appearance in the BBC's well-intentioned but ultimately ill-fated comedy sketch show *Revolver*, in which TV stars of earlier decades such as Melvyn Hayes, Gorden Kaye and John Inman worked with modern-day scriptwriters. Otherwise, Rodney Bewes seems to have spent much of his time either chasing work or performing in *The Diary of a Nobody* - his cheerful one-man show in which the delights of being a financially-strapped well-known father of four are entertainingly outlined. In 2006, he published his autobiography, *A Likely Story* (Arrow).

There was, however, to be one more twist to *The Likely Lads* story. It came when an all-time favourite episode, 'No Hiding Place', was remade in 2002, starring a couple of likeable Geordie favourites of a new generation, Anthony McPartlin and Declan Donnelly, better known as Ant and Dec. The special tribute version, in which Terry and Bob try to stay away from a football score so that they can watch the highlights later, also featured Mancunian comic John Thomson in the part of Flint, originally played by legendary Yorkshireman Brian Glover.

Although made with the best of intentions, the idea generally failed to satisfy. For one thing, to many older viewers, like the policemen on the streets, Ant and Dec looked too young for their roles. For another, the notion that an England international football match would not be shown live was blatantly incongruous in the wall-to-wall satellite era. Ironically, in an age of 'laddism' and the extremes of *Men Behaving Badly* - the groundwork for which, it could be argued, had been laid by *The Likely Lads* all those years before - the comedy seemed rather forced and twee.

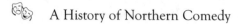

Not that it was all bad news. Showing admirable sportsmanship, the great Rodney Bewes himself made a show-stealing cameo as a one-legged newspaper vendor.

In fact, Bewes has never made a secret of his willingness to make another series of *The Likely Lads*, should the opportunity arise. And given the philosophical nature of the programme's time-passing theme, the ever-evolving political and cultural landscape of the north east itself and the fact that - at the time of writing - its principle creators and actors are all still drawing breath, here is one sequel that could just possibly work and work well. However, James Bolam's continued reluctance to tread over old ground must make such a venture unlikely.

Maybe that is for the best. In any case, during a BBC1 *Inside Out* programme to celebrate the 40th anniversary of *The Likely Lads*, shown throughout the north east and Cumbria in September 2004, writer Ian La Frenais was asked what Terry, in particular, would make of Newcastle today. 'Terry is going on a bit now,' La Frenais replied. 'He will probably be appalled by the Quayside and Bigg Market on a Saturday night and completely forget that he would be there if he was younger, one of the people arrested most frequently. He would find something to moan about but, like most north east people, he would see how the city has changed architecturally and culturally. He would be proud, particularly when talking to southerners.'

Although the end of *The Likely Lads* spelled mixed fortunes for the actors who played Bob and Terry, the programme was a wonderful career stepping stone for Ian La Frenais and Dick Clement. The duo went on to write or co-write a whole host of television comedy series, including *Thick As Thieves* (1974), a show that gave a major leg-up to John Thaw and Bob Hoskins, plus a couple of adaptations of Kingsley Amis's *Lucky Jim* in 1967 and 1982. Meanwhile, in the same year that *Whatever Happened To The Likely Lads* aired, the pair were also responsible for another show destined to enter the British sitcom hall of fame, *Porridge*. La Frenais and Clement's third big hit came ten years later, in November 1983, with the creation of *Auf Wiedersehen, Pet*, the first in a series of hugely popular comedy dramas in which the city of Newcastle was again to the forefront.

Television comedy in the 1960s, then, was fast becoming fertile ground for actors and specialist sitcom writers alike, although in the case of *Till Death Us Do Part* creator Johnny Speight, had it not been for the benign influence of one particular northern wordsmith, his own career might never have got going at all.

It was while working as an insurance salesman in 1955 that Speight - a 35-year-old wannabe writer - was introduced to Frankie Howerd at the Prince of Wales theatre. Howerd purchased a joke - 'I'm livid - they are pulling down my house to build a slum' - and promised to introduce him, in turn, to the well-known co-owners of a West London co-operative called Associated London Scripts - later to be known as 'The House of Fun'. A meeting was duly arranged and after a sample script of Speight's was received rapturously, the fledgling writer quickly packed in his day job and joined the company's books. Soon, Speight was contributing material to Howerd's new BBC radio show, upon which Eric Sykes, an ALS co-founder along with Spike Milligan, Howerd, Scruffy Dale, Ray Galton and Alan Simpson, would act as editor.

The significance of a female influence on the mindset of northern comedians is nowhere more evident than in the story of how Eric Sykes went from being runt of the litter to grade one national treasure. In Sykes's case, however, it was the absence of his mother, as well as her spiritual presence, that was a defining factor in the development of his dry, other-worldly and vaguely exasperated brand of humour.

Eric Sykes was born in 1923 among the cotton mills and hills of Oldham where, tragically, his 22-year-old mother, Harriet, died in giving him birth. Such a catastrophe would scar anyone, yet Sykes's endearingly cantankerous 2005 autobiography, *If I Don't Write It, Nobody Else Will* (Fourth Estate), revealed that his was a philosophical soul, emphatic in the belief that Harriet's spirit had subsequently guided his every career move. Doubling that early blow, his distraught father, a poorly-paid mill labourer, then farmed his baby boy out for two years, as he sought to build a new family with the woman who became Sykes's stepmother. Again, any grounds for lasting emotional disturbance are given short shrift by Sykes, who even cracks a joke about the results of being left in the care of the parrot who lived over his cot: 'Neither he [his father, who had eventually come to collect him] nor anyone else could understand what I was babbling about. Hardly surprising, as I'd never learned English but could speak fluent parrot.' In Sykes, the northern urge to make light of the most painful misfortune is writ large.

Like his ALS friend and colleague, Spike Milligan, Sykes discovered entertainment as a career option while serving in the armed services during World War Two, where he was a wireless operator in the RAF. Upon being demobbed, attempts to build on his membership of various concert parties and establish himself as a writer and performer faltered. His first potential break as a writer came through a chance meeting in London with Bill Fraser, later of *The Army Game* fame, who had been an RAF officer and a driving force in one of the concert parties to which Sykes had belonged. Fraser, a stage professional, commissioned his down-at-heel friend to pen him some funny lines, more as an act of charity than anything else. No actual scripts were ever forthcoming but, for Sykes, the idea of a life in comedy took root.

Initially, that meant floating around aimlessly in Oldham Rep' and the northern music halls, under the less-than-inspired stage name Rick Allen. Until eventually, in the late-1940s, Sykes had the good fortune to receive a telephone call out of the blue from a friend of Frankie Howerd, who was already by then a huge star on the wireless. While serving in the Army Welfare Services, Howerd had seen some of the former RAF man's work and enjoyed it. He wondered whether he could use some of it on *Variety Bandbox*? Several well-received and suitably eccentric scripts later, Eric Sykes was able to call himself a fully-fledged comedy writer.

Ahead of him were equally fruitful introductions to the likes of Tony Hancock, Harry Secombe and Milligan, whose own 1951 radio show, *Crazy People*, Sykes would describe as the best he'd heard on radio since *The Brains Trust*. As *Crazy People* evolved into *The Goon Show*, Sykes would play no small part in the development of that hugely influential programme himself, and he also contributed four award-winning years to the long-running *Educating Archie*. It was with Milligan that, in 1954, Sykes came up with the idea for Associated London Scripts.

The ever-prodigious Sykes's own writing output grew substantially in 1952, when he made the move to television with *The Howerd Crowd*, the two-series TV debut of Frankie Howerd. A year later, Sykes also wrote Max Bygraves' first headlining TV appearance, *A Good Idea - Son*, and two more television outings for Howerd, *The Frankie Howerd Show* and *Nuts In*

May, billed as 'a spring frolic'. In 1954, the year of ALS's launch, he wrote and co-starred in the first six Saturday night Variety shows to be shown on the new commercial channel ITV, along with Harry Secombe and the Liverpool-born comic Norman Vaughan. There was also a one-off special written for the out-sized gruff monocled comedian Fred Emney called *The Big Man* while, at the London Palladium, Sykes debuted as writer and director of the pantomime *Mother Goose*.

By 1956, TV's demands on Sykes's time were increasing rapidly and, in that year, he finally fulfilled a long-standing wish to perform in front of the cameras too. The show in question was *The Idiot Weekly, Price 2d*, a prototype Goons-for-the-telly effort that ran to five episodes and which primarily featured Milligan and Peter Sellers, with the latter as the editor of the bizarre Victorian magazine in the title. Alas, we will never know what northern audiences might have made of it, *The Idiot Weekly, Price 2d* was broadcast in the London area only. For Sykes, around this time there were also a couple of one-off Variety specials. The first, *Dress Rehearsal*, was based around a make-believe TV dress rehearsal. The second, *Opening Night*, celebrated the first night of the National Radio Show at London's Earls Court. Both allowed Sykes to develop a screen persona as a scatter-brained, harassed television producer. Yet it took a partnership with an old colleague from *Educating Archie* to launch him seriously on that road.

Having grown sick of appearing night after night in impresario Jack Hylton's *Talk Of The Town* West End stage revue, radio star Tony Hancock exchanged his stage contract for an agreement to launch his television career on ITV's London franchise with *The Tony Hancock Show*. The BBC, however, would not allow his usual radio writers, Galton and Simpson, to go with him. Instead, the pair were asked to script the BBC's own Hancock TV show that debuted five weeks after the first series of the ITV outing came to an end, a series written, in their absence, by the duo's ALS stablemate Sykes. The fact that this ITV vehicle employed a run-of-the-mill Variety sketch format, rather than the dramatic delineations of character favoured by Galton and Simpson, must be a big reason why this earliest of Hancock's TV incarnations has since been largely overlooked. More enduring was the rapport struck up between its writer and another of its former *Educating Archie* stars, the splendid Hattie Jacques.

Over the years to come, Sykes continued to combine writing and

performing to increasing effect. He made more of his mad Variety producer spoofs and became a regular in Val Parnell's *Saturday Spectacular* strand, despite debilitating hearing problems that would one day render him completely deaf. It was with the launch of *Sykes And A...* in 1960, however, in which he again teamed up with Jacques and co-writer Johnny Speight, that this great British comedy career really took off.

Despite Sykes's own northern English roots, *Sykes And A...* was set in East Acton, London, at 24 Sebastopol Terrace to be precise, presumably just up the road from Steptoe's yard. As a cohabiting brother and sister act rather than standard sitcom husband and wife, Eric Sykes and Hattie Jacques were an instant and unlikely hit. At the heart of the show was the wonderful visual gag brought about by the disparity in the duo's physical appearances. Accident-prone Eric, thin and wiry, was supposed to be the twin brother of fat, wide-eyed and bubbly 'Hat'. Their personalities were also a perfect blend, Hat's immense presence was matched by an equally big heart and a willingness to go along with Eric's childlike enthusiasm.

Speight relinquished his writing duties after the first series, and after Milligan and John Antrobus helped out on series two, the BBC persuaded Sykes to take over the writing of the show completely. Over the next two decades, Sykes went on to knock out well over one hundred episodes and while not every one of those was a comedy classic, there was always lots to enjoy in their homely brand of slapstick innocence. The beauty of *Sykes And A...* lay both in the quality of its writing and the fine comic timing of a cast that, at various times, also included Richard Wattis as snobby next-door neighbour Mr Brown, and Deryck Guyler in the role of neighbourhood policeman PC Wilfred 'Corky' Turnbull. The show's open-ended formula was another major boon.

With a title like that, every episode could be different. Sykes was free to explore the comic possibilities of whichever subject took his fancy, whether that be golf, elephants or chauffeuring a Rolls Royce. Among the best-loved episodes are surely *Sykes And A Mouse* (1963), in which the pair try to trap one such offending rodent, and *Sykes And A Haunting* (1962), which sees brother and sister spend the entire proceedings handcuffed together. One 1964 episode, *Sykes And A Plank*, was subsequently turned into both a 1967 film co-starring Tommy Cooper and a 1979 TV special featuring a line-up that reads like a who's who of 'seventies British comedy.

In 1961, with *Sykes And A...* already 24 episodes old, the comedian also had the distinction of appearing alongside Warren Mitchell in the first of those Galton and Simpson's *Comedy Playhouse* outings that led to *Steptoe And Son*. It was called *Clicquot Et Fils* and in it both men played crafty French undertakers. Yet it was for his own show that Sykes remained best known and by the time the ninth series came to a close with its sixtieth episode in 1965, both he and Hattie were now confirmed as huge stars, with Jacques developing a parallel career as a member of the *Carry On* team. After a brief lull, Sykes returned to the television front line two years later with a typically inventive and distinctly post-modern effort, *Sykes Versus ITV*, in which he attempted to persuade a courtroom that he should be allowed to make a one-hour comedy special for that channel! Hattie Jacques spoke in his defence, while the prosecution case was put by Tommy Cooper.

In 1969, Sykes was part of *Curry And Chips*, Johnny Speight's perhaps ill-conceived attempt to explore the racist attitudes he had first prodded away at with Alf Garnett. Aired on London Weekend Television and, ironically, the very first sitcom on that channel to be broadcast in colour, *Curry And Chips* was set in the staff canteen of Lillicrap Ltd, makers of seaside novelty items. Along with Sykes, who appeared as Arthur the foreman, a supposedly Liberal voice of sanity, the cast included a black-faced Spike Milligan, who reprised 'Paki Paddy', a cameo role from *Till Death Us Do Part*, otherwise known as Kevin O'Grady, an Asian man who claimed to be Irish on his father's side. The rest of the workforce included a couple of racist scousers played by Norman Rossington and Geoffrey Hughes (the latter going on to play *Coronation Street*'s Eddie Hughes and Onslow in *Keeping Up Appearances*), Sam Kydd as Smellie, and the black, Pakistani-hating Kenny, played by Kenny Lynch.

As with *Till Death Us Do Part*, Speight's intentions were honourable but even in those decidedly non-PC days the show was widely deemed to have missed its mark. As with Alf, the amount of swearing caused outrage in some quarters, although Speight insisted that it was all done in the pursuit of reality. Interestingly, the one character who did not curse was Arthur, simply because Sykes refused to do so. After six tortuous episodes, *Curry And Chips* was dropped from the ITV schedules never to return. Mind you, the indefatigable Milligan did attempt to breathe new life into the concept with his 1975 comedy, *The Melting Pot*. How's this for a pitch? Pakistani father and son (played, excruciatingly, by Milligan and John Bird) row a boat into Britain via Holland as illegal immigrants. Calling themselves Mr. Van Gogh and Mr. Rembrandt, so as to fit in more easily, they end up living in London, where their housemates are an Irish republican coalman Paddy O'Brien (played by Frank Carson) and his South African-raised daughter Nefetiti Skupinski; Luigi O'Reilly, a black Yorkshireman; Orthodox Jew Richard Armitage; former Indian army officer Colonel Grope; a racist Aussie named 'Bluey' Notts; Chinese Cockney spiv Eric Lee Fung; and Sheik Yamani, a Scottish Arab bank clerk. For some reason, the BBC got nervous and pulled it after one episode.

With that indigestible portion of *Curry And Chips* behind him, Eric Sykes retreated to less controversial waters and resumed his partnership with Hattie Jacques. After a couple of one-off comedy specials in 1971 - *Sykes And A Big, Big Show* for the BBC and *Sykes: With The Lid Off* for ITV - the pair appeared in 'A Policeman's Lot', a sketch written for the BBC's *Christmas Night With The Stars* later that year. These turned out to be precursors of the return of *Sykes And A...* after a seven-year absence, this time in colour and with a more succinct name, *Sykes*, in 1972.

Give or take a few details, such as a typically silly change of address from 24 Sebastopol Terrace to 28, the situation remained exactly the same. Eric, the boy who never grew up, continued to keep his big-hearted twin on her ample toes. In the supporting roles, Derek Guyler returned as 'Corky' and Richard Wattis, until his death in 1975, came back as snobby Mr. Brown, a character who was later replaced by Joy Harington as new neighbour, Mrs. Rumbelow. Hattie Jacques's *Carry On* colleague Joan Sims also made an occasional appearance as the seldom-seen Madge Kettlewell, owner of the local baker's shop and secret fancier of Eric, or 'Ricky' as she preferred to call him. Another cast member was Eric and Hattie's pet cuckoo clock cuckoo, Peter, spoken to as if he were made of real flesh, blood and feathers, rather than wood. Then again, perhaps Peter actually was a real bird. Who could be sure? Cuckoo indeed.

In terms of its longevity, the *Sykes* second coming proved even more durable than the first. Even the fact that many of the new shows were simply reworkings of scripts from the older black and white days didn't do it any harm. Although by the time *Sykes* finally did finish for good in

1979, as a result of the premature death of Hattie Jacques, the quality had dipped somewhat. Yet if anyone foresaw that as the end of Eric Sykes's television career, they were soon made to think again.

In 1977, when *Sykes* was still going its merry way on BBC1, the eponymous hero and his sister, 'Hat', had appeared in a couple of ITV shows alongside Peter Cook, that leading light of a whole new wave of comedians; evidence, if it were needed, that Eric Sykes has never been as far from the cutting edge as much of his ostensibly old-fashioned Variety-style projects might suggest. With Sykes, an undercurrent of anarchy is seldom far from the surface, gentle or otherwise. Building on his now well-established theme of theatrical chaos, *Eric Sykes Shows A Few Of Our Favourite Things* and, less unconventionally, *The Eric Sykes Show* were the first of seven such ITV specials over the next five years, culminating in *The Eric Sykes 1990 Show* in 1982! That latter programme and its immediate predecessors were, of course, made without the sadly-departed Hattie, who had died in the period between filming and screening of *Rhubarb Rhubarb* (1980), a small-screen adaptation of a Sykes big-screen effort from a decade before. Again, Sykes's capacity for surreal invention was on display; the only words spoken were those in the title.

Rhubarb Rhubarb came hot on the heels of 1979's star-studded version of *The Plank*. And Sykes followed that with *It's Your Move*, a similarly well-populated silent movie-style comedy in 1982. This time, Sykes and his old mate Tommy Cooper played a couple of Laurel and Hardy-esque removal men. By now Eric Sykes was almost 60 years old but, despite his rapidly deteriorating hearing, he battled on and by the end of the decade had made another television acting comeback as an undertaker in *Mr H Is Late*, a self-written tale of an attempt to get a coffin to church from the twenty-sixth floor of a block of high-rise flats. Comparable in feel to *The Plank*, *Rhubarb Rhubarb* and *It's Your Move*, *Mr H Is Late* again boasted a multi-star cast list in which roles were found for older stars such as Jimmy Edwards, Spike Milligan, Terry Scott and Jimmy James's sidekick Eli Woods, along with big 1980s names like Cannon and Ball, Freddie Starr and Paul Shane.

With the approach of the 1990s, and at an age when younger men would be settling in for a period of restful retirement, Sykes then popped up in another Johnny Speight sitcom, *The Nineteenth Hole*, set in a rather snobby, racist, chauvinistic and homophobic golf club. How do you mean, is there any other sort? As with *Curry and Chips*, its intended satire was not well received and it lasted a mere seven episodes in the summer of 1989. It did, however, lead to a perhaps unlikely stage show, in which Sykes went on tour in 1992.

In terms of sitcom starring roles, *The Nineteenth Hole* was to be Eric Sykes's swansong, although the old stager has continued to make occasional appearances on the small screen, and has regularly trodden the boards in high-profile theatrical productions by writers as diverse as Ray Cooney, Chekov, Moliére, Alan Bennett and Shakespeare, revealing a more dramatic string to his bow. Nowadays plagued by problems with his sight as well as his hearing, Sykes goes on seemingly undeterred, as a writer and performer. Aside from his autobiography, his book published in October 2003, *Eric Sykes's Comedy Heroes*, is a must read for any student of the subject. In 2001, a film CV which already contained such notable efforts as *Those Magnificent Men In Their Flying Machines* (alongside Jack Lemmon and Tony Curtis in 1965), *Monte Carlo Or Bust* (with Terry Thomas in 1969) and the Vincent Price horror spoof *Theatre Of Blood* (1973) was nicely added to with a role opposite Nicole Kidman in *The Others*. In 2005, Sykes also enjoyed a cameo as the elderly caretaker Frank Bryce in *Harry Potter and the Goblet of Fire*.

Suitably, one of Eric Sykes's more recent television appearances came in 2002, when he bade a funny and moving farewell to his old friend Spike Milligan in *I Told You I Was Ill*, a tribute to his late comedy-writing partner that once again featured a whole new generation of comics, including Eddie Izzard, Kathy Burke, Paul Merton and Harry Enfield. He also guested for Victoria Wood - a comedian for whom he has consistently had nothing but praise - in a 1998 episode of her culinary ensemble piece *dinnerladies*, which also featured Dora Bryan and Thora Hird.

Still active at the time of writing despite a stroke and a heart bypass operation, Sykes was awarded a CBE for services to drama in 2004. His penchant for making light of life's troubles remains undimmed. As he told the *Sunday Times*: 'I have to write in capitals, as I can't do joined-up writing any more; and I have a special light, but I can't see what I've written. Janey, my secretary, types it up and reads it to me, so I can change things. One day, I gave her a chapter [of his autobiography] on four foolscap sheets. She went to see Norma, my manager, saying: "I don't know how to tell Eric. There's nothing on this paper." My pen had dried up and I didn't know.'

8
Time for Tea and Meet the Wife

"What would Thora Hird do?"
- *Brian Potter, 'Phoenix Nights'*

So, the 1960s. A time of pushing the boundaries and social revolution; a changing world of writers and in-your-face realism in every entertainment genre? Well, yes, to a point. But, in comedy as everywhere, while the new and fashionable grabbed the headlines, a more traditional mainstream remained where it was at in terms of sheer weight of audience numbers. And although sitcoms like *Steptoe And Son* and *The Likely Lads*, plus a freshly burgeoning Oxbridge satire boom, helped the BBC to regain lost ground on its commercial competitors, as the 'sixties swung on it was ITV who garnered the most impressive viewing figures.

Was that achieved by appealing to the lowest common denominator? Or was it simply a reward for a total lack of elitism, with ITV's networks more in touch with the mood out there in the provinces, beyond the hip and happening in Carnaby Street and the Kings Road? New twists on an old debate reared back into view. And although, in 1962, ITV actually beat the BBC to the satirical punch by a month, with a show ironically called *What The Public Wants*, on the whole any commitment to breaking new ground was noticeable only by its absence. Certainly, when it turned

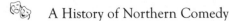

out that *What The Public Wants* was *not* what the public - or at least the ITV public - wanted, what was intended to be 'a weekly does of virulent, unrestrained satire' was swiftly dropped. In truth it was no great loss. The Parliamentary Television Act that governed ITV's output forbade mickey-taking of any kind when it was aimed at living, breathing politicians, and thereby rendered the show toothless. Had they wanted to, of course, the ITV bosses might have dared to challenge such a draconian ruling, in much the same way as BBC chiefs later stood up to the Government, for a while at least. But, in fact, they had no stomach for such a battle and it is not hard to see why. There were licences to worry about and, anyway, a comedy schedule stuffed with Variety entertainers and shows broadcast from London's best-known venues was doing very nicely, thank you.

Although the 'sixties were a decade of fundamental cultural upheaval, as ever, shifting social sands carried with them a simultaneous need for reassurance. In unpredictable times, it seems, the great British public does not much care to be challenged; it would far rather cheer itself up with a harmless chuckle at life's hardships. If that means more of those old-style northern Variety troupers, then send in the clowns. As a result, and boosted by the future arrival of colour TV, the 1960s brought a brand of bright and breezy light entertainment into the nation's living rooms which would dominate our television screens for the following two decades.

None of which is to deny that a dash of social revolution did not seep through the mainstream cracks. A more liberal attitude to sex, for example, paved the way for the *Carry On* films' bawdier moments, with the likes of *Carry On Screaming, Carry On Up The Khyber* and *Carry On Doctor* featuring more than a few performers with northern roots, including Jack Douglas, Roy Castle, Harry H. Corbett and an often over-looked member of that troupe, Peter Gilmore, raised in Nunthorpe, North Yorkshire and later to star in the BBC's nautical Sunday night drama *The Onedin Line*. The relaxed new public morality was also evident on the small screen, although not in Thora Hird's house.

After being established in the late 1950s, ITV's position at the top of the light entertainment pile was cemented throughout the early 1960s by the 'Cockney' comedian Arthur Haynes. And, in many ways, *The Arthur Haynes Show* was the junction between two eras. On the one hand, Haynes himself might be seen as the last hurrah of the old music hall coster comics. On the other, his Johnny Speight-scripted programme, which began in 1957, allowed Haynes's impressive knack for mimicry to originate the character comedy sketch format that, in future years, would make household names of Benny Hill, Dick Emery, Harry Enfield and, most recently, Catherine Tate.

Among Haynes's most popular characters was the mischievous Oscar Pennyfeather, who operated entirely in silence save for the urbane voice of his conscience, provided in the TV series by Haynes's Grantham-born sidekick Nicholas Parsons. Sadly, Haynes died prematurely, aged just 52, but his show set Parsons en route to a more enduring career. For the one-time public schoolboy and Clydeside engineering apprentice, a future half-century of film, TV, radio and theatre appearances went on to include a long-running role as straight man to Benny Hill; a stint as the cross-dressing narrator of *The Rocky Horror Show*; a twelve-year residency as host of the mega-popular Anglia TV quiz show *Sale Of The Century* ('... and now... from Norwich.... it's the *quiz* of the week'); and a still-running spell as the host of the BBC Radio 4 panel game *Just A Minute*, which has continued without deviation or hesitation since 1967.

If Arthur Haynes was king of the ITV castle throughout the first half of the 1960s, neatly tucked in behind him was the diminutive Dickie Henderson. Henderson, the son of a Hull-born music hall comedian, Dick Henderson III (1891-1958), a.k.a. 'The Yorkshire Nightingale' and equally popular in his day, made his first major public appearance at the age of ten in the 1933 Hollywood version of Noel Coward's *Cavalcade*. Five years later, he was taken under the wing of Lancashire impresario Jack Hylton and soon began to perform regularly alongside his twin sisters, Triss and Wyn, until their marriages broke the song and dance act up, forcing the versatile Dickie to go it alone.

Dick Henderson Sr., a rotund figure clad in a trademark tiny bowler hat, is said to have influenced generations of Variety comedians, if for no other reason than he pioneered the now-ubiquitous straight song after a comedy routine, in his case 'Tiptoe Through The Tulips'. The rest of his act was staple music hall foolery but so successful did he become that by the late 1920s the East Yorkshire comic had performed before the King in the Royal Variety Performance of 1926 and decamped to the United States, where he made a number of Vitaphone movie shorts.

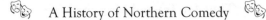

By the time young Dickie had followed up his role in *Cavalcade* with a part as his father's son in the 1935 UK offering, *Things Are Looking Up* (a film which also co-starred Max Miller and an, as yet, undiscovered Vivien Leigh), it was evident that the next in line to the Henderson family fortune was equally set upon a life in greasepaint. Back in England and now without his sisters, by 1951 he had built up such a head of steam that he was invited to follow in father's footsteps and star at the London Palladium, a venue that would henceforth play a huge part in his life.

In 1953, Dickie Henderson made his television debut on Henry Hall's *Face The Music*, followed by an appearance in Arthur Askey's *Before Your Very Eyes*. Given his family background, it was somewhat inevitable that America would again come calling and, in 1956, off he duly trotted on a transatlantic cabaret tour that culminated in a spot on *The Ed Sullivan Show*. Exactly thirty years after his father, Henderson returned to the UK for a spot in the Royal Variety Performance, a forerunner as it turned out to a soon-to-be regular spell as compere of Val Parnell's *Sunday Night At The London Palladium* - destined to become one of the most popular ITV shows of all time. A first ITV series of his own, *The Dickie Henderson Show*, began in 1957.

For Dickie, a song and dance man as much as a comedian, the idea of giving his television show a domestic setting was hardly obvious but, nonetheless, it worked. In *The Dickie Henderson Show*, his wife was played in the first instance by Anthea Askey, daughter of Arthur, and later June Laverick. Tragically, however, Henderson's real-life wife, Dixie, died in 1963, just as his TV career was at its height. He battled on gamely with the format for another two years and then took a sabbatical from sitcom, before eventually giving the genre another go, with *A Present For Dickie*, in 1969. This time, our eponymous hero had to contend with an absent wife, a nagging mother-in-law and the gift in the title, an Indian elephant named Mini. No one could ever describe that as unimaginative. Alas, few people described it as funny either and it only managed six episodes.

By the 1970s, Henderson was almost exclusively to be found in an altogether more traditional brand of Variety - or light entertainment, as it was becoming increasingly known. As the decade advanced, he formed a double act with fellow slick American-influenced gag merchant, Bob Monkhouse. *I'm Bob, He's Dickie* was followed by two solo specials, *I'm Dickie - That's Showbusiness*, an unselfconsciously stagy title that, all too soon, would only be got away with as ironic parody. As it was and, as we shall see, far from uniquely, time and the withering tides of public taste increasingly gathered against him. An apparent relic of a supposedly forgotten epoch, television work all but dried up and Dickie Henderson OBE died of cancer in 1985, shortly before his 63rd birthday.

An eye-catching stint as host of *Sunday Night At The London Palladium* also paid rich dividends for Liverpudlian comedian Norman Vaughan, whose debut solo TV show in 1964, *A Touch Of The Norman Vaughans*, sounds as though it ought to be rhyming slang for something unpleasant. Maybe it was. Vaughan's catchphrases, thumbs up, were 'Swinging!' and 'Dodgy!'.

Like many old-time Variety entertainers of the era, Vaughan's gentle comedic talents were nurtured in Second World War concert parties. His first TV appearance was on the BBC talent show *Showcase* in 1954, a spot which led to his appearance alongside Eric Sykes and Harry Secombe on ITV's opening Saturday night Variety shows. It was in those that all three became well-known for their 'marching to music' routine. In 1955, he co-starred in *The Harry Secombe Show* and, a couple of years later, landed a role in the Terry Scott BBC sitcom *Scott Free*. An archetypal 'stand-up' comic in the Ted Ray mould, Vaughan's talents were always better suited to the stage and *A Touch Of The Norman Vaughans* proved such a hit that an original six-show deal was extended to twelve and a move to the BBC soon followed, where *The Norman Vaughan Show* was shown in 1966. Appropriately enough, Vaughan's final TV comedy appearance came alongside Jack Douglas in *The End Of The End Of The Pier Show*, a 1981 children's programme wherein the demise of traditional seaside entertainment was lamented.

By then, it had long since become clear that, along with his hosting of the nation's favourite Sunday night Variety spectacular, Vaughan was destined to be best known for taking over from Bob Monkhouse on the highly popular Sunday afternoon game show, *The Golden Shot*, alongside Bernie the Bolt and blonde bombshell schoolboy fantasy figure Anne Aston. He was also the face of a much-loved advert for Roses chocolates, popularising the slogan, 'Roses grow on you'. In 2002, Norman Vaughan was killed in a road accident, aged 79.

It perhaps ought to be apparent by now - even if it wasn't back then - that despite a growing taste for realism, most mainstream television comedy throughout the 1960s continued to inhabit a world of its own. Take *Happily Ever After*, a 1961 sitcom starring the Lancashire character actor Dora Bryan, in which a scatter-brained wife puts her long-suffering husband through hoops. If that sounds familiar, it can only be because *Happily Ever After* was based on the legendary American show, *I Love Lucy*. There, however, all similarities end. Despite her dumb blonde act and tonsilitic voice, Bryan - born in Southport in 1924 - was no Lucille Ball. Nor, for that matter, was her husband Peter - played by the future Radio 1 DJ Pete Murray - any Desi Arnaz. Here was a show in which Bryan's character could insist that she and her husband are remarried, simply because she has somehow mislaid their wedding certificate. If they ever felt like defending such twaddle, the ITV programme-makers could usually point to the health of their viewing figures. Not this time. Just eight episodes and a pilot from the thirteen made were broadcast, before the programme was unceremoniously hauled off the air, although viewers in the north and Midlands were deemed undemanding enough to be shown the four missing episodes three years later.

At least dizzy Dora did have a happy ever after story of her own. A former member of ENSA and star of West End theatrical revues, her role in that ill-fated sitcom proved merely to be a blip in a sixty-year career that went on to include her own BBC sketch show, *According To Dora*, in 1968. By then, Bryan was already well known for her work in a plethora of British films too, including the classic Ealing police drama *The Blue Lamp* (1949), *Time Gentlemen Please!* (1952) and *Carry On Sergeant* (1958). After a BAFTA-winning display in Tony Richardson's *A Taste Of Honey*, in the same year that *Happily Ever After* flopped so badly, came an appearance as a dodgy headmistress in *The Great St. Trinians Train Robbery* (1966), before film work began to take second fiddle to theatre and television.

In the former, Dora had already had the notable distinction of being the first female to play a pantomime dame at the London Palladium, after already winning the Variety Club of Great Britain's Best Actress award for her role in *She Stoops to Conquer*. Notwithstanding her decision to take a break from acting in the 1970s to raise her children, she has continued to work in theatre and in 1996 was awarded an OBE for services to that profession. Since then, she has shown a gift for monologue in stage productions of Alan Bennett's *A Cream Cracker Under The Settee*.

Now over 80 years of age, although Bryan has not unreasonably slowed down a little, notable appearances in a medium in which she became the first person ever to be featured on *This Is Your Life* twice, go on. Modern-day roles include that of Roz, the sister of the late Thora Hird's character Edie, in *Last Of The Summer Wine*. Alongside Hird and Eric Sykes, she played Connie in Victoria Wood's *dinnerladies* and was also June Whitfield's friend Millie, in the 'last ever' episode of *Absolutely Fabulous* (1996), which turned out not to be the final episode at all.

Meanwhile, back in 1957, Alan Young, another comedian of northern heritage who, like Dickie Henderson, had nevertheless enjoyed an American upbringing, came back to his homeland to host *Personal Appearance*, an ITV Variety show broadcast live from London's Hackney Empire. The following year, at the bequest of Jack Hylton, the North Shields-born Young - born Angus Young in 1919 - returned and, this time, stayed for six shows. That must have been sweet for a kid who had emigrated to the US, with his parents, at the age of 13.

At which point, many a reader will doubtless be scratching his or her head and muttering, 'who on earth is Alan Young?' In which case, ask an American. Or maybe a friend of the equine persuasion. For, in 1961, Young landed the part of freelance architect Wilbur Post, owner of the world's most famous talking horse, *Mister Ed*. The show became a huge favourite with audiences on both sides of the Pond, running for over five years and leading to another phonecall from Granada Television, for whom Young returned to make a third show, *It's Young Again*, in 1963.

Still going strong at the time of writing, Alan Young also went on to appear alongside Eddie Murphy in *Beverley Hills Cop III* (1994), and has provided voices for such animated characters as Walt Disney's Scrooge McDuck and Haggis McHaggis in the *Ren And Stimpy Show*. The fate of Mister Ed - real name Bamboo Harvester - is less clear. Originally said to have died in 1979, in Oklahoma, it has since emerged that, after breaking a leg aged 19, he may have been put to sleep in California a decade earlier.

Mister Ed is just one example of the widespread American influence on ITV's comedy and entertainment schedules throughout the 1960s, as the commercial channels looked to capitalise on all those glamourous

transatlantic accents and glossy production values. And of all the franchises, Granada, based in Manchester, were the most innovative of the lot. It was they, for example, who gave the Jewish 'storyteller' Woody Allen his British TV stand-up comedy debut, after inviting Allen to showcase his act from their north west studios in 1965. As for London-based Thames Television, when *it* turned stateside for talent, it opted for a couple of out-and-out wise-crackers: Bob Hope and Jack Benny.

In November 1969, both ITV and BBC1 finally caught up with American technology and began to transmit their programmes in colour for the first time (although BBC2 *had* already been doing so since July 1967). One of the first ITV sketch shows to benefit from the bright new format was fronted by Oldham's very own Bernard Cribbins.

Already well known for his work in film and television, not to mention a recording career that included the top ten singles 'Right Said Fred' and 'Hole In The Ground', until ITV handed him his own series Cribbins had chiefly been a valued contributor in other folks' successes. In *Cribbins*, his individual versatility was up front and centre stage.

For much of the lengthy and busy career that followed, however, Bernard Cribbins, born 1928, would become known as a children's entertainer. That was thanks, in the main, to a sixty-episode run as narrator of *The Wombles* (1973-75), an even longer-running spell on the BBC's storytime programme *Jackanory* and a role as good-hearted Albert Perks in Lionel Jeffries's *The Railway Children* (1970).

Yet, in common with many a northern comic actor, 'good-hearted' would be a fair description of Cribbins's output in general, whether for children or adults. Ever a likeable presence, in 1971 he starred alongside Roy Kinnear in the BBC's north of England writing showcase *Get The Drift*, and other roles have come in a trio of ITV sitcoms: *Cuffy* (1983), the Yorkshire Dales-based *Langley Bottom* (1986) and *High & Dry* (1987). All in all, the nearest he seems ever to have got to aggression was as spoon salesman Mr Hutchinson in 'The Hotel Inspectors', a 1975 episode of *Fawlty Towers*. On film, an acting resumé that began as a 14-year-old, includes three *Carry On* films: *Carry On Jack* (1963), *Carry On Spying* (1964) and the terminally ill-advised *Carry On Columbus* (1992), which might now be viewed as a desperate attempt by certain alternative 1980s comedians to display new-found 'respect' for the British Variety tradition. Cribbins has played a couple of sidekicks to *Doctor Who* too; once, in the cinema, alongside Peter Cushing in *Daleks - Invasion Earth 2150AD* (1966), and most recently on television, as the star-gazing grandfather of Donna Noble (Catherine Tate) in 2007-08. Cribbins is the latest of many within these pages to have also appeared in *Coronation Street*, where he took a starring role as Wally Bannister, elderly seducer of Tracy Barlow, in 2003.

Generally throughout the 'sixties, ITV had a scattergun approach to attracting the largest audience figures possible. Throw everything at the screen and some of it is bound to stick, or so seemed to be their philosophy. Take the 1960 sitcom, *Our House*. In it, roles were somehow found for *Carry On* regulars Hattie Jacques, Bernard Bresslaw (although he hadn't yet made his *Carry On* debut), Joan Sims, Charles Hawtrey and Norman Rossington, while supporting roles went to the likes of Harry Korris and Hylda Baker, for good measure. Baker and Hawtrey also went on to star in 1963's less successful *Best Of Friends*, written and produced by the same team. Hylda Baker's most enduring 1960s legacy by far, though, is her partnership with Jimmy Jewel that began in 1968, in the aforementioned *Nearest And Dearest*.

If the 'simple northerner' persona of a George Formby or, latterly, Johnny Vegas is in danger of inducing a chippy cultural cringe, then the entire premise of *Nearest and Dearest* might be seen as a descent into cliché hell. That, however, would be to ignore the formidable comedic talents of Baker and Jewel themselves, who as Nellie and Eli Pledge - bickering brother and sister - combined to make it one of British television's most popular sitcoms of the next five years.

The dilemma faced by Eli and Nellie Pledge in *Nearest And Dearest* is one which, surely, every viewer will have struggled with at some stage in his or her life. Namely, just how *do* you run a struggling pickled onion factory once your aged father has popped his clogs, leaving you just £9 17 shillings and sixpence between the pair of you in his will? The downright silliness of that proposition was ideal for Baker's eccentricities. Nor did it do any harm that the show was set in deepest, darkest industrial Colne, Lancashire, with a script that was pure end-of-Blackpool pier.

Nearest And Dearest proved to be the perfect vehicle for Hylda Baker's

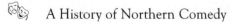

wonderfully daft malapropisms, sprinkled, as they were, with a dash of good old fashioned seaside double entendre. It also introduced another catchphrase into the Baker armoury to go with 'she knows, you know', the immortal 'have you been?', directed at feeble brother-in-law Walter (Eddie Malin), whose utterly silent hangdog expression belied a raging and presumably untrustworthy bladder. Yet what really kept the *Nearest And Dearest* comedy bubble aloft was the mutual hostility of its central pairing, a relationship that was as acidic off screen as it was on it.

In the show, Eli Pledge was portrayed as a womanising, leering, hard-drinking, flat-capped rogue, totally at odds with his chaste and domineering midget prude of a sister. Ironically, however, with the cameras off, in the pair's real lives away from Pledge's Purer Pickles, those character traits were all but reversed. We have already seen the levels of debauchery to which Hylda Baker has been accused of sinking. Whatever the truth of that, Jewel, fresh from his first solo TV appearance without Ben Warriss in the 1967 one-off playlet *Spanner In The Works*, did not drink and thought himself an altogether cleaner-living individual.

The result, it seems, was a whole barrage of insults off-screen and on. She was a 'knock-kneed knackered old nose bag', while he was a 'big girl's blouse'. Nellie: 'You remind me of that beautiful song from *The Sound Of Music*'. Eli: 'What? 'My favourite things'?' Nellie: 'No. Idleswine...' In the hands of Hylda Baker, even the weakest of puns could be amusing.

And here, as everywhere else in northern comedy, the shadow of *Coronation Street* fell. Walter's deadpan wife Lily was played by Blackburn's Madge Hindley, later to become Renee Roberts, née Bradshaw. Nothing Renee ever got up to in Weatherfield could match the episode of *Nearest And Dearest* in which Lily and Walter turn out not to be married at all, with the new bachelor joining Eli on a tour of 'the fleshpots of Colne' before Nellie contrives to return him to the registry office. Under starters orders for a lengthy spell as Bet Lynch, behind the bar of the Rovers Return, Julie Goodyear made an appearance as one of the chain-smoking Eli's many blonde girlfriends. And nor should we forget the admittedly historically unreliable claim that Baker actually considered suing the soap when the great Hilda Ogden began to refer to the 'muriel' on her living room wall. When informed that her own persona was dangerously close to Dickens's Mrs. Malaprop, Baker apparently threatened to sue her too.

Time for Tea and Meet the Wife

A more surprising fact, perhaps, is that after a 1970 summer season in Blackpool and a 1972 Hammer film version (truly bloodcurdling by all accounts, in which the cast, ahem, goes on holiday), *Nearest And Dearest* somehow found new life across the Atlantic. Still set in a pickle factory, but now starring Julie Harris and Richard Long as the renamed Nellie and Ernie Paine, the American version was re-titled *Thicker Than Water*. Coincidentally, that was also the name of Jimmy Jewel's next British sitcom, which we shall come to anon.

Although any sense of realism in *Nearest And Dearest* could hardly be described as gritty, another ITV sitcom launched in the same year did get decidedly closer to that mark. Jack Rosenthal's *The Dustbinmen* was topical too - chiming perfectly with a dustbinmen's strike of 1968. Through his story of everyday Fylde refuse folk, the Manchester-born playwright and future husband of Hull-born national treasure Maureen Lipman proved, like the writers of *Steptoe And Son* and *The Likely Lads* before him, that realistic and lifelike can also equal popular. Too frequently overlooked, Rosenthal's *The Dustbinmen* was an important point on a career path that would go on to include the seminal 1970s sitcom *The Lovers*, starring the Manchester-born Paula Wilcox and Nottingham's Richard Beckinsale.

In rattling the cage of the Mary Whitehouse brigade, *The Dustbinmen* was not in the same league as *Till Death Us Do Part*. Nevertheless it was ribald enough to merit a number of outraged complaints. After which, counter-productive notoriety did its usual trick and the first six editions of a twenty-two-show run, which began with a one-off 1967 play snappily entitled *There's A Hole In Your Dustbin, Delilah*, shot straight to the top of the viewing charts.

Riding up and down the Lancashire coast on a dustcart named Thunderbird 3, Rosenthal's protagonists were a motley crew. The beret-wearing Cheese and Egg (Jack MacGowran in the pilot and Bryan Pringle in the series) was foreman, and the rest of the gang included such well-drawn characters as Manchester City fan Winston (Graham Haberfield), the self-explanatory Smellie (John Barrett - destined for later glory as Eric Olthwaite's 'French' father), the witless Eric (Henry Livings/Tim Wylton) and smooth-tongued lothario Heavy Breathing (Harold Innocent/Trevor Bannister). All were sworn enemies of the Corporation Cleansing

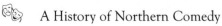

Department and, in particular, that organisation's inspector, the 'Bloody Delilah' of the original title, played by a couple of *Z-Cars* actors in Frank Windsor (pilot) and John Woodvine (series).

If nothing else, *The Dustbinmen* deserves a place in the British sitcom hall of fame for its origination of what has since become a standard genre device, namely the swearword that isn't. Where *Porridge* brought 'naffin' into the canon of comedic cuss and *Red Dwarf* 'smeg', *The Dustbinmen* begat the evocative and stench-filled 'pigging'.

As his career evolved, Jack Rosenthal was most often to be found in the field of comedy drama, where awards aplenty came his way for many a landmark television production. In the BAFTA-winning *The Evacuees* (1975) and *The Barmitzvah Boy* (1976), Rosenthal drew on his own Jewish, northern working class upbringing while, perhaps most famously, in *Spend, Spend, Spend* (1977) he turned his fine eye for painful and amusing everyday detail to the story of football pools winner Viv Nicholson. For the big screen, he wrote or co-wrote six feature films, including one he penned with Barbra Streisand, *Yentl*, in 1983. Another to spring from the *Coronation Street* talent well, he both worked on that soap as a scriptwriter and met his wife of thirty years there, after initially joining its makers Granada as a researcher in 1956. Jack Rosenthal CBE died from cancer, aged 72, in 2004. Wife Maureen, as we shall discover, lives and works on.

Keen not to be outdone, but outdone on the whole anyway, the BBC's battle to attract viewers went gamely on throughout 1960s. Amidst all the literary adaptations and *Comedy Playhouse* productions (less successfully aped by ATV's *Six Of The Best* strand), the Corporation also came up with a host of fledgling sitcoms of its own.

Usually, these were less frenzied affairs than ITV's, built around a single personality such as the Sid James vehicle *Citizen James* in 1961, and a trio of early sitcom outings for Benny Hill (1962), Lance Percival in *Lance At Large* and Bob Monkhouse as a DJ in *The Big Noise* (both 1964). Roy Hudd fronted his first major TV show *Hudd* in 1965. Occasionally, the Beeb teamed personalities up, as with Jimmy James and Bernard Bresslaw in *Meet The Champ* (1960), Jimmy Edwards and Beryl Reid in *Bold As Brass*, and Hugh Lloyd and Terry Scott in *Hugh And I* (1962).

Time for Tea and Meet the Wife

The BBC also enjoyed some success in emulating the sketch show format made popular on ITV by Arthur Haynes and, later, the likes of Des O'Connor, Charlie Drake, Dave King, Stanley Baxter, Graham Stark and, of course, Dick Emery.

Initially on ITV and then the BBC, Stanley Baxter would become a mainstay of the annual festive schedules, while the Wallasey-born Stark was one of those character actors whom everyone recognises but few can put a name to. Before landing a series of his own in 1964, Stark had *Goon*-ed extensively with Spike Milligan and Peter Sellers, with whom he went on to appear as Inspector Clouseau's assistant, Hercule Lajoy, in the latter's magnificent *Pink Panther* films (1964-82). During a ubiquitous cinema career, he was also among a cast of thousands in *Those Magnificent Men In Their Flying Machines* (1965).

Building on the Arthur Haynes tradition more directly than most, meanwhile, was the London-born Emery. His stock of wacky characters such as Lampwick the old soldier, Hettie the sex-starved spinster and the 'honky tonk' camp guy Clarence were a mainstay of British TV comedy for a whopping eighteen years, after the show's inception in 1963. No Emery creation was as popular as dumb blonde vox-pop victim Mandy, who would sense sexual innuendo in the most innocent of probings, before handing her interviewer off and tottering away up the street in her high-heels like someone with an uncomfortable wedgie. 'Ooh, you are awful... but I *like* you.' It was Emery's bovver boy skinhead, though, who gave the bloke playing his dad, Roy Kinnear, the chance to shine.

Born in Wigan in 1934, Kinnear's short and portly everyman frame endeared him to audiences everywhere. His father, Roy Kinnear Sr., had won sporting acclaim by playing rugby league for Wigan and Great Britain, and rugby union for Scotland and the British Lions. But there was little obviously athletic about his son. Educated in Edinburgh, Kinnear enrolled at RADA aged 17, before conscription and National Service interrupted his intended career route. Nevertheless, with the parade grounds behind him he returned to the stage and, in 1959, like Harry H. Corbett, joined Joan Littlewood's Theatre Workshop in Manchester. Spells with the National Theatre and Royal Shakespeare Companies followed, before the call came from a certain landmark television satirical show, of which more in the next chapter.

Another memorable character actor who came to prominence in this period was Derek Nimmo. With the 1966 clerical sitcom, *All Gas And Gaiters*, Nimmo first established the bumbling eccentric holy man persona that was to sustain him throughout his career. As the Reverend Mervyn Hoote, Nimmo, born in Liverpool and, like so many in that city it seems, a former fellow pupil of John Lennon at Quarry Bank School, formed a triumvirate with Robertson Hare's archdeacon and William Mervyn's bishop, all of them in perpetual conflict with John Barron's dean. *All Gas And Gaiters* was originally conceived as a one-off *Comedy Playhouse* offering, entitled *The Bishop Rides Again*. But its air of gentle mockery did well and it eventually ran until 1971.

Along with *Gas And Gaiters*, Nimmo simultaneously embarked on another religious role, that of the accident-prone apprentice monk Brother Dominic, in the BBC's *Oh Brother!*, broadcast between 1968-70. This ecclesiastical double-whammy led to a couple of chat shows, *If It's Saturday It Must Be Nimmo* and *Just A Nimmo*, as well as a sequel to *Oh Brother!* called, imaginatively enough, *Oh Father!* (1973). More such TV appearances followed throughout the 1970s and early '80s, including the equally religious sitcom *Hell's Bells* in 1986, but the best of Nimmo's later work came on the radio.

That ought to come as no surprise. In the far from gentle world of late-1980s television comedy, Nimmo's deceptively sly humour never had a prayer. Yet on the Radio 4 panel show *Just A Minute* he had the perfect niche in which to display his razor-sharp wit. In fact, Nimmo was in at the start of that long-running show in 1969 - hence the name of his chat show. Chaired by Nicholas Parsons, in *Just A Minute* contestants are asked to speak on a single subject for sixty seconds without being stopped by a fellow guest for one of three misdemeanors: hesitation, repetition or deviation. Given that Nimmo had a slight stutter and that among his fellow contestants were usually numbered the equally sardonic Clement Freud, Peter Jones and Kenneth Williams, hilarity was guaranteed.

Nimmo's involvement with *Just A Minute* straddled some thirty years until, in 1999, he died in hospital, two months after a fall at his home, aged 68. The show however lives on, enlivened these days by a list of regular panelists which includes Paul Merton, Ross Noble, Jenny Eclair and Graham Norton.

224

One of several *Comedy Playhouse* productions to make it to a full series, *Thicker Than Water* would, as we have seen, give Jimmy Jewel the chance to fillet his mackerel on the BBC at precisely the same time as *Nearest And Dearest* was pickling his onions on ITV. Yet Jewel was by no means first choice for the role of widowed fishmonger Jim Eccles, originally named Fred Holmes in the pilot, where the character was played by the Grimsby-born comedian Freddie Frinton.

Sadly, shortly after the BBC had given the series the thumbs up, fate gave Frinton the ultimate thumbs down. He died of a heart attack aged 59 while engaged in a Bournemouth summer season. Jewel was asked to step into the breach and provide a new focus for the attentions of the lead character's three unmarried daughters, not to mention his sex-starved next-door neighbour Aggie Plunkett, played by Jean Kent. As for Frinton, despite his premature demise, he had at least played a major part in the BBC's earliest 1960s mainstream success, *Meet The Wife*, to the extent that the show even merited a mention on the classic Beatles album, *Sergeant Pepper's Lonely Hearts Club Band*, in the lyrics of the song, 'Good Morning': 'It's time for tea and *Meet The Wife*'.

For Freddie Frinton, fame came late. Despite a lifetime treading the music hall boards, he was 55 years old when offered the role of plumber Freddie Blacklock, husband to Thora Hird's just as creatively-named Thora. Yet even after his death and now all but forgotten in his homeland, Frinton's name lives on in the most unusual of circumstances elsewhere.

As with *Thicker Than Water*, *Meet The Wife* was itself born of the *Comedy Playhouse* strand. Its own pilot, *The Bed*, was broadcast in 1963. Written by Ronalds Woolfe and Chesney, joint-creators of *The Rag Trade*, that the resulting series should have been as earthy and working class in tone as its forebear ought not to have been so shocking. Even so, some in the BBC hierarchy were said to be uncomfortable with its depiction of normal life, particularly as portrayed by Frinton's flat-capped, heavy-drinking Freddie, a man who was also partial to a spot of gambling if ever there was a bob or two to be made. And even his altogether more refined missus, Thora, a Hyacinth Bucket prototype, was quite willing to buy her way upwards on the never-never, with regular rounds of bingo *en route*.

225

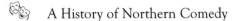

As usual, such corporate nervousness was in direct contrast to the response of viewers. They loved the show, a fact that had as much to do with the casting as it did the of-its-time scripts, from which Hird and the gap-toothed Frinton drew their inspiration. With their children having grown up and gone, the comedy revolved around the couple's attempts to navigate the waters of daily existence; Freddie just after a quiet life and Thora, twenty-five years of marriage notwithstanding, as dogged in her pursuit of social improvement as ever. It was a formula that would keep *Meet The Wife* at the top of the BBC schedules for almost three years.

If any actor was meant to play such a role, it was quite obviously Thora Hird. Before she got anywhere near it, and certainly in a vast array of such roles to come, she had revealed a gift for capturing the essence of a very distinctive kind of working class female pride that, in ordinary everyday life, was in common view right across England's north. Not that there was anything *remotely* common about Thora.

Her television career began with an appearance in the first episode of Jimmy James's BBC show, *Home James*, in 1956. Later that year, she took a similar role alongside the Battersea-born mustachioed comedian Jimmy Wheeler. Wheeler, born Ernest Remnant, took his stage name both from his entertainer father's double act, Wheeler and Wilson, and 'Lucky Jim', a nickname given to him by a certain George Formby Sr. during a music hall curtain call.

Yet by then, Thora Hird's entertainment career was already forty-five years old, if we count a debut stage appearance in her mother's arms, at just eight weeks of age. Either way, the fact that baby Thora was born next door to Morecambe's Royalty Theatre in 1911 was an omen in itself, and she was soon into her thespian stride. After a brief stint working in the local Co-op upon leaving school, she joined the Royalty Repertory Company and appeared in around 500 plays from 1931-41.

The story goes that her big break came during that latter year. While taking the part of a 60-year-old woman in a play called *As You Are*, she was noticed and admired by ukulele-playing member of the Formby clan, George Formby Jr., and it was he who suggested that Thora should head south for a screen test at Ealing Studios. The upshot was a seven-year contract and a part alongside Will Hay in his 1941 production, *The Blacksheep Of Whitehall*. More minor film roles followed.

Time for Tea and Meet the Wife

As with so many of her contemporaries, lasting fame came courtesy of the rise and growth of television. After *Meet The Wife*'s forty-episode run reached its conclusion in 1966, lead parts in a couple of ITV sitcoms underlined what a formidable force of nature Thora Hird could be. The first, *Ours Is A Nice House* (1969), lasted just two series and cast Hird as a boarding house landlady named - answers on a postcard - Thora. This Thora was a house-proud widowed mother of two children, the lazy Alan (Leslie Meadows) and trendy Vera (Caroline Dowdeswell). There were also regular turns from scrounging next-door neighbour Elsie Crabtree (Ruth Holden) and the show's writer, Harry Littlewood, who played Alf Whittle, one of a number of lodgers to come in and out of the place. Despite the show being set in Lancashire, usually those lodgers had a southern accent as *Ours Is A Nice House* was actually made by London Weekend Television, which may or may not account for its rather stereotypical northern feel. Veteran comedy actor May Warden, herself a former co-star of Freddie Frinton, played Thora's mother Mrs Potts, usually having neglected to put her false teeth in.

In Loving Memory was another story again. The original single pilot of that show, also made in 1969, had to wait a full ten years before being turned into a series and, by then, there was no longer any place for the original cast. Instead the role of undertaker's wife Ivy Unsworth, played previously by Marjorie Rhodes, went to Thora Hird. Her nephew (Harold Goodwin in the pilot) had a name change from Harold to Billy, with Christopher Beeny coming in. As for undertaker Jeremiah Unsworth (initially played by Edward Chapman), he was replaced by Freddie Jones. And even then, Jones's character wasn't able to see out the opening episode, unceremoniously pegging it before the first credits had rolled.

If the benign humour of *In Loving Memory* seemed tame in the harsh and highly-politicised comedic environment of 1979, Dick Sharples's tale of 1930s-based Lancashire funeral parlours nevertheless proved popular enough to see it through five series until March 1986. Furthermore, while such apparently lightweight fare was increasingly being met with derision at comedy's so-called cutting edge, setting it in the fictitious Pennine mill town of Oldshaw - in reality Luddenden - where horse-drawn hearses are on the verge of being replaced by motor cars, was actually a thoughtful and symbolic thing to do, comedy-wise. Not, you suspect, that the show's

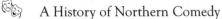 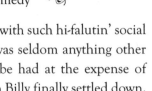

legions of fans would have been too concerned with such hi-falutin' social theorising. The humour of *In Loving Memory* was seldom anything other than slapstick and broad, with much fun to be had at the expense of unruly coffins and Billy's girlfriends. And when Billy finally settled down, his mother accompanied he and his new wife on honeymoon. Comedy trivia addicts, meanwhile, may care to note that the show not only featured *Royle Family* nana Liz Smith, it also gave a couple of walk-ons to Richard Wilson, half a foot in the grave away from Victor Meldrew.

Two years before *In Loving Memory*, in 1977, Thora Hird had already reunited with *Meet The Wife* writers Wolfe and Chesney to make *The Boys And Mrs B*, a *Comedy Special* pilot about a former northern textile factory manager named Mrs Battley, now relocated to the south, where she is the supervisor of an unruly London boys club. Among the tearaways in her care was one Tony Robinson, later to crunch turnips as the less-than-cunning Baldrick, heroically stupid sidekick of Edmund Blackadder.

While *The Boys And Mrs B* never made a full series, and as *In Loving Memory* continued to splash around happily in the mainstream, Dick Sharples developed another part tailor-made for Hird, that of Salvation Army Captain Emily Ridley in the 1983 sitcom *Hallelujah!*. As the over-devout and accident-prone Captain Ridley, pushed out of harm's way to the fictional Yorkshire town of Brigthorpe, Hird - whose own Christian faith was never a secret - had terrific fun with this interfering religious zealot, a character who found sin around every corner.

In fact, throughout her career and especially in her later years, Thora Hird's name became synonymous with a certain brand of common sense and unfussy religion. Largely, that was thanks to a seventeen-year spell as host of ITV's early Sunday evening show *Praise Be*. One more reason, perhaps, along with her age and the creakiness of those sitcom scripts, for the skill and truth at the heart of her performances not to receive the full recognition that they deserved. Nor, from 1986, did her role as Edie Pegden in the seemingly unstoppable *Last Of The Summer Wine* exactly endear her to the trainers and T-shirt stand-up set.

It seems hard to imagine Thora herself being particularly bothered by any of that, of course. And anyway, natural justice dictated that somebody somewhere must realise just what a priceless talent we had in our midst. Step forward Britain's greatest living playwright Alan Bennett who, along with the likes of Victoria Wood in future years, wasted no opportunity to give his friend the chance to explore the emotional depths of which she was time and again more than capable.

Happily, by 1998, a welcome new broom had swept through British comedy to the extent that Thora Hird, made OBE in 1983 and a Dame of the British Empire a decade later, was honoured with a richly-deserved lifetime achievement award. She had already won two BAFTAs for her roles in Bennett's *Talking Heads* television monologues, of which more later. And another soon followed for her brilliant depiction of the writer Deric Longden's mother Annie in the ITV drama *Lost For Words*, a story of failing health and senility in 1999. At one point asked by her son, played by Peter Postlethwaite, whether she wants to be buried or cremated, the reply is pure Thora: 'Oh, I don't know love - surprise me...'.

Proud of her Morecambe roots, as the subject of Melvyn Bragg's *South Bank Show* in 1994, the now Dame Thora insisted that her contribution should be filmed in the north west seaside resort's Winter Gardens, a venue of which she was soon to become a patron. Her last radio appearance came in *The Last Of The Sun*, a moving Alan Bennett monologue written especially for her and the new digital channel BBC7, in which she played pensioner and retirement home resident Dolly who, according to the writer, went down 'with all flags flying, game to the last'. Prior to broadcast in January 2004, Thora Hird died after having suffered a stroke in March 2003, aged 91. The day after her death, the BBC repeated *A Cream Cracker Under The Settee* as a poignant tribute.

At least, to adopt a suitably stoic northern catchphrase, Thora Hird had enjoyed a good innings. The premature death of her *Meet The Wife* co-star Freddie Frinton had denied Britain of another fine eye for age-related comedy that may have developed along similar lines if given the chance.

Like Hird, Frinton's talent to amuse was apparent early on. Born Frederick Coo, out of wedlock to a seamstress in 1909 and thereafter adopted, the first audience he entertained was colleagues at a Grimsby fish processing plant where, eventually, he was fired from his job. No matter, a liking for attention was awoken and it wasn't long before he took to the music hall stage and rechristened himself Freddie Frinton.

During the Second World War, Frinton's career as a comedian really took off, to the extent that by 1945 he was headlining in Blackpool, the resort in which he had first performed a sketch written in the 1920s that would one day see him enter German folklore. *Dinner For One* was its name and ritual was its game.

In it, lonely, upper class Miss Sophie is celebrating her 90th birthday with a dinner party for a quartet of former lovers: Mr. Winterbottom; Mr. Pommeroy; Sir Toby; and Admiral von Schneider. Clearly, this has become a regular event but, unfortunately, the guests she imagines to be there aren't present at all, having all died off in previous years. Undeterred, the party goes on and Miss Sophie's butler, James, played by Frinton, continues to navigate his way around a troublesome tiger rug and serve the empty places while surreptitiously polishing off the wine those absent guests have failed to drink. There are probably no better known lines in German culture than those delivered at the sketch's denouement, in which the now thoroughly sloshed butler accompanies his elderly mistress up the stairs: 'Same procedure as last year, madam?' - 'Same procedure as every year, James.'

Owing to how every time he performed *Dinner For One* Frinton had to pay out royalties to the original writer, at some stage in the 1950s - long before the Germans became interested - he decided to buy the rights to the sketch for himself. It turned out to be a very wise decision indeed. In 1963, Frinton and May Warden (as Miss Sophie) were invited to record the piece, in English, for the Hamburg-based German television channel Norddeutscher Rundfunk (NDR). The tipping point, however, did come until ten years later when, upon the sketch being re-shown on New Year's Eve, it proved to be so in tune with Germany's comedic sensibilities that a cult institutional phenomenon was born. And so it remains to this day, easily earning the highest TV ratings of the year.

Not only in Germany either. Picture the scene; every 31 December without fail, families right across continental Europe settle down to watch a couple of long-departed English music hall entertainers go through their paces, as often as five times in one night. *Dinner For One* can be seen on several different channels in many versions and languages, in black and white, touched-up colour, dubbed in dialect *Plattdeutsch* or whatever. German airlines even show it on their Christmas period flights, in order that no one should miss out on their annual festive fix.

Time for Tea and Meet the Wife

Subsequent years have also seen *Dinner For One* become hugely popular outside Germany, most recently in countries like Estonia. There have also been a number of remakes but, in Germany at least, the original eleven-minute production remains as much a signal for celebration as the midnight chimes of Big Ben or a wee dram of Hogmanay whisky in the UK. Disappointingly for Frinton's posthumous reputation in British comedy, the land of his birth has never shown the slightest interest.

After the success of *The Rag Trade* and *Meet The Wife*, the writers Ronald Woolfe and Ronald Chesney took their next project, rejected by the BBC, to the newly-launched London Weekend Television. The result was *On The Buses*, a similarly earthy but rather more raucous sitcom which, from its first first appearance in 1969 to its eventual demise in 1973, and taking in three big-screen incarnations, was nothing less than a major hit. Mainly that was down to a list of characters that, at the bus depot, included pompous and punctilious Inspector Blakey (Stephen Lewis), his troublesome driver Stan Butler (played by *Rag Trade* star Reg Varney) and Stan's womanising conductor mate Jack (Bob Grant). At home, meanwhile, middle-aged Stan lived with his mother (Doris Hare), his bespectacled disaster of a sister Olive (Anna Karen) and her layabout husband Arthur (Michael Robbins). Watching a repeat of the show today is like peering through a window onto a bizarre and uninhibited world.

Here, in essence, was the lack of so-called political correctness that, one day in the not too distant future, comedians who thought themselves alternative would delight in rebelling against. Fair enough, although, at heart, the *real* secret of the show's success lay in its old-style, non-political working class comedy roots. And while, by and large, most of the humour in *On The Buses* was indeed hoarier than the hounds of Hades, it would be wrong not to admit that there *were* some quality moments. How about the scene where Olive, sitting up in bed, is eating pickled onions directly from the jar (whether they are Pledge's Purer Pickles is, alas, uncertain). Beside her, Arthur, trying to get to sleep, chunters away at his wife's less-than-sexually alluring habits. Predictably, Olive then drops her midnight feast into the marital bed. Without her trademark jam-jar glasses, her frantic searches yield no result until, triumphantly, she grabs one of the crunchy offending items, only to be met with the anguished wail of her long-suffering husband: '*That's* not a pickled onion!'

231

Corny? Of course. Unreconstructed? For sure. Nor is there a doubt that the lack of sophistication on display in *On The Buses*, whether in terms of intention or actual production was, as the 'sixties turned into the 'seventies, a defining feature of mainstream ITV comedy. And yet the fact remains that when the wider British public wanted laughter it was usually to these sorts of programmes that it turned. This, let us not forget, was an era in which laughs could still be wrung from 'women's libbers' burning their bra in the back yard or, as we shall see, black people having the audacity to move in next door to white people.

Was that because of an inherent lack of intelligence in the viewing public themselves, or - as the enormous concurrent success of sitcoms like *Steptoe And Son* and *The Likely Lads* seem to suggest - merely down to complacency and a lack of imagination on the part of the programme-makers? Maybe there was simply nothing better to watch.

One thing is for sure, while such unenlightened attitudes did go relatively unchallenged in television comedy throughout the early 1970s - and indeed were the subject matter of choice in working men's Variety clubs - a mood of revolution was most definitely bubbling. And the seeds for that upheaval had been sown over a decade before.

9
Fringe Benefits

"Well, *we* used to have to get up at 12 o'clock at night
and lick t' road clean wi' t' tongue..."
- *Monty Python, 'The Four Yorkshiremen'*

At first, it had been a quiet revolution, based around the hearth and home. The radicalism of Eric Sykes and writers like him was all the more effective because, outwardly at least, it resembled so much of what had gone before. And the same was true for the man who had given Sykes his first big break on the wireless: Francis Alick Howard.

Though few would have him down as an archetypal northern comic, Frankie Howerd, as he later became known, was nevertheless born in a two-up, two-down terrace house in York in March 1917. With a Royal Artillery sergeant father and a mother who worked in one of the city's famous chocolate factories, Frankie's parents had seemed ideally suited to their location until a change in circumstances saw the family relocate to Eltham, South London, when Howerd was just two years old.

Young Francis got the showbusiness bug early, reportedly while on a pantomime outing to Woolwich Artillery Theatre with his mother. The theatrical world was a magnet thereafter. Although brought up alongside a sister (Bettina) and brother (Sidney), Howerd was a shy and lonely child who entertained himself, and presumably others, by writing little playlets

233

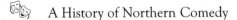

and performing them in the back yard for neighbours, whose kids were often dragged in on the act too. Later, despite suffering from a stammer, he rather courageously performed a Sunday School monologue and it was then that he inadvertently happened upon the distinctive, halting style that would be his trademark as a stand-up comedian, over a career that would go on to span around five decades. Or so the story goes.

Whatever the reality of his earliest origins as a performer, Howerd initially yearned to be a serious actor. He joined a number of amateur dramatic companies and, as a 16-year-old, applied for a place at the Royal Academy of Dramatic Art. To his great dismay RADA turned him down but, showing an aptitude for reinvention that would be a feature of his later career, he soon put that disappointment behind him and decided that comedy would henceforth be his route to fame and fortune.

Upon leaving school in 1935, Howerd - then still Howard - found a job in London's docklands and spent his evenings obsessively honing his act, often for no pay and in the unlikeliest of locations. Thus did the occupants of old folks homes join nightclub and Variety hall audiences in thrilling to the delights of *The Frankie Howard Comedy Revue* and *The Frankie Howard Knockout Concert Party*. Still, however, he struggled to win wider professional acceptance. With the arrival of World War Two, he began to perform in actual wartime concert parties, where those famous oohs, aahs and sarcastic audience asides had now become an established part of the routine. Still, though, the showbiz power brokers remained immune to the charms of a serving army soldier whose ambitions to join the cast of radio's *Stars In Battledress* were also resolutely knocked back.

Nor did matters improve upon his demobbing. Freshly back on the streets, Howerd was rebuffed by every London agent he approached, owing, they said, to his lack of professional experience. Until, that is, he played one last desperate card. Run by the Navy, Army and Air Force Institutes (NAAFI), 'The Stage Door Canteen' was situated in London's West End and a regular haunt of agents who went looking there for potential support acts among the British military personnel. Although he was no longer in active service, Howerd took the brave and actually illegal step of turning up there clad in his old army uniform, complete with a signed letter of reference from his one-time commander, the respected theatrical agent Major Richard Stone. His bluff did the trick and he was subsequently invited back for a second week, whereupon, finally, he was spotted by an agency rep who offered the wannabe funnyman his first professional contract. A subtle change of surname followed in a bid to distinguish himself 'from all the other funny Howards around'.

Frankie Howerd's debut professional appearance, therefore, came in the summer of 1946 when, in Sheffield with a touring revue called *Just For The Fun Of It*, his name appeared last on the bill alongside fellow novice Max Bygraves. Despite such lowly billing, as the tour continued it wasn't long before the BBC came knocking on *his* door. As with many of his contemporaries, the result was a spot on *Variety Bandbox* where, in double quick time, via the odd 'Ooh, please yourself...' and 'Not on your Nellie...', his stellar upward path crossed that of Eric Sykes, just one among many up-and-coming comedy writers desperate to work with this modern-day Prime Minister of Mirth.

In time, Howerd's talents would take him to television, where his dishevelled physical appearance and face like a startled donkey would be best appreciated. That, though, did not happen until 1952 and, even on radio, his rambling, long-winded and quirky conversational manner was immediately recognised for what it was: different and really rather wonderful. Sometimes, it seemed, Frankie had forgotten to end his story with a punchline - and even when he did stick a gag on the end, it was usually not worth waiting for. The journey was the thing. With the endlessly inventive Sykes on board, the Frankie Howerd phenomenon took an even more anarchic twist. Convention was there to be ignored.

Yet for all its originality, Howerd's comedy career was equally marked by the most remarkable ups and downs in popularity. Sykes himself was at the epicentre of the first of these dips; but he was also at least partly responsible for the first in a number of similarly emphatic rebounds too. Howerd's flop of a radio show *Fine Goings On* - scripted by Sykes and also starring a young Hattie Jacques - began the initial rot. And when that was followed by a disastrous attack of nerves in a Royal Variety Performance at the turn of the decade, Frankie was plunged into severe depression. Fragile of confidence at the best of times, the comic became convinced that his days in the spotlight were done. As ever, salvation was just around the corner.

It came courtesy of the Suez crisis and *Frankie Howerd Goes East*, in

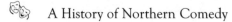

which he, Sykes and a group of BBC recording engineers set off on a tour of Libya, Egypt and Cyprus to entertain the troops. Along with writing the shows on the way out, the pair also picked up military personnel as support acts and threw all thoughts of decorum - for the time - out of the window. The result was a riotous wireless hit. Panned by the critics, distrusted by the BBC itself, but a massive success with listeners, *Frankie Howerd Goes East* re-invigorated Howerd's career to the extent that he received another huge boost to his self-belief upon his return.

This time it was that aforementioned television programme. *The Howerd Crowd (With The Beverley Sisters)* came into being on January 11 1952, the first of many TV shows to be written by Sykes and the boys at Associated London Scripts. 'I looked like a pasty-faced village idiot who needed a set of false teeth,' was Howerd's own reported assessment. For a while, though, the more popular and readily available radio remained where it was principally at, with Ray Galton and Alan Simpson further helping to cement Howerd's standing as a household name. The early 'fifties also saw a role in *The Runaway Bus* (1954), the first of several film appearances for Frankie, alongside Margaret 'Miss Marple' Rutherford and the starlet Petula Clark. When filming was complete, Howerd famously proved his worth as an ad-libber by improvising a conversation in a telephone box in order to add an extra three minutes to the running time, needed if the movie was to receive a West End screening.

And yet, as the 1960s hove into view, Frankie Howerd's comedy star had once more begun to wane. To an even greater extent than before, and a few bit parts in smaller films notwithstanding, the nation's taste in humour appeared to be changing and passing him by. Along with all the gritty social realism, there had emerged a form of comedy more obviously anarchic and challenging to those in authority than his own and, ironically, it had sprung from quarters very close to hand. In contrast to the antics of Spike Milligan and Co on the smash hit *Goon Show*, and the satire boom that it helped to inspire, the more traditional Variety shtick of Frankie Howerd looked tattier than his battered old welcome mat of a hair-piece. By 1962, bookings had all but dried up completely, so he finally 'quit' showbiz and began to look for a pub he could run. Woe, woe and thrice woe. Adding to his troubles was the death of his beloved mother but, shortly after her demise, fate again intervened for the better.

Fringe Benefits

To begin with, this second Howerd comeback took a conventional route. With his mother hardly laid to rest and a life of beer barrels and bar mats awaiting, Frankie was suddenly offered a return to television on ITV's *Alma Cogan's Star Time*. He couldn't resist and that appearance duly led to a spot on the *Billy Cotton Band Show*, whereafter he also returned to radio, in a series penned by a couple more writers of great contemporary influence, Barry Took and Marty Feldman. Crucially, too, this sudden burst of activity brought him to the attention of a certain comedy genius named Peter Cook, whose nightclub, The Establishment - privately-owned and therefore safe from the attentions of the censorious Lord Chamberlain - had just opened in London's Soho.

Primarily, to the wider British public at least, Cook was best known for his activities with the satirical Oxbridge stage revue *Beyond The Fringe*, alongside Dudley Moore, Jonathan Miller and northern-born national treasure-in-the-making, Alan Bennett. Together, that quartet had played - and would go on playing - no small role in redefining the capabilities of British comedy during an era in which widespread unemployment did not prevent a Government blithely telling its people: 'You've never had it so good'. *Beyond The Fringe* was, in many ways, an outward symptom of intellectual restlessness and hunger for modernity in a nation only just emerging from a cocoon of suffocating social conformity; a nation in which homosexuality was still a criminal offence; a nation burdened still by the strictures of class; a nation suffering delusions of grandeur on the world stage, where a certain type of smug and deep-rooted authoritarian self-satisfaction still held sway. In short, it ripped up the rulebook utterly. True, cracks in the British Establishment had first begun to surface during the Suez debacle in the autumn of 1956. Nevertheless, when Peter Cook not only impersonated but also had the temerity to ridicule Britain's then Prime Minister, Harold Macmillan, the sound of snapping taboos could be heard from Land's End to John O'Groats. Certainly, from the moment Frankie Howerd took to Cook's Establishment stage and performed a script written by ALS stalwart Johnny Speight, the idea that he was in any way *passé* had to be rapidly revised.

Culturally, the coming of *Beyond The Fringe* represented a sea-change

in the bigger picture too. Bolstered by its impact, the students of the Oxford and Cambridge University Footlight revues would henceforth take a grip on BBC comedy that shows little sign of loosening to this day. Given the desire of new Director General Hugh Carleton Greene for innovation, that the Corporation should have so eagerly embraced Oxbridge's fresh and exciting satirists ought not, perhaps, to come as any real surprise, especially as a sizeable chunk of its own employees were products of those same twin seats of higher learning. Nevertheless, given its remit as national public broadcaster, there were dangers in taking such an openly iconoclastic path, not least in the potential it held for political fall-outs. By the same token, however, ostentatiously intellectual satire ensured that the BBC maintained the cultural high ground over its more blatantly commercial rivals. And by the time *Beyond The Fringe* finally made it to British TV screens for a one-hour 'farewell special' in 1964, via a debut at the Edinburgh Festival in 1960 and stints in London and New York, a cathode Pandora's Box had been well and truly prised apart.

Although Britain as a whole was only belatedly able to see what all the fuss had been about, the influence of *Beyond The Fringe* on British television was nevertheless already immense. Most obviously, there was the launch, in 1962, of a topical revue show called *That Was The Week That Was*, or *TW3* as that programme became more conveniently known. With *TW3*, institutionalised deference toward the so-called British elite became a thing of the past. No person of high profile, political or royal, was safe from its withering gaze.

In fact, it was Hugh Carleton Greene himself who set the *TW3* ball rolling. Riding high on the positive outcome of the Pilkington Report, he came up with the idea of a weekly show that would 'prick the pomposity of public figures'. Significantly, however, instead of handing the project to the BBC's light entertainment department, he assigned it to current affairs. Freed from the necessity of adhering to the rigid and archaic rules and regulations of the Corporation's notorious Green Book - a draconian policy guide with an almost Biblical reputation for writers and producers of Variety shows throughout the 1940s and '50s - *TW3* was left free to lampoon pretty much anyone it liked.

Not that the influence of former Oxford and Cambridge graduates was in any way a new thing for the BBC. Not at all. Indeed, their ubiquity in the organisation at least partly explains how *Beyond The Fringe* was ever noticed in the first place. And, in fact, the man chosen to produce *TW3*, a one-time law student from Somerset named Ned Sherrin, had himself studied at Oxford's Exeter College before devising one of the BBC's earliest 'mobile television unit' broadcasts, *Oxford Accents* (1954), an 'intimate revue' presented by his university's Experimental Theatre Club. Sherrin's involvement with that pioneering broadcast clearly influenced him greatly as, instead of pursuing a career in the courtrooms, in 1957 he joined the staff of the BBC full-time. And when charged with bringing the Director General's concept to life five years later, he brought in a former Cambridge student, David Frost, as its presenter.

Otherwise, *TW3* was unique among television programmes in a number of ways. Provocative and controversial, it not only redefined what could be said about the country's leaders, thereby raising in public the idea that politicians might conceivably be up to no good, it did so in a lively and superficially accessible way. The majority of its writers may have been Oxbridge educated, but in front of the camera viewers were just as likely to encounter middlebrow entertainers like Millicent Martin - whose performance of the show's opening song, lyrics changed every week for added topicality, itself became a national institution - as the highbrow social commentary of newspaper doyen Bernard Levin. Through its Footlights-inspired mix of cabaret and acerbic political comment, *TW3* was, on one level, a well-intentioned attempt to cross traditional class boundaries. Yet in that ambition, at least, it was only partially successful. For all the show's longer-term importance in encouraging its viewers not to 'know their place', the on-screen existence of *That Was The Week That Was* was short-lived, its appeal largely middle class and the programme never quite enjoyed the widescale popularity that subsequent legend suggests. Partly, that may have been down to its late night slot in the Saturday schedules. Partly, it was simply ahead of its time. Certainly, the alacrity of its departure owed much to political pressure. And, whether it wanted to or not, *TW3* couldn't help but reinforce certain social stereotypes, even as it sought to undermine them.

Among the highest-profile performers of the show's weekly helping of satirical talk, songs, sketches and jaunty camera angles, all of it linked by the urbane Mr. Frost, were a couple of down-to-earth northern

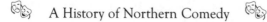

everymen in the Liverpool-born Kenneth Cope and Dick Emery's future sidekick, Roy Kinnear. While appearing in *TW3*, Cope was already a star of ITV's *Coronation Street*, where he played the loveable Scouse tearaway Jed Stone, best friend of Dennis Tanner and lodger of Minnie Caldwell, to underline his working class credentials. Cope's TV debut had come in 1958 alongside Jimmy Edwards in *Whack-O*. After Jed Stone was eventually given a nine-month jail sentence for handling stolen blankets, Cope would turn to disc-jockeying on Radio Luxembourg and, in 1969, he won still greater fame as Marty, the white-suited ghostly half of private investigators *Randall And Hopkirk (Deceased)*. In the 1970s, he also appeared in two *Carry On* films; *Carry On Matron* (1972) in which he got to drag up as a nurse and cuddle Barbara Windsor, and *Carry On At Your Convenience* (1971), when he played Vic Spanner, purveyor of good, clean lavatorial humour. By then, as a comedy writer, in 1968 he had already come up with London Weekend Television's first ever sitcom *Thingumybob*, set in Liverpool and starring Stanley Holloway. More recently, he has continued to pop up in programmes as diverse as *Doctor Who*, *Last Of The Summer Wine* and the truly dire 1994 BBC sitcom *Bootle Saddles*, in which he was lead northern cowboy. In 2008, after a break of forty-two years, Kenneth Cope and Jed made a return to *Coronation Street*.

TW3 was the door to a long and productive career for Roy Kinnear too, most often in television situation comedy but with over fifty film appearances thrown in for good measure. In *TW3*, Kinnear was usually cast as an average working class chap utterly bemused by Government and media double talk, whose ordinariness cut quite a contrast with the scholarly posturings of the bright young things around him. Small in stature and cheerful with it, that amiable persona followed him ever after and especially to sitcom, where Kinnear's infectious smile made him the perfect foil for others, while never quite winning him a starring role of his own. The part of Joe Jones, a building contractor in Thames TV's 1980 offering *Cowboys* was the closest he came to breaking that mould, although his role as George Webley, clerk at the Meanside and Beestly Savings Bank, in Keith Waterhouse and Willis Hall's Leeds-based 1968 sitcom *Inside George Webley*, also earned him credit.

As for cinema, a film career that began in 1962 with *Tiara Tahita* was never less than eclectic. It took in films such as *A Funny Thing Happened*

Fringe Benefits

On The Way To The Forum alongside Zero Mostel, Buster Keaton and Phil Silvers in 1967, *Till Death Us Do Part* (1968), *Taste The Blood Of Dracula* (1970), *Willy Wonka And The Chocolate Factory* (1971), *The Four Musketeers* (1975), *Herbie Goes To Monte Carlo* (1977), *Hawk - The Slayer* (1980), *Casanova* (1987) and his final feature, *The Return Of The Musketeers*, in 1989. Tragically, it was on location in Spain during the shooting of that latter film that Roy Kinnear was thrown from a horse during a comic chase and killed, aged just 54.

That Was The Week That Was ran for two series between November 1962 and December 1963; after which the Government - still reeling from the notorious Profumo Affair - persuaded the BBC to can it temporarily for the General Election year of 1964. And other than a one-off special to capitalise on that event, that ended up being that. Even so, throughout its short life, *TW3* had employed enough writers to fill a small telephone directory. Among an impressive list of regular contributors were Keith Waterhouse, Willis Hall, Christopher Booker, Dennis Potter, David Nobbs (of future *Reggie Perrin* fame), the great Peter Tinniswood, Jack Rosenthal, Richard Ingrams and Rochdale's favourite twitcher, Bill Oddie. Other credited writers included Peter Cook, Kenneth Tynan, John Betjeman, Malcolm Bradbury, Anthony 'Scouse git' Booth, John Braine, Roald Dahl, Frank Muir, Dennis Norden, Eric Sykes (of course!), Peter Schaffer and another pair of up-and-comers, John Cleese and Graham Chapman. Quite a line-up.

Ned Sherrin's inclination to give talent its head was further evident in his response to Frankie Howerd's appearance at The Establishment club. He offered him a guest spot on *TW3*. The upshot, on 6 April 1963, was a twelve-minute monologue, again written by Johnny Speight, in which Francis - titter ye not - tore into the Chancellor of the Exchequer's recently announced Budget speech with aplomb. As enjoyable as it was unexpected, the turn thrust a man whose only previous TV appearance in three years had been on Galton and Simpson's *Comedy Playhouse* right back into the limelight. The following October, Howerd was invited back for that aforementioned one-off and reflected on the General Election.

Yet again, Frankie Howerd's apparently ailing career had risen from its deathbed - and how. Offers of work came in at a torrent. He went on to make two television series with Galton and Simpson, still widely regarded as being among his best stuff and, on the stage, appeared as Pseudolos, a Roman slave, in a London production of the smash hit Broadway show *A Funny Thing Happened On The Way To The Forum*.

Notoriously useful road builders those Romans and, for Frankie, that particular production would be another big turning point, although not instantaneously. The tale goes that whilst on holiday in Italy a number of years later, the BBC's head of comedy, Michael Mills, was on a sightseeing trip to the Roman ruins of Pompeii when he joked to a friend how he 'half-expected to see Frankie Howerd come loping around the corner', as had been the case in the earlier stage show. From that light-hearted quip, it appears, came the idea for a sitcom.

Upon returning home, Mills contacted Talbot Rothwell, a writer of great experience who had just worked with Frankie on *Carry On Up The Jungle* (1970), along with the likes of Arthur Askey and Ted Ray in earlier years. Rothwell was so keen to be involved that he dropped all other projects, knocked out a few scripts and asked Howerd to star.

Along with satire and music, of course, the 'swinging sixties' were equally notable for sexual freedom and Frankie Howerd's brand of bawdy and saucy innuendo had proved well suited to the times. *A Funny Thing Happened On The Way To The Forum* got the ball rolling in that direction and the first of two *Carry On* film roles came in 1968, in *Carry On Doctor*. An appearance in the first of that team's annual small screen festive offerings, *Carry On Christmas*, followed in 1969, after which Howerd was asked by producers Gerald Thomas and Peter Rogers to take over from Kenneth Williams in *Carry On Up The Jungle* as Professor Inigo Tinkle, who is leading an expedition through the African jungle in search of the rare Oozalum bird (rare because it keeps disappearing up its own backside). Howerd proved to be an equally eccentric replacement for Williams but any chance of him becoming a long-term regular in the troupe was scuppered by Rothwell's approach. Oddly, given his usual material, Howerd was initially worried about the risqué jokes, so a pilot episode was made to gauge audience reaction. When everyone but clean-up campaigner Mary Whitehouse and her acolytes seemed to enjoy it, a first full series of *Up Pompeii* duly appeared in March 1970.

Fringe Benefits

As Lurcio, slave to government senator Ludicrus and his well-endowed wife Ammonia, Howerd was an instant hit. Each show began with a rambling prologue that also featured the appearance of a doom-saying old woman, Senna, she of 'woe, woe and thrice woe' fame and was quite post-modern in feel, maybe even Brechtian. There was never any pretence that any of this was in any way real; wobbly 'Roman' scenery was mocked for actually being in Shepherd's Bush; Howerd himself stepped in and out of character on a whim; the writing and acting was constantly rubbished by Lurcio. In fact, the only genuinely traditional thing about *Up Pompeii* was a Tiber-like flow of bad puns and double entendres. Described as a sort of 'Carry On Up The Forum' by the *Radio Times* listings magazine, the names of an ever-changing cast of characters included James Bondus and Pussus Galoria, Ambi Dextrus, Bumshus, Hernia, Scrophulus, Nymphia, Mucus, Tittia, Lecherus...

For all the indelible mark it made, only two full series of *Up Pompeii* were ever produced and those 13 episodes were shown over the course of a single year. There were, however, three rather forgettable films of which the first, *Up Pompeii* (1971), is generally considered to be the best. The TV show's early demise was at least partly down to Talbot Rothwell's ill health and, certainly, the BBC's next tailor-made sitcom for Howerd, the short-lived *Whoops Baghdad* (1973), was *Up Pompeii* in all but togas and laughs. Sadly, its demise heralded another retreat to the showbiz margins. In 1975, Howerd made a one-off Easter Monday special called *Further Up Pompeii*, and a similarly disappointing Christmas effort for ITV, *A Touch Of The Casanovas*, was still-born after its pilot episode. Otherwise, a role alongside his old pal Eric Sykes in *The Plank* was as good as it got. And come the politically correct 1980s, Howerd's conversational lasciviousness seemed irredeemably out of fashion, although his next chance of a comedy lifeline, the wartime-based sitcom *Then Churchill Said To Me*, was only shelved by the BBC when real war broke out in the Falkland Islands.

Thankfully, by the 1990s, younger comedians were increasingly more likely to be open in their appreciation of past traditions, as the 'rules' of comedy once more began to loosen. This owed much to the rediscovery of irony, a useful device that now endorsed guilt-free enjoyment of previously 'sexist' material. If anyone benefitted from such a cultural sea change it was Frankie. His one-man stage show *Frankie Howerd Bursts Into*

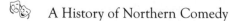

Britain began to garner rave reviews and it wasn't long before Britain's newest television network, Channel 4, gave him his own headlining show: *SuperFrank!*, a live concert in Weston-Super-Mare, recorded in 1987. Suddenly and although now over 70 years of age, Frankie Howerd was a wanted man on every University campus in Britain. In 1990, London Weekend Television filmed one such Oxford outing, *Frankie Howerd On Campus*, wherein just about everyone seemed to be clad in trendy 'Titter Ye Not' T-shirts. This latest upturn in popularity inspired a poignant contribution to the BBC's *Arena* documentary strand, *Oooh Er, Missus! The Frankie Howerd Story*, in which the comedian's loveable public persona was neatly contrasted with his private and lifelong battle with depression.   There was still time, though, for one final and probably best-forgotten go at resurrecting *Up Pompeii*; a one-off LWT production set in the time of Caligula, in which a now free Lurcio is landlord of the Bacchus wine bar, with slaves of his own. Much better and certainly more appropriate was Howerd's role as the 'God of Comedy', among the last TV appearances he ever made, dispelling useless advice to gobby Scottish comic Craig Ferguson in Channel 4's *The Craig Ferguson Story* (1991).

On 19 April 1992, while in the middle of filming his final television series, *Frankie's On...*, Frankie Howerd died of a heart attack, aged 75. Even then, public fascination with this most unique of British comedians continued. In recent years, his never very well hidden homosexuality and alleged predilection for pouncing upon young men in his dressing room have been the subject of television documentary and docu-drama. For Frankie Howerd, it seems, comebacks can even be launched from the grave. Death? Oh, shut your face.

Among the writers responsible for the triumphant *Frankie Howerd On Campus* was the Leeds-born Barry Cryer, a now recognisable face who, like Eric Sykes, began his career in the closing credits.

Born in Leeds in 1935 and one of two children, Cryer's life got off to a tragic start when, aged just five, he suffered the death of his father. To compound his sense of isolation, his older brother then departed for the merchant navy before eventually finding a job as a civil servant in London, ostensibly leaving young Barry an only child in a single-parent family. It was a lonely childhood, lit up mainly by the wireless and the likes of Tommy Handley, whose verbal dexterity young Barry admired greatly. Upon winning a scholarship to Leeds Grammar he became involved with amateur dramatics, and henceforth went on to Leeds University. While there, Cryer failed his English Literature degree (the outbreak of World War Two being the culprit, according to one account: 'Sixteen years before, but it upset me very deeply'). He did, though, win parts in student revue and it was after being spotted in one such production in the mid-1950s that Cryer was offered a week's work at the City Varieties, venue of Hylda Baker's TV launchpad *The Good Old Days*. While there he again had the good fortune to be noticed, this time by a London agent who put his stand-up comedy routine bottom-of-the-bill in a nationally touring nude revue. Fortunately, Cryer himself remained fully-clothed throughout, which was probably just as well given that, at the time, he suffered terribly from eczema. That dreadful skin condition only cleared up when he met and married his future wife, Terri.

Already displaying something of a talent for being in the right place at the right time, in 1957 Cryer's career curve took its biggest upward turn yet with a successful audition to appear with Bruce Forsyth at London's Windmill Theatre, a venue more famous for its employment of fan dancers and near-naked showgirls than the comedy, sketches and music it was ostensibly there to provide. During World War Two, the Windmill had been notorious for cocking a snoop at the nightly German bombers, allowing it to revel in the catchphrase: 'We never closed'. Now, however, and over a decade before abolition of stage censorship in 1968, largely male audiences were flocking in for rather more salacious reasons. As a result, comedy talents like Peter Sellers, Jimmy Edwards, Benny Hill, Tony Hancock, Tommy Cooper and Norman Wisdom struggled to divert the audience's attention from the on-stage nude tableaus.

For a comedian, then, working the Windmill Theatre was almost as gruelling as life on the road had been for the music hall comics of all those years before. After seven months of performing six shows a day, six days a week, Cryer finally had enough and left to take up a short-lived spell in pop music in which he appeared alongside Millicent Martin in *Expresso Bongo*, a musical that satirised the modern obsession with rock 'n' roll and, remarkably, had a number one hit single in Finland with the

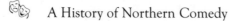

Sheb Wooley novelty song 'Purple People Eater'. 'They gave away a car with every record,' was Cryer's typically self-deprecating verdict. A career as Scandinavia's answer to Elvis Presley, however, would prove to be beyond him and soon he began to turn his hand to writing. The impetus for which was a meeting with the actress Anna Quayle, soon to appear alongside the Beatles, Wilfrid Brambell and the Liverpool-born comedy character actor Norman Rossington in *A Hard Day's Night* (1964).

Rossington, the son of a Liverpudlian landlord, played the Fab Four's road manager Norm in the film, by which time he was already a well-known face in cinema and television. As bumbling Private Cupcake, he had first come to public attention in *The Army Game* and from then on was scarcely off the screen. Born in 1928, Rossington had left school as a 14-year-old to work in the Liverpool Docks. While there, he appeared in a church hall sketch, just for a laugh, alongside his friend, the future *That Was The Week That Was* star Kenneth Cope. Discovering a taste for the stage, Rossington then went into amateur dramatics and was soon accepted at the Bristol Old Vic theatre school.

As a professional actor, the West End stage would be his main stomping ground, not least in musical theatre. During the 'fifties, 'sixties and 'seventies, however, Rossington's face was most widely seen on celluloid: *I Only Arsked* (1958), *Nurse on Wheels* (1963) and *Those Magnificent Men In Their Flying Machines* (1965) being three of his better known films. He also enjoyed a trio of *Carry On* roles, including a part in the first, *Carry On Sergeant*, in 1958. His crowning moment, however, was a straight role. As the pragmatic pal of Albert Finney's working class rebel in the prototype 1960s kitchen sink drama, *Saturday Night And Sunday Morning*, Norman Rossington was superb. Attributing the length of his career to scouse soup, 'cheap, nutritious and growing up in Liverpool we ate plenty of it', he died of cancer in 1999, aged 70.

As for Anna Quayle and Barry Cryer, it was the former who provided the latter with his next big career leap forward when she asked him to write a couple of revue pieces for her, to be performed at the Fortune Theatre, soon-to-be London venue of *Beyond The Fringe*. In the audience one night was well-known female impersonator Danny La Rue. So impressed was he with Cryer's talent that he too asked the writer for a couple of shows of his own. So began a thirteen-year collaboration at La

Fringe Benefits

Rue's Hanover Square nightclub, which itself boasted regular audience luminaries like Princess Margaret, Noel Coward, The Kray Twins, Richard Burton, Elizabeth Taylor, Judy Garland and any number of passing Hollywood movie stars. For Cryer, however, it was former *That Was The Week That Was* host David Frost who proved most important. Frost invited the writer to contribute to his latest TV show, *The Frost Report*, thereby launching a career in television that continues to this day.

Broadcast for the first time in 1966, *The Frost Report* lasted two series and was its eponymous presenter's third such TV outing, with a thrice-weekly 1964 show *Not So Much A Programme, More A Way Of Life* sandwiched between it and *TW3*. It also followed a programme on which Frost had worked solely as a writer, *BBC-3*, aired in 1965 and pretty much the last hurrah in the BBC's 'sixties satire boom. How edgy that title must have seemed at the time. Most famously, *BBC-3* was where theatre critic Kenneth Tynan first uttered the world 'fuck' on British television. One day, maybe, the modern BBC3 will become the first British TV channel where 'fuck' is the *only* word used. Equally pivotal in the field of human endeavour - as far as the history of northern comedy is concerned anyway - *BBC-3* also gave Alan Bennett his second TV appearance, after that final televised performance of *Beyond The Fringe* almost ten months before.

If the Cambridge-educated pair Peter Cook and Jonathan Miller might be seen as the ostentatiously cerebral components of *Beyond The Fringe*, then Oxford graduates Dudley Moore and Alan Bennett were the rather awkward feet that kept it pinned to the ground. As we will see, the notion that humour of the light blue variety was more intellectual than its earthier dark blue counterpart was an idea that would hang around the Oxbridge fraternity for years to come. And for sure, in the case of Cook and Moore - who later formed a volatile and equally historic double act partnership of their own - the former Radley public schoolboy's devastating wit and cruel ingenuity were the perfect counterpoint to Moore's apparently less complex and more emotional working class Dagenham little guy. That is, of course, if we leave aside the complicating factor of Moore's musical reputation as a piano virtuoso. In this, perhaps we find further evidence that the universal appeal of 'simple' northern-style comedy is as much about class as geography.

Dud did still like to show off, though, didn't he? And it would be fair to suggest that out of all the *Beyond The Fringe* troupe, the earnest, bespectacled northerner, Alan Bennett, cut the least charismatic figure of all. In contrast to the trio of extroverts around him, Bennett's rueful public persona, one part outgoing performer, nine parts in-growing toenail, gave him a downbeat air of owlish introversion. Yet from such an, on the face of it, unpromising theatrical start, Bennett would develop the most profound and certainly longest-lasting contribution of all.

Born in Armley, Leeds in 1934, Alan Bennett was the youngest son of shy and socially withdrawn working class parents. Dad, a somewhat unwilling butcher, and mam a housewife. Despite his relatively humble origins, Bennett was a bookish child and a talent for wry observation set in early, as chronicled in his hugely enjoyable collection of autobiographical writings originally published in the *London Review of Books*, *Writing Home* (Faber and Faber, 1994). A typical passage relates how, as a boy, Bennett delivered meat to a woman named Mrs. Fletcher whose daughter, Valerie, would one day move south and marry T.S. Eliot. Years later, with his dad now having sold the butcher's shop but with the family still living in Leeds, Bennett's mam reports that she has just run into her husband's former customer down the road. However, she wasn't with Mr. Fletcher, she was with another man: '...tall, elderly, very refined-looking. She introduced me and we passed the time of day.' Afterwards, Bennett realises with a start that his mam has just spoken to the great poet himself. The excited son tries, in vain, to explain the significance of the meeting, citing *The Waste Land* and Eliot's winning of the Nobel Prize. The latter achievement, at least, catches Mrs. Bennett's attention:

> 'Well,' she said with that unerring grasp of inessentials which is the prerogative of mothers, 'I'm not surprised. It was a beautiful overcoat.'

Such exchanges have long been a feature of Bennett's work. The ear for a seemingly trite, yet actually revealing phrase; the eye for the minutae of everyday detail. It is certainly no surprise that a sizeable chunk of his upbringing was spent in the company of a particular type of northern woman, one social step 'up' from that portrayed by Norman Evans and, later, Les Dawson, quite often with pretensions to refinement. Picnics to local Yorkshire beauty spots such as Bolton Abbey and Pateley Bridge, along with trips to seaside resorts like Filey, Morecambe and Scarborough have also provided a well of richly melancholic inspiration. Like many of his generation, Bennett's earliest encounters with comedy came via the family wireless.

Bennett himself has said that while growing up he had little time for the 'relentlessly cheerful' patter of comedians like Tommy Trinder and Tommy Handley. The *ITMA* character with which he most identified was Mona Lott, the morose charlady. Heroic pathos and out-and-out silliness were more his thing. In his 2005 anthology *Untold Stories*, he writes that: 'A child of the north, I don't care for cockneys or their much-advertised Blitz-defeating cheerfulness: all that knees-up, thumbs in the lapels down at the Old Bull and Bush cockney sparrerdom has always left me cold.' Bennett goes on to deride such 'cheeky chappiness' as 'overwhelmingly male', writing that '...there is not a breath of camp to it. It's perky, aggressive, wisecracking and a routine. It's seldom subversive and it caters to prejudice rather than running counter to it, its current exponents Bernard Manning and Jim Davidson.'

Later in *Untold Stories*, Bennett recalls how he and his family used to go to the pantomime at the Theatre Royal, Leeds, where he would often gaze in wonder upon comedians like Frank Randall, Albert Modley and Norman Evans:

> 'It may seem fanciful to claim that remarks like "Leave that cat alone! Do you know, I could taste it in t' custard" were closer to real life than the gags purveyed by Tommy Handley, but so it was and I thought the dame hilarious. It was a lesson, though I didn't realise it at the time, that comedy and real life were in some relation.'

Whatever his childhood favourites, an upbringing shaped by the second-hand Bakelite Philco wireless bought by Bennett senior 'through the Miscellaneous column of the *Yorkshire Evening Post*' would come in handy years later when, in 1992, upon answering a knock on his front door, Bennett found he had a new neighbour, the flamboyant Mancunian rock star Morrissey. 'Quite ridiculously early on in the conversation,' Bennett told the 2003 Channel 4 documentary *The Importance Of Being Morrissey*, 'he asked me whether I knew anything about a comedian called Jimmy Clitheroe. Morrissey was fascinated by this figure. Well, I gave him tea in my house and then he would give me tea in his house. We never went anywhere or really talked about anything other than Jimmy Clitheroe.'

Apart from a free pot of tea, perhaps Morrissey was drawn to Clitheroe - and indeed Bennett himself - by an aura of northern mystery. Theirs, after all, is a world where little is ever fully explained and things are often not quite as they seem. Most obviously, Morrissey's debt to Alan Bennett is evident in his own writing style. It is there that we see a shared fascination with the loneliness and longing that so often lies beneath the surface of ordinary lives. Both Morrissey and Bennett operate in a hinterland of hopelessness, under cover of twee banalities like cream crackers under settees or coastal towns 'that they forgot to close down'. Crucially, they tread a fine line between stoicism and existential despair while being very, very funny while they are at it. And as a description of where Alan Bennett is coming from, literally and creatively, the lyrics to the 1995 Smiths single 'How Soon Is Now' are surely spot on: 'I am the son, And the heir, Of a shyness that is criminally vulgar. I am the son and heir, Oh, of nothing in particular...'.

Bennett's parents felt their class and awkwardness in social situations keenly, wishing they had 'more off' and the confidence to 'be themselves' in public. The answer to this problem, they said, was education. So it was that young Alan was encouraged to get some, first at Leeds Grammar, then being packed off on a scholarship to Oxford, where he spent much of the 1950s obtaining a first-class degree in medieval history. It was there, while writing and performing revue sketches and parodies, that Bennett first met Cook, Moore and Miller. Yet even as *Beyond The Fringe* exploded onto the scene, this rather dour young chap from Leeds found his northern roots more of a hindrance than a help. As Bennett relates in *Writing Home*, after the revue's successful move to New York in 1962, towards the end of the following year the team decided to update their show and add some new material. It was then that Bennett first made a conscious decision to 'speak and write in a voice that was my own, rather than putting one on. I was going to be myself.'

Fringe Benefits

For his subject matter, Bennett alighted upon a topic that lay firmly within the reach of all: death. A universal theme indeed, although his audiences on Broadway didn't quite see things that way, given that the monologue in question did not concern itself with death in New Jersey or the Hamptons, but rather with death in the north of England and, more specifically, Morecambe and Blackpool. Drowning nightly in a sea of embarrassed indifference, Bennett battled on gamely with his routine for the best part of six months until *Beyond The Fringe* eventually died a natural death of its own. Stung, Bennett shied away from writing about the north of England for almost a decade.

Instead, he stuck to political satire, as his subsequent involvement with *Not So Much A Programme, More A Way Of Life* and *BBC-3* testifies. He did a bit of television acting too. The creative team behind *BBC-3* were also responsible for the Ned Sherrin-produced 1965 comedy *My Father Knew Lloyd George*, in which Bennett played an oily Victorian villain. A year later, Bennett was the ideal Dormouse in Jonathan Miller's inventive adaptation of *Alice In Wonderland*, alongside the Nottingham-born John Bird, Peter Cook, Peter Sellers, Wilfrid Brambell and quite a few more. He also wrote his first solo television show, the highly-acclaimed *On The Margin*, which was aired in November 1966.

The extent to which Bennett's northern voice had been temporarily silenced can be seen in an ongoing *On The Margin* sketch, 'Streets Ahead'. It took as its subject matter the 'life and times in N.W.1' of a London media couple, the Stringalongs, busily 'knocking through' in Camden Town. Otherwise, the show seems to have been an intriguing mix of songs, poetry and clips from old music hall archives. We say 'seems to be' because the show lasted for just six episodes and, although the BBC repeated *On The Margin* twice within six months of its first run, it became yet another victim of the BBC's self-inflicted curse of the wiped tapes, leaving modern audiences to take history's word with regard to its quality. Bennett did salvage some of it using original scripts on Channel 4's 1990 archive celebration, *The A-Z Of Television*.

Rather than launching Alan Bennett into a television comedy acting career, *On The Margin* instead turned out to be something of a full stop. With the exception of the occasional outing - he joined in with Miller's Amnesty International benefit gig, *Pleasure At Her Majesty's*, as writer and performer in 1976, for example, and took part in an ITV Christmas special, *Julie Walters And Friends*, fifteen years later, when the eponymous actor performed sketches written by writers who she saw as having shaped her career (Bennett, Victoria Wood, Willy Russell and Alan Bleasdale) - small screen acting roles, though by no means non-existent, were from then on few and far between. Increasingly, Alan Bennett was known first and foremost as a writer. In that line of work, he would be responsible for some of the most important theatre and television dramas of the late twentieth century and, when he turned his attentions to the movies, he enjoyed notable success there too.

Bennett's debut stage play, *Forty Years On*, a nostalgic literary parody, came in 1968. As the writer himself admits in *Writing Home*, it had 'much more to do with art than life'. A positive reception, however, did at least give him the confidence to go looking for that northern voice again. The result was *A Day Out*, the story of a Halifax cycling club set in 1911, written in 1969, and eventually broadcast by the BBC three years later.

Wistful and dreamy, *A Day Out* would now be seen as quintessential Bennett in that its benign setting - a trip to the ruins of Fountains Abbey - disguises darker truths just out of view. That is never more apparent than when Boothroyd, played by the actor-wrestler Brian Glover, already well-known as the over-competitive sports master in Ken Loach's northern masterpiece *Kes* (1969), confidently declares that there will never be another war. This, of course, is just three years before the cataclysm that would obliterate most of the characters on our screen; two of whom, incidentally, were played by a Rotherham club comic named Paul Shane and Bolton's best-known folk singer, Bernard Wrigley.

As with most of Alan Bennett's work, *A Day Out* overflows with apparently inconsequential dialogue. The viewer doesn't so much watch as eavesdrop. One such conversation allowed Bennett to explore the so-called battle of the sexes from a traditional male perspective. 'There's no nobility about them, women,' says Shorter (James Cossins). 'It's all mundane - one day to the next. No large view, no theory, all practice.' A view that would have been shared by many of Al Read's characters and one which might very well be tossed at northern comedy too.

Despite the fact that the BBC had been capable of broadcasting in colour for some time, *A Day Out* was nevertheless shot in black and white, both as a result of a low budget and the desire for an authentic period feel. Bennett had originally wanted to film it in sepia. Its director, meanwhile, was the Leicester-born Stephen Frears and its producer Innes Lloyd, two men with whom Bennett would collaborate on many occasions throughout the coming decade, including his next major television production, shown in 1975.

This time broadcast in full colour as part of the BBC's long-running *Play For Today* strand, *Sunset Across The Bay* was, if anything, even more bitter sweet than its predecessor. A little more personal too. The retired couple who relocate to their favourite holiday location of Morecambe, only to become swiftly disillusioned and homesick for the Leeds they have left behind, have more than a touch of Bennett's own parents about them. There is the usual humourous observation, of course, mainly at the expense of family tensions and the less-than-exotic appeal of those northern seaside resorts so beloved by Morrissey. There is also that aforementioned cameo appearance by Albert Modley. Otherwise, the prevailing almost elegiac mood is one of regret, both at the passing of time and at life's missed opportunities. You would have to go a long way to find a more perfectly-realised scene than the one in which the well-wrapped up 'Mam' (Gabriella Daye) waits outside a seafront toilet with a growing sense of fear and isolation as 'Dad' (Harry Markham) takes far too long to spend his penny.

Though Alan Bennett's work was invariably blessed with a northern sensibility, it just as often transcended strict geographical boundaries. Of more interest to Bennett, it seems, was the landscape of the mind and the ways in which culture, class and background impacted upon it. Future stage plays would deal less explicitly with the north and include *Getting On*, *Habeas Corpus*, *The Old Country*, *Kafka's Dick* and *The Lady in the Van*. As a writer for television, his biggest breakthrough to date came with a six-play series written for London Weekend Television, shown in 1978-79. *Me! I'm Afraid Of Virginia Woolf*, *Afternoon Off*, *Doris And Doreen*, *One Fine Day* and *All Day On The Sands* were all aired to great public and critical acclaim, although the final production in the sextet, *The Old Crowd*, co-written with one-time cinematic *enfant terrible* Lindsay Anderson, was met with a bewilderment best be explained by its experimental plot. A middle-class couple move into an Edwardian house in London and throw a party

to celebrate, whereupon their furniture is sent to Carlisle and the wife has her toes sucked by the butler.

When Bennett next returned to the BBC, the works that followed enhanced his reputation as a supreme chronicler of ordinary life under a looking glass. In 1982, a series collectively entitled *Objects Of Affection* was first broadcast, with the focus once more on everyday people. The subject matter - *Intensive Care* and *Rolling Home* dealt with dying fathers; *Marks* with unemployment; *Our Winnie* and *Say Something Happened* with the old and confused - allowed Bennett to further explore the psychology of crippling social isolation and desperate inner confusion. The series also featured a quite superb monologue performed by the Birkenhead-born actor Patricia Routledge, called *A Woman Of No Importance*.

In Routledge, Bennett had found his perfect Peggy, a rather boring middle-aged woman with a fascination for group status, especially with regard to her works canteen. It soon becomes apparent that Peggy's view of herself as an organised righter of wrongs and dispenser of happiness is completely at odds with reality. To the viewer, Peggy appears intolerant, bossy and thick-skinned. Until, that is, the realisation dawns that her infuriatingly narrow outlook is also a defence mechanism, distracting her from the essential futility of her existence.

At that point in TV history, single scene dramatic monologues to camera were rare but, some six years later in 1988, Bennett expanded upon that earlier one-off production and came up with a new set of six. The result was *Talking Heads*, his crowning television achievement to date and a genuine tour de force.

Along with the pin-point precision of the writing, each *Talking Heads* monologue was distinguished by emotional claustrophobia and a darkly amusing mood. There was some exceptionally fine acting on display too. Bennett himself was terrific in *Chip In The Sugar* and the team of actors who made up the numbers would be part of his 'repertory company' for many a year to come, something in the style of a Yorkshire Woody Allen (only without the clarinet and adopted Korean daughter/wife). Patricia Routledge returned to take the part of a maliciously nosey poison-pen letter writer in *A Lady Of Letters*. Julie Walters was on the casting couch in *Her Big Chance*. In *A Cream Cracker Under The Settee*, Thora Hird, probably the actor most closely associated with Bennett in the popular imagination, played a lonely, house proud old woman who has broken her hip in a fall. There were also roles for Stephanie Cole (*Soldiering On*) and the inimitable Maggie Smith, who gave the finest performance of the series - and that is saying something - as the alcoholic vicar's wife who rediscovers her sense of self-worth via an affair with an Asian shopkeeper, in *Bed Among The Lentils*. When Bennett came up with six more *Talking Heads* a decade later, Hird, Routledge and Walters all returned, and were this time accompanied by Eileen Atkins, Penelope Wilton and David Haig, in a bleaker if no less poignant collection.

Had Alan Bennett never written another word, he would have already done more than enough to justify his status as a legend of British television. As it was, before the first series of *Talking Heads* had so much as reached the airwaves, he had already embarked on a parallel career as a film screenwriter that would dovetail perfectly with his work on stage and small screen, where he continued to write successful one-off plays such as the biographical pieces *An Englishman Abroad* and *The Insurance Man*, based upon the lives of Guy Burgess and Franz Kafka respectively.

Of the four films Bennett is chiefly noted for, it is the second - a biographical take on the life and murder of 1960s playwright Joe Orton, *Prick Up Your Ears* (1987), that is the most workmanlike. Then again, it does face some pretty stiff opposition. His most recent, *The History Boys*, an adaptation of Bennett's Olivier Award-winning stage play, was voted among the top ten films of 2006. A 1994 film adaptation, *The Madness Of George III*, re-titled *The Madness Of King George* for American audiences, won Oscar nominations for himself and lead actor Nigel Hawthorne. Yet it was with his 1984 screenwriting debut, *A Private Function*, that Bennett was most obviously able to train his gaze back upon England's north.

In Alan Bennett's hands, words are always layered with meaning, not least in his instinct for a title. *A Private Function* was no exception to the rule. In its central role of Gilbert, a meek podiatrist (and notwithstanding a scene-stealing pig), it starred a fellow Yorkshireman of Bennett's who, along with five Oxbridge friends, had earlier picked up where *Beyond The Fringe* had left off: the Sheffield-born Michael Palin. Among a formidable list of co-stars - many of them northern - were Maggie Smith, Denholm Elliott, Alison Steadman, Pete Postlethwaite, Liz Smith, Bill Paterson, Jim

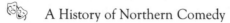

Carter and Richard Griffiths, and there was another northern comedy cameo, this time from Jimmy James's old partner, Eli Woods. A highly evocative tale of post-war food rationing and black market pig smuggling set in the semi-rural spa town of Ilkley, *A Private Function* allowed Bennett to indulge his ongoing fascination with class aspiration, the struggle for human dignity, his own upbringing and the flimsy facade of figures in authority. And when Maggie Smith's social-climber Joyce berates her husband for bringing his work home with him, it also featured one of British cinema's finest ever lines: 'Don't bring feet to the table, Gilbert.'

In more recent years, Bennett's small screen appearances have tended to be confined to documentaries, either about himself or subjects dear to his heart, such as the three-part tribute he made for the BBC to Westminster Abbey, *The Abbey*, in 1995. And in 2000 he did perform a series of ten short autobiographical monologues for Channel 4, *Telling Tales*. His best documentary outing to date, however, remains *Dinner At Noon* (what *other* time would northern folk eat dinner?), a sublime and highly personal fly-on-the-wall study of a day in the life of the Crown Hotel, Harrogate, first shown in 1988. In creating a programme out of overheard conversation, reminiscences and sociological asides, Bennett may even have helped to invent reality television.

Meanwhile, back in the 1960s, and it was as a result of finding work on *The Frost Report* that Barry Cryer felt able to take the plunge as a full-time writer - a decision which subsequently led to a 40-year-plus radio and TV career (and counting) of a most prolific nature. Today, the wiry-haired wag is probably best known as a resident panelist on BBC Radio 4's anarchic and Sony Radio Award-winning parlour game, *I'm Sorry, I Haven't A Clue*, but rare is the comedy or quiz panel show that has not benefitted from Cryer's expertise at some point or other, in either genre.

Cryer's all-pervasive role in the story of British comedy will be apparent many times over before this book reaches its own punchline. For now, it will serve merely to list a sprinkling of the more notable contributions on an action-packed CV. It was in the 1970s, with Tim Brooke-Taylor and John Junkin, that Cryer wrote and appeared in *Hello Cheeky*, a sort of prototype *Fast Show* but with excruciating puns rather than catchphrases, on both radio and television. Among his vast array of 'quiz' shows - including *Blankety Blank*, *Countdown*, *What's My Line*, *Give Us A Clue* and, most recently, *QI* - between 1969 and 1974, Cryer hosted *Jokers Wild* for Yorkshire Television, in which he attempted to keep guest comedians like Arthur Askey, Ted Ray, Jack Douglas and Les Dawson in check. And at the Edinburgh Festival in 1992 and 1993, he and fellow *Clue* star Willie Rushton performed a stage show, *Two Old Farts In The Night*, that went on a national tour of over forty venues before its sequel, *Farts 2 - The Musical*, returned to Edinburgh, ahead of another tour that culminated in Rushton's death, aged 59, in 1996. When producers have a leaking sink they ring a plumber. If they are after a few jokes they call Barry Cryer.

It was on *The Frost Report*, too, that Cryer first met a group of fellow budding writers and performers who would have a profound influence not only on his career, but on the course of world comedy as a whole. Among this bunch of upstarts was Alan Bennett's future leading man, Michael Palin.

One of the last programmes of its kind to be broadcast live and a combination of humourous sketches, monologues and music, *The Frost Report*'s performing cast included the still mutually independent Ronnie Barker and Ronnie Corbett, Sheila Steafel, Nicky Henson and a soon-to-be collaborator of Palin's, John Cleese, fresh-faced and gangly in his TV acting debut. One particular sketch, penned by Marty Feldman and John Law, in which the 6ft 4in 'upper class' Cleese lines up alongside the 5ft 8in 'middle class' Barker and 5ft 1in 'lower class' Corbett, remains an all-time British comedy classic, thanks to its neat visual encapsulation of the British class system. Cleese, from his lofty heights, looks down on Barker and Corbett. Barker looks up to Cleese but down on Corbett. Corbett, of course, can only look up to both men: 'I know my place'.

With Cryer among their original team of writers, messrs Barker and Corbett were destined to evolve into one of Britain's best-loved double acts. From 1971, their show, *The Two Ronnies*, became a BBC institution over 12 series and 97 episodes, until it was finally 'goodnight from them' with a one-off special in 1987. However, it was their lanky co-star, Cleese, who was destined to make the most revolutionary splash.

He did so alongside fellow members of a *Frost Report* writing crew in

which, for the first time, Cleese, Palin, Terry Jones, Eric Idle and Graham Chapman all worked together, amidst a string of other writers such as Feldman, Law, David Nobbs, Peter Tinniswood, Keith Waterhouse, Willis Hall, Frank Muir and Dennis Norden. Soon, the five of them - together with American animator Terry Gilliam - were to be responsible for what cinema historian and author George Perry describes in his 1983 book, *Life Of Python*, as 'a high-water mark in the development of British humour'.

Marching in on a blast of Sousa's 'Liberty Bell' and the words '...And now for something completely different', *Monty Python's Flying Circus* was first presented to an unsuspecting nation on 5 October, 1969. Broadcast in a late Sunday slot more usually devoted to religious discussion (rather ironically given what was to come), it hardly got off to a flying start, although an opening-night audience of around one million wasn't too bad an effort. From there, the show accumulated fans and detractors in equal measure, but when those initial viewing figures tripled by series end its future was assured.

When, in 2006, Michael Palin published his first volume of diaries, *1969-1979 - The Python Years* (Weidenfeld & Nicolson), a footnote early on at least partially explained the genesis of the Python name. 'Among other titles we tried unsuccessfully to get past the BBC,' Palin wrote, 'were *Whither Canada?*, *Ow! It's Colin Plint*, *A Horse, a Spoon and a Bucket*, *The Toad Elevating Moment*, *The Algy Banging Hour* and *Owl Stretching Time*.' A John Cleese-invented football forward line, *Bunn Wackett Buzzard Stubble and Boot*, was another brief contender. Mindful of the producer Barry Took's involvement in getting the team together in the first place, meanwhile, the Beeb's own internal memos gave the show a working title of *Baron von Took's Flying Circus* - later shortened to *Flying Circus* - on account of Baron von Richthoven's Flying Circus in World War One, rather than anything to do with the *Cambridge Circus* footlights revue in which Cleese and Chapman had earlier appeared. After Palin noticed the name Gwen Dibley in a local paper, she too assumed ownership of the flying circus in question, before a further group discussion came up with the names Monty - '...a shady sort of theatrical booker, the sort of man who fixes a fourth-rate act up with a week at Workington' - and Python, another variety of snake. So *Monty Python's Flying Circus* it was.

Fringe Benefits

Despite its Oxbridge roots, the north of England would never be far from *Monty Python*'s sights. In the team's most recent and probably final film outing, *The Meaning of Life* (1983), for example, it is the setting for one of the finest pieces of musical satire ever committed to celluloid. In the song 'Every Sperm is Sacred' ('...every sperm is great, if a sperm is wasted, God gets quite irate'), the Catholic predilection for large families is sent up brilliantly among the cobbled backstreets and outside toilets of Colne, Lancashire. And well before then, in the earliest years of *Monty Python's Flying Circus*, northern-influenced settings or characters, such as the 'pepperpot' Batley Townswomen's Guild, who re-stage Pearl Harbour in mud or perform *Wuthering Heights* in semaphore, were regular features. In *Python*'s second series, commonly held to be their best, it is a scene set in Jarrow, 'Trouble at t' Mill', which is rudely interrupted by the Spanish Inquisition. And few comedy sketches have ever nailed the tendency of a certain type of white rose male to wallow in his own miserabilism to such devastating effect as 'The Four Yorkshiremen': '...we used to have to get up at 12 o'clock at night and lick t' road clean wi' t' tongue...', even if that particular sketch was originally performed on *At Last The 1948 Show!* (1967), by Cleese, Chapman, Marty Feldman and Tim Brooke-Taylor.

So indelible was the mark made by *Monty Python* on British culture that the show spawned its very own adjective: Pythonesque. As a result, such absurd and surreal humour has come to be seen as an alternative to more traditional styles of comedy but, really, was the original programme all that different from what had gone before? For one thing, whether sending up the north, elderly women, judges, policemen or any other number of social staples, *Monty Python's Flying Circus* dealt almost exclusively in stereotypes. Until the team's 1979 film *The Life of Brian* anyway, any intellectual subtlety underpinning *Monty Python* humour was secondary to the silliness of the performance itself. Nor, one suspects, would the Pythons have ever claimed otherwise. In many respects, theirs was still the music hall world of Jimmy James, George Formby and *ITMA*. A place where northerners lived in back-to-back terraced houses, wore flat caps and clogs, spoke like Eddie Waring and, in all likelihood, reared whippets. And just like their zany forerunners, would the northern members of *Monty Python* have achieved anything like the same levels of comedic fame if they had not, at some point, headed south?

If there was one quality which marked *Monty Python's Flying Circus* as different and postmodern it was its unpredictable format and apparent lack of structure. Sketches would be randomly interrupted by characters from other scenes, BBC continuity announcements were falsified, closing credits were rolled at the start of the show etc etc. When combined with a distinctly dark edge - the scene in which an undertaker (Chapman) advises his client (Cleese) to eat his dead mother with broccoli, chips and parsnips, for example, still has the power to shock - that most certainly did feel new and daring. Yet watch the original shows today and, on the whole, it is a little difficult to see what all the fuss was about. Stylistically, the programme was indeed unlike anything else on British television at the time. But beneath the surface innovation, *Monty Python's Flying Circus* was actually born of the same irreverent traditions long established in British comedy; the very same traditions developed upon most recently by *Beyond The Fringe*, *That Was The Week That Was* and before them, *The Goon Show*. If it hadn't been for American cartoonist Terry Gilliam's wildly surreal animations, flying houses, carnivorous babies in prams, stamping feet and all, would the revolutionary mood of originality have been anywhere near as pronounced?

Of the remaining five members of *Monty Python*, two were graduates of Oxford - Michael Palin and Terry Jones - and three were graduates of Cambridge - John Cleese, Graham Chapman and Eric Idle. Jones and Palin had first appeared together in a 1964 revue that took the unpromising comedic subject of capital punishment as its theme, *Hang Down Your Head And Die*. Henceforth, the pair developed a working partnership that continued after Jones went down from Oxford later that same year, with Palin following in 1965. For Jones, BBC jobs weren't long in coming. Initially he worked as an assistant to Frank Muir and then embarked on an ultimately unsuccessful stint as a sketch writer on the BBC2 Friday night magazine show, *Late Night Line-Up*. Jones was assisted in that latter role by Palin, until both were unceremoniously dumped. 'I didn't come all the way from Gloucestershire to appear alongside this tripe,' the playwright Dennis Potter is said to have remarked.

Their saviour was *The Frost Report*, dedicated each week to the examination of a particular topic. Along with earning the princely sum of £7 per minute's material used, Palin and Jones now found themselves among writers like Cleese, Chapman and Idle. For Cleese and Chapman, the relationship with Frost first led to a collaboration on the screenplay of a film he was to produce, *The Rise And Rise Of Michael Rimmer*. And that was soon followed by *At Last The 1948 Show*, a Frost-produced ITV production that ran for 13 episodes over two series and contained many of the offbeat techniques soon to feature in *Monty Python*. Its leading lights were those aforementioned 'Four Yorkshiremen' Cleese, Chapman, Tim Brooke-Taylor and Marty Feldman as writers and performers, along with the archetypal blonde bimbo actress Aimi Macdonald, who operated under the mistaken impression that the show was all about her. Others to enjoy walk-on roles included Barry Cryer and Eric Idle.

While Cleese and Chapman were busy developing the style with which they were to become synonymous, Jones and Palin continued to earn their stripes on a John Bird-John Fortune programme, *A Series Of Bird's*. Following that, the duo appeared with fellow Oxbridge refugees Bill Oddie and Graeme Garden in an ill-judged attempt to take the *I'm Sorry, I Haven't A Clue* format to television, *Twice A Fortnight*. Meanwhile, in 1967, the producer of the radio version, Humphrey Barclay, was head-hunted for commercial television by the then-Rediffusion programme controller Jeremy Isaacs. Isaacs wanted Barclay to produce a comedy show for children and *Do Not Adjust Your Set* was the result, scripted and performed by Jones, Palin and Idle, with acting support from Del Boy-in-waiting David Jason, who was discovered by Barclay on the end of an Eastbourne pier, and Denise Coffey.

Although *At Last The 1948 Show* was only shown in parts of the UK, *Do Not Adjust Your Set* - subtitled *The Fairly Pointless Show* - was broadcast nationally and subsequently became an enormous hit. Ironically, given that its title was derived from an on-screen message which used regularly to flash up during transmission problems, the wrong tape was played on its first appearance owing to a technical cock-up, and the programme had to be cut short. From that moment on, though, it was upward all the way and *Do Not Adjust Your Set* won the Prix Jeunesse in Munich in 1968.

Shown at teatime - that's *northern* teatime - the guiding philosophy of *Do Not Adjust Your Set* was that it should be amusing to children without being patronising, an approach that soon led to it achieving cult status with parents who, it is claimed, regularly rushed home early from work to

catch its menu of satirical, surreal and downright silly sketches. There was music too, usually provided by the Bonzo Dog Doo-Dah Band and their majestically barmy lead singer Viv Stanshall, allowing Eric Idle a first meeting with the band's founder member and his own future collaborator, Neil Innes. Furthermore, the last few episodes before the show came to a halt in May 1969 featured drawings by Terry Gilliam.

In January 1969, Michael Palin and Terry Jones landed a first ever show of their own, *The Complete And Utter History Of Britain*, produced once again by Humphrey Barclay and an inventively anachronistic *1066 And All That*-type spoof in which major historical figures, such as William the Conqueror, were interviewed something in the manner of modern day news and sport reports. It was a good idea that for some reason never took off, running only to six episodes, but Jones and Palin didn't have long to dwell on its demise because, five months later, a large foot clipped by Gilliam from a painting by the Tuscan artist Bronzino fell from the sky and squished them.

As alluded to earlier, the man responsible for bringing together the six individuals who would go on to make *Monty Python* was Barry Took, a BBC comedy producer who, it seems, had long harboured a desire to see John Cleese and Michael Palin working on the same project. 'I thought that would be a magic combination,' he told George Perry. And in another footnote to his published diaries, Palin himself described Took in 2006 as Python's early 'father figure'.

Certainly, the physical differences between Cleese and Palin made for classic visual comedy; the toweringly thin Cleese contrasting neatly with Palin's less imposing everyman stature. Yet there was more to it than that. Geographically, the pair had enjoyed differing middle class upbringings; Cleese a tightly-repressed one in Weston Super Mare, Palin a somewhat freer northern affair in South Yorkshire, which appeared to show in their personalities and writing. Educationally, too, there seemed to be the same Oxford-Cambridge divide that had been evident in the *Beyond The Fringe* team; loosely defined as Cambridge - the comedy of the brain, Oxford - the comedy of the heart. That was further polarised with the addition of the pair's writing partners ('love me, love my dog,' as Took described it), Chapman and Jones. And when the proto-*Python* quartet requested that of a couple of loose cannons in Idle and Gilliam also be involved, the mixture was complete.

Fringe Benefits

It would not be stretching a point - or an owl - to suggest that while the contributions to *Monty Python* of Cleese and his Leicester-born sidekick Chapman might mainly be classified as cerebral - all convoluted verbal exchanges and scarcely concealed violence - the part played by Palin and Jones was rather more down to earth and traditionally 'northern'. Qualities of femininity as against the former's masculinity, you might say. For sure, of all the team, the one most usually to be found screeching in female clothing was Terry Jones. The others cross-dressed too, of course, but less often and where Cleese and his pipe-smoking chum Chapman looked utterly absurd in drag, somehow Jones - born in Colwyn Bay, North Wales - appeared to the manor born. Admittedly, to equate anywhere in Wales with northern England might be pushing a theory of northern comedy to its absolute limit, but Jones himself has described Colwyn Bay as being 'a suburb of Liverpool' and, although his father was Denbigh born-and-bred, his mother hailed from Bolton, Lancashire. In any case, his and Palin's temperaments were a perfect match.

The youngest of the *Monty Python* troupe, Michael Palin was born in Sheffield in May 1943. A cheeky-faced baby, in later life his ready and contagious smile would help to earn him a reputation as 'the nice one', a tag that dogged him like an over-friendly puppy. Educated at his father's old public school Shrewsbury - from where, incidentally, the satirical magazine *Private Eye* also sprang - Palin's childhood instilled in him a philosophy of making the best of life through laughter. In George Perry's *Life Of Python*, Palin relates how Shrewsbury, though a cold and physically austere place, was full of good humour, thanks mainly to the practical jokes of the masters, which 'enabled us to cope with the awful food and waking up in winter with six inches of snow on our beds'.

It was at Shrewsbury that Palin developed a talent for humourous writing and, after winning a place studying history at Brasenose College, he filled in the time between leaving school and going up to Oxford by joining a local amateur dramatic society and working in the publicity department of his father's firm, back in Sheffield. Once at Oxford, he began a lifelong friendship with an urbane young Londoner named Robert Hewison who, in turn, introduced him to the Oxford University

Dramatic Society and Terry Jones, who was already an eccentric and well-known university figure. The duo's first attempt at working together soon followed, on a revue show staged in a marquee, *Loitering Within Tent*.

In his second year at Oxford, Palin turned his hand to straight acting, appearing in a production of Harold Pinter's *The Birthday Party*, and he also made that debut trip to the West End with the revue, *Hang Down Your Head And Die*. *The Oxford Revue* at Edinburgh followed and in 1965, the year after Jones's departure, Palin made his own farewell performance in *The Oxford Line*, another revue characterised by zany surrealism. After which, paid employment as an advertising copywriter appeared to beckon until, thanks to his fresh face and clean cut looks, he landed a six-month spell as anchorman on the Bristol-based pop music show *Now*, broadcast across Wales and the west of England only. As a writer, he then graduated with Jones to *The Frost Report*, *Do Not Adjust Your Set* and one day took that fateful telephone call from Barry Took.

In *Monty Python's Flying Circus*, an atmosphere of creative tension was the norm; indeed it might very well be the secret of its success. Eric Idle and Terry Gilliam came up with their stuff individually, Jones and Palin wrote together, as did Cleese and Chapman, before all would come back and audition the material for the others, thereby ensuring the highest degree of quality control. Unsurprisingly, though, personality clashes ensued, not least between the super-analytical Cleese and the over-excitable Jones. Jones and Palin, it seems, had a need to squeeze as much pain and discomfort into their sketches as possible, an approach which clashed with their team-mates' preference for less stressful studio work. In *Life Of Python*, Palin puts that down to those old Oxbridge divisions: 'Oxford people can put up with far more discomfort,' he tells George Perry. 'The Cambridge people cannot intellectually justify why they should be so uncomfortable.... Terry and I always felt that we needed something extra, perhaps due to some deep-seated inadequacy in ourselves.'

In short, that meant that Palin and Jones (themselves influenced heavily by Spike Milligan's recently broadcast *Q5*) were largely responsible - along with Gilliam's groundbreaking cartoons - for Python's subsequent sense of visual outlandishness. While Gilliam added the animation, it was Palin and Jones who were chiefly responsible for the filmed inserts, frequently shot in some bleak outdoor location, such as the running '...and now for something completely different' gag, in which Palin's bearded hermit would crawl over coals to deliver the show's opening line. If there was an uncomfortable costume to be worn, then Jones and Palin would usually be to blame and it was theirs and Gilliam's shared love of remote history that led to *Monty Python And The Holy Grail*, the group's first 'proper' go at a movie, in 1974.

Directed by the Terrys, Jones and Gilliam, for whom a respective fascination with the gruesome and muck-filled 'dark' and middle ages would go on to play such a distinctive part in shaping their future careers, *Monty Python And The Holy Grail* nonetheless appears to have owed most to Michael Palin's fascination with Arthurian legend. The film was filmed in the wet and windy highlands of Scotland, and its one nod towards modernity was the arrival of the police who 'raided the set' and arrested its cast members at the end. Again, all the physical pain and suffering that went into creating such joyously amusing scenes as 'the knights who say ni,' 'bring out your dead' and 'bring me a shrubbery' came at the insistence of Palin, Jones and their ally in degradation, Gilliam. If subsequent accounts are anything to go by, few among the cast and crew enjoyed the process much but, for the viewer, at least, their discomfort was worth it. As well as being extremely funny, *The Holy Grail*'s visual qualities - filmed on a shoestring - are stunning. However, the internal tensions that were bubbling beneath the surface were evident in Cleese's departure ahead of a fourth and final *Monty Python's Flying Circus* BBC series, now called just *Monty Python* and a shade of its former self, later that same year.

With their television show over, the Pythons were now free to pursue individual careers of their own, while also making occasional returns to a highly-profitable franchise that has subsequently gone on to embrace books, records, cinema and, most recently, the West End and Broadway stage. Of them all, it was Graham Chapman who perhaps made least future impact and, sadly, he died from cancer in 1989, one day short of *Monty Python*'s twentieth anniversary. By then, though, Chapman had already penned a searingly honest account of his life, *A Liar's Autobiography*, published in 1980, and taken the starring role in the group's biggest and undoubtedly best foray into film, *Monty Python's Life Of Brian*, one of the greatest films - never mind comedy films - of all time.

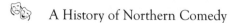

Eric Idle's outstanding legacy, meanwhile, must surely be musical. Born in South Shields in 1943, Idle's RAF-serving father was killed in a car crash when young Eric was just two years old. Aged seven, he was packed off to what he has since described as a 'semi-orphanage' in the English Midlands, although whether that had any influence on his future preference for working alone is probably best left to the psychologists. It certainly didn't do him any harm educationally. Upon following Cleese and Chapman down from Cambridge - where he was Footlights president in his final year of 1965 - Idle soon developed a reputation as a master of that brand of tongue-twisting wordplay so beloved of Ronnie Barker.

Among all the British Pythons, Eric Idle is the only one to claim not to have been particularly impressed by *The Goon Show*. In common with the rest, however, he was a devoted listener to Jimmy Jewel and Ben Warriss and their *Up the Pole* wireless show. Clearly, he must have also listened to a great deal of music. For who among us has not whistled along merrily, or tapped their feet, to the sweet refrains of *The Lumberjack Song*, *Spam* or *The Bruces' Philosophers Song* in their time? And on the big screen, without doubt Idle's supreme contribution to British cultural history must surely be his closing number from *Life of Brian*, 'Always Look on the Bright Side of Life', chirruped wistfully by crucified prisoners and destined thereafter to become a true timeless classic that will be forever sung by disappointed football crowds and the weeping relatives of 'resting' comedy fans who, like the dear departed Norwegian Blue before them, prepare to ring down the curtain and join the bleedin' choir invisible.

With his more regular *Monty Python's Flying Circus* commitments behind him, Idle was also able to utilise his gifts as a composer in the creation of a one-hour comedy Beatles parody that remains a cult classic to this day: *The Rutles* or *All You Need is Cash* (1978), written and performed in conjunction with Neil Innes and a spin-off from the pair's earlier BBC comedy, *Rutland Weekend Television* (1975-76).

Python-wise, Eric Idle has had his financial uses too. It is he who is responsible for the money-spinning and Tony award-winning musical comedy stage show *Spamalot* which, since 2005, has been 'lovingly ripping off' *Monty Python and The Holy Grail* in London and New York. And it is he who, back in the 1970s, was chiefly responsible for putting together those *Monty Python* books that were so popular among hormone-crazed

266

schoolboys. Who among us can ever forget the delight of removing the hardback dust jacket of *The Brand New Monty Python Bok* in 1976 to discover writhing naked female flesh and the words *Tits 'n Bums: A Weekly Look at Church Architecture* beneath? Alas, the softback reprint, *The Brand New Monty Python Papperbok*, complete with blood-stained thumbprints, boasted no such hidden treasures. Idle has also overseen an apparently never-ending stream of audio collections, each more blatantly contractual than the last. Away from *Monty Python*, he also made another long-lasting impact on television comedy by composing the theme tune - and playing a couple of cameo roles in - David Renwick's hugely popular *One Foot in the Grave* BBC sitcom of the 1990s.

Without doubt, however, Eric Idle's greatest contribution to the *Monty Python* legend - and perhaps the British film industry generally - lies in the role he played in getting *The Life of Brian* made at all. It was the former Beatle George Harrison, a personal friend of Idle's despite, or maybe because of, that mickey-taking in *The Rutles* and a long-standing fan of *Monty Python*, who agreed to bankroll the film when its original backers EMI developed cold feet at its so-called blasphemous nature and withdrew their interest. The independent company that Harrison formed to take over the project, HandMade Films, would go on to be responsible for a number of other Monty Python-related pictures too, such as *A Private Function, Privates on Parade* (1982) and *Nuns on the Run* (1990), in which Eric Idle appeared alongside the Scottish comic, Robbie Coltrane. Harrison sold the company in 1994 due to falling profits, but before that date it had also been responsible for the now-revered but then-ignored 1987 cult classic *Withnail & I*, starring Richard E. Grant and Liverpudlian actor Paul McGann. George Harrison died from cancer, aged 58, in 2001.

Of the rest of the *Monty Python* team, John Cleese will forever be associated with his TV sitcom creation of the 1970s, the monstrous Basil Fawlty, proprietor of *Fawlty Towers* through two short and magnificent series in 1975 and 1979, co-written with his then wife, Connie Booth. Nowhere is Cleese's ordered, systematic and cerebral approach to comedy better contrasted with Palin and Jones's more relaxed approach than in those twelve carefully layered and beautifully wrought half-hours. Similarly well constructed was Cleese's 1988 film *A Fish Called Wanda*, in which Michael Palin also starred, a self-written attempt to recapture the

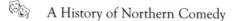

style of the Ealing comedies of the 1940s and 50s, directed by a doyen of that era, Charles Crichton.

Terry Gilliam has become an even bigger Hollywood player, albeit as a director and with an imagination larger than the financial budgets he has allegedly devoured in bringing astonishing films like *The Adventures of Baron Munchausen* (1988) and *Brazil* (1985) to the screen. Those films also featured appearances by Eric Idle and Michael Palin respectively and, in fact, none of the Pythons have been shy when it comes to including their former colleagues in individual projects. Gilliam's first major film outing, *Jabberwocky* (1977), for example, was a comical if patchy elaboration of the Lewis Carroll nonsense poem with Palin in the starring role as Dennis Cooper, a young man asked to kill the fearsome monster of the title, Terry Jones as a doomed poacher and an eclectic mix of comedy greats such as Harry H. Corbett, Warren Mitchell, Rodney Bewes, John Bird, Bernard Bresslaw, John Le Mesurier, Max Wall and the Bonzo Dog Doo-Dah Band member Neil Innes too. Gilliam's next film of note, the children's fantasy *Time Bandits* (1981), was produced by HandMade Films and featured brief cameos by Palin and Cleese, the latter on splendid form as a middle-class liberal Robin Hood.

Which leaves us with Palin and Jones. With the end of the *Monty Python* television series, the duo continued to write in tandem. Their first post-*Python* project was *Secrets*, a black comedy starring Warren Mitchell, in which human beings were used as confectionery fillings in a chocolate factory. For Palin, a role in Stephen Frears's television adaptation of the Jerome K. Jerome book *Three Men in a Boat* followed, after which he and Jones were asked by BBC director Terry Hughes to come up with a series. The subsequent pilot, a spoof of archetypal British children's literature called *Tomkinson's Schooldays*, received such a favourable reception on its debut airing in 1976 that an entire series was indeed commissioned as planned. Running over two series of six and three episodes respectively in 1977 and 1979, *Ripping Yarns* has become a cult television classic.

The visual quality of the series owes much to the fact that it was shot exclusively on film, but the success of *Ripping Yarns* was not down to production values alone. Each *Yarn* was a self-contained mini masterpiece of comic invention, displaying acute attention to authentic period detail and heaving with a bevy of 'proper' actors, not least Palin himself. The

Boys Own nature of the tales is perhaps best illustrated by episode titles that include *Roger of the Raj, Escape from Stalag 112B, Golden Gordon* and one adapted from a chapter in an earlier-published Palin and Jones book, *Bert Fegg's Nasty Book for Boys and Girls*, called *Across the Andes by Frog*.

It is the penultimate title on that list, *Golden Gordon*, which was the most directly autobiographical story however, concerned as it was with Palin's own love of football. It featured the exploits of Yorkshire Premier League side Barnstoneworth United and their supporter-in-chief, Gordon Ottershaw, a man who is so obsessed by the fortunes of his local side that he has named his son Barnstoneworth United and smashes up the family front room after every defeat (a regular occurrence since United haven't won in years). Gordon's long-suffering wife was played to perfection by *Duty Free* sitcom star of the future Gwen Taylor, while the role of the scrap metal merchant who intends to close the club down went to Bill Fraser, a childhood favourite in the Palin household thanks to his work in *The Army Game*. This particular episode also boasted an hilarious cameo from John Cleese, whose original suggestion for *Monty Python's Flying Circus - Bunn Wackett Buzzard Stubble and Boot* - was nicely resurrected as part of a former Barnstoneworth United line-up in homage.

Most memorable of all the *Ripping Yarns*, however, is *The Testing of Eric Olthwaite*, the second in the series and filmed in and around County Durham. If *Fawlty Towers* is rightly considered to be one of the funniest television comedies ever, then surely *Ripping Yarns* is the one that got away, certainly when it comes to mainstream popularity. None more so than this episode, wherein young Eric - the most boring man in Denley Moor - turns outlaw after being taken hostage by a bankrobber. As it turns out, the crook in question, played by a Mancunian actor who would go on to play Christ in *Life of Brian*, Ken Colley, shares Eric's interest in rain gauges and shovels, an especially fortunate development in the latter case given that Eric's neighbour, Howard Moulson, has just purchased a new one: '...an oak shaft, Spear and Jackson number three with reinforced brass handle.' 'Nickle scoop?' 'No, no. Steel scoop with copper-rimmed edging.' One of the 'gang's nocturnal bank raids leads to the newspaper headline: 'Olthwaites in Rotherham Bank Siege - Manager tells of night of boredom.' Nor can we forget Eric's sensational exchange with his black pudding-frying mother: 'Black pudding's very black today mother.' Not

unreasonably, Eric's coal miner father, played by the flat-capped John Barrett, would rather speak to his wife in French so as to avoid the possibility of a conversation with his tiresome son. Eventually, Eric's mum, dad and sister - 'oh, shut up, you boring little tit' - do a moonlight flit, taking the outside toilet with them.

Unfortunately, only nine episodes of *Ripping Yarns* were ever made as the BBC deemed it too expensive to produce. But if *Ripping Yarns* did little else, it alerted the world to Michael Palin's talents as an actor. At this point, creatively, Terry Jones and Palin largely went their separate ways, the latter as a performer and the former a full-blooded medievalist who, in recent years, has produced a number of fascinating books and historical documentary series - seldom missing an opportunity to give his old friends, the Romans, a verbal kicking. For Palin, television would play an even bigger part in his future, although perhaps not in the expected way. Sandwiched between appearances in *Jabberwocky* and *Time Bandits*, two years before his next hit film *The Missionary* in 1982 and four years before Alan Bennett's *A Private Function*, came a programme which sent his career spinning off in a different direction entirely.

A life-long lover of trains and exploration, Palin's one documentary in the BBC's *Great Railway Journeys of the World* strand was enough to tip the Corporation off as to his abilities as a travel presenter. Subsequently, he has wended his way *Around the World in 80 Days*, gone *Pole to Pole*, and *Full Circle*, via *Sahara*, *Himalaya* and *New Europe*. Nowadays, Michael Palin is more widely revered for transglobal jaunts than for being a northerner at the heart of a British comedy revolution.

10
On Behalf of the Committee

"How many Pakistanis can you get in a taxi?"
"Four. And possibly a small child."
- *Bernard Right-On (John Thomson)*

Something in the air there may well have been, but not everyone in the 1960s and '70s was keen to relinquish the old ways. One BBC sketch show, *Before the Fringe*, addressed this conservative urge absolutely. Led by the writer and performer Alan Melville and shown over two series in 1967, *Before the Fringe* replicated the less confrontational revues of a bygone era, long before all that satire and silliness from the bolshie Oxbridge set. It had original songs and sketches from the days of Noel Coward and the 1950s comic songsmiths, Flanders and Swann, plus a cast that featured Joan Sims, Beryl Reid, Thora Hird and Ronnie Barker, and the odd one-off spot from the likes of Stanley Holloway, Barbara Windsor and Wilfrid Brambell.

Driven by a similar impulse, although a good deal more low brow in comparison, were Britain's working men's clubs, whose output over the decade that followed came - in the minds of many - to signify the very notion of northern comedy in its entirety.

As we have seen, the glory days of the live Variety halls were moving to a close by the end of the 1950s, a slow demise that the death of Max

Miller in 1963 only seemed set to hasten. Even the annual Royal Variety Performance, still televised and very much a gig to be desired by the artists themselves, was losing its sheen with TV and newspaper critics, if not the actual viewing public itself. In the guise of light entertainment, television Variety continued to be popular and the vast majority of it had a natural home on ITV; no surprise given that two of Variety's best-known booking agents, Lew Grade and Val Parnell, together with Parnell's boss Prince Littler - owner of the Stoll Moss theatre empire - were on the board of the Independent Television Commission. With impresarios like Jack Hylton also in highly influential positions, and Lew's brothers Leslie Grade and Bernard Delfont major agents themselves, that most of the top acts should gravitate towards the ITV networks was therefore inevitable.

Instead of promoting the genre as a whole, however, ITV's success in capturing viewers helped - with the similarly disruptive advent of rock 'n' roll - to hammer the final nail into traditional live Variety's coffin lid. Increasingly, in a desperate attempt to get punters through the door, anxious theatre owners turned to staging the sort of naughty revues that featured touring acts like Rita Atkins' International Nudes (who, as Roy Hudd writes in his *Cavalcade of Variety Acts*, only really lived up to that moniker if 'Wigan, Warrington, Bolton etc. were international'). Thus was formed a vicious circle, in which the families who had previously populated the old Variety hall auditoriums now felt excluded.

Equally, the days in which British seaside holidays were thought to be exotic were melting like spilled ice cream on a Blackpool pavement. For *The Likely Lads* and just about everyone else, Llorett-de-mar rather than Llandudno was where it was at. No longer a sign that an entertainer's career was on an upward curve, a Golden Mile summer season had come to signify the exact opposite. On the bright side, at least those tired and tatty resorts hung on as places in which less fashionable Variety acts could eke out some form of semi-regular employment; as was also the case with the various holiday camps sprinkled up and down Britain's coastline, and that perennial winter favourite, pantomime.

On the whole, none of this was good news for a comedian like Liverpool's Jimmy Gay. According to Roy Hudd, Gay's reflective style was reminiscent of Robb Wilton puffing on a Capstan full-strength. After his theme tune, 'Have You Ever Caught Your Nuts In a Rat Trap?', Gay would yell out: 'Never!' Born in 1906, when he finally got his big break it was on the last-eve Variety bill at the Prince of Wales Theatre. After that, as Hudd says: 'There was nowhere for him to go.'

As the 'sixties advanced, time and the television age were, quite simply, catching many older entertainers up. Take Skeets Martin. Born Bernard Martin in Liverpool in 1886, this future Variety character comic had already fought in the Boer War when he became the youngest Army bugler in World War One. And in World War Two, Martin was one of the first performers to tour with ENSA. Yet nowadays he is largely overlooked. Having made his professional debut in 1906, Martin's final stage appearance came in Blackpool, a year before his death in 1970.

More happily, in the case of two more comedians, the demise of live Variety did not prevent them from bouncing back and using television to their own advantage much later in life, albeit in soap opera rather than out-and-out comedy. Then again, the characters they played in *Coronation Street* during the 1990s, Percy Sugden and his gravel-voiced romantic *bête noire* Phyllis, shared more than a few amusing moments anyway.

Born in Oldham and the son of a farmer, Bill Waddington - a.k.a. Percy - began his stand-up career in *Stars In Battledress*, complete with the *nom de plume* Witty Willie. Later, when Variety took a nosedive, Waddington retired from the stage and bred cattle instead, before being lured back as *Corrie*'s resident grumpy OAP. Meanwhile, as the off-spring of music hall comedian Marie Santoi and tightrope walker Alf Fuller, Honor Margaret Santoi Rozelle Fuller (a.k.a. Jill Summers - a.k.a. Phyllis) was born in Moncton Green, Lancashire in 1910. Her life in comedy began opposite her tenor brother Tom F. Moss, a double act that continued until her sibling's unreliability forced Summers to go solo in 1949. Summers's first encounter with Bill Waddington came in a 1955 revue at the Windmill Theatre, by which time she had already perfected her Variety act as a loud-mouthed female porter. A third comedian who appeared in that Windmill revue was also destined to be a future *Coronation Street* resident, the Leeds-born Tom Mennard, who also went on to host several wireless series, among them *Local Tales*, in which his talent for monologues was put to very popular use.

Generally, however, for most comedians, live Variety was becoming a career dead end. And increasingly, the one place where regular work could most often be guaranteed was in those aforementioned distinctly unglamorous working men's clubs. With an unpretentious, down-at-heel aura so affectionately sent up years later in Peter Kay's *Phoenix Nights*, if the supposedly revolutionary nature of the times is to be believed your average working men's club inhabited some sort of reactionary parallel universe. In these unashamedly working class bear pits, as the 'sixties grew into the 'seventies, flat caps, pints of bitter and Capstans were the order of the day, rather than the Afghan coats, marijuana and kaftans of popular metropolitan fancy. The nearest these places got to cutting edge modernity was chicken in a basket. And after having lurked in the background for years, with the Variety halls' demise working men's clubs came seriously into their own. Thanks to a couple of television shows in particular, it was not long before the style of comedy to be found there was almost exclusively being associated with the north of England.

While often epitomising all that is good about British working class culture, working men's clubs, like the music halls before them, could also exhibit a more parochial and less attractive gang mentality. An integral part of the communities in which they were located, the vast majority of working men's club displayed a distrust of anything that so much as hinted at individuality. And this inward-looking world view was, of necessity, reinforced by their chosen comedians, who were expected to deliver the same old reliable routines and bugger off before the bingo.

Although most working men's clubs were far from grand, a number of them did possess higher ambitions and attracted the headline grabbing performers to match. These venues, however, were more widely known as Variety rather than working men's clubs. And the most famous one of the lot was situated on the road out of Bradford, in the unlikely location of Batley, West Yorkshire.

The Batley Variety Club still stands, albeit a shadow of its former self and these days a vast aircraft hangar of a nightclub named 'The Frontier', chiefly used and abused by stag and hen parties. Back in its golden age of the late 1960s and early '70s, however, it not infrequently boasted a bill to put Las Vegas to shame. International stars of the calibre of Dusty Springfield, Roy Orbison, Eartha Kitt and Olivia Newton John regularly crossed its threshold, although Louis Armstrong was reportedly less than impressed by the surroundings, famously telling his chauffeur: 'Man, we done hit rock bottom' when he pulled up outside. With the best will in the world, the town's Fox's biscuit factory is no Hotel Bellagio, so why did they come? Two words: Jimmy Corrigan, a man of scant schooling born of travelling fairground and circus stock on Yorkshire's east coast, who earned his entrepreneurial spurs in local cinemas and bingo halls before taking over as the Batley Variety Club's owner and master-in-chief.

When, in 1966, Corrigan and his first wife Betty decided to set up the biggest cabaret venue outside Nevada on the site of an old sewage treatment works, it is easy to imagine the cynical disbelief with which the idea was met. What the couple had correctly surmised, however, was that there was no reason on earth why they shouldn't do exactly that. Once built and opened in March 1967, four months after Irish vocal sensations The Bachelors - Al Read's old upstagers - had laid the foundation stone, it was clear that they were onto something. Certainly, the club's bright neon frontage contrasted markedly with the dour industrial surroundings and nondescript trunk road along which the club stood blinking like a peacock in a coal mine.

Consciously or not, the Corrigans had come to much the same conclusion as Gracie Fields's ambitious mother, years earlier. Small town thinking would get you nowhere. It was one thing to appreciate your roots, another to 'know your place', as patronising and disabling a notion as was ever concocted. And never mind dreams, what about pragmatism? Folk were just as keen to be entertained and relieved of their lovely brass in the Heavy Woollen district as they were in the MGM Grand, weren't they? Give them enough big name acts and audiences were bound to come flocking. Which is exactly what did happen, until Corrigan's own money began to run out.

Before then, a night at the Batley Variety Club became a byword for affordable and pseudo-posh entertainment. Among a wealth of other fascinating facts, the Yorkshire historian Bob Preedy's book, *Live Like A Lord - The Jimmy Corrigan Story* (Yorkshire & Humberside, 2003), reveals that, to join, punters paid an annual membership fee of five shillings and six pence, roughly 27p today, a financial outlay that was hardly onerous and anyway offset by the pub-priced ale inside. Prior to opening, it had amassed some 30,000 members, a figure that quickly increased to 50,000.

Given the scale of the venue and, initially, the absence of anything

like it elsewhere, Corrigan had no trouble attracting the quality of act that his smaller contemporaries would have killed for. Predictably, that led to tongue-in-cheek references to the A653 as northern England's very own answer to Broadway. Corrigan is even reported to have tabled a bid to bring Elvis Presley to the town, only to be told by the singer's manager, Colonel Tom Parker, that while a mammoth £100,000 fee was fine for him, 'what about Elvis?'. Soon, however, similar paths were being beaten elsewhere. And with burgeoning competition in Wakefield, Sheffield, Manchester and the like, an the opportunity for acts to up their prices, cutting Corrigan's profit margins and pulling-power considerably.

Ironically, given the diminishing fortunes of the British seaside, the financial rot really began to set in for Corrigan when he invested in a Majorcan theme park, as he tried to capitalise on the growing popularity of Spanish package holidays. The venture flopped horribly, taking most of the Batley Variety Club's financial resources and its owner's hard-won personal fortune with it, leaving Corrigan with a £500,000 debt. In 1980, he was declared bankrupt and divorce soon followed. With his business and private life in tatters, Corrigan all-but vanished from public view although, in later years, the little town of Batley would display its gratitude with a special town hall tribute concert, during which a song, 'Hungry Eyes', written especially for the Corrigans by a musician of appropriate international standing, Neil Sedaka, was performed. In 2001, Jimmy Corrigan died in a nursing home, aged 74.

Along with all those international superstars and lorries thundering by, the green, turquoise and orange walls of the Batley Variety Club just as frequently shook to laughter produced by more humble turns, whose comedy was the product of venues where an original call for 'wholesome and constructive amusement' had long since fallen on deaf ears.

The concept of a club for British working men was first introduced in the 1840s, when examples could be found in Manchester, Birmingham and Brighton. But it was not until the creation of the working men's club and Institute Union (CIU) in 1862, that these providers of 'rational recreation' really became enshrined as part of wider popular culture.

Not surprisingly, given the period, the impetus for a movement that would soon see such organisations in the nation's every nook and cranny was lofty, philanthropic and grounded in self-help. The CIU's first general secretary was an archetypal Victorian social improver named Henry Solly, a London-born businessman who felt that true social harmony could only be achieved by educating the working classes into appreciating what was best for them. To that end, the original working men's clubs were places built on temperance, where the middle and upper classes were also encouraged to participate in order to generate an atmosphere in which they and the working classes could meet 'for conversation, business, and mental improvement, with the means of recreation and refreshment, free from intoxicating drinks' (as quoted in Solly's prospectus for the new union, written in 1862).

The emergence of such Institutes, Trade Unions and Co-operatives was absolutely nothing unusual in a Victorian society riven by poverty, crime and injustice, not to mention a recurring fear in well-to-do quarters that, if great care were not taken, bloody revolution may well be at hand. Superficially enlightened and well-intentioned individuals like Henry Solly were hardly rare, and a number of organisations created by such men proved admirably resilient in the face of an even more radical and unpredictable century yet to come. Few, however, experienced changes to their very fabric to quite the same extent as the working men's club.

For the words 'working class', of course, read 'working class men'. If one fact *didn't* change much over the next 150 or so years it was that women were by and large expected to keep out of the way. As recently as the last few years, the wives, girlfriends and daughters of working men's club members were strange and mystical beasts, best kept at arm's length. Until the ban was overturned at an annual conference in Blackpool in 2007, there were still around half a dozen clubs in England's north east who hung on doggedly to their 'right' to deny 'ladies' full national membership. Ironic that, and certainly revealing given the part otherwise played by women in wider working class northern society.

Happily, that particular roar was one of a startled dinosaur. In 2005, CIU clubs could boast around 406 female secretaries and the majority of those affiliated allowed women equal rights inside their own walls. Less happily, in these early years of the twenty-first century, there are roughly half as many working men's clubs than there were in the boom 1970s - a

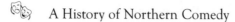

worrying statistic for a sector of the entertainment industry that, for all its troubles (a recent European smoking ban among them) continues to be one of the largest showbusiness employers in the United Kingdom.

Gender discrimination apart, in just about every other respect the working men's clubs of the 'seventies could not have been more different to their nineteenth-century forebears. For a start, middle class patronage was very firmly a thing of the past; the result, over a century before, of how a growing number of clubs and individuals had begun to resent their own gentrified and occasionally even aristocratic committees. That was bad news indeed for the concept of working men's clubs as a means of social control. What do you do when the working men you were set up to 'save' won't even come through the door? While Solly may have intended his clubs to be established less around authoritarian principles and more upon mutual co-operation, it seems that the folk on the end of his improving philosophies saw things rather differently.

Solly's high ideals of temperance had long been abandoned too, with a campaign for the sale of beer having been reluctantly agreed to in 1865. Showing admirable pragmatism, the alcohol-free philanthropist came around eventually to the argument that one reason why working men weren't joining his clubs in droves was that they would far rather be in the pub next door. Even the men who could be persuaded to come along would more often than not pop in for a gill or three on the way home. Once the beer barrels were rolled in, working men's clubs really did begin to take off, frequently on the initiative of the men themselves and especially, it seems, out there in the provinces. In London, meanwhile, nearer to the scrutiny of the Establishment classes, the issue of patronage appears to have been a more longstanding problem and club members developed a reputation - rightly or wrongly - for being far more politically active than was often the case elsewhere.

Generally, however, with their future increasingly in the hands of the working and lower middle class members themselves, working men's clubs proliferated rapidly. Like comedy itself, they developed into a comfortable and unpretentious means of escape from the grinding reality of everyday existence. With an atmosphere fuelled by comradeship, beer and irreverent joviality, as the twentieth century advanced they became a testing environment for performers indeed.

On Behalf of the Committee

For some of the older-established acts, reared on a more reverential Variety theatre crowd, the club circuit could be a challenge too far. At best it was a return to an environment they had hoped to have left behind; at worst a daunting, seedy and raucous endurance test. Jimmy Jewell and Ben Warriss, for instance, cited regular demands to perform 'blue' material as a major reason for pulling the plug on their partnership completely. And then there was the Hull-born comic Freddie Sales. Born into showbiz as Frederick Harry Walker in 1920, Sales debuted in revue aged 16 and thereafter performed as a Variety comedian in Australia, the Bahamas and Hong Kong, with a spell entertaining the American Forces in Okinawa thrown in for good measure.

Back in the UK, he was also a regular performer in seaside summer revues, for Billy Butlins burgeoning camp empire. Until one day, owing to the dearth of traditional Variety venues, his agent booked Sales on a tour of working men's clubs around the north east of England. Given how part of his act involved Sales cracking gags and playing soprano sax while clad in a royal blue suit, yellow cap and socks, we can only wonder at what the broon ale-swilling Geordies made of him. We do, however, know what he made of them. So little impressed was Freddie Sales with the levels to which Variety had 'sunk' that he made up his mind to throw in the towel completely. Then came a surprise offer from America, where a touring revue was searching for an English comic. Sales snapped their hand off and it wasn't long before he was heading the bill in Las Vegas as a 'poon-banging baby in a play pen, only returning to the UK upon his retirement in 1991.

The first opportunity to replicate on television what was being presented nightly in clubland - albeit in a heavily sanitised way - came courtesy of a Granada-produced show called *The Comedians*, first screened in 1971.

While there was nothing particularly new about any of the jokes - the majority had been around longer than the Manchester ship canal - the quickfire presentation was something else again. Opening to the foot-tapping sound of Shep's Banjo Boys, a Dixieland jazz band, each half-hour episode of *The Comedians* saw frilly-shirted club comics deliver a non-stop procession of gags (ad break notwithstanding), censored for foul language but with 'seventies-style racial and gender stereotypes intact.

The programme was the brainchild of Granada producer Johnnie Hamp, who made the show in tandem with director Wally Butler. The two men were the offspring of music hall entertainers themselves, Hamp's father being better known as the 'Great Hamp', a magician. The format of *The Comedians*, however, was strictly front cloth. This was straightforward working men's club stand-up, featuring 'the best thirty club comics in the land'. Terrifying sideburns were obligatory. The only things missing were beer and bingo.

In producing the show, each turn would record a twenty-minute spot after which Hamp and Butler would get out the scissors and begin cutting and pasting the results into the final quickfire format. In common with TV's earlier tendency to plunder music hall, Hamp took the comedians in question from the existing club circuit and the lucky ones soon became household names. Top of the bill was undoubtedly Manchester's favourite bad boy Bernard Manning, of whom more anon. Running him close, though, was Cockney 'sparra' Mike Reid who, in future years, would be even better known as Pat Butcher's errant husband Frank, in the BBC soap *EastEnders*.

Aside from Reid and the programme's resident barmy Irishman Frank - 'It's the way I tell 'em' - Carson, however, the bulk of the comics were as northern as nutty slack. There was the pathologically shy Ken Goodwin, whose stuttering style and catchphrase 'settle down now' won him as much sympathy as laughter. Goodwin's appeal was very much in the tradition of the grinning northern simpleton, his own showbiz career beginning somewhat appropriately as a George Formby impersonator. Like many of the era, he first came to wider public attention on the BBC talent show *Opportunity Knocks*. In more recent days, Ken Goodwin has followed the traditional Variety club comedian's route of cruise ship tours, seaside summer seasons and pantomime, together with the not so traditional route of singing with the BBC Radio Orchestra and releasing five easy listening (allegedly) LPs.

Liverpool-born comedian George Roper was probably best known for telling jokes about workmen in wellies. In hindsight, though, perhaps the most startling thing about him was his resemblance to the great 1990s American comedian, Bill Hicks. Like Hicks, Roper was predominantly concerned with the metaphysical futility of daily existence only, in his case, he maybe didn't realise it. Roper also smoked a lot of cigarettes and lost his life to cancer - albeit 37 years older than Hicks - at the age of 69, in 2003. When *The Comedians* came along, he had spent a decade touring the northern clubs and was one of the first comics to be approached by Hamp when he came up with the idea. With his 'seventies hair-do, portly figure, chubby bejeweled fingers and laid-back microphone technique, George Roper was old-school northern stand-up personified. Diagnosed with cancer in 1998, he nevertheless continued to perform throughout the five years of his illness - including a full Blackpool summer season in 2002 and a spot in the thirty-second *Comedians* reunion three months before he passed away. 'It wasn't necessarily the gags George told,' Hamp told reporters, at Roper's Manchester funeral, '...it was the face. There was always a twinkle in the eye.'

As was indeed the case with Barnsley's Charlie Williams. A former miner and professional footballer with Doncaster Rovers, Williams had a Yorkshire accent as broad as any coal seam. Of Jamaican descent, he also had a black face. In today's Britain, those qualities would most likely pass without notice, but on television in the early 1970s, it was an unusual combination to say the least. In short, Charlie Williams was the UK's first 'coloured' mainstream television comedian, some fourteen years after the first black person on TV, Cy Grant, had sung the news calypso-style on the BBC's *Tonight* programme.

Given the parochial nature of the working men's clubs in which the comedian earned his crust, not to mention the rabble-rousing antics of the right-wing British politician Enoch Powell, that Charlie Williams was a decidedly nonconfrontational figure ought not, perhaps, to be all that surprising. Along with their less than enlightened attitude towards female membership. as recently as 1963 many working men's clubs either had a limit on 'coloured' entry or barred black people from their premises absolutely. This, after all, was a society in which the Conservative party, while fighting a general election, could quite happily send children around the constituency of Smethwick in the West Midlands chanting: 'If you want a nigger for a neighbour, vote Liberal or Labour'. Against such a backdrop, the northern tradition of self-deprecation may well have felt very useful indeed. Nevertheless, in his own quiet humanistic way, Charlie Williams was as subversive as Bill Cosby or Richard Pryor.

The argument against Charlie Williams is that his material simply reinforced racial stereotypes, while feeding the prejudices of his audience. And certainly, on many a painful occasion, in retrospect, that does seem to be so. Williams himself, however, never saw it that way. Your average working men's club crowd was a gladiatorial beast; a comedian needed to keep it within his sights or he would never escape alive. And on top of that, there was the philosophical get-out clause employed by Alf Garnett - i.e. that the bigot was the one who came off worse in the end. Charlie Williams insisted that beating his audience to their own punchlines got them onside. It pulled the rug from beneath their feet and strengthened the notion of shared human experience. Of course it could also be argued that such a tactic might instead reinforce their delusions of superiority. Either way, that Williams spoke about the colour of his skin at all was a necessity. He may well have been constrained by the strait-jacket of social conformity, but his winning manner and cheeky smile helped him to unlock the doors that more blatantly radical comedians - black and white - would go on to kick down completely.

With 171 footballing appearances for Doncaster in the 1950s behind him, Charlie Williams began his showbusiness life as a crooner, although he discovered very early on that what his audiences really enjoyed were the gags he told between tunes. And black though he was, Williams also realised that the experiences of his own life were their experiences too - the austerity of the coal mines; the daily struggle to get by; the memories of war-time neighbourliness; the power of a local community etc etc. Furthermore, as an entertainer at least, the colour of a man or woman's skin was not necessarily a bar to individual popularity. As the bill of the Batley Variety Club confirms, for Britain's working class, their musicians of choice were not infrequently class acts like Ray Charles, Billie Holiday, Nat King Cole and Louis Armstrong. A feature by Roy Stone for on-line magazine *Ayup - The Best Of Yorkshire* also points out that the Hollywood actor Paul Robeson's 1940 film, *The Proud Valley*, was set in a Welsh coal mine, thereby ensuring he was very popular indeed down Barnsley way.

Where racism is concerned, nothing in the garden is ever free from sin. Nevertheless, throughout the 1970s, where ordinary black and white working class folk played and worked together in the same football teams, factories, coal mines and pubs, at least some semblance of happy integration often proved possible. Rather than contempt, *true* familiarity will often breed tolerance, albeit with strings of social uniformity and restriction attached. In other words, your average black sheep could only 'belong' to the flock by owning up to his or her incongruity within it. And maybe it was ever thus. The mind drifts back to the briefest of shots in one of those rediscovered Mitchell and Kenyon films, half a century or so before Britain's first official West Indian immigrants arrived on the *S.S. Empire Windrush* at Tilbury docks in 1948. One genuinely black miner grins mischievously at the camera from the middle of a bunch of coal and soot-blackened colleagues, freshly up from the pit.

As the 'seventies progressed and the political temperature rose, Charlie Williams summed up his attitude thus: 'Because I make jokes, it does not mean I'm willing to be walked over. I'm not saying that problems should be ignored. The great thing about this country is that justified complaints can be heard and get some action. There are a lot of things to complain about and put right for a lot of groups in Britain.' And despite falling foul of some with such a softly, softly approach, he has latterly won support from another black comic who got his own start using material that would nowadays be seen as beyond the social pale. Where Williams would crack jokes about 'rolling his eyes' to create light in a power cut, or threaten hecklers that he would move in next door, the Dudley-born comic Lenny Henry's George Formby-impersonations and a supporting role on a *Black And White Minstrel Show* tour led to him becoming the first ever black winner of the ITV talent show, *New Faces*. That achievement came two years after one of Henry's future 'victims', Trevor McDonald - a.k.a. McDoughnut - became ITN's first black news reporter in 1973.

'You have to understand that Charlie Williams was perfect for the time that he appeared,' Henry has since told the authors of *Windrush - The Irresistible Rise of Multiracial Britain* (Mike Phillips and Trevor Phillips, Harper Collins, 1998), the book of a BBC TV documentary of the same name. 'When he came along it was astounding to hear this bloke talking like: "Eh up, flower, eh. Hey, have you ever been to supermarket where they have the broken biscuits?" I think it was a huge culture shock for people. And Charlie exploited this to the full. He had the Roller and the big house and he was the king of comedy for a while and God bless him, good luck to him. Because at the time, nobody was doing what he was doing. He was playing the fat belly, bigoted northern comedian at their own game...'.

One thing is for sure. Charlie Williams's spots on *The Comedians* shot him into the comedy stratosphere. A couple of ITV specials in 1972 were accompanied that year by a Royal Gala appearance, a six-month stint at the London Palladium and an appearance on *This Is Your Life*. When, in 1973 he switched channels to make a one-off special for the BBC, *The Charlie Williams Show*, he might reasonably have expected that the only way was up. Sadly, after a best-forgotten spell following in the footsteps of Bob Monkhouse and Norman Vaughan on the Sunday afternoon quiz, *The Golden Shot*, as with so many of his comedy contemporaries, a cultural and political tide of change would wash him back to the unfashionable enclaves in which he had first made his name. Even so, he would never be forgotten completely. In 1999, Charlie Williams was awarded an MBE for his ongoing charity work and enjoyed the distinction of being named Doncaster Rovers' all-time cult hero by viewers of the BBC's *Football Focus*. In 2006, after a decade-long battle with Parkinson's Disease and dementia, he died, aged 78, at Barnsley General Hospital.

When former Accrington deputy headmaster and *Comedians* stalwart Jim Bowen made a racially insulting comment to a black woman on his BBC local radio show *The Happy Daft Farm* in 2003, the apologetic comic insisted that no offence had been intended and immediately announced his retirement from showbusiness. His announcement proved premature. With the rise to popularity of Peter Kay's *Phoenix Nights* and television nostalgia shows generally, Bowen was soon back in public favour.

Underpinning that renaissance was Bowen's triumphantly unlikely stewardship, from 1981, of an ITV Sunday tea-time show that picked up where *The Golden Shot* had left off. Its name was *Bullseye* and where Bernie the Bolt had prepared crossbows, Bowen's not infrequently bewildered contestants chucked darts, often with the prize of a speedboat at stake. A vehicle which, as Kay later pointed out, 'must come in handy if you live in Tamworth'. Under Jim Bowen's benign wing, losing contestants were always invited to see 'what they would have won' and could console themselves with a 'bendy Bully' booby prize statuette and brass tankard.

On Behalf of the Committee

Bullseye's enormous popularity was down to two things. One: The enchanting innocence of its host, whose favourite adjectives 'super', 'smashing' and 'great', were sprinkled liberally however appropriate the circumstances. Bowen: 'And what do you do for a living?' Contestant: 'I'm unemployed, Jim.' Bowen: 'Super.' And two: There was seldom anything else on. The result, an audience in the region of 12 million. 'Stay out of the black and into the red; nothing in this game for two in a bed.'

Bowen, born in 1939, put ten years of teaching experience to good use when he first braved the northern club circuit in the 1960s. Initially, that was on a part-time basis, until his dry and stony-faced style won him a spot on *The Comedians*. At that, the grammar school-educated comic put away his mortar board - assuming they wear mortar boards in Accrington - and turned fully professional. Thus was launched a career in which the bespectacled Bowen rode out the waves that sank so many of his comedy contemporaries and continued to pop up on many of British TV's most successful light entertainment shows - from *Summertime Special* to *Noel's House Party* - over three decades.

Another veteran of the club circuit still doing the rounds some forty years on is Duggie Brown, our latest link to the comedic maternity ward that is *Coronation Street*. The younger brother of *Corrie*'s notorious plastic surgery victim Lynne Perrie, well known from 1979 to 1994 as 'Poison' Ivy Tilsley (and marginally less famous as a residents association secretary in Diana Dors's 1970s sitcom *Queenie's Castle*), rare was an episode of *The Comedians* which did not feature Brown's squawked impression of a door-answering talking parrot: 'Who is it?' Born Duggie Dudley in Rotherham, like his sister (who was born Jean Dudley, nine years earlier, in 1931) young Duggie was stage-struck from the off. Originally, he toured as a member of a pop group called The Four Imps. Then, after turning to comedy, he won his way onto the *The Comedians*, where his fresh and cheery manner marked him out as one of its more memorable faces.

In common with many comedians, when called upon to try his hand at straight acting Duggie Brown proved to be a natural and film outings in such northern milestones as *Kes* (1969) (in which he starred alongside his big sister as a milkman) and *For The Love Of Ada* (1972) followed. In more recent years he has been a dependable bit-part player in television

285

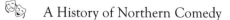

dramas like *The Bill*, *Minder*, *Common As Muck*, *Heartbeat* and *All Creatures Great And Small*. In fact Brown's latter career has had a predominantly thespian shape to it, including parts in three of Britain's four major sitcoms, *Brookside*, *EastEnders* and, of course, *Coronation Street*, in which he appeared as George Freeman in 1997. In 1999, he played the fool in *King Lear* for the northern Broadsides Theatre Company and, somewhat less challengingly, Vernon Sedgwick in the twenty-fifth season of *Last Of The Summer Wine*. Sadly, time ran out for his sister, Lynne Perrie, in 2006. She died, aged 75, from a stroke - ironically, the very same affliction that had carried off her fictional counterpart, Ivy.

One year after the television launch of *The Comedians*, the show was also adapted for the stage and it embarked upon well-received summer seasons in London, Great Yarmouth and Blackpool. Then, after having apparently come to an end after a seventh series in 1974, the TV version made three subsequent revivals in 1979, 1984 and 1992. En route, a further slough of northern comedy talent was unearthed that included Mick Miller, Stan Boardman and Johnnie Casson.

Hailing from Halifax and a naturally funny man, Casson is a classic example of a northern comedian who seems to have been denied greater national acclaim largely on account of the soon-to-become unfashionable nature of traditional club-style comedy, coupled with a determination not to be based in the south. Instead, he has preferred to reside in beautiful Brighouse, 'for tax reasons'. With *The Comedians* a distant memory, guest appearances on Des O'Connor chat shows and a reputation as a cracking after-dinner speaker were the best he could hope for.

Mick Miller, meanwhile, was a former professional goalkeeper with Port Vale. Born Michael Lawton in Dingle, Liverpool, in 1950, when *The Comedians* was first broadcast he had just changed career direction to become a Pontins holiday camp blue coat and bingo caller. By 1978, when Johnnie Hamp spotted Miller - no relation to legendary greyhound Mick the Miller - in a Blackpool summer season, his act was polished to the point where he had already won a heat of the television talent show *New Faces*, toured nationally with legendary rock 'n' roller Chuck Berry and performed his first summer season in Morecambe.

With his trademark bald pate surrounded by a moat of shoulder-length hair, Mick Miller's quirky visual presence proved perfect for the relaunched *Comedians*. And in 1982, he had his own half-hour special on Hamp's Granada showcase strand, *Success*. From there, it was TV light entertainment all the way, including spots in the Mike Smith-hosted Saturday night show *The Funny Side*, along with Cheryl Baker, Barbara Windsor and *The Sun* page-three girl Linda Lusardi, and numerous guest appearances on quiz shows from *Blankety Blank* to *They Think It's All Over*. These days, like Casson, he is a regular on the cabaret, cruise and after-dinner speaking circuit.

In 2004, when digital television channel E4 launched a reality show, *Kings Of Comedy*, the old-school acts to whom the producers turned were Miller and his fellow *Comedians* colleague Stan Boardman. Along with David Copperfield (or Stanley Barlow as he was christened), a Yorkshire comedian who starred alongside Lenny Henry and Tracy Ullman in the 1981 BBC series *Three Of A Kind*, Miller and Boardman were joined in a Bristol *Big Brother*-style house by five flatmates of more recent vintage, in experience if not in actual age.

Given that the flat-mates in question were BBC Radio 4's Hull-born eccentric Boothby Graffoe, the gay San Franciscan comic Scott Capuro, Irish stand-up Andrew Maxwell, 42-year old Glaswegian mum Janey Godley and a black former female prison officer named Ava Vidal, the most recent winner of the BBC's New Comedy Awards, the potential for fireworks was all too apparent. Particularly with Boardman on board, who, the pre-publicity helpfully pointed out, had once 'hit the headlines for making supposedly racist gags'.

Doubtless they were thinking of the 2002 occasion when, according to a report in the *Daily Mirror*, Boardman was booked to appear at an Elland Road function in honour of the then-Leeds United footballer of the year, Rio Ferdinand. Given how the club had just seen two of its star players, Jonathan Woodgate and Lee Bowyer, involved in a high-profile case at Hull Crown Court, in which Bowyer had been found not guilty of causing a young man named Sarfraz Najeib grievous bodily harm and Woodgate had been found guilty of affray, one of Boardman's opening gags might have been better judged. 'I see Woodgate and Bowyer are here,' he is said to have quipped. 'I hear they went to a club last night. When they came out, one said to the other: "I could murder an Indian".'

And that was probably the high point. When an Asian lawyer in the audience took offence and told Boardman that he was 'a disgrace', the comic was alleged to have responded: 'Fucking hell. I'm being heckled by Pakis now. Why don't you go back to your curry house or shop in Bradford?' To the reported 'dismay' of around 700 stony-faced guests, a procession of jokes aimed at the Irish and the aftermath of New York's September 11 atrocities followed, with Boardman later told in writing by the club that his act had been 'racist', 'inappropriate and unacceptable'.

When given an opportunity to explain himself by the *Mirror*, Boardman responded: 'I don't know what all the fuss is about. I tell jokes about everyone. This Indian guy heckled me so I heckled him back. He called out at me "sing, sing" and I said "Is that your name? Singh?" He insulted me by telling me to go back to Liverpool, so I told him to go back home and told him his elephant was waiting. If I am heckled, I'll respond no matter who that person is.'

As it turned out, the Boardman who took part in *Kings Of Comedy* two years later was comparatively well-behaved. In a show marginally less entertaining than the fat under your average student's cooker, Dubliner Maxwell was the eventual winner. But Boardman's participation in the first place and the fact that both he and Miller reached the last three on viewers' votes, at least showed the extent to which his 'German Fokkers' shtick, so popular on *The Comedians*, had struck an unpleasant national chord.

Stan Boardman was, like Mick Miller and Charlie Williams, a former professional footballer, apprenticed to hometown Liverpool. And like Miller, his showbiz career kicked off in the holiday camps, albeit Butlins in his case. At the insistence of Boardman's two children, the one-time welder and pipe fitter entered and won the regional heat of a talent contest while on holiday there. More successful heats followed before, eventually, at the London Palladium, he scooped first prize and a £1000 cheque in the grand final. A summer season as a redcoat followed before an equally successful TV break on *Opportunity Knocks*. That led to more telly work, culminating in a call from Johnnie Hamp to appear in *The Comedians*. It was on that show that Boardman really hit the heights, with his 'De Jeermans, dey bombed our chippies' line soon becoming a popular catchphrase.

All in all, Boardman's brash 'them and us' style sums up not only what has come to be recognised as archetypal northern club comedy, it also seems to epitomise what many people think of as traditional Scouse humour. And if every Liverpudlian is a comic, as the cliché suggests, then isn't Boardman merely one amongst many? Over-generalisation or not, his jokes do underline how the power of community - or indeed comedy itself - may not necessarily be a force for sweetness and light. And certainly, there will be those for whom Boardman's more recent absence from our screens will be viewed as just desserts for previous misdemeanours. De Jeermans have a word for it: *schadenfreude*.

Up at the better behaved end of town and a few years earlier, a one-time maths teacher named Tom O'Connor also came to prominence on *Opportunity Knocks* and, like Boardman, it acted as a springboard to *The Comedians*. In all other respects, however, O'Connor was a comparative saint. With his silver hair, dapper style and easy-going manner, he already stood out from the crowd, but it was the cleanliness of his material that ensured him longevity with family audiences. After *The Comedians*, he proved a natural at hosting Variety and quiz shows and, after the Royal Variety Performance of 1976, was asked to MC Thames TV's *Wednesday At Eight*. A half-hour ITV special, *The Tom O'Connor Show*, became a full series the following year. Future gigs included *Night Out At The London Casino* and the long-running *Name That Tune*.

Never mind northern, if there is one British comic whose influence has been consistently under-appreciated then it is surely Tom O'Connor. If anyone popularised the modern-day observational style, it was he. With his regular opening line of 'have you noticed how...' - and despite being clad in the same 'seventies clobber as everyone else - O'Connor was years ahead of the 'alternative' comedians who would follow in his platformed footsteps. Sure, he could do the tired old flea-ridden mother-in-law gags if he had to but that was generally left to his contemporaries. O'Connor's talent was for picking up on the humourous detail that had apparently passed everyone else by. It was an approach that began as a teacher and assistant headmaster, when he is said to have discovered that the only way to get through to the boys of the St. Joan of Arc School, in his hometown Bootle, was to make them laugh. After leaving teaching in 1974 and going full-time, initially as a singer, his eye for real life soon got him noticed.

Yet as with the rest of his bow-tied colleagues, the tide of comedy

trends would one day turn. And in many cases, it has to be said, not without good reason. Happily, in our own multi-channel days of digital and satellite television, lucky modern viewers may still catch an occasional glimpse of the original *Comedians* series on UK Granada Classic Gold Plus (or whatever it's called this week). Try it - usually after pub chucking-out time - and along with the better remembered names above, you may also be re-introduced to an array of frilly-shirted comics who were briefly in the spotlight before, on TV anyway, fading almost entirely to black.

Some, such as Blackpool's curly-haired giggler Lennie Bennett and the Irish-born host of *Catchphrase* Roy - 'it's good, but it's not right' - Walker, would at least go on to host afternoon quiz shows. A few others, like Russ Abbott, Les Dennis and Paul Squire, actually had prime-time careers in store. Yet soon, to the television watching nation as a whole, frilly-shirted comics like Kenny Cantor, Ray Fell, Pat Mooney, Charlie Daze, Jos White and Eddie Flanagan would be an extinct breed. And when the now-defunct Granada Plus satellite channel commissioned *The New Comedians*, yet another revival in 1997, the unknown northern club comics who were unearthed this time stayed unknown.

Also occasionally available for nostalgic late-night viewing on satellite TV - on the suitably 'seventies-entitled 'Men and Motors' - is Johnnie Hamp's follow-up to *The Comedians*: *The Wheeltappers And Shunters Social Club*.

Borrowing heavily from the list of comics who had lit up Hamp's original show - the Lancashire-born grape-crusher Stu Francis, for example - and featuring more than a few stars of the future who had not - such as up-and-coming double act Cannon and Ball - *The Wheeltappers And Shunters Social Club* completed the working men's club picture, by marrying stand-up with traditional Variety. Some of those turns, like the diminutive Middlesbrough magician Paul Daniels, were magical. Most were musical, including the piano-bothering first lady of clubland, Mrs. Mills, and the gold lamé 'cowboy' Eric Delaney, complete with his tubular bells and kettle drum. There was even a wagon wheel-twirling Canadian girl named Tina (a real wagon wheel, mind, not one of those chocolate-covered biscuit things that seem to shrink, year on year).

On Behalf of the Committee

Like any half-decent Variety show, it was an eclectic mix. Yet *The Wheeltappers* owed much of its popularity to its two hosts - both veterans of *The Comedians* themselves. In master of ceremonies Bernard Manning and chain-smoking chairman of the fictional entertainments committee Colin Crompton, the programme's producers had found the perfect duo to bring the no-frills atmosphere of a northern Saturday night out into living rooms up and down the land. On screen, the audience was served real beer at their doubtless sticky tables, from barmaids who at one point included Liz Dawn - a.k.a. Vera Duckworth - a future landlady of the Rovers Return. For more genteel members of the viewing public, it must have been like a David Attenborough natural history documentary, but with common folk where the meerkats should have been.

The Wheeltappers And Shunters Social Club originated in the touring stage version of *The Comedians* in which, to add some variety to the stand-up comedy, Johnnie Hamp introduced a working men's club skit to close the first half. The show had other segments too, including ersatz old-time music hall, hosted by Crompton in the manner of Leonard Sachs on *The Good Old Days*. The working men's club routine, meanwhile, chaired by Frank Carson, was given the name *Wheeltappers And Shunters Social Club*. Then, during rehearsals one day, Hamp switched the two comics around. It was an inspired move. With his cloth cap and dour demeanour, vacant expression and a comb-over that began at the back of his neck, the chain-smoking Crompton fit the bill perfectly. His deadpan interjections to 'Give Order!', accompanied by the ringing of his rotating bell, were soon the stuff of TV folklore: 'On behalf of the committee-eh, we've passed a resoluuuu-tion. Members are reminded that the signs in the gents toilets which say 'wet paint' are *not* an instruction.'

So convincing was Crompton's performance that, before long, the show's makers were fielding complaints from real-life club chairmen, affronted by his portrayal. The comedian, though, had an ace up his sleeve. As well as being a former Butlins redcoat whose TV debut had come some six years before *The Comedians* in the Liverpudlian comedian Johnny Hackett's 1965 BBC stand-up show *Let's Laugh* (which also showcased Norman Collier, Freddie Sales, Mike Yarwood, Keith Harris and another future *Comedians* regular, Mike Burton), he had once been a social club chairman himself, hence the brilliance of the characterisation.

Crompton wrote many of his own gags too - 'the first prize in the raffle is a diving suit... no, hang on.... a divan suite' - and delivered them in an understated style every bit as satirical as any Oxbridge revue.

Born in Manchester in 1931 and looking like Frank Skinner's dad, Crompton's dry and gormless manner had made him a firm favourite on *The Comedians*, as had his constant ribbing of the not quite so dry north west seaside resort of Morecambe, much to the dismay of its tourism board and residents. 'I went to Morecambe last week. It was shut.' 'There are some nice drives out of Morecambe. Mind you, *any* drive out of Morecambe is a nice drive...' and so on. Given the parochial nature of the British Film Industry in the 1970s, it wasn't long before Crompton also found his way to the silver screen, albeit in a less than glamourous 1977 soft-core porn comedy romp, *Confessions From A Holiday Camp*. Having already edited a series of little jokebooks under the name *Mini Ha Ha* in 1970, Colin Crompton's final contribution to the Wheeltappers phenomenon was his co-editorship of *The Wheeltappers And Shunters Members' Handbook* with Johnnie Hamp in 1976. A publican in later life, he died in 1995 from cancer, aged 54.

Although the charm of *The Wheeltappers And Shunters Social Club* was its essential innocence, as a show it was nevertheless also marked by a fair degree of knowing and often over-looked self-parody. In a period marked by social and political upheaval, strikes and unrest, out-and-out political diatribes were notable only for their absence, but the images on the walls were gently ironic portraits of Prime Minister Harold Wilson and Her Majesty the Queen. Patriotic communal sing-songs in the old music hall style were another frequent feature, as were good-natured jibes at your average working men's club's obsession with its own rules and regulations, as in the sign just over the chairman's shoulder: 'Hats will not be tolerated'. Crisis? What crisis?

In this, of course, *The Wheeltappers And Shunters Social Club* was merely following in the classic northern comedy tradition. If it was political ranting and raving you were after, you could get that at work or at home. Entertainment was there to help you forget about your troubles not add to them. In the not so very distant future, for a generation of new comedians and maybe even for the club committees themselves, such a notion would come to seem quaintly old-fashioned. After all, life is political, comedy is about life, ergo comedy *must* be political, even when it thinks it is not. And certainly, in the bigger picture, one of those 'organised channels of dissent' referred to earlier by Charlie Williams, the Trades Unions, were destined to be all-but quashed under the stewardship of a new Prime Minister, Margaret Hilda Thatcher. Soaring levels of unemployment were seeing a fall in actual 'working men' and, inevitably, the popularity of their social clubs also suffered. And while the alternative new comedians on the block were happy to vent their party political spleen in public, the old guard bumbled on regardless and never the twain would meet. With one side huffing that 'alternative' meant 'not funny' and the other apparently determined to toss them and their mothers-in-law out with Thatch's authoritarian bath water, the sadness is that actually they were all on the same side.

All that, however, is for another chapter. For now, let's acknowledge that *The Wheeltappers And Shunters Social Club* could be fantastic fun and a damn sight cleverer in design and delivery than its London-centric middle class critics ever gave it credit for. All traditional working men's club life was here. Crompton again: 'With regard to the £300 missing from club funds... we will have a word with the treasurer when he gets back from Tenerife.' And how could you *not* love a show in which star Americans like Bill Haley and the Comets, Howard Keel and Gene Pitney (of whom Bernard Manning remarked: 'It's a good job he was nice to me on the way up, I've just seen him on the way down...') regularly rubbed shoulders with The Grumbleweeds, Peter Gordino, Tony Christie and the Dooleys? Best of all was the energetic husband and wife comedy duo Ronnie Dukes and Rikki Lee who, according to Manning, '...need no introduction, because they already know each other.'

The Wheeltappers And Shunters Social Club ended its 39-episode run in 1978, by which time its host, Bernard Manning, was a household name and not always for the most positive of reasons.

By then, Manning was well on his way to becoming that rare beast in northern comedy, a hate figure, as universally reviled in some quarters as he was admired - and maybe even adored - in others. To a fresher breed of comedian, he was the epitome of everything that they wished to see changed; smug, or so they claimed, bigoted and stuck in his conservative ways. As for the old guard, while Manning had stuck the boot into many of them too in his time, he was more often than not commended both for his 'professionalism' and a steadfast refusal to alter his ways.

The roots of Manning's comedy style lay in both the working class insularity referred to earlier and the dog-eat-dog nature of the club circuit itself. Even in as benign an environment as *The Wheeltappers And Shunters*, as the ringmaster at a particularly rowdy circus your best mode of defence was attack. And that was a survival tactic at which this overweight and sardonic Mancunian proved particularly adept. In *The Wheeltappers* as elsewhere, nether the audience, the turns, the bar staff, the Union rep or his partner-in-crime Colin Crompton, would ever get the better of Bernard Manning. The savagery of his put-downs were cleaned up for television, but live on stage their brutality rose in relation to the levels of raucousness in the air. Yet, on the whole, his public knew what to expect and few openly took offence. To Bernard, any perceived weakness was fair game; be it colour, age, physical appearance, sexual leaning or whatever. If you had the misfortune of passing his eyeline, perhaps on an innocent trip to the toilet, then you needn't have bothered. The urine would have already been extracted before you had so much as left your table.

At least, that was how it was to begin with. As sensitivity to racial issues in particular increased, so did the capacity for insulted parties to answer back. Of the old school stand-ups, Manning was not alone in thrashing around like a bewildered tyrannosaur in the hinterland of just what was and was not socially acceptable. Like Stan Boardman, as far as he was concerned, there was an egalitarian defence for his humour. He took the mickey out of everybody, therefore how could he be accused of prejudice? In so far as Manning was willing to analyse his act at all, if his comedy had any philosophical motivation it was that no one should take themselves too seriously. He certainly didn't take *himself* seriously.

Unlike the majority of his contemporaries, however, and certainly those on television, Manning frequently operated in territory that most would have considered taboo. To him, there was no crevice of human existence into which the spotlight of comedy should not be shone, even if you did end up laughing at the bloke who was howling, battered and bruised, at the foot of the well. His was the realm of the too-soon-after-the-event sick joke, for example. Yet, in many ways, he did take the same vertiginous path on the outer edges of social acceptability as that trodden by American comics like Lenny Bruce, Dennis Leary, Richard Pryor, Eddie Murphy and one of Manning's biggest fans, Joan Rivers, whose own exploits earned them outright admiration from the very same trendy young comics who were at Manning's throat in the UK. If, across the Atlantic, such boundary-pushing humour might bring cultural cachet, in the shifting social climate of 1980s Britain, it was more likely considered way beyond the pale - especially when that boundary pusher was a fat middle-aged working class northerner, who closed his act with a song.

The real difference, if indeed there was one, is that in looking for comic capital, Manning most often followed that less than honourable working men's club tradition of going for the weakest target, i.e. anyone in a minority. There is a well known routine by the great Irish comedian Dave Allen who, when he died in 2005, was widely acknowledged as the father of stand-up political comedy (even if he did do it sitting down). In it, Allen informs his London audience that he tells Irish jokes and frequently gets in trouble for doing so but: 'Sod it! If you can't laugh at yourself, what's the point?' A quick burst of applause and he is on his way. 'Two paddies leave Dublin to find work in London. The collective IQ of Dublin halves overnight.' A big laugh. 'When the two get there, the IQ of London doubles overnight.' A not so big laugh. 'Hey, I thought we'd agreed that you're supposed to be able to laugh at yourself?' With Manning, the situation was more clear cut. If you couldn't take a joke, you shouldn't be in the building. To use his own words: 'A joke is a joke. Them that realise it's just a joke laugh. Them that don't, fuck 'em.' If the accusation that he made no effort to understand cultures other than his own had more than a ring of truth, could it not be said that those who were insulted in 'other cultures' made no attempt to understand his?

Bernard Manning's life and times were very well captured in a 2004 Channel Five documentary in the *Bad Boys of Comedy* strand, narrated by the *Father Ted* actor Ardal O'Hanlon, and from which the above quote is taken. In it, a sentimental Manning, described as 'the king of the working men's club', was taken on a tour of the Manchester streets in which he grew up and in which a monument to his reign there remains, his very own Embassy Club. Rare is the north of England amateur sportsman or

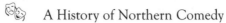

stag night guest who has not once been herded through those doors in nervous anticipation. Inside, Manning was in his element, king of his very own jungle. In his hands, the most vociferous drunken heckler was about as formidable as the dampest beer mat.

Born in Ancoats in 1930, in common with most of his neighbours, Manning's early years were marked by struggle. 'There used to be six of us in a bed,' he told his Channel Five documentarists, while standing outside his family's former Faulkener Street home in Blackley. 'Five used to piss themselves, so I learned to swim.' His upbringing did, however, spark a lifelong devotion to his mother which lasted until her death, aged 95. For his National Service, Manning spent two years stationed in Berlin where, among other duties, he was given the task of guarding Nazi war criminal Rudolph Hess. In the evenings, Manning crooned in bars and nightclubs, developing a talent that would prove useful and a less controversial bedfellow to his comedy routines over the years ahead. Returning to Manchester in 1952, the wannabe entertainer lined up a job as compere at the locally well-known northern Sporting Club, a home of wrestling, boxing and 'big-time' cabaret. He took to the role instinctively and, in 1959, persuaded his greengrocer father to flog the family shop and renovate the old billiard hall among the red-bricked terrace houses over the road. Thus did the Embassy Club come into existence, billed as 'World Famous' on the sign outside - evidence of the salesman in his genes - and a continued source of family employment for the likes of wife Vera and, eventually, a son, imaginatively christened Bernard.

Not that this archetypal northern 'self-made man' didn't range further afield when required, because he did. Manning had no problem juggling Embassy commitments with appearances far and wide, attracting the attentions of Johnnie Hamp in 1971 as he did so. On *The Comedians* and in the *Wheeltappers* he was always on his best behaviour, sticking to the script and only rarely throwing in the odd blue gag, knowing full well that it would be ditched in the editing. Elsewhere, though, Manning was more inclined to give his more controversial side free reign. And with every new comedic 'outrage' it grew increasingly obvious that a glittering future in TV comedy would always be beyond him. For producers other than Hamp, he was simply too hot to handle and an hour-long show, *Bernard Manning*, made for Granada in 1980, was his one and only solo television outing.

He was, however, still apt to pop up on the odd chat show, frequently trailing disaster in his wake. His 1977 appearance on the Saturday night institution that was *Parkinson*, for example, provided more than a hint of why television executives were apt to come over all dizzy at the mere mention of his name. After casually remarking that during a recent gig in Bradford he had felt like 'a spot on a domino', Manning was immediately rounded upon by a fellow guest, the *That's Life* presenter Esther Rantzen, who asked him: 'Why are all your jokes based on hate?' Never one to back away from a verbal tussle, Manning proceeded to shoot his unfortunate if gallant critic down in flames. 'There's no malice in me,' he countered, to the obvious approval of the studio audience. 'I believe that Jews, Christians, Methodists, everybody, should get together and (perfectly-timed pause) fight the Pakistanis.'

And there you have Bernard Manning in a nutshell. Do you give in to your baser instincts and laugh? Or do you follow your better instincts and shake your head sorrowfully in disapproval? For, make no mistake, if there was an ounce of racism in your body, then Manning was primed to find it. In that way, an old reactionary though he undoubtedly was, his was also a challenging style of comedy indeed; as uncomfortable for the hip young audiences of the 1980s and 'nineties, as their own, often outright polemic humour was to an older generation.

Furthermore, away from the stage, this apparent curmudgeon of a man might have come over as almost cuddly, if it wasn't for the way in which he appeared to lounge around in his out-sized white (of *course* they were white) Y-fronts all day. He was a lifelong supporter of any number of charities and a family man about whom no one in his immediate circle ever had a bad word to say. When contributing to a discussion in BBC Radio 4's *Great Lives* series in 2002, in support of Mother Teresa of Calcutta, he revealed that he prayed every day . 'A lady like Mother Teresa brings you nearer to religion,' he told the presenter, Francine Stock. 'What a wonderful person. All she had is what she stood up in - a bundle of rags. Holding children with all sorts of diseases, and loving them and kissing them - that's my kind of person.' Mind you, he also found time to squeeze in a defence of Adolf Hitler's economic abilities too: 'There were eight million unemployed in Germany when [Hitler] took over and he put them on their feet,' he said. 'That's not to say he didn't go the wrong way and went a bit potty at the end.' In so many ways, Bernard Manning was every northern working class enigma rolled into one.

Fellow Mancunian and *Royle Family* co-creator Caroline Aherne once described the BBC's supposedly groundbreaking Asian sketch show *Goodness Gracious Me* as being like Bernard Manning 'but without the timing'. It was in her 1998 guise as the elderly talk show host Mrs. Merton, however, that she came closer than most to revealing what really made Manning tick. As Mrs. Merton, Aherne admitted that while she and her audience of bussed in O.A.P.s wanted to like Bernard, they really did, they would like him a whole lot more if he would just stop being racist. Ever one to slam his own escape hatch shut, Manning obstinately refused to relinquish his ground. 'Are you racist?' Mrs. Merton goaded him directly. 'Yes,' he eventually admitted, backed into a corner of his very own making. Was that true? Or was he simply a 'bully' who refused to be bullied? At least someone was able to appreciate the essential silliness of the situation. Aherne's *Fast Show* colleague John Thomson, for instance, had long before developed a satirical character called Bernard Right-On. 'How many Pakistanis can you get in a taxi?' he would ask his audience. 'Four. And possibly a small child.'

Along with many Variety comedians, Bernard Manning had always harboured a love of the glitz and glamour of American showbiz, with Al Jolson and the great W.C. Fields cited as personal heroes. It should come as no surprise then that riding high on the success of *The Comedians* and *Wheeltappers* he decided to try his hand in Las Vegas. While Manning is fond of describing this period of his life in glowing terms, implying that he took the place by storm, if that 2004 Channel Five documentary is to be believed the level of success was rather more modest, as suggested by the size of the venues he played. Nevertheless, he did get to borrow Dean Martin's dressing room, a luxury of which he took full advantage: 'I had a slash in the sink'. Dubious toilet habits notwithstanding, Manning was invited back to Vegas but, characteristically, soon returned to the grim and gritty streets he knew best. For Bernard Manning, 'My Kind Of Town' was Manchester, not Chicago.

And, over the coming decades, it was in Manchester that he largely stayed, sometimes safely cocooned from the upheavals in social attitudes outside his familiar walls and at other times confronting it all head on, as in his notorious 45-second appearance on the opening night of Factory Records' Hacienda nightclub in 1982. On one particularly dramatic day - Friday 13th oddly enough - the Embassy Club burnt to the ground. When quizzed on how the fire had coincided with the venue's recent decline in popularity, Manning again resorted to his time-honoured technique of deploying a less-than-tasteful gag: 'Colonel Gadafi phoned and said, "sorry Bernard, wrong Embassy".' Whatever, the venue was soon back on its feet and when, in the 1990s, an ITV *World In Action* undercover investigator taped Manning entertaining a group of off-duty policemen there with distinctly off-colour jokes, its owner had the dubious distinction of becoming the first ever comedian to be criticised by a Prime Minister (John Major) in the House of Commons.

Before his death in 2007, aged 76, Bernard Manning was still insisting in countless newspaper and magazine articles that comedy's only job is to produce laughter, however that may be brought about. And, when he stuck to self-deprecation, it was a tempting philosophy: 'I could never be gay,' he once admitted. 'What? And be turned down by men as well as women?' Yet where Manning and comedians like him continually miss the point is in their insistence that it is fine to be as nasty as you like, so long as the majority of people in the room are having a good time.

Yet, for better or worse, when Bernard Manning was in the room, most of the predominantly white people there *did* have a good time. And at least, in 2003, he had enough sense to refuse an appearance at a British National Party rally, apparently agreed to by Manning's agent without his prior knowledge. After a lifetime of being accused of anti-semitism, in his self-penned obituary published shortly after his death in *The Daily Mail*, Manning also claimed to be descended from Jewish immigrants. A genuinely shocking development indeed from a man who had once 'joked': 'Don't mention Auschwitz to me, I lost a relative there. My uncle. He fell out of the machine gun tower.'

11

The Quality of Mersey

"Jimmy Tarbuck doesn't tell jokes, he just refreshes your memory."
- *Bernard Manning*

The 1970s: a decade of industrial unrest, economic instability, massive unemployment, three day weeks and soul-destroying three-star jumpers. The old social certainties creak, wobble and topple over. Post-war political consensus has reached a dead end. The revolutionary 1960s have fatally undermined automatic respect for Members of Parliament and other non-elected figures of authority. A mood of hopelessness blankets the nation, grey and grim, like a shroud over the bleakest of futures.

Yet switch on the telly, and you would think that we had never had it so good. For this was British television comedy's supposed 'Golden Age'.

When, during the miners' strike of 1973, the Government closed down all television services at 10.30pm as a means, they said, of saving electricity, cynics saw it as an attempt to further depress the population and bring an already volatile situation to a head. And for sure, like Marx's opium of the people, by now television had risen swiftly to feed a quasi-religious addiction in society. Families gathered around it, sat and kneeled before it, looked to it for sermons and stories, placed it on a pedestal and quite often viewed their own lives through the prism of that screen. And yet, in the field of light entertainment anyway, the depressing realities of everyday life were scarcely reflected back.

Structurally, there has never been such a period of calm in television broadcasting. From the arrival of BBC2 in 1964 (reaching the north in 1965) to the birth of Channel 4 some eighteen years later, three channels were your lot. In the geographical arena of ITV franchises, the three that were created in 1968 - Yorkshire Television, Thames Television and Harlech Television (HTV) - would be the last until the next round of franchises in 1982 brought forth Central Television, Television South (TVS), Television South West (TSW) and the new national breakfast time service TV-am. While the colour television sets invented in the late 1960s became more affordable and therefore increasingly prevalent as the new decade progressed, the only other technological advance of any note was the launch of ITV's teletext service Oracle in 1974, soon to be joined by the BBC's own Ceefax. Viewing figures too were steady away, as both companies enjoyed something approaching a fifty-fifty share.

That this stability should be echoed in the output itself, then, ought not to be so surprising. On the down side, such a cosy state of affairs was always likely to breed a fair degree of creative complacency. On the up side, this *was* a period in which time and funding were seldom in short supply, resulting in a sizeable percentage of TV comedy's funniest and most resonant moments ever being produced.

Without doubt, television comedy viewing figures have never reached such gigantic proportions, before or since. Partly, of course, that was down to simple lack of choice. For every British comedy classic like *Dad's Army*, *The Morecambe And Wise Show* and *Fawlty Towers*, there were at least ten others which really did not have to be all that wonderful to enjoy a reach the like of which today's shows can only dream.

Furthermore, it is fair to say that the vast majority of the very best stuff was produced by the BBC. On ITV, meanwhile, cheap and cheerful Variety shows in the manner of *Sunday Night At The London Palladium* continued to be more the thing, staffed by veterans like Ted Ray, Dickie Henderson and Arthur Askey. And if ITV's dependence on that more traditional format did nothing else, it provided high-profile employment for a never less than abundant stream of gag-crackers reared on the banks of the river Mersey.

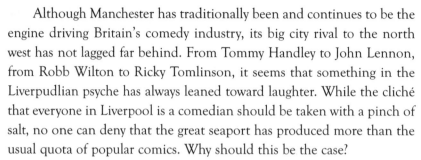

Although Manchester has traditionally been and continues to be the engine driving Britain's comedy industry, its big city rival to the north west has not lagged far behind. From Tommy Handley to John Lennon, from Robb Wilton to Ricky Tomlinson, it seems that something in the Liverpudlian psyche has always leaned toward laughter. While the cliché that everyone in Liverpool is a comedian should be taken with a pinch of salt, no one can deny that the great seaport has produced more than the usual quota of popular comics. Why should this be the case?

Is it because life in Liverpool is so much more terrible than anywhere else? At one time, quite possibly, but hardly any longer. Is it because that wry Scouse accent is just naturally amusing? Well, maybe today, although going back in time, both Hanley and Askey were forced to disguise that very same twang in order to gain national acceptance. Arthur Askey, in fact, tried to include references to his home city as long ago as the 1920s but was explicitly warned off doing so. More likely, Liverpool's humourous streak is mainly the result of it being such a heavily working class city. That does not quite account for its comedy's more stridently cocky and decidedly non-northern feel however.

Interestingly, as Stuart Maconie points out in his 2007 book, *Pies And Prejudice* (Ebury Press), there are many Liverpudlians who don't even consider that they live in the north at all. 'The opening line of the city's current official guidebook states: "Liverpool is not really the north. Not quite Midlands. Closer to Wales and Ireland. And definitely Atlantic. Or is it just a state of mind?".' Frankly, yes, a state of mind is exactly what it is. Liverpool is clearly part of the north of the England because, well, it's in the north of England, whether its inhabitants like it or not. And yet, to be fair, this feeling of it being somewhere apart does not only come from Liverpudlians. There is a sense in the rest of the country too that the place is maverick, determined to do its own thing.

It's true that, culturally, Liverpool is a law unto itself. Maconie likens it to New York - the city to which it has historically been tied by sea lanes - and there is something in that, not least in the swagger of its citizens. Being a seaport, Liverpool is characterised by a curious combination of cosmopolitanism and insular working class attitudes - manifested here in a brand of self-mythologising sentimentality that is ready to take offence at any slight, intended or otherwise - together with pride in its outsider status. It is a place where a large proportion of the population has, historically, come and gone and come back again, often on a whim. In the past, its place at the pinnacle of world trade gave it an attitude of strutting self-confidence rather than self-deprecation, which its people and institutions have been reluctant to shake off. In so many respects, then, Liverpool is a mini-London, with delusions of grandeur. A place where fashion and a certain type of showy individualism have mingled with community pride. A place, in the 1980s, capable of giving birth to Labour's flash, abrasive and suit-wearing Militant Tendency.

And then there is that competitive relationship with Manchester, its equally irascible but considerably less sensitive neighbour up the road. Owing to a glorious past, in which Liverpool usurped Manchester as the second most important city in the country before the Manchester Ship Canal came along in the late 1880s, not to mention both cities' huge contributions to the worlds of popular music and football, it is a rivalry that continues to bubble along nicely. If Manchester is going to be hailed as the capital of the north, then Liverpool would rather not play at all.

Asked for the Godfather of Liverpool comics, certainly throughout the 1970s and '80s, few would fail to nominate Jimmy Tarbuck. If at one point in his *Kings Of Comedy* reality show, Stan Boardman admitted wistfully: 'I see fun in tragedy', then the archetypal nine-iron swinging light entertainer 'Tarby' sidestepped all that with a cool and confident persona that glittered brighter than any shipyard picket line brazier.

Born the son of a bookie in 1940, the gap-toothed Tarbuck set his heart on a life as a performer from the outset and had already toured with a rock 'n' roll show and donned a Butlins redcoat when he was spotted as a 22-year-old by Val Parnell. That stroke of good fortune led to a TV debut on *Comedy Bandbox* and explains how Tarbuck, despite having made one of the earliest appearances at Bernard Manning's Embassy Club, managed to bypass the grittier slog of the working men's clubs. It also helps explain why, by the time George Roper, Jim Bowen, Duggie Brown and Co. were getting their first big break on *The Comedians*, his own star had long since left that particular firmament.

Tarbuck's major TV spurs were earned on Parnell's *Sunday Night At The London Palladium*, on which he was a regular guest in the early 1960s. Those eye-catching successes culminated in him stepping into the shoes

of Tommy Trinder, Dickie Henderson, Bruce Forsyth, Don Arrol and Norman Vaughan, by being given the resident compere's job in September 1965. Thus began a lengthy association with that long-term favourite and others like it, culminating in the *Live From Her Majesty's*, *Live From The Piccadilly* and *Live From The London Palladium* triumvirate that dominated ITV's Variety schedule throughout the 1980s.

His first solo television outing, however, came just over a year after his Palladium debut in 1964. *It's Tarbuck!* was a mix of sketches and stand-up produced for ATV, and also featured Ronnie Corbett, future *Coronation Street* star Amanda Barrie and a couple of Benny Hill stooges, Bob Todd and Henry McGee. Despite only running to six shows, the idea was nevertheless twice resurrected in 1970 and 1973, only this time with Tarbuck's long-time London-born stage collaborator, the versatile song and dance man Kenny Lynch in tow. A former pupil at the same school as John Lennon, Tarbuck has openly admitted that the parallel rise to prominence of the Beatles helped both his own career and that of fellow Liverpudlian contemporaries no end. 'The Beatles really put Liverpool on the map, and I was known as the fifth Beatle,' he told the local *Farnham Herald* newspaper, while promoting a show at Aldershot's Princes Hall in May 2003. 'It certainly didn't hurt to come from the area at the time. It started this crazy roundabout and I fell into it along with others like Cilla Black.'

In 1966, it was back to more familiar territory as compere of *Tarbuck At The Prince Of Wales*, again for ATV. Then came a rare dabble in sitcom. After Tarbuck appeared in an Easter 1967 *Till Death Us Do Part* special, writer Johnny Speight came up with a BBC *Comedy Playhouse* pilot for him, *To Lucifer - A Son*, in which he was son Nick to John Le Mesurier's Lucifer, a laconic (what else) Satan, thoroughly hacked off with Hell and bedevilled by the antics of his trendy offspring, who is busily intent on modernising the underworld. A premonition of New Labour if ever there was one. Maybe Tony Blair's future father-in-law Tony Booth had given Speight a tip-off.

For Tarby, however, his situation comedy career was to be brief. Henceforth, his credits read like a game of Variety broadcasting ping-pong, ITV one year, the BBC the next. In 1967, he returned to ATV and made, appropriately enough, *Tarbuck's Back*, another mix of stand-up, sketches and guest stars, this time alongside the Variety veteran Audrey Jeans, whose tragic destiny was to be killed by a hit-and-run driver in Paris, during her second honeymoon. Then it was back to the other side and *The Jimmy Tarbuck Show*, as part of BBC2's *Show Of The Week* strand, before a return to ATV with a show of the very same title in 1968.

Slightly more imaginative and entirely in keeping with the casual sexism of the era was Tarbuck's next solo project on BBC1, *Tarbuck's Luck*. The good fortune in question referred to how, each week, he would have a different female guest star by his side. Over seven episodes in 1970, those guests included, Joan Sims, Patricia Hayes, June Whitfield, Sheila Steafel, Miriam Karlin and Yootha Joyce. In 1973, it was back to ITV and *Tell Tarby*, in which he and his guests would focus on a single topic, for example the NHS, sex and the good old days (which, for some of us, amounts to pretty much the same thing - boom, tish). Also that year, Tarbuck made a one-off burlesque for the BBC called *The Tarbuck Follies*, set in a modern-day music hall and, from 1974, two series of another *Jimmy Tarbuck Show*, written by Dick Hills and Mike Craig, on ITV. Tarbuck's next ATV vehicle, *Tarbuck - And All That!*, in 1975, was written by the wonderfully gifted Liverpudlian writer Eddie Braben, of whom more later. That show featured early appearances by rising Liverpool-born actor Alison Steadman but, despite his and her best efforts, *Tarbuck - And All That!* failed to make much of a splash and, for Tarby, that was just about it in sketch-based TV comedy for almost a decade. There were, of course, his continued one-off Variety appearances and he also enjoyed a spell as a game show host, most notably in Yorkshire TVs long-running *Winner Take All*. But by the time Tarbuck returned to headline his own London Weekend Television series *Tarby And Friends* in 1984, old-style Variety comedy was yesterday's news.

Like many of his comedy colleagues, the rise of the alternative set had seen Jimmy Tarbuck cast into the unfashionable margins of celebrity golf tournaments and after-dinner speaking. All things, however, must pass. And, in the mid-1990s, like Frankie Howerd and others before him, he suddenly found himself 'rediscovered'. An LWT *Audience With...* special, screened in 1994, got the ball rolling, in which Tarby benefitted no end from the show's frequent cutaways to a celebrity-packed studio audience, among whom was modern day comedy Godfather Billy

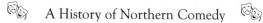

Connolly. Tarbuck's 1995 late-night chat show, *Tarbuck Late*, was shown only in the Granada and LWT areas however and, in any case, its potential was somewhat thwarted by the fact that every guest seemed to be one of the host's best mates. At least that's how they were introduced.

Not that everyone in hometown Liverpool felt quite so chummy. In his 2003 autobiography *Ricky* (Time Warner Books), for example, the future *Royle Family* member Ricky Tomlinson - a firebrand socialist to Tarbuck's Thatcherite Conservative - berates Tarbuck and Cilla Black, in particular, for 'not feeling as passionate about their roots' as he does, adding that: 'Some celebrities can't wait to get out of Liverpool or become "professional Scousers" trading on the accent and humour, but living elsewhere.' That's fine, he continues: 'People can live where they like... but it would be nice if some of the successful ones remembered where they came from and visited once in a while to do a charity gig, especially when you consider the tough time that Liverpool has had over the past twenty-five years.' He concludes: 'Maybe they got past Birmingham and simply lost their way.'

And a further indication of what Tarbuck, and others like him, were up against can be found in the following quote from Mark Steel's 1997 book, *Its Not A Runner Bean* (The Do-Not Press). In it, Steel, an ostentatiously clever Londoner of alternative comedy stock, described by one *Guardian* reviewer as 'the funniest Marxist since Groucho', muses: '...there's nothing more flattering than being invited to something you would never take part in on principle. For example I'm extremely proud of an invitation I received to be in the audience for *An Audience With... Jimmy Tarbuck*. Tarbuck is the latest in a line of buffoons who saw the way the wind was blowing towards comedians like Eddie Izzard and Jo Brand. These types of performers have been attracting a young mainstream audience, which the likes of Tarbuck must tap into if they're to remain stars. So they're desperately trying to re-invent themselves with a kitsch image by surrounding themselves with younger comics. The only stand to take was not to go. But on the other hand I'd have been well fucked off if someone I knew had got an invitation and I hadn't.' Which perhaps explains the empty seat somewhere to the left of Billy Connolly.

No one, however, friend or foe, could fail to acknowledge Jimmy Tarbuck's longevity. And if his reputation has been more marked by respect than fondness, that is at least partly because, like gag merchants everywhere, he has operated almost entirely behind other people's words. Not only are British comedians today and northern comics right back to music hall expected to say amusing things, it should at least *appear* as if they have written or thought of those amusing things themselves. In the public heart, obvious affectation rarely - if ever - equals affection. Nor was Jimmy your endearing northern archetype. Slick as you like, he knew that his comedy was an act and his audience knew it too. It is somewhat ironic, therefore, that on the night of Tommy Cooper's very public demise on stage at Her Majesty's Theatre in 1984, Tarby was hosting the show. That he handled the unfolding tragedy with total calm and dignity, despite the trauma of witnessing the death of a man who he always described as a personal hero, was admirable indeed. The ultimate pro', Tarbuck stayed behind the mask and managed a terrible situation with aplomb.

Nor should it be overlooked that Jimmy Tarbuck gave the comedy world a lovely daughter. Born around the time of her father's first London Palladium appearances in 1964, Liza Tarbuck went on to be a RADA-trained actor and a funny and talented performer in her own right. For her, a certain down-to-earth northern persona has very much been the order of the day and, since making her TV debut on the Liverpool-based sitcom *Watching* in the 1980s, she has added a number of impressive credits to her list - including a role as the eponymous *Linda Green* in the comedy drama of that name (in which her Jimmy made a cameo appearance in 2001), and a part alongside Ricky Gervais in *Extras* (2006), in which she 'starred' in 'When The Whistle Blows', a simple-minded, catchphrase-driven northern sitcom within its - of course- more knowing and wise London-based sitcom parent.

Were it not for the fact that it's Arthur, 'Variety' might well be Ken Dodd's middle name. A throwback to music hall's barmier days, 'Doddy', a.k.a. the Professor of Giggleology and Master of Applied Tickleology at Knotty Ash University, is also a one-man warning against generalisation. Far from being a typical Liverpool stand-up, his in-your-face flamboyance hardly marks him down as your traditional northern comedian either.

True, his rat-a-tat machine gun delivery may put him among the gag merchants rather than the character-driven comics. But that would be to ignore his distinctly 'feminine' side and be less than half the story. And where it could rightly be argued that, like all the great northern comics, his eccentric on-stage persona is his greatest comedic creation, ostentatiously clever wordplay has always been Dodd's thing; he is, remember, a self-styled professor. In short, with his tickling stick permanently set to erect, electric shock of a hair-do, unruly teeth and talk of jam butty mines, Ken Dodd walks alone and yet does *not* walk alone - just like the city of his birth. Still performing to sell-out crowds at the time of writing, Doddy might well be the last of the great stage clowns.

It can come as a surprise to those who know little of the area to discover that a place called Knotty Ash actually exists, albeit in a way less extraordinary than that portrayed by Dodd. Nevertheless, it is in this otherwise unremarkable Liverpudlian suburb that Dodd has spent just about his entire life. Indeed, he still lives in the same farmhouse in which he was born, the son of a coalman, in 1927 and where he used to perform Punch and Judy puppet shows in the backyard. Furthermore, the oddly-named Knotty Ash seems to have sparked a lifelong love of wordplay in young Kenneth and may also have tickled his formative mind in the direction of how humour can often reside in the gap between description and reality. One of his earliest alter-egos was one Professor Yaffle Chuckabutty, Operatic Tenor and Sausage Knotter, whose chief talent lay in funny renditions of famous contemporary songs.

Verbal invention and a penchant for crooning would be integral parts of the Doddy armoury. Nor, in the musical arena and in the best traditions of Victorian melodrama, has he been averse to indulging in a spot of melancholic mezzo-tenor warbling as a means of manipulating his audience's emotions. Tears of sadness; tears of mirth; it's all as one to Ken Dodd. In a highly successful recording career that ran parallel to his comedy throughout the 1960s and early '70s, his biggest hit was also suitably lachrymose. 'Tears' spent five weeks at number one and became the biggest selling pop single of 1965.

Now over 80 years old, Ken Dodd's touring *Happiness Show* has achieved legendary status, not only for the highly-individual brand of cheeky double-entendre - 'What a lovely day, what a lovely day for putting on a kilt, standing on your head outside the town hall and shouting: "How's that for a shuttlecock?"' - but also for a longevity every bit as impressive as his career itself. He may have an off-stage reputation for thriftiness but, where his and his audience's time is concerned, there is no doubting his generosity. Dodd will not leave the stage until he is good and ready, usually a couple of hours after the last bus home, five-plus hours after kick-off. And here again we find a competitive instinct more obviously at home in southern comedy - or maybe it's just that he likes a good natter! Doddy's audiences are battered into submission, if necessary with a big bass drum if he notices anyone nodding off. His public are dragged this way and that on waves of hilarity that only break with his trademark sign-off: 'Tatty bye, everybody! Tatty bye!', just as the milkmen are pulling on their trousers. The humour, with its references to Morris Minors, Vera Lynn and ham teas may be essentially nostalgic and escapist, but it is also essentially wicked too and you are going nowhere. As he himself has said, the Ken Dodd live show is: '...a feast of fun and a challenge to the kidneys.'

After swapping the life of a struggling door-to-door salesman for what might have been the equally insecure life of a full-time entertainer in 1954, Ken Dodd's first Blackpool summer season came the following year in *Let's Have Fun*, alongside that other comedian widely held to be careful with his wallet, Jimmy Clitheroe. It was a bill topped by up-and-coming comedy duo Morecambe and Wise and so well did Dodd go that a return visit was booked in 1956, in which he supported Jimmy James. By 1958, Ken Dodd had proved so popular that he was topping his own bill at the Central Pier in a show that also starred Josef Locke. Inevitably, it wasn't long before the talent spotters began circling and appearances at the London Palladium were followed by a break into television.

Thanks to his permanently astonished face, bizarrely unkempt mane and dodgy dentistry - the latter the result of a childhood cycling accident, by all accounts - Dodd and television were made for each other. His first BBC show in 1959, *The Ken Dodd Show*, ran to 35 episodes, including specials, over the following decade. It also co-starred a number of well-known names from comedy and music including, most regularly, Patricia Hayes and Graham Stark. In 1966, one year after BBC2 had used Dodd's show as a commemorative programme marking the extension of that

service into the north of England, Harry H. Corbett and Wilfrid Brambell also appeared, performing a short skit as Steptoe and son.

ITV, meanwhile, had to wait until 1967 before Ken Dodd headlined anything for them, *Doddy's Music Box*, which lasted for 18 episodes over two series. Otherwise, its main legacy was the creation of the nickname 'Diddy David' for Dodd's soon-to-be BBC disc jockey sidekick, David Hamilton. More importantly, both shows were co-written by the Liverpudlian scriptwriter Eddie Braben, whose own lunatic imagination matched that of Ken Dodd's beautifully.

More usually associated with Morecambe and Wise than Ken Dodd, Eddie Braben didn't so much *write* words as paint surreal pictures with them. 'When I was at school,' he had Dodd recall, 'I used to be teacher's pet. I sat in a cage at the back of the class.' Thus was Dodd's bizarre physical appearance echoed in his patter. Braben used spoken language like the best jazz trumpeters use musical notes; in nonsensical riffs that are nevertheless blessed with a certain inner logic, as in this later Eric and Ernie exchange: 'I think I curried her favours.' 'You very nearly casseroled her dumplings!' There was a fair portion of archaic language too - 'I have a long-felt want' - as Braben composed a self-contained world in which his subjects could play to their best advantage. Like the best writers, though, he allowed himself to be guided by the personality of the performer in front of him and, on the long and busy road ahead, would go on to help in the careers of comedians as diverse as Jimmy Tarbuck, Ant and Dec, Ronnie Corbett, Little and Large and Jim Davidson.

Eddie Braben's own northern working class background in Dingle left him with a distinct love of one comedian in particular, Dave Morris. Morris, it seems, provided a beacon of light for the aspiring writer as he scrawled jokes on brown paper bags while unhappily running a fruit and veg stall bought by his father, a butcher, in hometown Liverpool. 'He was very, very underrated, Dave Morris,' Braben told Graham McCann, author of the definitive Morecambe and Wise biography, *Morecambe & Wise* (Fourth Estate, 1998). 'Talk about being surreal - this man was surreal before most people knew what surreal was.' Braben goes on to recall an episode of *Club Night* in which the big mouth played by Morris tells his open-mouthed co-stars that they are looking at 'the greatest barrister that ever lived'. Braben: '...he'd say, "I defended Crippen! I got him off the murder charge, but they hung him for having his chimney on fire." They said, "Hung 'im?" and Dave said, "Yes, but I did appeal, but I lost the appeal - and just for spite they hung him again the following Friday!" I mean, that, to me, is brilliant. I loved that. I'd place him at least level with Jimmy James, because his humour was quite incredible. He was long, long before his time because most people didn't know what he was talking about.'

Braben knew what Morris was talking about. After the apparently obligatory, in Liverpool, unsuccessful football trial at Anfield, his first professional joke was bought by Charlie Chester. Emboldened, he then flogged the market stall for £100 and began a thirteen-year stint with Ken Dodd that took in stage, radio and television screen, including a record-breaking run at the Palladium. In their time together, an unconventional approach to comedy was not the only thing Braben shared with Dodd, whose scatterbrained persona belies an ironclad self-discipline that still sees him taking notes after each live performance on every single facet of his performance. 'When I was working with Ken, we used to aim for at least four gags a minute,' Braben tells McCann.

While years of tattyfilarious television appearances undoubtedly turned Ken Dodd into a household name, there is a feeling rare among modern-day comedians - although maybe Eddie Izzard is another - that he would still have enjoyed long-standing fame without it. Despite the fact that he once 'owned' his very own TV channel DDT (Doddy's Different Television), Doddy has always been best enjoyed live. Seeped in Variety history, he is fully aware of his own place within that tradition - 'It's an honour to play here tonight on this very special anniversary,' he tells his audiences in the Gods. 'It's one hundred years to the night since that balcony collapsed.' And there is more than an end-of-the-pier whiff about his constant companions, the Diddymen, originally there to entertain the kids, and willing workers at those aforementioned jam butty mines and gravy wells of Knotty Ash.

Whether as puppets, cartoon characters or, on stage, children in costume, Dickie Mint, Mick the Marmalizer, the Hon. Nigel Ponsonby-Smallpiece, Hamish McDiddy and Co. have seldom been far from their creator's side. In more recent years, however, it is their leader, Dickie, who is most often seen, in his occasional role as a ventriloquist's dummy.

In that particular part of the act, music hall melancholy is once again to the fore. The doll is a substitute for a son the ventriloquist never had, in a mournful musical duet that offers more than a nod towards Ken Dodd's own, often troubled, private life.

There is a revealing *Mail On Sunday* article written by the journalist Robert Chalmers in 2001, in which a then 73-year-old Dodd is tracked down on a punishing national tour of towns like Skegness, Eastbourne, Worthing and the down-at-heel resort once so favoured by Tommy Handley, New Brighton. In it, Chalmers finally manufactures a meeting with his comedy hero - 'a genius' - at the Whitley Bay Playhouse. It is soon obvious that after years of being in the public eye for the wrong reasons as well as the right ones, Ken Dodd has little love for the fourth estate. The death from cancer of his long-standing fiancée of 24 years Anita Boutin in 1977 and, more latterly, his 1989 trial for income tax fraud, during which it was alleged that the comedian had cash stashed away off-shore and in every conceivable hiding place, being foremost among the targets of, at times, quite cruel headline writers. To his credit, Chalmers does not let his subject's caginess get in the way of his own impartiality in a piece - still freely available online - that offers a fascinating, good-humoured and appropriately sentimental insight into the mind of this most singular of entertainers.

Well into the third decade of another unmarried relationship with current partner Anne Jones, Dodd continues to pepper his act with gags relating to those dark days at Liverpool Crown Court: 'I didn't owe the Inland Revenue a penny - I lived near the seaside!', being one such. This, though, is more likely to be good old-fashioned northern self-deprecation than anything else. For the record, Dodd won a full acquittal, albeit one with a sting in the tail. Along with the indignity of having the innermost details of his private life splashed all over the front pages, a huge bill for unpaid taxes and penalties rendered him virtually bankrupt.

More happily, he still had his comedy to fall back upon. And though he kept Chalmers at bay during their MoS interview like a lion-tamer in Blackpool Tower Circus, what he could not stop himself doing was holding forth on his beloved comedy craft itself. Most obviously he is unstinting in his praise of the great Variety comedians that went before, people like Handley, Robb Wilton and Frank Randle. 'If I could say I walked in their footsteps... I would be very proud. I think they left me to switch the light off. I am the last one. They've all gone. Frank Randle, Norman Evans. Max Miller. They're my heroes. They're my boys.'

When Chalmers tells him of a recent conversation with Johnny Vegas, in which the St. Helens new boy declared himself a huge fan and expressed astonishment at Dodd's capacity for physical endurance, the man himself laughs and reminds his interviewer that he holds the record for the longest ever run at the London Palladium, referred to earlier in relation to Eddie Braben: 'Forty-two weeks. Twice nightly, three times on a Saturday.' Besides, it seems, old age has given his act a new lease of life and opened up an entirely new jam butty mine of mirth: 'What do they give us on television? Frank Windsor appears saying "Have you paid for your funeral? Crack now, or we'll send you off in a bin bag".'

It would be nice to conclude here by revealing that, these days, Ken Dodd is putting his well-travelled feet up and taking it easy in a luxurious Knotty Ash retirement home, reflecting on a life packed with such awards as an OBE for services to showbiz and charity in 1982, a freemanship of Liverpool in 2001 and the beating of John Lennon and Paul McCartney into second and third place respectively in the 'Greatest Merseysider' awards of 2003. That, however, is never likely to be. In Doddy, the need to perform and make money is just too ingrained.

With his tax traumas behind him, in 1990 Ken Dodd made a triumphant one-off return to primetime television with a Christmas Day *Ken Dodd At The London Palladium* show for Thames. It followed an appearance alongside the bright young things of *Comic Relief* on the BBC charity telethon of the previous year, as he too won new-found trendiness. In 1994, Doddy became the latest in the line of *An Audience With...* hosts, so popular that it led to a five-minute standing ovation in the studio, some of the highest-rating light entertainment viewing figures of all-time and a second such outing in 2002. A more imaginative surprise came in 1996, when Dodd turned to straight-acting and played the role of court jester Yorick in Kenneth Branagh's 1996 film adaptation of *Hamlet*. And those skills were again to the fore in Channel 4's TV dramatisation of *Alice In Wonderland* in 2000, in which he played Mr. Mouse. In fact, Dodd had already made his Shakespearean debut as long ago as 1971, when playing Malvolio in *Twelfth Night* at the Royal Court Theatre, Liverpool. And through it all, the punishing live schedule continued unabated.

Although he ruled on stage and screen, Ken Dodd was far from the only eccentric northern comedian to enjoy huge popularity in the 1970s. The Hull-born comic Norman Collier, for example, was another whose offbeat style marked him out from the crowd.

Like Colin Crompton, Collier's first TV break came in Johnny Hackett's 1965 stand-up show *Let's Laugh*, before he became the original 'overnight success' after a show-stopping turn in front of Her Majesty the Queen and Princess Anne, in the 1971 Royal Variety Performance. His astonishing impact then and longevity since is all the more remarkable given that it is built upon one simple premise: a faulty microphone. Nevertheless, so completely did that stop-start routine catch the national imagination that, even today, hapless speakers who experience similar problems are said to be 'doing a Norman Collier'. Actually, come to think of it, to dismiss a long and distinguished career including countless summer seasons, pantomimes and TV Variety shows as one based around 'one simple premise' is unfair. No...m...n Col...r has also b..en kn...wn to dr...ss up as a chicken.

Equally offbeat, but showing a little more in the way of versatility, was the unmistakable Freddie 'Parrot Face' Davies. Despite being born in Brixton, South London, in 1937, Davies was very much raised in the England's north. The grandson of a music hall entertainer, he seems always to have been destined for a career on stage and, after a spell as a holiday camp entertainer, turned professional in 1964. If Davies's route into the business was largely conventional, his act itself was not. Adopting the stage name Samuel Tweet, the comedian's ready supply of corny gags about budgies were delivered to the accompaniment of a procession of lithsping rathspberrith, as in his catchphrase: 'I'm thsick, thsick, thsick up to 'ere.' An ability to contort his looks to resemble a parrot, earned him that celebrated nickname.

Like many who came to prominence in the 'seventies, Freddie Davies's initial burst of fame came courtesy of the BBC's long-running talent show, *Opportunity Knocks*. Together with guest appearances on *It's The Bachelors* and *Val Parnell's Sunday Night At The London Palladium*, winning that show ensured that vast swathes of the population quickly became aware of this most distinctive of comic personalities. With his weird way of talking and distinct physical appearance - bowler hat pulled down to the ears, long overcoat, sad eyes bulging - 'Parrot Face' was a once seen never forgotten play on the traditional concept of the innocent abroad. That was certainly central to Davies's BBC children's sitcom, *The Small World of Samuel Tweet,* in 1974. On stage, Freddie Davies had always been in a world of his own, on television, he was literally so. The fictional village of Chumpton Green was the setting, where our hero found himself among the great and good and working in a pet shop. With tall, skinny Cardew ('the cad') Robinson as Lord Chumpton and a veritable aviary of birds and other animals with which to entertain his young fans, *The Small World of Samuel Tweet* ran for two six-episode series.

For Freddie Davies that might well have been that, give or take a string of popular Variety show guest spots. But then, in 1995, he landed a role in one of the most scandalously under-rated films ever produced. Its name is *Funny Bones* and it also stars the legendary American comic Jerry Lewis, modern-day practitioner of slapstick Lee Evans, Hollywood supporting actor Oliver Platt, and a disparate group of character actors like Oliver Reed, Leslie Caron and Richard Griffiths. An at times bizarre and haunting exploration of what it actually means to be a comedian, *Funny Bones* is set in Blackpool, amid the fag ends of seaside Variety.

Although it is an unmitigated masterpiece, upon its release the film suffered a critical savaging. Yet visually, if for no other reason, the movie is stunning. Director Peter Chelsom, himself a product of that resort and earlier responsible for the more conventional Josef Locke biopic *Hear My Song* (1991), is clearly rooted deep in both subject matter and location. Presumably too challenging for some, *Funny Bones* perhaps also displays how perplexing a northern comedy with obvious intelligence and artistic integrity can be. Certainly, it eschews anything so predictable as regular linear narrative and swings back and forth in time, like two particularly dizzying hours on a Pleasure Beach Big Dipper.

As thought-provoking as it is, *Funny Bones* is also about mood. It is a film made *with* feeling *about* feeling, in which emotion and sense of self are pushed centre stage. Its plot revolves around young American comic Tommy Fawkes (Platt) who, after flopping on his Las Vegas debut, returns to the north of England of his early childhood. Once there he embarks

315

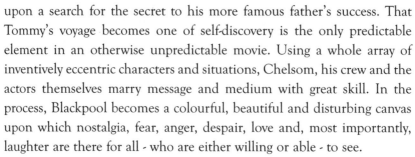

upon a search for the secret to his more famous father's success. That Tommy's voyage becomes one of self-discovery is the only predictable element in an otherwise unpredictable movie. Using a whole array of inventively eccentric characters and situations, Chelsom, his crew and the actors themselves marry message and medium with great skill. In the process, Blackpool becomes a colourful, beautiful and disturbing canvas upon which nostalgia, fear, anger, despair, love and, most importantly, laughter are there for all - who are either willing or able - to see.

Mostly, though, *Funny Bones* is just very, very funny and true. And nowhere - with the possible exception of Peter Kay's *Phoenix Nights* in the late 1990s - has the spellbinding everyday surrealism of Variety speciality acts been better represented. In one painfully amusing audition scene, in particular, we are introduced to characters as varied as 'Backward Talking Man', 'Bagpipe Playing Dwarf', 'Bastard Son of Louis XIV' and 'Plastic Cup Smasher'. And that's without mentioning the bloke who dances with biscuit tins on his feet and the woman with a synchronised barking poodle. Barking being the word.

Freddie Davies was surely born to play Bruno, one half of a once successful brotherly double act whose best routine, it later transpires, was long ago stolen by Tommy's father George (Jerry Lewis). With his 'Parrot Face' gurning days behind him, Davies's on-screen partnership with another entertainer for whom TV Variety was a regular home throughout the 1970s and '80s, the American comedian George Carl, injects just the right half-forgotten note of music hall melancholy into *Funny Bones*. It hints at the relentless tightrope walk of time and the ultimate strangeness of the performing urge itself, as exemplified in the comedy of both men in their prime. Whether it be in the halls, on *The Good Old Days* or alongside Ken Dodd in his one-off BBC stand-up show *Doddy!* in 1982, Carl's silent foolery had long been a sight to behold; once seen never forgotten. His very own speciality act tended to conclude with his clothes, hat, microphone and sundry limbs and digits inextricably entwined. Here, though, the inevitability of dying, both actual and metaphorical, was every bit as prominent as the struggle with life.

These days, Freddie Davies most frequently earns a crust as a straight actor, on stage and screen. In the same year as *Funny Bones* was released, on television he was a suitably bird-like Mr Heron in the well-received drama *All Quiet On The Preston Front*, a role sandwiched between parts in *Heartbeat*, the Rik Mayall light entertainment satire *Mickey Love* (both 1993) and *Hetty Wainthropp Investigates* (1997). More recently, there have been cameos in the BBC sitcoms *My Family* and *Last of the Summer Wine* (appropriately enough as a birdwatcher) and a brief film role as a talking portrait in *Harry Potter And The Prisoner of Azkaban* (2004).

In fact, it seems that whatever else fate had in store for Freddie Davies, somebody somewhere had him marked down as a children's entertainer from the start. Certainly, the childlike appeal of his gormless early persona would at one point see 'Parrot Face' adapted as a cartoon character in the kid's comic *Buster*. A year before *The Small World of Samuel Tweet*, he was a guest on *The Coal Hole Club*, another children's show this time hosted by five more northerners for whom *Opportunity Knocks* had also been a prime mover in turning professional. For the Leeds-based Grumbleweeds, however, their involvement had not been anywhere near as straightforward. In fact, so little did they trouble that show's notorious Clapometer as a musical group, that they resolved instead to turn to comedy and impressions, a decision that, for some of the troupe, continues to pay dividends.

With an original line-up of Maurice Lee, Graham Walker, Robin Colville and brothers Albert and Carl Sutcliffe, the Grumbleweeds also found guest slots in *The Coal Hole Club* for the likes of Stan Stennett and Ken Goodwin, as they finally found fame with the act that they had spent the past ten years flogging on the unforgiving working men's club circuit. Yet after a second series in 1974, this time simply called *Grumbleweeds*, guest appearances on other people's shows became the best they could hope for - on television at least. Radio was another matter. There, the group would find the ideal home for their cheerful, fast-moving and anarchic brand of zany and inoffensive spoofs. Playing and singing their own theme tune, 'We are the Grumbleweeds', they clocked up an impressive ten-year run on BBC Radio 2 from 1979-88, and were named 'Best Radio Show' in the prestigious Television and Radio Industries Awards of 1983 along the way.

Displaying admirable self-awareness and northern chutzpah, when they did make a headlining return to television on ITV in that award-winning year, it was with a Johnnie Hamp-produced Saturday tea-time series called *The Grumbleweeds Radio Show*, which reportedly attracted as many as 11.8 million viewers at one stage. These days, despite performing experience going back to 1962, The Grumbleweeds have to settle for appreciably less interest than that. The group continues, however, to tour the world as a live band, admittedly in truncated form. It was the showbusiness retirement of Albert and Carl Sutcliffe, better known to their fans as the Milky Bar Kid and Wilf 'gasmask' Grimshaw, that led to the demise of the Granada series, by then just *The Grumbleweeds Show*, in 1988. Ten years later, after bearded Bee Gee lookalike Maurice Lee opted to pursue his love of painting, founder-members Walker and Colville - a man who does a better impression of Jimmy Saville than Jimmy Saville himself - continued to perform as a double act. Like Freddie Davies, when not treading the boards these days, the pair can occasionally be found 'thesp'-ing on northern dramas like *Emmerdale* and *Heartbeat*. Most recently, Walker has appeared as a distinctly unsavoury farmer in the *Phoenix Nights* spin-off *Max & Paddy's Road To Nowhere*.

12
Britain's Got Talent

"I saw six men kicking and punching the mother-in-law. My neighbour said: 'Are you going to help?' I said: 'No, six should be enough.'"
- Les Dawson

In the deepest darkest recesses of television history, when Simon Cowell and others like him were still to emerge from their primordial sludge, for entertainers and comedians up and down the land opportunity knocked loudest on television talent shows. And the daddy of them all was indeed *Opportunity Knocks*.

Originally the brainchild of the Canadian radio announcer Carroll Levis, the *Opportunity Knocks* concept first suggested itself when, during a gap in a live programme, Levis invited a boy in the audience on stage to sing a song and fill in time. Later, Levis developed the idea into a highly popular theatrical Variety stage show in which, so he claimed, future stars such as Jimmy Edwards, Max Bygraves and Benny Hill were discovered. Unbeknownst to him, however, another Canadian-born personality had noticed its potential too. In the early 1950s, hosted by Hughie Green, *Opportunity Knocks* made its first broadcast appearance on wireless for the BBC and Radio Luxembourg.

Green's sophisticated blend of transatlantic charm and apparently heartfelt honesty - '...and I mean that most sincerely' - proved ideal for a

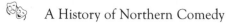

show in which the listeners were intended to be as much a part as the acts themselves. Once he had transferred *Opportunity Knocks* to Thames Television in 1956 (steamrollering Levis's own televisual ambitions in doing so), Green's ingratiating look to camera, one startled eyebrow higher than the other, broke the fourth wall. The relationship between television viewer and presenter was thus personalised - the audience at home were his 'friends'. As time went on, to some, Green's style grew un-nerving, if not smarmy, and easily mimicked, further helping to establish the show in the national consciousness. Even today, impersonators in wind-swept holiday camps are no doubt still trotting out their Hughie Green routines, along with well-worn renditions of Tommy Cooper and Frank Spencer. More recently, Hughie Green has perhaps become better known as the illicit father of 1980-90s youth TV presenter Paula Yates.

Although Green was the dynamo of a show that subsequently ran for over 22 years, the real spark in its engine came from the turns themselves. Each week, after being introduced by a personal sponsor, six acts were unleashed on an eager public who, at the end, would be asked to vote for their preferred winner by post (*Opportunity Knocks*, Thames Television, Teddington Lock, Middlesex). A more immediate sense of gratification was provided by the studio audience, who also had their say courtesy of that device before which the Grumbleweeds tumbled so horribly, the Clapometer. This venerable rather than venereal contraption claimed to gauge audience reaction scientifically, by deciphering the levels of noise generated and representing that auditory response in an on-screen visual graphic. All of which sounds rather more grand than the reality: some bloke backstage rotating a distinctly wobbly arrow by hand, until it reached a point that looked vaguely okay to him.

Each winning act was booked for a return appearance the following week, when they would face five new turns and get the chance to build unstoppable momentum in their quest for glory. As we have already seen, the likes of Ken Goodwin, Frank Carson, Freddie Davies and, later, Stan Boardman and Tom O'Connor found *Opportunity Knocks* the perfect springboard into the big time. Many of the biggest television names of the 'eighties also made their mark on it, including Freddie Starr, Little & Large, Cannon & Ball and The Black Abbots, a comedy revue group along the lines of The Grumbleweeds led by a certain Russ Abbot, soon to embark on a successful solo career of his own. Even for those who lost on the night - such as future sitcom star Su Pollard, famously beaten by a singing dog - an appearance on the show might lead to bigger and better things.

True to its Variety roots *Opportunity Knocks* broke straightforward musical turns too, from pop groups such as The Real Thing, Candlewick Green, Paper Lace, New World and Middle Of The Road, through actual middle of the road acts like The Bachelors, Bobby Crush, the visually-challenged vocal duo Peters and Lee, Mary Hopkin, Millican & Nesbitt, Tony Monopoly and the singing lorry driver Bernie Flint. Caroll Levis's original intention had been to showcase younger talent and, to that end, *Opportunity Knocks* was responsible for making child stars of Lena Zavaroni, Neil 'Mother of Mine' Reid, Grace Kennedy and the six-year-old Bonnie Langford, amongst others. For Hughie Green, though, age was no concern and speciality acts of varying vintage down the years also included west country poet Pam Ayres, Tony 'Muscleman' Holland and the somewhat longer-lasting Middlesbrough-born magician Paul Daniels. No one in that motley list can have been more entertaining than one of *Opportunity Knocks*'s very earliest contestants, the Lancashire cotton mill lass Gladys Brocklehurst, who would grab her husband Norman by the hair in the middle of a song and give him a slap, '...for the fun of it.'

Perhaps inevitably, by the time *Opportunity Knocks* had entered its third decade someone in the Thames corridors of power decided that its format, though obviously worth persevering with, could do with a bit of freshening up. The result was *New Faces*, a new type of talent show completely, in which performers were subjected to a panel of very visible and opinionated media professionals.

In Tony 'the Hatchet' Hatch and record producer Mickie Most, *New Faces* had experts every bit as brutal as today's millionaire Saturday night straight-shooters. In fact, given the otherwise benign nature of 1970s light entertainment generally, the impact of watching a nervous hopeful being torn to shreds by a self-styled showbiz guru was all the more shocking and profound. The same 'it's for their own good, showbusiness is a cut-throat world' line was peddled out, too, with humiliated acts frequently reduced to tears by quite ferocious attacks on their presentation, content and star quality. As a balance to such nastiness, each panel would also feature a couple of 'nice guys', like Ted Ray and Arthur Askey.

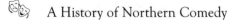

Launched in 1973, the initial series of *New Faces* - no relation to Granada's one-off *Max Bygraves Introduces New Faces* of 1967, which also featured the ubiquitous Grumbleweeds - was hosted by Derek Hobson who, more often than not, provided a friendly shoulder to cry on. Not that everyone needed consolation. In terms of sheer weight of numbers, if *Opportunity Knocks* launched a who's who of British entertainment, then despite being around for a much shorter period of time, *New Faces* isn't all that far behind. Among the comedians it introduced are Mick Miller, Lenny Henry, Jim Davidson (earlier knocked back by Hughie Green for needing 'more practice'), Michael Barrymore, Roy Walker, Les Dennis and a versatile Bury-born comedian/musician, Victoria Wood.

As with *Opportunity Knocks*, the majority of *New Faces* weekly winners were Variety-style turns, musical acts and wannabe child stars such as Showaddywaddy, Gary Wilmot, Aiden J. Harvey, Sweet Sensation, Patti Boulaye and scouse singing sensations, Our Kid. According to several scurrilous sources, ventriloquist Roger de Courcey had to change the name of his talking bear from 'Bollocks' to 'Nookie' after his audition, while nine-year-old chantreusse Malandra Burrows would return to our screens as an adult in the ITV soap opera *Emmerdale*. And then there were The Chuckle Brothers.

As a catchphrase, the Chuckle Brothers' 'to me..., to you...' may not be up there with 'that's another nice mess...', but the influence of Laurel and Hardy's removal men are plain to see and generations of British kids aren't complaining. Real-life brothers Paul and Barry Elliott have been regular tea-time favourites since their first pre-school children's TV show, *Chucklehounds*, was aired by the BBC in 1985. On the plus side, that has ensured a long career for the mustachioed, mullet-haired pair from Rotherham, South Yorkshire, whose first small screen success came with a *New Faces* win over a decade before in 1974. Less positively, it has also relegated them to the pigeon hole marked 'childish', on the face of it a not inaccurate description of their slapstick, seaside-style silliness.

Nearer the truth is that the end-of-the-pier humour championed by the Chuckle Brothers is no longer deemed worthy of grown-up audiences, by London-based commissioning editors at least. As they also proved with their attitude to Freddie 'Parrot Face' Davies and the Grumbleweeds, the modern-day Establishment-educated guardians of the British funny bone equate unpretentious with intellectually inferior. All too often, simplicity - a tough trick to pull off at the best of times - is confused with simple-mindedness, especially when the comedy in question carries echoes of Variety and hails from the north; *viz.* the sneering response to Rowan Atkinson's *Mr. Bean*. In the dog-eat-dog television corridors of England's south, likeability and inoffensive eccentric charm count for little.

The Chuckle Brothers' children's show *Chucklevision*, based upon their own fictitious TV channel, began in 1987. A year later, it was nominated for a Children's BAFTA in the Best Children's Television Series category. And with a reported audience of around three million, there is still no sign of the duo's continued appeal diminishing.

Despite regularly drawing ratings in excess of seven million viewers, *New Faces* reached the end of its original run in 1977. When ITV then decided to relaunch it from the Birmingham Hippodrome with a new host almost a decade later in 1986, it was to another former winner, the stick-thin, ginger-haired Marti Caine, whom the producers turned.

It was an inspired appointment. Caine, a Sheffield-born comic, was by now an established mainstream star in her own right. As the face of the show, she helped the revamped *New Faces* to attract huge audiences once more. And over the three series that followed until 1988, she made a catchphrase of her order to 'Press your buttons.... NOW!'. Although fewer household names were unearthed this time - most likely the result of Variety's dwindling influence on television generally - Caine's own popularity soared. *New Faces* mkII also reclaimed the dubious tradition of talent show unpleasantness by introducing the British viewing public to caustic *Sun* newspaper TV critic, Nina Myskow.

The show, though, remained Marti Caine's. Born Lynne Shepherd in 1945, having embarked upon a career in showbusiness Caine's future contribution to British comedy would be hugely important and too often overlooked. Even in the 1980s, an Englishwoman performing stand-up on television was a rare sight indeed. No wonder so many modern day female comedians point to her as a seminal influence. 'Growing up, the first and only woman I ever saw telling jokes on TV was Marti Caine,' says Jo Caulfield, on her website, www.jocaulfield.com. 'Most women

were comedy actresses or doing character comedy but she was just being herself and saying funny things about her life. She wasn't a foil to a male comic – she was the comic. I think watching her on TV definitely sowed a seed. There were lots of things that I used to find really funny but there are a few things, like seeing Marti Caine, that made me think – "maybe I could do that".'

After her initial success as a *New Faces* contestant, Caine's first major television appearance came alongside fellow winners Victoria Wood, Lenny Henry, Aiden J. Harvey and Trevor Chance in ATV's *The Summer Show* in 1975, intended to be an English version of the legendarily quick-moving and zany American comedy series *Rowan And Martin's Laugh-In*. The next year she had her own series, *Nobody Does It Like Marti*, in which guest stars like Arthur Lowe and Yootha Joyce joined her in performing comedy sketches and songs. The following year, 1977, was to be equally busy with two headlining shows, *Marti* for ATV and *The Marti Caine Show*, a one-off BBC2 special that eventually led to a long-running series which ended in 1984. There were a growing number of guest star slots too, including one alongside Little & Large in their Christmas special filmed in a Big Top in Belle Vue, Manchester, *The Little And Largest Show On Earth*.

In *Marti*, Caine's droll Yorkshire housewife persona was given a glamourous overhaul. Gone were dowdy run-of-the-mill threads and in came glittering spangly dresses with her trademark red locks primped into the stylish cabaret curls that would serve her so well when the *New Faces* producers again came calling. If anything, though, the cosmetic sophistication (and subsequent nose job) only helped to emphasise the warmth of the northern personality within, creating an oddly attractive impression of a rather gawky butterfly finally stretching her wings. As well as a mini-sketch segment of the show that hinted at situation comedy somewhere down the line, *Marti* also led to a six-episode series later the same year and lined its star up alongside another well-known Sheffield club comic, Bobby Knutt. Curly-haired Knutt's appeal, such as it was, lay in his bluff Yorkshire dourness. Certainly, his spell as a co-star in *Marti* was his finest hour although, as a character actor, he has since popped up in tried and tested drama series like *Heartbeat* and those twin northern soap opera giants *Coronation Street* and *Emmerdale*.

Marti Caine's sitcom future duly came to pass in *Hilary*, a two-series effort on the BBC in which, with less than glorious success, she played an absent-minded divorced TV researcher with a 19-year-old son, whose big mouth frequently landed her in trouble. Also in the show, which piloted in 1984 and then ran from 1985-86, was Jack Smethurst of *Love Thy Neighbour* infamy and the animal impersonator Percy Edwards who, throughout the first series, gave voice to Hilary's pet mynah bird, Arthur.

Despite her thespian ambitions, Caine's true appeal was in her interaction with audiences. And when her stint in charge of *New Faces* came to a close, a one-off special, *Marti Caine*, made for ITV in 1989, was recognition of that fact. Her co-star in that stand-up and sketch show was none other than American comedian Joan Rivers, a more than suitable choice given both women's pioneering credentials. Sadly, by the time the programme was broadcast, its British lead was already diagnosed with cancer. Against a backdrop of widespread public admiration and tabloid newspaper interest, Marti Caine battled gallantly on for over five years until the disease finally took her in 1995, around three years after her last television series, *Joker In The Pack*. In that somewhat convoluted offering, over 12 episodes from May to September 1992, she travelled the country urging 'normal' members of the public to tell jokes of their own. Though her death came cruelly early and her final show was hardly a high-water mark, it was nevertheless an appropriate way for this true woman of the people to leave the stage.

Although *Opportunity Knocks* originally ran from 1956 to 1977, as the once alternative comedy scene began to slip into cosy middle age and mainstream was no longer seen as such a dirty word - and doubtless prompted by the success of the reborn *New Faces* - the BBC relaunched and updated that show too in 1987.

For its own host, the Corporation turned to Bob Monkhouse, whose strong pedigree, it was hoped, would invest a brand that had already shown remarkable staying power with even more durability. Despite claims that the Beeb wanted to shake off the ghost of Hughie Green, there was more than a trace of the same overblown sincerity in Monkhouse. Not that it mattered. Its adoption of telephone voting and

biographical introductory film clips helped to make *Bob Says Opportunity Knocks* an immediate hit. Ratings were at a peak of 11.6 million come the 1989 final, after which Monkhouse decided that three series were enough and departed for pastures new. Into his shoes - following the precedent set by ITV with Marti Caine - stepped one of the show's best-loved former winners.

On the face of it - and *what* a face - Les Dawson may appear to have been a traditional bow-tied club comic with a mother-in-law who made married life a misery, but there was far more to him than that. And while his one and only series in charge of *Opportunity Knocks*, in the show's final year of 1990, was hardly a career high-point, the gurning and sardonic, existentially-challenged and surreally daft Dawson had by then more than earned his spurs as one of Britain's funniest-ever comedians. It is a reputation he totally warrants. Even allowing for a brief fall from favour with the 'seventies right-on brigade, only the most lumpen-headed could deny the talent and gargantuan depths of a man from whom a mere glance could draw paroxysms of laughter from a statue of Queen Victoria.

For one thing, there was Dawson's devotion to literary wordplay, a far from typical northern comedy trait in itself, but one built upon the region's surreal traditions and, for him, a survival mechanism in its own right. Then there was his musicianship. In other hands, his out-of-tune piano playing may well have come over as just another Variety-style piece of comedy business; a dodgy Norman Collier microphone, say, or a Jack Douglas twitch. When Dawson mangled those keys, however, the horrors were simply sublime. In his drag double act alongside future *Coronation Street* star Roy Barraclough, there were reverential nods in the direction of Norman Evans. And most of all, behind the sadness and frustration of those saddle-bag doleful eyes, there was more than a genuine glimpse of profundity; a heartfelt recognition of life's essential futility and a gallant determination to make the best of it anyway.

Les Dawson's roots were archetypically, perhaps even stereotypically northern. He was born, in February 1931, into poverty at Collyhurst, North Manchester, to a family for whom cobbled streets, soot-black grimy mills and daily struggle were everyday reality. His was an upbringing in which dreams of a life in showbusiness could hardly be admitted to. The young Les Dawson's world was one of hunger, unemployment, illness and strong women, who held hearth and home together while their menfolk's days and nights were divided between looking for work and taking shelter from their troubles in the local tap room. The Dawson household, like that of their neighbours, was an over-populated two-up, two-down terraced affair. An only child, Les shared that earliest home with his parents, Julia and Les senior, one lot of grandparents and an uncle, Tom. If that sounds like over-population, it was, although it also ensured that what the boy lacked in money and food was more than made up for in family affection. As in all working class communities of the time, folk rubbed against folk, with results both positive and negative; the line was often blurred between being cuddled and smothered. But Les Dawson never forgot where he was from; indeed his entire sense of humour was forged in that childhood of extreme contrasts; part harshness, part kindness. His background would serve him well.

When his father went to serve in the desert with the Eighth Army, Les and his mother spent the Second World War moving from one Manchester suburb to the next. It was a manner of living to which they were already accustomed, on the back of earlier moonlight flits timed to avoid the rent man or some other such financial predator, whenever Mr. Dawson, a builder's labourer, find work, money or both hard to come by. While at school, his son discovered a twin-talent for pulling faces and writing, the former enabling a child who was otherwise something of a social misfit to evoke laughter, the latter being no obvious use whatsoever. Nevertheless, as Mick Middles's book *When You're Smiling* (Chameleon, 1999) reveals, the moment that one of his teachers, Bill Hetherington, read an essay to his class from Dawson's text book, telling them that the pupil he had previously been chastising had 'the talent to be a fine writer', a flame was most definitely lit.

When employment became an issue for the 14-year-old Dawson, his mother pushed him towards what she intended to be a job for life, in the Drapery Department of the local Co-op. Hardly glamourous work, but then glamour did not come into it. Working there would, in later years, guarantee a pension. It paid a reasonable wage for the era and offered regular, reliable and clean work, unlike life on a building site. Despite Dawson's obvious brightness, though, things did not go well. He found the work boring and, one day, even had to fight off attempted rape by a male co-worker. The assailant was belted with a crowbar and the matter thereafter ignored. A departmental switch and equally dreary spell as an apprentice electrician soon followed, before he was whisked away again, this time to National Service in Catterick, North Yorkshire.

Those two years at Catterick proved significant. For all the day to day discomfort he and his fellow squaddies endured there, Dawson's mind was now alerted to the idea that life did not necessarily have to begin and end in Manchester. It awoke in him a taste for travel and adventure. Furthermore, while army life and all its hierarchical absurdities might have been one almighty pain in the neck, they also opened up a whole new way of thinking about human relationships and personal experience. In other words, Les Dawson was developing an ability to stand outside of himself and his surroundings and look in. If he hadn't quite yet worked out how to report the findings, it would only be a matter of time.

With National Service over Dawson returned to his job as a trainee electrician only to be sacked almost immediately. At the instigation of his uncle Tom, a former Manchester street-fighter, he then had a brief and ill-fated stint as a professional boxer. Despite his bulky, broad-shouldered physique, he proved too soft, although the episode might go some way to explaining the oft-repeated claim that his gurning abilities came as a direct result of breaking his jaw in such a bout. Afterwards, to the alarm of his family, he began to drift aimlessly, devoting his time to beer and women, while trying to banish the depression he bore through writing. That, of course, was done in secret. The open admission of such artistic leanings would have invited certain ridicule. Real working class men did not sit in their bedrooms penning stories and poems as Les Dawson did.

Which makes what he chose to do next all the more remarkable. Dejected by a constant flow of rejection slips from magazines unable, as he saw it, to recognise his precocious talent, Dawson took the radical and somewhat exotic option of heading for the Left Bank, Paris. There, he intended to become a fully-fledged professional writer, something in the manner of Ernest Hemingway, F. Scott Fitzgerald or Ezra Pound. In the event, what he actually became was a half-cut professional pianist, albeit one who twinkled the ivories as a diversionary tactic in a brothel, in exchange for a little money and as much vin rouge as he could pour down his ample throat. In contrast to the wine, that piano-playing residency meant that his writing all but dried up. And after four-months as a musical decoy in an empty bar he returned to Manchester and an equally temporary spell as an insurance salesman. At least, that was how Dawson himself described it. A Channel 4 documentary, *Les Dawson's Lost Diaries*, first broadcast in 2004, has subsequently revealed that pretty much the entire Paris episode is a myth. According to the comedian's self-penned accounts at the time, Dawson seems to have spent no more than ten days in the French capital, during which period he played piano in a bar and spent the rest of the time sightseeing.

Whatever the truth, the journey was not wasted. Not at all. For a start, it provided a first, small taste of what it was like to be in showbusiness. It gave Dawson the bug for performing before a live audience, even if that audience did not usually give him a second glance. And, upon his return, it also allowed him to engage in his first bout of self-mythologising. Take his legendary knack for duff piano playing. Was it a happy accident, as Dawson later claimed, coming about as a result of the comedian having had a few too many to drink one night? Or did it, as subsequent biographers have claimed, have its origins in Dawson discovering that if he played the odd jazz note ever so slightly off-kilter to humourous effect, he would suddenly become the centre of attention? Either way, until Paris, playing the joanna had merely been a hobby learned in the family home in the days before television. Now it could win him popularity. Kicking door-to-door insurance into touch, Dawson duly took those musical skills to a local pub where he earned ten bob for three hours' work, before eventually joining up with Manchester's Cotton Pickers' Jazz Band, when that form of music crossed the Atlantic in the Lindy-hopping 1950s. Having established a local reputation as a hopeless dreamer living in a world of his own, Les Dawson had finally hit upon his true path in life.

For a few weeks anyway. For after winning an audition to represent his home town in a talent contest at the Hulme Hippodrome, he suffered the intense humiliation of seeing his rather bizarre act fly completely over his audience's heads, to the extent that its finale was met with almost total silence. Mick Middles sums up that performance thus:

'He walked on-stage dressed as Quasimodo, complete with hump and scary leer. He crouched at a grand piano and proceeded to sing a song that was part off-key and comic, part childlike. He opened the piano lid and extracted a glass of coloured liquid, designed to look like some evil potion. Downing it, he fell into his gurning routine - which at least solicited a few embarrassed titters from the audience - and then crawled into the piano. He emerged from the other side of the piano wearing a ginger wig.'

His parents, who Les had invited along to watch, quickly vanished, with his mother telling him on his arrival home: 'Get in here before any bugger sees you. You are a bloody embarrassment to us.' Devastated, he resolved to turn his back on showbiz. Next stop, a career as a door-to-door hoover salesman.

If it is tempting to see Les Dawson as a comic artist ahead of his time, it is probably also reasonable to speculate that his talent show turn may just have been rubbish. Throughout his early years, he had constant difficulty tailoring his act for the audience to whom he was playing. In the future, such madcap lunacy would be commonplace in the humour of Eric Morecambe, say, and later Vic Reeves and Bob Mortimer, and indeed Dawson himself got plenty of mileage out of such out-and-out silliness as his career progressed. Deep in the industrial heart of England's north west in the 1950s, though, all it got him was bemused looks. When it soon became apparent that he had far too honest a soul to sell Hoovers that people neither needed or wanted, he once again hit the road, this time to London, where somehow - it has never quite been properly explained - he struck up a brief working friendship with the Variety clown par excellence, Max Wall.

It was under Max Wall's influence that Les Dawson began to think of himself as a singer. Possessed of a pleasant bass baritone voice, he impressed the veteran comic to the extent that he paid for him to take singing lessons from a voice trainer in Leeds. Back in London, with little or no money and living above a café in Battersea, a call came through one day from Wall offering his protégé what surely amounted to his big break. A musician's strike at the BBC meant that the usual singer on the bald-pated, loose-limbed one's television show had been forced withdraw;

could Les take his place? Alas, before he could get so far as the rehearsals, the strike ended, the original singer was recalled and Dawson's services were no longer required. Once again the young Mancunian's dreams had been shattered in the most cruel of ways and he was soon on his way back north.

Fortunately, it wasn't long before he again found employment and Dawson's spirits really lifted when he landed a job as a cub reporter on the *Bury Press* newspaper. If he couldn't be an entertainer, at least here was a sphere of work in which he could put his writing skills to good use. Besides, who needed showbusiness when you could have a career as a giant of literary journalism? As usual, things didn't quite turn out as hoped. Sent to cover a local alderman's funeral, the enthusiastic young scribe came back with a flowery account of 'tear-stained pavements' and 'glowering clouds'. His hard-nosed sub-editor was not impressed, declaring his efforts to be: 'a load of crap'. Utterly disillusioned, Dawson realised that a life of nuts and bolts reportage was not for him either. Newspapers working to deadlines value simplicity and a certain tightness of structure. And, in the relentless search for readers, attention-grabbing facts are the most priceless commodity of all. There is neither the time nor space to explore life's deeper complexities, yet it was to this interior aspect of human existence that Les Dawson was most instinctively drawn. There is, of course, more than a chance that his *Bury Press* piece was just pretentious twaddle, from a cub reporter trying too hard and overwriting, as cub reporters keen to stretch creative muscles are apt to do. Words, though, to Les, were ciphers to a level of meaning that lay tantalisingly beneath the surface. And whatever the reality, such a brutal dismissal of his talents left quite a scar, initiating a lifelong distrust of a tabloid press that would hound him horribly in the years ahead but, conversely, also reinforcing a faith in his own abilities as a 'proper' writer.

With his interest in a journalistic career over, it was to the stage that Les Dawson again turned and, more specifically, the northern clubland so well-parodied by Dave Morris and, later, the *Wheeltappers and Shunters* and *Phoenix Nights*. His act, though, was as verbally incontinent as ever and audiences used to quickfire gags from the usual stand-up suspects still didn't know what to make of him. From the point of view of appearance, he did his best to fit in. He wore the traditional garb of dinner jacket and bow tie, was suitably bling-ed in sovereign rings and gold bracelet, with a half-smoked fag never far from a face which he himself described as resembling 'a sack of spanners'. His material, though, was something else entirely. He dealt in clever observational flights of fancy, written and delivered like a true northern poet; each one marked by an attempt to find humour in the most mundane of circumstances and with a twist calculated to bring it all back down to earth at the end. To his intense frustration, much of this stuff flew directly over the heads of audiences who cared only for their next pint and the bingo, and whose response ranged from an almost charitable apathy to outright hatred. The most notable example of that latter reaction came in 1956 when, on a residency at the Hull Trawlermen's Club, Dawson was famously asked 'have you ever thought of being a bricklayer?' and loudly jeered night after night. By the end of his tim there, however, he had begun to win at least some of that crowd over. Armed with the knowledge that if he could survive that experience he could survive anything, he resolved to fight on.

Supported by more Hoover selling, that fight would continue for over a decade until, in May 1967, opportunity finally knocked for real. By then, Dawson had wed Margaret Plant, soon to be renamed Meg by her husband after their marriage in June 1960. And it was she who finally began to give the fledgling comedian the sense of direction that he had been lacking. Initially, she provided invaluable support when he quit the Hoover business in order to devote more time to pursuing his showbiz dream, although it was still necessary to flog the odd appliance from time to time to make ends meet. For much of the 'sixties, Dawson's occasional successes, such as a week compereing the *Billy Cotton Band Show* at the Manchester Opera House, were drowned in a sea of rejection slips from radio and television producers who saw nothing of use in his nonsensical ramblings, whether on stage or paper. Until, that is, one fell on the desk of the BBC's Manchester-based Head of Light Entertainment, Jim Casey, son of Jimmy James. Intrigued, he and former BBC writer and producer Mike Craig went to watch the letter writer at a club in Oldham and liked what they saw, even if the audience clearly did not.

Dawson, though, was now learning how to use that antipathy to his advantage. Rather than fight it, he began to work it into his act, infusing his very particular brand of humour with a self-deprecation that undercut any hostility the crowd might be feeling: 'I've seen the Grim Reaper get a better welcome than that.' To his enormous credit, Casey realised that a comedy style which relied so heavily on wordplay - '...in a series of coughs and barks, the primeval pantechnicon lurched away from the bus depot with all the grace of an arthritic gypsy fiddler with chilblains' - would be best launched on radio. A few brief spots on the Light Programme's northern output followed before, eventually, he was given his own short series, *Dawson - Man of Fiction*. He was by no means yet a star, but at least people in the business were beginning to take him seriously; even the great Kenneth Horne, whose comedy panel game *Strictly For Laughs* found a guest spot for Dawson as he finally spotted a route to leaving those formidable and merciless club audiences behind.

Then, one Sunday night as he and Meg played couch potatoes in front of *Sunday Night at the London Palladium*, with Jimmy Tarbuck apparently going down a storm, his wife suggested that he should write and audition for *Opportunity Knocks*. Reluctantly, he did so. The producer, Royston Mayoh, recognised Dawson's name on the letter from an otherwise forgettable television project the pair had worked on together with Mike and Bernie Winters, and suggested to Hughie Green that he might be worth a try. With the audition duly passed, Les Dawson was at last unleashed on the Great British public courtesy of a piece filmed at ABC's studios in Didsbury. His act went something like this.

Dawson (seated at piano): 'Tonight, I would like to play something from Chopin, but I won't. He never plays any of mine. Then I toyed with the idea of playing Ravel's 'Pavane Pour Un Enfant Défunte', but I can't remember if it is a tune or a Latin description for piles...'. This time his live audience lapped it up, the Clapometer reacted as if it had been injected with Viagra and although, as usual, there was a sting in the tail when Dawson lost the postal vote, there was also little doubt that he had finally arrived. As, by now, had a daughter, Julie, soon followed by a son, Stuart.

As a family man with bills to pay and the owner of a rather smart new bungalow in Bury, the radio shows and packed houses that followed his success on *Opportunity Knocks* were welcome, of course. But it was Les Dawson's show-stealing appearance alongside Dickie Henderson on television's *Blackpool Night Out* that really kept up the momentum and ensured that his biggest problem now was deciding which jobs to turn down rather worry about what was coming next. Put simply, as an ever-present face on the nation's TV screens, Les Dawson began to grow famous. He starred in his first pantomime - an entertainment medium with which he would become closely associated - in Doncaster, and was soon spending a summer on Blackpool's Central Pier. He wrote his debut novel, *A Card For The Clubs*, the first of around fifteen books published in his lifetime, and his contributions to Barry Cryer's much-loved show *Jokers Wild* were swiftly becoming the stuff of legend. Aside from the fact that he had also upped his drink intake as a means of keeping his nerves under control, life at last was good.

Then, after appearing in a Christmas show alongside Norman Collier in Leeds, he met a Yorkshire Television producer named John Duncan, a man with an eye for original talent who was already a fan of Dawson after hearing him on Cryer's panel game. Duncan had a vision of Dawson's dour, curmudgeonly persona as the perfect antidote to the starry glitz and glamour of what then passed for light entertainment. Thus, in 1969, was *Sez Les* born, a show unlike no other that played perfectly to the comedian's strengths while also sending up the genre into which he was now cast. It also first introduced Les to Roy Barraclough, with whom he launched a bosom-hugging double act, Cissie and Ada, in homage to the pair's lifelong hero Norman Evans. It originated as a bit of messing about between scenes, an audience warm-up, but proved so popular that it went into the show. Ada: 'Did you have the sheesh kebabs?' Cissie: 'Right from the minute we landed.' How could it fail?

By coincidence, like Dawson, the Preston-born Barraclough had also worked as a vacuum cleaner salesman. In his case, however, it was fictional, courtesy of an acting role in his second stab at *Coronation Street* in 1966. The year before, he had debuted as a window cleaner who sold his round to Stan Ogden and, by the time *Sez Les* was in full swing, had made his first appearance as Rita Littlewood's agent, the twittering Alec Gilroy. That was in 1972, but it was not until 1986 that Barraclough became a *Corrie* regular in that role. In between times, and in fact well before those dates, since kicking of his acting career in Huddersfield Rep', Roy Barraclough had honed his character comedy skills with the likes of Ken Platt, Hylda Baker and Albert Modley, while also appearing in numerous films and television programmes, including such sitcoms as *Pardon My Genie* (1972-73) and *Three In A Bed* (1972), with Syd Little and Eddie Large. There were also parts in *Nearest and Dearest, Love Thy Neighbour* and *Never Mind the Quality, Feel the Width*.

He was, then, a natural partner for Les Dawson, but the duo's two northern busybodies - one an affected social climber, the other a salt of the earth battler - were far from being the only attraction of *Sez Les*. Over an eleven-series run until 1976, the programme also starred John Cleese, who clearly knew talent when he saw it. Of its team of writers, Barry Cryer was just one who helped to create a show that established Dawson as one of the biggest names in British comedy. In the midst of *Sez Les*, Meg gave birth to a third child, Pamela, and after a brief lull in ratings around series four, an invigorated Les Dawson himself delivered a new character in the shape of the gurning, sex-obsessed Cosmo Smallpiece.

Guaranteed to raise a chuckle in all but the most tediously politically correct, this leering, wild-haired middle-aged grotesque, in jam-jar bottom spectacles, pin-striped three-piece suit and dickie bow tie, would sit in a grand leather armchair, alongside a vase of colourful carnations, pansies and geraniums, and begin to read a story. At the first hint of anything remotely sexual, the mention of a table leg, say, or perhaps a chicken breast, the most appalling gurn would spread across his face accompanied by an outburst of: 'Knickers, knackers, knockers!' As *Sez Les* progressed, Cosmo would occasionally leave his chair and meet actual women, in whose presence he would spectacularly crumble, a gibbering wreck. There was nothing remotely misogynistic in any of this. If anything, the exact opposite. In classic northern comedy tradition, it is the male who is the fool and Cosmo was just one among many. Dawson knew very well where the strength in most families lay. His was no exception.

Furthermore, although your standard mother-in-law joke was indeed getting a little stale by the mid-1970s, Les Dawson himself was hardly unimaginative in that area. It could even be argued that, more often than not, he was satirising the form itself. The language Dawson used was frequently inspired and as far removed from lazy cliché as it is possible to get. Take his now well-known skit on the great woman's imminent arrival: 'I can always tell when the mother in law's coming to stay; the mice throw themselves on the traps.' For a true indicator of his verbal invention,

 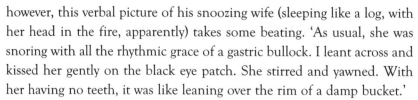

however, this verbal picture of his snoozing wife (sleeping like a log, with her head in the fire, apparently) takes some beating. 'As usual, she was snoring with all the rhythmic grace of a gastric bullock. I leant across and kissed her gently on the black eye patch. She stirred and yawned. With her having no teeth, it was like leaning over the rim of a damp bucket.'

Dawson's first Royal Variety Performance came in 1973. A massive success despite his nerves, it prompted these immortal opening lines: 'In 1645, Prince Rupert's mercenaries smashed Cromwell's left flank at Naseby and, in 1871, the Franco-Prussian war took a serious turn at the siege of Rouen and, in 1952, from the Kyles of Bute, came the first report of an outbreak of sporran rash. None of this has anything to do with the act tonight, but it just shows how your mind wanders when you're worried...'. A one-off ITV sitcom made for Yorkshire TV and written by Ray Galton and Alan Simpson, *Holiday With Strings*, followed in 1974. While the expected full series never materialised, it did give rise to a seven single comedies also written by Galton and Simpson, under the catch-all title, *Dawson's Weekly*, a pun on classified advertising newspaper *Daltons Weekly*. Those shows aired in 1975 and, like *Holiday With Strings*, again featured Roy Barraclough, along with John Bird, Kathy Staff, Patsy Rowlands, Avril Angers and Kenny Lynch. Both were mauled by the critics and subsequently sank without trace, despite Dawson rating them among his finest work.

Les Dawson's first sitcom role had been in *State of the Union*, a BBC *Comedy Playhouse* story of work relations in which he played a trade union secretary, one year after his *Opportunity Knocks* success back in 1968. John Duncan's intervention saw the next decade spent with ITV and Yorkshire in particular, with whom - apart from *Sez Les*, *Holiday With Strings* and *Dawson's Weekly* - the now nationally-renowned comic also made four hour-long specials, *Sounds Like Les Dawson* (1974), *Dawson's Electric Cinema* (1975) and a couple of festive show called *Les Dawson's Christmas Box* (1974 & '75). Also in 1975, there were three half-hour comedy playlets written by the Hull playwright Alan Plater, *Dawson's Complaint*, *Dawson's Connection* and *Dawson's Encounter*, all broadcast under the banner *The Loner*, along with another one-off *Les Dawson Show*. Then, in 1977, four hour-long specials entitled *Dawson And Friends*, in which Barraclough and Cryer were again prominent, were followed by a return to the BBC.

Dawson's motives for switching sides were rooted in a keen sense of artistic insecurity. Despite his undoubted mainstream popularity and ubiquitous presence on television, whether it be courting over-familiarity on those ITV programmes, chatting to Michael Parkinson and Des O'Connor or as just another Variety turn on the BBC's Saturday night *Summertime Special* seaside shows, what Les Dawson craved most was critical recognition. Whether he would admit to it or not, comedy to him *was* an art form and in those rip it up days of punk rock he had sniffed the revolutionary air and realised that the time was ripe to try something new. Unfortunately, his new BBC bosses turned out to be much like the last lot and the first programme he made for that channel, *The Les Dawson Show*, in 1978, offered more of the same. Ratings were poor and with a new wave of ageist alternative comedians breathing down his neck, what followed had better be good.

They need not have worried. So successful was *The Dawson Watch* when it was first broadcast in 1979, that not only did the public enjoy it, London's hard-to-please broadsheet critics did too. With sketches and routines based upon a different theme each week, the show ran for three series before finishing with a Christmas special in 1980. A year later, Dawson contributed to *Mussolini With Knickers*, a BBC documentary that looked at the history and meaning of mother-in-law jokes, and in which the comedian was able to perform a few such gags and offer some analysis of his own. It must have felt like validation. Where *The Les Dawson Show* had been as comfortable as a pair of old slippers, *The Dawson Watch* was more modern entirely. Its set was designed to look like a giant computer and its themes included transport, crime and the environment. The upshot being that Les Dawson became one of the few old-style comics to be considered trendy; a development largely down to his absolute grasp of irony, no better displayed than during his suitably sardonic spell as host of the BBC panel show *Blankety Blank* (1984-1989). By then, though, life had already delivered its latest major kick in the teeth for the lad from Collyhurst. Just when his career was at its highest and his confidence seemed indestructible, his beloved Meg was diagnosed with breast cancer.

For a while, he battled on regardless, and made another one-off *Les Dawson Show* for the BBC in 1981. A six-programme series by the same name aired the following year, along with a five-minute Christmas special,

The Funny Side of Christmas, before two more series of six half-hours in 1983 and 1984. However, by the time BBC Radio 2 disc jockey Terry Wogan handed over the *Blankety Blank* cheque book and pen to Dawson, the comedian's domestic life had deteriorated to the extent that his wife was in almost constant pain and he was about to be given shocking news of his own. In 1985, Dawson was diagnosed with prostate cancer and operated upon at Preston Hospital. The tabloid press, convinced he was not going to pull through, prepared his obituary. They were premature. Following the usual pattern of his life, Les pulled through and relatively quickly at that. Sadly, though, Meg's fight was lost. Inspirational bravery and the best treatment possible were not enough and she died in April 1986 at Manchester's Christie's Hospital.

Throughout his wife's illness and as soon as had recovered from his own, Dawson had continued to work - out of financial necessity as much as anything. A trip to New York to perform in cabaret, with Meg's blessing, was less than triumphant. 'He's interesting, but he sure needs a few piano lessons,' was one response documented by biographer Middles, as an American public proved stubbornly resistant to his downbeat style. He was now making regular appearances in pantomime too, as a very good dame in the old tradition. In fact, it was while in Manchester's *Babes In The Wood* panto of 1985-86, opposite the *Bergerac* actor John Nettles, who played the Sheriff of Nottingham, that one critic rated him: '...the finest pantomime dame of the century.'

As Meg's death drew closer, however, Dawson retreated out of the public eye and stayed closer to his family, in order to take care of his sick wife, and he poured his fears into a biography, *No Tears For The Clown*. Now resident in Lytham St. Annes, upon Meg's passing he began to drown his sorrows in that coastal town's St. Ives Hotel, where he found a shoulder to cry on in one of its barmaids, Tracy. Before long, Les and his new friend were photographed together at a Howard Keel Golf Classic Dinner: the cue for a tabloid feeding frenzy that only abated when the couple took the papers on at their own game, appearing on mid-morning television chat shows and telling their story via journalists they trusted. When it became clear that the public were on Les and Tracy's side, the papers had little choice but to switch tack. On tour in the farce, *Run For Your Wife*, and as alert to the benefits of irony as ever, Dawson sent his own situation up mercilessly. You've got laugh, or else you'll cry. Then, in 1987, he made another one-off *Les Dawson Show* special for the BBC and appeared in that year's *Royal Variety Performance*, his seventh and a watershed in so far as it also featured one-time alternative 'bad boys' Ben Elton and Rik Mayall. It was Les Dawson, though, who stole the show, supported by his unlikely troupe of elderly hoofers, The Roly Polys.

Again, however, the comedy times were changing. A new breed of comedian was once more knocking at the stage door. And where the last lot had mainly been southerners, this latest influx were from places like Manchester, Bolton, Middlesbrough and Leeds. Furthermore, while the alternative comedians of the early 1980s had been political to the soles of their training shoes, this latest wave, in keeping with their geographical roots, seemed intent on leaving the posturing, sixth form politics behind. Entertainers first and foremost, theirs was a no less surreal style of warm and even affectionate observational comedy that had more in common with Variety than speakers' corner. Nor was this new breed averse to tipping its collective hat in the direction of past performers who had influenced them as children. Had he been around today, Les Dawson would have slotted into the worlds of Vic Reeves, Steve Coogan, Peter Kay, Caroline Aherne and the League of Gentlemen with ease.

All that, though, was still to come. Despite the presence of the likes of Elton and Mayall on the Palladium bill, the traditional Variety game seemed to be up and Dawson chose to retreat to what he knew best. True, as the decade progressed, Ben Elton and Co. had grown noticeably less strident in their prior vilification of entertainers like poor old Benny Hill. Yet, on the whole, the television schedules seemed all but deserted by anyone over the age of 35. In fronting the still-popular *Blankety Blank* until 1989, the year in which he also made his fifth and last *Les Dawson Show* series for the BBC, Dawson remained an exception to that rule. Deep down, though, like so many of his contemporaries, he suspected that his time was gone and opted for a supposedly quieter life, in summer season at Blackpool Opera House.

Never given to self-aggrandizement, what Dawson had failed to realise was that his was a talent guaranteed to rise above the vagaries of fashion. Older entertainers may have fallen by the wayside but that was at least partly the result of their own complacency in the face of a new challenge. Dawson's ongoing willingness to try something new, coupled with his instinctive human empathy, put him on an altogether higher plane than the rest of the bow-tie and velvet jacket brigade. Yet still he threw himself into a seaside show that too few people were prepared to pay to see. The result was a heart attack and another lengthy spell of recuperation.

Even as he recovered from this latest blow, Les Dawson still kept on working, albeit in the relatively peaceful surroundings of the cruise ship circuit, so beloved of light entertainers seeing out their days. That fate, though, would be denied him by a call, in 1989, from *Opportunity Knocks*, a nice wedding present after his marriage to Tracy. The summer of 1990 also saw an eight-week revue in Paignton and there was a pantomime in Sunderland, but of greatest concern was the critical negativity accorded to his hosting of the talent show which had given him his first big break, a reaction that wounded him deeply. As ever, he put on a brave face and became a mainstay of TV chat shows for a while, introducing his verbal free-falling and trademark gurning to a whole new generation. And, like Frankie Howerd and Ken Dodd, just when he feared that his top-flight performing career was finished, he became something of a cult comedy hero instead. This new-found popularity resulted in a sell-out, record-breaking pantomime at Manchester's Palace Theatre.

Defying his health problems and a growing dependence on alcohol, it meant more television work too and a best-forgotten BBC game show, *Fast Friends*, in March 1991. He and Roy Barraclough also voiced an animated Post Office advertising campaign as Cissie and Ada. Most happily, here in later life, the artist in Les Dawson got his long-standing wish to be taken seriously. His next role married his skills as a pantomime dame with the literary impulse that had always been a part of Dawson's motivation. As the 100-year old South American grandmother, *La Nona*, in a BBC2 adaptation of the Argentinian playwright Roberto Cossa's allegorical black social satire of that name, Dawson excelled. And with the latest in a long line of novels, *Well Fared, My Lovely*, a northern take on the stories of Raymond Chandler, he was even to be found on high-brow discussion programmes like BBC Radio 4's *Start The Week*, hosted by Melvyn Bragg.

In January 1992, there was also an appearance on *This Is Your Life*, not representing himself (that had happened over two decades before in 1971) but honouring the leader of the Roly Poly troupe, Mighty Mo Moreland. Just to show that the old north-south divide was still going strong, Mick Middles quotes one London-based media critic's reaction: '...a gathering of horrendous northerners who had seemingly escaped from some seedy bingo hall. I had forgotten that the provinces were still crawling with dullards still labouring under a 1950s infatuation.'

Dawson had more important things to worry about. A combination of drink, cigarettes and a feeling of anxiety that he never quite managed to escape resulted in a second heart attack, this time in London. He stepped off the treadmill entirely for a while, a decision no doubt made easier by the birth of his fourth child Charlotte, his first with Tracy, in October of that year. Sadly, he would spend less than a year in his baby daughter's company. In June 1993, shortly after a return to the boards with *Run For Your Wife* in sleepy and sedate Bournemouth, Les Dawson was hit by a third and this time fatal heart-attack, while undergoing a hospital check-up. Working right to the end, his death came just days prior to a scheduled recording of his own planned contribution to ITV's *An Audience With....* series. With Les Dawson's passing, Britain lost an all-time comedy great; the epitome of how a gruff, northern exterior can belie a more fragile inward sensibility.

13
The Light Fantastic?

"You're playing all the wrong notes."
- *André Previn*
"I'm playing all the right notes.
But not, necessarily, in the right order."
- *Eric Morecambe*

The 1970s: Polyester decade of Watergate, Women's Lib, and the Raleigh Chopper. British television's 'Golden Age'.

This was an era when the opinion formers of today were either in their teens or leaving their teens, swapping Scalextric for Old Spice, Klackers for Aqua Manda. It was an era in which television itself came of age, leaving its formative years behind and moving into confident early adulthood. In a world of social and political upheaval, whether at home or abroad, television light entertainment was, for many British families, a calming reliable haven. It was a window into a less depressing reality; a place where three-day weeks, strike-torn collieries and shipyards, the IRA, power cuts and the death rattle of a discredited Labour government might safely be put aside, for a few blessed hours anyway. Television was a place of friendly faces and, once again in times of trouble, most of those belonged to comics born in the towns and cities of northern England.

In one particular instance, a good few of those 'faces' came courtesy of one man. Spotted in the pub and club circuit around Manchester by television producer Billy Scott, the Stockport-born impressionist Mike

The Light Fantastic?

Yarwood first made the leap from stage to small screen in a rarely seen 1961 episode of *Hancock's Half Hour*, before being featured among the newcomers on ITV's *Comedy Bandbox* in 1963. Future Variety-style spots in Johnny Hackett's *Let's Laugh* and on the bill of Val Parnell's *Sunday Night at the London Palladium* underlined his potential. And then, in 1967, the BBC placed Yarwood alongside the up-and-coming Glaswegian pop singer Lulu and comedian Ray Fell, when it launched a music and sketch show, *Three of a Kind*, pre-dating by fourteen years the programme of the same name which later provided a springboard for Lenny Henry, Tracey Ullman and, to a lesser extent, the Yorkshire comedian David Copperfield in the early 1980s. This original version of *Three of a Kind* lasted two series before Lulu and Yarwood plugged the plug, keen to front shows of their own.

For Mike Yarwood, in particular, that was a brave move which soon began to appear foolhardy. The solo vehicle he yearned for steadfastly refused to materialise. Instead, Yarwood spent much of the following year guesting for bigger name acts until, to his relief, Lew Grade's ATV network finally did offer him a show of his own. Even then, the resulting effort, *5/7ths to 7/7ths*, was shown only in the Midlands where, perhaps, a bizarre title relating to the channel upping its broadcasting output from five days a week to seven, presumably made some sort of sense. And even though his next effort, *Will the Real Mike Yarwood Stand Up?* (1968-69) - featuring guest stars of the calibre of fellow northern impressionist Peter Goodwright, Bob Monkhouse and Max Wall - actually did go national, so disappointed was Yarwood with it that he gave serious thought to chucking the towel in completely. It was a sign of things to come; seldom has there been a performer more wracked with self-doubt. And that lack of self-confidence was again to the fore in his third ATV outing, *The Real Mike Yarwood?* (1969), in which Yarwood, already wearying of hiding behind masks, ditched the impersonations and attempted unsuccessfully to concentrate on straightforward comedy.

It was a harsh lesson that Yarwood took fully on board when handed a return to the BBC in 1971. He could not have picked a better time to arrive. Over the early years of the coming decade, thanks to a cavalcade of popular entertainers like Frankie Howerd, Eric Sykes, Dick Emery, the follically challenged magician David Nixon, Bruce Forsyth and a couple

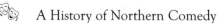

of first-rate northern entertainers to whom we shall shortly turn, a BBC bristling with self-assurance could regularly boast viewing figures in the tens of millions. *Look - Mike Yarwood*, too, soon joined those illustrious ranks. A blend of stand-up, music and sketches that ran to fifty shows over five years, the programme was destined to fly higher than just about any other, largely on account of the innovatory nature of Yarwood's act.

Although impersonations had long been staple fare in TV's Variety diet, until Mike Yarwood came along the victims had tended to be safe and universally-known subjects like classic Hollywood movie stars, most often long-departed and always uncontroversial; i.e. John Wayne, Charlie Chaplin and James Cagney. As early as that second ATV series, however, it was clear that Yarwood was set on a more potentially shocking route. If impressions operate via recognition, he reasoned, then the best figures to poke fun at must surely be those hogging the newspaper and television headlines. In the mainstream, at least, that was a rather revolutionary idea. And although Yarwood's humour tended towards gentle caricature rather than dark satirical savagery, it nevertheless carried a frisson of subversion in the arena of prime-time family viewing, as most obviously shown in the media fuss over his impression of H.R.H. Prince Charles. The public, though, lapped it up.

Yarwood had particular fun with politicians, including one of his earliest and most popular, the Labour Prime Minister Harold Wilson. Wilson's croaky Huddersfield tones were captured to perfection, or that's certainly how it seemed at the time. Heard now, it is hard to credit what all the fuss was about, as Yarwood's voices do tend to blend into one another after a while. Even so, *Look - Mike Yarwood!* was also turned into a BBC radio show called, wait for it, *Listen - Mike Yarwood* and, visually, Yarwood had hit upon a very neat concept indeed. Of crucial importance to each impersonation was at least one prop, whether actual or verbal. In Harold Wilson's case it was an ever-present pipe and Gannex raincoat, but just about every Mike Yarwood impression came complete with its own instantly memorable catchphrase and soon-to-be iconic wardrobe item. Whether it be the BBC political interviewer Robin Day's spectacles, periodically pushed up the bridge of his nose, or Chancellor of the Exchequer Denis Healey's explosively bushy eyebrows, which bobbed up and down as he called someone a 'silly billy', exaggeration was everything.

The Light Fantastic?

For Yarwood, it was not about what his chosen personality *actually* said and did, so much as what that personality *might* have said and done. And so well-conceived were these life-cartoons that once he had got his claws into you, there was really no point resisting. As far as the Great British public was concerned, that was how you would be remembered whether you liked it or not.

Throughout that first BBC series and the one that followed, *Mike Yarwood In Persons* (1976-81), which confirmed his decade-long status as a jewel in Auntie's crown, Yarwood found popular culture a priceless mine of material. He came up with impersonations that became so well established they would eventually morph into outright cliché. One such was the actor Michael Crawford or, more accurately, his accident-prone alter ego, Frank 'I've had a bit of trouble...' Spencer, complete with raincoat, beret and childlike twitches, a product of the much-loved slapstick sitcom of the time, *Some Mothers Do 'Ave 'Em.* A heavily-watered down Alf Garnett and his fellow comedy grotesques, Basil Fawlty and Harold Steptoe, were no doubt less than a stretch. And Yarwood did a fine line in genuine television eccentrics too, with the likes of Magnus Pyke, Patrick Moore, Jimmy Saville and Hughie Green ideal candidates for mimicry. Even more imaginatively for the time, Yarwood also made a highly-successful raid on the world of television sport, most famously through his impersonations of 'old big head' himself, the loudmouthed football manager Brian Clough, and the rugby league commentator Eddie Waring, a man frequently incomprehensible to anyone south of Workington (and they struggled to understand him there). Where Yarwood led, talents Rory Bremner, Alistair McGowan, Ronni Ancona and the *Dead Ringers* team would in later years follow.

Though quite revolutionary in its way, it is again worth stressing that Mike Yarwood's comedy was never seriously engaged in challenging the status quo. And, certainly, few of his targets complained - indeed they saw his attentions as confirmation of their celebrity, an honour even. During his second term of office, in 1976, Harold Wilson bestowed upon Yarwood an honour of his own, an OBE. Six years before, upon Wilson's first demise in 1970, Yarwood had coped admirably with the arrival of a new Prime Minister in the shape of Conservative leader Ted Heath, whose rocking shoulders and sailor's cap and jacket were soon another

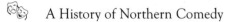

firmly-established part of the act. When Wilson again departed Downing Street and headed for retirement on the Scilly Isles, Yarwood once again rose to the task and re-invented his too-normal-by-half replacement, Jim Callaghan, although that characterisation proved much less memorable. Then, in 1979, came a Prime Minister who offered a different and ultimately insurmountable challenge entirely.

Never much of a one for credible female impressions, the arrival of Margaret Thatcher gave Mike Yarwood a real problem. After a brief and unsuccessful attempt at impersonating her himself, he was forced to pick up the phone and call in the well-known Scottish mimic, Janet Brown. That gave his writers the bright idea of pitting Brown's Iron Lady against Yarwood's Robin Day - a ploy that worked a treat. Potential disaster had been side-stepped to the extent that when Thames came sniffing around with the offer of more cash in 1982, like many other top-flight BBC entertainers of the day, Yarwood was gone, leaving nothing but a publicly-fuming Light Entertainment department in his wake.

Soon, though, it became increasingly apparent that the ascension of Mrs. Thatcher would have a more testing side effect entirely. The political unrest she engendered was now intruding on television entertainment. Despite running to two series and a handful of specials, Yarwood's new ITV show of the same name, *Mike Yarwood In Persons* (1983-84), felt old-fashioned when compared to the harder-edged and more overtly political and confrontational comedy that was now taking hold of the schedules, even with writers of the calibre of Eddie Braben, David Renwick, Barry Cryer and John Junkin. His amiable and at worst bumbling caricatures of public figures, and especially politicians, increasingly appeared toothless. For an old-school performer always lacking in self-confidence (his closing line - '...and this is me' - carried more than a hint of quiet desperation), this was a worrying development indeed. Yarwood, though, stuck to his guns and refused to stick the boot in. And that, coupled with anxiety and a hidden drink problem triggered by worry, overwork and homesickness, conspired to set him on a downward spiral. When the often-outrageously satirical puppet show *Spitting Image* launched in 1984, before going on to dominate Sunday evening viewing until 1996, the contrast could not have been more stark. To no one's great surprise, when his contract was due for renewal after a *Mike Yarwood Show* special in 1987, Thames declined the option.

The Light Fantastic?

It wasn't immediately over. In 1988, Yarwood was one among many in Eric Sykes's silent comedy, *Mr H is Late*. But after suffering from panic attacks while touring with a stage farce, *One for the Pot*, later that same year, the tour and an upcoming pantomime were cancelled. Hopes that Yarwood might be reinvented as a chat-show host also came to nothing; a pilot episode featuring the actor Anthony Hopkins never saw the light of day. His personal problems also brought about the end of his marriage.

In 1989, when Yarwood warmed up his Brian Clough impersonation for *Comic Relief*, it was the swansong to a once glorious television career. Nearly five years later, he hinted at a surprise comeback with a decent impersonation of yet another Prime Minister, John Major, during 1993's *Royal Variety Performance* but, in the longer term, it was not to be. A portrayal of Max Miller in the BBC's *Call Up The Stars* and an equally well-received appearance on the BBC's comedy news quiz *Have I Got News For You?*, both transmitted in 1995, seem, at the time of writing, to have brought down the curtain.

The extraordinary extent of Mike Yarwood's popularity is seen in how, upon the similarly ill-conceived departure to commercial television of our next couple of national institutions, it was he to whom the BBC turned to fill its most important slot of the year in 1978. Not only did Yarwood prove an adequate replacement for a pair of comedians who, even today, are generally held to be Britain's best-loved comedy double act of all time, he out-rated their first Christmas show for the opposition hands down.

It was some achievement. Throughout the 1970s, the BBC Christmas Day specials of Eric Morecambe and Ernie Wise had grown to become as traditional a part of the festive season as Charles Dickens, the Queen's Speech and over-stuffed turkey. In the year prior to their defection and Yarwood's elevation, by attracting an incredible 28 million viewers (over half the entire population) the duo had given British television what is still its most-widely watched comedy show in history; and a record unlikely to be broken any time soon. All that from an act whose original headlining show on national television back in 1954 had prompted one newspaper critic to pen the infamous 'Definition of the week: TV set. The box in which they buried Morecambe and Wise.' Little did they know.

The music hall and Variety tradition ran deep in Eric and Ernie's working class veins. By the time television came along, both had already enjoyed lengthy stage careers after originally making a splash as child stars, and therefore developed more than enough resilience to see them through the still greater challenges ahead.

Ernest Wiseman, born in Leeds in 1925, took his first on-stage steps alongside his father, Harry, a railway signal and lamp man by profession, later train driver and porter, in a modestly successful double act, 'Carson and Kid'. Subsequently, they would adopt the name 'Bert Carson and His Little Wonder' with seven-year-old Ernie, of course, taking the latter role, or 'The Two Tetleys', in honour of the Leeds-based brewery.

Ernie's mother, Connie, was a housewife who had earlier worked as a box-loom weaver in Pudsey. Married life was one of perpetual economic struggle for the Wisemans, for whom Ernie was one of four children, two boys and two girls, after a fifth child, Arthur, died from peritonitis aged two. Connie came from what would then have been termed respectable working class stock, but Harry's roots were altogether poorer and more 'common'. His own club singer father died when he was just 14 and his widowed mother was blind, which led Ernie's maternal grandparents to disown Connie and her new husband, despite Harry having won a medal for bravery during World War One. As a result, money was in short supply, a fact not helped by Harry's inability to grasp the seriousness of their situation, with each rare bit of spare cash falling into the hands of the local tobacconist, publican or spent on some unnecessary new gadget. Thanks to Connie's level-headed thriftiness, the family did manage to get by - just - and the family home seems to have generally been a lively and happy one, although young Ernest was left with a lifelong fear of debt.

Harry's outgoing nature did have its advantages. In an otherwise grey and dreary world marked by toil, worry and the tragic loss of a child, his was a quietly heroic and optimistic personality which held out the hope that some new and unconventional excitement might just be around the corner. For long-suffering Connie, who found her husband's financial fecklessness utterly exasperating at times, there was also the very real consolation that Harry's carefree attitude to life gave her imagination wings and fed dreams of better times to come. Though a competent pianist behind the walls of her own home, Ernie's mother was an otherwise quiet woman inclined towards social introversion. His father was a born extrovert, an instinctive showman, a walking bundle of fun.

Fortunately, Harry Wiseman was able to turn his innate talent for entertainment into an extra, if modest, source of income. Like his father before him, he spent his evenings performing on the local club circuit and, when young Ernest showed signs of a being a chip off the old block, he quickly made him a part of the act. The future Ernie Wise was a willing victim. The boy adored his father and was keen to soak up all the lessons that came his way, whether they be in tap-dancing, the singing of sentimental or rousing songs or comedy timing. Clad in a brimless black bowler hat, ill-fitting dinner suit and trousers, red clogs and occasional false moustache, he must have cut a droll sight indeed, and much of the duo's humour resided in the contrast between how Ernie looked and how he spoke and behaved. So well were 'Carson and Kid' received that, financially, things began to look up almost immediately. Through playing mainly at weekends, with Harry working on the railways through the week, the family income just about doubled.

In his highly-recommended biography of the pair *Morecambe & Wise* (Fourth Estate, 1998), the author Graham McCann describes how the only real downside to this subsequent glut of bookings was the way in which its increasing demands damaged Ernie's education. Occasionally, he fell asleep in class and his parents were brought into conflict with the local authorities. Eventually, Harry and Connie received a letter pointing out that 'exploiting juveniles was against the law and would have to stop immediately.' McCann then quotes Wise recalling: 'We played a game of cat and mouse: if the authorities spotted us in Leeds we moved our activities to Wakefield and if, after a while, they rumbled us in Wakefield we slipped quietly back to Leeds and Bradford. I'm sure in the end they turned a blind eye.' And it wasn't long before the boy had begun to strike out on his own.

With 'Bert Carson and His Little Wonder' now well-established in the towns and cities of what is today known as West Yorkshire, 11-year-old Ernie found himself performing in front of as many as 2,000 people when he took a leading role in the annual *Nignog Revue* at Bradford's Alhambra theatre. Despite the politically incorrect moniker, the Nignogs were then a quite innocent children's club run by the *Telegraph & Argus*,

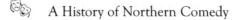

a local newspaper, to whom Wise paid his sixpence as an enthusiastic member. Organised as a charity event, that first revue and the ones that followed gave little Ernie the confidence to detect a future as a solo entertainer. This was no smoke-filled working men's club, this was one of the country's grandest Variety theatres and here he was, knocking them dead. And things notched up another level in 1938, when canny Harry heard that the impresario Bryan Michie was searching for a new juvenile talent and took his son along to the Leeds Empire.

For several months after that audition the Wisemans heard nothing, so it was back to the usual round of club appearances and talent contests, one of which was, tantalisingly, broadcast by the BBC. Then, one fine day as the year drew to a close, to the great excitement of his family, a letter arrived from an associate of Michie, the equally-influential Jack Hylton, inviting young Ernie to another audition in London. If ever there was a time to step up to the plate this was it and Ernie, bubbling over with confidence, did not disappoint. He sailed through what ended up being an impromptu audition in Hylton's own office and was thrust into his first major West End revue - a stage adaptation of Arthur Askey's *Band Waggon* - on Shaftesbury Avenue that very same night. As McCann recalls, it was in one of the rave reviews that followed that Ernest Wiseman - according to the *Daily Express* of 7th January 1939, the 'fair, perky-faced, quiffy-haired thirteen-year-old son of a parcels porter at Leeds Central Station' - became Ernie Wise. 'That in future will be his name. I believe you are going to hear it often...'

The reaction of Harry and Connie Wiseman to this was admirable. Having supported and, in Harry's case, performed alongside their son for so long and with so much modest success, it must have been tempting to try to cling on to and milk the double act. Certainly, for Harry, the boy might well have been a route to realising his own lifetime's ambition. Instead, and after having blubbed with pride through Ernie's astonishing debut, Harry took stock, put his personal hopes and ambitions to one side and made the best decision for his son. Declining an offer to stay on as Ernie's personal assistant, he left him under Hylton's care in London and went back to the rest of his family in Yorkshire. True, the Wisemans still stood to make money out of Ernie's new-found fame and, for a while, they did. But at an emotional level, the loss hit hard. After initially trying to keep the Bert

Carson and His Little Wonder act going with other youngsters, Harry quickly realised that, without his son, things were never going to be the same. With failing health from rheumatoid arthritis and no financial imperative to carry on, he quit the stage. After Harry's death, Connie confided in Ernie that coming home alone had been 'the breaking of him.'

Hylton, meanwhile, found Ernest Wiseman a London flat above an Italian restaurant in Covent Garden and provided him with a chaperone. He also took the *Daily Express*'s advice and renamed his young charge Ernie Wise, giving him a five-year contract worth twice as much a week as Harry was earning. While his real dad struggled away up north, Wise lapped up all the glamour and adulation under the tutelage of the man he would come to regard as a surrogate father, Jack Hylton. Out went the clogs, and in came black polished tap shoes and suit. Out when the vandalised bowler, and in came a debonair boater until, as McCann puts it: 'He now resembled more a cosmopolitan song and dance man than a parochial northern comic.' And later that year came a first view of the man - or at that stage 12-year-old boy - with whom he would share a large proportion of the rest of his life.

His name was John Eric Bartholomew, a resident of the North Lancashire seaside town of Morecambe, and the precociously-talented Wise first set eyes on him at another Hylton audition, held at a cinema in Manchester. Eric was up there on the stage, Ernie but an interested onlooker and despite Hylton's throwaway remark to the wannabe comic's mother, Sadie, that he would 'let them know', there was little doubt that he was going to be very funny indeed. Wise later confessed to having felt vaguely threatened by Eric's obvious talent, but with the outbreak of the Second World War he soon had more pressing matters on his mind. As a result of the initial closure of theatres, 14-year-old Ernie was invited to spend the duration out of harm's way at the Hylton family home in Sussex. It was a more than comfortable existence but, before long, guilt, homesickness or both drove him back to Leeds where, after a worrying few months as a coalman's labourer, a telegram dropped on the mat from Bryan Michie, offering the child prodigy a spot in his touring revue *Youth Takes A Bow*, then being presented at the Swansea Empire. Little Ern' high-tailed it to South Wales as fast as his short, but not yet fat and hairy, legs would carry him.

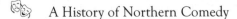

And who should be waiting for him when he got there? Among Michie's assembled discoveries, was the same John Eric Bartholomew whom Ernie had nervously admired at the Hylton audition in Manchester. This time, the boot was on the other foot. Where Wise had been out of the game for a while, the bespectacled young comic - at that stage still physically shorter than his future partner - was earning solid reviews having already joined the show in Nottingham. This interloper, older than Eric - or 'sonny' as Ernie helpfully called him - and with a reputation established alongside wireless greats like Arthur Askey, was viewed as the threat. Fortunately, his mother Sadie had other ideas.

Were it not for Sarah Elizabeth Bartholomew, there would be no Morecambe and Wise story to tell. Raised in Lancaster as one of six children, this determined stage mum sailed through life's choppiest seas like some pugnacious little gunboat. Blessed with a single-minded clarity of purpose to make lesser mortals quail, it was she who upon meeting her considerably more laid-back other half George Bartholomew, at a Winter Gardens dance in his hometown Morecambe, decided right there and then that she was going to marry the chap whether he liked it or not. It was she who persuaded their only child from that marriage, Eric, to take to the stage. And it was she who eventually suggested that while Eric and this new boy Ernie might very well have successful careers apart, together they would make an even more useful proposition.

As with the Wisemans, family life for the Bartholomews was a not uncommon one of financial hardship. In Sadie's case, that sparked a fierce determination to improve their lot. Having left school at 14, one of ten children, George Bartholomew had spent every working day since toiling as a labourer for the Morecambe and Heysham Corporation. Sadie, meanwhile, like many Lancashire lasses, began her working life as a cotton weaver until, after the couple's marriage in Accrington, she would supplement their small income by working as a waitress, among other part-time and poorly-paid jobs. With little John's arrival on 14th May 1926, suddenly she had a new focus in life, especially when the boy showed signs of being 'a born performer'. Walking and talking by his first birthday, 'Eric' as he became known, had a penchant for escaping the family home and entertaining anyone and everyone within earshot. Such talent, she decided, would not go to waste.

352

The Light Fantastic?

It may be hard to credit nowadays, and whisper it quietly or Colin Crompton will spin in his grave, but back in the 1930s Morecambe was considered a place of high excitement and northern showbiz glamour, second only to Blackpool. During his youth there, Eric was a regular entrant and winner of talent contests intended for holidaymakers. But, like Ernie, he also performed disastrously at school. To her credit, Sadie, determined that her son would enjoy a better life than she and his father had managed, chose to shove him on the stage rather than worry about academic qualifications, ignoring Eric's dream of being a professional footballer. It turned out to be a sensible move. As a soccer player, Eric was neither strong enough nor good enough, but on stage, well, that was a different matter. Eric himself, however, remained resolutely unambitious career-wise. Though a devoted fan of the movies, he was content just to sit and watch his favourites, Laurel and Hardy and Will Hay.

Sadie, though, had her sights on a film star closer to home. Inspired by the enormous success of George Formby, who had turned himself into Britain's biggest box-office attraction, she decided that if an apparently gormless Wiganer could do it, then her Eric could too. She bought him lessons on the piano, among other instruments, and took on extra work as a cleaner to pay for private dance lessons too. Before long, 'Master Eric Bartholomew - Vocal Comedy & Dancing' was warbling the Ella Shields music hall number 'I'm Not All There' in church halls and working men's clubs - business card and costume provided by Sadie Bartholomew, of course. Eric remained unhappy with his lot as a stereotypical northern simpleton and later recalled, rather ruefully, that in those days: 'it was a northern trait that a comic had to be dressed "funny" - to tell everyone, "look folks, I'm the comic!"'

His mother, still operating under the best of intentions, failed to realise the depth of Eric's disquiet and continued to drive him onward and upward. As far as she was concerned, her son loved being up there on stage, his periodic complaints were merely a normal feature of a relationship in which they always seemed to be disagreeing on something or other. Along with the weekend club work, for which George and Sadie had taken the sensible precaution, unlike Harry and Connie, of applying to the local Education Committee for a special licence, Eric was entered into more talent contests, with the most prestigious so far taking place at

the Kingsway Cinema, Birkenhead, in 1939. This wasn't just any talent contest, it was a regional heat of the *Melody Maker* music paper's national search for a star, and Eric's subsequent victory won him the right to try and impress Jack Hylton in Manchester.

From that date to the next occasion Eric and Ernie's paths crossed in Swansea, neither of their acts changed much. Under Sadie's guidance, Eric continued to trade as a droll and very young northern comic, while Ernie attracted the lion's share of attention as a Vaudeville-style song and dance man. And so it continued, as the pair became firm friends. The turning point in their relationship occurred six months later in Oxford. Unusually for him, Ernie arrived in town without having pre-booked any accommodation, an ill-judged decision that led to an unhappy evening wandering the streets. As the clock ticked toward midnight, with Ernie increasingly cold and distressed, at last he had the good fortune to bump into a fellow cast member, Doreen Stevens, with whom he tried the guest house that, unknown to him, was giving temporary residence to Eric and Sadie. Overhearing the landlady about to turn Ernie away yet again, Sadie ran to the door with an offer that the bedraggled young man could share Eric's bed - not for the last time as things turned out (although it is safe to assume that, on this occasion, Eric was yet to start smoking his pipe). At breakfast the following morning, Sadie proposed that henceforth it would make more sense if Ernie continued to travel with Eric and herself and her suggestion was eagerly accepted.

Thus began a three-way working relationship that served everyone well. For Ernie, away from his family and grown up before his time, Sadie became a surrogate mother, providing the support that his father, Harry, used to offer and matching his own drive and ambition yard for yard. For Eric, whose personality was closer to that of his laid-back father, along with a pal who would soon be more like a brother, Ernie had gained motivation and an example of might be achieved through hard work and determination. And for Sadie, as well as having a 'second son' under her wing, she found in Ernie a kindred businesslike spirit who she could trust to keep her boy on the straight and narrow if and when she was no longer around. Then came the big idea.

Trapped in a stationary tram carriage with the pair and intensely irritated by their banter en route to war-torn Coventry, the venerable Mrs.

The Light Fantastic?

Bartholomew asked in exasperation why, if they carried on like some sort of manic double act off-stage, they didn't formalise the scenario on it. Eric and Ernie as a double act. How about that?

The transition was not exactly smooth. Though they both liked the suggestion, the boys were already doing very nicely as solo artists on a bill that included Marie Lloyd's sisters, Alice and Rosie Lloyd, and a harmonica player who, many years on, they would incorporate into their television act, Arthur Tolcher, ('...not now, Arthur'). Still, as the boys worked through the idea and began to put together material, it became apparent they were on to something. After agreeing to a fifty-fifty split on this and any future earnings, before talking the idea through with Bryan Michie, Ernie, now 17, approached his former mentor Jack Hylton for permission to take things further. As a result, Variety theatre's newest double act, Bartholomew and Wise, made their debut at the Liverpool Empire in August 1941.

Owing to his more grown-up demeanour, Ernie at first took on the role of Eric's stooge. And presumably keen to throw of the shackles of overt northernness, the boys now used the sort of wisecracking repartee favoured by Bud Abbott and Lou Costello, among other American movie stars, with the odd Flanagan and Allen-style tune for good measure. Their Yorkshire and Lancashire accents temporarily disappeared too, to be replaced by a twang more Burbank than Batley or Bolton. Apparently on the advice of the American singer Adelaide Hall's husband Bert Hicks, they also ditched their Bartholomew and Wise tag, considered too clunky and nowhere near memorable enough by just about everyone. Hicks suggested that if the pair were looking for different surnames, then why not adopt the place of their birth? Thereafter, Eric became known as Eric Morecambe while Ernie - for a while at least - considered becoming Ernie Leeds until, according to Graham McCann: 'He realised that Morecambe and Leeds sounded too much like a return railway ticket, and thought better of it.'

So, full steam ahead to the big time? No, not quite. For just as things were developing nicely, box office takings slumped and Jack Hylton was forced to close the show. With no other offers of work on the table the pair drifted apart, Eric back to Morecambe and a distinctly unglamorous job in a razor-blade factory, and Ernie - via an unsuccessful attempt at

finding work in London - to his earlier coal round in Leeds. Despite staying in touch, they remained apart for three months until, utterly exasperated at the wartime lack of opportunities, Ernie once again set off blindly for the capital, but this time with Eric and Sadie in tow. Fortunately, what could have turned out to be a costly and disappointing fools' errand soon paid dividends, with a successful audition by the pair winning them a couple of solo spots in *Strike A New Note*, at the Prince of Wales Theatre. This was the show that provided a vehicle to stardom for the highly-regarded Birmingham comic Sid Field and his then straight-man Jerry Desmonde. Morecambe and Wise's double act did not fare nearly so well. Undeterred, they continued to work at it and made the move to radio when *Strike A New Note* hit the wireless in 1943. But otherwise, catching the attention of the right people as a team began to look like an insurmountable task. And when Ernie was served with his call-up papers in November of that year, before eventually joining the Merchant Navy, that really did seem to be that.

Eric, for his part, saw out the rest of the show's London run and joined the wartime entertainment association ENSA, where he played foil to Dave Morris's brother Gus for a while, prior to being called up himself for an aborted stint as a Bevin Boy the following year. Ominously, a touch of heart trouble soon saw him despatched back to Morecambe where, at first, he continued where he had left off in razor blades before, with his mother's assistance, hitting the road as a straight-man alongside the well-known pantomime dame Billy Revell, soon to team up with the Salford-born female comedian Pat Fields, as Revell and Fields. Ernie, meanwhile, kept his showbiz muscles in trim with small short-term appearances between postings and, upon his own discharge in 1945, he too set about re-building a solo career in Civvy Street. Or, more precisely, Regent Street. For it was there one fine day when, completely by accident, he bumped into Eric and Sadie, once again down in London looking for work. The double, nay, triple act was back in business.

Work, though, remained stubbornly tricky to find and when Sadie eventually returned to Morecambe, the lads took her departure as a cue to find themselves an agent. It did not prove easy, especially with so many former servicemen back in town and keen to pick up where they had left off before Hitler's intervention. Yet, as Barry Cryer would also discover, there was one possible exception. Namely, the Windmill Theatre, Soho, nude tableaus and all. Desperate to be noticed, Morecambe and Wise fared no better than anyone else in front of the venue's openly salacious audiences. The place, though, did attract agents, all of them keen to discover the next big thing. After passing an audition before the theatre's legendary owner Vivian Van Damm - a.k.a. VD for short - and being guaranteed a week's work, they managed to attract the attention of one such gentleman, Gordon Norval, who offered them a couple of spots in another nude revue, *Fig Leaves and Apple Sauce*, at the Clapham Grand the following Monday. As it happened, the offer came just in time. A distinctly unimpressed Van Damm had already served notice that he wouldn't be taking up the option.

The Clapham booking proved to be a successful one for the duo and under the guidance of Norval, with newly-written material, their profile began steadily to rise. And after they were recommended to impresario Reggie Dennis for a spot in his touring revue *Front Page Personalities*, Morecambe and Wise at last found themselves booked up solid for the next eleven months. By the end of it, Norval was amicably swapped for the hugely-influential Frank Pope who, as an agent of talent for just about everyone in the business, including the mighty Moss Empires, really set them on their way. Leaving the Abbott and Costello routines behind and opting to concentrate instead on more obviously British character-driven comedy, in which their own very obvious friendship played a major part, it wasn't long before they began an assault on the wireless too.

Well aware that, with the coming of the 1950s, live Variety was creaking dangerously, Eric and Ernie wrote to the Manchester-based producer Bowker Andrews, suggesting that their talents might be suitable for the BBC's North of England Home Service. A positive response led to a steady dribble of such appearances culminating, in 1952, in spots on *Workers' Playtime* and Ronnie Taylor's *Variety Fanfare*. Through his work with the likes of Al Read and Jimmy Clitheroe, Taylor had a reputation for nurturing talent and that continued with Eric Morecambe and Ernie Wise although, admittedly, an extended residency on *Variety Fanfare* owed more to fears that they were about to be poached by *Variety Bandbox* than any charity on his part. In fact, despite firing off a constant barrage of letters, they had consistently been turned down by the producers of that

more influential programme, apparently on one occasion for being too much like Jimmy Jewel and Ben Warriss. Nevertheless, it wasn't long before the duo were headlining their own show in the north, *You're Only Young Once*, otherwise known as *YoYo*, that ran from November 1953 to December 1954. By which time they had also launched a couple of new double acts on the side, Ernie finally getting around to marrying Doreen Blythe in January 1953 and Eric wedding a young dancer he met at the Edinburgh Empire, Joan Bartlett, six months after their first meeting in December 1952.

Morecambe and Wise had also made a brief transition to a third medium, television, making their debut in a BBC talent show, *Parade of Youth*, in 1951. That was followed by an appearance alongside Stan Stennett and Frank Randle's drinking buddy Josef Locke in the BBC Variety show, *Pantomime Party*. Two year's later, with that latter outing and the pair's now-regular radio spots continuing to provide good exposure, the BBC's Head of Light Entertainment Ronnie Waldman, knocked on their dressing room door at Blackpool's Winter Gardens with altogether more serious intentions. The show he proposed, *Running Wild*, was meant to be the stepping stone to greater things, a pathway to an exciting future on Britain's newest electronic mass media innovation. It turned out to be an enormous embarrassment which might very well have killed off their careers entirely, were it not been for the fact that, in 1954, the vast majority of British homes could not yet afford a television set.

Looking back, that Waldman managed to get the duo on air at all seems remarkable. His own inclination to break down the north-south divide does not seem to have been shared with other influential figures at the BBC's London HQ. For example, in *Morecambe & Wise*, Graham McCann quotes another of the show's producers, Bryan Sears, as telling the pair that none of their current ideas and ways of working would cut it 'down south'. 'They should be aware, he informed them, that they had a serious problem, and the problem was that they came from the "wrong" part of the country.' As McCann says, this must have come as something as a surprise to Eric and Ernie, given that their engagement book was stuffed with bookings in places as diverse as Brighton, Oxford and Norwich and that the BBC's own radio service increasingly had no problem in giving the duo national exposure via that medium.

The Light Fantastic?

Nevertheless, Sears remained convinced that, on television, such an ostentatiously northern style of humour would not appeal to southern viewers and set about fiddling with their act accordingly. The production team brought in a myriad of southern guests stars and writers, whose hastily-produced scripts suggested a lack of commitment to the idea of who Morecambe and Wise actually *were*, if indeed they had previously heard or seen their act at all. The result was unmitigated disaster.

Not only were the newspapers virtually unanimous in condemning a show that might more fairly have been labelled uninspiring rather than terrible, the fact that, in those days, British television output consisted of a single channel showing just a handful of carefully-rationed programmes per night, ensured no escape from the critical glare. To a press and public still unfamiliar with Eric and Ernie's stage personae - Bryan Sears, in his wisdom, insisted that Eric's audience asides about Ernie would not work on television - their corny old-fashioned gags were just that; corny old-fashioned gags. Even so, the intensity and maliciousness of the response left Eric and Ernie reeling; no allowance was made for their inexperience in the genre. It was a blow from which they felt they might never recover and the 'buried in a box' quip referred to earlier found a home in Eric's wallet to the end of his days. So heartbroken were the pair and concerned for their reputation that they begged Waldman to take the show off-air. He refused, insisting that they must honour their contract, and *Running Wild* limped on to the end of its six-episode run as planned.

True to form, Sears put the programme's failure down to Eric and Ernie's northernness, and Morecambe and Wise took time to lick their wounds before rebuilding their shattered egos in that part of the country as fourth on the bill at the Ardwick Hippodrome, Manchester. Only a few months before they might well have been the headline turn, but taking a deliberate step back was a good decision. Appearing once again as 'themselves' rather than scriptwriters' puppets repeating tired old lines, they went down a storm and it was apparent that very few people had seen the television series anyway. As their live reputation flourished so, again, did their confidence. Morecambe and Wise, doing what they did best, were back up and running.

Even so, it took them until 1956 to decide that they might like to give the now burgeoning television medium another go. And the chance

359

to do so came courtesy of the new commercial network which had begun broadcasting the year before, in a residency on ATV's *The Winifred Atwell Show*. Encouragingly, their writer this time would be the up-and-coming Johnny Speight, still to make his mark with Arthur Haynes, Frankie Howerd and Alf Garnett. Although a working class Londoner, Speight immediately twigged that their own, distinctly northern characters were Morecambe and Wise's strength and the audience, it seems, agreed.

A quickfire double for the BBC, first with a one-off appearance on the self-explanatory *Variety Cavalcade* and then as temporary hosts of a revue show named *Double Six* (1957), was the start of a five-year period in which they combined stage and screen to ever-greater effect. It was in 1959, however, upon their return from a six-month tour of Australia alongside Ms. Atwell and her tinkling ivories, that they finally saw which way the land was lying and again switched agents from Frank Pope to the more television-savvy Billy Marsh. By 1961, after countless appearances on Variety shows such as *Sunday Night at the London Palladium*, *Star Time*, *Let's Have Fun* and *Saturday Spectacular*, they were once again ready to take a deep breath and front their own show.

The pair's theme song would be a jaunty little Johnny Mercer number, 'Two of a Kind', and it was that title which ATV gave Eric and Ernie's most important television project since *Running Wild*. Also billed as *The Morecambe & Wise Show* in some quarters, in complete contrast to their earlier BBC debut the programme almost immediately established them as serious contenders for the title of Britain's most popular comedy double act. Yet it almost never happened. By the time ATV supremo Lew Grade had agreed to Marsh's suggestion that their obvious improvement since *Running Wild* meant that Morecambe and Wise should be given another go, the BBC were developing just such a series of their own. Called *Four Aces and a King* and written by comedy heavyweights Frank Muir and Dennis Norden, the Corporation had even got so far as asking Eric and Ernie to approve the scripts. In the end, though, the duo opted to go with ITV, and *Two of a Kind* it was.

Thus began an eight-year run in which the names Eric Morecambe and Ernie Wise became synonymous with enjoyable family entertainment. Much of that was not only down to the stars themselves but also the talents of their chief writers, Dick Hills and Sid Green.

Recommended to Eric and Ernie by the legendary double act Jewel and Warriss, Hills and Green certainly had the pedigree and were soon creating a whole new witty and unpredictable world for Morecambe and Wise to inhabit. Again, it did not start well and the show's stars fretted that their writers were trying to cram too much in, in terms of detail and actual bodies on screen. The critics, too, were lukewarm until an unexpected Equity strike suddenly rendered extra actors obsolete. Eric and Ernie were okay, they belonged to the Variety Artists' Federation rather than Equity, but scenes previously swarming with people had now to be stripped back to the bare minimum, resulting in a greater emphasis on Morecambe and Wise themselves and, most imaginatively, support appearances by Sid and Dick. The new naturalism worked a treat and, before long, Eric and Ern', one tall and daft, the other short and even dafter though, of course, he never quite knew it, were friendly and funny household names.

Over the coming decade, they seemed to be everywhere. On stage, there were summer seasons and pantomimes. In 1966, they had their own BBC radio show. They had singles and LPs in the 'hit parade'. Like Norman Evans, Eric and Ernie even appeared in America on *The Ed Sullivan Show*. British children could enjoy their comic strip adventures every Monday, in the pages of the popular Fleetway comic *Buster*. And they even broke into the movies, although none of the three of the films they made - *The Intelligence Men* (1965), *That Riviera Touch* (1966) and *The Magnificent Two* (1967) - could reach the quality of their TV series. That seems to have been particularly disappointing for Ernie, who continued to hold cinematic ambitions, but neither he nor Eric had time to dwell on it professionally. Another television series was now on the cards but, this time, back with the BBC.

It came as the result of a fall-out with Lew Grade who, despite the long-running success of *Two of a Kind*, had turned down flat the duo's demands of an improved financial deal and a commitment to producing their show in colour. Into the breach - with Lew's nephew and Billy Marsh's new partner Michael Grade acting as middle man - stepped BBC Head of Variety, Billy Cotton Jr. Offering an initial three-year deal, Cotton and the comedians came to an agreement that the shows would be shown first in colour on BBC2 and then repeated, in black and white, on BBC1.

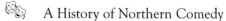

For the first series of *The Morecambe & Wise Show* (1968, eventually running to 1977), Eric and Ernie took Hills and Green with them. And on the surface at least all went smoothly, especially when the highly-capable producer John Ammonds - who in his younger days had provided sound effects for Tommy Handley's *ITMA* and, latterly, done much to shape the careers of Dave Morris, Harry Worth and Dave Allen - was also brought on board. The workload, though, was intense and, with the series over, a shock lay in store. In November 1968, while driving back from a midnight gig at the Batley Variety Club to a Leeds hotel, 42-year-old Eric Morecambe was hit by a major heart attack. Fortunately, a passer-by, one Walter Butterworth, was on hand to jump into the car and drive Eric quickly to intensive care. It had been a close-run thing and everybody knew it.

As Eric recuperated at home in Harpenden, the second series of *The Morecambe & Wise Show* went on hold, perhaps indefinitely. Even so, Bill Cotton and the BBC insisted that he take as much time out as necessary and confirmed that they would honour the original contract as and when he felt well enough to return. Without his partner, Ernie continued to tread the boards on behalf of the duo, taking care to split all earnings fifty-fifty and loyally turned down any offers of solo work. And when Eric Morecambe eventually did make his BBC comeback six months later, Cotton did not just honour the original contract, he improved it, allowing Morecambe and Wise an extra fifteen minutes per week in their second series and a luxurious amount of time in which to produce it. Less happily, when met with Eric's heart problems, Dick Hills and Sid Green had chosen not to stick around. By the time preparations for this latest *Morecambe & Wise Show* were underway, they had already returned to ATV. Their replacement was Eddie Braben, former wordsmith to Ken Dodd, and he would lift Eric and Ernie to another level entirely.

In his scripts for the duo, Braben blended perfectly all the madcap verbal lunacy of his 'Doddy' work with the more conventional reality-based scenario as previously developed by their earlier writers. Producer Ammonds, too, continued to be crucial. Already, he had introduced the pair to the potential of close-ups and a vaguely Shakespearian breaking of the fourth wall. And it was Ammonds who came up with the ingenious conceit that each show should open with a piece of front-of-cloth comedy business, with the set thereafter coming to resemble a Variety stage rather than a glitzy TV studio. In this way, Eric and Ernie appeared more at ease in their surroundings and an almost communal sense of immediacy was established with the audience, bypassing camera and screen entirely. For its millions of viewers, watching *The Morecambe & Wise Show* soon came to feel less like sitting in front of a television programme and more like having a convivial dialogue with friends, not least because it was usually watched with the rest of the family - young, not-so-young and downright ancient - with the hours afterwards devoted to recalling the best routines. In the 1970s, Eric and Ern' were an unmissable event.

At the heart of the phenomenon was the way in which Eddie Braben was able to strengthen and elaborate upon Eric and Ernie's individual characters. For Eric, this meant presenting him as an overgrown kid: always ready with a quip, usually apropos of nothing, enthusiastic, unable to concentrate on anything for long and with a twinkle of mischief behind those iconic and occasionally skewed black spectacles. Perhaps Braben's most significant contribution, however, was with Ernie. Here, all notions of him being an archetypal straight man, merely a feed for the funnier half's jokes, were dropped and in came a fully-formed comical personality of its own. Ernie's in-bred caution with money was made fun of, as was his diminutive frame, perched upon his apparently short, fat and hairy legs. An inherent moral decency was redrawn as prim propriety. And the drive and ambition that had sustained Ernie Wise in his showbiz career was caricatured into a loveable and pretentious dimwit, lacking in solid education but convinced that he is a genius, whose dreadful plays will surely cement a reputation - in his own head - as a literary great.

Having created such a character, it is a measure of Braben's skill that instead of openly pricking his partner's bubble - as would most likely have been the case in other comedy double acts - he allowed Eric instead to humour Ernie and become a willing, and knowing, accomplice in his self-delusion. In short, Braben learned to mine the deep well of personal affection that was already there in reality. Here were two men whose friendship had grown to the extent that they behaved, to all intents and purposes, like brothers. Or maybe a better analogy would be a long-married couple, for whom harmless teasing and the odd playful two-handed slap on the chops merely served as love tokens, along with a veritable 'Arsenal!' of family in-jokes: '...get out of that', '...you can't see the join', '...what's a Greek urn?' and so on. Equally amusing (and decidedly British) was the way in which the show's steady stream of big name guest stars - André Previn, Tom Jones, Cliff Richard, Shirley Bassey, Robert Morley and a fee-chasing Peter Cushing to name but a few - were also too polite to mention that anything might be amiss.

Interestingly, their biographer Graham McCann writes that a further explanation for the appeal of Morecambe and Wise may lie in the way that the duo were subtly, and sometimes not so subtly, engaged in '...their own private War of the Roses'. And certainly, Eric and Ernie did encapsulate a general English conception of Yorkshire and Lancashire personalities. Lancashire folk, it seems, are blessed with a quirky accent, playfulness with language and a gift for physical gormlessness that makes them perfect comedians. Your stereotypical Yorkshireman keeps a close eye on his wallet and is possessed of an altogether more dry, self-opinionated and maybe even conceited personality. In other words, the ideal straight man. In reaching his conclusion, McCann draws upon the work of the Bradford-born literary great J.B. Priestley who, in his seminal *English Journey* (William Heinemann Ltd/Victor Gollancz, London, 1934), reflected that Lancastrian speech was 'almost the official accent of music hall humour', adding that one its qualities was an ability 'to suggest either shrewdness or simplicity, or, what is more likely than not, a humourous mixture of both.' The Yorkshire accent was described by Priestley as 'quieter, less sociable and less given to pleasure.'

Here again, perhaps, we might detect northern comedy's roots in the Industrial Revolution. In the north west - the undoubted centre of national activity - much of the industry was based in cotton mills and other factories or, in Liverpool and the far north east, shipyards, i.e. above ground. The nearby West Yorkshire towns of Huddersfield, Halifax and, particularly, the city of Bradford were other areas of major textiles activity but, further afield east of the Pennines, the predominant industry was coal-mining. Life for your average working class Yorkshireman was spent cramped and huddled underground. Unless he was a sheep farmer or fisherman to the north of the county, of course, in which case his remained a largely anti-social existence, albeit one spent in the wide open air. No matter how sooty, noisy and rigidly disciplined, daily life for working class Lancastrians was an often roomier and more public affair. In a mill, there could be social interplay - however restricted - a mixture of age groups and sexes, and something of a performance atmosphere, with catchphrases and facial expressions a valued ingredient of existence. Why bother to 'perform' if you work in the bowels of a black, dark pit, or have only a few sheep as an audience on a windswept and lonely north country dale? Could this be why Yorkshire folk are traditionally thought of as dour, while Lancastrians are considered more cheery and 'up'?

For all their alleged differences, those two traditional old regional rivals Yorkshire and Lancashire share plenty of qualities too - not least a deep-seated mutual respect for community which can, more often than not, find combined shape in ostentatious friendliness and an initial distrust of strangers. The celebrity guests who wandered through Morecambe and Wise's TV apartment would have no trouble recognising that behaviour.

Nor, since George Formby senior's pioneering days, have many northerners baulked at playing up to the simpleton image when it suits them, deploying Priestley's mixture of 'shrewdness and simplicity'. And most obviously, there is that ingrained aversion to taking life too seriously.

'There used to be a big difference between north and south in humour,' admits Ernie Wise in William Kimber's book, Bring Me Sunshine: A Harvest of Morecambe & Wise (London, 1978) - '...there used to be a definite dividing line between "Oop fert cup" and all that.' Note the 'used to be'. In these days of shifting social, geographical and technological boundaries, the more enlightened and well-travelled among us like to imagine that those lines of distinction have become rather more blurred, if indeed they have not vanished all together. In just about every way that counts, that is most likely true. Maybe, though, in Wise's words, we hear the moment when, in comedy at least, north and south began to be so much less of an issue.

Maybe, back when those regional distinctions were clearer, when radio stars Arthur Askey and Tommy Handley had to temper or even lose their accents to gain a national audience, when Al Read felt he needed to link his Salfordian characters by talking all posh, maybe Morecambe and Wise's greatest achievement was to render such geographical limitations redundant, ironically using the very same qualities that were soaked up like a sponge through a lifetime swamped in the richest northern Variety traditions.

Whether you saw the Pennines as the backbone of the country or just a bunch of grim and grimy hills in some distant industrial no-man's land, post-Eric and Ernie that did not seem to matter anymore. No pair of comedians have ever been more 'northern' and yet it was easy to forget that they were northern at all. In their hands, the universal qualities of northern humour, with its emphasis on the struggling little guy, its profound juxtaposition of the real and surreal, and its recognition of the comfort of friendship amid the ultimate absurdity of human existence, were seldom more apparent. Whatever your age, whatever your gender, whatever your rank in society, whatever your cultural background and wherever you happened to live, Morecambe and Wise were fun. And the best thing of all was that we were invited to have fun with them.

Nothing made the intimacy of the pair's relationship more obvious than their trademark propensity for sharing a bed. The idea, an inspired one, was Eddie Braben's. At first, the duo weren't keen, worrying that it might carry homosexual overtones. But when Braben pointed out that sharing a bed had not done Laurel and Hardy any harm, the argument was won there and then. Anyway, given the cheerful innocence that lay at the heart of their act - not to mention the way in which Eric pensively puffed on his pipe during the routine, while Ernie scribbled away at his latest 'masterpiece' in a notebook beside him - raw man-on-man action was never likely to be high on the agenda. For Morecambe and Wise, sex and gender were just two more things in this world not to get quite to grips with; *viz.* Eric's insistence on addressing just about every woman who ever crossed his path as 'sir' or 'sonny'.

Gender confusion was but one example of how influential the old entertainment traditions were on *The Morecambe & Wise Show*. Along with the sets and front-of-cloth curtains already described, each and every programme was littered with references to the routines and turns of yesteryear. Eric's fourth wall-breaking asides and mock exclamations - 'What do you think of it so far?' - carried echoes not only of Laurel and Hardy but also the raucous days of early music hall. In a classic working class northern comedy way, Eric and Ernie were masters at putting their audience at ease by telling them: '...we are as daft as you are'. The singing, dancing, spoon-playing, overblown costumes and acrobatics that lit up each series would have been familiar in Variety or pantomime. Much of their still instantly recognisable funny business, Arthur Tolcher's aborted 'Spanish Gypsy Dance' on the harmonica for example, was either lifted directly or based upon the antics of a roster of performers who were stars when Morecambe and Wise were merely up and coming. In the surreal stupidity of their three-way conversations with their aforementioned celebrity guests, can't we hear at least a hint of Jimmy James - 'I'm not a complete fool.' 'Why, what part's missing?' In Eric's flights into useless ventriloquism, can't we see Sandy Powell? Alongside Glenda Jackson in Ernie's very own *Cleopatra* they even regurgitated Wilson, Keppel and Betty's sand dance. And what about that little hands behind the head shuffle to which they departed the stage at the end of every show, while singing their new theme tune 'Bring Me Sunshine'? A direct lift from that impeccable American vaudevillian, Groucho Marx.

All in all it was a comically potent brew and one made even richer by the quality of the BBC's own production values. Many of the musical sections - usually choreographed by the brilliant Ernest Maxin - became instant television classics. Scenes like Eric and Ernie preparing breakfast to the accompaniment of 'The Stripper'; the pair's memorable take on Gene Kelly's defining dance in *Singin' In The Rain*; the unveiling of newsreader Angela Rippon's legs; and the dancing assortment of sailor-suited and in some cases quite aged TV personalities - Eddie Waring, Michael Aspel, Frank Bough, Richard Baker and Barry Norman *et al* - performing acrobatic cartwheels and somersaults in a spoof of *South Pacific*, continue to feature on lists of the nation's favourite television moments to this day.

In fact, that final musical skit appeared on what would turn out to be the pair's very last BBC Christmas show in 1977. By then, if British light entertainment could claim two bigger stars than Eric Morecambe and Ernie Wise they would have been very hard to find. Not only were the weekly shows winning awards and pulling in millions of viewers, the draw of the annual festive outings was simply astonishing and led to the duo being awarded an OBE apiece in 1976. To a nation still hungry for more, there seemed no reason for any of that to change any time soon.

Behind the scenes, however, all was not well. Not only was Eddie

Braben over-worked and physically and emotionally stressed out, leading to the introduction of extra writers who couldn't quite paint Eric and Ernie as colourfully and completely as he had, the boys themselves were feeling tired, stale and ready for a change. Their much-trusted friend and advisor John Ammonds had already amicably departed the show in 1974, to further the career of a certain Mike Yarwood amongst other things, leaving Ernest Maxin in charge. And even though that latter gentleman would continue to create and produce some of Morecambe and Wise's best routines ever, there does seem to have been a feeling that the only way now for the pair was down.

A high-profile move to ITV and Thames Television must, therefore, have seemed like a good idea at the time. However it quickly became apparent how tricky the transition was going to be. Notwithstanding writers of the calibre of Barry Cryer and John Junkin, in this latest ITV incarnation the old BBC spark had gone, smothered by a 25-minute format and regular commercial breaks. As confirmed by that very public bloody nose administered by Yarwood and their old pal Ammonds on Christmas Day, 1978, viewing figures dipped alarmingly, with almost nine and a half million viewers jumping ship in the case of that festive edition. By the time Ammonds and Braben were drafted in to try and rejuvenate the show in 1980, an under-pressure Eric Morecambe had already suffered a second major heart attack, resulting in a further too-brief period of rest and a triple-heart bypass. The good old days were now fast becoming a golden memory, as implicitly recognised by their former employers, who began to broadcast compilations of Eric and Ernie's best-loved moments under the banner, *Morecambe & Wise at the BBC*.

Why, everyone wondered, had they made such a switch in the first place? At the time, an offer of five times as much money was blamed, although it has since become widely accepted that Bill Cotton and the BBC offered to match the ITV deal pound for pound. No, equally high on their agenda was a promise by Thames that its subsidiary company, Euston Films, would develop a cinematic vehicle for the duo, an idea that Ernie in particular had never been quite able to let go. In the end, that movie never materialised; the closest they ever got to it was in a Thames feature-length comedy *Night Train to Murder*, plus an unlikely starring role as themselves in a 1978 episode of popular ITV cop show *The Sweeney*.

Sadly, by the time that former project was finally shown on British television in 1985, as a result of a third and this time fatal heart attack seven months earlier, the 58-year-old Eric Morecambe was dead.

Despite private moans that he was by now fed up with the concept of Morecambe and Wise, and half-hearted threats to break the double act in two, with Eric's second return to television the pair had in fact carried on just as before. True, they had dallied with individual projects, Ernie alongside Bill Maynard in a revival of *The Odd Couple* and Philip Larkin-lookalike Eric in a couple of ITV programmes for Anglia, based around the poetry of John Betjeman, *Betjeman's Britain* (1980) and *Late Flowering Love* (1981), but it was the partnership which still commanded most of their attention. In a one-hour 1983 Thames TV special, *Eric & Ernie's Variety Days*, the duo reminisced over those early times touring the halls. Deep down, they knew that their audiences were never likely to accept them as anything else. So they battled on regardless, until an incident in which Eric accidentally collided with a wall during the making of the duo's 1983 ITV Christmas Show, resulting in another heart scare and a two-night stay in hospital, brought his health back sharply into focus.

That, it seems, was the trigger for Eric Morecambe finally to heed the warnings and retire. No more *Morecambe & Wise Shows*; instead just a peaceful life of golf, photography and any other physically undemanding activity that took his fancy. This period of Morecambe's life was later captured beautifully in a Channel 4 documentary, *The Unseen Eric Morecambe*, first shown, appropriately enough, during Christmas 2004. In a strand normally devoted to revealing the dark and often tawdry secrets of well-known comedians, the only 'secret' here was that there were no secrets, or dark and tawdry ones at least. Instead the programme revealed a devoted family man of integrity and good humour. Despite filling what seemed to be a mountain of dictaphone tapes with future comedy ideas, found in a home office which had remained unopened since his death, and embarking on no end of time-filling hobbies that also included bird watching, trout fishing and painting, the over-riding impression was of a man who had decided, temporarily at least, to prioritise his wife Joan, their two grown-up children Gary (later to write a number of books based upon his father's life), Gail and adopted son, Steven. That and writing comic novels; the first such book in question, *Mr Lonely*, the story of

former club comic Sid Lewis who stabs himself to death with a star-shaped showbiz award, being published to widespread positive acclaim by Eyre Methuen in 1981. He would also write two children's books, *The Reluctant Vampire* (Methuen, 1982) and *The Vampire's Revenge* (Methuen, 1983), a fishing manual *Eric Morecambe on Fishing* (Pelham, 1984) and a further unfinished novel interrupted by his demise, *Stella* (Severn House, 1986).

Appropriately enough, Eric Morecambe's final moments were spent making an audience laugh. Early in 1984, after a period of relative good health, frequent hospital visits again began to be a feature. When a stomach and chest complaint refused to go away, subsequently leading to breathing complications and another visit to the doctor, Morecambe again found himself on medication. That new dose of tablets seemed to do the trick but when an ECG examination shortly afterwards showed enlargement of the heart, he was booked back into hospital for precautionary tests. Before then, however, he intended to go through with a couple of personal obligations. There was the Spring Bank Holiday weekend wedding of a family friend and then, on the Sunday, he went as promised to a charity show in Tewkesbury, where he was to be a guest interviewee for his old friend, Stan Stennett.

At first, the show in the cosy little Roses theatre went well, with Eric clearly enjoying the opportunity to once again delight an audience without too much, if any, physical effort. Then, when his interview with Stennett ended and the band struck up, it all got a bit silly. His mother Sadie had been right, a born entertainer, he could not help himself. The more the audience lapped up his antics, the more energetic Eric became until, to the relief of wife Joan looking on from the auditorium, after no less than six curtain calls he gave them a wave and stepped back into the wings. There, almost immediately, Eric Morecambe caught his breath, fell to the floor and hit his head. He was rushed to Cheltenham General Hospital where, around five and a half hours later, he finally lost the fight to regain consciousness.

How the nation mourned. Britain had not seen such an outpouring of collective grief at the death of a popular entertainer since the demise of Tommy Handley. And as the tributes flowed, a bewildered Ernie came under growing pressure to say a word or two about his former partner. The task of speaking at Eric's packed funeral in Harpenden, however, fell to Dickie Henderson, who the great man had 'booked' in the role after seeing him performing it with such distinction at the funeral of Arthur Askey. 'I would like to be cremated and my favourite music is "Smoke Gets in your Eyes",' he wrote to Henderson after that event. Six months after his own funeral, a star-studded London Palladium Show was staged in aid of the British Heart Foundation, *Bring Me Sunshine - A Tribute to Eric Morecambe*, recorded and later re-shown as an ITV Christmas Day special. In 1999, fifteen years after his death, a bronze statue of Eric would be unveiled by Her Majesty the Queen in his hometown Morecambe, close to the spot where his mother and father, Sadie and George, had gazed across the bay all those years before. Fittingly, he is captured by sculptor Graham Ibbeson in the throes of the 'Bring Me Sunshine' dance, with which he and Ernie had become so instantly synonymous. Less appropriately, he is dancing by himself.

While television would continue to be kind to the memory of Eric Morecambe well into the 21st century - in 2005 he was voted the fourth greatest comedy act ever in *The Comedian's Comedian* - that would not be the case for the 'brother' he left behind. For when the BBC documentary makers came calling on Ernie eight years after Morecambe's death in 1993, to make a *40 Minutes* programme called *The Importance of Being Ernie*, he did not fare anywhere near as well.

Life without Eric was always going to be a struggle for Ernie Wise. Not only had he never known any other life but showbiz, he had spent 43 years of it alongside a man who was now gone. Furthermore, for all his undoubted contribution to the double act they had created together, there was no escaping the fact that little Ern' had essentially been thought of as the straight man. Eric had been the funny one. Eric without Ernie? Why not? Ernie without Eric? Unthinkable. Where could his career go now? Back to his roots was the answer, as a solo song and dance man on a short tour of Australia. After that, he took whatever opportunity came his way, including a one-off appearance in an American sitcom, *Too Close for Comfort*, and a starring role in a 1987 West End production of Charles Dickens's unfinished last novel, *The Mystery of Edwin Drood*. He took a role as a policeman in the Ray Cooney farce *Run For Your Wife* and there were numerous TV panel game appearances on the likes of long-running favourites *Countdown* and *What's My Line?* In 1990, he also published a

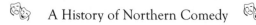

tellingly-titled autobiography, *Still On My Way to Hollywood*, before appearing on *This Is Your Life* the following year. For a man of retirement age, that wasn't a half bad workload yet, it seems, that wasn't quite enough for the makers of *40 Minutes* two years later. In a spiteful and quite nauseating display of presumably youthful arrogance, they took a twisted delight in portraying the now-elderly Ernie Wise as some sort of showbiz weirdo, lost in the past and foolishly unwilling to give up his dreams. Some forty years on, they were still trying to bury him in that box.

Wise, now 67, had made the mistake of growing old and living his life in the way he wanted - nay, needed - to live it. One newspaper review of the documentary echoed the cynicism of its makers perfectly: '...there could be no doubt, watching this programme, that "and Wise" was just as dead as Morecambe'. Never mind, you want to say, if you wouldn't mind waiting for just another eight months or so, his *actual* demise will begin to kick in. For it was then that Ernie Wise suffered the first of the two strokes which led, eventually, to official retirement on the occasion of his 70th birthday. Four years later, in 1999, he too was dead, the victim like his partner and friend before him, of a fatal heart attack.

But let us not leave Eric Morecambe and Ernie Wise on such a bitter note. The year 1999, after all, was also when Eric beat Tommy Cooper and John Cleese to the title of 'funniest man of the 20th century' in an internet poll. Repeats of classic *Morecambe & Wise* shows continue to attract large numbers of viewers and, in 2001, a West End play written by and starring Sean Foley and Hamish McColl, *The Play What I Wrote*, opened with assistance from Eddie Braben and was originally directed by Kenneth Branagh. Indeed, as recently as 2009, Tim Whitnall's one-man play, *Morecambe*, with Bob Golding in the starring role, blazed a trail through the Edinburgh Fringe. In it, the role of Ernie Wise goes - rather ingeniously - to a ventriloquist's dummy, whom the ghost of Eric kisses sweetly on the forehead as he lays him down to sleep. Ernie's father Harry would surely have approved.

14
They Don't Like It Up 'Em

"The central heating broke down and I had to
hold my pussy in front of it - it was frozen solid."
- Mrs. Slocombe, (Mollie Sugden), Are You Being Served?

While light entertainment glittered on gaily through the darkest days of
the 1970s, for television drama it was another story entirely, especially on
the BBC. In particular, many of the UK's finest future dramatists - such
as Ken Loach and Dennis Potter - were first showcased on *Play For Today*,
a strand which replaced *The Wednesday Play* at the turn of the decade. It
was on *Play For Today*, too, that Britain first squirmed its way through the
Manchester-born Mike Leigh's *Abigail's Party* (1977), a groundbreaking
comedy of embarrassment which lit a fuse for sitcom writers still to come.

For TV playwrights, a hard-hitting mood of 'sixties realism continued
to be *de rigeur*, as they shone a torch on nooks and crannies all too often
overlooked in polite society. But when it came to 'seventies sitcom - and
indeed for much of the 1980s too - although issues of class were very much
in the subtext, the nation preferred to pack up its troubles and smile. And,
as elsewhere, there were plenty of northern funnymen and women to help
it do just that. For all the ongoing and grittier glories of *Steptoe & Son*, *The
Likely Lads* and *Till Death Us Do Part*, in this defining decade for British
sitcom, escapism was the quality most frequently cherished.

It is safe to say that in the battle for television ratings in the 1970s, the BBC had a very good war indeed. And a major weapon in its artillery was its situation comedies, the most memorable among which being written by two men in particular. Their names were Jimmy Perry and David Croft and their first contribution to the cause, *Dad's Army*, was set on England's south coast during World War Two.

Manning the barricades for nine series and a number of Christmas specials between 1968 and 1977, in a reign which took in 80 episodes, a film, a stage show and three radio series along the way, after a wobbly start Walmington-on-Sea's aged and bumbling Home Guard grew into nothing less than a British institution. On the one hand, a nostalgic hymn to a bygone era of air-raid wardens, bicycle clips and church halls, *Dad's Army* was also a timeless and quietly subversive reflection on the English class system and the futility of war, which all the while recognised the latent heroism in the British character when called upon to do its duty. The perfect pick-me-up, in short, for economically stressful times.

The programme owed much of its popularity to the utterly perfect character acting of a cast that included John Le Mesurier (Sergeant Wilson), Clive Dunn (Lance Cpl. Jones), Ian Lavender (Private Pike), John Laurie (Private Frazer), Arnold Ridley (Private Godfrey), James Beck (Private Walker), Bill Pertwee (ARP warden), Frank Williams (the vicar) and doleful Mancunian Edward Sinclair (the verger). A fair amount of guest stars were brought in over the years too, many of whom, such as the Wakefield-born Janet Davies (Mrs Pike), Avril Angers, Oldham pair Eric Longworth and Caroline Dowdeswell and Durham comic Gordon Peters, had northern Variety backgrounds. Nor should we overlook the taciturn contribution of Wigan's Colin Bean who, as Private Sponge, appeared in 28 episodes as a member of the platoon's non-speaking back row!

There was no doubt, however, about the star of the show: Captain George Mainwaring, self-appointed leader of men and pompous pillar of the Walmington community. In the short and stocky, bespectacled and balding Arthur Lowe - born in Hayfield, Derbyshire in 1915, but raised in Manchester - Perry and Croft found the ideal actor to play their gruffly-officious Colonel Blimp of a bank manager. Yet he almost didn't get the gig. A high-profile ITV role as Leonard Swindley, the jilted paramour of Emily Nugent (later Bishop), in *Coronation Street* and a reprisal as Swindley in that soap's sitcom spin-offs *Pardon The Expression!* (1965-66) and *Turn Out The Lights* (1967), meant that BBC Head of Comedy Michael Mills was initially reluctant to cast him. Happily, the BBC's first choices, the St. Trinian's actor Thorley Walters and future *Doctor Who* Jon Pertwee, cousin of Bill, turned the part down and Mills was eventually persuaded to change his mind. How the comedy Gods rejoiced. With his grumpy, portly demeanour, and a chip perched comfortably on both shoulders, grammar school-educated Mainwaring, as played by Lowe, was the most comical of counterpoints to his second-in-command, the tall, languid and louche public school-educated Wilson, played with equally pained panache by Le Mesurier. Notwithstanding *Dad's Army*'s most obvious staples of slapstick and an avalanche of catchphrases - Jonesey's 'They don't like it up 'em' and 'Don't panic!', Frazer's 'We're doomed!', Mainwaring's put down of Pike: 'Stupid Boy!', the Warden's 'Put that light out!' and anything to do with Godfrey's geriatric sisters Cissie and Dolly (the latter played in three later episodes by Lowe's wife, Joan Cooper) among them - it was the inter-play between its two lead actors that produced many of the show's most sublime comedy moments.

The awkwardness in their relationship was established in the very first episode. Mainwaring: 'Get the first man in.' Wilson: 'Oh, very well. [Looks out of office door]. Would you mind stepping this way, please?' Mainwaring: 'Wilson, Wilson, come here, come here. I intend to mould those men out there into an aggressive fighting unit; I'm going to lead them, command them and inspire them to be ruthless killers. I'm not going to get very far if you invite them to step this way, am I? Quick march is the order.' And by the time episode 58 was aired in 1973, the pair were running like a well-oiled machine. Mainwaring: 'Where gave you been?' Wilson: 'Well, I went up to the golf club and had a bite to eat up there.' Mainwaring: 'The golf club?' Wilson: 'Yes.' Mainwaring: 'Who took you?' Wilson: 'Well, I'm a member.' Mainwaring: 'You're a member? Since when?' Wilson: 'Yes, well you see, when the committee heard about this title thing [the death of an uncle has moved 'The Honourable Arthur Wilson' even further up the social ladder], they asked me if, you know, I'd like to join.' Mainwaring [red-faced with fury]: 'I've been trying for years to get in there.' Wilson: 'I believe they're awfully particular.'

Yet it is another of the show's great strengths that while we are encouraged to laugh at Mainwaring's delusions of grandeur - and surely no comic actor was ever as adept at portraying punctured pomposity as Arthur Lowe - we are never allowed to forget the character's underlying honesty. For example, when a sherry party hosted by Mainwaring is gatecrashed by his black sheep of a travelling salesman brother Barry, also played by Lowe, in a 1975 Christmas special during which it emerges that the pair's father Edmund, who George has always referred to as belonging to The Master Tailors' Guild, actually ran a little draper's shop in Eastbourne, it allows both actor and writers to dig further beneath his bumptious surface. Captain Mainwaring is a flawed human being, but a human being nevertheless. And, ultimately, he has the courage to defend the values he holds dear (just as long as the dictatorial tyrant trampling all over them isn't his fearsome wife Elizabeth, of course).

Arthur Lowe's own father was a railway booking clerk, but the young Arthur showed no inclination to follow in his dad's tracks and began his working life as a stagehand at the Manchester Palace of Varieties. As a performer, he played in World War Two concert parties while stationed with the army in Egypt until, upon being demobbed, turning professional aged 30. A stage debut duly followed at the Hulme Hippodrome in 1946 and, by 1950, his talent was such that he had already taken bit-parts in six films, the Ealing comedy classic *Kind Hearts and Coronets* (1949) among them. In the years to come, Lowe would appear in literally hundreds of plays throughout London and the provinces, establishing a reputation as a character actor that eventually earned him roles in more than 50 films, perhaps most notably for the maverick director Lindsay Anderson in *This Sporting Life* (1963), *If....* (1968) and *O Lucky Man* (1973). His small screen debut came in 1951 and thereafter he found an increasing amount of work in that medium too, culminating in a seven-year residency among the cobbles of *Coronation Street* from 1960.

Unfortunately, the rapid rise of Lowe's own star was in direct contrast to the spluttering demise of his wife's. Since putting her own thespian ambitions to one side in order to raise a family, Joan, it seems, had begun to feel cut adrift from her husband's success. While Arthur worked up in Manchester, loved by millions, she was left to cope with the children at the family home in London and, as a result, began to drown her frustrations in drink. This personal pressure, when coupled with an intense workload and an uneasiness with stardom that would never leave him, Lowe fell hurtling into a major bout of depression. Realising he had to do something, he quit *Coronation Street* and set to work on patching up his marriage instead. Then, in 1967, came an invitation to lunch at the BBC from Jimmy Perry and David Croft.

When he first came up with the idea for *Dad's Army*, sitting on a commuter train bound for Stratford East, Jimmy Perry was a jobbing actor under Joan Littlewood's wing. He had, however, long held an ambition to write a television sitcom, not least because that was the only way in which he could guarantee himself a good part, or so he thought. And as a former member of the Barnes and Watford Home Guard, Perry knew the ideal subject. Thus were born 'The Fighting Tigers', a motley collection of hapless civilian soldiers; Britain's last line of defence against German invasion.

Although some twenty years after the event and deep in the swinging 'sixties, a comedy about the Home Guard was really not all that odd a concept. For one thing, the classic situation comedies *Bilko* and *The Army Game* were still fresh in the collective memory and continued to be much loved. Then there was the old Will Hay film *Oh! Mr Porter* which, as luck would have it, was receiving a television airing on the very same Sunday afternoon that Perry grappled with the mechanics of the set-up. 'One of the movie's strengths was the wonderful balance of characters,' Perry told Richard Webber, the author of *Dad's Army - A Celebration* (Virgin, 1997), '...a pompous man, a boy and an old man. The combination made for perfect comedy.' Upon completing a first draft, he put the script to one side before finally showing it to David Croft, already an established BBC director, on the set of a sitcom in which he had a bit part, *Beggar My Neighbour* (1966). Croft liked it and after the pair produced a second draft, Michael Mills was equally enthused, albeit proposing a change in name from 'The Fighting Tigers' to *Dad's Army*. With that done, the BBC's Head of Comedy gave the go-ahead for a first series of six episodes.

Far from hurtling straight into the comedy hall of fame, *Dads Army* took off in altogether less impressive style. And right up until the opening episode, there remained a danger that it might never be shown at all. The BBC was terrified that the programme might be deemed inappropriate or considered disrespectful and dismissive of the Home Guard and their

efforts during Britain's finest hour. In the end, these internal doubts were only allayed by an agreement that the cast would take part in a prologue ahead of the first episode, filmed in the present day, in which they would openly declare support for an 'I'm Backing Britain' campaign. Furthermore, the now familiar 'You have been watching...' closing credits, with which this and subsequent Perry and Croft collaborations have become so instantly recognisable, only came about after the original version - featuring actual war scenes, tanks, guns, refugees, vast ranks of marching Nazi troops *et al* - was objected to by the controller of BBC1, Paul Fox. Less controversial was *Dad's Army*'s cheery theme tune, 'Who Do You Think You Are Kidding, Mr Hitler?' Rather than being a genuine wartime song as many assume, it was in fact written by Jimmy Perry and Derek Taverner, and the last song to be recorded by Bud Flanagan, one half of the 'Crazy Gang' double act Flanagan and Allen, shortly before his death in 1968.

Nor did the show's content meet with universal acclaim. While a few newspapers gave it time to develop - 'I cannot say I cracked a rib, split my sides or even raised a good hearty belly laugh,' wrote the *Daily Express*, 'but some instinct is still telling me that the BBC is about to come up with a classic comedy series' - the majority were not so sure. Said the *Sunday Times*: '...the balance between humour and nostalgia seemed to be held uneasily.' 'Jimmy Perry's and David Croft's inaugural script was pretty feeble,' declared the *Sunday Telegraph*. While first prize in the 'Don't Give Up Your Day Job' awards of 1968 must surely go to the *Daily Mail*, whose TV critic loftily declared: 'The trouble with this is that it isn't situation comedy or character comedy, it's only gag comedy, the easiest to write and the quickest wearing on the ear.' It wasn't long before those words were being loudly eaten. As the audience grew to know and love the characters, so the humour developed and ratings increased.

It has since come to light that, originally, Jimmy Perry wanted Arthur Lowe to play Sergeant Wilson, while his original choice as Captain Mainwaring was the St. Helens actor Robert Dorning - who in the end had to make do with a cameo in a later show as a bank inspector. Jack Haig was in line for two roles - Jack Jones the butcher and his twin brother, George. Joe Walker, the spiv, was the part that Perry had originally written for himself, although he was soon elbowed out of the picture by the lure of music hall legend Arthur English. Of the final cast, only the respected Shakespearean actor John Laurie, *Hugh and I* sitcom star Arnold Ridley and the up-and-coming Ian Lavender lined up as expected from the start, as the dour Scottish undertaker Frazer, doddery incontinent pensioner Godfrey and Wilson's gormless young 'nephew' Pike respectively. Haig, having accepted a role in the children's TV show *Whacky Jacky*, was replaced by Clive Dunn as the now solo Jack Jones after impressing as an old man in *Bootsie and Snudge*, James Beck came in as Walker and, most wonderfully of all, John Le Mesurier landed the role of Pike's 'Uncle Frank', Mainwaring's number two. 'Michael Mills suggested John Le Mesurier and wanted him to play the captain,' recalls Croft, in Richard Webber's anthology. 'But then we came up with the idea of switching the classes, and he was cast as Sergeant Wilson.'

However they all got there, the team of all talents was now assembled and, over the years ahead, it became impossible to conceive of any *Dad's Army* member being played by anyone else. The unexpected death of James Beck cast a brief pall of gloom in 1973, after the actor fell victim to a burst pancreas while being operated on for a suspected stomach ulcer. Ironically, Beck had been one of the youngest cast members but, for a show whose very idea revolved around the notion of age, death was always going to be an occupational hazard. Somewhat remarkably then - and contrary to the so-called 'curse' of the programme - with the exception of verger Edward Sinclair, who died of a heart attack shortly after filming the final episodes, the rest of the protagonists hung around gamely until *Dad's Army* was last broadcast in November 1977. Appropriately enough, it all ended with raised mugs and a real life toast that carried echoes of that opening-day prologue, only this time by a team who had long ago made any original doubts look ridiculous. Wilson: 'Excuse me, sir. Don't you think it might be a nice idea if we paid tribute to them?' Mainwaring: 'For once, Wilson, I agree with you. To Britain's Home Guard.' All: 'To Britain's Home Guard!'.

Subsequently, John Laurie died of emphysema aged 83 in 1980. John Le Mesurier 'conked out' - as his self-written newspaper obituary put it - aged 71 in 1983. A year later, Arnold Ridley said goodbye at the grand old age of 88, while Janet Davies (Mrs Pike) died in 1986. Of the rest, Frank Williams, Bill Pertwee and Clive Dunn were all still around though

understandably taking life easier at the time of writing, while Ian
Lavender has since regained his status as a household favourite in the
long-running BBC soap opera *EastEnders*. As for Arthur Lowe, like the
rest of the surviving cast, with the finale of *Dad's Army* he had little choice
but to move on to pastures new.

Not that work was hard to come by. Indeed, he enjoyed great future
success with another couple of comic creations, the incorrigible meddler
Redvers Potter in *Potter*, a sitcom in which he starred for the BBC in
1979, and the cunning Irish priest Father Duddleswell in *Bless Me, Father*
(1978-81) for London Weekend Television the year before. In a busy
period generally, Lowe had also trodden the boards alongside Sir John
Gielgud in *The Tempest* at the Old Vic, popped up in numerous TV
dramas and, from 1974, been suitably delightful as the narrator of the
animation series, *Mr. Men*, based on the children's books of Cleckheaton-
born writer Roger Hargreaves. Wife Joan, though, remained unhappy.

By all accounts possessed of a personality not dissimilar to that of
Captain Mainwaring, in so far as he was a proud man of principle (in
Dad's Army, for example, Lowe's contract featured a clause that he should
never appear without his trousers and he refused to bring scripts into the
family home), he increasingly began to turn roles down unless a part
could also be found for his wife. Such loyalty was bound to limit his
employment prospects and, as a consequence, when he should have been
taking it easy in the many film and television projects that continued to
be put his way, Lowe instead developed an increased dependence on
more arduous, hectic and less well-paid theatre work, usually in smaller
provincial productions, staged outside London.

Until, in 1982, having made just two series of *Potter* and shortly after
filming his final sitcom for ITV, an adaptation of the HF Ellis books and
Punch magazine articles featuring the kindly public school maths teacher
A.J. *Wentworth*, BA, prior to performing alongside his wife in the play
Home At Seven at Birmingham's Alexandra Theatre, he suffered a fatal
stroke, collapsed in his dressing room and died the following morning in
hospital. Sadly, despite his enormous on-screen popularity, few people
attended his funeral. Uncomfortable with fame, perhaps he would have
appreciated the privacy. A more surprising absentee, though, was his wife,
Joan. As her husband was laid to rest, she was over the Irish Sea in

Belfast, continuing in the run of *Home At Seven* as planned. The show, it seemed, must go on until Joan herself passed away in 1987.

For all his many achievements in theatre, film and television, it is for Captain Mainwaring that Arthur Lowe will be most fondly remembered. His delight in playing Walmington's very own Napoleon, as his arch-nemesis Warden taunted him, was there in every disgruntled little pause and raised eyebrow. Maybe that was because so many of Mainwaring's characteristics were his own, and Lowe made no secret of the fact that the portrayal was based on the uppity Mr. Muddlecombe J.P., Robb Wilton's magistrate of all those years before. Yet whatever the world threw at him, however tattered his dignity, Captain Mainwaring was essentially a decent man who tried to do his best. And we can surely all relate to that.

For Jimmy Perry, then, *Dad's Army* did provide a hoped-for stepping stone into the world of television comedy writing. And as Walmington-on-Sea's Local Defence Volunteers continued their adventures, Perry came up with two more sitcoms of his own, the rather less memorable *The Gnomes of Dulwich* for the BBC in 1969 and *Lollipop Loves Mr Mole* for ITV in 1971. However, it was when he and David Croft put their heads together again on a new project in 1974 that popular success once more came calling. The result was a second show set against a military backdrop but which was, this time, based in the jungles of India and, later, Burma.

Another ensemble piece, *It Ain't Half Hot Mum* made the music hall influences detectable in *Dad's Army* explicit, in that it revolved around the antics of a Royal Artillery Concert Party whose number included Bombardier 'Solly' Solomons, played in the first two series by Bradford actor George Layton (who, as a writer, had contributed to *Doctor In The House* and, from 1986, would create *Executive Stress*, the ITV sitcom that gave the actor Nigel Havers his first big television role). Other members of the troupe included Gunner 'Gloria' Beaumont (a usually dragged-up Melvyn Hayes), the cultured Gunner 'Lah-de-dah' Graham (John Clegg) and a couple of upper class officer twits, Colonel Reynolds and Captain Ashwood, played by the Manchester-born Donald Hewlett and *Dad's Army* bit-parter Michael Knowles respectively. Most controversially, until his death in 1978, the part of head servant Rangi Ram was played by the

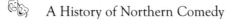

Indian-born but otherwise very white actor Michael Bates, replete with blacked-up face and turban. The remaining 'native' roles in *It Ain't Half Hot Mum* went at various times to Babar Bhatti as Punka-Wallah Rumzan, Dino Shafeek as Char-Wallah Muhammed and Andy Ho as Ah Syn, the cook. Those of a 'politically correct' persuasion should look away now.

While each member of the supporting cast played a part in helping *It Ain't Half Hot Mum* to last eight series from 1974 until 1981, without ever coming close to the critical high regard enjoyed by *Dad's Army*, it was Welsh actor Windsor Davies (Battery Sergeant-Major Williams) and his diminutive Mancunian stooge Don Estelle (Gunner 'Lofty' Sugden) who struck the loudest chord with the British public. So much so that when the duo recorded a cover version of the old Ink Spots hit, 'Whispering Grass', in 1975, it went straight to the top of the pop charts and stayed there for three weeks. Only 4ft tall in his stocking feet and with a physique like a little beer barrel, the bespectacled and cheerfully vacant Estelle - the concert party's unlikely lead chanteur, but with a voice like a nightingale - played foil to Windsor's mustachioed and bullying braggart, whose chest-out, overbearing machismo - catchphrase, a bellowed 'Shut up!' - was under threat from the 'bunch of pooftahs' under his command.

In keeping with Perry and Croft's tendency to employ a loose sort of repertory company, Estelle's own big television break had come courtesy of four bit-parts in *Dad's Army*. Until then a part-time club singer who had made a handful of walk-ons as an extra in *Coronation Street*, he had Arthur Lowe to thank for his first speaking role. Estelle, it seems, met Lowe on the set of the Granada soap and was advised by him to write to David Croft. This Estelle did with the result that, in 1969, he delivered a naval gun to Walmington-on-Sea in a Pickfords removal van. The following year he was asked back, this time to make the first of three appearances as Gerald, an assistant to Bill Pertwee's power-mad warden, Hodges.

Meanwhile, back in *It Ain't Half Hot Mum*, Don Estelle's fellow Mancunian, Kenneth MacDonald (Gunner 'Nobby' Clark), was one of four characters who gave the impression of making up the concert party numbers. The others were Stuart McGugan (Gunner Mackintosh), Mike Kinsey ('Nosher' Evans) - who was elected Labour party councillor for Greenhill in the London Borough of Harrow in 2002 - and Christopher Mitchell (Gunner 'Parky' Parkin), who Sergeant-Major Williams thought was his son and therefore favoured accordingly. In reality, Mitchell was actually the son of a Sheffield-born comedy actor named Norman Mitchell, who had himself appeared in a 1969 episode of *Dad's Army* as Captain Rogers. Tragically, after a career that spanned just about television comedy show imaginable over five decades, Mitchell senior died in 2001, only twenty-five days after his son Christopher passed away from cancer. The career of Kenneth MacDonald, meanwhile, reached its apogee in 1981, when he began a thirteen-year stint as pub landlord Mike Fisher in the hugely successful BBC sitcom *Only Fools and Horses*. He too died in 2001, aged 50, of a heart attack while holidaying with his family in Hawaii.

After another solo effort for ITV, *Room Service* (1979), had limped its way to a disappointing seven episodes, the Perry and Croft partnership hit its third consecutive piece of pay dirt with the launch of holiday camp comedy *Hi de Hi* (later, souped-up with hyphens and a dog's dick as *Hi-de-Hi!*). This time the era was the 1950s, but otherwise all the familiar traits established with *Dad's Army* and *It Ain't Half Hot Mum* remained in place: fine ensemble acting with class conflict a recurrent theme, a keen eye for nostalgic detail, a catchy theme tune ('Hi-de-hi-de-hi, ho-de-ho-de-ho, go, go, go, do the holiday rock...'), a stock troupe of amusing character actors in which northern comedians were again to the fore, echoes of the music hall and so on. And all of it mined from the personal experiences of Perry and Croft, who were respectively a former Butlins Redcoat and holiday camp summer show producer between them. And two bit-part veterans from *Dad's Army*, Felix Bowness (as the jockey Fred Quilly) and Jeffrey Holland (the wannabe comedian Spike Dixon), now had major billing.

Although it limped home in 40th place during a televised BBC poll searching for *Britain's Best Sitcom*, in its finest moments *Hi-de-Hi!* matched anything that *Dad's Army* had to offer. Unfortunately, those finest moments didn't come around with anything like enough regularity. True, over the first four series, there was lots to enjoy in the interplay between Maplin's Entertainments Manager Jeffrey Fairbrother (the moon-faced Simon Cadell) and his Yellowcoat-in-chief Gladys Pugh, whose sing-song in-house radio announcements elicited an increasingly weary communal response of 'ho-de-ho' as time went by, thereby giving the show its name. Gladys was played with formidable Celtic forcefulness by Ruth Madoc,

the one-time wife of actor Philip Madoc who, as a German U-boat captain in a 1973 episode of *Dad's Army* memorably demanded a certain cheeky young Private's name only to be met by Captain Mainwaring's immortal retort: 'Don't tell him, Pike.' For all its comedy value, however, the class divisions that kept Jeffrey and Gladys apart lacked the subtlety of the Mainwaring-Wilson dynamic, and the humour only got broader with the arrival of David Griffin as Squadron Leader Clive Dempster, when Cadell headed back to theatre before his untimely death from cancer in 1986. Generally, *Hi-De-Hi!* had a tendency to lay the comedy and pathos on with a trowel.

Not that any of that affected its ratings. Perry and Croft's ability to marry engaging characterisation with brilliant casting again proved not only timeless but priceless too, with veteran actor Leslie Dwyer, as the child-hating Punch and Judy man Mr. Partridge, and the married (yet quite clearly gay) frustrated hoofers Yvonne and Barry Stuart-Hargreaves (Perry's sister-in-law Diane Holland and Barry Howard) helping to attract regular audiences of some 15 million viewers. A pantomimic atmosphere was further reinforced by a clutch of appropriately vacuous Yellowcoat girls and boys (principally, the under-dressed Nikki Kelly and Rikki Howard, with Chris Andrews and the Webb twins, Stanley and Bruce, wearing the white flannel trousers). And best of the lot were Yorkshire comedian Paul Shane as resident camp comic Ted Bovis and a madcap actor from Nottingham named Su Pollard who, as Peggy the chalet maid, held an ambition to one day become a glamourous Yellowcoat herself. All in all, it was an appealing brew that began with a successful pilot in 1980 and continued through eight massively popular series until 1988, ensuring 20 years of unbroken success for its creators.

Legend has it that the Rotherham-born Shane - christened George Frederick Speight in 1940, and whose television debut came in 1972 in Alan Bennett's aforementioned TV play *A Day Out* - beat the challenge of ex-Goon Harry Secombe among others to win the part of Bovis. Either way, with his gruff northern demeanour and ample proportions wrapped tight in a brown-checked suit, replete with dickie bow and red carnation, Shane was the perfect choice as the surly Brylcremed comedy pro with a heart of gold. He certainly had several years' experience of his own to draw upon, out there on the South Yorkshire club circuit.

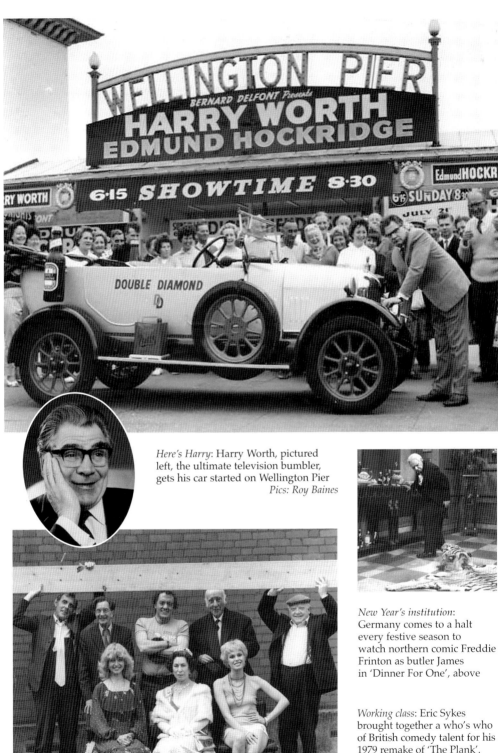

Here's Harry: Harry Worth, pictured left, the ultimate television bumbler, gets his car started on Wellington Pier
Pics: Roy Baines

New Year's institution: Germany comes to a halt every festive season to watch northern comic Freddie Frinton as butler James in 'Dinner For One', above

Working class: Eric Sykes brought together a who's who of British comedy talent for his 1979 remake of 'The Plank'. Clockwise - Eric Sykes, Charles Hawtrey, Harry H. Corbett, Wilfrid Hyde-White, Arthur Lowe, Joanna Lumley, Jeanette Charles, Liza Goddard.
Pic: FremantleMedia Ltd/ Rex Features

She knows, you know: Hylda Baker and Jimmy Jewel star as Nellie and Eli Pledge in the 1973 ITV sitcom 'Nearest and Dearest'   *Pic: ITV/Rex Features*

The Good Old Days: Oldham's Bernard Cribbins performs before an amateur dramatics crowd on the stage of the City Varieties Music Hall, Swan Street, Leeds
                                        Pic: Nev Jopson/City Varieties

Life's a drag: The legendary duo Eric Morecambe and Ernie Wise line up with guest star Leonard Rossiter during the pair's less successful ITV show.
Pic: FremantleMedia Ltd/ Rex Features

Revolutionary impressionist: Mike Yarwood's shows were enjoyed by millions

King of Knotty Ash: Ken Dodd and his Diddymen took every entertainment medium in the 'sixties and 'seventies by storm - including the jigsaw industry!

Laundry day chit-chat: Les Dawson, right, and Roy Barraclough appear as Cissie and Ada during Dawson's show, 'Sez Les'
Pic: ITV/Rex Features

It's the way they told 'em.: 'The Comedians' line up for the first series in 1971. Pictured clockwise from back - George Roper, Ken Goodwin, Duggie Brown, Frank Carson, Bernard Manning, Charlie Williams, unknown and Paul Melba.   *Pic: ITV/Rex Features*

Rock on!:
Cannon &
Ball, above,
were a breath
of fresh air
 Pic: Bobby Ball

If the hat fits...: Liverpool's prince of stand-up Jimmy Tarbuck meets the one and only Freddie 'Parrot Face' Davies   *Pic: www.freddiedavies.com*

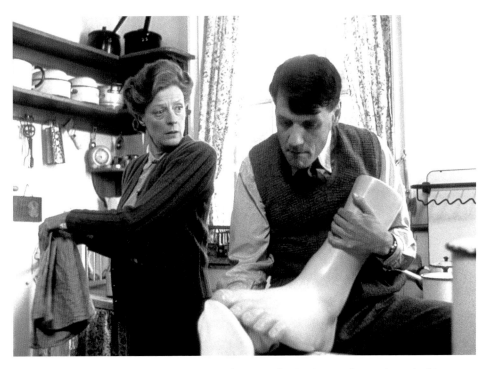

Don't bring feet to the table...: Maggie Smith and Michael Palin put chiropody on the big screen in Alan Bennett's 1984 film, 'A Private Function'. *Pic: c.Island/Everett/Rex Features*

Unique folk: The late great Jake Thackray, pictured left, and Chorley's inimitable Phil Cool - the man of a million faces
*Pics: www.jakethackray.com
& www.philcool.co.uk*

New Faces: Victoria Wood, Nicky Martyn and Marti Caine get a hair-do apiece in 'The Summer Show'
*Pic: ITV/
Rex Features*

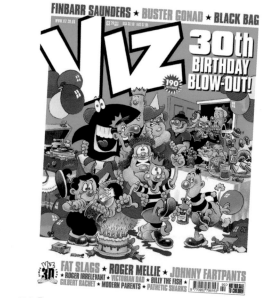

Anarchy in the UK:
Rik Mayall and
Bradford-born
Ade Edmondson,
in their early guise
as the Dangerous
Brothers, above

Comic cuts:
Viz comic was
a publishing
phenomenon
thanks to a
host of ribald
stars like the
Fat Slags, left,
and Sid the
Sexist, right

*Pics &
characters:
copyright Viz*

Master craftsman: Sheffield
superstar John Shuttleworth
is a maestro of the banal
*Pic: John Baucher, a.k.a. Moochin
Photoman on www.flickr.com*

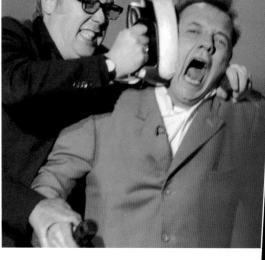

*It's about this time in the evening that I like to iron my
friend's face...*: Vic Reeves and Bob Mortimer
unleashed on 'Des O'Connor Tonight'
Pic: FremantleMedia Ltd/Rex Features

Masterpiece: The stars and
creators of The Royle Family,
pictured in 1998. Clockwise
from back - Ralf Little,
Caroline Aherne, Craig
Cash, Liz Smith, Ricky
Tomlinson and Sue Johnston
Pic: ITV/Rex Features

When giants collide - aha!:
Chat-show legend Alan
Partridge (Steve Coogan)
comes face to face with 'Last
of the Summer Wine' veteran
Nora Batty (Kathy Staff)
Pic: ITV/Rex Features

Peter, Paul and merry: Two modern-day northern favourites go head to head as Peter Kay appears on Channel 4's 'The Paul O'Grady Show' in October 2009   *Pic: Ken McKay/Rex Features*

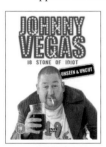

Not so daft: Johnny Vegas is far from the only comedian to utilise his character's marketing potential through the regular release of dvds

Silver fox: Dave Spikey is the master of a microphone
Pic: Bighook Ltd

Count Arthur Strong *To Dear Sonny it's Tony only a little one! Arthur*

Back to the future: Former Variety trouper Count Arthur Strong, above, deserves to take his place in the pantheon of greatness
Pic: www.komediaentertainment.com

Like so many from that part of the world, Shane's working life had begun down the pit, in his case at Silverwood Colliery, until an accident in the pit-head baths left him with a double-slipped disc and pensioned off at the tender age of 27. It was a blessing in disguise. Two years later, Paul Shane had reinvented himself as a professional entertainer, initially as a singer and then a comedian, a development that anyone who saw his unintentionally hilarious rendition of the Righteous Brothers classic 'You've Lost That Loving Feeling' on the BBC1 lunchtime show *Pebble Mill* in 1996 would surely endorse wholeheartedly. And if you didn't see it then, it is probably still available on *You Tube*. Sixteen years earlier, with his sackless protege Spike perched firmly under his wing and engaged in a constant battle of wills with Fairbrother, whose job he covets, the bombastic and pig-headed Ted was a splendid figurehead for a show whose entertaining exploration of thwarted human desire and aspiration, personal and professional, is too often overlooked.

For along with all the playground humour, *Hi-de-Hi!* was never afraid to grapple with the restless sensitivity of the human soul, particularly where thin-skinned and needy showbiz-types are concerned. On its own terms, Joe Maplin's camp was simply a place of unthreatening family fun, an oasis of innocence before the flamenco dancers of Llorett de Mar and Benidorm came stomping over the horizon, spreading their visions of package holidays, paella and chips in the Mediterranean midday sun. For the invisible tyrant's yellow-coated employees, meanwhile, it signified something else entirely. To them, Maplin's was in some ways a prison camp of the cliché, a cage, and a metaphor for lives and ambitions unfulfilled. At best, that tatty old camp might be one small step on a ladder heading for the stars. At worst, it put a glass ceiling on all their hopes and dreams. And worse still - we as viewers knew what was coming next. Not only was the slow lingering death of the annual British seaside holiday just around the corner, but the end of live Variety entertainment itself. That the characters in the show were unaware of any of this, and continued to dream their dreams and hope their hopes anyway, lent the *Hi-de-Hi!* set-up a profound level of insight usually found in only the very best situation comedies.

And of them all, who knew more of hopes and dreams than Peggy Ollerenshaw? Downtrodden in equal measure by her unseen boss Miss

Cathcart and Gladys, and overlooked by those with whom she craves to be considered a peer, Su Pollard's lovably enthusiastic and goodnatured, if distinctly potty, chalet maid soon became the heartbeat of the show.

By the time *Hi-de-Hi!* came along, Susan Georgina Pollard - born 1949 - had already appeared in one BBC television sitcom, as one half of a hippy partnership with the actor Paul Nicholas in the short-lived squatters comedy *Two Up, Two Down* (1978). Before that, her TV debut had come four years earlier, when her version of 'I'm Just A Girl Who Can't Say No' from the Oscar and Hammerstein musical *Oklahoma*, was beaten into second place on *Opportunity Knocks* by a singing Jack Russell, as already described. Between those two career high points she retreated to the stage, a place where, if her own website is to be believed, she made her first public appearance in a school nativity play aged six: 'Whilst standing on a box announcing the arrival of the Angel Gabriel, she fell through the lid. Everyone roared with laughter.' Well you would, wouldn't you? As a 16-year-old, Pollard began singing in working men's clubs - brave girl - and developing her craft at Nottingham's Arts Theatre, where she completed the dramatic apprenticeship that served her so well when given the chance to play Peggy.

Carried along by Pollard's talent for gurning - a somewhat unusual approach in a female comic even today - and the sterling efforts of the rest of a cast that was never less than wholehearted, *Hi-De-Hi!* was nevertheless looking long passed its best by the time the finishing line came into view, some eight years after its original outing. Yet with the end in sight, the programme raised its game again and the impetus for this new-found energy was the closure of the Maplin's camp itself. For all their shared longings of improving their lot, its inmates were finally about to be confronted with the unpredictable and harsh new world outside those soon-to-be crumbling walls. In the light of which, their previously limited but comfortable existence didn't seem too bad an option at all. Time, as ever, was moving on and the message was clear: strive to be better by all means, but in the meantime appreciate the life that you have. Because nothing - absolutely nothing - lasts forever.

And then came a trademark stroke of Perry and Croft's genius. As the show's principal characters say their last goodbyes and depart to the station on a specially hired coach, the one who has most to lose from the

They Don't Like It Up 'Em

Maplin's closure is not even allowed to share the same vehicle. Instead Peggy, whose dreams of becoming a Yellowcoat are now irreparably dashed forever, is told to stay behind and clear up. As the programme enters its closing titles, with the melancholy mood enhanced by a slowly retreating camera shot in which the emotionally crushed chalet maid wanders forlornly towards the centre of the camp alone, what might have been the most downbeat of finales suddenly takes a different twist. Standing in the dead square middle of a camp now shrunk to panoramic proportions, the tiny figure of Peggy suddenly leaps into the air and yells *Hi-de-Hi!* from the depths of her not inconsiderable lungs.

With the chalets shuttered up and the buckets and spades left to rot on the sands, Jimmy Perry and David Croft again turned to three of the stars of *Hi-de-Hi!* when planning a fourth assault on the sitcom hall of fame. Su Pollard, fresh from a national tour of her one-woman show and the ghastly hit single, 'Starting Together', theme tune to BBC reality TV show *The Marriage*, returned to the fray. Paul Shane and Jeffrey Holland came back too. And the show in question was *You Rang, M'Lord?*, the pilot for which launched in 1988.

Again it was a period piece and again it dealt primarily with class. This time, though, the period was the roaring 'twenties and the setting a well-to-do London household, in which the toffs lived upstairs and their servants downstairs. The first in a four-series run began in 1990, with Shane, Holland and Pollard duly employed as Alf Stokes the butler, head servant James Twelvetrees and parlour maid Ivy Teasdale respectively. In keeping with Perry and Croft's repertory instincts, there were also roles for *It Ain't Half Hot Mum* pair Donald Hewlett and Michael Knowles, as Lord Meldrum and his nice-but-dim brother, the Honourable Teddy, and a regular walk-on for *Dad's Army* stalwart Bill Pertwee as the officious PC Wilson. If ever a show looked promising on paper this was it. Alas, for *You Rang, M'Lord?* looking promising on paper was as good as it got. Unusually for a Perry-Croft sitcom, the main problem was that few, if any, of the characters were likeable or even sympathetic. In a convoluted set-up, Stokes was actually an undercover crook who, in partnership with Ivy (secretly his daughter), intended to rob Lord Meldrum (with whom he

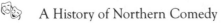

had gained employment, along with the non-criminal but over-deferential James Twelvetrees, after saving the life of Meldrum's brother Teddy in the First World War trenches a decade before). The show also had strong elements of sexual farce. Just about everyone was chasing or attempting to escape the clutches of one suitor or another, usually across accepted class boundaries. And in Katie Rabett's ironically-named Cissy, monocle and all, *You Rang, M'Lord* featured British sitcom's first openly lesbian character. It added up to a far darker experience than anything the writers had come up with before.

If the concept was good, the production qualities were too, but the British public remained stubbornly reluctant to warm to a sitcom that never hit the mark with anything like the required consistency. And when the last of its 26 episodes aired in 1993, that effectively brought an end to a partnership that had, once upon a time, struck television comedy gold. Even before that date, however, Perry had continued to plough his own parallel furrow and, in 1989, launched another writing relationship with the producer Robin Carr on an ITV sitcom *High Street Blues*, which was fortunate to last one series. Nor did Croft have much luck when, in 1995, and in association with a number of writers that did not include Jimmy Perry, he brought the *Hi-De-Hi!* trio of Shane, Pollard and Holland back together for a third time for his take on the British railway closures of the 1960s, *Oh, Doctor Beeching!*. Again, it was a terrific idea that, despite a well-received pilot, didn't really catch on, hitting the sitcom buffers after two disappointing series in 1997.

By which time, David Croft had also spent around a quarter of a century embroiled in a second comedy writing partnership that, in terms of longevity, paid even richer dividends than *Dad's Army*. With the adventures in Walmington-on-Sea in full flow and *It Ain't Half Hot Mum* a twinkle in his and Perry's eye, he had also begun to collaborate with the established actor and writer Jeremy Lloyd, whose scriptwriting experience already extended to working with Harry Secombe, Dickie Henderson and Roy Castle. The show the pair created, *Are You Being Served?*, confirmed Croft's nose for timeless situation comedy and underlined his matchless knack for talent spotting. And here too, much of that talent was born of the north of England.

Croft's own career as a writer and producer began in 1961, when he produced and contributed episodes to a seven-episode BBC sitcom based around the exploits of a group of students, *The Eggheads*. For his next trick, Croft produced the fifth series of the increasingly popular *Benny Hill Show* later that same year. By the time he teamed up with Jimmy Perry to produce *Dad's Army* around six years on, he was a BBC fixture and fitting, a state of affairs that led to his appointment as producer of the first series of Frankie Howerd's *Up Pompeii!* in 1969. Two years after that, the BBC received an idea in the post from the now out-of-work Lloyd, freshly returned from writing and appearing on the legendary American sketch show *Rowan And Martin's Laugh-In* (during which spell, jet-lagged, he had slept in and missed the party that ended in the Charles Manson-inspired massacre of Roman Polanski's pregnant wife Sharon Tate, plus four of her Cielo Drive house guests). With *Dad's Army* now comfortably up and running, after seeing Lloyd's proposal for a series set in a department store, the BBC asked the industrious Croft if he wanted to be involved. A request to which they doubtless received the answer: 'I'm Free!'.

Never have the origins of such a benign piece of sitcom fluff been accompanied by so much death and destruction. For along with Lloyd's own close-shave, it was only thanks to the horrifying kidnapping and massacre of Israeli athletes by Palestinian terrorists at the 1972 Olympic Games that *Are You Being Served?* went to air in the first place. Until that point, Croft and Lloyd's pilot sat ignored on a shelf in somebody's office awaiting a possible berth in the next series of *Comedy Playhouse*. Yet when the tragic events in Munich unfolded, leaving the BBC with no sport with which to fill their schedules, that tape was brought in to plug a gap. Once shown, it won widespread acclaim and a full series was duly made.

From its launch proper in 1973 to its tenth and last series in 1985, *Are You Being Served?* enjoyed phenomenal popularity, not only in the UK but overseas too. Somewhat appropriately, given its taste for excruciating double entendres, there were 69 episodes in all, plus a 1977 feature film, a stage show, a less successful sequel - *Grace and Favour* - in 1992 and, bizarrely, a CBS-driven American version of the show, *Beanes of Boston*, that lasted one episode in 1979. An Australian remake in 1980, this time with the original *Are You Being Served?* title and written by Croft and Lloyd, enjoyed 16 episodes down under. Even today, the antics of the

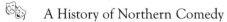

Grace Brothers sales staff continue to be a surefire ratings winner on cable channels across the world.

When the *Are You Being Served?* lift doors slid open, David Croft again continued to take the ensemble approach that was serving *Dad's Army* so well. The likes of Arthur Brough (the elderly tailor, Mr. Grainger) and Harold Bennett ('young' Mr Grace) had both made cameo visits to Walmington-on-Sea church hall in their time and the original choice for Private Walker, Arthur English, was the irreverent maintenance man, Mr. Harmen. As usual, a well-crafted theme tune - 'Ground floor: perfumery, stationery and leather goods, wigs and haberdashery, kitchenware and food. Going up!' - kicked things off, followed by plenty of quintessential class-based Britishness, in which everyone was respectfully addressed by their title while simultaneously peddling a music hall brand of innuendo that sailed daringly close to the wind during family primetime.

Chief in that department was Mrs. Slocombe's pussy, the trials and overnight tribulations of whom were shared in eye-watering detail upon her entry to the store - 'the least sign of danger and my pussy's hair stands on end.' As the head of ladies fashion and the owner of that aforementioned cat (at least we must *assume* she was talking about a cat), Mrs. Betty Slocombe (maiden name Mary Elizabeth Jennifer Rachel Yiddell Abergavenny) was destined to become one of British sitcom's true comedy grotesques. With her garish rinses, outrageous double entendres and pretensions to refinement, this middle-aged force of nature was played to perfection by a Keighley-born actress who was already a doyen of British sitcom by the time *Are You Being Served?* came along.

Born Mary Isobel Sugden in Riddlesden in 1922, Mollie Sugden trained at the Guildhall School of Music and Drama, before honing her skills for many years in repertory theatre. It was there, in 1956, that she met her husband, the actor William Moore, best known for his role as Ronnie Corbett's father in the sitcom *Sorry!*. Sugden's television comedy debut came with the Croft-produced *Hugh And I* in 1962 and she was soon equally well known as the arch-gossip Nellie Harvey in *Coronation Street*. Reprising her stage role as Jimmy Clitheroe's mother, Mollie also featured in an ill-fated attempt to take the diminutive comic's radio show to TV, via the children's sitcom *Just Jimmy* in 1964. However it was when she landed the role of Mrs. Hutchinson, the snobbish and domineering mother of Sandra in the Liverpudlian sitcom *The Liver Birds*, that she really began to make her mark. And from there it was but a small step to even greater stardom on the floor of Grace Brothers, where she forged a fine double act with her bubble-headed protégé, Miss Brahms, played by the Middlesbrough-born but London-raised Wendy Richard, another who had once enjoyed bit-parts in *Dad's Army*, in her case as Private Walker's girlfriend. In later years, Richard would be even more familiar as the altogether dowdier Pauline Fowler, matriarch of Albert Square in BBC soap *EastEnders*. And ironically, as closely associated as Sugden and Richard were in sitcom, so they became in death. When Mollie Sudgen died, aged 86, after a long illness in July 2009, after having never quite recovered from the loss of her husband William nine years earlier, her departure came only weeks after the death of Wendy Richard, who passed away with cancer in February of that year, aged 65.

Along with Mrs. Slocombe, the second great cult comedy figure spawned by *Are You Being Served?* was played by yet another northerner, the Preston-born actor John Inman. And not since the days of Julian and Sandy in *Round The Horne* has there been a more unworldly purveyor of gay innuendo than Mr. Wilberforce Humphries. Whether tottering down the stairs from the store's central escalator on glam rock platform shoes, clad in a biker's black leather jacket or dressing down for the day in a little boy's sailor suit, Mr. Humphries's response to the probing of floorwalker Capt. Stephen Peacock RASC (Frank Thornton) - 'Are you free, Mr Humphries?', 'I'm Free!' - entered catchphrase folklore. Inman, Croft and Lloyd have all subsequently insisted that the character was camp rather than homosexual, a less than credible position in so many respects. That they felt the need to be so defensive over the inclinations of a fictional character at all owed much to the criticism regularly aimed at the programme throughout the politically correct 1980s, on account of its supposedly crude and out-of-date stereotypes. Watched today, however, and the abiding impression is one of innocence matched by a still quite shocking daring. *Are You Being Served?* is unsettling, but in a good way.

Well before his days of inside leg measurements, as John Inman revealed in an edition of the BBC Radio 4 programme *That Reminds Me* in 2001, the future Mr. Humphries took his first fledgling steps on stage at the prompting of his sewing machine factory worker mother, who paid half a crown a week for his tap-dancing lessons. An equally useful patron was his stagestruck headmaster who sent the young hoofer - already a frequent performer in his mother's back yard - to audition for a repertory company aged just 13, leading to employment on Blackpool's South Pier and a later job sweeping the stage. He began acting upon it as a school-leaver. From there, Inman embarked on numerous tours up and down the country and began a pantomime career with his friend, the *Hi-De-Hi!* star Barry Howard, with whom he appeared in more than forty productions. Real fame came, however, with his elevation to the staff of Grace Brothers although, as Inman himself told Radio 4, the initial response of BBC chief Bill Cotton to the pilot did not augur well. 'Yes, we'll have more,' Cotton is said to have told David Croft. 'But get rid of the puff.' Needless to say, thanks to a threat from his co-creator that if 'the puff' went, so did he, the senior sales assistant of Grace Brothers menswear was granted a reprieve and Inman was duly voted the funniest man on television by readers of the listings magazine *TV Times* in 1976. When Grace Brothers finally closed its doors in 1985, John Inman continued to work in television and theatre, where he already had a reputation as one of the best pantomime dames in showbiz. He died from complications with Hepatitis 'A', aged 71, in 2007.

On the face of it the north west's answer to *The Likely Lads*, but with a couple of single girls instead of boys in the lead roles, even at the end of the so-called swinging 'sixties *The Liver Birds* was somewhat unique in putting two young female flatmates centre-stage; mild-mannered 'good girl' Sandra (Nerys Hughes) and her loud-mouthed working class friend Beryl (Polly James). Having said that, a show which, like *Are You Being Served?*, began as a *Comedy Playhouse* pilot in 1969 was not entirely without precedent. In 1963, another *Comedy Playhouse* one-off penned by *Hugh And I* writer John Freeman called *The Bachelor Girls*, starring Tracey Reed and Anna Palk, had aired without a follow-up series. And two years before that, *Winning Widows* also featured two female characters on ITV. Given that the stars of *that* production were the battleaxe character actor Peggy Mount and her on-screen sister Avice Landon, however, it seems safe to say that the liberated Sandra and Beryl were always going to be a different proposition entirely.

Just about latching on to the final dregs of 'sixties Scouse trendiness and with a theme tune sung by Paul McCartney's brother Mike McGear of pop-poets Scaffold - 'Are you dancing?', 'Are you asking?', 'I'm asking', '..then I'm dancing...' - *The Liver Birds* was as ballsy an idea for a sitcom as had, until then, been seen. Written by a couple of Liverpool housewives, Myra Taylor and Carla Lane, it captured the aspirational realism of the times, thanks to its high-energy originality. The weekly plotlines revolved around the lives of these two independent young women and their luck - or otherwise - with a succession of prospective boyfriends, one of whom, incidentally, was played by the future creator of *Yes, Minister*, Jonathan Lynn. Most amusingly to modern audiences, perhaps, as the series unfolded, the characters adorned themselves in the height of flamboyant 'seventies fashion, particularly Beryl, who looked like an explosion in a Bootle hot-pants factory.

To begin with, in the 1969 pilot and a four-episode first series shown later that year, *The Liver Birds* (the name a pun on the sculptures that sit atop the Royal Liver Building on the Mersey pier head) were Beryl and Dawn, the latter played by Pauline Collins. When Dawn moved out, Sandra moved in and that was how it stayed until series five, when Beryl departed and Nerys Hughes's character teamed up with the altogether dippier fashion victim Carol (Elizabeth Estensen). When Carol brought the rest of her large and eccentric family with her, albeit living in their own house, including her rabbit-loving brother Lucien (played by the Liverpudlian actor Michael Angelis - that's the brother, not the rabbit), it added yet another twist to a show that was by then at the mid-point of an enormously popular nine-series run. Indeed, its impact could still be felt in 1996, a full 17 years after the original programme finally ended, when a less successful comeback in which the lives of Sandra and Beryl were brought right up to date was broadcast over seven episodes.

Along with being a landmark in British sitcom, for one half of its creative partnership, Carla Lane, *The Liver Birds* also provided a pathway to a respected career in sitcom writing. Given her and Myra Taylor's inexperience, the original scripts had been produced in tandem with the respected sitcom writer Lew Schwarz, while no less a figure than Eric Idle, of *Monty Python* fame, was brought in as script editor for series two. With Taylor's departure after series three, Carla Lane pretty much took sole

responsibility as writer-in-chief and it soon became evident that hers was a special talent. In and amongst its wilder moments, *The Liver Birds* was also a subtle exploration of the small-scale personal woes that are so often at the heart of everyday life. And as the show progressed, aided no end by the arrival of Carol's Catholic hordes, Lane's interest in the dynamics of family relationships was increasingly to the fore. Presciently, the surname of Carol and her clan was Boswell.

More immediately for Lane, the success of *The Liver Birds* led to employment on the archetypal 1970s ITV sitcom, *Bless This House*, to which she contributed twenty-five scripts after the show's creators, Vince Powell and Harry Driver, had got it up an running for Sid James, Diana Coupland and family in 1971. A less bombastic approach to relationships was prominent in her next BBC outing, *No Strings* (1974), which, after yet another *Comedy Playhouse* pilot, became a one-off series starring 1960s kitchen sink movie starlet Rita Tushingham and a Yorkshire-born actor set for bigger sitcom things, Keith Barron. And when the BBC failed to commission a series from the atrociously-title 1975 pilot *Going, Going, Gone...Free?*, in which Pauline Yates played a newly-divorced woman, Lane took her place alongside an army of TV comedy writers - including Keith Waterhouse, Willis Hall, Richard Waring, Dick Clement, Ian La Frenais, John Esmonde, Bob Larbey, Jilly Cooper and Alan Coren - in contributing material to Diana Rigg's 1967 sketch-based showcase, *Three Piece Suite*. It was with the arrival of *Butterflies* in 1978, however, that her big solo breakthrough occurred.

Here, Carla Lane was truly able to marry a talent for dry wit with an ability to convey the hopes and desires of well-rounded female characters. In this case, the lead role of Ria Parkinson went to Wendy Craig, born in Sacriston, County Durham, and until then considered something of a blonde airhead having made her name in the lightweight ITV comedies, *And Mother Makes Three* (1971), *And Mother Makes Five* (1974) and the BBC's *Not In Front Of The Children* (1967). The choice of someone so closely associated with middle-class housewife dippiness was no accident. From the beginning, *Butterflies* undermined such lazy stereotypes in style. Though in almost every respect a traditional chintz and sofa sitcom in which the apparently happily-married Ria is mother to two sons, Russell and Adam (played by Andrew Hall and the future Rodney Trotter,

Nicholas Lyndhurst), and the wife of terminally-content dentist Ben (the incomparable Geoffrey Palmer), all is not what it seems. Suffocating in her family role, Ria is deeply depressed and frustrated at the waste of her years. Wifely duties do not come easy, hence the running gag of her disastrous cooking, as self-evident a metaphor as ever there was. One day, while out walking in the local park, she meets businessman Leonard (Bruce Montague), and a whiff of adventure enters her life. Yet somehow, torn and conflicted, she can never quite bring herself to take advantage of the opportunity and, instead, contents herself with daydreaming.

Though it never quite attracted audiences on the scale of *The Liver Birds* or, indeed, another Liverpool-based Carla Lane sitcom still to come, *Butterflies* has since come to be seen as a British sitcom classic built, as it was, around the pathetic pursuits of marital boredom and jogging. Less obviously, before the end of its four-series run in 1983, *Butterflies* also reflected Lane's tendency to give heavy-handed moralising a wide berth. We are all of us flawed human beings, she seemed to say, it is how we deal with that and relate to each other that really matters. Another child of Liverpool, with her own independent streak.

With the demise of the BBC's back-to-nature sitcom *The Good Life* in 1978, that show's four stars - Richard Briers, Felicity Kendal, Penelope Keith and Paul Eddington - were cast to the winds. For Kendal, that meant an appearance as the human doormat Gemma Palmer in Carla Lane's next bitter-sweet exploration of the female psyche, *Solo*, the first of two series of which began early in 1981. Running almost simultaneously was Lane's first attempt to look inside a newly-single fifty-something male head in *The Last Song*, which starred Wendy Craig's *Butterflies* husband Geoffrey Palmer. A writer who never lacked the courage to experiment then came up with three more relationship-driven shows that were more comedy drama than sitcom: *Leaving* (featuring Keith Barron in 1984), *I Woke Up One Morning* (the story of four recovering male alcoholics in which Michael Angelis loomed large) and *The Mistress* (with Felicity Kendal again, fulfilling many a male fantasy) in 1985. All of those lasted two series each, with the uneasy subject matter a mitigating factor in their failure to draw significant audiences. Then, in 1986, Carla Lane suddenly cheered up, went back to her roots, and toasted some *Bread*.

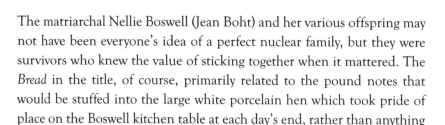

The matriarchal Nellie Boswell (Jean Boht) and her various offspring may not have been everyone's idea of a perfect nuclear family, but they were survivors who knew the value of sticking together when it mattered. The *Bread* in the title, of course, primarily related to the pound notes that would be stuffed into the large white porcelain hen which took pride of place on the Boswell kitchen table at each day's end, rather than anything produced in a bakery.

While much of the show's appeal lay in the amusing antics of a relentless hunt for quick bucks, as usual with a Carla Lane sitcom there was more to it than that. The emotional subtlety of *Butterflies* was notable only by its absence, but characterisation and a telling eye and ear for the interdependence of human relationships once again gave the show its depth. Elder son Joey (Peter Howitt) was expected to be a surrogate father for his absent, feckless and unfaithful wild-haired dad Freddie (Ronald Forfar). Newlywed youngest son Billy (Nick Conway) couldn't quite let loose of his mother despite only living about three doors away. The poetic third son, Adrian (Jonathon Morris), dreamed of a professional life of literary creativity, while fourth son Jack (Victor McGuire), a wannabe salesman, seemed permanently confused. And just about every member of the cast - with the possible exception of ungrateful granddad next door (played by Huddersfield's Kenneth Waller who, as store owner 'Old' Mr. Grace in *Are You Being Served?*, was actually 28 years younger than Harold Bennett's 'Young' Mr. Grace) - was fiercely protective towards the Boswells' only daughter Aveline (Gilly Coman). It was a mixture that worked and viewers were drawn in by the million. So much so that one episode, the marriage of Aveline and Oswald (Giles Watling) in 1988, attracted an audience of 21 million, a phenomenal rating for its time, confirming that *Bread* had become not so much a sitcom as a fully-fledged soap opera.

It was certainly not that way at the start. In 1986, the first episodes of *Bread* were met with outright hostility from many within the city in which it was based, owing to a preponderance of scrounging Scouse stereotypes. The critics had a point. The DHSS office provided a regular set-piece arena in which Joey, in particular, would do his best to outsmart the acerbic official Martina (Pamela Power) rather do anything as obvious as actively seek bona fide employment. His strawberry-nosed father

Freddie, meanwhile, was a waster, more interested in the boozer and his piece on the side, 'Lilo Lil', than looking after and providing for a family who also boasted a cousin called 'Shifty' (Bryan Murray). For the Irish Catholic Boswells, who lived in a terraced house on a cobbled hillside, the system was there to be exploited and *Bread* featured just about every Liverpudlian cliché in the book. Yet somehow, as Lane's characters began to take hold, all of that came to matter less, replaced by admiration at the family's sheer indefatigability. With fearsome mother hen Nellie pulling the strings, the Boswells would not be pushed around by anyone, least of all the men in suits. And all of that was merrily helped along by a script that, at its best, fairly crackled with Liverpudlian wit and ingenuity.

Inevitably, in time, the glory days grew fewer, the jokes became more predictable and the stories increasingly stretched credibility. And by the time *Bread* reached its seventh and final series in 1991, not only were three of the show's pivotal characters now being played by different actors - with Graham Bickley having a virtually impossible job to replace Peter Howitt as the leather-clad Joey, Melanie Hill taking over from Gilly Coman as Aveline and Hilary Crowson coming in for Caroline Milmoe as the lachrymose Billy's bolshy wife Julie - but British society was in the midst of another recession. Margaret Thatcher was out, John Major in, and unemployment suddenly wasn't funny anymore. As a result, *Bread* looked stale, even if it did stagger on for a while as an unlikely London stage show.

For Carla Lane, it would be her last major success to date. The sitcom which followed, *Screaming* (1992), harked back to her less popular comedy dramas of the mid-1980s in that it was almost exclusively about the lives of three middle-aged women (Gwen Taylor, Penelope Wilton and Jill Baker as Annie, Beatrice and Rachael), and seemed merely to bewilder everyone, schedule planners included. Her most recent effort for ITV, *Searching* (1995), set in a Voluntary Therapy Centre for young women with special psychological needs, fared even more poorly and was dropped after just seven episodes. In between came the more impressive *Luv* (1993), a sort of Liverpudlian *Butterflies* but with added venom, starring Michael Angelis and future *Royle Family* favourite Sue Johnston. Running to two series, *Luv* met with critical praise for its unflinching treatment of a marriage gone wrong, but never quite won over the public.

By then, the lead female characters from her four most popular sitcoms, *The Liver Birds, Solo, Butterflies* and *Bread*, had already made a joint appearance in a 1989 *Comic Relief* special, *The Last Waltz*, confirming their iconic status in at least three of those cases with the viewing public. Nowadays, Carla Lane is a vocal champion of the cause of animal rights.

However much the new breed of comics disdained it, *Are You Being Served?* bestrode the 1970s like a saucy seaside landlady and, by 1979, drew in a biggest-ever audience of over 22 million. It was during that year, that Trevor Bannister - the randy Mr. Lucas, junior to Mr. Humphries, who spent much of his time chatting up Wendy Richard's Miss Brahms - left a show that had already seen the departure of Arthur Brough in 1977, to be replaced at various times by James Hayter, Alfie Bass and Benny Lee. Bannister's spot on the floor was taken by the former pop star Mike Berry who, as Mr. Bert Spooner, carried on Mr. Lucas's sexist traditions until, after 13 years of references to what must by now have been a somewhat bedraggled pussy, the Grace Brothers doors finally clanged shut. To paraphrase 'Young' Mr Grace: 'They all did very well.'

For the never less than hard-working Mollie Sugden, the demise of *Are You Being Served?* simply made room for another sitcom, *My Husband And I* (1987), wherein the former Mrs. Slocombe appeared alongside her real-life husband, William Moore. This was a follow-up to her earlier ITV series, *That's My Boy* (1981), one of several situation comedies in which Sudgen took part while ostensibly employed by Grace Brothers. In 1972, she had appeared in the *Comedy Playhouse* pilot, *Born Every Minute*, with *Dad's Army* spiv James Beck. Later that same year her forthright personality was put to good use as John Alderton's mother in *My Wife Next Door*. In 1973, she played Terry Scott's widowed mum in *Son Of The Bride*, before making her first move to Yorkshire Television to star alongside Les Dawson and Roy Barraclough in *Holiday With Strings* (1974). And, in 1977, she was handed the lead role of Gertrude Noah in David Croft and Jeremy Lloyd's imaginative if poorly-received science fiction sitcom pilot, *Come Back Mrs Noah*.

Based in the year 2050, *Come Back Mrs Noah* was an unusual proposition featuring Sugden as a middle-aged housewife mistakenly blasted off into space after winning first prize in a cookery competition. The humour, such as it was, resided in the attempts to get her and a crew that included Croft veterans Ian Lavender, Michael Knowles and Donald Hewlett - plus another actor soon to join that canon, Gorden Kaye - back to earth. After a single series in 1978, the concept was jettisoned. Also unable to take flight was the Ray Galton and Johnny Speight comedy *The Tea Ladies* (1979), in which Sugden, Dandy Nichols and Patricia Hayes spent 30 minutes brewing up in the House of Commons tea-bar.

As for David Croft and Jeremy Lloyd, with Mrs. Slocombe and Co. behind them, the pair continued to write, produce and direct material together, alone or, in Croft's case, with Jimmy Perry. In 1980, Croft and Lloyd co-wrote *Oh Happy Band!* for Harry Worth. Around 14 years later, their World War Two-based pilot for ITV, *Which Way To The War*, also fell at the first hurdle. In between, though, they had their biggest hit since *Are You Being Served?*.

When *'Allo 'Allo!* first keeked oeuf in 1982, it too met with not a little resistance. How, enquired its detractors, could anyone find comedy in Nazi-occupied France, scene of many of the most brutal episodes of the twentieth century? Well, leaving aside humanity's psychological need to find humour in any situation, however terrible, *'Allo 'Allo!* did no such thing. Using high farce and low innuendo, and with an aperitif of outrageous national stereotypes, it instead set out to spoof the clichéd ways in which the region and period were depicted in TV and film, most recently in the BBC drama series, *Secret Army* (1977-79).

'Allo 'Allo! was 'about' the French Resistance, therefore it must be set in a café. Every Frenchman, no matter how old, must be having an affair. The French waitresses must wear stockings and suspenders. The actually quite stupid German Gestapo officers must make regular visits and be oblivious to underlying plots that, in the tradition of farce, become more complicated as events unfold. Two hidden British airmen who wait to be smuggled home must speak in received pronunciation and be possessed of stiff upper lips. And with the arrival of a feather-hatted strutting Italian, Captain Alberto Bertorelli, cowardice, a latin temperament and a vast array of medals for servicing Fiats should be in the mix.

Critics sniffed, but audiences loved it. From the start, *'Allo 'Allo!*'s harmless silliness and corny catchphrases caught the fancy of a public who stayed with it in huge numbers throughout a decade that took in the 1982 pilot, a nine-series run from 1984 (including one mammoth series of 26 episodes between 1988-89), two Christmas specials and a stage show that got as far as Australia. Nor was the popularity of *'Allo 'Allo!* confined to the UK. Making a mockery of the notion that it might prove offensive on the European mainland, the programme also became a massive hit across the continent and, especially, in France. And even since Liberation arrived for the fictional village of Nouvion in December 1992, repeats of *'Allo 'Allo!* have continued to be shown on TV sets the world over.

At the heart of the show's lively cast was the likeable Huddersfield-born actor Gorden Kaye, whose hangdog looks were put to great use as world-weary café owner René Artois, a man blessed with outstanding diplomatic skills and a demeanour that women, inexplicably, find attractive. Christened Gordon Kaye (the latter spelling apparently an Equity card typing error) and born in the less-than gallic Moldgreen in 1941, Kaye made his TV debut as Elsie Tanner's nephew, Bernard, in *Coronation Street* in 1968. After which, the route to René featured a procession of theatre work, supporting roles in films such as *Jabberwocky* and *Brazil*, plus sitcom appearances in shows like *Are You Being Served?*, *It Ain't Half Hot Mum*, *Oh Happy Band* and *Come Back, Mrs Noah*. The part of René's wife, Edith Artois, went to the veteran comedy actress Carmen Silvera, while René's mistress was Yvette Carte-Blanche, a leggy waitress played with charming cod Frenchness by Vicki Michelle.

A major ingredient in *'Allo 'Allo!* was its clever way with language. For example, Croft and Lloyd decreed that whenever French characters spoke French to each other they should do so in English, but in a caricatured accent: 'Leezen verrry carefully, I weel zay zis only once...' etc. On the other hand, when the same characters spoke English, they should adopt the overblown Public School tones of the posh upper classes. Likewise, when English characters spoke English, they talked in an appropriate English accent for the part which they were playing. When they tried to speak in French, it would again be English but tinted with strangled Fronch Lingwidge vowel sounds. Hence Arthur Bostrom's Crabtree who, in his disguise as village gendarme, was invariably 'just pissing by' before uttering the greeting that became one of *'Allo 'Allo!*'s most recognisable lines: 'Good moaning.'

If farces are distinguished by the convoluted nature of their plots, then *'Allo 'Allo!* is surely a contender for the most distinguished of all. Unusually for a sitcom, it was presented in serial format which allowed René to set the scene for each show with an introductory recap: 'As you will remember...'. That was just as well given the deliberate complexity of the story. René's yearning to escape Edith ('You stupid woman!') was matched only by his desire for Yvette and a constant succession of 'love' tangles with other waitresses, resistance agent Michelle (clad in mac, beret and red lipstick, naturally), Michelle's all-female gang of fellow Communists and the camp Lieutenant Gruber, driver of 'little German tanks'. In fact, the show's Germans were a nuisance all round. These included Gestapo leader Herr Flick, his ice maiden Helga and diminutive sidekick Englebert Von Smallhausen, all of them embarked upon a never-ending hunt for a missing work of art, 'The Fallen Madonna (With The Big Boobies)', painted by that notable Dutch master, Van Clomp, and hidden, where else, in a giant garlic sausage. The rest of the Germans were a positively docile bunch by comparison, with Colonel von Strohm, General Von Klinkerhoffen and, for the first three series, Captain Hans Geering (the Manchester-born actor Sam Kelly), providing unwanted business at the café. Among the smaller French parts, until his death in 1989, Jack Haig, the *Dad's Army* Corporal Jones that never was, played Monsieur Leclerc, an elderly master of disguise (in his own mind) whose catchphrase was: (raised spectacles) 'It is I, Leclerc'. The veteran soprano Rose Hill appeared as Fanny 'Fifi' Lafanne, Edith's elderly mother and Leclerc's future wife; while *Carry On...* regular Kenneth Connor was Monsieur Alfonse, the amorous village undertaker who wanted Edith for himself.

It was Gorden Kaye, however, who held it all together and nowhere was the affection for the show and its lead star more apparent than when the actor was involved in a dreadful road accident in 1990. During a particularly violent storm, a loose wooden hoarding smashed through Kaye's windscreen and pierced his skull. That he was not killed instantly was a miracle but, even so, the immediate prognosis did not look good. After a six-hour operation it remained touch and go whether he would survive and the actor spent a lengthy period in a coma. Happily, with the help of medical staff, family and friends, he eventually fought his way

back to a full recovery and went on to make two further series of '*Allo* '*Allo!*. Most recently, in March 2007, Kaye was one of several actors to reprise their earlier roles in a one-off special, *The Return of 'Allo 'Allo*, filmed in Manchester and shown on BBC2.

Another of Gorden Kaye's earliest sitcom appearances came in the hundredth episode of what is officially the longest-running British sitcom of all time. *Last of the Summer Wine* began life as the tale of three old codgers who wile away their autumn years in the West Yorkshire village of Holmfirth, high in the Pennine hills over Huddersfield. And it is still going - if not strong, then at least still going - to this day.

The manner in which *Last of the Summer Wine* has meandered over Britain's televisual landscape for almost 40 years, virtually unchanged by death, pestilence and fashion, is entirely appropriate. From the opening strains of its mournful theme tune, to spend half an hour or so in its company is to be wrapped in a heavy woollen comfort blanket, safe in its stately embrace from the fast, furious and, ahem, occasionally funny real world outside. In *Last of the Summer Wine*, wisecracks and smart-aleckery are replaced by philosophical whimsy and drollery, based upon growing old, disgracefully or otherwise. Since 1983, when the show first took the traditional day of rest as its own, its runaway vehicles on wheels, madcap contraptions gone wrong, mischievous pranks and fearsome roost-ruling women have come to be as closely associated with Sunday night telly as the *Antiques Roadshow*. As such, *Last of the Summer Wine* does not so much rage against the dying of the light as give it a bit of a run for its money.

The Last of the Summer Wine was first shown in 1973, as a *Comedy Playhouse* pilot. When a first full series was commissioned to be shown later that year, the definite article was dropped. The programme's creator was the Austerfield-born former schoolteacher Roy Clarke who, until then, had mainly written television and radio drama. With *Last of the Summer Wine*, it became apparent that Clarke had a fine ear for the humour in everyday northern dialogue, qualities which have subsequently stood him in good stead. Not only has Clarke written every single episode of the sitcom that began it all, he has also penned at least three other landmark shows in a grand total of seventeen.

They Don't Like It Up 'Em

Last of the Summer Wine wasn't Roy Clarke's first go at sitcom; in 1970 he had written *The Misfit*, which lasted two series starring the actor Ronald Fraser. But it was in dreaming up Cyril Blamire (Michael Bates), Norman Clegg (Peter Sallis) and Compo Simonite (Bill Owen) that he really found his niche. In the original pilot episode and throughout the first two series, trouble-maker in chief was Blamire, played by *It Ain't Half Hot Mum*'s blacked-up Bates. When Bates was forced to leave by the illness that would soon take his life, the similarly manipulative Foggy Dewhurst came in. Foggy, played by the Lancastrian actor Brian Wilde, was a former army man whose military approach to planning the trio's day unfailingly resulted in minor catastrophe. His air of good-natured and bumbling superiority contrasted nicely with Clegg's laid-back middle-class fatalism, while Compo's easily-led little man usually came the most spectacular cropper of all. To begin with, the show was a class act, in every sense of the phrase and an almost eerie modern-day echo of the legacy of Winky and the rest of the Bamforth family's 'Holmfirth Hollywood' enterprise of some sixty years earlier.

When he landed the part in 1976, Wilde was already a recognisable sitcom face, having appeared in Jack Rosenthal's *The Dustbinmen* in 1970 and, most notably, starring as a mild-mannered prison officer named Mr. Barrowclough in *Prisoner and Escort*, one of seven one-off comedy pilots showcasing the talents of Ronnie Barker, in 1973. When that show evolved into Ian La Frenais and Dick Clement's *Porridge*, Wilde immediately became one of the best-known actors in the country. Yet it was Foggy who provided him with his longest-running role over a 21-year stretch that included a five-year leave of absence during which he appeared in a BBC sitcom of his own, *Wyatt's Watchdogs*, before returning to replace the man who had filled the gap - Michael Aldridge, as barmy inventor Seymore Utterthwaite - in 1990. Commonly considered *Last of the Summer Wine*'s classic combination, Foggy, Clegg and Compo's last appearance together came in 1997, when Wilde once again departed to be replaced, this time, by *Are You Being Served?*'s Frank Thornton, as former policeman Truly Truelove.

Somewhat ironically, Brian Wilde is the only member of any *Last of the Summer Wine* triumvirate to originate from the north of England. Bill Owen, for example, who donned the wellies and iconic woolly hat as scruffy little Yorkshireman Compo, actually hailed from London. You would never have guessed it. As Compo, Owen - a snappy dresser in real life - slotted into the Holmfirth landscape better than the Emley Moor mast. His character's heroically unrequited passion for Nora Batty, wrinkled stockings and all, was northern comedy's love affair with big women and little men writ large; the stuff of television folklore. Pinafored Nora was a battleaxe supreme. Played by the Dukinfield-born actor Kathy Staff (born Minnie Higginbottom in 1928), she rebuffed her amorous admirer's advances like a formidable broom-wielding Yorkshire Boudicca. Holding forth atop the stone steps which led to her terraced weavers' cottage, Nora would rent the air with demands of 'get along with you, you daft beggar,' as Compo stubbornly refused to heed the message.

Before *Last of the Summer Wine*, Staff's battle-hardened features were already well known to the British public through her role as Doris Luke in the long-running and unintentionally hilarious ITV soap *Crossroads*. Yet so deep an impression did she make as Nora that she became almost exclusively known as a character comedy actor from that point onward, enjoying supporting roles alongside Les Dawson in *Sez Les* and *Dawson And Friends*, Eric Sykes in *Mr H Is Late* and Freddie Starr, along with a headlining part in a BBC sitcom of her own, *No Frills*, in 1988. In it, Staff played Molly Bickerstaff, a newly-widowed grandmother from Oldham who moves down to London to help her divorced daughter Kate raise her own daughter Suzy. Staff's gift for obstinate cantankerousness was given full reign in a show that was supposed to find fun in the north-south divide, but it only lasted one seven-episode series. After a lengthy acting career that also took in soap operas like *Coronation Street* and *Emmerdale Farm*, and after making her final appearance in the 29th series of the sitcom with which she was most closely associated, Kathy Staff died in December 2008, just nine months after Foggy, Brian Wilde, who passed away in March of that year.

The show, however, went on... and on. And undoubtedly the most telling example of *Last of the Summer Wine*'s robust indefatigability came with the sad demise of Bill Owen, from pancreatic cancer, in 1999. Given Compo's huge popularity and it may have been assumed, irreplaceability, it seemed certain that the programme must now at last come to an end. As his one-time co-star Wilde later told on-line Yorkshire magazine *Ayup!*: 'I treasure the memory of us sitting in the churchyard where Bill is now buried. It was a nice sunny day and Compo was looking around at the tombstones and their inscriptions. He asked, "I wonder what they'll put on my grave when I'm dead?" and Foggy replied, "something very heavy I hope!"' Convinced that, without Compo, there was no need for Nora to exist anymore, Kathy Staff herself departed - temporarily as it it turned out - to return to her earlier role of Doris Luke in an ill-fated revival of *Crossroads*. For the producers, though, shutting up shop was just not an option. Before Owen's death, three episodes of the show's 21st series had already been filmed, with an obviously ill Compo prominent. Heavy of heart but otherwise undaunted, Roy Clarke set about re-writing the remaining seven episodes, in which the little Tyke was given an emotional send-off and a new character introduced in his place. Enter Compo Simonite's long-lost son Tom, played by Bill Owen's real-life offspring of the same name. *Last of the Summer Wine* was now free to trickle on with the same gentle inevitability as ever, albeit branching off from its original three-way remit in more recent times into more of an ensemble piece.

Although the star trio in *Last of the Summer Wine* were seldom northerners, that was certainly not the case in a constantly changing and evolving supporting cast down the years. You didn't have to be born in the north of England - as the inclusion at various times of guest stars like Norman Wisdom, Ron Moody, Cardew Robinson and even John Cleese (operating under the pseudonym Kim Bread) testifies - but it did help. For every Smiler (Stephen Lewis, the former *On The Buses* inspector Blakey) or Alvin Smedley (Brian Murphy of *George And Mildred* fame), there was an eccentric Danny O'Dea, who played Eli Duckett, the short-sighted bumbler until his death in 2003 and a couple of useless policemen (Ken Kitson and Tony Capstick, the latter replaced after his death that year by former *Brookside* actor Louis Emerick). By far the most prominent supporting northerners, however, have been Thora Hird (Edie Pegden), the Salford-born Gordon Wharmby (Edie's husband Wesley, until his death in 2002), Dora Bryan (Edie's sister Roz) and the Liverpudlian actor better known as *Coronation Street*'s Hilda Ogden, Jean Alexander (Auntie Wainwright). Nor should we forget the brown bread and butter-voiced Joe Gladwin, Nora's put-upon husband Wally before his death in 1987, and Gladwin's fellow Mancunian John Comer (1924-1983) who, as cafe owner Sid was husband to Jane Freeman's terrifying Ivy, a stalwart of the show still.

One particularly imaginative piece of casting surrounds Bert Kwouk, a Manchester-born actor of Chinese heritage, perhaps best known as Peter Sellers's karate-mad house servant Cato in the *Pink Panther* films. After underlining his comedic credentials in the 1990s alongside the surreal Harry Hill, Kwouk went on to become a *Last of the Summer Wine* favourite as Entwistle, an electrician and fortune-teller from Hull who, despite his oriental looks, has changed his name from McIntyre to avoid being thought of as a Scotsman.

For all that its cast has altered down the years, the one true constant in *Last of the Summer Wine* - apart from the stark majesty of the Holmfirth countryside itself, of course - has been the Twickenham-born actor Peter Sallis. And once again, that is entirely appropriate given that it is his character, Clegg, who is supposed to be the steady away middle man. Whatever scheme the pompous one of the trio comes up with, whatever trouble Compo or his descendents land themselves in, it is Clegg, solid, reliable Clegg, who holds the gang together and ensures that the creaky-limbed overgrown schoolboys live to fight another day.

Now in his 80s, Sallis is an occasional rather than full-time presence as *Last of the Summer Wine* strolls on into the 21st century. Yet away from the camera and behind a microphone, his dreamy tones have become just as well known as northern cheese-loving inventor Wallace, the talkative half of Nick Park's Aardman Animations double act, Wallace and Gromit. After voicing four meticulously put together (and very funny) films - *A Grand Day Out* (1989), *The Wrong Trousers* (an Oscar winner in 1993), *A Close Shave* (an Oscar winner in 1995) and *Wallace And Gromit: The Curse Of The Were-Rabbit* (2005) - Sallis made his first ever visit to the Academy awards to watch the fourth film in that list collect yet another Oscar in Los Angeles in 2006. It was a long way indeed from when the Preston-born National Film and Television School student Park first sent the actor a begging letter and a promise of £50 towards the charity of his choice if he would participate in a ten-minute short, made with clay, that he had first begun working on in 1982 and eventually finished four years after joining Aardman Animations in 1989. While *A Grand Day Out* was merely nominated by the Academy, another Nick Park creation released simultaneously, the brilliant animal vox pop *Creature Comforts*, was the film that actually earned the self-effacing animator his first Oscar in 1990.

They Don't Like It Up 'Em

It was in playing Clegg that Peter Sallis first came to Park's attention as someone who could do good old-fashioned northern English decency. 'I didn't actually know he wasn't northern,' Park admitted on a 2006 edition of *The South Bank Show*. 'It really surprised me when we met.' And it was as Clegg that Sallis first got to speak the words of Roy Clarke. No surprise then that when, in 1988, Clarke came up with a prequel to his magnum opus, *First of the Summer Wine*, the only member of the original show's 'grown-up' cast to feature (unless you count Yorkshire character actor Joe Belcher, who appeared in three episodes of the former and one in the latter as a Mexican admiral) was Peter Sallis.

Cast as as Mr. Clegg, father to his *Last of the Summer Wine* character Norman (played here in his younger guise by David Fenwick), in a show that was set against the impending arrival of World War Two in 1939, Sallis again hit just the right note of honourable dignity. His understated instinct for melancholy was ideal in a programme that began with the older Norman reading from his diary and ended having allowed Clarke to further explore the relentless movement of time and the noble futility of human mortality, with a handful of pratfalls thrown in for good measure. As such, *First of the Summer Wine* was far more in tune with *Last of the Summer Wine* in its original guise, when the programme was less the knockabout pantomime of its later years, and more an almost Beckettian reflection on Andrew Marvell's winged chariot. Of the rest of the young cast, the remaining future *Summer Wine* characters were played by Paul Wyett (Compo), Richard Lumsden (Foggy), Paul McLain (Seymour), Helen Patrick (Nora Batty), Gary Whitaker (Wally) and Sarah Dangerfield (Ivy). After the initial success of its pilot, it ran to two series of six episodes each and concluded in 1989.

As for Roy Clarke himself, the positive reaction to *Last of the Summer Wine* allowed him to develop yet another northern-based classic sitcom which, like *Porridge*, had first been part of that 1973 Ronnie Barker showcase, *Seven Of One*. But where the philosophical reflections of Foggy, Clegg and Compo were wrestled with amid the rugged windswept Pennine foothills, the existential m-musings of st-stammering corner shopkeeper Albert Arkwright took place under the stars, as he packed up for the night beneath the black velvet skies of deepest darkest Doncaster.

Open All Hours was classic Roy Clarke. A perfectly observed essay in northern thrift and stoicism, its gentle mix of homespun philosophy and daft set-pieces (i.e. the too-eager till which slams viciously shut on unwary fingers, much like Arkwright himself) was further seasoned by a regular supply of miserable customers, including Kathy Staff as the suitably dour Mrs. Blewitt and future Alan Bennett favourite Stephanie Cole, as the equally menacing Mrs. Featherstone. In shop assistant Granville, given a wistful exuberance by David Jason - a future sitcom giant and the former co-star of Eric Idle, Michael Palin and Terry Jones in *Do Not Adjust Your Set* - it had the loveable dreamer who yearns for exciting escape but is either too comfortable or too apprehensive to do anything about it. The poor lad can't even bring himself to ask out the milkwoman he secretly adores (Barbara Flynn), despite his apparent depression at his routine of daily drudgery in the employ of his manipulative uncle. Meanwhile, old Arkwright's own relentless hounding of Nurse Gladys Emmanuel - played in the pilot by Sheila Brennan, but immortalised thereafter in the buxom shape of Urmston-born actor Lynda Barron - was about small horizons and a yearning for exotic adventure too. This particular would-be lothario, of course, was played by Ronnie Barker, justifiably hailed as one of Britain's finest ever character actors well before his death in 2005.

Although Bedford-born, Barker slipped naturally into the role of an archetypal grasping northern miser whose chief concern is whether he can get away with swindling his equally canny customers for another ha'penny on their bag of apples. And why wouldn't he? There was plenty for him to get his teeth into here, not least Arkwright's st-stuttering vocal tics. Barker, a true comedy craftsman who, since making his TV debut in 1956, had worked with just about everyone, not least Ronnie Corbett and John Cleese in *The Frost Report*, was already five years into the enormously successful BBC Variety sketch show *The Two Ronnies* (1971-1987) alongside Corbett. Versatility might well have been his middle name and not only front of camera. As a secret writer, he adopted a number of pen names including 'Bob Ferris', who had nothing to do with *The Likely Lads* but who did contribute regularly to *The Two Ronnies*, before anonymously penning Barker's final myopic sitcom *Clarence*, before his too-premature retirement in 1988. By then, Ronnie Barker had not only starred in *Going Straight*, a short-lived sequel to *Porridge*, he had also collaborated again with Roy Clarke. However their Welsh-based 1984 effort, *The Magnificent Evans*, proved nothing like as enduring as *Open All Hours* and was dropped after just six episodes.

While 84 Cooper Street, Doncaster, has never quite enjoyed the level of celebrity allotted to the more scenic Holmfirth - where Sid and Ivy's cafe, Nora Batty's house *et al* still draw in coachloads of tourists to this day - the corner of Lister Avenue in which *Open All Hours* was based was nevertheless destined to become something of a landmark in its own right. However, visitors expecting to see a grocer's shop were to be disappointed. For over 40 years, the building had actually been a hairdressing salon, latterly called 'Beautique', and one which, in 2006, was in danger of being knocked down all together after a compulsory purchase order was made on the property ahead of a £35 million regeneration scheme by the local Town Council. A petition to halt the demolition was subsequently signed by David Jason and other well-known faces such as Bernard Cribbins, Terry Wogan, David Frost, Ben Elton, Richard Briers and Stephen Fry. It worked too, although when the site of a show which throughout its four-series run from 1976-85 used to regularly attract upwards of 17 million viewers was put up for auction in November 2008, it failed to find a buyer. Perhaps they were afraid of Arkwright's till.

After the launch of *Open All Hours*, in 1974 the industrious Roy Clarke came up with his next couple of *Comedy Playhouse* pilots, *It's Only Me - Whoever I Am*, again starring David Jason, this time as a Rochdale mother's boy named Quentin, and *Pygmalion Smith*, a vehicle for Leonard Rossiter that would be dug up and reworked as *The Magnificent Evans* for Ronnie Barker fourteen years later. While no immediate series ensued from either of those, Clarke did fare better with his next project *Rosie* - known in its first 1975 series as *The Growing Pains Of PC Penrose* - the tale of an idealistic and naive young police constable, played by the Stockton-on-Tees actor Paul Greenwood. Set in the fictional Yorkshire town of Slagcaster, this latest Clarke sitcom was again informed by the writer's own employment experiences (after an early spell as a teacher, he had also worked in a corner shop and as a policeman) and found much of its humour in Clarke's now well-established knack for matching the idiosyncratic rhythms of northern speech with the wistful reflections of well-drawn characters.

Of those, a good number departed before the programme adopted Penrose's nickname for its second series and became simply *Rosie* in 1977. The PC's randy young pal PC Butress (David Pinner) had left for a start, as had the pair's despairing superior Sergeant Flagg (the Staffordshire-born but Bolton-raised character actor Bryan Pringle). Others to leave were PC Toombs (Alan Foss), WPC Dean (Catherine Chase) and Inspector Fox (Christopher Burgess). Such sweeping changes were made necessary by the relocation of Clarke's eponymous hero to the coastal town of Ravensby owing to the, deliberately inaccurate as it turns out, news that his mother is about to pop her clogs. Despite or maybe even because of the switch in surroundings, *Rosie* lasted five series and by the time its final episode came along in 1981, it had made something of a star of PC Penrose's latest sidekick, PC Wilmot. Played by the prolific Liverpudlian actor Tony Haygarth, Wilmot soon became a favourite to the extent that, in its latter days, the show was based more around this uniformed double act rather than the adventures of Rosie himself. Particularly popular was the catastrophically short-sighted Wilmot's habit of rearranging his wedding tackle in public environments. In supporting roles, Avril Elgar gave fine service as Penrose's interfering (and perfectly healthy) snob of a mother Millie, for whom the police force was beneath her sensitive boy, as did his Aunt Ida (Lorraine Peters) and Rosie's spoilt marriage-hungry girlfriend Gillian (Frankie Jordan).

After joining Carla Lane in contributing an extended sketch to Diana Rigg's *Three Piece Suite* in 1977, Clarke's next creation was his 1979 Arthur Lowe sitcom, *Potter*, the story of a - physically, not emotionally - retiring confectionery magnate named Redvers Potter. Most notable now for the deaths - ahead of a third series - of Lowe and his second-series co-star Harry H. Corbett in 1982, *Potter* was nevertheless a well-crafted, thoughtful and amusing take on old dogs with too much time on their hands. As usual, Arthur Lowe was immaculate as a *Daily Telegraph* reading dinosaur, whose inclination to assist all and sundry is undermined by his own incorrigible nature. So much so that, with Lowe's demise, it seemed unthinkable that the show could continue. Yet as with the death of Bill Owen years later, Roy Clarke was not about to let the Grim Reaper put him off his stride. Despite the calamitous loss of Lowe and Corbett, with another fine character actor to whom we will shortly turn our attention,

Robin Bailey, drafted into the lead role, *Potter* struggled through a third series before limping to a close in August 1983.

Although *Last of the Summer Wine* sailed on like a stately Yorkshire galleon throughout the decade, the latter half of the 1980s were generally less than fruitful territory for Roy Clarke. Not uncommonly in those aggressive and go-getting days, the essential tranquillity of his work came to be viewed as archaic. Sitcoms like *The Clairvoyant* (starring Roy Kinnear and borne of the same BBC2 pilot strand that launched Marti Caine's *Hilary* in 1984), *The Magnificent Evans* and the downright bizarre *Mann's Best Friends* (led by that other *Porridge* great, Fulton Mackay, in 1985), proved to be out of tune with the national mood. However, as the 1990s arrived and with just about every generation growing weary of being told what they could and could not laugh at, Clarke scored a minor hit with *First of the Summer Wine* and the television world seemed once again ready for his idiosyncratic charm.

That Clarke hardly rocked the sitcom boat in *Keeping Up Appearances* ought not to disguise the fact that it broke one very significant mould indeed. As played by the Birkenhead-born actor Patricia Routledge, interfering mega-snob Hyacinth Bucket (pronounced 'bouquet' by the woman herself) was a rare creature indeed - namely a middle-aged female able to milk slapstick every bit as energetically as any male counterpart. Hyacinth was a grotesque in the grand tradition of Basil Fawlty, Alf Garnett and Albert Steptoe, even if her scripts never quite reached such exalted heights. *Keeping Up Appearances* boasted many of the traditional Roy Clarke calling cards, including recurrent routines such as the dog in the rusted old Hillman Avenger which regularly forces Hyacinth into her sister's council house privets, lovingly crafted dialogue - 'I hope you are not going to spoil things with lower middle class humour' - and nicely-drawn characters, but the mood was almost zany when compared to his earlier work. In thick-skinned Hyacinth, however, for whom the value of the people around her is judged purely on the basis of whether they can help or hinder her upwardly-mobile social trajectory, he had a triumph.

Hopefully assisting Hyacinth in her ambitions were the Major, Mrs. Councillor Nugent, the vicar and other local big wigs who happened to cross her path. Her mild-mannered husband Richard (the Liverpool-born Clive Swift) and equally long-suffering neighbours Elizabeth and her brother Emmet (John Inman's cousin Josephine Tewson and *Hi-De-Hi!*'s David Griffin) had their uses too, so long as they took off their shoes when they came in and didn't brush against the wallpaper. Chief among Hyacinth's obstacles were her very own family, not least her sister and brother-in-law Daisy and Onslow, played with sublime slobbish aplomb by Judy Cornwell and Stan Ogden's former *Coronation Street* oppo and future *Royle Family* regular Geoffrey Hughes, who usually came to call just when it was most inappropriate. Nor did it help that Daisy and Onslow's arrival was inevitably heralded by the backfiring of their patched-up, seen-better-days Ford Cortina, and that Daisy's conversation tended to revolve around the lack of fornication on offer from her baseball-capped, beer-bellied other half. Sex was a major preoccupation for the third sister too. Maintaining the floral theme - and underscoring Hyacinth's unique pronunciation of their surname - Rose, as played by Shirley Stelfox in the first 1990 series and Doncaster-born Mary Millar (1936-1998) from the second series on, threw her leg over any man who stayed in one place long enough. Then there was the very senile 'Daddy' (George Webb), whose troublesome escapes from Daisy and Onslow's back bedroom inevitably brought further disrepute on the Bucket family name. Finally, a fourth sister, Violet (Anna Dawson), was deemed to be not so bad, possessed as she was of... 'a Mercedes, a sauna and room for a pony.'

From her palace on Blossom Avenue, Hyacinth Bucket became a huge hit at home and abroad. *Keeping Up Appearances* attracted enormous viewing figures in the UK and was also a perhaps unlikely success on cable in the USA, where a projected remake set in class-conscious Boston never quite materialised. In Britain, the show lasted five series before ending with a fourth Christmas special in 1995 when its star, Patricia Routledge, opted to leave the chintz curtains, hand-painted periwinkles and indoor-outdoor luxury barbecue with finger buffet behind. Even Roy Clarke couldn't get around that one.

Although Clarke would go on to write four short-lived BBC sitcoms - *The Sharp End* (1991) with Gwen Taylor as the inheritor of her father's debt collection agency in the fictional Yorkshire town of Rawthorne, *Don't Tell Father* (1992) with Tony Britton as Vivian Bancroft, a sort of male Hyacinth Bucket, *Ain't Misbehaving* (1994), a story of adultery starring former *Doctor Who* Peter Davison, and the ultra-whimsical *Spark*

412

(1997), with *Vicar Of Dibley* star James Fleet in the lead role - *Keeping Up Appearances* is his last major contribution to the British sitcom canon to date. Even so, at the time of writing, Roy Clarke OBE continues to write *Last of the Summer Wine*, ahead of a freshly commissioned 31st series of six episodes scheduled to be broadcast in 2010.

'*Last of the Summer Wine* started two years after we did and we thought then that it was the geriatric *Goodies*.' Thus spoke another comedian who signed the aforementioned petition to save Albert Arkwright's shop, Tim Brooke-Taylor, in an interview with *Word* magazine, in March 2005.

He had a point. While it's doubtful that Clarke had that particular trio in mind when coming up with his own creations, the two shows were certainly on a par popularity-wise, despite being targeted at opposite ends of the age-range spectrum. And where *The Goodies* were a product of the Oxbridge Footlights generation, like the *Monty Python* team before them they had a very distinctive flavour of the north of England, not least because one of their number, the bearded future ornithologist Bill Oddie, hailed from the wilds of Rochdale.

Oddie and Brooke-Taylor were joined in *The Goodies* (1970-82) by fellow Cambridge University graduate Graeme Garden. Together they were responsible for 77 of the silliest television programmes ever made. It was on *The Goodies* that the Great British public first learned of a dance called the 'Funky Gibbon', watched a giant rampaging pussycat named 'Kitten Kong' knocked over the Post Office Tower, and hooted as rugby league commentator Eddie Waring ran off with a golden egg, among many other such moments of visual tomfoolery. The celebrated Queen of Northern Soul, Black Pudding Bertha, found a home there, as did the ancient Lancastrian martial art, Ecky Thump. In short, *The Goodies* was a live-action cartoon, harking back to the days of silent movie slapstick, but with an added bucketful of wildly imaginative 1970s sound and colour.

Despite *The Goodies*'s enormous popularity - it twice won the coveted Silver Rose of Montreux award and enjoyed the healthiest of peak-time viewing figures - critics did tend to compare it unfavourably with its most obvious rival, *Monty Python's Flying Circus*. And it is true that while the best *Monty Python* routines were what might now be termed 'water cooler

moments' in colleges, universities and sixth forms, the most natural territory for *The Goodies* was school playgrounds. Indeed, for the younger generation, your preference for the former over the latter became a badge of honour where aspiring teenage intellectuals were concerned. *Python* silliness, more ostentatiously wordy and clever, was stuffed with ego-polishing references to Descartes, Proust, Oscar Wilde and Mao Tse-Tung that nevertheless demanded no real knowledge of their lives and work. *The Goodies*, on the other hand, lacked any such pretentiousness. And maybe it was those forays into stereotypical northernness that helped to give the show its more 'simple' reputation. With them, you were more likely to see three fully-grown men toppling off a specially converted tandem every week or, perhaps, being chased through London by a giant Dougal, the dog from *Magic Roundabout*. It was a situation sent up nicely by John Cleese's cameo appearance as a grumpy genie in *The Goodies and the Beanstalk*, a 1973 Christmas special where, after appearing in a puff of smoke from a baked bean tin and announcing '...and now for something completely different', the great man grumpily harumphs: 'kids' programme!' In switching on a TV set and being met by the *Python* opening credits in another 1973 episode, Garden returned the compliment: 'Damn! Missed Moira Anderson!'

Oddie and his colleagues were widely known in BBC circles when Head of Comedy Michael Mills gave the show the go-ahead in 1970. That he should have done so despite the flimsiness of their original proposal - i.e. that it should be about an agency of three men who 'do anything, anytime' - perhaps tells us all we need to know about the usefulness of an Oxbridge school tie in launching a comedy career with the British Broadcasting Corporation. On this occasion, Mills's benevolence was justified when *The Goodies* soon began to take the nation by storm.

Born in Rochdale in 1941, but raised mainly in Birmingham, as a child William Edgar Oddie was primarily cared by his father when his mother was placed into long-term psychiatric care, a fact which only became public knowledge in 2004 when, during filming for the BBC's genealogy documentary strand, *Who Do You Think You Are?*, in which celebrities are followed as they uncover the roots of their family tree, Oddie discovered that his mother had not abandoned him in childhood as he had always assumed. Oblivious to this at the time, the young Oddie

414

immersed himself in a world of egg-collecting and bird-watching. A bright and inquisitive youth with a penchant for music, he would eventually go on to study English Literature at Pembroke College, Cambridge, where he wasted little time in becoming a busy member of the Footlights Club.

Aside from the sheer fun of performance, the first major perk of that membership was a call to write for David Frost on *That Was The Week That Was*, while Oddie was still studying. Post-graduation, he had a first credited front-of-camera spot with Bernard Braden in *On The Braden Beat* (1964), a fore-runner to Esther Rantzen's consumer-cum-entertainment show *That's Life!*, followed by an appearance on the soon to be infamous *BBC-3*. Regular radio work was further supplemented by a minor part in ITV's *At Last The 1948 Show*, a programme that had also given a TV debut to fellow Cambridge Footlights product and future *Goodie* Tim Brooke-Taylor in 1967. Alongside Cleese, Graham Chapman and Marty Feldman, the amiable Brooke-Taylor, born in Buxton, Derbyshire, and a former Footlights president of 1963, caught the eye. Appearances with Feldman and John Junkin on *It's Marty* (1968) and the Easter special *Marty Amok* (1970), sandwiching a 1970 Yorkshire Television sitcom, *His And Hers*, further cemented Brooke-Taylor's growing reputation.

Aberdeen-born Graeme Garden, meanwhile, had made his first brief TV appearance as part of ATV's response to *Beyond the Fringe*, a half-hour sketch show, *Footlights '64*, alongside Eric Idle and Miriam Margolyes, shown in the year of his presidency of that organisation. More substantial was the Scot's first TV appearance with Oddie on the BBC sketch show *Twice A Fortnight* (1967), in which Michael Palin and Terry Jones also took part while formulating plans for their *Complete and Utter History of Britain*. *Twice A Fortnight*, a television version of the radio show, *I'm Sorry, I'll Read That Again* - itself a spin-off of the Footlights revue *A Clump of Plinths*, in which Oddie, Garden and also Brooke-Taylor loomed large - was a rowdy affair that did, nevertheless, allow Oddie and Garden to develop a shared taste for visual anarchy in the shape of comically speeded-up routines, unusual camera angles and unexpected jumps from one scene to another. When *Twice A Fortnight* juddered to a halt after ten episodes in December 1967, a more lasting working relationship was just around the corner.

At first, Bill Oddie appeared as an occasional guest on *Broaden Your Mind* (1968-69), described by its publicity as 'part quiz, part educational

programme' but really just a traditional sketch show whose conceit was that it was an 'encyclopaedia of the air', spoofing the collect-in-parts knowledge building beloved of book and magazine publishers. All of which meant a different theme each week, a format that allowed for the appearance of guest artists, of which Palin, Jones and Oddie were three. Most importantly, along with Graeme Garden, another of its full-time contributors was the man who came up with the concept in the first place, Tim Brooke-Taylor. When Bill Oddie was promoted from special guest to regular cast member for the second and final series, three men who had already been in one and other's orbit for a number of years were finally assembled as a team in their own right. There was still time for Brooke-Taylor to turn to traditional sitcom with *His and Hers* and for Garden to take a small role as a TV director in an ill-fated BBC *Comedy Playhouse* pilot, *The Valley Express*, set in a South Wales newspaper office. Oddie too acted opposite Leslie Phillips in a one-off Ray Galton and Alan Simpson ITV sitcom, *The Suit* while, as writers, Oddie and former medical student Garden worked together on the first two series of *Doctor In The House* (1969-70). And when all three got back together for the opening episodes of *The Goodies*, originally due to be known as *Narrow Your Mind* and then *Super-Chaps Three*, it too followed a conventional sitcom format of sorts.

Initially, the trendy open-plan office suite in Cricklewood that, to *The Goodies*, became their home, was merely the place to which potential customers came in order to employ the trio's services. *The Goodies* were given a problem, they solved the problem and that was that. But by the third series the show had an altogether more surreal and cartoonish air. Nothing was safe from caricature, including the personalities of the performers themselves. 'Bill', a short and hairy environmentalist, became a faintly aggressive northern loudmouth, full of his own opinions and campaigns, determined not to be pushed around. 'Tim' was a chronically nice, fey and ever-so-slightly toffee-nosed Tory Establishment figure in a patriotic Union Jack waistcoat, prone to making inspirational speeches with strains of 'Land of Hope and Glory' playing in the background. And 'Graeme' was a tweedy bespectacled mad scientist-type, forever coming up with new ideas and inventions such as the three-seated 'trandem' that *The Goodies* rode around on and which soon became their trademark.

Nor was the television process itself immune to the team's lightly satirical touch. Along with all the special effects and dangerous moon rabbits, a comical if devoutly BBC attitude to commercial television was there in the spoof advertising breaks that punctuated every unpredictable episode, among the most memorable of which was Tim Brooke-Taylor's terminally put-upon Heinz Beanz kid. And as with Morecambe and Wise, a regular supply of family friendly BBC celebrities like David Dimbleby, Magnus Magnusson, Michael Aspel and the mercilessly mocked Radio 1 DJ Tony Blackburn further confirmed *The Goodies'* mainstream appeal. It was a recipe that, during the show's salad days from 1973-76, took the show to enviable heights of popularity. More problematically, it all came at a high financial cost too, and when the Light Entertainment special effects budget finally ran dry in 1980 - allegedly as a result of the TV adaptation of Douglas Adams's radio series *The Hitchhikers's Guide to the Galaxy* hoovering up all the cash - *The Goodies* trooped off to LWT for a one-off special, *Snow White 2*, in 1981. While there, they also made a disappointing ninth and final series before the money again ran out and the future BBC boss, John Birt, pulled the plug for good a year later.

If Eric Idle was the musical linchpin in *Monty Python*, in *The Goodies* that role fell to Bill Oddie. Responsibility for the majority of writing fell to himself and Graeme Garden anyway, so when music was called for it seemed only natural that Oddie should provide it, especially as he had already filled that role with some aplomb on *I'm Sorry, I'll Read That Again*. In that landmark radio show, Oddie was one of the first performers to openly parody rock songs, most notoriously reworking the Beatles' 'With A Little Help From My Friends' as Yorkshire's 'national' anthem 'On Ilklah Moor Baht 'At', as sung by Joe Cocker. Upon the death in 2005 of another one-time *Goodies* guest star, John Peel, a recording of that tune was discovered among the legendary DJ's most treasured box of singles.

In fact, Oddie's musical contributions to the *The Goodies* became a lucrative sideline in their own right. A host of records - among them 'The Inbetweenies', 'Funky Gibbon and 'Black Pudding Bertha' - not only earned memorable appearances on *Top of the Pops* and *Crackerjack* for the trio, they were out-and-out chart hits. Of them all, their cover version of the Troggs' 'Wild Thing' - 'So come on, hold me tight. Not. Quite. That. Tight...' - was probably the best although, in 1975, *The Goodies* enjoyed no

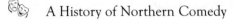

less than five hit singles in only twelve months. As with *Monty Python*, there were several amusing spin-off books too and the trio did at least claw back some credibility back with their fellow Oxbridge intelligentsia by appearing in the 1976 Amnesty International fund-raising concert, *A Poke In The Eye (With A Sharp Stick)*, filmed for the BBC's *Omnibus* strand as *Pleasure At Her Majesty's*.

These days, while Graeme Garden and Tim Brooke-Taylor continue to entertain on BBC Radio 4's *I'm Sorry, I Haven't A Clue* amongst other radio and television offerings, Bill Oddie appears to have put the comedy on the back burner and has practically re-invented himself as an enthusiastic presenter of highly entertaining natural history programmes, in the eccentric British tradition. Indeed, he was awarded an OBE for services to Wildlife Conservation in 2003.

It is as a *Goodie*, however, that he and the rest of the triumvirate will doubtless be best remembered, not too bad a legacy if the sad fate of 50-year-old Kings Lynn bricklayer Alex Mitchell is anything to go by. So amusing did Mr. Mitchell find one 1975 episode of *The Goodies* that the poor man is said to have literally died laughing. Newspaper reports at the time claimed that the guilty episode was 'Kung Fu Kapers', in which Tim Brooke-Taylor, clad as a kilted Scot, is engaged in the well-known Scottish martial art of Hoots-Toot Ochaye by a psychotic black pudding wielding Ecky Thumper (Oddie). Faced with impending peril, Tim proceeds to defend himself with a set of bagpipes, to devastatingly hilarious effect for one man at least. According to Mr. Mitchell's widow, her late husband spent the next 25 minutes convulsed with helpless mirth until his heart, unable to take any more, finally gave up the fight. 'Thank you for making his final moments so pleasant,' she is said to have told the cast in a letter.

To die laughing was not a fate ever likely to befall Uncle Mort. The elderly, flat-capped and positively morose star of *I Didn't Know You Cared* must be a candidate for one of the most miserable sitcom creations of all-time. He made Victor Meldrew look like Timmy Mallett, and the rest of his grim northern tribe weren't far behind either.

Based on three comic novels by the Liverpool-born writer Peter Tinniswood - *A Touch Of Daniel* (1969), *I Didn't Know You Cared* (1973) and *Except You're A Bird* (1974) - the TV version of that middle title was first aired by the BBC in 1975. Like the books from which four subsequent series sprang, a television show which has never been given the posthumous recognition it deserves dealt with the trials and tribulations of Yorkshire's Brandon family, an extraordinarily downbeat collection of individuals who are seemingly never really happy unless they are unhappy. Despite being born on the banks of the Mersey in 1936, Tinniswood actually grew up above his mother's dry-cleaners in Sale, Manchester, where he would by all accounts sit under the counter honing his future writing skills by listening to the chatter of her customers. Doubtless his Lancashire origins also explain how he came to form the view shared by many in that county that a monumental dreariness is the defining characteristic of their rivals on the other side of the Pennines.

After starting working life as a journalist in Sheffield, and then moving on to Cardiff, Liverpool and London, Tinniswood's television writing career began on *That Was The Week That Was*, a more than useful gig that led to him spending the rest of the 1960s providing material for David Frost, Dick Emery, Lance Percival and Roy Hudd before coming up with his first sitcom for ITV, *Never Say Die*, in 1970. Based around his days as a hospital porter while a student, it was a short-lived effort that ran to just one single series. Happily, when Tinniswood's parallel career as a humourous novelist gave him another chance five years later, he was ready to make far better use of it.

An extended family member only, Uncle Mort - as played by Robin Bailey - was nevertheless the philosophical heart and soul of *I Didn't Know You Cared*, a position that came into sharper focus when the character contracted cancer. In the first series, the show's plot revolved around the doomed struggle of Mort's distinctly dopey nephew Carter to avoid marriage to girlfriend Pat, on the surface at least. As its title suggests, though, what was really under the microscope in *I Didn't Know You Cared* was an ongoing battle of the sexes, wherein the menfolk hid away in the pub, discussing rugby league, football and how best to ensure a quiet life, while the women and their burnt meals waited not-so-patiently at home. There was only ever one winner in the inevitable confrontation that followed and they did not wear trousers. A continuation of the grand caricatured male-female traditions of northern comedy, then? To a point, yes. But *I Didn't Know You Cared* was also an ingenious mixture of witty, truthful and frequently surreal observations on day-to-day married life, and all of it busied along by Tinniswood's absolutely cracking dialogue.

The skillful writing of dialogue is one thing; you also need actors who are capable of doing it justice and in the show's figurehead Robin Bailey, Tinniswood was blessed with a very fine actor indeed. Born in Nottingham in 1919, Bailey had enjoyed a long and varied career in both film and television before being cast as Yorkshire's grumpiest man, and he would go on to have an almost equally long and varied career afterwards, until his death in 1999. Such experience was put to wonderful use in the part of Mort, a newly-widowed pensioner who is ready to offer an opinion, always pessimistic, on any given subject - but especially women - at the drop of a beer mat. As indeed is his brother-in-law, Carter's father Les, played with similarly fatalistic woe by John Comer, otherwise known as *Last of the Summer Wine*'s cafe-owner Sid. Carter's mother, meanwhile, was the horrendous acid-tongued Annie (another top-notch performance from Liz Smith). And completing the Brandon clan was Auntie Lil (Gretchen Franklin), whose knitting needles clatter like there is no tomorrow, and Uncle Stavely (Bert Palmer, later Leslie Sarony), the only male Brandon able to enjoy anything like a peaceful life on account of him being completely ga-ga and apparently deaf. Along with carrying his best friend's ashes around in a cardboard box, Uncle Stavely is best remembered in certain circles for his regular outburst: 'I heard that! Pardon?'.

Of course, those 'certain circles' were mainly in northern England, where the dedicated regionalism of *I Didn't Know You Cared* rang truest. After all, this wasn't the UK's usual 'we're all feeling miserable so let's laugh at a northerner' scenario. The Brandons weren't in the cheering up business, they had quite enough misery of their own to contend with, thank you very much. Maybe that is one reason for the show's otherwise inexplicable absence from any 'classic TV sitcom' list in recent memory. Since the demise of *I Didn't Know You Cared* in 1979, it appears to have sunk without trace. Why should that be? There was nothing wrong with the quality. Most disappointingly, perhaps we saw a similar phenomenon at the start of the 21st century too, when two series of the equally splendid Craig Cash and Phil Mealey situation comedy *Early Doors* also struggled to gain popular recognition.

Still, the short-term popularity of *I Didn't Know You Cared* did at least persuade the BBC to broadcast two 15-minute monologues written by Peter Tinniswood in 1980. The resulting *Tales From A Long Room* were based on Tinniswood's best-selling books of cricket stories and were once again performed by Robin Bailey. The concept also won a home on BBC Radio 4 where, in August 1981, Bailey read five more tales from the same works before, three years later, Channel 4 recognised their on-screen potential and extended the format to 13 episodes over two television series, in which Bailey again waxed lyrical from the village of Witney Scrotum. Back on radio and, in 1992, another full series was made called *Tales From The Brigadier*, which now boasted Richard Wilson as narrator.

Sitcom-wise, Tinniswood's next port of call was ITV where, in 1983, he tried to replicate his *I Didn't Know You Cared* success with another northern family saga, *The Home Front*. Again based upon one of his comic novels, this time the family in question were the Places; namely the bossy and interfering Mrs. Place (Brenda Bruce) and her three grown-up children, Avril (Cherith Mellor), Garfield (Malcolm Tierney) and Hallam (Warren Clarke), in whose lives she is incapable of not interfering. Son Hallam is particularly interesting here in that he is a television comedy scriptwriter, based in London, and therefore felt by Mrs. Place to be 'contaminated'. When *The Home Front* ground to a halt after only six episodes, another ITV adaptation of a Tinniswood novel, *Mog*, fared equally poorly. It worked to an unusual and, frankly, perturbing premise wherein the eponymous Mog (Enn Reitel) was a burglar who lived in a mental hospital, from where he escaped on a nightly basis to commit his crimes. Tinniswood's next project, *South Of The Border*, made for Yorkshire Television in 1985, was just as short-lived. In it, Brian Glover was typecast as an archetypal big-mouthed Yorkshireman, Edgar Rowley, whom unemployment drives to London, and who abuses his new neighbours re. their lack of northern grit. Nowhere near as excruciating as it sounds, by all accounts, the show was nevertheless put to sleep after only seven episodes and, in the unlikely event that any of them noticed, all them 'southern softies' could once again rest unmolested in their feathery home counties beds.

From that point on, apart from contributing a single episode to Richard Wilson's ill-fated LWT sitcom *Duck Patrol* in 1998, Peter

Tinniswood pretty much left television sitcom behind. Instead, he turned to theatre and radio where Uncle Mort and Carter were resurrected for the highly entertaining BBC Radio 4 series *Uncle Mort's North Country* (1987-89) and *Uncle Mort's South Country* (1990-91). On those programmes, Mort was for some reason played with a Lancashire accent by Stephen Thorne, and his nephew's role was shared between the Bury-born singer-songwriter Peter Skellern and *'Allo 'Allo*'s Sam Kelly. Displaying an admirable lack of parochialism, in 1996 the pair's roaming brief was further widened by *Uncle Mort's Celtic Fringe*. By then, echoing Uncle Mort's own misfortune all those years ago, the pipe-smoking Tinniswood had been diagnosed with the oral cancer that would not only render him unable to speak, but which sparked a creative surge in radio and theatre output that is still to be fully utilised to this day. Some of that work, he claimed, was his best ever. After a long struggle with the disease, Peter Tinniswood died in a London hospice, aged 66, in 2003.

15
Love Thy Neighbour

"It's quite a nice view, now they've painted the gasometer."
- Rupert Rigsby (Leonard Rossiter), Rising Damp

In 2005, the digital television channel BBC 3 launched *The Last Laugh*, a competition to find up-and-coming situation comedy writers. In 2006, that same search sparked a follow-up programme in which the host, Irish comedian Dara Ó Briain, made the following quip: 'So, what makes a good sitcom? The short answer is, of course, not ITV.'

Well, they do say that the secret to comedy is truth. And certainly, when it comes to sheer weight of numbers, the classic-to-turkey ratio of the BBC is far healthier than that of its commercial rival. In a 2004 poll, admittedly carried out by the BBC itself, every single member of the eventual top ten was made by the national broadcaster. The resulting TV show, *Britain's Best Sitcom*, in which celebrity representations were made on behalf of each of those finalists, revealed them as (in eventual order of merit): *Only Fools And Horses* (342,426 votes), *Blackadder* (282,106), *The Vicar Of Dibley* (212,927), *Dad's Army* (174,138), *Fawlty Towers* (172,066), *Yes, Minister/Yes, Prime Minister* (123,502), *Porridge* (93,902), *Open All Hours* (67,237), *The Good Life* (40,803) and *One Foot In The Grave* (31,410). The best commercial television could manage was Channel 4's *Father Ted*

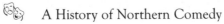

(11th) and *Drop The Dead Donkey* (26th), with ITV's top-ranking entrant *Rising Damp* limping in at an outrageous 27th.

As the above list and our previous chapter implies, in terms of quality alone, the BBC were - and to date remain - sitcom kings. The time and support given by the Beeb to the vision of writers like *Only Fools And Horses* creator John Sullivan has frequently paid off handsomely. In Sullivan's case, not only did he deliver what must surely qualify as the best mainstream sitcom of recent times, running over fifteen years from 1981 and complemented by a series of massively successful Christmas specials, he made even greater audience-grabbing stars of David Jason and Nicholas Lyndhurst, aka Derek and Rodney Trotter, than they already were. Class actors and intelligent scripts were also a feature of Sullivan's next couple of hits, *Just Good Friends* (1983) and *Dear John...* (1986), with Paul Nicholas, Jan Francis and Ralph Bates to the fore, and other substantially popular BBC sitcoms like *Ever Decreasing Circles* (1984), *Birds Of A Feather* (1989), *May To December* (1989) and *Waiting For God* (1990) were of similarly solid stock. Yet that really is only part of the story.

Although the BBC did tend to have the really big hits - in 1981, for example, the Penelope Keith and Peter Bowles comedy of manners *To The Manor Born* drew a record 24 million or so viewers for its final episode - in terms of actual viewing figures, the Corporation was given a far more vigorous run for its money, certainly throughout the 1970s. Cheap and cheerful shows like *Bless This House* (from 1971), complete with scripts by Carla Lane and starring *Carry On* favourite Sid James and the Leeds-born Diana Coupland as the harassed parents of a couple of teenagers, was at the forefront of the television ratings war for around five years. The equally unstuffy *Man About The House* (1973) proved highly popular too, as did *Get Some In!* (1975), a National Service sitcom initially set at the fictional RAF base Skelton, starring Ilkeston-born actor Robert Lindsay as the gobby London Teddy Boy, 'Jakey' Smith.

Nor were they on their own. Among other regular entrants in ITV's own JICTAR[1] (Joint Industry Committee for Television Advertising Research) ratings throughout the 1970s were *The Dustbinmen* (1968-70), *On The Buses* (1969-1973), *My Good Woman* (1972-74), Richard Gordon's *Doctor* series (1971-75), *The Muppet Show* (1976-81), *A Sharp Intake Of Breath* (1977-81), five Eric Sykes specials (from 1977) and *Only When I*

Laugh (1979-82), showing that the viewers were happy enough even if the critics most usually were not. ITV's long-held Variety tradition continued unabated too, with camp *Generation Game* host Larry Grayson launching a sketch show based upon his catchphrase *Shut That Door!* in 1972, and enormous audiences were guaranteed for Ken Dodd, Jimmy Tarbuck and company. For all that, there remained a widely-held conviction that, with adverts, standards dropped. The BBC had Morecambe and Wise. ITV had Mike and Bernie Winters.

ITV's reliance on low-brow Variety was also reflected in its sitcoms; saucier and less worthy, on the whole. ITV comedies had a brashness and bravado about them that seemed more in tune with the socially-turbulent times, but at the cost of leaving them looking outdated in the eyes of future audiences. Where the best-remembered BBC sitcoms dealt mainly in timeless middle-class themes (with any working class characters usually looked down upon, however fondly), ITV was a place where racial and social stereotypes were strung out like council estate washing, on a breeze of brazen music hall cheekiness. To supporters of the BBC, that spelled aiming for the lowest common denominator. A somewhat lofty position, given that ITV was ruled by commercial considerations which the BBC had the luxury of avoiding, although the Beeb did still deliver audiences in huge numbers.

In short, ITV, tended to stick to what it knew best and if that meant being fresh, colourful and unselfconscious, then so be it. On the thorny subject of race relations, for example, while the BBC was quite capable of producing *It Ain't Half Hot, Mum*, Alf Garnett and the supposedly satirical *The Black Safari*, in which four black 'explorers' go on an expedition up the Leeds-Liverpool canal in search of the centre of Great Britain, it largely escaped critical censure. Similar subject matter in the hands of ITV, meanwhile, quite often had the feel of an excruciating and bitter-soaked tap room discussion about it. The zenith of such vulgarity is

---

[1] *Re. television ratings, both organisations collected their figures differently until August 1981, when the BBC and ITV together came up with the Broadcasters Audience Research Board, or BARB as it is known. Before, the ITV-commissioned JICTAR ratings were widest published and calculated by attaching electronic measuring equipment to a select number of household television sets. The BBC preferred to deal in the watching habits of single viewers rather than entire homes and used a more selectively publicised system of individual telephone interviews and diary entries.*

generally said to be the notorious *Love Thy Neighbour*, which lasted eight series from 1972, before shuddering to a halt four years later. Then again, isn't saying so just contributing to an elitist and snobbish view, wherein such a blatantly commercial organisation as ITV must intrinsically be incapable of rising above the uncouth? It is certainly true that, culturally speaking, the commercial networks were on a hiding to nothing. When Johnny Speight sought to ridicule bigots on the BBC, the result was the critically respected chairman Alf; on ITV it took shape as Speight's widely-panned collaboration with Spike Milligan, *Curry And Chips*. Same writer, two different reactions entirely. Why is that the case? Can it only be because *Till Death Us Do Part* was actually funny?

You won't often hear the adjective 'funny' used these days in relation to *Love Thy Neighbour*. Yet it would be dishonest in the extreme to deny that it struck a very profound nerve at the time, and that vast swathes of the population lapped up the antics of the rabidly chauvinistic 'white honky' Eddie Booth (Manchester's Jack Smethurst) and his 'Sambo' next door neighbour Bill Reynolds (Rudolph Walker), a free-market Tory to Eddie's old-school Labour. And while the show was undeniably keener to draw laughs from gratuitous racial insults than come up with anything genuinely insightful, it did have its amusing moments. If the joke was on anyone, the writers made sure it was über bigot Eddie, the abject personal humiliation of whom was a reliable denouement to the show. The supporting cast, too, was generally a more liberal bunch than received wisdom allows. The friendship of long-suffering wives Joan and Barbie, played by Kate Williams and Nina Baden-Semper, is relatively peaceful despite their spouses' intolerance. And Eddie's drinking buddies Arthur, Nobby and the rest of the regulars down at the Lion And Lamb would rather enjoy a peaceful pint (or in the cloth-capped Jacko's catchphrase: 'I'll have 'alf') than participate in World War Three. For one half of the Mancunian writing partnership behind *Love Thy Neighbour*, at least, social division does seem to have been a comic obsession.

Building on their shared Variety roots on the Manchester club circuit as the comedy double act Hammond and Powell, Vince Powell and Harry Driver were a perfect fit for ITV's unreconstructed 'seventies. Their writing career had begun, at first separately, in 1955, when Driver contracted polio and was henceforth confined to a wheelchair. Soon the pair were, individually, contributing stage and TV routines to entertainers as diverse as Billy Dainty and Frankie Howerd. Writing together, a seriously big break came in 1960, when BBC Manchester commissioned a script for Harry Worth's show, *Here's Harry*. Buoyed, Powell and Driver began to provide scripts for *Coronation Street* too, before Powell's involvement with that soap came to an end in 1964, unlike his colleague who continued to be involved at one level or another until his death in 1973. The duo also dabbled in drama, most famously on five episodes of the BBC's imaginative time-travel fantasy *Adam Adamant Lives!*. Comedy, though, was where the real money was at. And after Driver cut short another already prolific television writing partnership with Jack Rosenthal to join Powell in writing Arthur Lowe's *Corrie* spin-off *Pardon The Expression* in 1965 - at which point Powell himself had ended a similar partnership with a third *Here's Harry* writer, Frank Roscoe - the Vince Powell and Harry Driver partnership would go on to be responsible for no less than ten more ITV sitcoms over the following eight years.

That one of them should have been *Never Mind The Quality, Feel The Width* (1967-71) could hardly be more fitting. For one thing, the show was set in a Whitechapel tailor's firm, a branch of industry in which both men had had experience themselves. Next, its title is as apt a summation of ITV's sitcom output as there is. Thirdly, the central relationship in *Never Mind The Quality, Feel The Width*, between Jewish Manny Cohen (played by John Bluthal) and his Irish Catholic employee, Patrick Michael Kevin Aloysius Brendan Kelly (Joe Lynch), is one of ethnic strife, a defining feature of Powell's later work in particular, though seldom dealt with quite so subtly or successfully again. Both Cohen and Kelly fall out regularly on the grounds of religion and differing life philosophies while, in a symbolic twist, Manny's skill lays primarily in making jackets while Patrick's forte is trousers. Without which two items, of course, no suit would ever be complete.

Not that racial intolerance was the only arena of human interaction explored by Powell and Driver. In their second sitcom, *George and The Dragon* (1966-68), class loomed large, with Sid James and Peggy Mount playing chauffeur and housekeeper respectively to John Le Mesurier's retired army officer. Industrial relations were a feature of *Spanner In The Works*, the one-off *Comedy Playhouse* pilot that gave Jimmy Jewel his first sitcom start after the split with Ben Warriss and also featured Norman Rossington in 1967, while north-south politics were dealt with in *The Best Of Enemies* (1968). As we have already seen, in *Nearest And Dearest*, a show created by Powell and Driver but largely written by others, Hylda Baker and Jewel tore each other to shreds in the name of the family. And much the same was true in *Bless This House*, although the conflict was of a more cross-generational variety there. In *For The Love Of Ada* (1970-71), where pensioners Irene Handl and Wilfred Pickles found romance, age was the predominant theme. And those two issues were combined in *Spring And Autumn* (1972-76), an equally gentle sitcom which gave Jimmy Jewel his final big success in the role of 70-year-old northerner Tommy Butler, a newly-bereaved widower who goes to live with his daughter and son-in-law in a high-rise flat down south. Doubtless there would have been some off-screen conflict, too, when the pair dreamed up *Mike And Bernie*, a not very good sitcom for the feuding Winters brothers, who were willing but unable to emulate the success of Eric and Ernie in 1971.

Yet it was with *Love Thy Neighbour* that Vince Powell and Harry Driver won their longest-lasting fame or infamy, depending upon your point of view. So much so that having co-written the first four series with Driver, who died in 1973 at the tragically premature age of 42, Powell not only went on writing *Love Thy Neighbour* (and *Spring And Autumn*) alone, he continued to develop its controversial themes in the nine new sitcoms created by him that followed.

At the time of his partner's death, Powell was already working as a script editor on *Thirty Minutes Worth*, the sketch show which resulted from Harry Worth's move to ITV in 1972. And come 1975 he was ready to launch three solo efforts. The first of those was *The Wackers*, a show that produced more tabloid newspaper headlines than laughs through its portrayal of a down-to-earth Liverpudlian family, the Clarksons, who live in the then-notorious district of Bootle and are split roughly fifty-fifty in terms of religion and favourite football teams. One half of the family is Catholic, the other Protestant. One half follows Liverpool, the other Everton. The authenticity of the show was further enhanced by plenty of toilet humour (its characters were regularly visitors to an outside loo) and a cast that had more real scouse in it than a dockworker's belly. Former prisoner Billy and his wife Mary, the parents, were played by real life husband and wife team Ken Jones and Sheila Fay. There were roles for future *Brookside* actor Bill Dean and long-time northern favourite Joe Gladwin too, who had first come to prominence alongside Dave Morris in *Club Night* back in the 1950s. Since then, Gladwin had also played Northtown football supporter Arnold Birtwistle in Powell's unsuccessful *Comedy Playhouse* pilot, *The Mascot*, written with Frank Roscoe, in 1964. Of Billy and Mary's three children - named Tony, Bernadette and Raymond - the first was played by David Casey, the second by another Liverpudlian actor with a growing reputation, Alison Steadman, and the third by a future children's entertainer named Keith Chegwin, destined to reveal his willy to the world in the 'action oriented game show for nudists', *Naked Jungle*, in 2000. *The Wackers* lasted six half-hour episodes.

Next in Powell's 1975 repertoire was - oy vey - *My Son Reuben*, starring Lila Kaye and Bernard Spear as Fay and Reuben Greenberg, stereotypical Yiddish mother and son, the latter comprehensively controlled where the acquisition of a suitable Jewish wife is concerned. Again it limped through just six half-hour episodes. At least Powell's next effort, *Rule Britannia!*, stuck around for seven. This one was basically an extended Englishman, Scotsman, Welshman and Irishman joke featuring a quartet of characters named George, Jock, Taffy and - you're ahead of me, aren't you? - Paddy. In short, *Rule Britannia!* was the type of show to give the airbrushing of history a good name. And nor was he finished yet. In 1977, Powell hit stereotype overload with *Mind Your Language*, the mere mention of which can give your average Commission for Racial Equality officer a nosebleed.

At the time, all critical accusations of gratuitous offence were batted away with reference to the show's scrupulous evenhandedness. And it is true that, with the possible exception of Venezuelans, Eskimos and Skokomish tree people, no single nationality escaped ridicule. In that regard, the *Mind Your Language* evening school was most definitely a hotbed of equal opportunities. Every student, whether Chinese, French, Pakistani, Indian, Spanish ('por favore?'), Japanese, Swede, German, Italian, Russian or Greek was as mercilessly caricatured as the next, along with, to a lesser extent, their English teacher Jeremy Brown (Barry Evans). All of which might well have saved its reputation if the jokes had been any good. Unfortunately, as with *Love Thy Neighbour*, there was never any

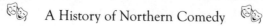

real attempt to rise above comic cliché. Yet also like *Love Thy Neighbour*, audiences at home did not give a stuff. Critical opinion counted for little as *Mind Your Language* straddled three series and 29 episodes before being scrapped by London Weekend Television deputy controller Michael Grade, at the dawn of a new comedy age in 1979. Even then, Powell and his producer Albert Moses, who also played Indian student Ranjeet Singh, briefly resurrected it on four ITV networks, Central, Granada, HTV and Ulster in 1986, although Granada alone broadcast the full 13-episode run and original broadcaster LWT wouldn't touch it with a baghlah pole. The concept was then sold to America where, with an emphasis on Russians and Mexicans, it was remade as *What A Country!* in 1986. Somewhat ironically, *Mind Your Language* was among the first British TV programmes to be broadcast in South Africa when, with the demise of apartheid, actors' union Equity lifted its boycott in the 1990s.

Along with contributing an episode to Bill Maynard's short-lived sitcom, *Paradise Island*, Vince Powell's other 1977 effort was John Inman's decidedly poor *Odd Man Out* which, with its emphasis of effeminacy and sticks of Blackpool rock, also brought homosexuality into the equation. Meanwhile, another successful international market for both *Mind Your Language* and *Love Thy Neighbour* was Australia - never the most politically correct of countries - where Powell developed another couple of sitcoms in 1980. Their names were *Home Sweet Home*, which took the clash of cultures brought about by the emigration of an Italian down under as its theme, and *Love Thy Neighbour In Australia*, which did exactly what it said on the tin. In this latter show, Jack Smethurst was again the star, having, as Eddie, emigrated to the fictional Sydney suburb of Blacktown. But this time, in a neat twist, it is he who is the 'outsider' or the 'bloody pommie poof', as his neighbour takes to calling him. Alas, neat or not, the underwhelmed Aussies were unimpressed and tossed *Love Thy Neighbour In Australia* into the dunny after just seven episodes.

Powell had better luck with a British series that also aired in 1980. The easier going *Young At Heart* starred that fine old thespian John Mills as Albert Collyer, a 65-year-old Stoke-on-Trent pottery worker newly in retirement. Albert's wife, Ethel, was played in the show by the equally venerable Megs Jenkins, fresh from playing the mother of a certain Selwyn Froggitt and co-star of the now septuagenarian Mills in his 1949 film, *The History of Mr Polly*. However, against a backdrop of fundamental change in British comedy, the writer of *Young At Heart* spent much of the rest of the 'eighties working on the projects of other people, beginning with the final series of *A Sharp Intake of Breath*, after that show's creator and writer-in-chief Ronnie Taylor died in 1980. By the end of the decade he had also written for the Windsor Davies and Donald Sinden antique (in every sense) comedy *Never The Twain* (1981) and co-authored the religious comedy *Father Charlie*. Rather gallantly, in a perverse way, in 1984 Powell also had one last bash at rekindling former ITV glories with *Bottle Boys*, in which a team of milkmen, led by the soft core *Confessions of...* film star Robin Askwith, entertained an array of big-busted London housewives. At least *someone* was entertained. Miraculously, *Bottle Boys* made it through two full series.

Vince Powell's contribution to British comedy history may not have been to everyone's taste, but his sheer longevity and work ethic are surely deserving of both recognition and admiration. Nor could anyone deny the courage and indomitability of his former partner Harry Driver who, it is said, when originally struck down with polio, dictated his lines from an iron lung. When relocated to a wheelchair, Driver then switched tactics and rattled out scripts with a knitting needle clenched between his teeth. Which, when you think of it, is quite apt, given that most of his and Vince Powell's more liberal critics endured their situation comedies in almost exactly that same way; through gritted teeth.

In any case, the ITV programme planners of the 1970s and 'eighties were responsible for levels of shoddiness far outweighing anything dreamt up by Vince Powell and Harry Driver.

Who, for example, will ever forget *Don't Drink The Water*, a downright shocking 1974 sequel to *On The Buses*, in which Blakey and his spinster sister Dorothy (Pat Coombs) decamp to Spain? Well, just about everyone, actually. Or how about *Yus My Dear*, the sequel to *Dad's Army* star James Beck's *Romany Jones* (1972), featuring Arthur Mullard as Cockney bricklayer Wally Briggs? And there were plenty more where they came from. At least those two shows were marked by a sort of witless innocence. By the end of the following decade, ITV's situation comedy

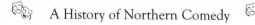

chiefs were still quite clearly strangers to shame, as shown by the risible yuppie sitcom, *The Two Of Us* (1986-1990), which starred Nicholas Lyndhurst and Doncaster's Janet Dibley as Ashley and Elaine, a couple of terminally dull and self-satisfied live-in London lovers, marginally less thrilling than gout. And not that this was in any way a north-south thing. *My Brother's Keeper*, written by and starring *It Ain't Half Hot Mum's* George Layton in 1975, has hopefully since been buried in a lead-lined box while, four years later, *Take My Wife* gave former *Comedians* stalwart Duggie Brown the chance to display his acting skills as northern club comic Harvey Hall, who cracks gags at the expense of his mother-in-law. Which must have been quite a stretch.

So, it's official then? All the terrible sitcoms were on ITV? Well, no, not quite. For in and amongst all that commercially produced garbage, and distracted by the good stuff, the amount of smug middle-class drivel also put out by the BBC during this period is often overlooked. Admittedly, though banal, *Terry And June* was nowhere near as bad as it has since been painted, and the fact that it lasted from 1979-1987 ought to win its star performers, Terry Scott and June Whitfield, a begrudging pat on the back at least. Otherwise, and with the obvious exceptions of *The Good Life*, *Reggie Perrin* and, later, *One Foot In The Grave*, the trials and tribulations of suburbia were by and large as an excuse to leave originality and invention back in the office with the boss. Oh, and did we mention that he and his wife are coming to dinner? Gaze upon these at best middling efforts, ye mighty, and yawn: *Rings On Their Fingers* (1978), *Second Time Around* (1974), *Partners* (1981), *Tears Before Bedtime* (1983) and *Don't Wait Up* (1983). At least most of the rubbish on ITV had a bit of life to it.

Among a plethora of long-forgotten 'seventies and 'eighties BBC sitcoms set in the north, the only interesting aspect of *That's Your Funeral* (1971), in which Bill Fraser was a pompous funeral director, is that some poor fool also saw fit to make it into a film. Or how about Mike Stott's *Pickersgill People* (1978), in which the delightfully dozy northerners of that fictional town were a few bags of nutty slack short of a colliery? Even with a cast of talents like Bernard Hill, Antony Sher and Prunella Scales, it was doomed to be little more than a passing fancy. Equally swift to fade from the memory was *Sink or Swim* (1980), in which northerner Peter Davison goes to live on a London houseboat. A touch more imaginative and well-intentioned, but every bit as obscure now, was *Lame Ducks* (1984), in which Bradford actor John Duttine played itinerant hermit Brian Drake (geddit?), who collects an assortment of fellow oddballs on his travels. And who but the most devoted comedy historian could, without the aid of the *Radio Times Guide to TV Comedy*, recall *Sharon And Elsie* (1984) - in which the structured habits of Manchester-born Elise, played by Rodney Bewes's *Likely Lads* missus Brigit Forsyth, are turned upside down by the arrival of Janette Beverley's less predictable Sharon?

One area in which ITV very definitely did come up trumps in comparison to the BBC was children's television comedy, where the commercial channel's less staid approach paid off nicely. For those kids whose parents let them watch it, ITV in the 1970s and 'eighties was home to a wide range of decent after-school series. There was *Pardon My Genie* (1972) and *Robert's Robots* (1973), both invented by Bob Block, the man soon to be responsible for the BBC's *Rentaghost* (1976). Future *Brookside* creator Phil Redmond was on the writing staff of the perkily irreverent *The Kids From 47A*. The long-running *Sooty Show* showed no sign of stopping when the Shipley-born Harry Corbett's son Matthew assumed responsibility for sticking his hand up the eponymous bear's backside and being periodically abused by a water pistol in 1976. Back among the humans, no less a northern light than Jim Bowen hosted *You Must Be Joking!* (1975), a sketch show for kids which discovered future *Birds Of A Feather* stars Pauline Quirke and Linda Robson. From 1985, Tyne Tees's *Supergran*, made in Tynemouth, was another big favourite for children of all ages, as it says on board game lids.

And although ITV did not have the same amount of critical success enjoyed by the BBC with their adult sitcoms, they nevertheless did have more than is allowed for by conventional wisdom. In 1979, for example, one of British television's longest-running sitcoms ever began in *Shelley*, the story of an eponymous London layabout played by Hywel Bennett, which drew consistently large audiences until its demise in 1992. By and large, however, most of ITV's big guns in this period were either set in the north, endowed with a northern influence in either the writing or the cast, or all three at once, beginning with Vince Powell and Harry Driver's aforementioned *For The Love Of Ada* at the start of the decade.

The male lead in that programme, Wilfred Pickles, had first come to public attention as long ago as 1938, when he landed a job as a radio announcer on the BBC's northern regional service, where he had already made his first broadcast as an amateur actor on *Children's Hour* in 1927. Born in Halifax in 1904, Pickles soon began to make a name for himself as a newsreader and, from 1941, appeared on the National programme in that capacity too, jockeying for position with Bradford's J.B. Priestley as the first BBC broadcaster to speak with a regional accent. Unusually in those days of received pronunciation, Pickles made no attempt to disguise his broad Yorkshire dialect. In fact he played up to it and would even close bulletins with the words, '...and to all in the north, good neet.' If that alarmed the traditionalists, it was lapped up by a wartime public in need of a comforting down-to-earth voice and Pickles was soon a bona fide media celebrity. His fame grew still further with the opportunity to present the audience participation game show *Have A Go* on the BBC Light Programme in 1946. His warm personality and a ready supply of catchphrases like 'Give him the money, Mabel', directed to his wife, Mable Myerscough, helped to make *Have A Go* one of the most popular radio shows of all time. It also earned Pickles an OBE in 1950, some 17 years before the show reached the end of its run in 1967.

In maintaining his radio presence, Pickles also continued to indulge his dramatic leanings, in the theatre, on the wireless and in film, where perhaps his best known role was as the father of Billy Fisher in John Schlesinger's film version of Willis Hall and Keith Waterhouse's *Billy Liar*, released in 1963. He developed a presence in the fast-growing medium of television too and would later present ITV's long-running religious show, *Stars On Sunday*. A first sitcom opportunity came in 1958 with a short-lived BBC effort, *Caxton's Tales*, in which Pickles and Myerscough played husband and wife printers Wilfred and Mabel Caxton, whose problems included contending with a Cockney next-door neighbour. But another 12 or so years would pass before the next. Blessed with a quiet revolutionary charm, *For The Love Of Ada* proved well worth the wait and a far more popular proposition to boot.

This story of love among the tombstones featured retired Cockney widow Ada (Irene Handl), who begins and then continues an affair with Walter Bingley (Pickles), the similarly elderly Yorkshireman who buried her husband. Lasting for 28 episodes, it hung around until a Christmas special on Boxing Day 1971 shortly before, in true 'seventies style, a movie spin-off was made a year later. *For The Love Of Ada* was also notable for introducing its writers, Powell and Driver, to Jack Smethurst who, as Ada's Manchester United-supporting son-in-law Leslie, provided solid support along with Barbara Mitchell, who played Leslie's wife and Ada's daughter Ruth. Already nearing his 70th year when *For The Love Of Ada* came to an end, Pickles's final role came in Arthur Hopcraft's award-winning TV drama, *The Nearly Man*, in 1974. Though a northerner through and through, in his latter years Wilfred Pickles lived in Brighton and it was there where he died in 1978. His body, however, was returned to Manchester, where he was buried alongside his son, David, who had died in childhood from the very disease which had taken Harry Driver's life less than five years before; polio.

More youthful and groundbreaking in their amorous antics were Beryl and Geoffrey, the trendy couple of lovebirds played by Paula Wilcox and Richard Beckinsale in Jack Rosenthal's Manchester-based sitcom, *The Lovers*.

First screened in 1970, *The Lovers* was controversial fare indeed, in that it was driven quite unashamedly by sexual behaviour, prompting accusations that it perpetuated the permissive society that had apparently taken hold in the 1960s. In fact, *The Lovers* was a witty and clever attempt to reconcile the legacy of the so-called swinging 'sixties with the reality for the young British majority. Namely, how did one navigate promiscuity, sexual freedom and old-fashioned good behaviour, especially as a female. Week by week, this problem was reflected in the plight of Beryl, as she semi-reluctantly fought off Geoffrey's physical ardour. In the Manchester-born Wilcox and her co-star Beckinsale (Ronnie Barker's future *Porridge* cellmate, Lennie Godber), Rosenthal struck it lucky. Wilcox, all big eyes and innocence, was entirely believable as an apparently liberated single woman who nevertheless harbours traditional dreams of marriage, a lovely home and bouncing babies. And the Nottingham-born Beckinsale too was full of boyish charm, with his consistently awkward attempts to relieve his girlfriend of her underwear. Driven by Rosenthal's fine scripts (in the first series, anyway, Geoffrey Lancashire took over on series two), it was a formula guaranteed to catch the attention. It also spawned a better than average movie spin-off, written by Rosenthal in 1972.

For Paula Wilcox, Beryl was followed by Chrissy in ITV's rather less psychologically insightful but even more popular flatshare sitcom, *Man About The House* (1973) where, alongside Richard O'Sullivan and Sally Thomsett, she helped to lay the ground for spin-offs *George And Mildred* (1976) and *Robin's Nest* (1977). After which, she was an unmarried mother in the less salubrious *Miss Jones And Son* (1977). And to show that the passing years had not dulled her gifts, in 2004 Wilcox was wonderful as Lillian McNab, a divorcee intent on enjoying her new-found freedom, in the BBC sitcom *The Smoking Room*. Richard Beckinsale, meanwhile, went from *The Lovers* to *Porridge* to *Rising Damp* to *Going Straight*; and were it not for his premature death from a heart attack at the age of 31 in 1979, while filming his final BBC sitcom *Bloomers*, he would surely have risen to still greater heights.

Along with class, the battle of the sexes was an equally predominant theme in ITV sitcom throughout the 'seventies and 'eighties and real-life married couple John Alderton (born Lincolnshire) and Pauline Collins (born Exmouth, raised near Liverpool) contributed fully to the fight. Alderton first came to prominence as bumbling schoolteacher Bernard Hedges in John Esmonde and Bob Larbey's children's comedy series *Please Sir!* (1968-71), which sparked both a sequel *The Fenn Street Gang* (1971) and a prequel *Bowler* (1973). In 1972, he starred alongside Mollie Sugden in *My Wife Next Door* but it was with his missus, with whom he had also starred in the second series of the television drama *Upstairs, Downstairs*, that Alderton became most closely associated. Through that show and their sitcom *No - Honestly* (1974), the pair came perilously close to being the Posh and Becks of their day. A whimsical show about a marriage told in flashbacks, and with a theme tune sung by girl of the moment Lynsey de Paul, *No - Honestly* blurred the edges of fiction and reality. Collins was particularly amusing as the ditsy children's book illustrator Clara. So all-consuming was public interest in the couple's private life that when a sequel, *Yes - Honestly*, came along in 1976, Alderton and Collins had decamped, leaving Donal Donnelly and Liza Goddard to pick up the marital baton.

Whether together or apart, in television or cinema, John Alderton and Pauline Collins have continued to portray positive images of northerners on screen. In 1983, Alderton played a northern writer living

436

down south in the otherwise forgettable ITV sitcom *Father's Day*. In the film *It Shouldn't Happen To A Vet* he played the novelistic Yorkshire vet James Herriot and, most recently, took a bit-part in Womens' Institute nudist comedy *Calendar Girls* (2003). But it was Collins who made the biggest splash in the movies. As *Shirley Valentine*, she gave hope to middle-aged housewives everywhere in the 1989 film of that name, adapted from Liverpudlian writer Willy Russell's stage play.

Less subtle by far, but possessed of no less distinguished a dramatic lineage, was *Oh No - It's Selwyn Froggitt*, written by the prolific Jarrow-born but Hull-raised playwright Alan Plater. Like so many of the sitcoms of the era, *Oh No - It's Selwyn Froggit* (single 't') began life as a comedy pilot, this time for Yorkshire television in 1974. The infuriatingly inept, bumbling Froggitt graduated to a series of his own in 1976 (collecting an extra consonant, a pint of cookin' an' a bag of nuts along the way). Thus was a catchphrase '...magic, our Maurice' born, as Froggitt (Bill Maynard) became an unlikely television icon. With thumbs aloft, a beaming smile and Herculean talent to annoy, Selwyn Froggitt, a *Times*-reading serially-accident prone labourer in the Scarsdale Council Public Works department, was cultural self-delusion personified. As clueless as he was irrepressible, the middle-aged Froggitt still lived with his mother and brother (the Maurice of the catchphrase) and drove his family and drinking pals daft by turning every molehill into a mountain. Over three series and two years, *Oh No - It's Selwyn Froggitt* was a big silly hit for ITV.

As situation comedy monsters go, Selwyn Froggitt may not be up there with Albert Steptoe and Basil Fawlty, but were he a BBC creation he would certainly give Hyacinth Bucket and Frank Spencer a run for their money. Another reason why *Oh No - It's Selwyn Froggitt* is so frequently overlooked, however, may be its flop of a 1978 sequel, *Selwyn*, in which our anti-hero was relocated as a holiday camp entertainments officer. Only Maynard remained of the original cast and it featured no contribution at all from Alan Plater. In more recent times, Surrey-born surrogate northerner Maynard played loveable rogue Claude Jeremiah Greengrass who, from 1992, was a regular on ITV's nostalgic Yorkshire Dales-based Sunday night show, *Heartbeat*.

Alan Plater has produced a stream of usually humourous television screenplays throughout his long career that have included *Trinity Tales*,

the story of a group of Wakefield rugby league fans on their annual pilgrimage to Wembley in which Maynard also starred in 1975; *The Beiderbeck* trilogy, in which James Bolam played such a big part; plus episodic contributions to the drama series *Midsomer Murders*, *Dalziel And Pascoe* and *Maigret*. His last traditional television sitcom, *The Middlemen*, was broadcast in 1977.

Another ITV sitcom to score highly with audiences and critics alike was *Agony* (1979), wherein Mrs. Jack Rosenthal, Maureen Lipman, played Jane Lucas, a wisecracking magazine and radio agony aunt. Though *Agony* was not set in the north (the lead character was a London-based Jewish wife and mother), Lipman herself is of common sense Hull stock and she shone as a woman who is able to solve everyone's problems but her own.

With real-life agony aunt Anna Raeburn as co-creator and first series writer, *Agony* was a liberal taboo buster that sailed perilously close to the prevailing conservative wind. Its acceptance of homosexuality as normal, as depicted in the relationship between Jane's neighbours, Rob and Michael, (the sanest characters in the show until, in the final series of three, Michael commits suicide) was particularly daring. The popularity of *Agony* also proved that if the material is strong enough there is indeed an audience for intelligent comedy on ITV. Some fourteen years after it left our screens, the long-standing impact of the show was confirmed when the BBC produced a less successful sequel, *Agony Again*, in which Lipman returned as the central character in 1995.

Born in 1946, the daughter of a Jewish tailor and encouraged onto the stage by her mother Zelma, Maureen Lipman made her first TV appearance of any note on a 1969 BBC sketch show, *Don't Ask Us - We're New Here*, alongside the Surrey-born but Liverpool-raised Richard Stilgoe. By then, she had already landed her first cinematic role in the classic 'sixties kitchen sinker *Up The Junction* (1968). After a spell in TV drama and another film appearance in Stephen Frears's *Gumshoe* (1972), Lipman was then cast as Marjory in a Ray Galton and Alan Simpson one-off TV comedy, *You'll Never Walk Alone* (1974). Her husband was played by Brian Glover who, as Maurice Pouncey, leads an attempt to convert a trio of non-football fans while heading to Wembley for the FA Cup final on a train. Lipman's first continuous sitcom, *A Soft Touch*, came in 1978, but although she caught the eye as Alison, the wife of an unemployed dreamer, the series itself was short-lived and only ran to seven episodes. Even so, regular television work had by now made her a recognisable face. And *Agony* sent her star well and truly into orbit.

When that series ended, more film work followed in *The Wildcats of St Trinian's* (1980) and *Educating Rita* (1983), another Willy Russell play adapted for the big screen in which she won a best-supporting actress award for her part as Trish alongside Julie Walters. There was plenty more television work too, including her next ITV sitcom, *All At No. 20* (1986), where Lipman played a cash-strapped widow awash in a sea of lodgers. Ironically, though, perhaps her best known role throughout a period that also included parts in one-off plays and comedy dramas like *The Knowledge* (1981), *Smiley's People*, *Outside Edge* (both 1982) and a Channel 4 adaptation of the popular stage farce *See How They Run* (1984) was Beattie, a somewhat stereotypical Jewish mother and grandmother who appeared in a series of thirty-two commercials made for British Telecom from 1987 - catchphrase: 'You got an 'ology?' Possibly, Beattie was based upon Lipman's own maternal dynamo who she later described as 'very funny, without knowing why'.

In Maureen Lipman, the gene for a more knowing but equally dry brand of feminine northern wit has lived on, within whatever medium she operates. Along with authoring a number of entertaining books, in the theatre she performed a critically-acclaimed one-woman tribute to the legendary Joyce Grenfell, *Re-Joyce*, adapted for television in 1991. In 1996, a video called *Maureen Lipman: Live And Kidding* was released of her stage show filmed live at the City Varieties, Leeds. Less happily, she was one of several in a cast that must cringe with embarrassment whenever *Carry On Columbus* (1992) is given another airing on satellite TV. Almost a decade before that, she enjoyed the distinction of appearing in Arthur Askey's final TV appearance, *The Green Tie On The Little Yellow Dog*, in which she, Askey, Barry Cryer, Leonard Rossiter, Cilla Black and others recited classic monologues once written and performed by esteemed masters of the genre like Billy Bennett, Gracie Fields and the Cockney coster comic Albert Chevalier, on Channel 4.

Following in the footsteps of husband Jack, in 1999 Maureen Lipman

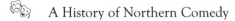

was awarded a CBE and, in 2002, followed that up with a best supporting actress award for her role as the mother in Roman Polanski's *The Pianist*, the same year in which she put in a sentimental show-stopper as landlady Lillian in the soap to which her hubby once provided scripts, *Coronation Street*. Since Rosenthal's death in 2004, Lipman has continued to work prolifically on a career that has never lacked variety. Her most recent projects include a bit-part in the BBC's classic science fiction series *Doctor Who* in 2006; *Glorious!*, her own stage celebration of the life and talents (in that word's loosest sense) of American soprano Florence Foster Jenkins; and, with Anne Reid, the very funny epistolary ITV sitcom *Ladies of Letters* (2009), adapted from a popular BBC Radio 4 series of the same name.

As ought to be obvious by now, quality actors and ITV sitcoms most definitely did mix. And that was certainly the case in *Chance In A Million* (1984), a contender for the most bizarre and overlooked ITV sitcom of all time. In it, Simon Callow played Tom Chance, a man plagued by unlikely coincidence to a miraculous degree. You would not have guessed it at the time, but both Callow and his co-star, Brenda Blethyn, were destined for then equally unlikely film stardom. More conventional than *Chance In A Million* and graced by already-established theatrical nobility was *A Fine Romance*, in which real-life husband and wife thespians Judi Dench (born in York in 1934) and Michael Williams (born in Liverpool in 1935) endured the trials and tribulations of middle class matchmaking and, ultimately, marriage over four series from 1981-84. An American off-shoot, made in 1983, lasted only one pilot episode, but it did star no less a contemporary comedic figure than Julie Kavner as Laura, the part played by Dench in the British version. These days, Kavner is more widely recognised as the voice of Marge Simpson.

With the demise of *A Fine Romance*, both Dench and Williams had other situation comedy hits too. Indeed, for Dame Judi, the long-running *As Time Goes By* was an even bigger hit from 1992, this time on the BBC. Williams, meanwhile, made *Double First* (1988) for the BBC and, in 1993, returned to ITV with *Conjugal Rites*, adapted from a Roger Hall stage play which also starred the Derby-born actor Gwen Taylor. Despite the apparent conventionality of its setting, in which a long-married couple suddenly begin to grow apart with the departure of their grown-up children, *Conjugal Rites* was another likeable effort that lasted two series.

Its high point was undoubtedly Toby the talking dog, whose thoughts were audible only to the viewer and whose hobbies included urinating on parked cars. Also in 1993, Williams starred opposite Tracey Ullman in *Tracey Ullman - Takes on New York*, a trio of mini comedy playlets based in that city made for the cable channel HBO, in which Ullman played three wives to three different husbands, another of whom being Dan Castellaneta, nowadays the voice of Marje Simpson's other half, Homer. After the busiest of careers in theatre, TV, cinema and radio, Michael Williams died from cancer, aged 65, in 2001.

If we were handing out awards for the most under-rated ITV sitcom of all time, then up at the front of the stage, tearing open the little gold envelope and gushing praise on writers Julian Roach and John Stevenson, would surely be the cast and producers of *Brass* (1983). Set in the fictional north country town of Utterley, *Brass* was indeed an utterly superb twin parody of both the glamourous American soap operas that infested the airwaves throughout the 1980s and the traditional northern period-piece dramas that had long since bordered on the stereotypical. Utterley was a grim cobbled world where shoulder pads were replaced by flat caps, 'Greed is Good' braces by leather belts, the oil wells of *Dallas* by the textile mills of Ramsbottom, and the dynastic Colbys and Carringtons by the Hardacres and Fairchilds (Agnes of that downtrodden clan being played, appropriately, by one Barbara Ewing, now a best-selling novelist).

In true soap opera style, the plot and family relationships in *Brass* were complex - ludicrously so - but the secret to its success was that it was all played straight. The viewers may have known that this was a comedy, but that was most definitely not the case for its participants. Chief among those was the renowned classical actor Timothy West who, as despotic self-made 1930s industrialist Bradley Hardacre, blustering owner of t' local cotton mill, shipyard and coal mine, ravager of lower order women, smoker of Churchillian cigars and ruthless exploiter of the working classes, owes his rise up the social ladder to 'good honest hard work', rather than his seduction of and subsequent marriage to a baronet's daughter, Lady Patience Hardacre (Caroline Blakiston). Unfortunately, Lady Patience is now confined to a wheelchair - a voluntary tactic, it turns out, to escape her odious husband's sexual advances - and spends her life as a gin-soaked pent-up ball of sexual frustration on wheels, totally useless

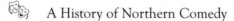

to her four grown-up children, namely the nymphomaniac red-haired Isobel, her idealistic socialist sister Charlotte (given to ripping off her blouse in the name of medicine at any moment) and brothers Austin and Morris, one as ambitious as his father and the other a gay refugee from *Brideshead Revisited*, destined to become a Russian spy. A third son, Bentley, is deceased as the opening episode begins, as confirmed by his memorial stone.

Meanwhile, down with all the poor people in the terraced back-to-backs, live the front-line factory fodder Fairchilds, whose father, George, is a forelock-tugging working class dimwit, grateful for work no matter how degrading or dangerous. As played in the first couple of series by Geoffrey Hinsliff, soon to be known as Ivy Tilsley's one-legged husband Don Brennan in *Coronation Street*, he won't hear a word of criticism against his monstrous employer at the top of the hill. However George's wife, the aforementioned Agnes, is a woman possessed of both a magnificent bosom and militant feminist leanings, who encourages her two sons, the rebellious Jack and poetic Matthew, to murder Hardacre while simultaneously providing him with sexual favours herself. It further transpires that Matthew may, in fact, be Bradley Hardacre's son as a result of that relationship, that Jack and Isobel are secretly conducting an affair, and that Charlotte is the result of a clandestine romp between Lady Patience and the aged Lord Mountfast, to whom Isobel has latterly been betrothed. Charlotte, on the other hand, marries Matthew, who the teddy-bear hugging Morris holds a torch. In the words of the American sitcom *Soap*: 'Confused? You will be...'

For all its innovation and classy production values, *Brass* was rather more popular with the critics than the public, although for its makers, Granada, viewing figures were nothing to be ashamed of. After a couple of 13-episode series in 1983 and '84, it made a welcome and unexpected return on Channel 4 six years later. This time, the story was set against the outbreak of World War Two, where it managed another six episodes during which the opportunistic Bradley Hardacre made even more brass through his strategically vital ammunition factory. With *Brass* behind them, Roach and Stevenson came up with another popular sitcom, *The Brothers McGregor*, about a couple of money-grabbing Liverpudlian half-brothers, Wesley and Cyril, one black, the other white.

Love Thy Neighbour

Although ITV comedy was not a total disaster zone throughout the 'seventies and 'eighties, then, it must be admitted that the vast majority of its comedy output was distinctly forgettable. The 1980s sitcom *Thicker Than Water*, for example, also dealt in nostalgia, with Yorkshire again the backdrop for a 1920s-based sitcom in which Josh Ackland starred as Joseph Lockwood, a stereotypical widowed Tyke adrift in a world of whippets, flat caps and cobbled streets, but without anything like the self-mocking irony of *Brass*. Also in 1980, Dick Sharples, writer of *Thicker Than Water* and *Z Cars* among much else, moved a trashy family of criminals named Nesbitt, first seen in that latter BBC1 cop show, across the great divide. At least *The Nesbitts Are Coming* had the virtue of being imaginatively conceived, with the troublesome clan wreaking havoc across the north of England to the accompaniment of music composed by Sharples himself. But that didn't stop Mr. and Mrs. Nesbitt and their corrupt children, the cowboy-hatted Len, sex-mad Marlene and punk rocker Tom from being condemned to obscurity after just six episodes.

Another bizarre ITV sitcom offering, this time of the early 1970s, starred Britain's very own answer to Marilyn Monroe, Diana Dors, born in Wiltshire but here with a Yorkshire accent. Its name was *Queenie's Castle* and it was written by Keith Waterhouse and Willis Hall. Set in a northern high-rise tower block, Margaret Rose House, ruled over by the light ale-supping Queenie Shepherd of the title - played by the now middle-aged and more buxom than ever one-time screen goddess herself - *Queenie's Castle* also featured Hull-born playwright Barrie Rutter as one of Queenie's three sons. Waterhouse and Hall dropped out of the show for its third and last series, but a spin-off of sorts followed in 1973, *All Our Saturdays*. This time Dors played the equally formidable Di Dorkins, aka 'Big D', the manager of a textile firm who also runs the company's amateur rugby league team, Garsley Garments, later rebranded by Di as 'The Frilly Things'. It did well to last six tackles.

Another Waterhouse-Hall production was the similarly short-lived *Our Kid* (1973), in which Barrie Rutter again appeared, here alongside Leigh music hall veteran Ken Platt, a man known in his younger days as 'the Pocket George Formby'. The pair were Bob and Ben Buslingthorpe, a couple of cohabiting brothers, one getting on a bit, the other young and industrious, who inherit their now-deceased mother's house in Halifax

and have their loyalties tested by the arrival of a fiancée (Sylvia Brayshay). In his pomp, Platt was best known for his catchphrase: 'I won't take me coat off - I'm not stopping.' He died in 1998.

A more significant example of the Waterhouse-Hall *oeuvre* was the television adaptation of Waterhouse's novel *Billy Liar* which began later that same year and starred Jeff Rawle as the eponymous dreamer, Billy Fisher, in the part originally played on stage by the Salford-born actor Albert Finney in 1960 and on screen by Hull's Tom Courtenay (1963). Much later, Rawle would be even better known as harassed newsroom editor George Dent, in Channel 4's over-rated topical comedy of the 1990s, *Drop The Dead Donkey*. Unfortunately, the identity crisis at the heart of *Billy Liar* was nowhere near as effective as it had been in either book, theatre or cinema, but there were plenty of enjoyable moments, not least from the head of the Fisher family. As Billy's father Geoffrey, whose obsessive use of the word 'bloody' created something of a frisson when aired at 8.30pm - George A. Cooper made for a spectacularly grumpy Yorkshireman, delivering a performance almost on a par with Wilfred Pickles in the film. In 1979, *Billy Liar* was also reincarnated on American television as *Billy*, where *Policy Academy* movie favourite Steve Guttenberg took the starring role. That followed a stage musical, in 1974, which starred Michael Crawford and gave a West End debut to the soon to be ubiquitous Elaine Paige adapted, interestingly enough, by sitcom legends Dick Clement and Ian La Frenais. Willis Hall died, aged 75, in 2005, while his octogenarian writing partner and legendary Fleet Street journalist Keith Waterhouse passed away in September 2009.

There was yet more Yorkshire drollery in *Sounding Brass* (1980), in which Brian Glover appeared as Horace Gilbert Bestwick, the musical director of Ettaswell Town brass band, whose ambitions of overtaking the likes of Brighouse and Rastrick and Black Dyke Mills were consistently thwarted. In 1982, Barry Jackson played joke shop attendant *Horace*, a Yorkshireman with the mind of a ten-year-old (anyone west of Keighley can insert their own punchline) and a constant source of consternation to his poor mother. And in 1986, *Coronation Street* legend Pat Phoenix swapped the cobbles of Weatherfield for the boarding houses of Bridlington in *Constant Hot Water*, a real throwback to the sitcoms of the previous decade in which the former Elsie Tanner made for an equally formidable landlady. Regrettably, *Constant Hot Water* ran cold when Pat Phoenix died from lung cancer in the September of that year.

Meanwhile, on the soggy side of the Pennines, a Watford-born *Coronation Street* scriptwriter called Geoffrey Lancashire created *The Cuckoo Waltz*, a sort of *Man About The House* without the belly laughs.

Along with his duties on the soap, Lancashire had already helped out on *Pardon The Expression!* and *The Lovers*, but this was his first solo sitcom and he set it in the county of his name. Chorlton-cum-Hardy was the location and this time it was about two men and a woman, with the ensuing sexual tension more realistically portrayed than in its stablemate *Man About The House*. Lewis Collins - destined for later fame in the ITV cop show *The Professionals* - played the cuckoo of the title, Gavin Rumsey, a wealthy and untrustworthy lodger who has his eye on Fliss, the wife of his best friend, with whom he shares a bedsit. Bradford-born actor David Roper played the friend in question, an underpaid and overworked local newspaper journalist named Chris Hawthorne for whom life is a constant struggle to make ends meet, not least because Fliss (Diane Keen) has just presented the couple with a pair of newborn twins.

Adequate rather than hilarious, the show nevertheless progressed through four series before its last waltz in 1980, by which time the twins had reached school age and Collins had departed to be replaced by the equally caddish Ian Saynor. During this time, Roper simultaneously appeared opposite *Last Of The Summer Wine* stalwart Peter Sallis in the Bolton-based insurance office comedy *Leave It To Charlie* (1978) before disappearing off the sitcom map more or less completely, with the exception of brief one-off appearances in the likes of *Birds Of A Feather* and *A Bit Of A Do*. His screen missus Diane Keen, meanwhile, also moonlighted in the forgettable and forgotten BBC sitcom *Rings On Their Fingers* (1978) opposite Martin Jarvis, before following up *The Cuckoo Waltz* with a starring role in Geoffrey Lancashire's next sitcom attempt, the even less inspiring *Foxy Lady* (1982). In that, Keen played Daisy Jackson, feisty female editor of the northern weekly newspaper, 'The Ramsden Reminder', a subject close to the heart of Lancashire, who was himself a former newspaper reporter. Diane Keen's last starring sitcom

445

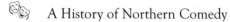

role came as Tim Brooke-Taylor's newly-successful wife in the BBC's *You Must Be The Husband* (1987). Since then, like David Roper, she has mainly appeared in television drama.

With a handful of exceptions then, ITV sitcoms throughout the 1970s and '80s were indeed ordinary at best. From the Nottingham-born Leslie Crowther's first sitcom *My Good Woman* (1972) to the Bolton-based *A Kind Of Living* (1988) - in which a splendid cast led by Frances de la Tour, Richard Griffiths and Tim Healy ought to have produced comic gold but did not - uninspired schedule fillers were the norm. Echoing the title of a 1986 Manchester-based ITV effort, in which Sam Kelly played a newly redundant middle-aged husband full of schemes to get rich quick, the attitude could be summed up thus: *We'll Think Of Something*. If ITV went for originality, the result was most often lazily written or considered tacky. If they tried to copy the BBC, a self-satisfied exercise in tedium like *Chintz* (1981) would ensue, set in leafy Cheshire and as thrilling as a 4x4 ride in Knutsford. Even a show as well written and performed as *Watching* (1987), which starred Jimmy Tarbuck's daughter Liza and lasted seven series and four specials until 1993, is barely remembered now.

There was, however, one enormous exception to the rule; a timeless classic up there with anything produced by the BBC. Its name was *Rising Damp*, and it was created by the Grantham-born writer Eric Chappell.

When the grasping, opinionated, carnally-frustrated and downright chauvinistic northern landlord Rupert ('The permissive society doesn't exist; I should know, I've looked for it') Rigsby first hit the small screen, he was already known to theatre audiences as the anti-hero of Chappell's 1971 stage play, *The Banana Box*, albeit then under the name of Rooksby. On the boards, Rooksby was originally played by no less a figure than Albert Steptoe himself, Wilfrid Brambell, although it wasn't long before a Liverpool-born actor named Leonard Rossiter took over the role, first in Hampstead and then at London's Apollo Theatre in 1973. Rossiter, by this time, was already a West End star in his own right, acclaimed among other things for his 1969 depiction of the Adolf Hitler-like protagonist of Bertol Brecht's satire, *The Resistible Rise of Arturo Ui*. But it was while starring in *The Banana Box* that Rossiter was seen in the part by a representative of Yorkshire Television. Soon the play had moved from stage to television courtesy of a 1974 pilot, in which Richard Beckinsale, still impressing as Godber in *Porridge* on the other side, replaced his stage predecessor Paul Jones in the role of Rigsby's innocent and endearing lodger, Alan Moore. Frances de la Tour and Don Warrington, Rossiter's co-stars in the theatre production, continued as Rigsby's middle class love interest Miss Jones and Alan's African room-mate Philip respectively, to complete a formidable lead quartet. A full series followed three months later.

It was clear from the start that ITV and Eric Chappell were onto a winner. For Chappell, whose television outings thus far were confined to a one-off comedy called *The Spanish Dancers* (shown only in Wales) and another 1974 pilot of a sitcom that eventually ran to three series, the office politics-based *The Squirrels*, *Rising Damp* was the cue for a sitcom writing career that would also take in more mundane, if high-rating, efforts like *Only When I Laugh* (1979), *Misfits* (1981), *The Bounder* (1982), *Duty Free*, *Singles* (both 1984) and *Home To Roost* (1985). Of those, the latter - starring the Manchester-born John Thaw and Normanton's Reece Dinsdale as a warring father and son - was the best received critically, leading to an American version *You Again?*, part-scripted by Chappell, in 1986. In the terms of popularity, however, the package holiday farce *Duty Free*, developed in association with Chappell's assistant Jean Warr, was second only to *Rising Damp*. Set in Marbella, filmed in Leeds and starring the very northern pair Keith Barron and Gwen Taylor as David and Amy Pearce, one of two romantically entwined holidaying couples, *Duty Free* also began life as a stage play - *We're Strangers Here*. On television, its unlikely three-season run - surely the longest Spanish holiday of all time - culminated in an hour-long Christmas special in 1986. Chappell also went on to write two less successful sitcoms, *Haggard* (again featuring the Mexborough-born Barron and Reece Dinsdale in 1990) and accountancy comedy *Fiddlers Three* (1991), which despite having Paula Wilcox in the cast was about as funny as, well, accountancy. Then again, after *Rising Damp* anything might be considered a disappointment.

The key to its success was surely Leonard Rossiter's virtuoso display as Rigsby, an ignorant sex-starved self-delusional grotesque in the best British sitcom tradition. As the miserly owner of a shadowy dilapidated northern bed-sit, forever crashing uninvited into his tenants' rooms, eavesdropping private conversations, leering at Frances de la Tour's coyly

vulnerable Ms. Jones or unloading racist bigotry on the true object of her affections, Philip - who despite having the surname Smith is thought by Rigsby to be the son of a tribal chief with ten wives - he gave nothing less than one of the finest television performances ever. As the theatre critic Milton Shulman put it after watching *The Banana Box* for the London *Evening Standard*: 'His eyes darting about like fireflies, his hands playing frantic games in his pockets when they are not scratching his bottom, his conversational stance angled as if everyone he talks to has halitosis, his mouth falling slack in alternating spasms of surprise and contempt - Mr Rossiter hilariously personifies the pinched little souls who make up the Soho mackintoshed brigades...'. There aren't many gasometers or slag heaps in Soho, but you take his point.

Yet not only is Rossiter very funny, he also renders his ghastly alter ego if not likeable then, at least, vaguely sympathetic. In tandem with a physical ability to clown and gurn broad comedy with the best of them, Rossiter also gets beneath his character's surface awfulness to hint at the existential angst that lurks within, turning what could have been a two-dimensional pantomime into something altogether more profound and, therefore, satisfying. Beneath his threadbare cardigan, Rigsby, a grotesque money spider in a web of his own making - a metaphor underscored by some quite spectacularly dingy scenery, all dark and dreary greens and browns - is a frightened, lonely human being who has lost grip on what really matters and a warning to all. Jealous of youth, his is a life wasted. At heart, he is vulnerable and in pain. And in comedy - and particularly northern comedy - that is fertile ground for laughter indeed.

Before treating the UK to *Rising Damp*, Rossiter's saturnine features had been best put to use on cinema screens as Shadrack, the rodent-like funeral director employer of Billy Fisher in the 1963 film version of *Billy Liar*. By then, he had also appeared in another couple of gritty, northern kitchen-sinkers, *This Sporting Life* (also 1963), in which he played a rugby league journalist, and the seminal *A Kind of Loving* (1962), where he was cast as the wonderfully named Whymper, a dour and phlegmatic worker, intent on keeping his head down and avoiding trouble. Future feature film projects would include Lionel Bart's Dickensian singalong *Oliver!* (1968), in which Rossiter played another undertaker, Mr Sowerberry, a man with a coffin-shaped snuff box; Stanley Kubrick's *2001: A Space*

Odyssey (also 1968) and the same director's eighteenth-century romp *Barry Lyndon* (1975). As Superintendent Quinlan, there were also a couple of supporting roles alongside Peter Sellers in *The Pink Panther Strikes Again* (1976) and *Trail Of The Pink Panther* (1982), although in that latter production the deceased Sellers was present only in archive footage.

Rossiter's theatre career, meanwhile, began in 1954 when he quit his job in an insurance office, aged 27, to become a professional actor. It was a brave move to make because Rossiter was hardly of theatrical stock. Robert Tanitch's 1985 biography, *Leonard Rossiter*, reveals that the nearest his parents got to showbusiness was when his father, John, boasted of having played golf with George Formby senior. Sadly, John Rossiter was killed while working as a voluntary ambulanceman during a 1942 air-raid, leaving Leonard's mother Elizabeth to bring her son up alone. Financially stretched, Rossiter was therefore forced to forego the university education he so badly craved and was forced, by necessity, into earning a wage amid the claims and accidents at the Liverpool-based Commercial Union. It was while working there that he became interested in amateur dramatics, a hobby that was soon an all-consuming passion. Subsequently, Rossiter appeared in over thirty amateur productions and emboldened by an avalanche of good reviews - Tanitch quotes the *Liverpool Echo* thus: 'This actor has a keen feel for comedy...I found his timing and reactions to so many amazing situations irresistibly funny' - he eventually auditioned for Preston Rep', for whom he won a small part in a play called *The Gay Dog*. Fourteen productions later and he was off to Wolverhampton, where he was directed by a future co-star who didn't get where he is today without directing the Wolverhampton Repertory Company, John Barron (1920-2004). Then, in 1959, after building a reputation as a solid performer of comedy and drama, he arrived at the Bristol Old Vic. Rossiter's two-year spell there was later described by the actor himself as 'the bedrock' of a career in British theatre which bestrode the next three decades.

In and amongst all this theatrical and cinematic work, in 1963 there came a major break in the medium that would truly turn Leonard Rossiter into a household name, television, when, as the sly Detective Inspector Bamber, he appeared in eight episodes of the BBC police drama *Z Cars*. The following year, Rossiter landed his first sitcom bit-part as the church-lead stripping, Bible-quoting 'Welsh Hughie', opposite the

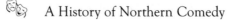

original Rupert Rooksby, Wilfrid Brambell, in an early episode of *Steptoe And Son*. Henceforth, almost ten years of one-off comedy roles followed until, in 1972, he returned to Steptoe's yard as an escaped convict who, along with his older accomplice, in a mirror of the show's central relationship, takes refuge while on the run from Wormwood Scrubs. So miserable an experience is it, that he chooses to go back. By this time, the producer of *Steptoe And Son* was John Howard Davies, who obviously liked what he saw in the guest star because when David Nobbs, another sitcom writer with a journalistic background, set about adapting his darkly humourous novel *The Death of Reginald Perrin* for the BBC in the mid-'seventies, intending Ronnie Barker to take the lead role, Davies instead drafted in Rossiter who, since 1974, had spent the last two years making a more lasting impact as Rigsby in *Rising Damp*.

Born in South London and raised in Kent, Cambridge graduate David Nobbs began his writing career as a reporter on the *Sheffield Star* newspaper in 1958. It was a short-lived position. After two years of door-stepping in the steel city, he again went south to write unstaged plays, work in advertising and return to the media on the *St. Pancras Chronicle*. Until, in the early 1960s, as a result of contacts made in the Cambridge Footlights, Nobbs had the first of several jokes and sketches accepted by *That Was The Week That Was*. From there, he began to provide scripts for Les Dawson, Frankie Howerd, Jimmy Tarbuck and Ken Dodd, while also knocking out the odd novel. It was during a stint as a sketch-writer on *The Two Ronnies* that Nobbs came up with the book which would eventually become *The Fall And Rise of Reginald Perrin*, hence his initial preference for the services of Ronnie Barker.

From 1976, *The Fall And Rise of Reginald Perrin* gave *Rising Damp* more than a run for its money by means of inverting the usual sitcom trick. Instead of everything revolving around one monstrously exaggerated ego, as was most often the case, here the central character was the only sane person in the programme and just about everyone else was barking mad, at least to begin with. An exasperated everyman in the eye of the storm, by the original show's final episode in 1979, Reginald Iolanthe Perrin - R.I.P. - had not only faked his own suicide, he had persuaded his family and friends to do so too, attracting audiences of over 11 million along the way. And in another magnificently judged performance from Leonard

Rossiter, Reggie's growing eccentricity over two wonderful and one not quite so wonderful series stayed just the right side of caricature, the better to satirise the repetitious and mundane insanity of modern-day living. As with Rigsby, Rossiter's subtlety of performance as Reggie brought humanity to the theory, and he was helped by a wittily-written cast of supporting characters who, between them, were responsible for the biggest influx of catchphrases into the English language since *ITMA*.

The world of Reginald Perrin, while recognisably our own, is a place where everyone and everything operates in precise metronomic routine. Reggie leaves for his job as a senior sales executive at Sunshine Desserts at exactly the same time every day. He kisses his wife Elizabeth (Rossiter's fellow Liverpudlian Pauline Yates) goodbye as goes, meeting her request in the hallway that he should 'have a good day at the office' with a wearily resolute 'I won't'. He walks to the train - which is, as usual, precisely eleven minutes late - and sits in the same carriage, with the same fellow commuters, attempting the same *Times* crossword puzzle. His route to the station has taken him through the same tree-lined suburbs, whose streets are tantalisingly named Coleridge Close, Tennyson Avenue, Wordsworth Drive and so on; surely a nod at the power of poetry to free the human soul. In fact, poetic metaphors are highly relevant in describing *The Fall And Rise of Reginald Perrin*. Not only with regard to how poems impose discipline upon those who would operate within their steady rhythms of form, but also owing to their capacity to paradoxically release and yet contain flights of fancy and self-expression. As such, *The Fall And Rise Of Reginald Perrin* may well be as close to poetry as any situation comedy is likely to get.

And speaking of rhythm, what repetitive form of dialogue could be more rhythmic than catchphrases? As Reggie's boss C.J., a pompous old bore whose self-regard borders on the fetishistic, Rossiter's former colleague in rep', John Barron, had perhaps the most memorable: 'I didn't get where I am today without knowing a winner when I see one,' *et al.* C.J.'s obsequious sales lackeys Tony and David weren't far behind, every suggestion met with the word 'great' from one and the other 'super'.

Nor were the catchphrases strictly verbal. Characters and situations recurred regularly in *The Fall And Rise Of Reginald Perrin* too. From the now-iconic opening title sequence in which a silent movie-style speeded

up Reggie throws off his clothes on a Dorset beach before dashing off into the rolling surf, the comedy of recognition is remorseless. There is even a new take on the tried and tested mother-in-law joke, with an image of a hippopotamus wobbling towards a water hole whenever Elizabeth happens to mention her. The equally hoary secretary-boss affair scenario is another old chestnut to be given a shakedown via Reggie's fantasies of congress with his bespectacled factotum Joan, played by future *Coronation Street* actor, Sue Nicholls, of Audrey Roberts fame. Just as Laurel and Hardy can leave us giggling at a set-up sign-posted a good thirty years ago, so does *The Fall And Rise Of Reginald Perrin* raise a chuckle with running gags like C.J.'s farting chairs ('sorry, C.J...'), Reggie's failure to understand telephones and his inability to hit a coat-stand with a brolly.

The bizarrely predictable antics of the supporting cast are best illustrated in Elizabeth's militarily deranged brother Jimmy, as played by Geoffrey Palmer, who eventually reprised the role in a spin-off also written by Nobbs, *Fairly Secret Army* (1984), albeit then known as Harry Kitchener Wellington Truscott. For cash-strapped and hungry Jimmy, for whom there was 'a cock-up on the catering front' and an undercover enemy around every corner, outward conservatism was matched only by mental anarchy, as in this sublime exchange with Reggie:

> REGGIE: Come on, Jimmy. Who are you going to fight when this balloon of yours goes up?
> JIMMY: Forces of anarchy. Wreckers of law and order. Communists. Maoists. Trotskyists. Neo Trotskyists. Crypto-Trotskyists. Union leaders. Communist union leaders. Atheists. Agnostics. Long-haired weirdos. Short-haired weirdos. Vandals. Hooligans. Football supporters. Namby pamby probation officers. Rapists. Papists. Papist rapists. Foreign surgeons. Head shrinkers, who ought to be locked up. Wedgewood Benn. Keg bitter. Punk rock. Glue sniffers. Play for Today. Squatters. Clive Jenkins. Roy Jenkins. Up Jenkins! Up everybody! Chinese restaurants. Why do you think Windsor Castle is ringed with Chinese restaurants?

REGGIE: Is that all?

JIMMY: Yes.

REGGIE: I see. You realise the sort of people you are going to attract, don't you Jimmy? Thugs. Bully boys. Psychopaths. Sacked policemen. Security guards. Sacked security guards. Racialists. Paki-bashers. Queer-bashers. Chink-bashers. Basher-bashers. Anybody-bashers. Rear admirals. Queer admirals. Vice admirals. Fascists. Neo fascists. Crypto-fascists. Loyalists. Neo loyalists. Crypto-loyalists.

JIMMY: Do you really think so? I thought support might be difficult.

Other equally lunatic characters in *The Fall And Rise Of Reginald Perrin* included Reggie's privet wine making, briar pipe smoking liberal son-in-law Tom ('I eat a lot of fish. I'm a fish person'). This mild-mannered boring new age zombie, married to Perrin's daughter Linda, was thought by Reggie to be 'a bearded prick' who made his grandchildren, Adam and Jocasta, 'eat garlic bread the minute they were off the breast'. And as Perrin's own mental state deteriorates, so too does his physical well-being, as symbolised to great effect by the giant yellow letters on the company's Sunshi e Dess rts sign, which droop and drop off like middle-aged body parts. All of which means regular visits to Doc Morrisey, a confused works doctor in whose surgery Reginald Perrin is asked the immortal question: 'Do you find you can't finish the crossword like you used to? Nasty taste in the mouth in the mornings? Can't stop thinking about sex. Can't start doing anything about sex? Wake up in a sweat in the mornings and keep falling asleep during *Play For Today*?' 'How extraordinary, doc' says Reggie. 'It's exactly how I've been feeling, yes.' 'So do I. I wonder what it is?'

When the third and, for now, final series of *The Fall And Rise Of Reginald Perrin* drew to a close, with Reggie having previously faked his own death, returned in disguise as the curly-haired Martin Wellbourne, owned up, fallen into the old routine as Reggie, worked in a piggery, risen to great heights as the creator of Grot (a shop-turned-corporate giant of a company which earns him a fortune on the back of openly selling useless products) before departing the rat race once more - along with Elizabeth

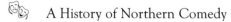

and C.J. - and establishing his own personal commune, David Nobbs headed back to ITV and an all together less salubrious (and complicated) sitcom, *The Glamour Girls* (1980). Despite the efforts of *The Comedians* regular Duggie Brown and *The Likely Lads*'s Thelma, Brigit Forsyth, it was something of a disappointment as, indeed, was his next BBC effort, *The Sun Trap*, a story of Spanish expats which, according to the writer himself on a 2004 edition of the BBC's *Comedy Connections* strand, produced '...the lowest recorded audience for sitcom in the history of BBC1.'

Eric Chappell had better luck in 1980 with a surprisingly passable full-length feature film of *Rising Damp*, made shortly after the death of Richard Beckinsale. Christopher Strauli, the actor who took over from Beckinsale in the fourth and final series of that sitcom in 1978, was recast as the art student, John. The film, essentially three *Rising Damp* episodes strung together, also benefitted from the not inconsequential talents of Denholm Elliott and, amongst other things, revealed that Rigsby's so-called African prince, Philip, was actually from Croydon. For David Nobbs, meanwhile, the rest of the decade television-wise amounted to an assortment of forgettable sitcoms such as the long-distance lorry driver comedy, *Dog Food Dan And The Carmarthen Cowboy* (1982), *Fairly Secret Army* and the equally unremarkable *The Hello Goodbye Man* (1984), before coming to a close on a much happier note with his nicely observed series of ITV comedy playlets, *A Bit Of A Do* (1989).

Based upon his own 1986 novel of the same name, *A Bit Of A Do* was the story of various functions attended by the Simcocks, an extended family of down-to-earth Yorkshire folk. Head of that family is David Jason's no-nonsense Ted, married to Gwen Taylor's Rita and owner of the Jupiter Foundry, makers of the finest coal scuttles, door knockers and toasting forks in England. The first such 'do' - i.e. 'party' in Yorkshire-speak - is the marriage of Ted's youngest son Paul (David Thewlis) to the rather less earthy but distinctly pregnant Jenny (Sarah-Jane Holm), only-daughter of dentist Laurence Rodenhurst (Paul Chapman) and his wife Liz (Nicola Pagett). Thereafter, *A Bit Of A Do* revolved around funerals, christenings and unlikely charity fund raisers over 13 episodes and two series. In 1991, Nobbs set another sitcom, *Rich Tea And Sympathy*, in the same county, wherein two more Yorkshire families, the Merrygroves and the Rudges, fought it out against the backdrop of a biscuit factory. These days, David Nobbs is perhaps best known for his literary fictional hero Henry Pratt.

As for Leonard Rossiter, after Rigsby and Reggie were laid to rest he enjoyed still more success with an advertising campaign for the alcoholic drink Cinzano during which, over ten television commercials shown between 1978 and 1983, he contrived to spill vermouth on the glamourous British screen actor Joan Collins in just about every way possible. The locations for those adverts varied, taking in such venues as a ski lodge, a roller disco and a couple of aeroplane seats, but the result was always the same. With a witless (or was it cunning) smile, Rossiter's louche and clumsy oaf would deposit said drink down the front of the unimpressed Hollywood star, shattering any illusion of sophistication completely.

Such was the impact made by the Cinzano ads that, upon Rossiter's untimely death, a BBC news report declared that the actor would be best remembered for them, a statement as bold as it was surely crass. Good as they were, how could a string of adverts match Rupert Rigsby and Reggie Perrin? And what about all that film and theatre work? Indeed it was in that latter genre, having just finished filming opposite Michael Caine on the Dick Clement and Ian La Frenais movie *Water* (1985), that Rossiter took his final curtain call. The play in question was a 1984 production of the Joe Orton farce, *Loot*, in which he played the bent and incompetent Truscott of the Yard, while simultaneously appearing as a supermarket manager in his final ITV sitcom, *Tripper's Day*, a role soon to be taken over by Bruce Forsyth. While in his dressing room at London's Lyric Theatre, Leonard Rossiter suffered a massive heart attack and died, aged 57.

For Reginald Perrin, however, that was still not the end of the story. Firstly, some 12 years later in 1996, Nobbs had a go at relaunching the Reginald Perrin franchise with a fourth series, *The Legacy of Reginald Perrin*, in which Rossiter's importance to the concept was reinforced absolutely. Despite an all-star original cast with the catchphrases and idiosyncrasies to match, Perrin Mk4 was but an empty shell without its lead star. And when the entire concept was then remade as *Reggie Perrin* in 2009 with, unthinkably, *Men Behaving Badly* star Martin Clunes this time suffering Rossiter's mid-life crisis, although the result was actually not half bad, an over-riding impulse to ask 'yes...but what's the point?' was all-but impossible to fight off. Sorry, C.J.

16
The Dying of the Light?

"Name a seaside resort on the south coast."
- *Les Dennis, Family Fortunes.*
"Rio de Janeiro."
- *Contestant.*

To begin with, there was little indication of the upheaval to come. As the 'seventies prepared to make way for the 'eighties, in television sitcom and Variety alike, complacency was afoot. Politically, areas of Britain remained a tinderbox, apt to burst into flame at the slightest provocation. In music, the rip-it-up vibrancy of punk had all-but deposed the rock and pop old guard and a revolution in desk top publishing had led to an upsurge in fanzines, football or otherwise. If you want a thing doing right, then do it yourself, as a certain incoming female Prime Minister might have put it, albeit in terms less than agreeable to an equally revolutionary counter-culture. In one way or another, the nation was set on change.

Someone, however, forgot to tell the makers of Saturday night telly. In time, even here, the lure of a more youthful audience would prove irresistible. Eventually the penny - such as it was - would drop. Although, as the sitcoms of our previous chapters confirm, old school mainstream entertainment would never be banished entirely, a less reverential and more belligerent mood would soon begin to take hold. Yet for now, the BBC's light entertainment department in particular, heady with the

456

recent past glories of messrs. Yarwood, Morecambe and Wise, sailed as blithely on as it had before. And to be fair, audiences - or at least a certain *type* of audience - continued to tune in faithfully. The old adage, it seemed, held true: in uncertain times, Britain appreciated its traditional northern comics more than ever. And of this latest stock, the biggest (and littlest) were Syd Little and Eddie Large.

Little and Large were a double act in the now well-established family-friendly mould and their shows stretched across the BBC's early evening Saturday schedules through 76 episodes, eleven series and eight specials, between 1978 and 1991. The 'funny' one of the two was big, jovial, cheeky Eddie - born Edward McGinnis in Glasgow in 1941 - whose main claims to fame were his weight and impersonations. Syd, short of stature but huge in spectacles, was the straight man to end all straight men in that he appeared to be devoid of any noticeable personality of his own and seemed purely to be there as the butt of Eddie's ribbing. While his rotund pal cracked corny jokes beside him, grinning Syd, eyes like Bambi under glass, hovered nervously, as if he had just wandered in off the street.

With a scriptwriting team down the years that included Eddie Braben, Barry Cryer (of course) and *One Foot In The Grave* creator David Renwick, Little and Large were quite obviously intended as replacements for Eric and Ernie. Alas, they would never manage that but, then again, who could? And their longevity in the face of that approaching sea of change does suggest that they must have tickled the funny bone of somebody somewhere. While, at their worst, the duo's shows were formulaic and lazy, at their best they were harmless fun. Their problem - if it *was* a problem - was one of being in the right place at the wrong time. Comedians like Syd Little and Eddie Large did not set out to change the world. Along with thousands of comedians before them, their ambition was simply to have a decent showbiz career. Whatever else that is, it is hardly a crime against humanity (although Eddie's primetime Deputy Dawg impersonation might reasonably be regarded in that light).

Little and Large's act originated in a Wythenshawe pub in 1963. Eddie, whose family moved to a red-brick terrace house near Manchester City's old Maine Road ground when he was ten, was among the audience for a one-man show in which the performer sang to the strains of an electric guitar - strain presumably being the operative word. Unimpressed,

he began to heckle the poor crooner with the result that he was invited up to see if he could do any better. So well received was the impromptu performance that the pair are said to have received rapturous applause, although whether that occurred while they were on the stage or leaving it is unclear. Be that as it may, a 'turn' was born and it rarely shifted from that same essential formula: useless musician interrupted by annoying plump comic. That pub singer, of course, was one Cyril Mead, destined to be known as Syd, born in Blackpool in 1942. Initially known as 'Cyril Mead and Friend', the ensuing double act soon changed their names to Syd and Eddie, before finally settling upon Little And Large.

In now time-honoured tradition, Little and Large's television break came courtesy of winning *Opportunity Knocks* in 1971, a victory which led to a one-off ITV sitcom the following year called, somewhat alarmingly, *Three In A Bed*. The man who gave them their chance on *Opportunity Knocks*, the producer Royston Mayoh, was the force behind it and Syd and Eddie played a couple of darts team regulars preparing to take on a rival pub, in a big local derby. Roy Barraclough also starred. No full series followed and the duo had to wait until 1976 before their next leap forward, when Mayoh again produced and directed the pilot of *The Little And Large Tellyshow*, which was developed into an ITV series in 1977. That same year, the duo also enjoyed a sell-out Blackpool summer season. However, as so often, it was with a move to the BBC that the television career of Little And Large really got underway.

It began with a 1977 Boxing Day special, *The Little And Largest Show On Earth*, filmed in a Manchester circus big top and also starring Cliff Richard and Marti Caine. Five months later, another one-off special, *Little And Large*, took to the air, followed by a first full series later that year. From that moment on, throughout the following decade, *The Little And Large Show*, as it was now known, became a fixture and fitting.

As, in fact, was the case with another northern double act on the opposite channel. Tommy Cannon and Bobby Ball had shared billing on at least three occasions with Little and Large at Bernard Manning's Embassy Club in Manchester, well before fame and fortune came calling. Nor did the similarities end there. Like Little and Large, the Oldham-born Cannon and Ball were also apt to plough the 'singer interrupted by comedian' furrow. Unlike that pair, however, both Cannon and Ball were possessed of fully-fledged personalities in their own right and, until the demands of mainstream knocked off their rough edges, a shock value that on first viewing could be genuinely hilarious.

The key to their popularity was little Bobby, a manic mustachioed bundle of anarchic energy, prone to twanging his braces and yelling 'Rock on, Tommy!' or 'You little liar!' at inappropriate moments during his partner's vocal renditions. The naughty boy who has never grown up, Bobby Ball was a gust of fresh air, certainly in the duo's regular appearances on *The Wheeltappers And Shunters Social Club*. Their own first small screen audition on *Opportunity Knocks* in 1968 had not gone quite so well. They came last. In some ways, Bobby's tourettes-like outbursts were an omen, a sign of things to come for comedy in general. They certainly gave him an air of unpredictability and danger that, all too soon, was tamed by a cosy twelve-year tenure on Saturday night TV.

Robert Harper - aka the perpetually-grinning Bobby Ball - was born in 1944. His more urbane partner Thomas Derbyshire beat him to the maternity ward by six years. Both men began their working lives as welders in the same Oldham factory, before forming a musical duo, Bobby and Stevie Rhythm, in 1964 and heading out into the pubs and clubs of Lancashire. After being dropped down the bill at the Batley Variety Club, the pair reinvented themselves as a comedy double act. With humour came three name changes: the Sherrell Brothers, the Harper Brothers and eventually - with Tommy named after the rock and roll singer Freddie Cannon and Bobby named after, well, a ball - Cannon and Ball. Despite those sporadic early TV dates - culminating, in 1977, with a *Cannon And Ball At The Wheeltappers* concert special, introduced by Manning and Colin Crompton - the duo spent much of the 1970s polishing their live act, an area of activity in which they have since broken many a box office record in pantomime and seaside summer season. However, it was after filming sketches for the ITV Variety show *Bruce Forsyth's Big Night* - ironically, never used - that they landed a series of their own, almost immediately attracting around 12 million viewers in 1979.

For an ITV network out to make inroads into the BBC's Saturday evening monopoly, this was good news indeed and it owed much to an irreverent blend of stand-up, sketches and celebrity guests in the pattern set down by Morecambe and Wise. Ironic, given the brief of their ratings-war adversaries, Little and Large, to whom they would have posed an even bigger threat had that first series not been interrupted by an ITV network strike. As it was, when the industrial action ended, the duo continued to attract sizeable audiences and *The Cannon And Ball Show* continued in one format or another until August 1990, including a brief London-based sitcom between 1986-87.

At the height of their popularity in 1983, Cannon and Ball starred in their one and only film, *The Boys in Blue*, described in *Halliwell's Film Guide* as a 'horribly incompetent remake of [Will Hay's] *Ask A Policeman*', also starring Eric Sykes, Roy Kinnear and Jack Douglas. In the film, the duo play a couple of village coppers whose station, like the half-empty cinemas in which it was shown, seemed doomed to closure. Better received were Variety guest spots on Jimmy Tarbuck's *Live From The Palladium* and the BBC's *Seaside Special*. Until, in 1991, with their long-running television series over, Tommy and Bobby had another attempt at sitcom in what was intended to be a group of six pilots going under the banner *Cannon And Ball's Playhouse*. Only three were actually made: *Free Every Friday* (based in the offices of a fictional local paper, the 'Althorp Claxton and Advertiser'), *Growing Concern* (about a couple of newly fired maintenance men) and *Plaza Control*, in which the pair played Bernard and Trevor, two particularly useless shopping centre security guards. And unusually, having ditched the remaining three pilots, a full six-episode series of *Plaza Patrol* was produced made instead. It flopped and, amid off-screen problems with their relationship, Cannon and Ball (temporarily) went their separate ways.

If we are looking to sum up mainstream light entertainment during this period we might well alight on the adjective 'zany' - a perhaps safer and more manageable attempt to harness the revolutionary riotousness currently bristling like an underground rumour. And if Bobby Ball and Eddie Large were zany, then what did that make Freddie Starr?

Born Frederick Fowell in the Liverpool of the wartime 1940s, Freddie Starr was one of many light entertainers in the 'eighties who came to national attention on London Weekend Television's *Who Do You Do?* Having the same format as *The Comedians* but with impressions, *Who Do You Do?* was a similarly quickfire concept, in which turns were whizzed on and off with brutal rapidity. From its first series in 1972, the show hung around over five series and two specials until 1976, when Little and Large and future John Cleese-lite Michael Barrymore belatedly joined it for the final run. And where Bernard Manning was the star of the stand-up version, there is little doubt who stole the show for the mimics. Despite steady support from the likes of Peter Goodwright, Janet Brown, Faith Brown and another couple of comics who were also regulars on *The Comedians*, Johnny More and Paul Melba, together with stars of the future like Russ Abbot, Les Dennis and Dustin Gee, Starr's manic and madcap impersonations of Hitler, Max Wall, Elvis Presley and Tarzan made him a clear favourite with the public.

Married at 17, the young Freddie's showbusiness career had begun as a rock 'n' roll singer in the mid-1950s, before he won an uncredited part as a Teddy Boy in the 1958 crime film, *Violent Playground*. With the arrival of the 'sixties, he became lead singer with Howey Casey and the Seniors, a group credited with being the first from Liverpool to play in Hamburg, Germany. When financial problems brought about their demise, Freddie Fowell joined a similar set-up called The Midnighters, with whom he released three now obscure records on the Decca label and, like a certain drummer also destined for Hamburg, adopted the moniker 'Starr'. By then, an ingrained talent to amuse was very much in evidence and after he joined another group, The Delmonts, in 1965, irreverent gags and impersonations began to dominate. Having turned solo, Starr was invited onto the bill of the 1970 Royal Variety Performance where, despite only having three minutes in which to strut his stuff, he became the first act in 47 years to perform an encore after tearing down the house as Mick Jagger.

Like Frank Randle, Barrymore, Bobby Ball and others before him, the diminutive Freddie Starr - 5ft 5" in his stocking feet - dwelt firmly in the realms of the loveable rogue. As the six-year-old son of a bricklayer who spent his leisure time bare knuckle boxing, the young master Fowell spent a portion of his childhood without the power of speech. Although Starr himself has described his upbringing as 'tough but fair', his father is said to have dropped the youngster from a table with a promise to catch him, before reneging on the deal. Whatever the truth, a psychosomatic illness was blamed for the speech loss, with the result that young Frederick was sent away to a children's home for two years to recuperate. When he returned it was with a stammer that he continued to struggle

with throughout his early years. All in all, it was an event that had a major psychological impact on the wannabe young performer. It also awoke in him the comedic potential of what, in those less enlightened days, was seen as mental and crazy behaviour. It is perhaps safe to assume that there would have been a fair degree of anger in there too. Either way, with his rugged good looks, wild twinkling eyes, cheeky smile and tousle of blond hair, a Freddie Starr performance was always one tantalising step away from outrage and audiences thrilled to the spectacle.

While still a regular on *Who Do You Do?*, Starr's solo television debut came in 1974. *Ready Freddie Starr*, again made by LWT, was a one-off sketch and stand-up show, as straightforward as any Freddie Starr show can be. It was followed by two more specials, this time for the BBC, both simply called *The Freddie Starr Show*, in which impressions were very much to the fore. In 1978, it was back to ITV for *The Freddie Starr Experience* while Starr's next LWT project, *Freddie Starr's Variety Madhouse*, an even zanier proposition, arrived the following year. From there, it was lunacy all the way, via *Freddie Starr On The Road*, a documentary of sorts following the comedian on one of his many live tours; his own talent contest, *The Freddie Starr Showcase*, filmed in the unlikely showbiz setting of Harrogate, Yorkshire; a 1984 New Year's Eve special called *Freddie Starr At The Royalty*; and *The Freddie Starr Comedy Express* 12 months later. All of which confirmed their eponymous star as a British comedy original.

Yet for all that he was nothing short of a phenomenon in his day, whether in his own shows or disrupting someone else's (in which regard, the crooner Des O'Connor was a regular victim), Freddie Starr has never quite reached the levels of acclaim accorded to many of the comedians among whom he might once have been expected to join in comedy's hall of fame. The reason for that, perhaps, is his reputation for being every bit as unpredictable and edgy away from the screen as he was on it. Certainly, few British comedians have provoked anything like the *Sun* newspaper's now infamous headline: 'Freddie Starr Ate My Hamster'. It accompanied a front-page story that told (wrongly) of how the comedian had placed said rodent between two slices of bread and proceeded to tuck in, live on stage, in 1986. On its own, that would not have done much damage. In fact, such outrageousness flogged tickets. More damaging were allegations made by a number of TV producers and former co-stars, repeated in the

The Dying of the Light?

Channel 4 documentary *Freddie Starr Ate My Hamster* in 2001, that bad and allegedly violent behaviour had made him impossible to work with. Not surprisingly, the man himself - filmed largely at the Spanish villa in which he lived with his third wife - denied this and a somewhat bizarre hour of TV ended with its clearly bitter subject laying a symbolic wreath to mourn what he described as the death of British comedy.

Certainly, after appearing alongside Cannon and Ball and the rest in Eric Sykes's *Mr H Is Late* in 1988, Freddie Starr pretty much vanished from the small screen until ITV again decided to take the plunge with a couple of hour-long specials under the banner *Freddie Starr* in 1993. A full five-episode series of that name began in May the following year, although there was a two-month gap between the first and second programmes, on account of that year's football World Cup. By now, however, it was clear that television companies were struggling to deal with the self-destructive dynamo in their midst. Starr's popularity with audiences was still intact, as shown when he fronted his own contribution to ITV's *An Audience With...* strand in 1996, and subsequently became one of the few to return for a second bite in *Another Audience With... Freddie Starr* two years later. In between came two more series of *The Freddie Starr Show*, inspired by that success. But after a final seasonal special in 1998, Freddie Starr's reign as the clown prince of TV light entertainment was at an end.

One beneficiary of Freddie Starr's tendency not to settle in one place for too long was Russ Abbot, born Russell Roberts in Chester in 1947, whose performing career also began as the funny member of a musical group.

Abbot had been a drummer with The Black Abbots, a cabaret band formed by the comedian himself, as the name suggests. The Black Abbots won a first recording contract in 1977 and Abbot subsequently spent 15 years with the group, during which time he made some of those early appearances on *Who Do You Do?*. In 1980, they made a couple of music and sketch shows, *The Black Abbots*, for Yorkshire Television. Keen to pursue a solo career, their founder had by then already turned up alone on shows like *The Comedians*, *What's On Next?* (1976) and *Bruce Forsyth's Big Night*, before being deposited in *Freddie Starr's Variety Madhouse*. When that show came to an end in 1979, it was Abbot - until then a mere co-star, along with Norman Collier and rotund funny lady Bella Emberg - who took over the naming rights. Thus was born the highly-popular *Russ Abbot's Madhouse*, running over six series and six seasonal specials from 1980 until 1985.

Having resigned from the Black Abbots after a gig in the Fiesta Club, Stockton-on-Tees, Russ Abbot was soon the new the king of Saturday night slapstick. With an appeal that bridged the generation gap, his shows were in many ways a mainstream equivalent of *Monty Python's Flying Cricus* and seldom received the critical attention they merited. Boundaries of comedy structure were tested and crossed. Sketches ended prematurely. In this way was Abbot the unheralded post-modern renaissance man of 'eighties light entertainment.

Certainly, the *Saturday Madhouse*, as it also became known, caught the public's imagination from the start, with Abbot's wacky array of alter egos like Jimmy McJimmy (an Irn Bru-headed Scot with an accent broader than the Firth of Forth) and private detective Barratt Holmes (plus his sidekick, Dr. Wimpey) among the favourites. By now, Norman Collier had left to be replaced by Michael Barrymore, Les Dennis and Dustin Gee. Bella Emberg, though, stayed and the spirited atmosphere continued courtesy of such characters as Irish rocking chair crooner Val Hooligan, Spanish smoothie Julio Doubleglazius, World War Two air ace Boggles, German lunatic Fritz Crackers, quiffed rock 'n' roller Vince Prince, Sid the Spiv and Cooperman, an inept superhero whose powers extended to an ability to say 'just like that...' in the manner of you know who. Not surprisingly, given such silliness, *Russ Abbot's Madhouse* was a big hit with children too, another reason, perhaps, why its Pythonesque quality was overlooked.

In any event, by the time the quality conscious BBC came knocking on his door in 1986, Russ Abbot was firmly established as a Saturday night mainstay. However, a name change to *The Russ Abbot Show* - on account of mental health sensibilities, no doubt - could not disguise how the new vehicle was moving down the same tracks as before, albeit with Jimmy McJimmy renamed CU Jimmy (in accordance with his catchphrase), 'Secret Agent X' now known as Basildon Bond (complete with diving flippers, balaclava and naval jacket) and a healthier budget all round. Making the transition with Abbot to the other side were Bella Emberg and Les Dennis, the trio again making six series and six specials together, this time until 1991, when the Beeb suddenly decided their former golden boy was now old hat and declined to offer him another contract.

In 1994, Abbot returned to ITV and picked up where he left off, introducing new characters like the Clueless Cleric, Percy Pervert and a family called Noisy who, er, made too much noise. On the whole, they were less well received than his earlier creations and this latest ITV show finished after two series and a 1996 special. As with many who made their mark in the mid-to-late 1970s and 'eighties, the prevailing comedy winds were against him. Perhaps wisely, it was now that Russ Abbot opted to change course, instead concentrating on acting, both in situation comedy and straight drama. He had already played widower Ted Fenwick who decamps to Blackpool in the 1993 ITV play *September Song* and, with the curtain about to come down on *The Russ Abbot Show*, his next step in that direction was as Ted Butler, the father of a particularly unpleasant family in *Married For Life* (1996), a British adaptation of the popular American hit comedy *Married... With Children*. Unfortunately, the Butlers were not the Bundys and the show was scrapped after just seven episodes. Abbot enjoyed better reviews when he appeared as a wheelchair-bound OAP, complaining about the young folk and their gadgets, in the second series of *TV To Go* (2002), a technological sketch show written by Bill Bailey and Sean Lock among others, which also starred Mrs. Doyle from *Father Ted*, Pauline McLynn, and *The Office* territorial, Mackenzie Crook.

Yet *The Russ Abbot Show* was not quite done yet. In that same year, 2002, a radio series in which many of the original TV sketches were re-recorded - the fifth such since 1997 - was broadcast on BBC Radio 2. These days, Russ Abbot is more likely to be found popping up in West End theatre productions than indulging in madcap tomfoolery.

It was on *Russ Abbot's Madhouse* that those other two *Who Do You Do?* graduates, Dustin Gee and Les Dennis, first appeared as a bona fide double act, and again in our story the influence of *Coronation Street* looms large. Having impressed Abbot as solo performers, when invited to join the *Madhouse* Gee and Dennis married their talents in an impersonation of Vera Duckworth and Mavis Riley, respectively. The routine proved such a hit with viewers that the duo struck up a double act full-time.

Most immediately, that meant a move to the BBC for *The Laughter Show* (1984), initially a five-way effort that also included fellow up-and-

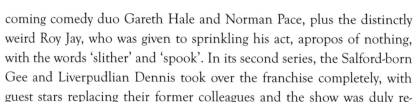

coming comedy duo Gareth Hale and Norman Pace, plus the distinctly weird Roy Jay, who was given to sprinkling his act, apropos of nothing, with the words 'slither' and 'spook'. In its second series, the Salford-born Gee and Liverpudlian Dennis took over the franchise completely, with guest stars replacing their former colleagues and the show was duly re-named *Les And Dustin's Laughter Show* from series three.

Tragically, after only one episode, Gee suffered a heart attack and died, aged 43, in January 1986; and a promising partnership had come to a premature halt. A fortnight later, Dennis elected to complete the final six programmes alone before, once again, pitching in as support to his old mate Russ Abbot, when he too made the move to the BBC the following May. And when *The Laughter Show* concept surfaced again twelve months later, this time it was re-branded *The Les Dennis Laughter Show* and also featured the comedian-cum-drag act, Joe Longthorne. Former Russ Abbot regulars Bella Emberg and Jeffrey Holland (of *Hi-De-Hi!* fame) were included too, but it was Longthorne who turned the exposure into a one-off stand-up show of his own, the provocatively-named *Joe Longthorne Entertains*.

The Hull-born Longthorne had first appeared on television as long as 1969 when, as a 14-year-old, he won an episode of the Yorkshire TV talent show for children, *Junior Showtime*. Subsequently, he spent two years hosting the programme but, aside from that and another winning appearance on one of its adult counterparts *Search For A Star* in 1981, the northern clubs seemed destined to be his chief stamping ground. His stint alongside Dennis, however, changed all that and a growing number of guest slots on other television Variety shows, including Royal Variety Performances, reached their apogee with *The Joe Longthorne Show* in 1988. That stretched across three whole series before coming to a resounding thud in what shaped up to be old-style Variety comedy's 'year dot', 1991.

With or without Abbot, Gee or Longthorne, the fresh-faced Les Dennis, born Leslie Dennis Heseltine in 1953, continued to amuse the licence fee-paying public until his own five-series run of musical skits, impersonations and family-friendly comedy was unceremoniously yanked from the schedules, also in 1991. With *The Les Dennis Laughter Show* behind him, Dennis was free to appear in the second and final series of *The Russ Abbot Show* on ITV. Yet, by now, the traditional days of light entertainment comedy, all shiny floors and brightly-lit sets, were fading fast. Henceforth, the television genre that would pay richest dividends for Les Dennis and countless other out-of-favour Variety comedians, was the one to which he had already turned in 1987: the quiz show. For Dennis, that had meant taking over from Max Bygraves on *Family Fortunes* which, our survey says, at least had the virtue of being one of the funniest shows of all time, even if much of its humour was entirely unintentional.

If the contestants who eventually appeared were the brightest of the bunch to apply, then one can only wince at the potential carnage of the auditions. In each show, a couple of families were lined up against each other and asked, two by two, to provide their own answers to questions previously given to members of the public, as fast as they could and in supposed order of popularity. The results were frequently as magnificent as they were intellectually-challenged. Question: 'Name something Father Christmas does when he comes to your house.' Answer: 'Feeds your pets.' Question: 'Name a word used to describe a very hot day.' Answer: 'A very hot day.' Question: 'Name an animal with horns.' Answer: 'A bee.' Question: 'Name a sign of the zodiac.' Answer: 'April.' Question: 'Name something that makes you scream.' Answer: 'A squirrel.' Question: 'Name a dangerous race.' Answer: 'The Arabs.' And so on and so forth. Dennis himself contributed to an ironic celebration of the programme, *Family Misfortunes*, in 2000.

Family Fortunes kept Dennis busy until 2002, by which time he had shown a disarming talent for self-deprecation, whether as a guest on that last hurrah of mainstream light entertainment, Noel Edmonds' *House Party!* (1996) or the shows of younger and trendier comics like Harry Hill, Vic Reeves and Bob Mortimer. Indeed, Mortimer and Dennis went head to head in a charity boxing match staged specifically for *Sport Relief* - an athletic *Comic Relief* spin-off - in 2002, which Mortimer won, before another bout was set up between Ricky Gervais and former *Blue Peter* presenter Anthea Turner's husband, Grant Bovey, in which comedy was again the victor, the following year. For Dennis, that *Sport Relief* slot had come on the back of his memorable 2001 *Celebrity Big Brother* appearance in which, reeling from off-screen relationship problems with his actress wife Amanda Holden, funnyman Les - as the tabloids would have it - conversed with chickens in the name of charity. Best by a mile, though, was his sensational send-up of his tabloid self in Gervais's BAFTA-

winning masterpiece *Extras* in 2005. Condemned to a life in provincial panto, with the glory days a distant memory and troubled by a glamourous and ambitious young wife who is having an affair behind his back, this particular Les Dennis was a perfectly-portrayed combination of pathos and humour; a northern comedian at the top of his game.

Along with Cannon and Ball, Little and Large, Freddie Starr, Russ Abbot and Les Dennis, the decade's other big Saturday night superstar (in terms of ratings) was comedy magician Paul Daniels.

Born in Middlesbrough in 1938, the diminutive sorcerer was a mainstay of the BBC's Saturday night schedules with *The Paul Daniels Magic Show* from 1979 until 1994, rendering his oft-repeated catchphrase, 'You'll like this - not a lot...' common currency. Less memorable was his squeaky-voiced 'That's magic!', although later it did reappear as one of Dave's impressions in the couch-bound *The Royle Family*. Daniels, who began his working life as a local government official and reportedly turned to magic as a way of making friends, owed his early success to the rapport he built with his audience. At first, his mild admonishments of the volunteers who took part in his tricks seemed simultaneously naughty and endearing although, in time, they would often be seen as supercilious and patronising. Maybe that is why, for some people, their most treasured televisual memory of Paul Daniels is from 1997, when he was duped by *Brass Eye* satirist Chris Morris into making an appeal on behalf of an East German elephant, whose trunk had become lodged up its own anus.

Among the era's more minor light entertainers, Lennie Bennett's double-act partner Jerry Stevens, Roger Kitter and Aiden J. Harvey were three more comedy impressionists who owed all-too brief moments in the sunshine to *Who Do You Do?* The Lancashire comic Harvey also appeared in *Go For It*, LWT's short-lived go at reviving the concept in 1984, alongside Gee, Dennis, Johnny More and rising impressionist Bobby Davro. Equally lukewarm was *Copy Cats* (1985), in which Davro led a team that included Harvey, More, Gary Wilmot, Andrew O'Connor and Allan Stewart. And the Liverpool-born impressionist Faith Brown was another to get her television start on *Who Do You Do?*, where she first caught the eye as Dolly Parton in 1975. A year later, she (and her ample bosom) were promoted to *Ken Dodd's World Of Laughter*. Faith Brown wasn't the first well-known female Liverpudlian impressionist by any means - wireless star Beryl Orde beat her to that honour by almost half a century - but she was certainly the first to land her own ITV programme, *The Faith Brown Chat Show*, which launched in 1980. By which point, a certain Margaret Thatcher had been added to a CV that already boasted such glamourous female figures as Barbra Streisand, Mae West, Zsa Zsa Gabor and Hylda Baker.

Among other Saturday night Variety staples in the 'eighties, a BBC show called *The Main Attraction* ran for two series, in which Les Dennis, Dustin Gee, Dickie Henderson, Bernard Manning, Marti Caine, Norman Collier, Les Dawson, Aiden J. Harvey, Bobby Knutt and more all lined up alongside luminaries of the calibre of Shields and Yarnell, Adrian Walsh, Charlie Daze, Dave Wolfe, Lew Lewis and Mike Newman. Who? Well, quite. Leicestershire-born camp comic Duncan - 'Chase me!' - Norvelle also received welcome (for him) early exposure, as did the fast-rising Brian Conley. In fact, the 1980s schedules were bloated with then-popular faces who are now most likely to be found on cruise liners.

In ITV's *Funnybone* (1982), for example, Birmingham's Malc Stent was joined by two northern comics who rejoiced in the worst comedy double act name of all time: Barry Cheese and Mike Onion. *Funnybone* did well to last five episodes. Another northern club scene product, Paul Squire, saw his name in lights no less than three times via, ITV's *The Paul Squire Show* (1981), the BBC's *Paul Squire, Esq* and ITV's *PS It's Paul Squire* (both 1983), the first of which also featured Bobby Knutt. Squire would soon return to the relative anonymity of the club circuit, but not before his name was used as an ironic charades clue in the last ever episode of *The Young Ones*, a programme to which we shall return in due course.

There was also a single stand-up show for Liverpudlian *Search For A Star* winner Fogwell Flax, whose *A Foggy Outlook* (1982) coincided with a 30-week run in the disappointing final series of ITV's Saturday morning kids show *Tiswas*, to which Lenny Henry, Chris Tarrant, Liverpudlian ventriloquist Bob Carolgees, Spit the Dog and former Scaffold member John Gorman were by now but memories. But perhaps the most unusual of the traditional Variety performers shortly to be overthrown at this time was the St Helens-born ostrich botherer, Bernie Clifton.

Poor old Bernie has come in for a lot of undeserved stick down the years, thanks mainly to his habit of pretending to ride around on a rather forlorn example of what the Greeks call a 'sparrow camel', a routine subsequently copied to 'hilarious' effect by charity fundraisers in the London Marathon and Great North Run to this day. Born in 1935, young Bernard Quinn left school as a 15-year-old and is said to have developed his vocal chords by singing in empty bathrooms while working as a corporation plumber. After an RAF National Service stint, he moved to Doncaster and turned professional entertainer, grinding out a career on the northern club circuit until, now known as Bernie Clifton, he won a 1971 spot on *The Good Old Days*. Appearances on *The Comedians* followed, as did the three series of the childrens TV show *Crackerjack* that built upon the crazy prop-based act he had developed in summer seasons, pantomime and cabaret tours, in the UK and overseas. It was around this time that he discovered Oswald the ostrich and a destiny as an archetypal northern comic, supposedly fit only for entertaining kids, was assured.

Even so, Bernie Clifton continued to plug away on and off screen and after appearing in the *Royal Variety Show* of 1979 he finally got to make a programme of his own, a half-hour ITV special, *Bernie Clifton On Stage*, broadcast in 1980. Otherwise, apart from a role as a theatre owner in the third series of the BBC childrens sitcom *Tricky Business* (1989), the rest of the 1980s, television-wise, were limited to rare guest spots. On radio he fared a little better. In 1986, he was the proprietor of *Bernie Clifton's Comedy Shop* for BBC Radio 2 and went on to host BBC Radio Sheffield's afternoon show. Most recently, along with marching down a certain corridor, he has appeared in the BBC's comedy drama *Love Soup* (2007). Plus, whether on dry land or at sea, he continues to perform live and in 2006 won heartwarming critical acclaim on the Edinburgh Fringe.

An earlier review by *Guardian* journalist Charlie Skelton was equally gushing in its praise. In that piece, Clifton is described as 'a certifiable genius' by a writer who paints a lovely picture of his talent for visual lunacy. 'Between wrestling a giant inflatable deep-sea diver and doing the bossa nova with biscuit boxes on his feet,' Skelton writes, 'he found time to perform an avant-garde balloon dance, have his dancing marked on stage by a dog, and stick an ostrich beak up his arse.' The review continues: 'Certainly this warm, uncynical lunatic in the funny suit is the spiritual father of Vic Reeves, Harry Hill and Johnny Vegas. Aahh! You say, but Reeves and Vegas are ironic, postmodern cabaret entertainers. Well, nothing could be more ironic and postmodern than Bernie Clifton, shaking his head as a young girl led the dance-scoring dog off the stage, and muttering: "What an earth is she going to put on her CV?" Clifton knows damned well how daft it all is. He's not just a nutter with a flightless-bird fixation. Au contraire: Clifton is God.' In February 2005, Harry Hill himself told *The Independent*: 'Look at Bernie Clifton. He does a prop act, which includes a 20ft inflatable sausage that he throws out over the audience. A lot of that sort of stuff - prop acts, ventriloquism, eccentric dancing, falling over, dressing-up boxes - originated in music hall. No one does those things any more, they've fallen from memory. But they're still terrific.'

Bernie Clifton or no Bernie Clifton, the year 1991 did indeed mark a watershed for television light entertainment; a development to which the progress of one particular entertainer testifies. In that same year, as a half-hearted shove rather than a raging at the dying of the light, the BBC launched perhaps its last traditional Saturday night Variety sketch show, *You Gotta Be Jokin'*, in which five young comedy 'hopefuls' were given a shot at the big time. Although it only ran to eight episodes, for two of the featured comics it was nevertheless a more than handy career boost. One of them was the cheeky cockney lad about town Shane Richie, destined for much later fame in *EastEnders,* among much else. The other was Leeds-born *New Faces* finalist of 1986, Billy Pearce.

Though neither Richie or Pearce were as raw to television as the *You Gotta Be Jokin'* publicity suggested, they were certainly helped by the primetime exposure. Pearce, for instance, would go on to prove himself a heck of a crowd puller on stage where, in 1991, he took part in his first Royal Variety Performance and, by 1994, had won a British Comedy Award for Top Theatre Variety Performer, beating Ken Dodd and Michael Barrymore to the prize. Over the years ahead, whether in pantomime, musicals or one-man extravaganzas, seats in theatres where Pearce played were filled, tours sold out and punters sent home happy, an achievement that should not be underestimated in this electronic media-obsessed world. As such, it seems reasonable to assume that if light entertainment had been as high on the television agenda then as it was

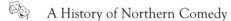

in the 'seventies and early 'eighties, a family-friendly entertainer like former Butlins Redcoat Billy would surely have become a very big name indeed. As the man himself told trade newspaper *The Stage* in 2004: 'I suppose I have come along at the wrong time.'

Come the dawn of the 1990s, then, television comedy had long been heading in a more daring and confrontational direction. For old-style Variety turns, the casualty rate had been high. Performers now acted as if they had a right to take over a corner of your living room, rather than behaving as the benign and respectfully-attired guests they had appeared to be before. Their subject matter too had drawn closer to the bone and comedians had increasingly come to be judged on *what* they said as much as *how* they said it. How had that happened? In hindsight, it was a trend that had quietly taken root in the mid-1970s, before gathering pace and, ultimately, gaining predominance in the decade that followed.

The more obviously manufactured style of TV light entertainment comedy had initially been challenged by a loose collection of story-telling folk artists, to whom our story will turn in a while. But there were equally revolutionary - if a little less down to earth - boundary pushers on radio too. The king of these was Kenny Everett, a Liverpudlian disc jockey with the face and sense of humour of an irreverent imp. In time, Everett would create an even bigger splash on the small screen, all but reinventing the visual language of that medium, too.

Kenny Everett first came to national prominence on the pirate radio station Radio London, alongside his then double act partner Dave Cash, shortly after turning down an offer from the BBC's more prestigious - and legal - Light Programme in 1962. A determined individualism would be a key feature of this latest Liverpudlian funnyman's career; most immediately three years later, when he was fired from Radio London for broadcasting outspoken comments about religion live on air. Such was his popularity, however, that a couple of months later the station took him back, before Everett - born Maurice Cole in 1944 and renamed after his boyhood Hollywood hero Edward Everett Horton - once again flew the coop, this time to Radio Luxembourg in 1966. With the launch of Radio 1 the following year, it was back to blighty, where an interview with fellow Liverpool exiles The Beatles, timed to coincide with the release of *Sgt. Pepper's Lonely Hearts Club Band*, led to a regular role with the BBC's fledgling pop music station.

At the time, Radio 1 itself was fresh, new and exciting, though to nothing like the same extent as Everett, whose cut-and-paste madcap wit and zany jingles soon established him as a genuine radio maverick. In some ways, he was an heir to the throne of Tommy Handley, though no one would have quite seen it that way at the end of the swinging 'sixties, when this comic upstart from Crosby seemed so irreverent and original. So much so that it was always likely that Radio 1, explicitly set up by the Government to suffocate the burgeoning independent pirate voices drifting in off the North Sea, would struggle to contain a personality that was 'out there' from the start. And so it proved. In 1970, after suggesting that the current British Transport Minister's wife had bribed her driving test instructor, Kenny Everett was once again shown the door, only to return to Broadcasting House two years later on the proviso that all his material would henceforth be pre-recorded - shades of the Jonathan Ross 'Manuelgate' affair in 2008. But in 1973, Everett was off again, this time to the first legal commercial radio station in England, London's Capital Radio, where he remained - on and off - for the rest of the decade. In 1981, Everett returned to the BBC for a weekly Saturday lunchtime Radio Two show, before once again taking up a final, longer-lasting residence at Capital Radio between 1983 and 1994.

Kenny Everett's impact on the presentation of popular music radio was heard most immediately in his Radio 1 successor, the derivative and excruciating Adrian Juste, whose attempts to imitate Everett in a similar slot served only to prove how gifted his predecessor had been. A longer-lasting range of influence can perhaps be traced through the likes of Steve Wright ('In The Afternoon' or otherwise), satirists Chris Morris and Victor Lewis-Smith, and, most recently, Everett's northern wireless brethren Chris Evans, Chris Moyles, Mark and Lard (Radcliffe and Riley), plus a whole host of less talented national radio wannabes on local stations up and down the land, for whom amusing characters and inserts have become, in many cases, more important than the music. Yet for Everett himself, the medium that gave him his start in the entertainment industry was only part of the story.

If Kenny Everett rewrote at least a chapter of the radio rule book, his influence on the lingua franca of mainstream television was every bit as profound - although profound may not be the best word to use in the circumstances. Of those who witnessed it, for example, who will ever erase the inflating buttocks of pseudo Scottish rocker Rod Stewart from their memory? That particular routine - in which gravel-voiced Rod was, of course, played by Everett himself, resplendent in skin-tight leg-ins and peroxide wig, gently floating away backside first - would reduce anyone to a quivering wreck. And that was just one such skit among many which first peppered ITV's *The Kenny Everett Video Show* and then *The Kenny Everett Television Show*, a delightfully unpredictable and popular mainstay of BBC Variety entertainment from 1981-88.

By then, Kenny Everett's TV career was already over 13 years old. It began in 1968, with a suitably anarchic spot alongside Oxbridge feminist icon Germaine Greer and *Candid Camera* japester Jonathan Routh. *Nice Time*, a lively audience participation effort, was made by Granada, who later added a fourth presenter in *Coronation Street* and future Steve Coogan co-star, Sandra Gough. When its two series were done, London Weekend Television swooped for Everett who, fresh from being given the boot at Radio 1, was handed a TV show, *The Kenny Everett Explosion*, in which the hottest property on radio crossed mediums with imaginative aplomb. Several of Everett's Radio 1 characters made the move too, ensuring that his quirky mixture of pop and silliness would be every bit as effective visually as it had proved to be aurally. Eager to emphasise its own youthful relevance in opposition to Everett's former employers - and no doubt seeking a contender to the *The Goodies*, also launched in 1970 - ITV ran *The Kenny Everett Explosion* over the following twenty-five weeks, while also making another couple of shows with Everett, the diminutive *Ev* (nine episodes) and *Making Whoopee* (six) in the same year. In the first, pop-hungry teenagers heard the latest sounds from the 'hit parade', held together by the host's unique and playful brand of nuttiness. In the latter, Everett was on-stage presenter to the poor man's Bonzo Dog Doo-Dah Band, Bob Kerr's Whoopee Band, at a nightclub in Putney.

In 1972, Everett's talent for satire was first put to use on BBC TV in *Up Sunday*, a spin-off of the weekday evening current affairs and arts show, *Line-Up*, to which the likes of Clive James, Willie Rushton, Eric

The Dying of the Light?

Idle, Viv Stanshall and Ivor Cutler also contributed as writers, performers or both. It wasn't until the arrival of *The Kenny Everett Video Show* in 1978, however, that Kenny Everett was fully able to translate his radio genius to the small screen.

A major clue to the levels of technological wizardry aspired to by Everett and his writers, Barry Cryer and Ray Cameron, lies in the title. Video, although commercially available, was a recent innovation indeed in the late 1970s, with the majority of the Great British public - when it wasn't worrying about the fall of civilisation on account of 'video nasties' - not yet having quite made up its mind whether to go with Betamax or VHS. *The Kenny Everett Video Show* had no such anxiety. Instead, it clasped the possibilities of the format to its bosom, pioneering a colourful, snappy and ostentatiously electronic style of presentation, pre-dating the still-to-be founded MTV by at least three years. Again, there was a steady supply of pop musicians to complement Everett's own outlandish characters, but here style was married absolutely with content. Banks of television screens, solid white backdrops, whizz-bang graphics and an abundance of ultra-modern special effects reinforced the wild creativity that had always been at the heart of Everett's comedy. And, as Rod Stewart's swollen backside would show very well, there was still lots of room for outsized body parts and old fashioned slapstick, much of it loudly and audibly appreciated by the production crew. 'Zoo' television for adults had arrived.

In fact, in *The Kenny Everett Video Show*, the art of the shamelessly physical was all-pervasive. Notoriously, among a cast of breathtakingly risqué characters that included such legends as Cupid Stunt, the large-breasted, leg-swinging Hollywood actress (catchphrase: 'It's all in the best possible taste!'), Brother Lee Love (a gospel minister with absurdly large hands), Sid Snot the punk and Angry of Mayfair (a furious moralistic city gent, with a penchant for stockings and suspenders), were Hot Gossip, a scantily-clad dance troupe who bumped, grinded and titillated like refugees from a soft core porn movie. Another weekly regular was cartoon superhero Captain Kremmen, first established on Everett's Capital Radio show, whose antics were also made into an animated film voiced by Everett, *Kremmen - The Movie*, in 1980. Ironically, in exactly the same year as *The Goodies* moved in the opposite direction, after three seasonal specials and a fourth ITV series now re-titled *The Kenny Everett Video*

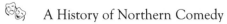

Cassette, Kenny Everett himself jumped ship and crossed back to the BBC where, if anything, *The Kenny Everett Television Show* proved to be an even bigger ratings winner.

While Cricklewood's best-known tandem-riding trio struggled on ITV before being put of their misery in 1982, Everett's move to the Beeb resulted in another seven years of success in which the old characters carried on very much as before, albeit with Sid Snot renamed Gizzard Puke, until the curtain came down with a fifth and final series in 1988. For Everett, that heralded a return to relative national obscurity on Capital Radio. Or, at least, obscurity might have been the outcome had he not then contracted the terrifying disease that would take his life. For, in 1995, at the end of a spell in which his homosexuality and unorthodox marriage arrangements had kept newspapers in headlines for months, a battler to the end, Kenny Everett lost his very public fight with AIDS.

Another northern-born television comedian who very much came out of left field during the 1980s was Chorley's Phil Cool, christened plain Phil Martin, a hugely original impressionist blessed with a face like an over-used trampoline. Where others in that line might treat an audience to impersonations of James Cagney, Frank Spencer, or, since the days of Mike Yarwood, assorted politicians and the royal family, Cool was more likely to mimic Quasimodo, the Pope or the aliens of hit science fiction drama *V*. Furthermore, while props had long been an important part of any impressionist's armoury, the only prop Cool needed was his face.

That approach was not entirely without precedent. American comics Frank Gorshin and Rich Little had done similar things, both across the pond and for British audiences in the early-'seventies series *Kopykats* (not to be confused with 'eighties show *Copy Cats*). Cool, however, was something else again. His remarkable rubbery visage seemed able to travel every which way at once and didn't so much pretend to be someone else as physically inhabit them, to an extraordinarily exaggerated degree. Even a relatively clichéd 'victim' like Rolf Harris took on new qualities. Nor did Cool only do people. Cars and other inanimate objects were turned into living and breathing caricatures too. This was gurning with a purpose.

Phil Cool made his national television debut on the 1980 Yorkshire

476

The Dying of the Light?

Television talent show, *Rock With Laughter*, which itself led to a residency on *Saturday Stayback*, Chris Tarrant's second attempt at getting an adult version of his kids show *Tiswas* up and running early in 1983. Following in the footsteps of the disappointing *O.T.T.*, it too was a bit of a let-down and Cool retreated to a job as warm-up man for the satirical puppet show *Spitting Image*. While there, he was invited on to the BBC's lunchtime magazine show *Pebble Mill At One*, which in turn led to a series of his own, *Cool It*, shown on BBC2 in 1985. So well received was it that a second series was commissioned, which won the Royal Television Society Award for Most Original Television achievement. A former electrician who turned professional in his mid-20s, for Cool a decade spent working in obscure pubs and clubs was finally paying off. And that was thanks, in no small part, to the fact that pushing his cause in the background was no less a figure than highly influential Birmingham comic Jasper Carrott, himself then helping to redefine Saturday night telly for the BBC with his irreverent live stand-up (or more accurately sit-down) show *Carrott's Lib* (1982), to be followed in future years by the even more successful *Carrott Confidential*, *24 Carrott Gold* and *Canned Carrott*, amongst other such carotene-based punnery.

Jasper Carrott had slipped into the mainstream courtesy of the same 1970's folk tradition that had introduced the likes of Billy Connolly, Max Boyce and Mike Harding to the world of popular British entertainment. The unflashy, earthy and usually regional approach adopted by that new breed of troubadours - Bristol's Fred Wedlock and London's Richard Digance were two others - might now be seen as the most immediate ancestor of what would come to be termed alternative comedy. Be that as it may, there is no doubt that the naturalism which followed had more in common with Harding and Co than the sideburns and bow-tie brigade.

The hirsute, welly-wearing and expletive-laden Billy Connolly, or the 'Big Yin' as his hometown Glasgow patois would have him, not only built an act around his formative experiences as a welder in that city's shipyards, but upon the folk music that helped to give meaning to his early life. Indeed, Connolly's first steps towards fame and fortune came as a useful banjo player with his band the Humblebums, in which he was later joined by the now well-known Scottish singer and songwriter Gerry Rafferty. Mike Harding's performance background, meanwhile, was also

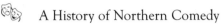

in music. Born in Crumpsall in 1944, of working class Irish Catholic stock, his childhood was another to be characterised by hardship, largely as a result of his father being killed while returning from a World War Two bombing mission, only four weeks before his son was born. Not surprisingly, that event coloured Harding's formative years in post-war Manchester considerably, with much of the work that followed carrying echoes of those bygone days.

Harding's original stage forays came as a member of the folk, skiffle and rock bands with whom he played as a means of supporting himself financially while studying for a degree in Education in the 1960s. It would have been good fun too, of course, for a young man who now lists his influences as Lonnie Donegan, Jesse Fuller and the Lancashire folk singer Harry Boardman. Before strumming his guitar in the pubs and clubs, Harding had also worked as a dustman, bus conductor, carpet fitter and road digger, so to find himself sharing bills with The Beatles, Gerry and the Pacemakers, The Hollies and the rather less glamourous sounding Eric Spanner and the Rhythmaires, seems to have set his blood pumping. The upshot was that all plans for a teaching career were put to one side and it was during a 1967 gig at Leeds University, with the Edison Bell Spasm Band, that Harding began filling in the gaps with surreal little stories, as the group tuned its instruments. The bespectacled, self-effacing 'Rochdale Cowboy' was on his way.

Even so, it would take him quite a while yet to arrive. Until 1975, in fact, when after making an impression alongside the likes of Beryl Reid, Ken Dodd and the cartoonist Bill Tidy on *The Stuart Hall Show* the year before, he recorded a song whose reputation has dogged him ever since, Its name was the aforementioned 'The Rochdale Cowboy' and it was a hit in a year when comedy novelty records fell into the charts like leaves. For 1975 was also the year in which *The Goodies* had five hit singles in twelve months. It was when Billy Connolly, fresh from a career-cementing turn on the chat show *Parkinson*, rode high with one of several pop smashes of his own: a spoof version of country diva Tammy Wynette's contribution to the campaign for adult literacy, 'D.I.V.O.R.C.E.' ('...she sank her teeth in my B.U.M. and called me an F.N.C...'). Harding's tale, meanwhile, was one of northern hardship unmatched in the annals of musical history before or since: 'It's hard being a cowboy in Rochdale. T' spurs don't fit right on your clogs. It's hard being a cowboy in Rochdale. 'Cos people laugh when I ride past on our Alsatian dog.' Poetry in anyone's language, as confirmed by the fact that it came in with a bullet at number 22 and never rose any higher.

It did, however, lead to many a mainstream television appearance, initially alongside a group of fellow Lancashire folkies, The Fivepenny Piece, with whom Harding became closely associated in a series of BBC shows, filmed live, known variously as *MH & 5p* and *Mike Harding And The Fivepenny Piece* from 1977, before both acts were eventually given their own series. It was also during this time that Harding set a record for the longest joke ever told on British television. It was about a budgie and it lasted for an entire programme, which must have been quite a Trill. The following year saw another BBC series, *One Night In Lincoln*, in which six 30-minute episodes were wrung out of a single evening's performance there. In 1984, there was another such venture filmed over the Irish Sea, *Mike Harding In Belfast*, but that proved to be something of a dead end, television comedy-wise. Harding's next BBC project was *The Harding Trail*, shown in the same year, a forerunner to the nowadays ubiquitous comedian-travelogue genre popularised by Michael Palin's *Around The World In 80 Days* from 1988, in which he indulged a lifelong passion for cycling and the open air on America's Appalachian Trail. Nowadays, Mike Harding is a regular host of BBC Radio 2's annual Folk Awards, the station on which he also presents his own weekly folk show.

As for Phil Cool, after three series of *Cool It* - on which his mentor Jasper Carrott was associate producer and unofficial script editor - he made two *Comic Relief* appearances and returned with a Sunday night show, this time for ITV, entitled *Cool Head* in 1991. Yet unlike its BBC incarnation, this and a similar series recorded live a year later called simply *Phil Cool*, failed to win anything like the same attention. And in 1993, after being filmed backstage in Channel 4's documentary strand *A Day In The Life...*, Cool inexplicably vanished from British TV screens as suddenly as he had arrived. Today, replete with acoustic guitar and describing himself as a 'faceologist' rather than impressionist, he can most often be found performing in theatres or at comedy festivals. And if his personal website is anything to go by, he still harbours a dream of playing 'Jim Carrey's dad in a Hollywood blockbuster.'

Music and monologues, then, were the stock-in-trade of folk comedians in the 'seventies, more often than not in a comical regional accent. Again, this was hardly a new phenomenon. In the latter case, the north country drollery of one Marriott Edgar - born in Kirkcudbright, Scotland in 1880 and the brother of crime writer Edgar Wallace - had been a cherished source of joviality for years. And as Edgar's birthplace suggests, his world famous monologues were also an object lesson in just how utterly northern comedy can outgrow its geographical roots.

For not only was Marriott Edgar himself anything but a working class northerner, the actor Stanley Holloway, undoubtedly the most famous performer of Edgar's work in the 1930s and beyond, was a product of London's East End. Holloway had actually studied opera in pre-First World War Italy and was a relative stranger to the delights of music hall before Gracie Fields suggested that he might perform some of Edgar's stuff on a Variety tour. Of these, the best known was 'The Lion and Albert', a classic piece of dialect-driven humour wherein young Albert Ramsbottom is devoured by said king of the jungle while on a trip with his matter-of-fact parents to Blackpool Zoo. Another was 'Old Sam', in which Holloway made famous the phrase 'Pick Oop Tha' Musket...'. Edgar's talents were many and varied. As we have seen, he also worked as a scriptwriter for Will Hay and Arthur Askey among others, knocking out a grand total of 41 films from 1936, including a co-writing credit on Hay's *Oh, Mr Porter*.

In the art of the monologue we see northern comedy distilled to its storytelling core, as such it is a genre particularly suited to the humour of the region. And certainly, the dry distinctive rhythms of Marriott Edgar's blend of realism and surrealism have proved particularly timeless in that regard. Listen again to Mike Craig's splendid BBC series *Marriott's Monologues* for example where, to gentle piano accompaniment, Bernie Clifton, Roy Castle, Thora Hird, Les Dawson and others each take it in turns to recite such lines as the following from 'Three Ha'pence A Foot' (the price of the maple wood needed to build Noah's Ark in Bury, of all places): 'The rain showed no sight of abating; t' water rose hour by hour; 'til the only dry land were at Blackpool; and that were on top of the tower.'

The Dying of the Light?

More recently, the Sheffield-born ex-Pulp front man, Jarvis Cocker, has turned his tongue to Edgar's tales too. But perhaps the most prolific modern-day performer of monologues - whether written by Marriott Edgar or himself - is the 'Bolton Bullfrog', aka the wonderful Bernard Wrigley; living proof that being a twenty-four-carat star is about much more than millions of people being able to put a name to your face at the meat counter in Tescos, or gulping down grubs in the Australian bush.

After starting out as a folk singer who was not averse to writing his own tunes, Wrigley went on to develop a twin career in drama, including a spot on the highly eccentric *Ken Campbell Roadshow* in 1970. From there he moved on to appearances in a handful of Alan Bennett television plays, including *Sunset Across The Bay, Afternoon Off* and *Me, I'm Afraid Of Virginia Woolf*. His debut telly appearance had come on Kenny Everett's *Nice Time* in 1968 (in which he played a sailor's hornpipe on his teeth). Since then he has walked the Holmfirth hills in *Last of the Summer Wine*, turned up in *Cold Feet, Coronation Street* and *Emmerdale*, and played everything from a bloke with a ferret down his pants in a 1990 Webster's Bitter advert to a Walls sausage-loving convict in television commercials. In the cinema, he appeared in Steve Coogan's under-rated 2001 film *The Parole Officer*, Alan Bennett's *A Private Function* (1984) and, as a harassed schoolteacher, Andrea Dunbar's *Rita, Sue And Bob Too* (1986). On stage, a 1997 appearance in Southport's Christmas pantomime, *Snow White And The Seven Dwarfs*, has jostled on his CV with more substantial roles as Estragon to Mike Harding's Vladimir in Samuel Beckett's *Waiting For Godot* at Bolton's Octagon Theatre in 1991, and parts in other critically acclaimed productions such as Jim Cartwright's *Road* in 1995 and Barrie Rutter's *Passion Play*, staged by the Northern Broadsides company in 1998. Looking not unlike Bobby Ball's cuddlier big brother (except in earlier photographs, where he bears an uncanny resemblance to the Yorkshire Ripper), Wrigley's friendly and lived-in face has character actor written all over it. If a producer is looking for a curly-haired Lancastrian union official or a chatty milkman, Bernard Wrigley is usually their man.

Perhaps the Bolton Bullfrog's most charming trait, however, is his growling Boltonian burr, in which a chuckle is never far from the surface. For that reason, he can also be counted upon to whip up a storm on radio, whether in BBC Radio 4 afternoon plays or, most recently, alongside Mark

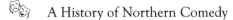

Radcliffe, on whose Radio 1 show with Lard, Wrigley first broadcast his 'Fairly Truthful Tales'. These were self-written witty monologues in the tradition of Marriott Edgar but with a modern sensibility, and have been amply added to since, among them: 'Robin Hood And The Bogey Rolling Contest' and 'The Tripe Ships Of Wigan'. On CD in 2000, Wrigley released his eleventh album, *Magnificent Monologues*, which contained his own versions of Edgar's 'The Lion And Albert', 'The Battle Of Hastings' and 'Magna Charter', along with less well-known efforts by Robb Wilton and Al Read. In the early twenty-first century, Bernard Wrigley remains a prolific hawker of humourous wares in every medium, whether that be books, concerts with the Oldham Tinkers or Houghton Weavers, mp3s for internet download, inflatable bouncy penises on Peter Kay's *Phoenix Nights* or his own shows on BBC Radio Lancashire. Long may he continue.

The magnificent Jake Thackray, on the other hand, was most adept at telling his comical little stories in song. Yorkshire's heavy-lidded answer to Noel Coward, Thackray was born John Philip Thackray in Leeds in 1938, the working class product of a strict Jesuit upbringing. In the world of work, he found his earliest employment in France, spending four years there as a teacher upon graduating from Durham University in the late 1950s. It was in that fine country that Thackray fell under the spell of the legendary *chansonniers* Jacque Brel and Georges Brassens, two men in the troubadour tradition who would later influence his own music greatly.

Upon returning to England and a job teaching English in his native city, Leeds, in 1963, Thackray taught himself to play guitar and soon became a regular on the local folk scene. In turn, that led to numerous television appearances, first regional and then national, on enormously popular current affairs programmes like *Nationwide*, *The Frost Report*, *The Braden Beat* and *That's Life!*. Jake Thackray, however, would never grow comfortable with the demands of fame.

As we have seen, music was an inherent component of the 'seventies folk comedy tradition, as also shown by the likes of Tony Capstick, best known to modern audiences, before his death in 2003, as one of the useless policemen double act in *Last of the Summer Wine*. Yorkshireman Capstick it was who, in 1981, enjoyed massive success with his musical monologue 'Capstick Comes Home', a parody of the old Hovis brown bread adverts, in which the eponymous protagonist recalls his father's homilies to the sound of Dvořák's Symphony No. 9, *From the New World*. 'He said as 'ow workin' folk should have some dignity an' pride an' self respect, an' as 'ow they should come home to summat warm an' cheerful. An' then he threw me mam on t' fire...'. It reached number three in the charts and led to a brief Channel 4 series, *Capstick Capers*, two years later, before Capstick himself retreated to the relative anonymity of an often controversial thirty-year broadcasting career on BBC Radio Sheffield.

In time, anonymity would be a state craved for and enjoyed by Jake Thackray too, although such was his talent and impulse to create that it would be a forlorn hope when his renown was at its height. With his Roman emperor-like good looks, dour, lugubrious tones and ear for a catchy tune, Thackray was ideally suited to small screen familiarity. Audiences loved both his deadpan delivery and the wonderfully inventive words of his songs, more often than not self-written and, on the face of it anyway, supposedly autobiographical. Thackray's blending of exotic gallicism and earthy northern charm, was further blessed with a healthy dollop of the rude vulgarity so beloved of traditional English folk culture. Accusations of misogyny notwithstanding, some of his funniest and - to some - controversial material dealt with the battle of the sexes. Perhaps the best known in that regard is 'On Again! On Again!', which bears the classic opening lines: 'I love a good bum on a woman, it makes my day. To me it is palpable proof of God's existence, *a posteriori*. Also I love breasts and arms and ankles, elbows, knees. It's the tongue, the tongue, the tongue on a woman that spoils the job for me.'

The Yorkshire countryside and farmyard animals also loomed large, as Thackray - a genuine example of the literary cliché 'wordsmith' if ever there was one - followed in the tradition of George Orwell's *Animal Farm* in using beasts of the field as a satirical social metaphor. *Viz* 'The Bantam Cock', during which the amorous bird of the title - 'a grand upstanding bantam cock, so brisk and stiff and spry' - lays sexual waste to every feathered creature in the vicinity: 'He ravished my fan-tailed pigeons and me lily-white columbines, and while I was locking up the budgerigar, he jumped my parrot from behind. She was sitting on me shoulder at the time.' Other Thackray favourites, as witty as they are wicked, include *The*

Widow Of Bridlington, The Castleford Ladies' Magic Circle and a beautifully understated song, *Kirkstall Road Girl*. Modern-day fans and champions of Thackray's oeuvre include the Barnsley poet Ian McMillan and the gifted Arctic Monkeys lead singer and songwriter, Alex Turner.

While Jake Thackray's lyrics were at once amusing, subversive, moral, sad and funny, they would not have been anywhere near as effective without his fine acoustic guitar playing, unfussy melodies and distinctive chord sequences. All topped off by a singing voice that was part irritable tap room regular, part romantic Pudsey postman. Not unusually, there was an element of nervousness to be detected in there too. Thackray was a notoriously uncomfortable performer, particularly in front of large live audiences. And as his career progressed, he became ever more uncomfortable in a manufactured and impersonal TV environment. No matter that he had played in a Royal Variety Performance at the London Palladium, natural shyness and a tendency toward self-deprecation meant that he much preferred playing in the 'real' environment of pubs and clubs. An anti-authoritarian to his bones - as an English teacher he had regularly halted lessons for a sing-song - these smaller arenas better suited his low-key demeanour, as did the recording studios in which he made seven albums between 1967 and 1991. In each of those, honesty triumphs over falsehood, modesty over pomposity, and the absurdity of life is revealed at every turn.

It couldn't last. Disillusioned with life as an entertainer and having by then moved to Wales, Thackray gave up performing completely in the 1990s. He did, however, contribute a humourous newspaper column to the *Yorkshire Post* newspaper and took up a new hobby, bell ringing, in his local church in Monmouth. After a bout of bad health and financial problems, which culminated in bankruptcy, Jake Thackray died on Christmas Eve, 2002, aged 63. In the summer of 2005, a musical play based on that 'right funny nun', Sister Josephine, and other Thackray characters, *Sister Josephine Kicks The Habit*, (written by Ian McMillan) celebrated his life and times. Victor Lewis-Smith, meanwhile, followed up a radio documentary for BBC Radio 2 with a similar television tribute broadcast in 2006, *Jake On The Box*. In it, among other delights, was a 1980 performance of *The Bull*, whose chorus is a neat summation of Thackray's steadfastly northern attitude to 'whoever looks down on you from a height. 'Beware of the Bull,' it begins. 'The bull, the bull is the biggest of all. He is the boss, he is, because he's big and we are small. But the bigger the bull, bigger the bull, bigger the balls. The bigger the bull, the bigger and quicker and thicker the bullshite falls.'

And so we come to the performer who most neatly bridges the traditions of the old and the shock of the new. A comedian whose big TV break came amid old-school glitter and stardust, but who has taken - and indeed is still taking - her own unique journey down a more grounded musical path. When Prestwich-born, piano-thumping Victoria Wood first popped up on *New Faces* as a chubby 20-year-old back in 1974, who could have guessed how resilient and pervasive her knowing brand of observational, reality-based humour would become?

Yet behind that apparently shy and angelic exterior was a wit and intelligence as astute as anything possessed by the Oxbridge set. The same themes of unfulfilled lives and suburban shells which line the work of, say, Alan Bennett, were as plentiful as cockles on Morecambe Bay sands here too. But toss in a dash of unrequited love, ill-matched relationships and weight issues, plus previously untouchable gags about hysterectomies, fabric conditioner and the sexual potential of a rolled-up *Woman's Weekly*, and there you had it, something entirely her own. And there you *almost* had it. For as well as acting, writing and directing, Victoria Wood also composed and performed her own songs, playing a mean joanna as she went. If all that wasn't enough, for a while she was the most popular stand-up comedian in the country bar none, helped rather than hindered by a succession of improbably colourful coats and the grin and haircut of a ten-year-old boy.

Victory in her particular round of *New Faces* appeared to indicate that Birmingham University drama student Wood had grasped her big chance and was now on her way. So she was, although it didn't seem that way to begin with. Television producers sought a pigeon hole in which to put her in vain - what *was* she supposed to be exactly? A cabaret turn? A novelty act? Further TV offers did not exactly flood in.

Nevertheless, in the year following her debut, Wood did return to television as one of five victorious *New Faces* heat winners - the others being Marti Caine, Lenny Henry, Aiden J. Harvey and Trevor Chance - in an ITV sketch and song based offering called *The Summer Show*. After

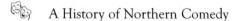

which, apart from a radio gig on BBC Radio 4's *Start The Week*, that was pretty much it until, like Jake Thackray, she had the good fortune to land a spot on the consumer-protection show *That's Life!* in 1976. To a British public receptive to regional singer-songwriters (and, indeed, poets in the case of Pam Ayres) Wood was a natural fit. Looking not unlike a vicar's daughter with her innocent eyes and twee middle-aged lady's shampoo and set - the trademark basin cut still being some way off at this stage - her wry little ditties about everyday life and its troubles earned her a level of popularity up there with dogs who growled 'sausages' and penis-shaped turnips. If her singing voice wobbled a bit, so what? She was funny, from the north, and everybody loved her.

Wood's full versatility, however, was not yet known. In 1978, she was asked to contribute to a musical revue at London's Bush Theatre, *In At The Death*. Among the cast was an actor named Julie Walters, whom Wood had already briefly met while attending an unsuccessful audition for Manchester Polytechnic's English and Drama department as a 17-year-old. In the BBC's 2006 series *Dawn French's Girls Who Do Comedy*, Walters recalled how Wood had been so nervous that she threw up in a bucket. In a 2006 edition of the BBC's *Comedy Connections* documentary strand, meanwhile, Wood herself recalled writing a sketch for *In At The Death* in which Walters was a librarian. During it, a character was asked: 'Where are you in t' menstrual cycle?', answering 'Taurus'. According to Wood: 'That was when I felt I had clicked into a sort of voice that I felt was really only mine.' Victoria Wood and Julie Walters would feed off one and other in such a fashion through four decades and counting.

Most immediately, the director of the revue, David Leland, asked Wood to provide him with a full-length play to be staged at Sheffield's Crucible Theatre. Appropriately enough, it was called *Talent* and won its writer a Most Promising New Writer award, while catching the attention of Granada television's Head of Drama, Peter Eckersley. On Eckersley's insistence, the production was duly adapted for the small screen in 1979 with Walters - for whom the lead part of brassy talent show contestant Julie had originally been written - taking the place of Hazel Clyne, who had filled that role alongside Wood's less outwardly confident character Maureen in the theatre. An elderly fellow contestant was played by the no longer quite so rubber-limbed Nat Jackley. Eckersley then commissioned two more television plays, *Nearly A Happy Ending* (1980) and *Happy Since I Met You* (1981), in which Walters again appeared. In the latter, there was also a sizeable role for a Bradford-born actor named Duncan Preston. In these early days, the nucleus of what would later be seen as Wood's very own repertory group was already being formed.

However, there was no doubt about who were the stars of the show. In Wood and Walters, British television had found that rare thing - a female comedy double act - and one that was every bit as appealing to mainstream audiences as the 'alternative' new breed of comics currently making their way in the clubs of London. Their on-screen relationship was confirmed when Eckersley suggested an ITV series, the eponymous *Wood And Walters*, which began with a one-off special *Two Creatures Great And Small* in 1981, before properly taking flight the following year. Alas, Peter Eckersley died before production on that had even begun on and so never reaped the rewards of his vision.

Although patchy by her later standards, *Wood And Walters* confirmed Victoria Wood as a voice of true originality. On the face of it, a traditional light entertainment TV show like any other, with the duo addressing their audience from a buffed-up shiny showbiz set before a flight of those useless chat show steps with lightbulbs on the risers, it turned out to be anything but. For a start, here were two women; women clad in suits and ties and wearing a couple of unflattering 'eighties mullets admittedly, but women none the less. Thus far, to see one female stand-up on television was unusual, two was virtually unheard of. And the somewhat androgynous appearance that Wood would continue to adopt did have a point. Wood and Walters challenged their audience to recognise the trials and tribulations of gender, but also to go beyond all that, from a female point of view. The duo seemed happy to mine their sexuality for laughs, but were less keen to be defined by it. For them, good comedy was about shared experience, male and female. Or maybe they just liked wearing trousers. Anyhow, they struck a nerve.

For all its promise, *Wood And Walters* only managed that single series of seven episodes before Julie Walters' talents were put to higher profile use, first in Alan Bleasdale's seminal TV drama *Boys From The Blackstuff* (1982), where she played the pressured wife of *Liver Birds* regular Michael Angelis, and then Willy Russell's Oscar-nominated film, *Educating Rita*

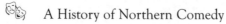

(1983). Meanwhile, Victoria Wood continued to forge ahead on her own. She followed *Wood And Walters* - and a perhaps unlikely simultaneous spell providing musical interludes for Little and Large on BBC Radio 2 - with a return to her first love, live stand-up comedy. Although, by the early 'eighties, there were more female stand-ups around, to earn a living in such a hard-nosed, male-dominated environment remained as difficult as ever. A niche Wood duly began to carve anyway, helped by the exposure brought about by a big money BBC offer to return to television.

The show in question was *Victoria Wood: As Seen On TV* (1985), a hugely successful sketch-based programme for which Walters put her burgeoning solo acting career on hold to take part, and in which that soon to be familiar troupe of Victoria Wood regulars really did come to the fore. They included the steely blonde Susie Blake - another future *Coronation Street* regular - whose deadpan continuity announcer uttered, among other barbed insults, the immortal phrase: 'We would like to apologise to our viewers in the north. It must be awful for you.' Still to be discovered portraying Hyacinth Bucket, Patricia Routledge was the suburban middle class housewife Kitty, sweet sherry in hand, waxing lyrical from her comfortable armchair. Celia Imre was another favourite, with her smouldering Calvinistic demeanour and breath of Caledonia. And there was a regular place for Duncan Preston, too, most often in spoof fly-on-the-wall documentaries well before the days of *The Office* and *People Like Us*. It was in one such lonely hearts parody that the widow of Peter Eckersley, Anne Reid, made *her* Victoria Wood debut.

Yet there is no doubting which part of *Victoria Wood: As Seen On TV* proved most enduring. From its wobbly opening credits to the botched cliffhanger at the end, 'Acorn Antiques' was Victoria Wood at her most satirically inspired. A simple enough premise - the terrible old ITV soap *Crossroads* parodied to a merciless degree - was lifted via rattling scenery, missed cues, visible microphones and acting not so much wooden as, well, antique, into the ranks of television comedy at its finest. Again, one of the most enjoyable performances came from Julie Walters, whose Mrs. Boadicea Overall, the stooped, hump-backed, tray-wielding char lady, a premature ejaculator of lines and starer at cameras best left unnoticed, became a legend in her own teatime. And Mrs. Overall had a first rate supporting cast too. Imre, as Manchesterford boutique owner Miss Babs, had the incongruous soap opera glamour off pat. 'Looks like we won't have to go out of business after all. I've just been offered Leonard da Lisa's *Mona Vinci* at a very reasonable price...' and '.....that's 87p change - enjoy your antiques!', being just two memorable lines among many. Preston's leading man Clifford, meanwhile, was at risk of Dutch Elm disease and Wood's own turn as the terminally bewildered Miss Berta equally well judged. Indeed, so completely did *Acorn Antiques* capture the imagination that its creator was able to reinvent as a West End musical, starring much of the original cast including Imre and Preston, in 2005.

It's hard to credit, given its impact, that *Victoria Wood: As Seen On TV* ran for just two series. But it did and, after a Christmas special in 1987, the woman herself was back on ITV in *An Audience With... Victoria Wood*. Six BBC comedy playlets followed before, in 1991, Julie Walters returned the favour and included Wood among her guests in LWT's *Julie Walters And Friends*, the same Christmas special in which she performed sketches by the four writers who had most influenced her career, i.e. Wood, Willy Russell and Alans Bleasdale and Bennett. In 1992, *Victoria Wood's All Day Breakfast* was another seasonal special, this time taking the mickey out of breakfast television. And then came *Pat And Margaret* (1994), a movie screenplay until the BBC stepped in with a rescue package, after film companies declined to show any interest.

Pat And Margaret bore close resemblance to a *Comedy Playhouse* pilot, *Once In A Lifetime*, which had starred another talented female actor, Kate Robbins, the year before. Robbins, the most high-profile member of a Liverpudlian family that also includes well-known brother Ted (later to star as the villainous Den Perry, destroyer of Bolton's most famous social club), was first seen on television in *Crossroads*. Her real talent, though, lay in impersonations, which is how she also came to appear alongside Mike Yarwood towards the end of his TV career, 'doing' Prince Andrew's Sloaney wife Sarah Ferguson. In time, Robbins would also find work in *Spitting Image* and a one-off special, *Robbins* (1986), in which she shared a spotlight with fellow clan members Ted, Jane, Emma and Amy. Less than a year later, Kate and Ted got together for *Kate And Ted's Show*, a harmless Saturday night fling, followed by a 1987 Boxing Day special, *Christmas Robbins*. In 1988, *The Kate Robbins Show* saw its eponymous star go solo before her talent for voices was further put to use in *The Staggering Stories of Ferdinand De Bargos*, wherein

the BBC archives were raided in 1989. One day, Kate Robbins too would become a member of Victoria Wood's 'rep' company.

That, however, was for the future. For now Wood concerned herself with *Pat And Margaret*, a sensitive and intelligent drama comedy pitched somewhere between pathos and laughter, that critiqued a growing cult of celebrity along the way. Initially part of BBC1's drama strand, *Screen One*, Victoria Wood regulars Reid, Imre and others were again in evidence, while Julie Walters took the role of Pat Bedford, a successful American soap star reunited with her dowdy and distinctly dull sister Margaret, whom she has not seen for twenty-seven years. Bedford is the star of a Saturday night light entertainment show, 'Magic Moments', clearly based on Cilla Black's *Surprise, Surprise*. Duncan Preston played Margaret's boyfriend Jim, still living at home with his elderly mother, a suitably majestic northern turn by the one-and-only Thora Hird.

Despite her television work Wood did not leave stand-up behind. And her growing command of it is no better illustrated than the way in which, in 1996, she was able to sell out London's Albert Hall on fifteen consecutive nights. That is a record which has remained unmatched since and her tour across the rest of the country proved equally popular.

In 1997, Victoria Wood was awarded and accepted an OBE (she was also made CBE in 2008), by which time, along with her old *New Faces* colleague Lenny Henry, she had become a mainstay of the *Comic Relief* crowd. Henry's wife, Dawn French and her double-act partner Jennifer Saunders - of whom more anon - were high-profile attendees of her critically well-received *Audience with...* ITV show for example and, despite her less than hip showbiz origins, Wood had long since been accepted as a member of the fashionable brigade. Even so, she has never denied that her own attitude to comedy is firmly rooted in the traditional.

Certainly, when Victoria Wood decided to have a go at something different on television in 1998, she chose the not so edgy genre of studio-based situation comedy. Her taste in such matters had already been made apparent when, in 2000, she researched and presented *Don't Panic! The Dad's Army Story*, a celebration of the Walmington-on-Sea Home Guard. With *dinnerladies* (deliberately lower case, she somewhat bizarrely told *Comedy Connections*, because she wanted it to resemble the, er, capitalised American hospital drama *ER*), the group dynamic in both *Dad's Army* and her own earlier work was again prominent. As might have been expected, to tell this everyday story of - mainly female - catering folk, Wood again drafted in her tried and tested team of all talents. Duncan Preston played the overly fastidious odd-job man Stan. Celia Imre was back as Philippa, the steadfastly liberal and virtually clueless human resources manager, while Julie Walters put in the occasional appearance as Petula Gardeno, the scabrous mother of Wood's own character, the relentlessly cheerful Bren. And in among the old familiar faces there was a whole new ensemble, all of them to the Victorian manor born.

Forming a competitive double act with Anne Reid's Jean was one-time *Corrie* stalwart Thelma Barlow, as the blunt-speaking, self-obsessed Dolly, erasing the memory of her wittering former alter-ego Mavis Riley entirely. A year or two short of her own *Coronation Street* debut was Shobna Gulati, who played Anita, an Asian bimbo as northern as anyone else, with the possible exception of the sublimely dim Twinkle, a performance of sheer downbeat brilliance from Maxine Peake, soon to shine equally brightly in *Early Doors* and Paul Abbott's *Shameless*. The canteen's long-suffering male supervisor and Bren's love interest, Tony, was played with deadpan grace by Andrew Dunn, and there were cameos from the likes of Eric Sykes, Thora Hird, Dora Bryan and Bernard Wrigley. It was now that Kate Robbins entered Wood's orbit, too, as other-worldly Babs, in from planet Urmston. Metaphorically, *dinnerladies* was equally clever: this dreary works canteen was, contradictorily, both a prison and a means of escape. Everyone was avoiding something, whether emotional or, in Tony's case, physical (and not since *I Didn't Know You Cared* was cancer used to such comic effect). Yet, in the final analysis, *dinnerladies* was a curate's egg of a show that, though entertaining, was never quite as satisfying as it might have been.

In *Comedy Connections*, Wood, always her own biggest critic, laid the blame for its less than spectacular reception on it being out of touch with changing times. And it's true that when the second and, as it turned out, final series of *dinnerladies* was shown in 1999, a certain other ensemble sitcom called *The Royle Family* was indeed redefining the possibilities of what might be done in the genre. However, there will always be more than one way of skinning a cat and perhaps a more prosaic truth about *dinnerladies* is that it was just a little too formulaic. One hesitates to be too critical because there was lots to enjoy and it was certainly a step up from your average sitcom, but whenever the scene-stealing Julie Walters wandered on set, for example, half-pissed, farting like a vagrant and with an unlikely toy boy in tow, the comedy levels lifted noticeably. The rest of the time, it was apt to feel as if the actors knew they were in a 'Victoria Wood production' and delivered their lines accordingly. The result: a stilted procession of 'Wood-isms' rather than graceful comedy flow. Then again, in these high-paced days of five-second attention spans, maybe we have all been brainwashed into believing that anything which moves at a pace statelier than 2 Fast 2 Furious is just not slick enough.

If dinnerladies can be said to have almost attained greatness but not quite, that verdict can most definitely not be delivered on Victoria Wood herself. These days a bona fide national treasure, in 2005 she was rewarded with a televised BAFTA tribute night all of her very own, at which French and Saunders, Barry Cryer, Lenny Henry, Eric Sykes, Ted and Kate Robbins, Craig Cash, the League of Gentlemen and Peter Kay were notable for either their presence, tributes or both. In the same year, both Wood and Kay appeared as a suitably regal Queen Mary and an unseen servant respectively in The League Of Gentlemen's Apocalypse. In fact, since the days of Pat and Margaret, Wood has retained a desire to see her own work up there on the big screen. And she would have done just that had the Disney Corporation not pipped her to the post when the opportunity to make a film about the naked members (so to speak) of a North Yorkshire women's institute came along. To add insult to injury, when the house of mouse-produced Calendar Girls made it to cinemas in 2003, it not only starred Julie Walters, but Celia Imre too.

For all her continued popularity - fellow comedians voted her among the all-time top 50 comedy acts in 2005, when Reader's Digest subscribers also dubbed her the funniest comedienne ever - since dinnerladies any new television series by Victoria Wood has been notable only by its absence. And certainly, her Christmas special Victoria Wood With All The Trimmings, broadcast in 2000, was essentially a satire on the dumbing down of that very medium. In December 2006, however, she was back with a vengeance with the BAFTA-winning Housewife 49, an ITV drama based upon the war diaries of Barrow housewife, Della Last. It was a tale by turns amusing, thought-provoking and moving, and confirmed her as Alan Bennett's heir apparent - there were even a few Bennett-like digs at George Formby,

The Dying of the Light?

Gracie Fields and *ITMA!* Even more exciting for fans of her comedy and bringing her story bang up to date, meanwhile, it was announced towards the end of 2009 that another BBC seasonal special was in the pipeline, *Victoria Wood's Mid-life Christmas*, her first in nine years.

Victoria Wood, then, remains very much in business. But as the dorsal fin of alternative comedy cut a swathe through the blood red tide of the early 1980s, many other talent show refugees were not quite so fortunate. Once-ubiquitous primetime presences like Cannon and Ball, Freddie Starr and Little and Large would these days be absent from our screens completely, were it not for reality television. In 2004, for example, Freddie Starr found himself appointed team captain on ITV's *Celebrity Fit Club*, while Faith Brown went so far as to actually win Living TV's *I'm Famous and Frightened!* Bespectacled Syd Little turned up in something called *Trust Me, I'm A Holiday Rep* in 2005, the same year that Cannon and Ball lit up the fifth series of *I'm A Celebrity, Get Me Out Of Here*. Alas, Tommy was the first to be voted off and Bobby rocked on to finish fifth. Still, that story did at least have its happier side. For during their earlier pomp, the pair had fallen out to the extent that the only place where they could stand to speak to each other was on stage. A couple of decades on, Cannon and Ball were reconciled as born-again Christians - Bobby's conversion coming in 1986, Tommy six years behind in 1992.

Since recovering from a heart transplant in 2002, Syd Little's former partner Eddie Large has supplemented regular after-dinner speaking gigs with spots on the likes of *Win, Lose Or Draw*, *The Weakest Link* and *Today With Des And Mel*, along with acting cameos in *The Brief* and *Blackpool*. Paul Daniels, meanwhile, developed a natty line in daytime quiz shows, namely *Odd One Out*, *Every Second Counts* and *Wipeout*. With his wife Debbie McGee (a former magician's assistant whom he married in 1988 and who was notoriously asked by Caroline Aherne's Mrs Merton: 'So, Debbie McGee, what first attracted you to short, balding millionaire Paul Daniels?'), the diminutive prestidigitator too has since become no stranger to reality TV. Mr. and Mrs. Daniels were the first to be eliminated in ITV's *The X Factor: Battle Of The Stars* in 2006, while Paul also popped up on Channel 5's agricultural reality show *The Farm* (2004), in which David Beckham's one-time personal assistant Rebecca Loos masturbated a pig. The pig liked that. Not a lot. But he liked it.

17
The Young Ones

"People often theorise about why the music hall died out. I'll tell you why
it died out; because it was crap. Ladies and gentlemen, Ken Platt and his
talking Pond...That's why they had a war every thirty years, rather than go
to the bloody music hall. 'Do you want to go to the music hall tonight?'
'No, I'd rather get blown up in a trench on the Somme.'"
- *Alexei Sayle.*

A strip joint in Soho is an incongruous location from which to launch a
comedy revolution. Especially when that same revolution is supposed to
be offering an alternative to the lazy casual sexism that went before. Yet
such were the contradictions of alternative comedy.

For there indeed, in the now-legendary Gargoyle Club, beneath an
'exotic' dancing haunt called the Nell Gwynne and just a hop, skip and
right-on jump from Peter Cook's old Establishment club in Greek Street,
was alternative comedy's first official home. Known as the Comedy Store,
it was a raucous, gladiatorial live entertainment venue like no other and
its impact is still being felt on popular British culture to this day. When
its doors swung open for the first time in the early summer of 1979, a
Pandora's Box of comic possibilities spewed forth, into a nation riven by
punk rock, economic strife and a new Conservative Government; a world
where who you *were* mattered far less than who you *were not.*

At least, that is the theory. For while it's true that shouty political
sloganeering was a radical departure for British stand-up comedy, clubs
like the Comedy Store were not without historical precedent. In some

ways, the emergence of live and 'dangerous' entertainment carried echoes of the wild, rowdy and ungovernable days of music hall and beer gardens over a century before. Looked at like that, alternative comedy was simply a cycle completed. It was about rebirth and the inevitable replacement of a complacent and comfortable older generation with a younger, vibrant and occasionally over-intense new wave. And just as in popular music, this new wave shook things up, challenged the status quo and turned the existing order upside down. Alternative comedy was loud. It was brash. It sneered. More often than not, it was ostentatiously political. The one thing it most definitely was not, on the whole, was northern.

Established by one-time club comic Don Ward who, in partnership with a former life insurance salesman named Peter Rosengard, was freshly returned from a holiday in California and determined to open a similar alternative comedy venue to the ones he had seen in Los Angeles, the Comedy Store quickly built a reputation for presenting what might be termed a more eccentric brand of entertainer. Initially, adverts placed in the likes of *The Stage*, *Private Eye* and London's *Evening Standard* for wannabe comedians brought plenty of response, but not much of it was inspiring. Then, wrote Rosengard in a letter to the *Independent* newspaper in 2005: '...as I was despairing of finding anyone with any comedy potential at all, in walked a Liverpudlian called Alexei Sayle; and the rest is comedy history.' Soon, acts were invited to try their hand on stage, with a gong sounding whenever a notoriously tough audience grew bored or disenchanted. Lions, Christians and the Glasgow Empire spring to mind.

For those whose ambition was to outlast that gong, a useful survival mechanism was originality. Acts who churned out crusty old mother-in-law jokes, or had a go at the Irish or Pakistanis, were lucky to last ten seconds. And as soon as the London listings magazine *Time Out* began to champion the Comedy Store, it became a honeypot for radical trendies, with the more predictable turns denied time even to introduce themselves. Far safer to tread a path of apparent anarchy and aggression or tap into a political zeitgeist whose lead villains were 'Thatch' and Norman 'cricket test' Tebbit than risk a thumbs-down from the braying mob. Then again, given the state of the nation, there was plenty to get upset about. And this socially relevant line of comedy also had its roots elsewhere. Namely in America, where stand-ups like Lenny Bruce and expletive-laden disciples

such as Richard Pryor and Eddie Murphy (with Steve Martin and Robin Williams picking up the tab for out-and-out craziness) had long since courted mainstream controversy. Of those British comedians who saw the lie of the land, Sayle, Keith Allen, Rik Mayall, Ade Edmondson, Nigel Planer, Dawn French and Jennifer Saunders would be most prominent.

By the time the Comedy Store moved from Soho to Leicester Square in 1982, the likes of Ben Elton, Clive Anderson, Chris Barrie and Paul Merton could be added to that list of showbiz royalty-in-waiting. And, as the decade advanced, they would be joined by Arthur Smith, Jack Dee, Rob Newman, David Baddiel, Jo Brand, Julian Clary, Eddie Izzard, Lee Hurst, Mark Lamarr, Harry Enfield and others for whom the Comedy Store would be but a stepping stone into a less edgy comedy career. Back in the late 'seventies, meanwhile, those comics who nightly braved the slings and arrows of outrageous heckling couldn't even agree on a name for the movement.

In fact, the comedian credited with having first coined the word 'alternative' in this regard (the original phrase being 'alternative cabaret') is the now-relatively unknown Tony Allen, whose confrontational nature is perhaps best summed up by the title and contents of his book on the subject published in 2002, *Attitude - Wanna Make Something Of It?* (Gothic Image Publications). In it, Allen writes that '...a bunch of my mates were editing the info-directory *Alternative London*, so that name was in my head when I booked our cabaret package to a promoter who'd rung up to book me solo. When he asked me for a name, I just plucked Alternative Cabaret out of the air as a meantime ting [sic]. In the following weeks, no one came up with anything better, more gigs started coming in, and the name stuck. Alternative Cabaret soon becomes Alternative Comedy when referring to a show that features a bunch of comedians...'.

Born into an atmosphere of civil unrest, massive unemployment and widespread disquiet, and exacerbated by an equally radical Government intent on modernisation whatever the individual humanitarian cost, the prevailing mood inside the Comedy Store was one of Marxist belligerence. Yet here, too, there were contradictions. As Alexei Sayle himself admitted on the BBC documentary *When Comedy Changed Forever* in 2006: 'We did hate Mrs. Thatcher, I suppose, or at least say we did in a sort of unthinking way... but on the other hand she was making me rich and famous, so I'm doing her a disservice in a sense.' Furthermore, for all that the new wave was ostensibly on the side of the trade unionists, strikers and anyone else prepared to put up a fight against the Iron Lady and her cronies, those comradely instincts did not quite extend to the older comedians who had traditionally entertained those very same working class antagonists. It was a situation nicely recognised by the *Guardian* comedy critic William Cook who, in his book, *Ha Bloody Ha - Comedians Talking* (Fourth Estate, 1994), notes that: '[Ben] Elton and his showbiz brothers back Labour and the unions, but they made it big by short-circuiting the [mainstream light entertainment] system rather than juggling gerbils in front of kindergarten kids in a grovelling attempt to get an Equity card and paying their dues on the windswept seaside circuit.' These self-motivated alternative comedians, suggests Cook, had more in common with the strike-breaking 'scabs' of Wapping and Orgreave than they might care to admit.

And unlike the traditional comics they usurped, only a very small proportion of this new comedy breed was actually working class at all, however much the impression given was otherwise. Quite often they were helped in their deception by the way in which any further education had usually occurred at red brick universities, polytechnics and provincial art colleges, rather than beneath the BBC's previously beloved dreaming spires of Oxford or Cambridge. Indeed, the Oxbridge tradition was also doomed, initially at least, to be met with a disdain that bordered on the antagonistic, as Cambridge-educated comedian David Baddiel revealed in a BBC4 interview with the journalist and broadcaster Mark Lawson in 2006. As a fledgling stand-up, fresh out of university, Baddiel told how, whenever he telephoned the Comedy Store or venues like it looking for a gig, they would ask for details of past experience. If the young tyro was so honest as to admit that he had been vice-president of the Cambridge Footlights they would not infrequently put the phone down.

Undoubtedly, the success of the Comedy Store led to a boom in London's live comedy scene in general. True, Tony Allen's *commedia dell' arte*-style travelling band of squatters, clowns, musicians and 'rough theatre' thespians had in some respects already laid the groundwork for a more challenging brand of humour on their tours of the capital pubs and student unions, as indeed had 'folk comics' like Billy Connolly and Mike Harding on TV. But it was with the arrival of the Comedy Store that other purpose-built alternative comedy venues began to spring up in the city like ducks in a fairground shooting gallery. The most famous of these was the Comic Strip, a Soho neighbour of the Comedy Store and brainchild of another of its pioneers, Peter Richardson. It too had a less than right-on setting: the pornographer Paul Raymond's Revue Bar. And other such dens of comedic iniquity included the Woolwich Tramshed and the infamous Tunnel Club, Rotherhithe, home to the most 'alternative' alternative comedian of all, the irrepressible, inimitable Malcolm Hardee.

Sadly, for Hardee, last orders rang in 2005, when the 55-year old was found dead in the Thames. By then, along with running the Tunnel Club and several other future comedy venues, this Lewisham-born alternative comedy guru could also boast cheque fraud, burglary, imprisonment and the theft of Queen singer Freddie Mercury's birthday cake on his CV. Perhaps best known for his membership - so to speak - of a balloon dance troupe named the Greatest Show On Legs, with whom he impersonated French general Charles De Gaulle with his genitals, his last club was the aptly-named Up The Creek, in Greenwich. It also served as the venue for a celebratory show paying tribute to Hardee, who fell from a dinghy while returning from his Wibbly Wobbly floating pub to his houseboat on the opposite bank of the river.

That the strident world of alternative comedy was London-centric, then, is in no doubt. Yet while northern accents were as rare as parking spots in Piccadilly Circus, the northern influence - although minor in terms of sheer weight of numbers - did have its part to play. For one thing, those red brick educational establishments referred to earlier were quite frequently located at the upper end of motorways one and six. Ben Elton, Rik Mayall and Ade Edmondson, for example, all went to university in Manchester. Of a slightly later vintage, the 'investigative comedian' Mark Thomas is a product of Bretton Hall drama college in Wakefield, and the wonderful Linda Smith - tragically taken by cancer in 2006 - was a student in Sheffield. The provinces were not to be shaken off that easily.

Most clearly, the northern influence can be seen in the aforementioned Alexei Sayle, alternative cabaret contemporary of Tony Allen and Jim Barclay (another Comedy Store pioneer, whose best-known future role would be Geordie football manager 'Jossy' in the 1986 BBC childrens soap *Jossy's Giants*). And how appropriate it is that when this most 'un-northern' of comedy movements took a northerner as its figurehead, it should be one of those fiercely noncomformist Scousers. *From* the north, but not quite *of* the north. With his intimidating, confident manner and natty line in breakneck revolutionary Socialist patter, Alexei Sayle was the perfect Comedy Store compere. He swiftly became a bristling, snarling symbol of the new comedy's confrontational ethos.

Born in Anfield in 1952 to a Russian mother and Liverpudlian father, themselves a couple of Jewish working class Communist Party members, Alexei Sayle's life was tinted with creativity and ideology from childhood. After brief membership of the Young Communist League, he moved still further to the left and joined something called the Merseyside Marxist-Leninist Group, an act, he later said, of rebellion. In time, the eleven or so members of that group became the Liverpool branch of the Communist Party of Great Britain and, politically, he was on his way. Creatively, after being asked to leave his school's sixth form, he embarked upon a two-year arts foundation course in nearby Southport. From there, it was off to the Chelsea College of Art and Design in the city that would thereafter exert the greatest pull on his fortunes, London. It was while at Chelsea that Sayle first turned his radical views into actual performance, finding it an enjoyable and fulfilling experience. A series of 8mm comedy films made there led to a number of applications to film schools, all of whom turned him down. Instead, he was forced to find a job as a clerk with the Department of Health and Social Security, before falling into five-years' worth of dead-end jobs and part-time teaching. It was at the latter end of this period that Sayle joined a Brechtian touring company, run by an old school pal. Before long, it dissolved into a political comedy trio from which Sayle would eventually go solo, before replying to one of those early Comedy Store ads in the *Evening Standard*.

Given Sayle's angry, bolshie and domineering stage character, it was perhaps inevitable that he would be employed as the Store's first MC. It was equally inevitable, in the contemporary climate, that his gift for the outspoken gab would not go unnoticed by the comedy industry at large. A year after landing the job, Sayle was spotted at the Edinburgh Festival by his future manager, Martin Lewis. Not long afterwards, came a show on London's Capital Radio, in which Sayle was further able to develop a style of radio delivery and manic agitprop inventiveness that would define his work for years to come. The show in question was the Sony Award-winning *Alexei Sayle and the Fish People*, from which an album - *The Fish People Tapes* - was also spawned, that included Sayle's 1982 hit "Ullo John! Gotta New Motor?". Sayle's soon-to-be trademark look was also perfected on that disc: mod wide boy, clad in suit, tie and pork pie hat, the latter too big, the former several sizes too small.

His singular visual presence notwithstanding, radio and Alexei Sayle would continue to work well together; with the highlight being his role in Marcus Berkmann's inspired take on football comics, *Lenin of the Rovers* (team-mates Terry Trotsky and Stevie Stalin), broadcast by BBC Radio 4 in 1988. However it was on television where Sayle's menacing charisma had its greatest impact. Martin Lewis's most important contribution in that regard lay in directing his client towards Peter Richardson's Comic Strip club where, along with fellow Comedy Store refugees Nigel Planer, Ade Edmondson, Rik Mayall, Jennifer Saunders, Dawn French, Arnold Brown and Richardson himself, Sayle again became a core performer.

By then, Sayle, Planer, Richardson, Mayall and Edmondson had already taken a first tentative step into television courtesy of a late-night BBC2 show whose intentions were explicit in the title. Yet when *Boom Boom...Out Go The Lights* (as in light entertainers, geddit?) aired in October 1980, it seemed that the only people watching it were the acts themselves. Along with the quintet mentioned, the other Comedy Store regulars featured were the two Allens, Keith and Tony, Pauline Melville and Andy de la Tour, brother of Frances, better known as Miss Jones in *Rising Damp*. Produced by a fledgling BBC producer named Paul Jackson, with its confrontational and often scurrilous take on the world *Boom Boom...Out Go The Lights* was certainly a long way different to anything else on the box at that time. A solitary follow-up show in May 1981 fared equally poorly, ratings-wise.

Nevertheless, the seeds of future popularity were sown. *Boom Boom... Out Go The Lights* featured a first televised appearance for a couple of comical student characters, Planer's woolly-hat clad, guitar-wielding hippy Neil - typical line: 'this is a number about a massive depression I had, 30 minutes ago' - and Mayall's Rick, inspired by a woeful performance poet at the Edinburgh Festival who became angry when the audience didn't

500

take him seriously. Otherwise, all was patchy at best and a throwaway gag that Sayle had grown fond of using - 'I'm an alternative comedian - I'm not funny!' (a line subsequently adopted by the deposed old guard *ad nauseam*) - sums up the underwhelming reaction. An alternative platform, however, had been laid; and such widespread apathy in the face of the 'new' comedy was but a temporary blip.

That it was soon overturned owed much to the BBC's canny retreat to a more cautious middle ground and the sketch-show format it knew best. Most immediately, that meant *A Kick Up The Eighties* (1981-84), in which Rik Mayall again featured, but here alongside less dangerous colleagues like Miriam Margolyes and Tracey Ullman. In fact, Essex-born Mayall's monologues as the swivel-eyed, inadequate Brummie private investigator Kevin Turvey were the best thing in it, bestowing instant fame on the performer who can now be seen as the first alternative comic to make the leap from trendy obscurity to fashionable success. And while irreverence was a touchstone of *A Kick Up The Eighties* its structure was far from revolutionary. Although itself spawning carbon-copy BBC Scotland productions like *Laugh??? I Nearly Paid My Licence Fee* (1984) and *Naked Video* (1986) - from where Gregor Fisher's Glaswegian drunk Rab C. Nesbitt wobbled forth in 1989 - the self-consciously topical *A Kick Up The Eighties* was a blatant throwback to a show that had laid more convincing claims to originality two years before: *Not The Nine O'clock News*.

Described by *The Radio Times Guide to TV Comedy* as bridging the gap between 'the zany mania of the 1970s and the anarchic cynicism of the alternative comedy of the 1980s,' *Not The Nine O'clock News* was indeed a mixture of innocent silliness and social relevance which snuck up on the blindside of more traditional light entertainment fare that, lest we forget, continued to hog the primetime slots for much of the coming decade.

Conceived of and produced by the radio producer John Lloyd and BBC current affairs man Sean Hardie, as the name suggests, *Not The Nine O'clock News* was originally intended to be a fast-moving spoof news revue and was scripted accordingly. Scheduled to kick off in April 1979, just as Peter Rosengard and Don Ward were about to start sifting through the Comedy Store applications of unemployed Butlins redcoats and angry

young men (and wimmin) in Soho, the programme's initial team sheet contained Christopher Godwin, John Gorman, Willoughby Goddard, Jonathan Hyde and two television newcomers in Chris Langham and Rowan Atkinson, who had nevertheless already performed alongside assorted Monty Pythons and others to great acclaim in the 1978 Amnesty International benefit concert, *The Secret Policeman's Ball*. With a General Election looming, however, the BBC top brass suddenly developed cold feet over the new show's explicitly political nature and yanked it from the BBC2 schedules, giving Lloyd and Hardie six months to come up with a more suitable format.

Which is exactly what they did; only this time with most of the cast going the same way as the original news bulletin concept (the title stayed on account of the real *Nine O'clock News* being broadcast simultaneously over on BBC1). Langham and Atkinson remained and they were joined in the new four-person line-up by the morose and tonsorially-challenged Mel Smith, along with Pamela Stephenson, a funny, beautiful and smart Antipodean destined to be the future wife and biographer of one Billy Connolly. Although having such a talented female in the cast was an inspired decision on any level, it later emerged that Stephenson had not actually been Lloyd's first choice. That honour, it seems, went to Victoria Wood. However, when asked, Wood said she preferred to concentrate on her solo stand-up career and turned the offer down. Even without her, the first series of *Not The Nine O'clock News*, aired in October 1979, was received healthily enough. Behind the scenes, however, things were going not nearly so well and another major rethink was deemed necessary for its second series in 1980.

This time, the cast member to depart was Chris Langham. Having already penned scripts for Spike Milligan and been the only British writer on the hugely popular *Muppet Show*, for the London-born Langham *Not The Nine O'clock News* should have represented his first major break in front of camera. Instead, after just six episodes, he was summarily fired, with the show's producers claiming that he did not quite 'fit in' with the rest of the team. In recent interviews, Langham himself has pointed to an over-fondness for alcohol and cocaine as the real reason for his departure. In any event, although his subsequent personal life has not exactly been devoid of trauma and controversy, Langham did at least go on to win huge professional acclaim for his contributions to landmark television comedy milestones such as *People Like Us*, *Help* and, most recently, *The Thick Of It*, for which he won a BAFTA in 2006. His replacement on *Not The Nine O'clock News*, meanwhile, was Welsh Cambridge graduate Griff Rhys Jones who, along with his Oxford counterpart Mel Smith, would go on to form one of the most enduring (and financially lucrative) double acts of the 1980s in their own right.

With the new team in place, *Not The Nine O'clock News* really began to hit its stride. So much so that its second-series blend of topical satire, musical spoofs and digs at authority won a Silver Rose at the Montreux Festival. A team of writers that included such future sitcom stalwarts as David Renwick, Andy Hamilton and Richard Curtis, their ears tuned firmly to prevailing cultural winds, ensured that its cutting edge nature made the show a hit with a younger, more politicised audience. And they weren't the only ones. Even at their most biting, satirical send-ups of subjects like institutionalised racism in the police force or health service cuts were carried off with such panache and likeability that viewers were attracted from across the generational spectrum. The cosy familiarity of *Not The Nine O'clock News* settings - local high street, television studio, the Conservative Party Conference etc - plus an air of almost childlike surrealism at times made many a serious point re. the absurdity of much contemporary political ideology but, crucially, in a non-threatening way.

As a result, many of its best sketches slipped effortlessly into British comedy folklore. Where Michael Palin and John Cleese had their 'Parrot Sketch', *Not The Nine O'clock News* had Gerald the Intelligent Gorilla: 'Wild? I was absolutely livid!' Where Palin and Cleese had a shop devoid of cheese, Jones and Atkinson berated customer Mel Smith for his lack of knowledge when it came to mega-trendy Bang and Olufsen hi-fis: 'You want a gramophone?' And if *Monty Python* could send up BBC continuity announcers, then why shouldn't they do that too? Thanks to *Not The Nine O'clock News*, it was once again possible for television comedy to be mocking, outrageous and daft, and with a point to it too.

And yet even here, amid all the spiky smartness and ostentatiously bright ambitions, the most popular contributor by far was a northerner best loved for his funny faces and silly voices. With his distinctive, rubbery features and vocal gymnastics, rendering even the most mundane

three-letter word amusing, Rowan Sebastian Atkinson, a Consett-born son of the north East, had the look of a Gerald Scarfe cartoon sprung to life. Or, perhaps, an amiable priest who may be inclined to viciousness if left too near the Holy Communion wine. In fact, Atkinson was the ideal incarnation of northern comedy's long-held capacity for using superficial shallowness to mask a deeper and more profound angst-ridden existential pit. In a programme whose chief delights were puncturing pomposity and savaging sacred cows, his disarmingly geeky demeanour was more than useful. And thanks to a face simultaneously capable of simplicity and complexity, etched all the while in a semi-permanent ache of distaste, the line between a smile and a sneer was never drawn so fine.

Born in 1955, Rowan Atkinson's childhood was a rural one and life on a Northumberland farm gave little indication of the performing career to come. Naturally shy, with a slight stutter, upon his entry as an 11-year-old to Durham's Chorister School - future British Prime Minister Tony Blair being a couple of years above him - he is said to have been teased mercilessly about his unusual appearance. Though possessed of innate theatrical ambitions, the young Atkinson's abilities tended more obviously towards the technical. So, when the time came to leave, he took an electrical engineering degree at Newcastle University and scored the highest marks in his year. In 1976, he set off to Oxford.

The move south proved liberating. Upon arrival, this quiet young man with the features of a washed-out Smurf, who had seemed destined for a distinctly unglamorous life in nuts, bolts and metal, headed pretty much straight to an audition for that year's Oxford University Revue, where his eye-catching routine of mime and monologue, based around the driving of a car, brought instant attention and led to a meeting and friendship with *Not The Nine O'clock News* co-writer Richard Curtis, then a fellow student. That meeting of minds begat a double act - writing off stage and performing on it - wherein Curtis was usually straight man to Atkinson's occasionally cruel cohort. It was a relationship later parodied in Curtis's debut screenplay *The Tall Guy* (1989), directed by Mel Smith and starring Atkinson as a career-obsessed, downright nasty funnyman who makes the life of his partner (the terminally laid-back American actor Jeff Goldblum) a misery. Trivia fans might also like to note the presence of John Inman in a cameo role.

With their collaboration still in its infancy, the Oxford Revue was taken to Edinburgh where Atkinson's solo routine was spotted by *Not The Nine O'clock News* creator John Lloyd. This wasn't Atkinson's debut at the Festival - he had once performed there as a 17-year-old - and nor was Lloyd the only comedy producer who knew potential when he saw it. Some six months before the launch of *Not The Nine O'clock News*, Atkinson would make his first television appearance on ITV, in a one-man show called *Rowan Atkinson Presents...Canned Laughter*. Nevertheless, it was not until he threw his lot in with Lloyd and the BBC that his first serious steps to the top were taken.

With *Not The Nine O'clock News*, one less than successful and three hugely successful series ensued, setting a benchmark for future television comedy in the process. Nothing - with the possible exception of *Last of the Summer Wine* - lasts forever, however. And in 1982, at the height of their powers, the quartet opted to move onto projects new. For Atkinson, Curtis and Lloyd, that meant *The Black Adder*, a bawdy historical send-up written by Curtis and Atkinson in which the latter played the cowardly and foolish youngest son of Richard IV, a character with no redeeming qualities whatsoever. Richard IV was, of course, a fictional conceit; i.e. one of the princes supposedly murdered by Richard III in the Tower of London who, it transpired, had not actually been killed at all. So far, so good. The production values and casting were first rate too. Doubtless, the plaster-shattering bombast of veteran South Yorkshire-born classical actor Brian Blessed could be heard back in Mexborough and, played by Tony Robinson and Tim McInnerny, the 'Black Adder' of the title had a pair of handy sidekicks in Baldrick and Percy. Nevertheless, after a less than spectacular reception, it was only when *The Black Adder* won a 1983 international Emmy award for popular arts that the BBC somewhat reluctantly agreed to a second series. Here, Atkinson concentrated on the acting, while another writer was brought in who introduced a more coherent structure, transforming the programme's fortunes entirely.

The writer in question was Ben Elton, by now supplementing his stand-up routines with an even more prolific career as an imaginative and prolific television comedy scriptwriter. The location filming of the first series was now ditched in favour of the studio, primarily as a cost-cutting measure, a move which had the happy result of focusing more attention on the scripts. And what scripts! Through the three further series and trio of specials which followed, in which the original Black Adder's equally untrustworthy descendants (and his closest allies) were genetically re-implanted upon various stages of British history, but now with the family name Blackadder, the gags fairly glinted like lovingly-crafted gems. Rowan Atkinson's ability to find humour in the emphasis of a single consonant - 'B-o-b' - was given full reign. As was his knack for cruel verbal dexterity, best exemplified in the vulgar and convoluted insults directed at his smelly, turnip-loving underling Baldrick who, though full of cunning plans, seems destined to be tied to his self-obsessed schemer of a master in eternity. Indeed, the rhythm of those insults, marked by a logical if nonsensical repetition of words and phrases, would be a much-mimicked ingredient of humourous English conversation thereafter: 'He's madder than Mad Jack McMad, the winner of this year's Mr. Madman competition,' for example, or '...she's as wet as a fish's wet bits'. Less formulaic but just as ubiquitous were Blackadder's withering surrealisms: '...if a hungry cannibal cracked your head open there wouldn't be enough inside to cover a small water-biscuit,' being one such. Or how about, '...he's got a brain the size of a weasel's wedding tackle' and, in referring to the Scarlet Pimpernel, '...he's the most overrated human being since Judas Iscariot won the AD 31 Best Disciple competition.'

With the idiot Black Adder now replaced by his bastard great, great grandson, all ruffs, goatee beard and black hair, looking not unlike an overdone toasted currant teacake, curled and blackened at the edges, Rowan Atkinson really began to flex his comedic muscles. In so doing, he (and Elton) turned Edmund Blackadder into one of the great British sitcom characters of all time. His supporting cast wasn't bad either. For *Blackadder II*, in which the Southport-born Miranda Richardson was simply stunning as Queen Elizabeth I, a spoilt, childish Tudor brat, one moment declaring her love for Edmund, the next threatening to have his head chopped off, Tim McInnerny's Percy, though still dim-witted, was reincarnated as a Lord. In a third series, *Blackadder The Third* (1987), Blackadder and Baldrick were relocated to Regency London, where the former was employed as a butler to the Prince Regent, George, as simple-minded as the most simple-minded simpleton in Simpletown, played with appropriate foppishness by Hugh Laurie. Of the rest, back in the England of the 1560s, Stephen Fry shone as Edmund's rival to the Virgin Queen's favours, Lord Melchett, before in later episodes returning as Charles I and First World War General Hogmanay Melchett, a dangerous, upper class military nincompoop whose Tourettes-style grunts and 'Baaaaah!'s allowed him to challenge Atkinson's previously unassailable reputation as a purveyor of amusing noises. Completing the court of Queen Elizabeth, meanwhile, was the bovine Nursie, played with a simplistic glee by Patsy Byrne, udders on stand-by. Other recurring cast members included Rik Mayall as dashing Lord Flashheart ('Woof!'), Ade Edmondson as the evil Baron von Richthoven, Nigel Planer as Lord Smedley and Robbie Coltraine as Dr. Samuel Johnson and the Spirit of Christmas. In the third and fourth series, Miranda Richardson returned as cross-dressing highwayman and a spying nurse, respectively. Warren Clarke (Oliver Cromwell), Miriam Margolyes (Queen Victoria) and Jim Broadbent (a very entertaining Prince Albert) also joined in the fun.

Of those aforementioned one-off specials, an episode was made for the opening of London's Millennium Dome in 2000. *Blackadder Back & Forth* was a tale of time travel and intrigue, beginning on the last day of the twentieth century and subsequently featuring Tony Robinson, Tim McInnerny, Stephen Fry, Hugh Laurie, Miranda Richardson, Patsy Byrne and a whole host of historical characters like Robin Hood (Rik Mayall), Maid Marian (Kate Moss), Shakespeare (Colin Firth) and Napoleon (Simon Russell-Beale). Over a decade previously, *Blackadder's Christmas Carol* (in which Comedy Store pioneer Pauline Melville appeared as Mrs. Scratchit) and a Comic Relief short, *Blackadder: The Cavalier Years*, both aired in 1988, but it was the final full series that followed which can now be seen as the true high-water mark.

The Blackadder character had fleshed out considerably since that uneven first series. Indeed, he had begun to take on contemporary traits entirely in keeping with the times. At his worst, Edmund Blackadder was a dark personification of the entrepreneurial 'eighties; a thrusting money-driven era when fellow feeling was merely an obstacle to personal gain. In *Blackadder Goes Forth* (1989), that penchant for self-preservation is back, albeit in more sympathetic form. Here, World War One Army officer Captain Blackadder, Private Baldrick and Lieutenant George Colthurst St. Barleigh (a vacant Hugh Laurie again) find themselves rather too close to the front line for comfort. And although an Army captain, Blackadder remains as steadfastly averse to danger as ever. Far from being a gallant warrior, he is a time-serving soldier caught in a mess not of his own making, yearning for as peaceful and easy a life as possible. Yet faced with the insane disorganisation of war, his schemes to escape the trenches (hindered, of course, by Baldrick's cunning plans), feel less like cowardice than common sense. In contrast, the lifestyles of Stephen Fry's monstrous warmonger Melchett and his sycophantic assistant Capt. Kevin Darling - 'Don't slouch, Darling...', 'Come on, Darling, we're leaving...' et al - appear positively decadent. Even here, however, the broad brush humour disguises a more subtle truth. As played with a chilling and mounting desperation by McInnerny, Darling's obsequiousness, too, comes to be seen for the survival mechanism it is. All in vain, of course. Once Field Marshall Haig (Geoffrey Palmer) and his mouthpiece Melchett have assigned him an active role in their war games, Darling has as much chance of seeing his wife and children again as a homesick fly going towards the light in a doner kebab shop.

At the end of six wonderful episodes, how easy it would have been for Richard Curtis and Ben Elton to have scripted in a last-minute escape act, perhaps one of Baldrick's cunning plans which this time, shock upon shocks, actually works after all. Phew, what a relief! To their enormous credit, the temptation - if it ever existed - was resisted. Instead, in possibly the most moving closing imagery ever employed by a situation comedy, Blackadder, Baldrick, George and Darling go over the top as planned. Baldrick: 'I have a plan, sir.' Edmund: 'Really, Baldrick? A cunning and subtle one?' Baldrick: 'Yes, sir.' Edmund: 'As cunning as a fox who's just been appointed Professor of Cunning at Oxford University?' Baldrick: 'Yes, sir.' Edmund: 'Well, I'm afraid it'll have to wait. Whatever it was, I'm sure it was better than my plan to get out of this by pretending to be mad. I mean, who would have noticed another madman around here?' To the gentle piano accompaniment of the show's by now iconic theme tune, upon Blackadder's whistled command the quartet climb the trench walls and emerge, slow motion, into a smoky nightmare world of mud, bullets, barbed wire and shells. The picture then freezes before fading to reveal that same field today, complete with row upon row of blood red poppies, the tranquil sound of birdsong in the air.

Rowan Atkinson would later work with Ben Elton again on the latter's police-based sitcom *The Thin Blue Line* (1995), an open attempt on Elton's part to get back to the good old days of *Dad's Army*, *'Allo 'Allo* and other traditional ensemble sitcoms with a dash of political correctness thrown in. More immediately, when *Blackadder Goes Forth* reached its haunting denouement, Richard Curtis and Atkinson then reinvented a silent character that had long been a part of Atkinson's repertoire for a 1990 New Year special. His name was Mr. Bean and he would not only be an enormous hit in the UK, but in over 245 territories worldwide.

A true international phenomenon, Mr. Bean is a wordless, childlike odd-ball who drives a lime green mini and runs into difficulties doing the most innocuous things, changing into his swimming trunks, for example, or stifling a sneeze in church. If ever he does try to speak, what comes out instead is a high-pitched funny noise. His best friend is a teddy bear. No wonder high-brow (and indeed quite a few low-brow) critics grow sniffy at the mention of his name. Here again, in essence, is the northern comedy conundrum. Belying a surface simplicity that encourages universal appeal is an ingeniously-constructed joy, at best, with antecedents in Buster Keaton, Charlie Chaplin, Jacques Tati's Monsieur Hulot and early Benny Hill. Thanks to its essentially harmless fun for audiences of all ages and - going by endless airline repeats - altitudes, the adventures of *Mr. Bean* took him through fourteen shows for ITV bearing such titles as *The Curse of Mr. Bean*, *Merry Christmas Mr. Bean* (watched by a British TV audience of 19 million), *Mr. Bean Rides Again* and the final such outing, *Tee Off, Mr. Bean* in 1995. There have also been a couple of films: *Bean - The Ultimate Disaster Movie* (1997), which took an astonishing £152 million at the global box office, and *Mr. Bean's Holiday* (2007). And in 2002, Mr. Bean was turned into a similarly profitable animated series.

It might be argued that, in Rowan Atkinson - brilliantly cerebral satirist on the one hand, physically inept character-comic on the other - we see the moment in British entertainment history when the northern and southern comedy traditions finally start to merge, or at least become less rigid. Certainly, in the wider picture, this was the decade in which Margaret Thatcher's Conservative Government commenced its organised destruction of British manufacturing and all it had previously stood for, favouring, instead, less heavily-unionised service industries, investment in global financial markets and the like. In effect, the nation was at the tail end of the very phenomenon that had given birth to recognisably modern northern comedy in the first place: the Industrial Revolution. Motorways were now commonplace, telecommunications much improved, travel no longer any problem whatsoever. There is no such thing as society, once-proud northern communities forged in over a hundred years of steel, wool, coal, shipbuilding and sweat were casually informed. Need a job? Then get on your bike.

A further and suitably business-driven example of how Rowan Atkinson - and others like him - have further shaped modern British comedy lies in their interest in independent production companies, those privately-run fun factories which nowadays fill the schedules not only of the BBC and ITV, but also the channel most responsible for taking alternative comedy on its next major leap into the mainstream. Atkinson's own involvement began with a reported fifteen per cent stake in Tiger Aspect, one of a number of such companies able to take full advantage of the launch of Channel 4 in 1982.

The birth of Britain's first new television channel in twenty-seven years owed much to supply and demand. Over the previous decade, the number of TV licences in circulation had risen from 15 to 18 million and, with the coming of the 1980s, the average family was said to watch over five hours of television per day. Radio's glory years were behind it and cinema attendances, too, were around a quarter of what they had been in the 1960s and falling. Into this scenario stepped a Thatcherite Government intent on championing free markets and deregulation. The key word, for them, was choice. And if water, transport and electricity companies could undergo privatisation, then why not the television industry too? The upshot was the 1981 Broadcasting Act, which dictated that rather than making its own programmes, as had primarily been the case since the medium's invention, the UK's newest channel must commission them instead, from a range of independents. In light of an ongoing ideological struggle between this upstart, cash-oriented new breed of Conservatism and its paternalistic control-hungry forerunner, however, a number of checks and balances were inserted in the remit.

First and foremost, Channel 4 should pursue diversity. Its programming must provide an alternative, distinctive voice to that which was currently on offer elsewhere, catering for as many different audiences as possible. Here again, we have the irony of a cocky new wave of comedians, writers and programme-makers being given the mother of all helping hands by the anti-Establishment figure they most volubly claimed to detest - the Rt. Hon. Margaret Thatcher.

Not that the irony all went one way. The brash, youthful new kid on the block ruffled feathers from its launch. Well, almost from its launch. In fact, the first programme broadcast was the innocuous game show *Countdown*, a now well-established teatime treat with students, OAPs and comedy historians alike, hosted by the Bradford-born presenter Richard Whiteley (who, on account of famously being bitten by a ferret rather than his trademark terrible puns, warrants a mention in any history of northern comedy in his own right). Yet as Channel 4's opening night progressed, so did a tendency towards controversy. Most obviously, that came via the channel's very own alternative soap opera *Brookside*, made by the Liverpudlian writer and producer Phil Redmond's Mersey Television. Set in his home city and bedevilled with a brand of colourful language previously unimaginable at 8.00pm, *Brookside* stories were unflinchingly realistic. Rape, unemployment, drugs, incest, child abuse, homosexuality, AIDS, murder, prostitution - no subject was deemed too taboo. It even had the world's first sighting of Alan Partridge, albeit a completely different character of that name played by the Todmorden-born actor Dicken Ashworth. Eventually, the swearing was dropped and *Brookside* would grow into a phenomenal success, turning actors like Ricky Tomlinson, Sue Johnston and Anna Friel into well known stars.

For the moment, though, all it did was get newspapers like *The Daily Mail* hot under the collar. And that was a trend continued elsewhere. In *The Tube*, Channel 4's Friday-night alternative to *Top of the Pops*, acts and presenters were frequently pilloried for bad language and lack of taste as, from 1990, was the case with 'yoof' show, *The Word*. A short-lived current affairs programme, *The Friday Alternative*, was lambasted for consistent left-wing bias, as on the occasion it dared to criticise Thatcher's decision to sink the Argentinian troop ship *Belgrano*, with devastating loss of life during the Falklands War. More controversies erupted when the channel

turned its attention to sex, whether straight in Margi Clarke's *Sex Talk* (1990) or gay in *Out On Tuesday* (1988), among others. For a while, a red triangle became on-screen shorthand for levels of explicit sexual activity guaranteed to have the likes of Mary Whitehouse and 'Disgusted' of Milton Keynes reaching for their green ink.

But back to opening night and once *Countdown*, *Channel 4 News*, *Brookside* and the rest were out of the way, viewers were treated to the talents of alleged Australian funnyman Paul Hogan and a hard-hitting Stephen Frears drama, *Walter*, itself the start of an institution that was to become known as *Film On Four*. The most memorable programme of the evening, however, was still to come. For it was at 10.15pm on Tuesday 2nd November 1982, that *The Comic Strip Presents...* first hit TV screens in the shape of the Enid Blyton *Famous Five* spoof, *Five Go Mad In Dorset*.

Like the venue from which it took its name, *The Comic Strip Presents...* was very much the pet project of Peter Richardson who, along with his stage partner Nigel Planer, had initially been one half of a Comedy Store partnership called 'The Outer Limits'. Treading those very same boards, of course, were Rik Mayall and Ade Edmondson, whose own double act set standards of manic violent invention to rival *Tom and Jerry*. Edmondson and Mayall originally met at Manchester University in '20th Century Coyote', a five-man drama-student troupe that was soon whittled down to two. As a duo, highlights of their fledgling act included the pair hanging from the ceiling in a couple of pink Brentford Nylons duvet covers, pretending to be God's testicles. There was also a routine called 'Death on the Toilet', in which Death came to collect his latest victim only to find him otherwise engaged.

While disaffected youths weren't exactly thin on the ground in the late 1970s, the Bradford-born Edmondson had perhaps more reason to feel alienated than most. Born in 1957, his childhood was spent travelling the world in thrall to his father, a teacher in the Armed Forces. After spells in Cyprus, Bahrain and Uganda, at 12 years of age Edmondson was shipped off to boarding school in Pocklington from where, he told Paul Jackson in a conversation broadcast on BBC Radio 4 in 1999, he went on to Manchester University because he 'daren't go to drama school.' In the same interview, Edmondson also pointed to emotional insecurity as the chief reason for a resulting short-lived marriage. Whatever the downside

512

of this rootlessness, a lack of a settled background did have one positive outcome for a young man who was, by any definition, something of a loose cannon. Paradoxically, self-destructive feelings fuelled his creativity. And with the youth phenomenon that was punk rock at its lawless zenith, upon graduation in 1978, and in tandem with Rik (the 'c' being dropped for punkish effect) Mayall, '20th Century Coyote' headed south.

En route to London, the duo self-funded a twenty-four-date tour of provincial church halls before eventually drifting up at the Comedy Store. From there, and known now as Adrian and Richard Dangerous (aka 'The Dangerous Brothers'), the pair took their act around the capital's growing comedy circuit before, in 1980, transferring their allegiance to the Comic Strip. It was a wise move. When Peter Richardson was approached by Channel 4 with a view to adapting the alternative comedy club concept for TV via six specially commissioned films, Edmondson and Mayall - by now nibbling around the edges of small screen exposure themselves - were on hand to lend support. As indeed, in the first instance, were Dawn French (George) and Jennifer Saunders (Anne) who, with Richardson (Julian), Edmondson (Dick) and Timmy the 'licky' dog, made up that inaugural *Comic Strip Presents...* quintet.

Though hardly northerners in the strictest sense - French's origins are in Holyhead, Wales, and Saunders is a native of Sleaford, Lincolnshire - it would certainly be true to say that if any act injected the aggressive, politicised world of alternative comedy with the subtler charms of character and observation, then French and Saunders were it. After meeting at London's Central School of Speech and Drama in 1977 and half-heartedly joining the stand-up cabaret circuit, when the chance of a career in television came their way it was grabbed with both hands. While most of their male contemporaries were hitting one another over the head with shovels or ranting against the wicked Tory government, French and Saunders were happiest pointing their shiny torch of ridicule at family relationships and, horror of horrors, their own imperfect selves. It was a knack that would serve - and indeed continues to serve - them in good stead, whether together or apart, in shows as diverse as *Girls On Top*, *Absolutely Fabulous* (wherein the gormless office airhead Bubbles, as played by Rawtenstall-born actress Jane Horrocks, was a very northern fashion victim), *The Vicar of Dibley*, *Psychoville* and *Jam and Jerusalem*. And

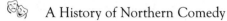

it all began with *Five Go Mad In Dorset*, in whose cast they were also joined by Daniel Peacock, Robbie Coltraine, *Crossroads* actor Ronald Allen and the soft core 'seventies sex-movie star Fiona Richmond, presumably as a result of the live venue's unusual location.

Much to Channel 4's delight, *Five Go Mad In Dorset*, with its spoof-fifties moralising, smutty stereotype-busting innuendo and lashings of ginger beer, was a huge and instant hit for the new broadcaster. And in its wake came no fewer than thirty-eight such freestanding comedies, in which each of those performers - and others like them - reappeared with varying degrees of regularity and success. In a long and distinguished list, Rik Mayall, Nigel Planer and Keith Allen were most ubiquitous, although there were several roles for the likes of Alexei Sayle, Miranda Richardson and Phil Cornwell too. In fact, the only Comic Strip club regular *never* to appear on screen was Arnold Brown. Dawn French's future husband Lenny Henry appeared in a couple, Kathy Burke made three and there were a range of memorable one-off roles for old-stagers like Peter Cook (a hitman), Nicholas Parsons (his target), Leslie Philips and Beryl Reid too. The worst *Comic Strip* productions were so painfully 'politically correct' that the message seemed, on occasion, to take precedence over the humour. The best reached heights of intelligence and satirical brilliance that would have been unimaginable in television comedy only a few years earlier. Of these, *Bad News Tour* (1983), *Fistful of Travellers Cheques* (1984), *The Strike* - a Golden Rose of Montreux-winning take on the coal miners dispute of 1984, as seen through the eyes of Hollywood, in which Mr. and Mrs. Arthur Scargill were played by Al Pacino (Richardson) and Meryl Streep (Saunders) - and *Mr. Jolly Lives Next Door* (both 1988) were among the finest. There were also a couple of full-length feature films in the shape of *The Supergrass* (1985) and *Eat The Rich* (1987), in which Peter Rosengard himself made an on-screen appearance as an Israeli ambassador.

Meanwhile, five months after the Falklands War ended and in the very same week that messrs. Richardson, Edmondson, French, Saunders and hound were embarking on the first *The Comic Strip Presents...*, the BBC, its thrusting young producer Paul Jackson and one member of that Channel

4 cast, Edmondson, were belatedly ready to broadcast the most significant alternative comedy show of them all. Preceded by its manic Cliff Richard-inspired theme tune, *The Young Ones* would turn the cosy suburban world of mainstream British sitcom on its head.

The roots of this madcap half-hour of mayhem, music and cartoon-like devastation lay in Jackson's first foray into alternative comedy, *Boom Boom...Out Go The Lights*. For it was there, as we have seen, that the viewing pubic got its first taste of Neil the hippy and Rick, leading Mayall to contemplate how it might be if those characters, plus a couple of others played by Edmondson and Richardson, lived together in the same house. Edmondson, he thought, could reprise his lunatic, gratuitously violent Adrian Dangerous persona from 'The Dangerous Brothers', while Richardson would make a splendid if other-worldly straight man. Assisted by his girlfriend at the time Lise Mayer, the daughter of one of his former university tutors, Mayall duly produced a script which Jackson considered interesting, if a little on the rough side. Unperturbed, Mayall knew the very person to tidy it up.

Back in Manchester, studying the same drama course but two years below Edmondson and himself, had been a young writer and comedian named Ben Elton, whose plays Mayall had admired at the Edinburgh Festival. With Jackson's approval, Elton was added to the team, although Richardson, in contrast, was swiftly rejected as a result of his 'creative differences' with the producer on *Boom Boom...Out Go The Lights*. In his place as Mike, the so-called cool one, came Christopher Ryan, a former London drama student and the only member of the group possessed of no particular comedy background. As the dysfunctional tenants of the lazy, abusive and barking mad East European landlord Jerzy Balowski (the characteristically grotesque and malevolent Alexei Sayle, who wrote his own sections), the quartet was now complete. A pilot episode was shot, which Jackson very much liked. His BBC bosses, however, could make head nor tail of it and the project was discreetly shoved to one side.

Before it could be lost to history, however, Jackson took the liberty of showing the tape to the Corporation's head of youth programming, Mike Bolland. So impressed was Bolland that upon becoming Channel 4's youth and entertainment commissioning editor two months later, he immediately set about grabbing a piece of the alternative action. Thus,

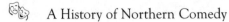

when Peter Richardson subsequently shuffled into his office with a list of films he would quite like to make, was born *The Comic Strip Presents....* And thus, with the BBC finally awoken to the spirit of the age by one of its usual bursts of sheer competitive nervousness, were *The Young Ones* finally given their overdue green light.

With explosions galore, bizarre homicidal assaults and an occasional attack on more obviously traditional situation comedies like *The Good Life*, *The Young Ones* was an immediate favourite with one section of the BBC audience at least. For while many of the older generation were left utterly bemused by all the slapstick comic violence, and a supporting cast list that included smelly socks, a talking bannister called Roger, assorted rodents and a fly on the wall documentary film crew made up of real houseflies, the young of age and heart lapped it up. Here, it seemed, was something completely fresh and original. And so, in many ways, it was, although again not without a hint of what had already gone before.

For sure, that Penelope Keith might kick her own decapitated head up a railway line may previously have been something of a long shot (and speaking of flies on the wall, how fascinating it would have been to be one when Ade Edmondson eventually acted alongside another star of *The Good Life*, Richard Briers, in a short-lived BBC sitcom, *If You See God, Tell Him*, in 1993). Nevertheless, beneath that brash aggressive exterior lurked a recognisable - and even traditional - sitcom sensibility. For a start, in order to qualify for the greater funding given to BBC variety shows, *The Young Ones* took care to feature a traditional musical interlude - Madness, Dexy's Midnight Runners, Motorhead *et al*. A sitcom repertory company of sorts was established too, with old pals like Keith Allen, Tony Allen, Pauline Melville, Jim Barclay, Andy De La Tour, Daniel Peacock, Stephen Frost, Arnold Brown, Gareth Hale and Norman Pace all afforded regular cameos. Most obviously, there was the set itself: an admittedly poxy sitting room but complete with obligatory sitcom sofa; a device as familiar as the genre itself. Finally, in the four lead characters, we had a nuclear family if ever there was one; the controlling, aloof Mike as father; the put-upon, long-haired Neil as mum; and Rik and Ade - renamed 'Rick' and 'Vyvyan' - as the squabbling, unruly children. As Ben Elton himself later admitted during a BBC *Comedy Connections* documentary broadcast in 2004: 'Of course [*The Young Ones*] falls into the rules of sitcom. We had sets, we had characters and we had a situation. *Dad's Army* is probably a more weirdly original idea.' According to Lise Mayer, even Rick's *bêtes noires* in the police force became devoted fans.

Nor was *The Young Ones* averse to a dig at trendy political youth culture itself, satirising the very people who held the programme in such high esteem. After all, what are Rick's limp attempts at rebellion if not a send-up of easy student sloganeering and an opportunity to have fun at the expense of an ideological mindset whose grasp on the complexities of the real world is shaky indeed. 'You will be hearing from my solicitors in the morning. I am going to write to my MP.' 'But Rick, you haven't got an MP. You're an anarchist.' 'Well, then I shall write to the lead singer of Echo and the Bunnymen.' In Rick, as in so many teenage radicals, there is a married, mortgaged to the hilt middle-aged conformist just waiting to get out. A rebel without a clue, he is 'on board the freedom bus heading for good time city - and I haven't even paid my fare!'

Yet while *The Young Ones* secretly did conform to the demands of the sitcom genre, it would be perverse to deny its over-riding influence as a pioneer in the field. An instant cult hit, the first series of six episodes was repeated almost immediately. And when a second batch of programmes came along in 1984 - after a twenty-three-date tour the previous year - audiences really did rocket. Tellingly, however, that second series began with a now classic spoof of the long-standing *University Challenge* quiz show, in which our riotous quartet - representing 'Scumbag College' - took on a team of 'Footlights College' toffs, played by Stephen Fry, Hugh Laurie, Emma Thompson and Elton. Griff Rhys Jones was quizmaster 'Bambi' Gascoigne and a later episode in the series featured the former *Monty Python* star Terry Jones as a drunken vicar. It was clear that, despite all the on-screen antagonism, the dividing line between Footlights-based comedians and the red-brick new wave was dissolving fast. Increasingly part of the television Establishment themselves, were the so-called alternative lot already mellowing?

Once these six episodes of *The Young Ones* were over, and very much against the wishes of the once-reluctant BBC suits, Edmondson, Mayall and Elton chose to ignore the enormous ratings and called it a day. The end, when it came, was suitably berserk. In the twelfth and final episode, 'Summer Holiday', a boring summer's day, enlivened only by the odd

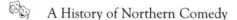

bout of senseless violence, culminates in disaster. The red double-decker bus on which Rick, Vyvyan, Mike and Neil are escaping, after having robbed the Fascist Pig Bank, hurtles through a roadside billboard image of a certain Peter Pan of Pop ('Look out! Cliff!') before plunging over the precipice in question and exploding.

In 1986, *The Young Ones* did get back together to record a cover of Cliff Richard's 1959 hit *Living Doll* for Comic Relief, alongside the man himself and Shadows guitar guru Hank Marvin. The same team - minus Christopher Ryan - also produced, wrote and starred in the ill-fated *Filthy, Rich and Catflap* (1987), which this time fired its arrows at the world of Light Entertainment directly. Written as a reaction to the burden of fame and fortune brought about by the success of *The Young Ones* (the notion of simply leaving showbiz behind and finding a normal job presumably being too 'alternative' to contemplate), it stalled after one series.

From 1987, Rik Mayall enjoyed an almost equally huge solo hit as the rabid, immoral Thatcherite politician Alan B'Stard - Tory MP for the North Yorkshire constituency of Haltemprice - in Laurence Marks and Maurice Gran's delicious satire *The New Statesman*. Originally blessed with the working title 'The B'Stard File', *The New Statesman* proved perfectly in tune with the sleazy, cash-obsessed times and ran over four ITV series and a couple of specials, the last shown on the BBC in 1994. And when Ben Elton was drafted in as a co-writer on *Blackadder*, there were guest spots for Mayall and Ade Edmondson in those series too.

As a double act, however, their next major turning point after *The Young Ones* came when they returned to their thespian roots in Samuel Beckett's *Waiting for Godot* on the West End stage in 1989. Not only was that production rapturously received by audiences and critics alike, Beckett's bleak existentialism had long seemed a close cousin to situation comedy - see *Hancock's Half Hour* and *Steptoe & Son* for example - and its shadow was most definitely cast on the duo's next television series together, *Bottom* (1991). According to Edmondson in his aforementioned 1999 chat with Paul Jackson, a show characterised by pointlessness, time-wasting, squalid immorality and violent juvenile slapstick was originally going to be called 'My Bottom'. But after BBC boss Alan Yentob realised that his continuity announcers would have to utter the immortal phrase, '...and now, here's My Bottom', the possessive pronoun was no more. In

The Young Ones

any event, despite the fact that the show's slobbish central characters, Eddie Hitler and Richie Richard, were clearly just Vyvyan and Rik with a few more years and a couple of tatty suits on them, *Bottom* turned out to be not bad at all. Its joyous malevolence went some way to picking up where *The Young Ones* had left off and inspired several equally successful live stage tours, before coming to an end after three series in 1995.

It was on one of those tours that Edmondson and Mayall wrote the script that later became the less-than inspiring movie *Guest House Paradiso* (1999), in which Richie and Eddie were now hopeless owners of a hotel next door to a nuclear power plant. Its quality aside, that the film should have been made at all was a minor miracle. In April of the previous year, Rik Mayall was very nearly killed in a quad bike accident in the grounds of his Devon family home. Serious head injuries left him several days in a coma; a good chunk of that time on a life support machine. Happily, he made a good recovery. Marginally less painfully, Adrian Edmondson's future television work also landed him in hospital, in his case courtesy of the utterly unremarkable BBC sitcom *Doctors And Nurses* (2004) and the medical drama *Holby City* (2005-2008).

Confirming the English alternative scene's debt to America, in 1985 came Channel 4's next big contribution to the British TV comedy revolution, *Saturday Live*. Based on NBC's groundbreaking *Saturday Night Live* - a launchpad for Chevy Chase, Dan Aykroyd, John Belushi, Bill Murray and just about everyone else who ever made it big in Hollywood comedy - the Channel 4 version began as a one-off special before going on to enjoy the first of two full series the following year.

Again produced by Paul Jackson, the mood of unpredictability at the heart of *Saturday Live* guaranteed it a reaction from the start, and a positive one at that in the case of younger audiences. In its first series, the regular cast list included Ade Edmondson and Rik Mayall, Stephen Fry and Hugh Laurie, Comedy Store favourites Mark Arden and Stephen Frost ('The Oblivion Boys') and a spangle-suited Ben Elton who, from show number eight, took over as host. On an apparent one-man mission to bring down the hated 'Thatch' and infuriate the tabloid press, 'loony lefty' Elton used his weekly soapbox to develop an on-screen stand-up

519

persona that hit its greatest heights in his own BBC show *The Man From Auntie* in 1990. More immediately, *Saturday Live* also brought southern comics like Harry Enfield, Paul Merton, Julian Clary, Jeremy Hardy and, later, Jo Brand to widespread public attention.

Boasting nothing like the viewing figures of its American forebear, the British *Saturday Live* was an energetic mixture of music, supposedly humourous polemic and character-driven comedy, in which latter genre Harry Enfield was particularly effective. Rather oddly, given the newly-developed aversion to racial stereotypes, the character with whom Enfield made his name was Stavros, an Arsenal-loving kebab shop owner - catchphrases: 'Allo everybody peeps' and 'Up the Arse!' Indeed, the keen reaction to the character might be taken as an indication that comedians and their audiences were already growing weary of philosophical strait jackets. And when *Saturday Live* then morphed into a third such series named *Friday Night Live* in 1988, Enfield's next creation - written, once again, in association with a thus far silent partner named Paul Whitehouse - was a brilliantly unreconstructed marriage of the political and observational.

If any comedy character can be said to symbolise British society in the late 1980s - a 'me first' dash for cash stock market, property market and cattle market in three parts equal measure - then it must surely be Loadsamoney, Enfield's mammon-obsessed (Essex) plasterer who gets his kicks from waving wads of dosh at the unemployed and regaling all and sundry with loudmouth tales of his fiscal good fortune. Perhaps inevitably, he became something of an 'eighties Alf Garnett, in that the very people whom Enfield and Whitehouse had intended to satirise began, without any trace of the original irony, to adopt the catchphrase for themselves. Never slow to dump a character when he grew tired of it, Enfield was soon developing other alter egos too, most notably Buggerallmoney, a north Eastern antidote to the original creation whose defining feature - apart from 'drinking beer and smerking tabs' - was the fact that he was permanently skint and reduced to dodging his fare on the Newcastle Metro and spending his holidays in Whitley Bay. As his career progressed, the north would continue to be a rich breeding ground for Harry Enfield who, though Sussex-born, was educated at York University. Among future favourites in shows like *Harry Enfield And Chums* (1994-98) would be the South American footballer with the Tyneside accent Julio Geordio (played by Whitehouse) and Enfield's shell-suited, curly-permed, mustachioed Scousers, a send up of the ultra-argumentative residents of Brookside Close.

The contributions of Enfield and Elton apart, *Saturday Live* and *Friday Night Live* rosters were seldom lacking in talent and originality. Into a mix that also, from time to time, included such comedy veterans as Peter Cook, Spike Milligan, Frankie Howerd, Dame Edna Everage and Jasper Carrott (the latter chastised by Ben Elton for joking about women drivers - presumably Elton's own gag about how women always pinched your chips after telling you they weren't hungry was fine) dropped the occasional humourous poet too. Among the best known of these was Liverpool's Craig Charles who, together with the likes of Benjamin Zephaniah, Attila the Stockbroker and fellow northern wordsmiths Mark Miwurdz (Mark Hurst) and Seething Wells (Steven Wells), were perfectly positioned to take full advantage of comedy's shifting sands.

Thanks to the British performance poet tradition pioneered, to a large extent, by Roger McGough and his Mersey colleagues in the 1960s, a tradition that was itself both built upon and shaken up by the 'Bard of Salford' John Cooper Clark the following decade, poetry was no longer seen as the sole preserve of dusty university libraries and twee little Lake District cottages. There was no reason, now, why a poetry reading could not have all the fun and vitality of stand-up comedy. Both could be similarly adversarial - the gallant Cooper Clarke, born in 1949, had achieved prominence while supporting the likes of the Sex Pistols, Elvis Costello and the Buzzcocks during the original punk explosion - and both were a good way of sneaking truth and social relevance in on the blind side. Clarke, still going strong, didn't so much read his poems as chant them, a cappella. A demented pipe-cleaner of a performer, all drainpipe trousers, winkle pickers and out-sized shades, his sooty Mancunian tones and spinning mule delivery carried the contradictions of the north in every syllable.

As for Craig Charles, born in 1964, he too cut his teeth as a warm-up for local bands, before making his way to television, first as a guest on the chat-show *Wogan* and then on *Saturday Live*, where his winning smile and cheeky Liverpudlian manner won him many admirers. A spell on the BBC's Manchester-based pop programme, *The Oxford Road Show*, followed

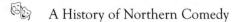

and around this time he also enjoyed a stint as the presenter of *What's That Noise?*, beginning an association with children's television that would serve him well. However, Charles's poetic ambitions took a backseat when he landed the part of super slob Dave Lister in a proposed new BBC science-fiction sitcom, *Red Dwarf*.

In 1988, the year of its first broadcast, the idea of a sitcom in space didn't sound all that promising. And despite getting off to respectable start in terms of viewing figures, with over five million people tuning in for the first episode, the numbers soon fell away dramatically. Even so, in terms of overseas export sales, *Red Dwarf* was destined to become BBC2's most profitable comedy ever. At home, it became a grade one cult, akin to *Star Trek* and *Doctor Who*, spawning geeky fan conventions and over-intense analysis from legions of devoted 'Dwarfers', ensuring a long and healthy shelf life long after a supposedly final series span off into infinity in 1999. In fact, *Red Dwarf* is one of those programmes which has never quite gone away. Rumours of a big screen version and-or brand new series have been rumoured for years and, in 2009, a three-part mini-series, *Red Dwarf: Back to Earth*, was indeed shown on the satellite channel Dave. In it, in a post-modern twist, the real Craig Charles, in his present role of taxi driver Lloyd Mullaney in *Coronation Street*, was tracked down by the fictional *Red Dwarf* crew. At the time of writing, a tenth series was planned, with filming reportedly scheduled to commence in 2010.

Once again, the man responsible for lifting *Red Dwarf* off the launchpad was executive producer Paul Jackson. The show's writers and creators, however, were the Salford-born Rob Grant and his Mancunian childhood friend Doug Naylor who, during their schooldays, claim to have suffered the attentions of a prefect called Rimmer and a bully called Kochanski. After leaving Liverpool University, while working in a range of dead-end jobs, Grant and Naylor began writing scripts, whereupon, in 1981, they hit upon *Son of Cliché*, an award-winning BBC Radio 4 show. It was during its second series, in 1983, that the listening public first met a character by the name of 'Dave Hollins Space Cadet', the last man alive in the universe. Soon, his sketches were adapted and reworked into the pilot television script that, five years later, would rise from the interstellar soup as *Red Dwarf*.

Based on John Carpenter's satirical space comedy movie *Dark Star*, that *Red Dwarf* was made at all owed plenty to the fact that Grant and Naylor had followed *Son of Cliché* with contributions to Jasper Carrott's TV show, *Carrott's Lib,* also produced by Jackson. The Red Dwarf of the title was a twenty-first century deep space mining ship in which a radioactive leak has killed every crew member but one, the Liverpudlian everyman Lister, who survived by dint of being in a state of suspended animation as disaster struck. Ironically, he was there as punishment for smuggling his pregnant pet cat Frankenstein into the cargo hold.

Upon waking three million years later (the original sentence having been for 18 months), Lister discovers that while he is the only human being left on board, he is not alone. For a start, after three million years' worth of evolution, the cat's offspring is now walking around on two legs. As played by the ultra-cool Danny John-Jules, this humanoid feline, Cat, is himself the last known survivor of the race *felis sapiens* and acts accordingly. Then there is the ship's talking computer Holly, responsible for returning Lister to consciousness when radioactivity levels were sufficiently decreased and who, though active, is showing signs of senile dementia. In the first and last couple of series, Holly was played by the downbeat Norman Lovett, while Hattie Hayridge gave him or her a more upbeat sex change in between. The most irritating crew member of all, however, is Lister's former bunk mate and shift leader Arnold J. Rimmer or, rather, his hologram. Though strictly speaking no longer there, he nevertheless retains the anally retentive, bullying, rule-obsessed attitudes of the original, much to Lister's consternation. The cowardly Rimmer - named after a) Grant and Naylor's old school nemesis or b) an unspeakable sex act, take your pick - was played with bureaucratic élan by Chris Barrie, another refugee of *The Young Ones* and *Saturday Live.* Barrie had already voiced Hab the computer in 'Dave Hollins Space Cadet'. As a third series progressed, the *Red Dwarf* team was joined by Robert Llewellyn as the sanitation mechanoid Kryten (David Ross having briefly played the character during series two), and the second of Grant and Naylor's alleged school bullies, Kochanski, was reborn as Kristine Kochanski, Lister's ex-girlfriend, played in the first two series by 1980s pop singer Clare Grogan and in the final two by Chloe Annett.

Despite its cosmic setting, at heart *Red Dwarf* was, like *The Young Ones* before it, as traditional a British sitcom as *Steptoe & Son,* mining laughs from social status and a claustrophobic environment. And like many a traditional sitcom, it also had the distinction of bringing a new word into the English language, however briefly. Just as *Porridge* was responsible for 'naffing' as its expletive of choice, so did *Red Dwarf* give the world 'smeg'. Thus, an idiot is a 'Smeghead'. Enemies are told to 'smeg off' and a spoof of the popular BBC cookery series *Can't Cook, Won't Cook* for a tribute evening of special programming called *Red Dwarf Night* in 1998, becomes 'Can't Smeg, Won't Smeg'. When quizzed on the origins of the word in an on-line fanzine interview, Doug Naylor replied coyly that it was: '...Latin for clean; also there's an Italian washing machine company called Smeg. ...Each of the letters stand for smelting metal... something to do with the washing machine process.' A less innocent reading might note that 'smeg' is also alarmingly close to smegma, i.e. secretions found on and around human genitalia. Whatever the truth, a debate over the exact origins of the word is entirely in keeping with the show's penchant for attracting the anorak tendency.

The influence of *Saturday Live* also lives on. Along with kicking open flood gates earlier nudged apart by *Not The Nine O'clock News*, *Boom Boom... Out Go The Lights*, *The Comic Strip Presents...* and *The Young Ones*, Channel 4 attempted to repeat the concept with a similar combination of music and stand-up, *Saturday Zoo*, in 1993. Hosted by Jonathan Ross, it featured a whole new generation of comedy upstarts including Steve Coogan, Graham Fellows and John Thomson, of whom more later.

Irreverence apart, perhaps alternative comedy's most lasting contribution to the development of British entertainment lies in the way that, all of a sudden, comedians were expected to produce their own material rather than rely on professional gagsmiths or, worse, steal jokes off each other, as had almost universally been the case before.

Again, there was nothing *fundamentally* new about such creativity. There had existed, after all, a clear personal imprint on the routines of comedians like George Formby Sr., Frank Randle, Jimmy James, Robb Wilton, Al Read, Hylda Baker, Les Dawson, Tom O'Connor and others, even if, as their fame grew, their actual scripts were increasingly crafted elsewhere. The so-called folk comedians who pre-dated the alternatives owed their success, too, to an ability to mould personal experience into original and self-revelatory little stories. *The Goons*, the *Beyond The Fringe* team and *Monty Python's Flying Circus* had originality as their middle name. And back in the mainstream, while their best scripts were penned by Eddie Braben, even the legendary Morecambe and Wise only began to scale Olympian heights when they gave up pretending to be Abbott and Costello and went for the personal touch instead. In America, Lenny Bruce, Woody Allen, Joan Rivers and Co. had been exorcising their inner demons in public for years.

Nor, in discussing self-authorship of funny lines, should we forget Ireland's laconic rebel Dave Allen, widely hailed as the 'Godfather of alternative comedy' upon his death, aged 68, in 2005. The epithet was deserved. Perched on a stool, holding court with a whiskey glass in one hand, a slow-burning Gauloise in the other, and with the fourth finger of his left hand severed at the knuckle, Allen's absolute fearlessness in the face of those twin Establishment bastions political authority and religion, during an era when savage religious satire was virtually non-existent, was truly groundbreaking, particularly from a man born and raised Catholic. An act in which he routinely referred to nuns as 'the Gestapo in drag' or portrayed the Pope as a stripper, left him never far from controversy. Yet despite his aversion to organised religion, Allen's own life philosophy was far from dogmatic. 'Goodnight, thank you,' he would close his BBC shows in the early 'seventies, 'and may your God go with you.'

There is little doubt, however, that with the coming of alternative comedy, the balance of writing responsibility began to tip most definitely in the direction of the comedians themselves, as a matter of course. The ground rules, on the whole, had shifted. Soon, the majority of comics were as keen on relating some sort of personal truth as they were on making their audiences laugh - the ideal, of course, being both at once. Although the intention was undoubtedly admirable, in effect it no more guaranteed quality than the well-thumbed joke books had before. In fact, the very opposite could be argued. For while an artistic genius might well thrive on a long leash, is an average singer-songwriter necessarily better off than a musician who, for example, interprets the words of Cole Porter or Irving Berlin? Would Eric and Ernie have been as effective without a skilled craftsman like Eddie Braben putting in the hours? Would Kenny Everett's wild and wonderful television shows have been anything like as effective and disciplined if Barry Cryer hadn't been in the background? After all, for every Dara Ó Briain there is a Sean Hughes or Patrick Kielty. For every Billy Connolly, a Craig Ferguson or Helen Lederer. Unabashed, as the 1980s progressed, the BBC, Channel 4 and, to a lesser extent, ITV positively wallowed in this nirvana of youthful creativity. A determination to engage unflinchingly with contemporary issues edged ever closer to the centre-stage, accompanied by an easier acceptance of 'bad' language, a knowingly ironic (some may say smug) style of delivery and the evolution of a London-based comedy Establishment every bit as cliquey as that which had gone before.

In fact, over much of the 'eighties and early 'nineties, England's north was the region that, comedy-wise, dare not speak its name - or, if it did, it must expect to be greeted with contempt. True, there was the odd bucking of the trend. The Newcastle-born Richard Morton, for example, was a very bubbly regular on the stand-up circuit who happily explored his roots. Morton began his comedy career as one half of a musical double act, 'The Panic Brothers', in tandem with guitarist friend Reg Meuros. Indeed, the pair were one of the first to be represented by the new comedy agency, Avalon, a further indication of the entrepreneurial careerism behind alternative comedy's proletarian facade. When Meuros returned to music, Morton continued in stand-up alone, primarily as support to the very grim-down-south Jack Dee. A greater contrast in style is hard to imagine. Yet for whatever reason, the glittering television career that awaited other comics was subsequently denied to Richard Morton. Maybe this little potted biography in William Cook's 1994 book *Ha Bloody Ha - Comedians Talking* (Fourth Estate) can give a clue why. 'It only remains for him to shed his supporting role for a full-length show in Edinburgh,' Cook writes, 'where his tendency to lean a little too heavily on his Geordie heritage would be mitigated by the residence of his fundamental *joie de vivre*.'

In fact, *Ha Bloody Ha - Comedians Talking* is a mine of information with respect to the attitudes of both the comics themselves and the London-born, public school-educated *Guardian* critics who wrote and indeed still write on the subject in Great Britain. Take this peach from Cook's introduction: 'One constant theme on the London circuit is the out-of-town comic (who has usually had to move to London to make his living) telling his audience (increasingly made up of folk who've also moved to the capital to find work and can't wait to leave it every weekend) what a miserable shit-hole their adopted city is. This is in stark contrast to trad comics whose winsome celebrations of their economically devastated hometowns constitute the cornerstones of their shamelessly parochial acts.' On the one hand, bemoaning the lack of newspaper column inches devoted to coverage of live comedy, Cook can make such a clear-sighted observation as: 'Fans of third division football must feel similarly frustrated when their favourite broadsheet prints lengthy reports of rugby union matches whose attendances amount to only a few hundred. The reason for this imbalance is impure and simple: class.' And then, just a few paragraphs along, state that: 'Alternative comics loathe London, but at least they don't come on all cutsie-pie about their small-town origins. Thankfully, they've nous enough to know that narrow streets breed narrow minds.' Sometimes, Mr. Cook. Only sometimes.

Scottish comedians were more often than not exempt from such critical disdain. Right from the start, thanks to Arnold Brown, Gerry Sadowitz, Stu Who, Bruce Morton, Fred MacAulay, Phil Kay and more, alternative comedy had a flavour as strong as Cullen Skink. Partly, that may have been down to the on-going influence of the Edinburgh Fringe and, partly, it may simply have been that comics from Scotland were less of a threat to an innate southern English superiority complex. northern comedians, after all, had long been able to cut through all that pompous social posturing and laugh at the vulnerable human condition beneath. Maybe this dislike of northern experience was a manifestation of guilty conscience or motivated by out-and-out jealousy of a community to which, owing to accidents of birth and geography, its critics could never belong? Whether it was openly admitted or not, the comedians, writers and audiences of the north had, historically, been the glue that held the entire British comedy industry together. And who, in London, wanted to be reminded of that? Or maybe it was just down to relief, that in such a watchful atmosphere, aim could still be taken at one area of British society, safe in the knowledge that here, at least, nobody would complain.

Still, as ever in alternative comedy, there remained fun aplenty to be had with stereotypes, from whichever direction they hailed. In a live 1983 election-night offering on Channel 4 for example, *The Nightwatchman,*

Comedy Store stalwart Keith Allen - father of modern-day pop star Lily - played a homosexual security guard named Gerry Arkwright, who sits outside an old factory reflecting on his hatred of southerners and democracy, all the while musing upon how his father was gay 'and his father before him was gay'. Shades of the reversal in *Monty Python's* classic playwright sketch, in which Graham Chapman's north country-accented father taunts his visiting son (Eric Idle): 'Hampstead wasn't good enough for you, was it? You had to go poncing off to Barnsley, you and yer coal-mining friends...'.

When viewed in hindsight, and for all its contradictions, the dawn of alternative comedy did usher in a liberating wind of change right across the television spectrum. The retreat from stuffiness cleared the way for a more anarchic approach to children's television, as evinced by ITV's hugely popular Saturday morning kids show *Tiswas*, for example, a bucket of water in the face of the oh-so staid and well-behaved *Swap Shop* on the other side. Puppetry was put to coruscating Sunday night use in *Spitting Image* which, from 1984, gave a career boost to countless up-and-coming talents. The era's fixation with politics was further reflected in its variety shows, wherein *Sunday Night at the London Palladium* might take second place to *An Evening For Nicaragua* (Channel 4, 1983) or *First Aids* (ITV, 1987), one of a number of concerts intended to raise awareness of Aids. And beyond the nation's living rooms, the new breed of comedian was more likely to be found alongside Billy Bragg, Bob Geldof or Paul Weller in events like *Live Aid* (1985) and various Red Wedge concerts - organised to support the Labour Party ahead of its ultimately unsuccessful 1987 General Election campaign - than in any working men's club or Butlins seaside holiday camp.

TV drama was a beneficiary of the new mood too but this time eager to engage with England's north and all who sailed in her. And, as with comedy, much of it had opposition to the effects of a Tory Government at its heart. Playwrights such as Liverpool's Alan Bleasdale came to the fore, with a brand of darkly amusing northern working class realism that began with unemployment saga *Boys From The Blackstuff* in 1982 (derived from his own single play *The Black Stuff* in 1980). Such efforts as John Byrne's *Tutti Frutti* (1987) and Jeanette Winterson's *Oranges Are Not The Only Fruit* (1990) followed, along with less gritty comedy-dramas like Ian

La Frenais and Dick Clement's *Auf Wiedershen, Pet*, which began in 1983 and ended after four series and a couple of specials in 2004. Peter Flannery's *Our Friends In The North* (1996), *Dockers* (co-written by Jimmy McGovern and Irvine Welsh in 1999), the four series in a Manchester textile factory that were *Clocking Off* (2000-03) and, more recently, the Burnley-born Paul Abbott's *Shameless* (2004-present) are but a few direct descendents of that dramatic trailblazing.

In British cinema too, a new taste for realism such as that reflected in 1960s kitchen-sinkers took hold. Prior to the arrival of *Film on Four*, and its brief to fund and develop independent productions that had its first success with Hanif Kureishi's *My Beautiful Laundrette* in 1985, mainstream hits like Bill Forsyth's *Gregory's Girl* (1981) and Willy Russell's *Educating Rita* (1983), had shown that down-to-earth explorations of British working class life could still find an audience. And as the influence of *Film On Four* spread, begetting much artistic worthiness along the way, a simultaneous increase in independent production companies and audience hunger for innovation and social critique yielded still more box office hits. Among the earliest was Alan Clarke's 1986 adaptation of Bradford playwright Andrea Dunbar's stage play *Rita, Sue and Bob Too*, which chronicled the exploits of a married man and his teenage babysitters. Hot on its white stilettoed heels came Bruce Robinson's quirky *Withnail & I* (1987), a cult classic in the making that starred Paul McGann, Richard E. Grant and Cumbria's Lake District. Willy Russell's next Liverpudlian escape story *Shirley Valentine* (1989) and Ken Loach's *Riff-Raff* (1990) also did well, with the latter winning a Felix Award for Best European Film on account of its portrayal of northerners (and others) at work on a London building site. Yet it was not until the end of the 'nineties that the now post-industrial north found itself truly positioned as the resurgent British film industry's location of choice.

Thanks for that can be laid at the door of Keighley writer Simon Beaufoy, whose Sheffield-based, Oscar-winning tale of hope, desperation and exhibitionist steel workers, *The Full Monty* (1997), put millions of bums on seats and not all of them female. In its wake came a string of similar cash-generating projects of varying quality: among the best of which were *East Is East* (1999), *Billy Elliott* (2000), Nick Park's animated *Chicken Run* (2000) and *Calendar Girls* (2002).

Size, however, isn't everything and often the fruits of such fecundity were felt - in the north at least - to reinforce regional stereotypes. Among a number of potential suspects in this area, Mark Herman's brass band and coal-mining comedy *Brassed Off* (1996) pre-dated *The Full Monty* by several months without scaling anything like the same heights. Nor, metaphorically apart, did Beaufoy's follow-up yarn, *Among Giants* (1998), a tale of Yorkshire pylon painters, or his 2001 hair-dressing tale, *Blow Dry*, set in his home town. A clunking adaptation of John Godber's otherwise enjoyable rugby league stage romp, *Up 'n' Under* (1998), was disappointing too. Faced with such fare, national audiences could hardly be blamed for concluding that, if these rude mechanicals were anything to go by, it was indeed grim up north. On the plus side, at least fine actors like Bernard Hill, Jim Broadbent, Liz Smith and Jane Horrocks weren't short of work. And apart from the already eulogised *Funny Bones* (1995), the late 'nineties northern film explosion reached a high point with Herman's *Little Voice* (1998), in which Horrocks, Brenda Blethyn and Michael Caine fairly dazzled as a shy and reclusive music-loving daughter, her blousey widowed mother and the seedy talent scout who sees the girl as his ticket to the big time, all set in the exotic surroundings of Scarborough.

Meanwhile, back in the 'eighties, and while alternative comedy and the birth of Channel 4 had shaken every television genre to its roots, the impact on Light Entertainment was most marked. The 1980s, for example, was the decade in which *Comic Relief* was born, comedy's response to Geldof's *Live Aid* phenomenon of the year before. In fact, the original 1986 *Comic Relief* programme was a compendium of three sell-out live shows, staged at London's Shaftesbury Theatre and held together by 'ringmaster' Rowan Atkinson, shown as part of the BBC arts show strand *Omnibus*. The idea was the brainchild of former MENCAP charity worker Jane Tewson, whose organisation, Charity Projects, co-ordinated the event. Tewson had set up Charity Projects with the intention of pooling resources and expertise as a means of raising funds, primarily for the Sudan. Her project won support from a wealth of comedic talent, including Rik Mayall, Ben Elton, French and Saunders, Lenny Henry, Billy Connolly, Stephen Fry and Rory Bremner, leading the BBC to detect a promising idea in the making. In 1988, the Corporation devoted an entire Friday evening's viewing schedule to the cause and a national institution was up and running.

The first *Comic Relief* telethon proper was presented by Lenny Henry and Griff Rhys Jones, who had to contend with regular interjections from Harry Enfield's Stavros, reporting on the huge wads raised, innit? Here again, however, when the Light Entertainment industry needed to rally the nation to a cause, it looked north. Although *Comic Relief* was very much fronted by comedy's new Establishment, in a pragmatic nod to the generation-crossing appeal of old-style Variety, space was also found on the bill for Little and Large, Cannon and Ball and Ernie Wise, by now in all other respects *passé*. Slightly 'cooler' were alternative forerunners Phil Cool, Victoria Wood and Michael Palin, while special editions of already well-known sitcoms were also produced; in 1988 that honour fell to *Blackadder* and *The New Statesman*. Most recently, the crowd-pulling power of a good northern funnyman was shown by the astonishing reaction to Peter Kay's 'Amarillo' video, which helped to attract a ton of cash in 2005.

Despite the vast amounts of money raised and put to good use in the UK and abroad, *Comic Relief* has never been everyone's cup of tea. Alexei Sayle, among others, has pointed out that the people who do best out of the concept tend to be the entertainers themselves, a rather grouchy and beside-the-point criticism which has also been levelled at *Live Aid*. But although Sayle's confrontational style was very definitely an indicator of changing comedy times (albeit, with the added rider that Liverpudlian comics have always done their own thing anyway), in all other respects he remained as traditionally northern a comedian as they come.

One of the saddest sections of Eric Sykes's autobiography, *If I Don't Write It, Nobody Else Will*, features Sykes being given an award for services to television at the Montreux Festival. While there, he attempts to pitch a handful of fresh ideas to the late Bill Cotton, then the BBC's Head of Light Entertainment and a man who, to quote the book, is the 'son of my old mate on whose band shows I had made several appearances.' According to Sykes, Cotton will not so much as acknowledge his presence before finally applying the killer blow: 'Your day's gone, Eric. We're now into alternative comedy.'

Chances are that Cotton would not have quite put it like that. In any case, without being in the room ourselves, how would we know? But, that is certainly how old trouper Eric heard it and nor is it hard to see why.

Yet the irony is that the comedy of Eric Sykes and Alexei Sayle isn't really all that far apart, not when you get down to it. For while the aggressive delivery of Sayle is indeed predominantly political and calculated to make the hackles of his opponents rise, his comedy is also stuffed full of silly, everyday surrealism and self-deprecation of the type often overlooked in Sykes's own work.

For all his soapbox theorising, Sayle's most resoundingly successful solo shows by far - *Stuff* and *The All New Alexei Sayle Show* - were a lively combination of inventive set-pieces, spoofs and good old-fashioned physical tomfoolery. Like Rowan Atkinson, then, he embodies a blurring of traditional boundaries, a growing up of sorts and greater fluidity between north and south in every sense, as the streak of iconoclastic and radical dissent that has always been a feature of the northern psyche finally began to seep into its comedy. And, perhaps coincidentally, this process had run parallel to a more 'masculine' shift in the social position of women at large; no better exemplified than in the spirit of the Prime Minister herself. Henceforth, although recognisably 'northern' humour would endure, the act of pigeon-holing it as such became much less straightforward.

As for Alexei Sayle personally, since the second and final series of *The All New Alexei Sayle Show* in 1995, he has moved away from stand-up and built a respected career as the author of more often than not dark and biting novels and short stories. During his higher profile 'angry' years, he performed a routine in which his musings on the demise of the music hall led him to conclude that, rather than socioeconomic and political transformations or technological innovation being to blame, it actually died out because it was 'crap'. Yet around the same time, already lurking in the more offbeat fringes of the London circuit, a double act was emerging who would turn such an idea on its head and all-but rescue a moribund Variety genre as they did so. Appropriately enough, they again had their roots in the north of England.

18
They Wouldn't Let it Lie

"This is a local shop for local people, there's nothing for you here..."
- *The League of Gentlemen.*

Blown in on a wave of youthful exuberance and polemic, the alternative crowd of the late 1970s and early 'eighties had been out to start a comedy revolution. Soon, it would no longer be good enough for writers and performers merely to go through the motions and expect a job for life.

Yet come the 1990s, those once-trendy revolutionaries might also be said to have formed a tired and predictable Establishment of their own. As ever, a new generation jostled for its own seat at the table, with once hard-won distinctions between what was acceptable comedy fodder and what was not again up for grabs. To this new species of comedian and consumer, the grim grey days of 'seventies strikers, scabs and industrial and economic unrest were on a par with grainy wartime Pathé newsreels for their Baby Boomer parents. And while irreverent sitcoms like *The Young Ones* and *Blackadder* were revered, so were the more mainstream Saturday night anarchists of their youth, comedians like Russ Abbot, Freddie Starr and Michael Barrymore, and the too-often ignored harder-edge they brought to family entertainment. For this up-and-coming gang of humourous young bucks and their audiences, comfortable and

533

relatively wealthy on the whole, outrageous comedy felt like a birthright. Culturally and politically, it seemed, liberal arguments had won the day. In such a confident atmosphere, it wasn't long before so-called political correctness was viewed as a less than useful comedy accessory.

If the fate of the mystifyingly controversial BBC sitcom *A Small Problem* (1987) is any indication, such a reappraisal was long overdue. Starring Christopher Ryan (Mike in *The Young Ones*), *A Small Problem* was an interesting attempt to satirise the notion of prejudice via a particular concentration on height. In a Britain ruled by 'heightism', anyone under 5ft tall was shipped off to a ghetto south of the Thames. Such was the outcry that the show was lucky to limp through one equally short series, owing to a veritable deluge of complaints from the vertically-challenged. What would they have made of Jimmy Clitheroe?

British comedy's PC retreat from the late 'eighties onward has been directly attributed, by some, to Margaret Thatcher's return for a third term in office, as a result of the Conservative party's General Election victory of 1987. And certainly, there were many of a left-wing persuasion who, reeling from the hammer blow of unexpected defeat, doubted if the country would ever have a Socialist government again. At this moment, it is theorised, the vast majority of comedians who might otherwise have been that way inclined relegated 'social activism' to the box marked 'youthful idealism' and concentrated on wringing the most fun and money out of life's sponge instead. Thatcher's children, no less.

Doubtless, as the subsequent explosion in the commercial potential of comedy merchandise would attest, there may be something in that. But nor should that greater comfort (complacency?) with regard to archaic attitudes toward race, feminism and sexuality be overlooked. Although in no way eradicated completely, public displays of prejudice were much less socially common or acceptable than they had been a decade or so before. In that sense, there was an unspoken agreement that stringent political correctness was no longer quite so necessary; it had already done its job. In the unreconstructed 'seventies, Bernard Manning had been able to tell jokes about 'Pakis' and 'wogs' and get a big laugh. Try that in front of a audience today and, most likely, you would be met with embarrassed silence. Why bother, then, to manufacture a line in the sand? Comedy, as ever, can be trusted to reflect a society's attitudes back at itself, can't it?

Oh, hang on. What about the former scaffolder, hod carrier, steelworker, barrow boy and petty crook, Roy 'Chubby' Brown?

Born in 1945 in the shadow of a smoke-belching steelworks on an impoverished council estate in Grangetown, near Middlesbrough, Brown - real name Royston Vasey - left a volatile family home aged just 15. By then, constantly in trouble with the law, he had already been abandoned by his mother, aged eight, and would spend his remaining formative years either stumbling through dead-end jobs, living rough or serving in the Merchant Navy (where he was stabbed by an apparently gay chef off the coast of Malta). By his early twenties, this trouble-seeking missile had also found time to get married and divorced, spend a couple of years in the UK's toughest Borstal, Portland, and serve three stretches in prison. The rest of the 1960s and early 'seventies were as harsh, grim and eventful.

Fortunately, along with having a talent for crime, young Roy Vasey was also a nifty drummer, with skills honed in the Thornaby Boys Band. A natural flamboyance as a performer was also made evident when he volunteered to support an elderly female pianist at a local pub, after which he began to take the idea of a career in showbiz more seriously. In Brown's entertaining autobiography *Common As Muck!* (Time Warner, 2006), he recalls that: 'Nancy would sit in the lounge, drinking pints of Guinness (which surely didn't help), and lifting her backside off the stool as she played the piano, farting all the while.' Meanwhile, with their regular drummer away on holiday, his cousin Derek's rock 'n' roll band The Pipeline were looking for a temporary replacement. Roy stood in and did so well that the original incumbent's services were no longer needed. Along with so many groups like them, the newly-named Four Man Band spent the next two years knocking out pub and club standards before reaching the conclusion that more money could be made with comedy in the act, in which the artist soon to be known as 'Chubby' took the lead.

When the Four Man Band split up, Vasey formed a madcap comedy-musical duo with a pal called Mick Boothby, Jason and Everard, which soon filled out into an equally zany group, The Nuts, a band whose dress sense might best be described as surreal - no frilly shirts and dickie bow ties here. For all that he was in a traditional working men's club world, Vasey was already displaying the sort of eye-catching sartorial originality that would mark him out as different to the rest. And crucially, rather

than 'borrowing' everyone else's material as was the usual clubland mode of behaviour, he was also writing his own gags.

In the originality-averse 'seventies northern clubs, of course, that was not necessarily a good thing. In *Common As Muck!*, Brown lays the blame for a dwindling number of dates on the fact that much of The Nuts' stuff was 'utterly tasteless, telling jokes about shit and sex.' It seems equally likely that an act which featured 'a talking bucket that had a big pair of tits painted on the side' might also have gone over one or two heads. Either way, their reputation began to precede them and bookings dried up. With the group disbanded, Roy and two fellow band members reformed as a trio named, somewhat perversely, Alcock and Brown, in honour of celebrated aviators Captain John Alcock and Lieutenant Arthur Whitten Brown, who had first flown the Atlantic non-stop in 1919. The name was further inspired by Roy's recent habit of wearing an old flying helmet on stage. Nor was it long before another soon-to-be familiar item of costume was introduced. Sick of having pints thrown at him by disgruntled punters, Vasey took to wearing a suit made entirely of beer towels, shortly to be replaced by a multi-coloured patchwork job, because 'it looked more professional'. Then, in 1974, the Alcock 'half' of the partnership opted to form a less-stressful part-time act and Brown was left to go it alone.

As it happened, that parting of the ways coincided with Vasey's debut television appearance. Already performing the occasional live solo stint, the one-time jailbird found the tables turned as the policeman who arrested Hartlepool's infamous hung monkey, in a humourous skit for a Tyne Tees show, *Sounds of Britain*. In the event, the item proved even funnier than expected. To the mirth of all but the victim, the chimp in question, borrowed from Scarborough zoo, grabbed the fledgling comic by the testicles and refused to let go. Upon his eventual release, the show's sympathetic producers offered Vasey a studio spot by way of recompense on which, clad in helmet and suit, he performed a version of the Bonzo Dog Doo-Dah Band's 'Jollity Farm'. When asked for a name to go on the programme's credits, he kept the name Brown from Alcock and Brown and threw in his regular nickname Chubby. Roy 'Chubby' Brown had his first official billing.

The original mixed-up kid was finally on the straight and narrow, in a manner of speaking anyway. After having little or no discipline in his youth, from somewhere had arisen enough self-will to read the newspapers and write down at least ten new, original gags per day. Almost entirely, these dealt with the everyday lives of bottom-of-the-heap working class people: '...there was no point in trying to make them laugh with smart-alec jokes and sophisticated witticisms,' Brown admits in *Common As Muck!*. 'Like me, they used humour as a way of getting away from the miserable realities of their lives.' Soon, advice from local north East club comic Johnny Hammond resulted in fewer gags and more stories. Even so, success hardly arrived overnight. An earlier audition for *Opportunity Knocks* had come to naught (largely as a result of his use of the word 'arse'), and soul-destroying gigs in Cumbrian rugby league clubs, down-at-heel social clubs and pit village WMCs hardly hinted at an assault on Butlins Skegness - never mind Las Vegas - anytime soon. Then, in 1976, Chubby Brown had another go at a television talent show: *New Faces*.

This time he sailed through the audition and it proved to be a pivotal moment. Yet it wasn't success that changed the course of Brown's career - he finished second to a country band, Poacher - it was failure. Realising that there was little chance of him ever finding fame or fortune as one clean frilly-shirted comedian among many, he elected to go in the opposite direction entirely. If I cannot get noticed with mainstream material, he reasoned, why not make a name as the crudest, rudest and bluest comedian around? Thus was created a comic persona who would see more people walk out of his shows in disgust than walk *in* elsewhere. A man who has had alsatian dogs set upon him, drink poured over him and who has actually been arrested for fending off audience members - all in the name of comedy. For Chubby Brown, no subject matter would be sacrosanct, with women and their biological workings somewhere near the top of his agenda, most often in far from complimentary terms. An unreconstructed old bigot, then? Well, yes. And no.

For one thing, there is the sheer eccentricity of his image. Not for Chubby Brown, the velvet suit and bling-filled fingers of the standard WMC funny man. Clad in his flying helmet, goggles and harlequin-like suit, here is a comedian who is truly alternative, whatever we may think of his supposed opinions. Perhaps such extreme attire is ironic with a capital 'I'. Although, on the face it, the victims of Chubby Brown gags are

more often than not women, the real targets of his humour are surely himself and the inadequate men in whose confidence he seems to be. 'The thing that swung it for me,' he writes, 'was realising that I had a talent for being filthy - or rather, the Chubby Brown character I'd created could get away with being crude and rude because my stage persona was a hapless fool, a lecherous Billy Bunter who boasted about his virility but was quite obviously a dead loss with women.' And on the subject of size, isn't there at least a hint of Alexei Sayle in the way Brown's live act always opens with the crowd chanting: 'Who ate all the pies? You fat bastard!' Just who is ridiculing who here?

Nor ought it to be ignored that, despite Brown's apparent misogyny, locating women as it does in either the kitchen or the bedroom, his act *is* carried along on an undercurrent of female working class reality. Maybe that is why he attracts such a large percentage of the so-called 'fairer sex' to his shows. The comedy of Chubby Brown is one of self-deprecation and, in his case, foul-mouthed recognition, with the focus on gender relations rather than beer and football. A Chubby Brown concert is said to make for a much better hen night than stag do. A true northern phenomenon then? Well, again, yes and no. As the comedy critic Ben Thompson not unreasonably points out in his book *Sunshine On Putty* (Harper Perennial, 2004): 'The dividing line in terms of Brown's popularity is traditionally portrayed as the soft south versus the naughty north. In fact, it's a class barrier not a geographical one. Chubby has been big in London for years, packing out the Dominion and Hammersmith Apollo...'. And what sizeable audiences they are too. Few comedians, TV stars or otherwise, come close to matching Chubby Brown's ticket sales. For a while there he even outgrew the working men's club and pub circuit, rising stratospherically to the level of a marquee act, largely under the command of a brutally effective agent, George Forster.

Prior to being struck down with throat cancer, from which he has since recovered, Brown's only obvious concession to the old ways was an annual summer season in Blackpool. Otherwise, he spends much of his time engaged upon sell-out national tours, with venues packed primarily through word of mouth. Given the controversial nature of his act, since the days of the Hartlepool monkey television has long been a route less well travelled. Not that Brown himself is worried about that - why should he be? As a producer of his own material, that on-going absence from our screens simply installs him as the first comedian since music hall to enjoy the luxury of not being over-exposed. On top of that, like the less original Bernard Manning before him, his bad lad status merely increases his must-see factor.

And anyway, all of that pre-supposes the ongoing power of traditional television companies, currently in danger of wilting in the white heat of competing technologies. The internet aside, for those in possession of a DVD or video player, for example, there are other ways of watching a favourite comedian on telly. And throughout the 1990s, as comedians and canny agents like George Forster awoke to the wonders of recording live shows, nobody was more prolific in that department than Chubby Brown. The year 1990 saw his first effort, *From Inside The Helmet*, and just about every year since has been marked by the release of a similar best-selling and sexual pun-laden effort. A random selection might include: *The Helmet's Last Stand* (1992), *Jingle Bollocks* (1994), *Clitoris Allsorts* (1995), *Saturday Night Beaver* (1996) and *Too Fat to be Gay* (2009). In 1993, Brown even wrote and appeared in a film, the critically-mauled *U.F.O.* (as in 'You Fuck Off', rather than Unidentified Flying Object), in which he was kidnapped by aliens in Blackpool. Though even its own star described it as 'crap', it did at least include one immortal line, delivered when Brown is asked by a young girl to record a cassette message for her brother, who is lying deep in a coma. 'Get out of bed, you lazy c**t,' the unfortunate youth is told.

The live popularity and exclusion of Chubby Brown notwithstanding, those comedians who did enjoy television exposure throughout the 1990s were far freer than their forebears in terms of what could and could not be joked about on the small screen. As a result, early-seventies-style victim-based humour was soon back on the agenda, covered in a cloak of post-modern irony, although whether or not you got away with it depended a) to which social group your victim belonged or b) the age of the assailant.

All in all, after decades of unpleasant social upheaval, by the early 1990s Britain was finally moving onto something like an even keel, culturally at least. This time, it seemed, the country really *had* never had it so good. And even when the divisive Mrs. Thatcher was hounded from

office in 1990, into her shoes - figuratively speaking - came the personable, cricket-loving and ultimately rather nondescript John Major. Evidence of the extent to which the nation was weary of revolution and just yearning for a bit of peace and quiet came with the General Election of 1992, Major's first as Conservative Party leader. And ironically, it was to be another northern comedy show - Neil Kinnock's infamously over-the-top April Fools Day rally in Sheffield - that would be blamed for snatching yet another Labour defeat from the jaws of victory, as the opposition again fluffed its chance amid too much Nuremberg-style triumphalism.

In the year prior her departure, Thatcher's deregulatory activities had taken further shape in the establishment of satellite television and, more specifically, Rupert Murdoch's Sky TV, which began transmissions in February 1989. Initially, the venture was met by a similar atmosphere of derision to that of the launch of ITV in the 1950s, both with regard to the manner of its funding - i.e. subscription, programme sponsorship, advertising and private ownership - and the quality, or otherwise, of its programming. The BBC's attitude was perhaps best exemplified by a, with hindsight, quite shameless piece of comedy propaganda, *KYTV* (1989), which satirised its satellite competitor on the twin grounds that it was rubbish and that no one would ever watch it anyway. In the *KYTV* line-up were Angus Deayton, the Cheadle Hulme-born Helen Atkinson Wood and future BBC Head of Comedy Geoffrey Perkins, plucked from the latest batch of Oxbridge graduates. Not for the first time, Auntie was wide of the mark - in terms of audience potential at least. Multi-channel viewing would indeed become the norm even if, for now, the BBC and ITV retained their place as market leaders. Even so, by the end of its first year, Sky boasted one million subscribers and, after a merger with British Satellite Broadcasting (BSB) in April 1990 resulted in the formation of a new company, BSkyB, by 1997 that figure had grown to four million, a total which had itself more than doubled to nine or so million by 2009.

Cable television too began to make in-roads, though in nothing like the same initial numbers, and with the birth of Channel 5 in 1997, digital television in 1998 and digital radio in the early 2000s, British broadcasting had discovered a new watchword: choice. By the decade's end, literally hundreds of television and radio channels were available, with over 70 per cent of British homes able to access more than the four traditional terrestrial channels by 2006. Subsequently, a surge in internet and broadband communication technology has ensured that the fragmentation of television, film and radio output continues unabated.

All in all, then, in comedy as elsewhere, Britain remained a land of plenty. And the mood of social complacency only increased with the election of 'New Labour' in 1997, as John Major's government imploded in a welter of scandal, sleaze and corruption, bringing down the curtain on eighteen years of Conservative governance. Under the stewardship of youthful democrat Tony Blair, whose so-called 'third way' meant building upon Thatcherism and Major's talk of a classless society, the atmosphere turned positively hedonistic, as a nation high on pop music and football wallowed in the epithet 'Cool Britannia', a short-lived burst of patriotic and economic self-confidence unseen since Victorian times.

And once again, as in those far-off days of music hall, if you were a British comedian intent on making a national name for yourself, there was one place you needed to go. As England's capital city, London had never stopped being the centre of attention. All the major broadcasters and theatrical impresarios continued to be based there. For a wannabe comic, the explosion in live clubs sparked by alternative comedy in the late 1970s meant that this was where the agents and bookings were, and where a commissioning editor might just be in every audience. Equally, the rise of comedy as a cultural phenomenon meant that capital-based national newspapers and magazines now employed comedy critics who, Edinburgh-apart, rarely wandered further north than Stevenage.

With the approach of the 1990s, the end result of all this London-centric introspection was a certain staleness of style and a disinclination on the part of comics to take genuine risks. Although superficially brash and cutting-edge, live British comedy had become boring. The time was ripe for something less predictable. And, lo! What is that light, glinting from the north? Can it really be two chivalric knights-errant riding into Brixton and beyond on the backs of geese, ducks and other domestic waterfowl? Why, it is! It's Vic Reeves and - at this stage still waddling some distance behind - Bob Mortimer.

At first, few people noticed their arrival. But one who did was the comedy critic Bruce Dessau, in whose biography of the pair, *Reeves &*

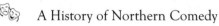

Mortimer (Orion, 1998) he recalls: 'By 1988, Vic and Bob's weekly Thursday evening Big Night Out at the Goldsmiths Tavern in New Cross had become a ritual for South Londoners with a well-defined sense of the absurd.' Ushered on stage by a cassette recording of the Sex Pistols, or maybe a Gregorian chant and always some 'seventies heavy metal, Reeves - '..suited, booted, his hair greased back - he claims with whale blubber' - and his troupe of comedy chums would bodge their way through a manic array of surreal skits and catchphrases, convincing all who were present that they were in on a cast-iron cult, for three hours at a time. Dessau goes on: '[Even] when it wasn't brilliant it was startlingly different from the post-Ben Elton right-on humour that dominated many clubs,' before stating that: 'Even Vic's northern accent made him stand out.' The small but devoted audience, remembers Dessau, usually left confused and delighted at having been part of something highly original.

Original? Well, to a large extent it was - certainly in contrast to the jeans and T-shirt brigade in other London venues. But then again, as we have seen, the juxtaposition of the sacred and mundane had long been a feature of northern English comedy, as displayed in the antics of *Monty Python*, *The Goodies*, Jimmy James, Bobby Thompson, Chubby Brown and the rest. And while Vic and Bob would indeed rewrite the rule book for late-twentieth-century light entertainment, their avant-garde humour had undeniable echoes of a century or so before. Mass consumption - though by now an entirely different phenomenon from that which had carried George Formby Sr. and contemporaries out of this world - was not the only piece of Victoriana enjoying a comeback.

Consider these two musical hall turns popular in the early 1900s. The first, going by the name Artemus and his Gang, were according to *Roy Hudd's Cavalcade of Variety Acts*, a knockabout slapstick magic act. The eponymous Artemus (Arthur Hayes) and his 'Incompetent Assistants' would indulge in a frenzied onstage roustabout as bizarre as it was fun. Among their routines: 'The scruffy boy holding a block of ice throughout the act, the lady sleepwalking across the stage and the boy in the audience sitting on a needle....'. Or how about Burnley's Bob Nelson - born Rupert Lambert in 1893 - whose best-known catchphrase was: 'Aren't plums cheap?' Nelson, presumably adopting the nearby town of that name as his stage moniker, was a real character. 'He would open by staggering on stage carrying a huge cannon ball,' writes Hudd's co-writer, Philip Hindin. 'This he would drop onto the stage (and almost through it). Later he would spend time trying to catch it on the back of his neck. The rest of his turn was taken up with a futile attempt to climb up a pile of chairs.'

Come the 1990s, of course, the antics of Artemus and Nelson were all but forgotten, so the gleeful reaction to the novelty of Vic and Bob was entirely understandable. And given that they were performing in London rather than Blackpool or Bridlington, the capital's comedy cognoscenti were bound to catch on eventually. The result of that interest, in May 1990, was a spot for *Vic Reeves Big Night Out* on television.

From the start, *Vic Reeves Big Night Out* shook TV comedy to its cuban-heeled boots, dividing generations and opinion in equal measure. The more open-minded, young and old, considered its weird flights of fancy inspired. Lines like 'I don't stock [the chocolate bar] Curly Wurlys, I find them far too elaborate' would surely have done Les Dawson proud. Others saw the show as self-indulgent clap-trap. Either way, fronted by a well-dressed fop who styled himself Britain's 'top light entertainer and singer', and boasted a look that was part Andy Williams, part Las Vegas era Elvis and part Batley Variety Club refugee, there was nothing else like it in the schedules. Whether it be giant digestive biscuits, a foul-mouthed fox named Allan Davidson or Spandau Ballet laughing at an orphan who had fallen off his bike, no everyday object or mainstream television star was too banal for ridicule.

Given its Friday night broadcasting slot of 10.30 p.m. on Channel 4, the level of outrage and antagonism whipped up by *Vic Reeves Big Night Out* is nowadays hard to fathom. And certainly, out-and-out revolution seems never to have been part of the plan. Both Reeves and Mortimer have insisted that, far from seeking to overturn any existing formula, they were simply trying to make each other laugh. So when a man who played a major role in the rise of Vic Reeves to television prominence, Jonathan Ross, declared that *Vic Reeves Big Night Out* '...marked the end of comedy having to be about something' during the somewhat hysterical BBC documentary *When Comedy Changed Forever* in 2006, he was surely on to something. Although Jimmy James's lion in a box might beg to differ.

Vic Reeves - aka James Roderick Moir - was born in Leeds in January 1959. According to his characteristically idiosyncratic autobiography,

543

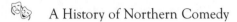

Me:Moir (Virgin, 2006), young Vic - or Rod as he is known to his family, and Jim to his friends - was of an unorthodox mein from the get-go. He yearned to own a pet crow, hid uneaten vegetables in his pockets before depositing them down the lavatory and rather more conventionally, on more than one occasion fell out of a tree (not the same tree, obviously). Self-written in the style of one of Spike Milligan's better literary efforts, *Me:Moir* is a highly recommended treat.

In 1964, after father Neill left his job as a linotype operator with the *Yorkshire Post* and found work on the *Northern Echo* instead, the Moir clan upped sticks and left Leeds for Darlington, the same town, interestingly enough, where that other great absurdist Lewis Carroll, though born in Cheshire, spent many of his formative years. For Reeves, it seems to have been an idyllic childhood marked by hearty country walks, laughter in the home and a bunch of friends who, going by his own account, were just as puddled as he was. As a red-haired teenager he discovered a taste for music and what can only be described as unusual modes of dress, along with a talent for art that continues to serve him well to this day. As with many of his generation, the most influential televisual event of these early years was the arrival of *Monty Python's Flying Circus* in 1969. In Darlington as elsewhere, public displays of lunacy were now worn like a badge of honour. Even so, other than a brief and unlikely spell as a teenage pig castrater, there was little to mark Rod Moir as a comedy star of the future. And with his schooldays over it was off to SAB Brake Regulators in nearby Newton Aycliffe, to serve a five-year factory apprenticeship.

Despite winning Apprentice of the Year and, he later revealed in *Me:Moir*, inadvertently loading the lorry of the Yorkshire Ripper, steady employment and Jim Moir were not to be comfortable bedfellows. Having by now learned to play the guitar and later the saxophone, the membership of bands increasingly took up his time. One initially non-musical group of which he was a founding member became known (among themselves anyway) as the Fashionable Five, a collection of fellow Darlington Technical College students with whom an already outlandish sense of humour veered more obviously towards actual performance. In 1979, with Reeves having quit the factory and the Fashionable Five now operating as an experimental musical group, the quintet decided to try their luck in London. Band member Graham Bristow, in the pay of the

Civil Service, got his pals work in the Brixton department of the DHSS and all five lived together while they decided what to do next. It was while on long weekends at East Anglia university during this period, visiting an old friend from Darlington, that Jim's path first crossed with a student named Charles Higson - of whom more in a nonce.

In time, when the Fashionable Five dissolved as a performing group, four of its members would either return north or embark upon some other road to conventional middle-age. Jim, meanwhile, having now left the DHSS and a job as an aircraft parts inspector in Croydon, gained employment in the Charing Cross Road branch of Our Price records where, in 1981, he met Tom Fawcett. Fawcett, the store manager, was also the member of an Indie band whose single was currently a favourite of John Peel on Radio 1. Soon, the pair produced music cassettes of their own, before forming a duo, Fawcett and Moir, and then a band, Design for Living, followed by live gigs and their own record label, Boy Smells. When all that turned sour, Reeves began to drift aimlessly from group to group and indulge himself in noise-based performance art. Still, though, no sign of out-and-out comedy. Then he moved to New Cross.

At first, life continued to meander in pretty much the same aimless and indisciplined way. Increasingly a well-known eccentric figure around town, he changed bands as frequently as his hair colour. He even worked for a time as an art gallery assistant, displaying his own artistic endeavours in a Lewisham council-backed exhibition. 'It all seemed to be based around large, overweight pigs,' the owner's wife, Jo Gapper, tells Bruce Dessau in *Reeves & Mortimer*. 'But there was no theme to it except that everything he did had a twist. It was very bizarre, very *Monty Python-y...*'. The comedy voice, it seemed, was calling and, during Christmas 1985, Jim Moir took a first tentative step in that direction at an alternative cabaret night in the Goldsmiths Tavern's Parrot Café.

Even then, although his offbeat combination of poetry and stories did well enough to earn repeat bookings, music was still the ambitious Reeves's route to the top of choice. In 1986, he took over as manager of Winstons, a night club in a wine bar in Deptford. Unfortunately, filling the place on a regular basis proved trickier than expected and it was only when he decided to jump on the band wagon and start a comedy night, during which he himself took to the stage under the pseudonym *Vic*

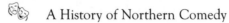

Reeves Variety Palladium, that its doors were more consistently troubled. Even then, at first, Winston's customers did not quite know what to make of a northerner in ruffs, holding a stick in the air that had a carrot perched on its end. Adrift in an ocean of right-on blandness, the comedy-going public of South London struggled to understand. Not, in truth, that there *was* much to understand. Anyway, the comedian now known as Vic and his zany co-star pals seemed to be enjoying themselves. And it wasn't long before enough people were tuned to his wavelength to suggest that something exciting might be in the air. So much so that, buoyed by his growing fame, when the Winston's residency came to an end Reeves retained his new comedy persona. Under the title *Big Night Out*, he began a Thursday night spot at the scene of his earlier debut, Goldsmiths Tavern, where for an audience fuelled by a late-night drinks licence, amusement finally began to banish bemusement.

On its opening night, the crowd at that venue included a hard-up Middlesbrough-born solicitor named Bob Mortimer, there to see what all the fuss was about. Despite their shared geography, the orbit of Reeves and Mortimer had thus far failed to collide, although, as a chapter in *Me:Moir* relates, it later turned out that they had unknowingly attended the same prog-rock Camel concert in the mid-1970s, in which the seeds of a future Vic and Bob favourite, the 'Dove from Above', were sown. More importantly, they also had a mutual friend, Bob's former school mate Alan King, who now also lived in South London and was an occasional member of Vic's team, most memorably in the guise of 'seventies electropop icon Jean Michel Jarre, complete with miner's helmet and torches. It was King who invited Mortimer along to see the *Big Night Out* where, despite an approximate audience of twelve, Bob was immediately won over. Unlike Reeves, whose comic influences tended to begin and end with *Python*, *Stingray*, the countryside champion Jack Hargreaves and assorted black and white Will Hay comedies, Mortimer was also clued up on contemporary comedy. Like Reeves, he had a typically northern predilection for the absurd and, despite having displayed no previous ambition as a performer, was soon up there on stage himself.

Born in May 1959 and the youngest of four brothers, Bob Mortimer knew better than most how illogical life can be. His father, Charles, had been a sales representative who died in a car crash before his son had reached 10 years of age. Thereafter, Bob's mother, Eunice, worked and raised their four children alone. Mortimer's juvenile years were divided between football, the usual mischief and playing in rocks bands, echoing his future comedy partner's own upbringing (minus the football). Later on, he worked for a while as a dustman before, in 1977, heading off to study law at Sussex University and then moving back to the north East to take up a job at Stockton Law Centre, specialising in housing. After which, he completed his higher education in Leicester and Manchester and washed up, somewhat disillusioned and penniless, in London. Once introduced to the man who, at that stage, was still only 'the north East's top light entertainer', an unshakeable friendship began, on stage and off.

By the time of his first trip to the Goldsmiths Tavern, Bob Mortimer had grown somewhat disenchanted with the law courts. Consciously or otherwise, he was itching to put his oratory skills and quick wit to more imaginative use. In the end, it took him about six weeks to find the courage to give it a go but, when he did, one of his earliest contributions was memorable indeed. Step forward the 'Man with the Stick', whose bizarrely illustrated paper mask and catchphrase 'What's on the end of the stick, Vic?', would become the stuff of comedy legend. For the time being, however, Mortimer continued with his 'real' job during the day.

Nevertheless, it was soon apparent that the Vic and Bob dynamic was blossoming, despite the presence of a whole host of pals and drinking buddies in the line-up. The best known of these was Fred Aylward who, as the bald, silent Les, fearful of chives but given strength by the sight of a spirit level, enjoyed great popularity. The extent to which ex-law student Bob's influence was being felt, meanwhile, can perhaps best be seen in the arrival of Judge Nutmeg, punisher of random crime, whose fluffy wheel of justice would be spun, spun, spun to cries of 'comb its hair'. Influenced by Winston's comedy night regular Jools Holland, by now a friend, a greater emphasis on sartorial elegance became a feature too. And, as the duo's confidence in the format and Mortimer's disciplined influence grew, a wealth of new nonsensical characters spewed forth like silent clowns Talc and Turnip, Graham Lister, Pippin (later Morrissey) the consumer monkey and Wavy Davy, who waved at everyone and everything and was finally revealed to be Satan. Most, if not all, of those and more came with their very own catchphrases - 'You couldn't (later,

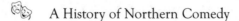

wouldn't) let it lie' and 'very poor', being among them. It all gave *Big Night Out* the chaotic, but now more structured, air of the post-modern Variety extravaganza it was always intended to be.

For all Bob's steadying input, Reeves remained the headline act; as confirmed when, in 1986, Jools Holland gave the lad from Darlington his debut television break on Channel 4's music show, *The Tube*, recorded in Newcastle, which Holland fronted with Paula Yates. As host of a spoof quiz insert, 'Square Celebrities', suspended on wires and clad in white jacket with a black DA, Reeves - ahead of his time as usual - cut a suitably offbeat figure but made no lasting impact. Still, the idea of firing silly questions at minor celebrities would not go away and nor would Reeves himself, who immediately threw himself back into the world of the South London comedy scene where his reputation for eccentricity continued to grow. Then, in 1988, he was introduced to the burgeoning media bigwig, Jonathan Ross.

Playing middleman between the pair was Ross's brother Adam, a comedy entrepreneur at whose club Reeves had dee-jayed. After a shaky start, in which Jonathan apparently mistook Bob for Vic's boyfriend, Reeves was invited to perform a cameo on the Channel 4 show *The Last Resort* whose presenter, Ross himself, was currently being touted as Britain's answer to David Letterman or at least a 1980s Simon Dee. Here, Reeves was a farmer chatting about odd-shaped vegetables but, once again, the supposed comedy backfired and left his audience baffled.

Fortunately, just as Vic's fledgling television career was fizzing like a catherine wheel on a Tijuana donkey, the live *Big Night Out* experience took another big leap forward. It moved from the Goldsmiths Tavern to the way more theatrically impressive Albany Empire in Deptford, where a comely desk now appeared on stage in place of the previous lectern. A house band, too, was introduced, allowing Vic to sign off with a nightly burst of his easy listening classic 'Oh! Mr Songwriter' ('write me a song, on your trumpet...'). Installed at the Albany, the *Big Night Out* rocketed in popularity. So much so that, at the instigation of one of his Channel X production company colleagues, Ross was soon sniffing around again. Prompted by that appearance on *The Tube*, Charlie Higson, having long since left East Anglia and by now contributing scripts to Harry Enfield's television show, was another to turn up in the company of writing partner Paul Whitehouse. Whitehouse later told Bruce Dessau: 'They stood out because there weren't any northern, working class voices in comedy then.' After seeing the final *Big Night Out* gig at the Goldsmiths Tavern, Higson and Whitehouse started to join in themselves, whether as contestants on the 'talent show' Novelty Island or in some other supporting role. As anarchic as ever on the surface, a show that had once been one man and his gang was becoming distinctly professional.

And soon, thanks again to Ross, Vic had a third TV appearance to contend with. In 1989, *One Hour With Jonathan Ross* was launched, a chat-cum-Variety entertainment comedy spectacular. The format, no doubt inspired by Reeves's own stage show, was perfect for the up and coming cult comic and this time Bob took part too (as a bearded social worker, amongst other things). The *Celebrity Squares*-style quiz that passed without notice on *The Tube* was revised and renamed 'Knock Down Ginger', the name of an American prank wherein children knock on doors and run away. Only, in this case, instead of being run away from, each inhabitant of what appeared to be a block of council flats was subjected to a surreal, insane question from Vic.

Though hardly the greatest television comedy moment of all time, 'Knock Down Ginger' did provide the key to a door marked 'own series'. To the men in suits, he looked suspiciously like the next big thing. For the moment, Vic Reeves was neither nationally famous nor infamous. But all that was about to change. At the end of a protracted bidding war between Michael Grade's Channel 4 and Alan Yentob's BBC in May 1990, the first series of *Vic Reeves Big Night Out* took its place in the Channel 4 schedules, co-produced by Jonathan Ross and Alan Marke, his Channel X co-founder. For Reeves, fame was fast becoming reality and an indication of the anticipation shared by long-time fans of the live show was most obviously seen in the way that, earlier that same week, the *New Musical Express* newspaper went so far as to plaster his face across its front cover; an unprecedented honour for a comedian. Never mind the north East, here indeed was a candidate for the epithet Britain's top light entertainer as advertised. Comedy, with Vic Reeves at the forefront, really was about to become the new rock 'n' roll.

Given the profound influence of *Vic Reeves Big Night Out*, it might be expected that initial ratings for the show were tremendous. In fact, as

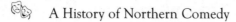

with *Monty Python's Flying Circus* two decades before, the very opposite was true. As with the stage show, the programme's immediate reputation was built upon word of mouth and the feeling among those who did tune in that they were privy to a weird and wonderful secret. Nevertheless, despite its innovatory feel, the old-fashioned premise of *Vic Reeves Big Night Out* - recorded at a studio in Wandsworth, complete with Morecambe and Wise-style stage and curtains for that true Variety feel - was there from the opening credits. To the backing of a cheesy theme tune, Vic, Bob and Les cavorted in cartoonish triplicate before an urbane announcer intoned: 'Ladies and Gentlemen, Britain's top light entertainer, Vic Reeves.' Whereupon Vic, seated behind a small lounge bar decorated in horse brasses, would introduce turn after ridiculous turn, many played by Bob, but with sterling support from Fred Aylward as Les and occasional turns from Charlie Higson, Paul Whitehouse and a landscape gardener-turned-comedian Simon Day. The latter had been another contributor to those earlier live productions in London and, much later, he paid tribute to Vic's courage: 'It was like me going to Wigan and starting a Cockney knees-up,' he told Bruce Dessau.

On television, it was difficult at first to say just who was supposed to be Vic's sidekick, or whether he actually had one at all. Bob enjoyed the greater screen time, but wasn't Les supposed to be Reeves's assistant? In the pilot, never shown, Aylward's character had been described as Vic's 'partner', but on the intervention of script editor Jack Docherty the Reeves and Mortimer combination soon began to dominate. For Bob, that was just as well. He had taken a twelve-week sabbatical from his job as a solicitor to make the show and, as things turned out, never returned. Fred Aylward, however, was not so lucky. In *Reeves & Mortimer*, Dessau quotes an interview which Aylward gave to the London listings magazine *Time Out* in 1993, in which Vic's former assistant claims to have been passed a note saying: 'I just want to work with Bob.' Not surprisingly, the beneficiary of that decision sees things differently: '...you couldn't gather a load of people and take them along for ever.' Aylward, it seems, was just one of many who, by the time the second and final series ended in 1991, had outlived his artistic usefulness.

They Wouldn't Let it Lie

Whatever anyone else thought about it, for Vic and Bob it was onward and upward. A New Year special was followed by an appearance on *Comic Relief*, a second series of *Vic Reeves Big Night Out* and, in June 1992, the making of a sitcom, *The Weekenders*, the reaction to which was entirely in keeping with the reaction to everything else so far. Viewers and critics were divided roughly down the middle, usually, though by no means exclusively, on a generational basis. On *Vic Reeves Big Night Out*, for example, promised guests such as 'a family of trained puffins' or, even less likely, Sean Connery had seldom arrived as billed, with cardboard cut-outs maybe taking their place. Some found that amusing. Others, such as future Reeves and Mortimer collaborator and *Little Britain* co-creator Matt Lucas, did not. It has since been reported that Lucas, then a student, was outraged by such antics after watching the first show and rang in to complain. By week three, he was a self-confessed addict.

Easier to laugh at was the duo's penchant for daft costumes and a brand of slapstick violence that, for imagination, matched Rik, Ade, Tom *and* Jerry. For Vic and Bob, physical assault with a frying pan or some other household implement was an occupational hazard, usually leading to profoundly bizarre injuries. Very early on in the *Big Night Out*, the pair explicitly recognised their debt to Eric and Ernie too, most obviously when Vic, clad in raincoat, flat cap and carrier bag in hand, enters stage left, glasses askew, before shouting 'wahay' and slapping his very own 'little Ern' Bob (or is it 1980s pop warbler Rick Astley?) roundly about the chops. In the stage show, Bob had returned the compliment dressed as a giant lobster. Yet for all their devotion to the Variety format, given the decade of ridicule for traditional light entertainment just passed, it was perhaps inevitable that such homages would not be taken in the spirit intended. In a televised tribute show in September 2000, for example, no less a figure than Ronnie Barker took umbrage at their version of Eric and Ernie's celebrated 'Yeah, Yeah, Yeah' routine, performed with its original guest, the Welsh singer and underwear collector Tom Jones. Though forgiveable, Barker's criticism was wide of the mark. Behind all that obscure messing around, Vic Reeves and Bob Mortimer were about nothing less than a return to the old values.

Ronnie Barker was not alone in failing to get the joke. Mainstream audiences, in general, were often blind to the affection that lay at the

heart of these latest young upstarts' act. And those who saw Vic and Bob simply as purveyors of self-indulgent tosh found more ammunition in *The Weekenders* when it aired. Contributing one episode to Channel 4's *Bunch of Five* pilot sitcom strand (which also featured efforts by Higson and Whitehouse, and Frank Skinner), Vic and Bob - or Jim and Bob as they were called in the programme - had high hopes of the idea running to a full series. Why it never did so must remain a mystery. Certainly, by Vic and Bob's standards, the outline was conventional enough: two friends visit a meat festival in a field and buy a sausage from Human League frontman Phil Oakey. A passing trio of aliens then try and steal said snorker, in order to feed it to their queen.

The setback would be survived - and how. The pair's pulling-power had already been confirmed by a wildly popular tour towards the end of 1991. *The Big Night Out Brown Tour* ran in tandem with a move into pop music that Vic had begun with his suitably eclectic album, *I Will Cure You* and a cover of the Matt Monro standard, 'Born Free'. When Reeves then released a remake of Tommy Roe's 1969 hit 'Dizzy', made in association with the Wonder Stuff, the single actually reached number one in the UK charts - heady heights for a man who used to work in a record shop. Later, in 1995, a cover of the Monkees' 'I'm A Believer', this time helped along by the Indie dance band EMF, gave him a third hit single. It was now clear that the younger generation, in particular, saw Reeves and Mortimer as something akin to pop stars, especially in the provinces. As Charlie Higson later put it on the BBC's *Comedy Connections*: 'It has always slightly mystified me that Vic and Bob were seen as this impenetrable weird surrealist act. I think that was mainly the perception of southerners. Northerners always accepted them as just a couple of funny guys.' But whatever the whys and wherefores, one-time Variety theatres were again packed to the rafters for big-time comedy and, as awake as ever to a chance missed the first time around, the Beeb soon muscled back in.

Despite or maybe even because of the often hysterical public reaction to *Vic Reeves Big Night Out*, on tour or TV, its two stars were wearying swiftly of the catchphrases and characters that had thus far served them so well. There seems also to have been a lingering disgruntlement towards Channel 4 who, rather than developing and promoting *The Weekenders* as a natural progression, wanted nothing more than a third series of the show already in their schedules. So when Auntie came calling, she found the duo in receptive mood. The upshot, in 1993, was *The Smell of Reeves and Mortimer*, in which Bob now joined Vic behind the desk, *Two Ronnies*-style, and earlier *Big Night Out* favourites were culled mercilessly. There were two survivors, Donald and Davey Stott, a pair of bickering northern brothers with masking tape moustaches. But even then, they had to wait until the second series in 1995 before rejoining the repertoire. A song about the weird and wonderful things the pair liked to sniff, performed in that original never-aired *Big Night Out* pilot, called 'Let's Have A Look At It' was also rehashed as the theme tune. Otherwise, it was out with the old and in with the new.

Owing to greater BBC resources, *The Smell of Reeves and Mortimer* had an altogether classier look than its predecessor. The main set, resplendent with classical Ionic pillars set off by the giant black letters 'R' and 'M', was almost wholly white, while the improved production values also allowed for Pythonesque inserts, such as the inspired 'Slade In Residence', a spoof of pioneering reality show *The Family*, wherein Vic, Bob, Whitehouse and Mark Williams masqueraded as the glam rock band in question, arguing like spoilt children and addicted to Cup-a-Soup. Other new characters included a pair of aggressive bra-wearing Geordies, Pat Wright and Dave Arrowsmith, the folk-singing duo Mulligan (complete with breasts) and O'Hare, farting French Petomanes Le Corbusier et Papin, and miniature agony aunts Otis Redding and Marvin Gaye, who lived in a cupboard. In the second series, around eighteen months later, the roster was bolstered by corrupt Aldington On Sea councillors Cox and Evans, the Stott brothers and optimistic children's entertainer Tom Fun. Adding to the lunacy across both series was a bloke who wandered around in search of booze for his baby - eliciting the horrified response, 'you can't give booze to a baby' (although sometimes Bob would give it a cigarette) - and the wild-haired, wrinkled and distinctly unnerving Uncle Peter, aka former Butlins comedian Charlie Chuck.

How to describe Charlie Chuck? As he roamed here and there in his battered jacket and moth-eaten bow tie, ejaculating the catchphrase 'Donkey!' and other such random incomprehensibles, Chuck (real name Dave Kear) was a sight to behold. Goodness only knows what the happy campers at Skegness and Filey made of him. Maybe that's where he got

another of his lines: 'Stop it, you're frightening me.' By the early 1990s, this most individual of comedians had somehow made his way to the Edinburgh Fringe, which is exactly where Bob Mortimer found him playing to a baffled audience of virtually none. The act, such as it was, largely consisted of him waving a large plank around and smashing up a drum kit (in perfect four-four time). Once ensconced on *The Smell of Reeves and Mortimer*, Charlie Chuck spent much of his time begging not to be sent back 'to t' dark place' and appeared to be in relentless pursuit of something called a 'cakey pig'.

Another feature of *The Smell of Reeves and Mortimer* was its penchant for ridiculous musical numbers and equally absurd send-ups of television staples like *Food And Drink*, in which expectorating wine buff Oz Clarke was portrayed as a love-struck owl. Most memorable in that department was a second-series spoof of competitive cookery show *Masterchef*, Vic and Bob's finest television hour to date. With Vic as the Bostonian restaurant critic Lloyd Grossman, all strangulated vowels and hovering one and a half inches above the ground, here was the ultimate marriage of parody and surreal weirdness. Visually, it was astonishing; nothing less than a grotesque live-action Ralph Steadman cartoon. Grossman, for example, had a bulbous air-filled head and cutlery for fingers. Bob played one of the contestants, a creepy-looking spiv with a tiny button nose unfeasibly close to his forehead who baked a shoe cake. Matt Lucas, now on the road to superstardom himself after also being 'discovered' by Mortimer during an open-mike spot at a North London club called the VD clinic in 1992, was a toff in a dinner suit who lifted a silver salver to reveal Charlie Higson's bare backside, and Scottish comedian Morwenna Banks played a woman whose severed ears were an ingredient in a dish representing Jesus.

Although ratings for *The Smell of Reeves and Mortimer* were healthy, it could not yet be judged to have made a mainstream breakthrough. Even so, thanks to Vic and Bob, a dam of sorts had been broken and into the surreal breach flowed Harry Hill (a former Albany devotee, whose eponymous show on Channel 4 from 1997 was pretty much *Vic Reeves Big Night Out* without Vic and Bob), Graham Linehan and Arthur Mathews's *Father Ted*, and a national institution waiting to happen: *The Fast Show*.

They Wouldn't Let it Lie

A scatter-gun collection of characters and catchphrases and the bastard offspring of *ITMA*, from its launch in 1994 *The Fast Show* gave a showcase to a number of performers who had been or would become a part of Vic and Bob's entourage. Chief among them were the show's originators, Charlie Higson and Paul Whitehouse. Simon Day and Mark Williams were in there too, as was a brilliant young Mancunian named Caroline Aherne, who had made a very brief appearance on *Vic Reeves Big Night Out* in 1990. Aherne's national TV debut proper was in the guise of her comical nun, Sister Mary Immaculate, on the BBC stand-up show *Paramount City* (1990-91), which also, in its second series, featured Day's music hall comic Tommy Cockles. Making up the numbers were Arabella ('Does my bum look big in this?') Weir and Aherne's fellow Mancunian emigrée, John Thomson.

As with Caroline Aherne, Thomson's talents came to the attention of *The Fast Show* creators on *Paramount City*, when he performed in the same edition as Whitehouse and Day. Though a fairly conventional stand-up in those days, he nevertheless had an ability to put an appealing, irreverent spin on received comic wisdom - alternative and traditional - through his aforementioned Bernard Manning-esque character, Bernard Right-on. Thomson's primary ambition, however, was to act and as he would many years later tell an episode of *Comedy Connections*, the only reason he was doing stand-up in the first place was to get an equity card: 'I didn't want to do some sad clowning act.' Initially, those thespian muscles were stretched on Vic and Bob's *The Weekenders*, in which Thomson played a police constable, Day a slow-motion copper and Whitehouse - in his own proper acting debut - an attitudinally-challenged bus driver.

Born Patrick Francis McAleer in 1969, John Thomson was adopted as a child and grew up around Preston. Upon leaving school, he studied drama at Manchester Polytechnic and while there met a fellow student who would go on to have a key role in his future, Steve Coogan. Soon, Coogan and Thomson were partners-in-comedy and, in time, began to contribute voices to *Spitting Image*. Eventually, that led to a 1994 role for Thomson as Fat Bob in *The Paul Calf Video Diary*, a New Years Day special which fleshed out Coogan's earlier appearances as Calf - a student-hating northern waster, catchphrase: 'bag of shite' - on shows like *Paramount City*

and *London Underground* (1992). Thomson reprised Fat Bob in Coogan's full-length sequel *Three Fights, Two Weddings And A Funeral* the following Christmas. And his acting abilities were put to further good use in *The Fast Show*.

Perhaps John Thomson's best known contribution to a programme crammed with instantly memorable routines - Ted and Ralph, 'jumpers for goalposts', 'suit you, sir', phlegm machine Bob Fleming, 'very, very drunk', Swiss Toni among them - was his super smooth Jazz Club host Louis Balfour. Adrift in a sea of cigar smoke and beneath his ill-fitting pudding bowl wig, the terminally laid-back Balfour greeted every screech and blare with a solitary 'great' or 'nice'. Rather more in the way of acting was required as long-suffering husband Roy, perpetually embarrassed by his atrocious wife Renee (Caroline Aherne) who, with her Su Pollard hair-do, outsized specs and cutting tongue, would probe him with a 'what did I say, Roy?' while engaged in one-way conversations with total strangers. Thomson's other characters included American hippy science Professor Denzil Dexter, a deaf stuntman named Chip Cobb and Yuppie football fan Roger Nouveau. As well as with Renee, Aherne played a Spanish weathergirl for whom every day was 'Scorchio!'; the optimistic if sackless Janine Carr; a supermarket check-out operative who loudly discusses the merits of every purchase ('Ribbed condoms? Very thoughtful') and a dim-witted barmaid for whom the most obvious things are a mystery.

Well before the eventual demise of *The Fast Show* in 2000, both Aherne and Thomson had built fine comedic reputations in their own right. For Caroline Aherne, that was largely down to her involvement in a sitcom that had every bit as groundbreaking an effect on that genre as Reeves and Mortimer would manage on Variety. For John Thomson, it was the result of an increasing presence in comedy drama, most notably in the hugely popular ITV series *Cold Feet* (1997-2003), *Blackpool* (2004) and, most recently, the Sunday night Stephen Fry vehicle *Kingdom* and - of course - *Coronation Street*.

Meanwhile, back in 1993, and shortly after the debut series of *The Smell of Reeves and Mortimer* had reached its conclusion, Vic and Bob were entrusted with an entire evening of Boxing Day programming on BBC2. This one-off festive special was entitled *At Home With Vic and Bob* and it allowed the eponymous duo to link favourite old television programmes, intermingled with homegrown characters like Mulligan and O'Hare, bra-wearing Pat Wright and Dave Arrowsmith, 'Slade at Christmas' and more. And staying true to Mortimer's predilection for offering a helping hand to left-field talent, one other contribution - 'The Christmas Orphan' was provided by Yamaha PSS680 maestro John Shuttleworth, otherwise known as Graham Fellows.

Fellows, whose childhood was spent in Sheffield, had first had a sniff of the big time as long ago as 1978, when his novelty single 'Jilted John' reached number four in the charts. A simple story of thoroughly fed-up teenager John, ditched by his girlfriend Julie in favour of the cool, trendy and moronic Gordon, 'Jilted John' chimed perfectly with the prevailing punk mood. Alas, his follow-up concept album, *True Love Stories*, was less successful and thereafter Fellows poured his efforts into a straight(ish) acting career. Like Thomson and Coogan, he had prepared for it at the Manchester Polytechnic School of Theatre only, in his case, at exactly the same time as Rik Mayall and Ade Edmondson were busy hanging from ceilings in that city's university. Acting work, though, proved tricky to come by, despite a couple of stints on *Coronation Street* in 1979 and 1982. And eventually a future in comedy was born when, in the 1980s, Fellows was given some demo tapes to listen to by a record company A&R man. As revealed on his alter ego's official website, the cassettes in question were full of nervous middle-aged hopefuls introducing themselves thus: 'Hello, here are some songs which I hope you will consider with your professional ear..'. Terrible as they were, Fellows also concluded that there was 'something very noble, magnificent and honest about these attempts.' After recording a spoof tape of his own, he was encouraged to take the idea further.

In 1993, rebranded as the older but hardly wiser John Shuttleworth, a fifty-something ex-security guard and wannabe singer-songwriter, in roll neck sweater, leather coat and national health glasses, Fellows returned to the nation's television screens with a regular spot on *Saturday Zoo*, after having been shortlisted for a Perrier Award in Edinburgh the year before. By now, and again largely as a result of Reeves and Mortimer's influence, the prevailing comedy mood was one of offbeat fun rather than politics, so again his highly original blend of musical self-delusion and provincial mundanity was ideally suited to the times. So much so that, in October of that year, he and his fictional family were unleashed upon BBC Radio 4 in *The Shuttleworths*, an epic wireless comedy that ran to four series and nine specials over the following decade. In 1994, Fellows made six weekly hour-long shows for Radio 1 called *Shuttleworth's Showtime*, along with numerous guest spots alongside Mark and Lard and another Radio 4 series, *Radio Shuttleworth*, in 1998 and 2000. And the great man appears to have plenty of life left in him yet. In 1996, *John Shuttleworth's Open Mind* consisted of five half-hour Radio 4 shows in which our hero turned his attentions to such long-standing mysteries as ghosts, vampires, fairies, UFOs and the Bermuda Triangle.

Though Shuttleworth is far and away his finest creation, Graham Fellows has other characters in his repertoire too. His part-time lecturer in media studies, Brian Appleton, for example, is another splendid example of the comically deluded. Appleton's monologues, broadcast on radio as *Brian Appleton's History of Rock 'n' Roll*, in which he outlines his own massive influence upon the history of popular music, all the while complaining about how he has been ripped off by just about every rock and pop star imaginable, verge on the sublime. Take this gem, lifted from a lecture in which Appleton relates how the late Pink Floyd member Syd Barrett, out of his head on LSD, had gone home, fed the cat and locked his girlfriend in the spare room for three days, feeding her nothing but cream crackers under the door. 'Mind you,' Appleton reasons, 'what else could he have fed her? Ryvitas, I suppose, but she wasn't on a diet...'. Dave Tordoff, a builder and concrete floor specialist from Goole, is an equally imaginative combination of everyday northern observation and surreal lampoon.

Immaculate attention to detail is the key. In Shuttleworth's case, the listener is lured into a world also inhabited by John's wife Mary, teenage offspring Karen and Darren, and his untrustworthy manager and agent Ken Worthington, aka 'TV's Clarinet Man' (the result, we are told, of an ultimately unsuccessful appearance on *New Faces*), each voiced by Fellows himself. The Shuttleworth family home is one marked by DIY, porcelain splash-backs and ping pong. It is a place where a full-scale domestic crisis might be brought about by two simultaneously open cartons of margarine and where objects and situations which would dip beneath the radar of most sane individuals assume Biblical proportions. Like Alan Bennett,

Victoria Wood and Vic Reeves before him, the language of John Shuttleworth is awash with the stilted, everyday provincial poetry of pub carvery, Comet salesroom and out-of-town garden centre. Nowhere is that more apparent than in his song titles, which bear such legendary epithets as 'Pigeons In Flight' (a failed Eurovision Song Contest entry), 'Incident At Snake Pass' (located on the A57 between Manchester and Sheffield, rather than Arizona) and a deep psychological treatment of mood swings, 'Up And Down Like A Bride's Nightie'.

A further flavour can be found in the early *Shuttleworths* episode, 'Mini-Break in Giggleswick', wherein John is left to his own devices at the B&B while wife and daughter go on a shopping expedition to Skipton. As he contemplates going for a lager with Ken, Shuttleworth composes a song, 'The Bee And The Wasp', inspired by son Darren's swatting of a bee in the bay window (note, not just *any* old window - a 'bay' window). 'Go down on your knee to the honey bee, for she is very nice,' John warbles to the accompaniment of cheesy samba rhythms. 'Before you kill her, with a rolled up *Mirror*, think twice. How will that bee's mother feel when she finds out her child is a ghost? Kill the bee, and ultimately, you'll have nothing to spread on your toast.' Your wasp, on the other hand, devoid of all such apiarian delights, is expendable.

In 2005, Shuttleworth, the ultimate cult, even appeared in his own feature film, shot by the renowned stills photographer Martin Parr. In *It's Nice Up North* that hypothesis is put to the test when our intrepid social commentator travels all the way up to the Shetland Islands in his trusty Austin Ambassador. So dryly convincing were his exploits to some that the Edinburgh Film Festival declined to show the movie, having already filled their slots, they said, in the documentary section. Ultimately, however, Graham Fellows's greatest achievement may well be the way in which his one-man flights of fancy have helped to reinvigorate radio as *the* place to find superbly-drawn character comedy. It is unlikely that the listening figures for *The Shuttleworths* or any other contemporary offering will rival *The Goons* or *Around The Horne* any time soon. But at least this modern-day throwback to Jimmy Clitheroe and Al Read reopened the door to the medium best suited to painting pictures in our minds.

Collectively known as The League of Gentlemen, a quartet of writers and performers named Jeremy Dyson, Mark Gatiss, Steve Pemberton and Reece Shearsmith also found radio to be an excellent imaginative canvas. And while their own humour was a good deal darker than that of Fellows, it too was marked by the northern comedy traditions of surrealism and observation. Here, though, along with the Alan Bennett and Victoria Wood-like ear for everyday dialogue - 'it's not everybody who can make a lasagne out of half a dozen Pot Noodles and a Dairylea' - were less prosaic flights of fancy, topped more often than not by a macabre twist. This team of Bretton Hall-educated friends (the exception being Dyson, who studied philosophy in Leeds) drew upon every last drop of popular culture soaked up during childhoods spent in Leeds, Sedgefield, Blackburn and Hull respectively.

Following a first gig together in Brighton, the League of Gentlemen officially took flight at London's Cockpit Theatre in 1995, when their first professional sketch show under the name was staged. Subsequently, they won a residency at the Canal Café Theatre in Maida Vale and then debuted at the Edinburgh Fringe where, in 1996, bearing black tuxedos, Brylcreemed hair and Sellotaped porcine noses, they hit the limelight with an idiosyncratic clatter. For once, the BBC acted quickly and signed them up for radio, by which time the League's self-contained universe of freaks, weirdos and assorted social misfits, often cloaked in the veneer of outward suburban respectability, was almost fully-fledged. The outcome, broadcast the following year, was the Sony award-winning Radio 4 show *On The Town With The League Of Gentlemen*, which boasted six masterfully crafted episodes that were as funny and clever as they were bizarre. Upon returning to Edinburgh in 1997, the four friends added to their growing prestige by winning the Perrier award.

If their rise thus far might be termed meteoric, it was about to shoot still higher. Soon, Dyson, Gatiss (both born 1966), Pemberton (1967) and Shearsmith (the youngest arrival at Wakefield's Bretton Hall, born 1969), along with their radio producer Sarah Smith, had a commission to adapt their ideas for television. Given the fanciful tapestries weaved on radio, there were doubts about the transition, both in terms of cost and quality of realisation. However, all concerns were banished on sight of the first episode which, renamed simply *The League Of Gentlemen*, was broadcast on BBC2 in January 1999. To begin with, the location was inspired. Filmed in dour windswept Hadfield, high in Derbyshire's Peak District, the League's collection of grotesques were seen to reside in a town as disturbingly creepy as its residents. The four settled on it after touring the north in a minibus, looking for a place that felt isolated and hard to leave. With its dreary shop fronts, unremarkable high street and elevated position, surrounded by a countryside of bleak rolling moors so particular to that part of the world, Hadfield guaranteed *The League Of Gentlemen* a haunted look before any of its population had so much as opened their dentally-challenged mouths.

On radio, the fictional town in which the League's creations lived was known as Spent. On television, it became Royston Vasey, the real name of Roy 'Chubby' Brown. Such nuggets of cultural cross-reference and homage would be a staple ingredient; some obvious, others less so. The very name, League of Gentlemen, for example, was a tip of the hat to the 1960 crime caper of that name starring Jack Hawkins as the leader of ex-army bank robbers. And in the very first episode, when an ill-fated Scottish policeman (Gatiss) enters the lonely hillside shop especially created for the TV series run by husband and wife serial killers Edward and Tubbs, in search of a missing hiker, a suggestion of the cult 1973 horror classic *The Wicker Man* is inescapable. As the sign on the moors says: 'Welcome to Royston Vasey - You'll Never Leave'. Edward and Tubbs turn out to be merely the tip of a very sinister iceberg.

Cunningly, we viewers are introduced to the charms of Royston Vasey through the eyes of that unfortunate hiker's friend, Benjamin, a perfectly sane young man who has the intention of staying overnight at the home of his aunt and uncle, Harvey and Val Denton, and meeting up with his now deceased hiking partner later. And the scene-setting routine in which Benjamin reads a letter while travelling into town on the train must rank as one of the most beautifully judged openings to any sitcom ever. 'Dear Benjamin,' we hear the female voiceover say, 'we are so glad you are coming to stay with us, if only for the night...'. The camera then pans out to reveal a nosey old lady who is actually reading the letter out loud. 'Excuse me, do you mind?' grumbles its recipient. 'This is private!'.

Having disembarked from the train, Benjamin is then transported to his relatives' unremarkable Barratt-style house by Barbara, a half-viewed

hairy-armed taxi driver who, by his or her own unflinching account, is undergoing a sex change: 'I've only been on the hormones eighteen months, my nipples are like bullets.' Once ensconced with the Dentons, Benjamin's unease is further deepened by the amphibian-faced Harvey's obsession with order and personal hygiene - 'In this house, we leave our shoes in the front porch, underneath the barometer' - before realisation dawns that the couple are intent on his imprisonment. We also discover that Harvey has a fascination with toads (batrachianism, apparently) and that the couple have two young daughters, Chloe and Radcliffe, a pair of mind-reading refugees from the *Village Of The Damned*.

Though *The League Of Gentleman* is heavy with horror and science fiction film references - other spooky motifs will go on to include a man trapped inside a scarecrow, Edward and Tubbs's howling, monstrous offspring and, creepiest of all, Shearsmith's raspy-voiced carnival man, Papa ('...you're my wife now, Dave') Lazarou - the whole is a complex mixture of the Gothic and the mundane, snappily written and performed by a cast willing to ham it up whatever their personal discomfort. Of its four writers and creators, only the camera shy Dyson doesn't appear on screen (give or take the odd cameo). The rest, talented actors all, go for it big time whether in drag, anorak or shell suit, under some of the finest make-up ever seen in television comedy. In fact, the production values in general are marked by superb attention to detail. Top-notch camera work gives the show a classy filmic quality and Joby Talbot's musical score, all brass and dissonance, adds another rich layer of eccentricity.

A quick roll call of Rosyton Vasey's other main inhabitants gives a further illustration of the high levels of creativity. There is the sweet-natured vet, Matthew Chinnery (Gatiss), whose good intentions are consistently undermined by his knack of killing the very animals he is supposed to be saving, often in the most horrifying and bloodthirsty ways. There is the camp German tour operator, Herr Lipp (Pemberton), a veritable stream of teutonic gay double entendre, whose eye for a nice young man never wavers ('..put yourself in my fist. *Alles klar?*'). There is vindictive job restart officer Pauline Campbell-Jones (Pemberton), with her fixation on pens and determination to ensure that the unemployed charges under her wing remain that way, especially her gormless buck-toothed favourite, Mickey 'love' (Gatiss). No British sitcom would be complete without some sort of take on the class system and, in *The League Of Gentlemen*, the honour falls to Mrs. Judee Levenson (Shearsmith) and her cleaning lady, Iris (Gatiss), who taunt each other with stories of middle class luxury and working class sexual activities respectively. The over-familiarity of husband-wife relationships are explored through Stella (Shearsmith) and Charlie (Pemberton), a constantly bickering pair who nevertheless cling together on to the wreckage of a marriage adrift in a sea of boredom and simmering bitterness. Of the rest, violent domineering small-time businessman Pop (Pemberton), constantly playing his sons Al and Rich off against one another; the former 'pop star' rhythm guitarist Les McQueen (Gatiss), whose band Creme Brulée, we are told, made the heats of the Eurovision Song Contest in 1981; the right-on touring community theatre group Legz Akimbo; and Royston Vasey's diabolic butcher Hilary Briss (Gatiss), whose 'special stuff' might very possibly be human flesh, all merit a mention.

Again, thanks to its clever blending of the self-consciously intellectual and the daft, *The League Of Gentlemen* was a further example of the ways in which still recognisably northern comedians were now wider-ranging in their ambitions while, simultaneously, exerting just as much influence on up-and-coming comics in other parts of Britain and the world. The old geographical walls, it seems, were now guides rather than boundaries and almost unnoticed ones at that, with the interchange in ideas very much two-way traffic. Most immediately, that could be seen in a show quite blatantly inspired by *The League Of Gentlemen* - Matt Lucas and David Walliams's *Little Britain*, which followed on radio in 2001 and TV in 2003 (initially boasting Mark Gatiss as script editor). In some ways, the reaction to the two carried echoes of 'seventies attitudes to *Monty Python* and *The Goodies*. One, *The League Of Gentlemen*, was seen as more artistic and grown-up, the other, *Little Britain*, for the kids. An ironic state of affairs when you come to think about it, given that with their respective geographical origins, traditionally, it would have been the other way around.

In other ways, however, *The League Of Gentlemen* and *Little Britain* conformed entirely to type. Although both shows set out to shock with copious bodily fluids, catchphrases and busted taboos, amidst all the mock-horror and buckets of entrails, only in *The League Of Gentlemen* did the actors seem genuinely affectionate toward the characters they played.

In his portrayal of Les McQueen, for example, niceness and shattered dreams personified, Gatiss brings depth and pathos to a character who, elsewhere, would most likely have been a caricature. There was plenty of heart, too, in the way the League lovingly plundered the Hammer films and other pop cultural icons of their youth. All of it topped off by a twisted brand of northern realism, much of it blacker than coal, as with the flowers on the back of a hearse arranged to spell 'bastard'.

At least one cast member has since played down the importance of northernness to *The League Of Gentlemen* and, for sure, what is the shibboleth, '...this is a local shop for local people, there's nothing for you here', if not a well-aimed jibe at small-town parochial attitudes. In a rather grumpy interview with *The Scotsman* newspaper in 2005, the journalist doing the questioning refers to the group as being influenced by the 'grim northern towns..of their youth', to which Reece Shearsmith reportedly retorts: 'Well, you couldn't get four more anti-northerners than us. We don't like the idea of flat caps and whippets, or whatever the north is. So I hope that's not our legacy.' For any creative person, such defensiveness in the face of a handy pigeon-hole is entirely understandable and maybe even necessary in the relentless battle against stereotypes and accusations of so-called 'professional northernness'. Yet whatever their oddities, the fact remains that the residents of Royston Vasey *are* both northern and a recognisable (if hardly close-knit) community in a way that the characters in *Little Britain* simply are not. The northern influence *is* there - albeit to a less obvious extent than ever before - for good or ill.

In any case, in the end it all added up to the same thing. A universal popularity that saw *The League Of Gentlemen* top the Best Entertainment category at the Golden Rose of Montreaux awards in 1999 and win a BAFTA for Best Comedy the following year. And this from a bunch of television novices. Almost exactly twelve months after that first series aired, a second came along by the end of which, as the village fell victim to a plague of mysterious and deadly nose bleeds, Mr. Royston Vasey himself, Chubby Brown, had put in an appearance as the town Mayor. 'Thank you, Mr. Mayor,' says a member of the press, upon grilling said official, who has just kept his word not to swear on camera. 'It's a fucking pleasure,' comes the reply.

After a sell-out live UK stage tour in October 2000, *A Local Show For*

Local People (which also ran at the Theatre Royal, Drury Lane for six weeks early in 2001), the League of Gentlemen produced an equally well-received Christmas special which took as its inspiration old portmanteau horror films, as made by Amicus and the like. Then, after the first of several spells working apart on solo projects, the team reunited for a third television series, broadcast in September 2002. Rather than employing a random series of sketches, linked or otherwise, this time six individual stories were told, leading to a simultaneous road accident. A number of new characters were introduced too, like wannabe street magician Dean Tavalouris (Shearsmith), owner of a dog cinema Kenny Harris (Gatiss) and sexually adventurous swingers, Alvin and Sunny Steele (Gatiss and Shearsmith). Of existing Royston Vaysarians, the confused and frustrated businessman Geoff Tipps (Shearsmith) who, along with colleagues Mike and Brian had been there from the radio days, was given his own episode, 'Turn Again Geoff Tipps', in which he pursued his lifelong ambition to become a stand-up comedian despite having no talent whatsoever. Again, the series as a whole was a critical success, winning the *South Bank Show* Award for Best Comedy. And although, for some viewers, the playfulness of spirit apparent in the first two series now felt angrier and more cynical - in reaction to the burgeoning success of Ricky Gervais's mockumentary *The Office*, it was suggested - this latest *League of Gentlemen* remained streets ahead of just about everything else in the comedy schedules.

Also in 2002, just as the third series was reaching its conclusion, Gatiss, Pemberton and Shearsmith followed a long line of comedy actors by appearing in the West End play, *Art*. This would herald a lengthier period in which all four team members went off and did their own thing in just about every area of the entertainment industry, all the while insisting that the *League of Gentlemen*'s return would come as and when circumstance dictated. The event to spark that reunion was the chance of realising the team's cherished ambition to write and star in a film of their own. With funding finally secured from Film Four, the result was *The League Of Gentlemen's Apocalypse* (2005), a contender with Simon Pegg's *Shaun Of The Dead* for the title of best British comedy spin-off since *Monty Python's Life Of Brian* (with little competition in the interim, admittedly). A enjoyable post-modern romp through time and metaphysical space, in which the inhabitants of Royston Vasey leave their fictional world in the

hunt for their real-life alter egos in ours (in order to avoid the *League of Gentlemen* series being killed off), along with cameos by Pegg and Peter Kay, it also featured no less a figure than Victoria Wood as Queen Mary.

Since when, apart from a pantomime-inspired tour *The League Of Gentlemen Are Behind You* in 2005 (and voicing the Vogons in the movie version of Douglas Adams's *The Hitchhiker's Guide To The Galaxy*), the four League members have predominantly flown solo, although Pemberton and Shearsmith did co-write and star in their quite magnificent sitcom *Psychoville* in 2009, along with Gatiss (in one episode) and Dawn French among others. These days, Jeremy Dyson concentrates largely on a writing career that has seen him co-create the BBC3 sitcom *Funland* (2005) and become a reliable spinner of quirky and often dark short stories in collections like *Never Trust A Rabbit* and *The Cranes That Build The Cranes*. Mark Gatiss, too, has been prolific, whether contributing scripts to and appearing in *Doctor Who*, writing novels, or putting his acting skills to good use in such diverse successes as the cruelly funny Julia Davis sitcom *Nighty Night* and the 2006 celebrity chef biopic *Fear Of Fanny*, in which he was a monocled Johnny to Davis's Fanny Craddock. Acting, too, has dominated the output of Steve Pemberton and Reece Shearsmith. For the former, that has meant roles in programmes like *Blackpool*, *Shameless* and the hit ITV sitcom *Benidorm*, a throwback to the old mainstream northern comedy traditions if ever there was one. Shearsmith's more edgy television work includes absurdist medical sitcom *tlc*, surreal sketch show *Monkey Trousers*, *Max and Paddy's Road To Nowhere* and *Catterick*.

Where the writers of the final sitcom in that list *Catterick* are concerned, Reeves and Mortimer, back in 1993 their career direction was about to be propelled further by a distinctly unpromising spoof quiz inserted into *At Home With Vic and Bob*. It went by the name 'Shooting Stars'.

By way of encouraging audience participation, ridiculous questions had long been a part of the *Big Night Out* live experience: 'True or false - film producer David Lean is responsible for the Findus range, Lean Cuisine?', being one such. 'Shooting Stars', however, imposed more structure. It also helped immeasurably to broaden Vic and Bob's appeal, pitching them, as it did, alongside supposed contestants who were already well-known mainstream faces. In its original outing, the team captains were the pair's long-time patron Jonathan Ross and all-round music factotum Danny Baker. Alongside Ross was *Are You Being Served* veteran Wendy Richard and Martin Clunes - aka Gary in the laddish sitcom *Men Behaving Badly* - who, it could be argued, with Stafford-born actor Neil Morrissey, had all but entirely applied the killer blow to politically correct comedy. On Baker's side, meanwhile, were Slade singer Noddy Holder (the real one this time) and former TV-AM weathergirl Ulrika Jonsson.

There were those, like Ross, who considered 'Shooting Stars' to be just one more short-lived piece of throwaway fun. But the BBC saw things differently. When a repeat of the insert drew a remarkable audience of over two million, a full series was commissioned and it went to air - with one or two subtle changes - in 1995. Most obviously, along with classier graphics, that meant two new captains in pilot team member Jonsson and the terminally morose 'fifties throwback' Mark Lamarr, a hard-edged Swindon stand-up drafted in from Channel 4's yoof TV show, *The Word*. Former foe turned fan Matt Lucas, fresh from a cameo on *The Smell of Reeves and Mortimer*, was introduced as George Dawes, the world's biggest baby, while, behind the scenes, Charlie Higson combined his role as associate producer with an occasional walk-on part.

The all-new *Shooting Stars* was not dissimilar in look to *The Smell of Reeves and Mortimer*. It opened with a song ('...welcome to *Shooting Stars*, welcome whoever you are, the stars are all greeted, successfully seated....), after which Vic and Bob, as dandily clad as ever, would retreat behind a desk framed by a red, white and blue target, in the centre of a white set. The superficially familiar quiz show format was further underlined by the presence of archetypal B-list celebrity Jonsson, who had been spotted as a comedian in the making by Bob, when he saw her being 'Gotcha'-ed on *Noel's House Party*. Come 1997, the Swedish lovely - mercilessly teased by Bob on account of her alleged predilection for professional footballers and the male of the species generally - was such a part of the Vic and Bob furniture that the duo wrote her a comedy sketch show of her own own, *It's Ulrika!* A critical flop, it could at least lay claim to having given future *Little Britain* stars Lucas and Walliams their first shared on-screen appearance.

Equally traditionally, the questions on *Shooting Stars* were split into

rounds - picture rounds *et al* - while an eclectic combination of guests could include household names like Russell Grant, Carol Smillie and Vanessa Feltz, or more alternative names designed to appeal to the youth vote like Louise Wener, lead singer with the band Sleeper, her fellow Brit-pop icon Jarvis Cocker or Robbie Williams. Yet however accessible it appeared, *Shooting Stars* was as subversive as anything Vic and Bob had done before, redefining the game show genre too as it went.

Again, ritualistic behaviour and a ready stock of surreal catchphrases were at the heart of the humour. Uttered by Bob, the name Ulrika morphed into 'Ulrika-ka-ka!'. The startling entry of the bald and chubby Lucas in outsized pink babygrow - 'he's the man with the scores - George Dawes' - en route to his drum kit, was greeted by a raucous chorus of 'he's a baby!'. Contestants were informed during the quickfire buzzer round that 'we really wanna see those fingers'. And there were the strangely mythical words Eranu and Uvavu, delivered in ghostly detachment by Vic, together with routines like the clump of tumbleweed that rolled silently across the stage whenever Reeves cracked an awful pun; the club singer round in which the lyrics and tune as rendered by Vic were utterly indecipherable; and the arrival of the Dove from Above, charmed down by a barrage of beckoning and cooing.

That it worked so well owed much to the pleasure of watching television personalities out of their comfort zone, utterly bemused in an alien world. Most of them at least partially got the joke but, even if they didn't, as was the case with American soap actor Larry Hagman and the voluminously-breasted British glamour model Jordan, well that just made it all the funnier. Instead of attempting to compete with Vic and Bob in the comedy stakes - a mistake made painfully by Danny Baker (twice) - the wiser guests let their hosts get on with it and simply played along. Some, however, were made to work harder in this department than most. Namely, those unfortunate ladies seated immediately to the right of Vic, who were forced to endure Vic's lecherous rubbing of his own thighs. If that became a visual catchphrase, then so did each week's finale when one lucky celebrity was asked to undergo a physical challenge as bizarre as it could be humiliating. The episode in which Lamarr tried to repel the 'charge' of a giant stuffed bear, armed only with a toy shield, must rank as one of the most amusing comedy moments of the 1990s.

They Wouldn't Let it Lie

Given that the first series of *Shooting Stars* had attracted twice as many viewers as *The Smell of Reeves and Mortimer*, catapulting Vic and Bob well and truly into the mainstream, that the BBC wanted a second series came as no surprise, especially when the show's 1995 Christmas special was entered at the Montreux Television Festival. In the event, (complete with subtitles) it won the Silver Rose, and a second run (minus subtitles) began in September 1996. Coinciding with that broadcast, however, was an arduous *Shooting Stars* tour and, once that was over, an out-of-steam Reeves and Mortimer initially decided that enough was enough, only to be tempted back by a third series the following year. But once that came to an end, the duo did indeed finally call time on *Shooting Stars*, for the next few years anyway. Because now they had yet another self-devised quiz show in mind and it aired, rather ambitiously, on BBC1 in August 1998.

If *Shooting Stars* had boosted Vic and Bob's recognition factor with family audiences, *Families At War* was an even more overt attempt to turn Reeves and Mortimer into the new Morecambe and Wise. Sitting pretty in an early Saturday evening slot, the new venture was intended to be a *Generation Game* for the 'nineties. Here, though, replacing Bruce Forsyth's 'didn't she do well?' and Larry Grayson's 'shut that door', was a new catchphrase: 'I am the spider.' The period when this was said - i.e. as contestants attempted to guide Vic, dressed and suspended like the arachnid in question, to prizes sprinkled across a web known as The Cubiscus, accompanied by Bob (aka The Water Boatman) on keyboards - was the funniest bit of the show. Particularly when those prizes were as coveted as a hoover or foot spa. Unfortunately, the rest of the 40 minutes wasn't quite so enticing. Nevertheless, the pilot, in which opposing family members performed bizarre competitive tasks, was promising enough for the BBC to commission a full series that aired early in 1999, at which point consumer affairs journalist Alice Beer had replaced *Big Breakfast* presenter Denise Van Outen in the female co-host role. Sadly, such lunacy was ahead of its time. Ratings were disappointing and the show was ditched after just eight episodes.

By then, on New Years Day 1999, the pair had already returned to their own comfort zone with the sketch show *Bang Bang It's Reeves And Mortimer*. As if in response to the relative lightness of *Shooting Stars* and *Families At War*, its six episodes featured some of Vic and Bob's most

569

surreal antics yet. In many ways a continuation of *The Smell of Reeves and Mortimer* but with a darker edge, *Bang Bang It's Reeves And Mortimer* contained a weekly docusoap routine called 'The Club', set in a Hull nightclub whose talent show host, Kinky John Fowler (Reeves), owed not a little of his look to Malcolm Hardee. The squeaky-voiced Stott brothers reappeared as bizarre celebrity interviewers - memorably leaving the Irish chanteuse Sinead O'Connor stranded alone on stage at one point - and there was a disturbingly strange running gag featuring two very poor car parkers. Yet for all its originality, and many still consider it one of the best things they have ever done, *Bang Bang It's Reeves And Mortimer* also lasted just one series before the pair's next project saw them move off in a more traditional if equally less successful direction. Namely, to a BBC remake of ITV's stylish 1960's private detective caper *Randall and Hopkirk (Deceased)*, scripted and produced by their old pal Charlie Higson. Despite sounding like a perfect vehicle for a couple of comics whose friendship and shared devotion to popular culture made them ideally suited to the roles, the show unfortunately completed a triple-whammy of programmes that showed how, despite their popularity, Vic and Bob could still soar over the average viewer's head at twice the speed of sound. Somehow, *Randall and Hopkirk* limped its way through two series, before ending in 2001.

Given those setbacks, Vic and Bob's decision to resurrect *Shooting Stars* at this particular point in their career may well have been pragmatic. But anyone expecting them merely to go through the motions would have to stand corrected. A popular ingredient of *Shooting Stars* over its first three series had been the slapstick visual gags that peppered the show, particularly by series three. Hitting each other on the head with everyday household objects and sticking broom handles in unorthodox places had been a feature of *The Smell...* and *Bang Bang It's Reeves And Mortimer* too. So when *Shooting Stars* arrived back on BBC2 in 2002 - after a dry-run on satellite channel BBC Choice - cartoonishly violent trade-offs were even more prominent. The spruced-up new version also had more of the pre-filmed clips that had been such a reliably strong feature of series three. Many of those, such as the sublimely ridiculous renditions of *Billy Elliott* and *Carry on Camping* were little masterpieces in their own right.

Personnel-wise, Matt Lucas returned as George Dawes and, very occasionally, as George's mother Marjory - soon to become a regular on

Little Britain herself. He now also got to perform a range of his own songs, containing subject matter as diverse as hip-hop, peanuts and lesbians ('recognised as a minority, funded by the local authority, some drink coffee, some drink tea, a handy metaphor for sexuality...'). Mark Lamarr, now fronting an irreverent if rather more savage quiz show of his own in *Never Mind The Buzzcocks*, was replaced as captain of team 'A' by the, if anything, even more bilious novelist Will Self. With his air of intellectual superiority and elite smart-arsery, the provocative Self sent himself up in fine style, while directing cascades of erudite insults at two very naughty boys. The Dove from Above too was gone, replaced by 'the wonderful, wonderful car', as *it* had taken over from Donald Cox, the sweaty fox. Ulrika Jonsson, however, remained as captain of team 'B', where she would henceforth be assisted on a weekly basis by a loudmouthed overweight comic from St. Helens, who was partial to a drop of stout.

When interviewed on BBC television in 2006, Johnny Vegas described *Vic Reeves Big Night Out* as 'my *Monty Python*'. So it is safe to assume that when messrs. Moir and Mortimer invited said comedian to become a *Shooting Stars* regular, his ample frame will have wobbled in delight.

Born Michael Joseph Pennington in St. Helens in 1971, when Vic and Bob came knocking, Johnny Vegas had established a comedy persona of frenzied and unpredictable brilliance. On the face of it an unkempt northern slob with three unshaven chins and beer belly to match, Vegas's angst-filled bouts of passionate soul-searching were already the stuff of stand-up legend. Although a mild-mannered and intelligent soul off-stage, Pennington's outrageous alter-ego with an ironic showbiz name ranted like a booze-addled madman on it, frequently causing offence. And often the ones most offended were his fellow northerners. To some, the Johnny Vegas persona was a cliché that reinforced ignorant southern stereotypes. Wasn't he just the latest in a long line of northern comedy simpletons? Well, in terms of perception, perhaps. But there was always much more to him than that.

In essence, Johnny Vegas - as distinct from Michael Pennington - is a deeply wounded individual who feels himself to be one of life's outsiders, especially with regard to his relationships with women. His is an over-

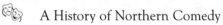

sensitive and troubled soul, flailing in a sea of self-inflicted blubber, wracked by self-doubt and full of barely concealed anger and misery. In short, he is the creation of a very fine actor indeed.

The youngest of four children and the product of a devout Catholic upbringing, Johnny Vegas's childhood had a healthy share of laughter. In 2004, he told BBC Radio 2's *Talking Comedy* that the family's favourite comedians had been Tom O'Connor, Les Dawson and Ken Dodd; the latter pair for their inventive use of word play ('Can I have some sleeping pills for my wife?' asks Dawson, in a clip to illustrate the point. 'Why?' 'She's woken up...') and the former for his preference for stories over gags. Tommy Cooper's physicality would also prove influential on the budding comic, although no one - least of all young Michael himself - knew that at the time. In fact, as an 11-year-old, Vegas seemed destined for a career in the priesthood and went so far as to enter seminary school before having second thoughts and returning home to St. Helens some eighteen months later. Aged 24 and thoroughly depressed, he left for Middlesex University, where he studied art and ceramic design. And in 1996, when he finally made the leap from audience to comedy club stage, he worked his skill on the potter's wheel into the act.

The Johnny Vegas persona appears to have initially been no more than a happy accident. As the comedian himself told the writer Poncho Steele in an online interview: 'I'd written some stuff that I thought was funny [for his first comedy open mic gig]. When I got to the pub I realised I was going to die. In a drunken panic I got up and went "I'm not a comedian, I'm an entertainer. I don't do jokes." I started coming out with some horrible things that had happened in my life... Johnny Vegas was really born out of that gig.' The BBC's drama website, meanwhile, states that the epiphanic moment came at his home town's Citadel arts centre. It was there that Pennington heckled a comedian and was invited to see if he could do better. Soon, as Vegas, he was the regular compere.

Whatever his exact origins, in this rambling dishevelled emotional loser of a man, Pennington had actually unearthed a winner. And after entering Manchester's well-respected City Life Comedy Awards - and coming second to some Boltonian fellow called Kay in the final - the following year he took himself off to Edinburgh's Fringe. The deliberately shambolic one-man show he performed there, an innovative mixture of humour, sing-songs and pottery, met with such acclaim that he won the Festival Critics' Award outright. He might also have collected the 1997 Perrier Award had The League of Gentlemen not also been nominated. With one or two uncomfortable stumbles, as audiences subjected to his verbal abuse struggled to work out whether or not the chaos inflicted by this hoarse drunkard's ramblings was for real, his live act bloomed. An array of manic television guest appearances also followed, but it took a series of popular adverts to really turn Johnny Vegas into a household name. The product was ITV Digital; his partner a puppet monkey voiced by the former Cambridge Footlights comic Ben Miller. And nor did it diminish his new-found fame when 'monk-eh' and company went belly up. As ITV Digital went into administration, Vegas put his energies into a 'proper' TV career that had not developed as smoothly as it might have.

Apart from an uncredited appearance as a fresh-faced contestant on the afternoon quiz *Win, Lose Or Draw* back in his student days, Johnny Vegas's first television comedy appearance had come in one of four ten-minute Channel 4 shorts under the combined name *The Comedy Slot*, filmed on location at the Edinburgh Fringe in 1997. The other three were made by fellow up-and-coming comics Owen O'Neill, Tommy Tiernan and the Southport-born Lee Mack. Though more of a slow burner than Vegas, Mack - christened Lee McKillop - was destined to make a national name for himself too, primarily as a very witty panelist on shows like *Mock The Week* and *Would I Lie To You?* a decade or so into the future.

More immediately, either side of his appearance on *The Comedy Slot*, the scrawny stand-up hosted two series of Channel 4's comedy showcase *Gas*, whose impressive line-up of rising stars included Julian Barratt, Noel Fielding, Hovis Presley and Peter Kay. In 2001, Mack joined Tim Vine, Ronni Ancona, Jim Tavaré and the Barrow-in-Furness born Karen Taylor in bringing us ITV's *The Sketch Show*, which also had the then unknown Ricky Gervais in the writing credits and was produced by Steve Coogan's production company Baby Cow. In 2005, Mack was the only original cast member to also appear in a short-lived American version of the show produced by *Cheers* and *Frasier* star Kelsey Grammar.

In Britain, to begin with Lee Mack's most regular home was radio, where he appeared as a security guard in Barratt and Fielding's BBC Radio 4 comedy *The Mighty Boosh*, while also enjoying an eponymous

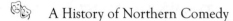

Radio 2 series *The Lee Mack Show*, billed as 'a Variety show for the twenty-first century'. Then came the chance to take over from Nick Hancock as host of long-running television sports quiz, *They Think It's All Over*, also in 2005. Given that, by that time, its puerile schoolboy humour had long since passed its sell-by date, it was perhaps unsurprising that the plug was pulled after a nineteenth and final series. Fortunately for its new host, he and fellow *The Sketch Show* co-star Tim Vine had simultaneously reunited for a BBC sitcom pilot with the fate-tempting title, *Not Going Out*. A gallant attempt at rejuvenating a supposedly ailing genre, it was written in association with award-winning writer and broadcaster Andrew Collins and turned into a first full series in 2006.

Having had a first taste of television exposure on *The Comedy Slot*, Johnny Vegas was given a full 45-minute Channel 4 show of his own as a Christmas present. Its title, *The Johnny Vegas Television Show*, was the only unimaginative thing about it, as drunken tormented Johnny, yearning for lost days as an all-round entertainer in Skegness, pestered real life friends and neighbours like some demented wraith with tales of what might have been. It was a critical success but anyone eagerly anticipating a follow-up was to be disappointed. Foremost among those was the man himself, as a blistering quote at the 2002 British Comedy Awards revealed: 'I'd like to thank Channel 4 for putting my career back five years.' Vegas referred to the blow of losing a series promised by outgoing commissioning editor Seamus Cassidy, and then cancelled by his replacement Kevin Lygo, who declared that the humour in the Christmas show had been 'too dark'. The comedian was distraught and many within the industry feared that his star had all-too quickly burned out.

In fact, the wait he had to endure after *The Johnny Vegas Television Show* was more like two years, although a role in Simon Munnery's short-lived surreal effort *Attention Scum*, broadcast on BBC2 in 2001, hardly looked like a significant shift forward. Munnery, aka the League Against Tedium, imparted weird words of philosophical wisdom from the back of a parked van, while Vegas and another comedy star waiting to happen, Catherine Tate, were in support. But as his appearance at the following year's Comedy Awards confirms, Vegas would soon make up for lost time and put his Channel 4 troubles behind him.

The main impetus behind that upturn in fortunes was his part as the pathetic Charlie, permanently drunk friend of the chief protagonist in *Happiness* (2001-03), Paul Whitehouse's first solo BBC sitcom and a good one at that. In it, Whitehouse played the actor and micro-celebrity Danny Spencer, who undergoes a mid-life crisis after the unexpected death of his wife and is best known as the voice of Dexter, a cartoon bear. For Vegas, his performance in *Happiness* led to him winning the Royal Television Society's best newcomer award for 2002, a misnomer given his track record but what the heck. He was again being noticed. Other future big hitters in Danny's circle of equally creaky mates included Mark Heap of *Spaced*, *Big Train*, *Jam* and *Green Wing* fame, Pearce Quigley, star of the Manchester-based hair-dressing drama *Cutting It*, and Bury-born Fiona Allen, one third of a virtually all-female sketch show, *Smack The Pony*.

Fiona Allen it was too who played Sandra, one half of a Geordie good-time girl double act, in the 2004 British comedy film *Fat Slags* (Sophie Thompson playing Sandra's mate Tracey), a simply atrocious adaptation of the shag-happy creations of a comic named *Viz*.

A product of the fevered minds of Newcastle trainspotter Chris Donald, his brother Simon and their friend Jim Brownlow, *Viz* had begun life as a twelve-page black and white pamphlet, price 20p, in 1979. Born in an age of punk rock and alternative comedy, after a shaky start, its anti-establishment take on life, disrespect for established conventions and pervasive use of foul language made it a hit with the Geordie pub and club-going public and the city's artier students alike. In *Viz*, swearing may not have been big, but it was certainly clever. Its vast array of cartoon oddballs - Johnny Fartpants, Sid the Sexist, Biffa Bacon, Buster Gonad, Newcastle's very own superhero the Brown Bottle, Terry Fuckwitt and the rest - weren't just fresh and hilarious in their own right, they struck a witty cultural chord.

In keeping with classic comic tradition, several characters seemed possessed of special abilities merely because it rhymed with their names, i.e. foul-mouthed Roger Mellie, the Man on the Telly; Paul Whicker the Tall Vicar; Finbarr Saunders and his Double Entendres and so on. Some, like mullet-haired Fulchester United footballer Billy the Fish, the right-on Millie Tant, surreal Roger Irrelevant ('he's so hatstand') and the Pathetic

Sharks were openly parodic. And all of them, in true northern comedy style, hid such intelligence behind a mask of frequently coarse and down-to-earth alliterative smut; Tina's Tits anyone? It was a recipe for success.

The Donald brothers' artistic leanings appear to have been inherited from their wheelchair-bound mother, Kay, an artist and window dresser by trade, who was struck down by multiple sclerosis in 1963. Their humour came from their dad, Jimmy, a working class oil salesman who used comedy as a way of lightening his family's otherwise heavy load. In Chris Donald's *Rude Kids: The Unfeasible Story of Viz* (HarperCollins, 2004), the author reveals how Jimmy introduced his three sons - Steve was the third - to Laurel and Hardy, The Goons and Morecambe and Wise. When the family moved to leafy Jesmond, a well-to-do suburb of Newcastle, in order to improve Mrs. Donald's ailing health, Donald sr. would take amusing verbal pot-shots at his trendy, CND supporting left-wing middle-class neighbours. And other family members were equally adept at undermining pretension. 'Nana Donald,' writes her grandson, 'took to calling my Uncle Jack "Lord Shite" after he got himself a job as a chauffeur for the Lord Mayor and started dressing in fancy suits.'

Alas, the sales figures for Donald's first magazine, *The Lily Crescent Locomotive Times*, which he 'published' as a 15-year-old in 1975, have gone unrecorded. It is safe to assume, however, that they will not have come anywhere close to the 1,366,350 copies at which *Viz* would peak in 1990. Such astonishing figures officially made *Viz* Britain's third-highest selling magazine title behind the *TV Times* and *Radio Times*. Its scurrilous and ribald assortment of cartoon strips, spoof tabloid news stories ('Cabinet Minister had SEX with dolphin!'), fake consumer tests and surreal games and competitions ('Kill some animals! Play our fabulous FREE Royal Hunting Game..') had turned it into something of a national institution. The comic was certainly at home in a celebrity-obsessed comedy climate straddled by Vic Reeves and Bob Mortimer. The pair even produced a DVD in association with its advice pages, *Viz Top Tips - With Reeves And Mortimer* (1996), wherein helpful pieces of advice along the lines of 'to deter children from resting their elbows on the table, sprinkle it with broken glass' were dispensed to a grateful public. In 2002, Johnny Vegas famously sold his wedding photos to the publication for the princely sum of £1. Its roots, though, were of an altogether less glamourous nature.

Whatever anyone thought of the music, one undoubted side-effect of punk was the equally hands-on philosophy it bred with regard to the creation of fanzines, cheaply-produced DIY mags usually typed up and stapled together in a spare bedroom and then sold at live concerts or local record shops. In time, *Viz* would itself influence a whole host of such publications across many different genres, most notably football. Chris Donald's first foray into this territory came when he asked to contribute cartoons to a heavy rock fanzine. Upon its appearance, *Bad Breath* proved so awful that Chris and Jim withdrew their services and set up their own publication instead. Putting music to one side, the pair went exclusively down the comical route and after Newcastle label Anti-Pop let them flog it at their gigs in return for a back-page advert, *Viz* duly underwent its first 150-copy print-run (printing bill: £41.52).

By issue two, that figure had increased to 500, with each copy sold by hand, pub to pub, by Donald himself. Fast forward still further to Christmas 1984 and, by issue 12, the presses were rattling to the tune of 5,000 copies, a figure that had serious implications distribution-wise. If he was to cope with *Viz*'s burgeoning popularity, Donald needed a plan. And given that the Newcastle branch of Virgin Records had sold over 1,000 copies of the previous issue, he came up with the idea of writing to that company's owner, Richard Branson. Branson himself did not reply, but a chap called John Brown, from his book division, did and a deal was swiftly done. When Brown left Virgin to go it alone seventeen months later, he persuaded the Donald brothers to let him take the *Viz* contract with him. Subsequently, a print run of 29,000 climbed to over 60,000 by the end of 1987. A year later, it was 500,000. In 1989, the average sale was 680,000. Mail order income from T-shirts, beach towels, boxer shorts and baseball caps added to the financial windfall, along with spin-off annuals bearing names like *Spunky Parts* and *The Dog's Bollocks*. From entering the decade trying to extract 20p from bolshie passers-by, the *Viz* gang were about to leave it richer than they could have ever imagined. Nor was that the end of the spurt. In December 1989, the print run finally passed the million mark thanks, largely, to the appearance of San and Tray, those aforementioned Fat Slags.

As the creations of two more cartoonists who had since joined the team, Graham Dury and Simon Thorp, the kebab-munching pair,

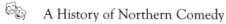

bedecked in all-weather low-cut dresses and white stilettos, with a penchant for jumping on any male in sight, were an immediate and long-lasting hit. So much so that when, some fourteen years later, the idea of a *Viz* film was aired, San and Tray seemed like the perfect candidates for the job.

Of course, as with any British success story, after scaling such heights of trendiness the slippery slope is never far away. And *Viz* duly became a victim of its own success. Despite having spent the past decade mocking celebrities like Michael Winner and Shakin' Stevens, those same 'stars' were increasingly eager to be in on the 'irony', as was also the case on *Shooting Stars*. Politicians saw a chance to trumpet their 'street cred'. The Conservative Students' Association leaked a story to the papers that it had placed an advert in its pages. In his book, Donald recalls how, in the summer of 1991, even the Lord Mayor of Filey got in on the act, telling the *Scarborough Evening Gazette* that he was highly delighted after *Viz* reported Kylie Minogue's intention to purchase 'a static caravan in the unfashionable Yorkshire coastal resort'. And pale imitations of the comic began to proliferate. The rebels, it appeared, were in danger of becoming fully-fledged members of the establishment themselves and sales began to fall. By 1995, the figures had 'slumped' to the half-a-million mark, still remarkable but on a downward trend in comparison with the glory days. A disinclination to 'gracelessly flog the magazine to death' didn't prevent Donald from continuing to edit *Viz* until 1999, when an editorial cabinet of brother Simon, Graham Dury, Simon Thorp and new recruits Davey Jones and Alex Collier took over, before Simon left too in 2003. Since then, the sales of *Viz* - now part-owned by Felix Dennis - have settled into a steady 100,000 per issue and, in 2009-10, an exhibition of the comic's artwork, *30 Years of Viz*, was staged at London's Cartoon Museum.

As his Royal Television Society award proved, with *Happiness* people were awoken to the notion that inside Johnny Vegas was an actor waiting to get out. Supporting roles in television dramas like *Tipping The Velvet*, where the world's best known St. Helens rugby league fan played music hall singer Gully Sutherland, and the football drama *Staying Up* followed in 2002. An appearance as Bottom in a BBC adaptation of Shakespeare's *A Midsummer Night's Dream* was equally well-received, as was his turn as the spontaneously-combusting Krook in Charles Dicken's *Bleak House*, both broadcast in 2005. On radio, five years earlier, there had been a role in the Radio 4 adaptation of Marcel Pagnol's play, *The Flump*, and in 2002 an apparently autobiographical Radio 4 comedy drama *Night Class*, in which he played a pottery teacher and former Butlins redcoat. In 2004, he appeared as *Norman* in Mike Stott's radio play of that name. Those fledgling days as a struggling stand-up seemed a long way off indeed.

These days, when he isn't livening up tedious award ceremonies with apparently impromptu rants or hijacking talk shows in similar fashion, he can mostly be found in sitcoms. Of these, *Benidorm*, in which he stars alongside the League of Gentlemen's Steve Pemberton, is most accessible, and *Ideal*, in which he was the small-time cannabis dealer Moz ('I deal' - geddit?), least. And in 2005, Vegas hosted his own anarchic Friday night Channel 4 show, *18 Stone Of Idiot*, a throwback to those live audience-participation days. On the big screen, he appeared in Mel Smith's 2003 bowling comedy *Blackball* and the critically-savaged *Sex Lives Of The Potato Men* (2004), which mistook pointless crudity for comedy and made *Fat Slags* look like *Citizen Kane*. Earning him rather more in the way of artistic credibility was his role as the poet Sackville, opposite grade a Hollywood movie star Johnny Depp, in the 2005 film *The Libertine*.

Meanwhile, in 2002, instead of capsizing a well-oiled ship as might have been feared, he slipped in alongside Vic, Bob and the rest of the relaunched *Shooting Stars* contestants effortlessly. Whether through his beery half-cut asides or his contribution to the pre-recorded video rounds - his parody of former Manchester assistant-chief constable John Stalker's garden patio awning adverts being a particular treat - the programme was rejuvenated by his presence. Indeed, so at home did he become that, on occasion, even that ostentatious brainbox Will Self seemed to enjoy his eccentricities.

As for Reeves and Mortimer, when *Shooting Stars* reached the end of this latest incarnation with a fifth series at the end of the year, as a double act the pair again chose a route of experimentation. The result was the resolutely surreal and really rather splendid comedy drama *Catterick* (2004), the strange saga of absent father Carl Palmer (Mortimer) who, aided by his hirsute idiot of a brother Chris (Reeves, looking like a cross between the Yorkshire Ripper and Oddbod in *Carry On Screaming*) returns to that North Yorkshire town in search of the son he last saw as a four-year-old. Not only did *Catterick* give the pair the chance to have a go at 'proper acting', a challenge which Mortimer in particular met with aplomb, it allowed them to utilise the services of Charlie Higson, Matt Lucas, Morwenna Banks, Julie T. Wallace and the Geordie actor Tim Healy in an array of weird and wonderful supporting roles. Reece Shearsmith was in suitably unnerving form as Carl's now psychopathic son Tony, and there was also a cameo for his *League of Gentlemen* colleague Mark Gatiss. Bob's eagerness to promote fresh-faced talent found form here in the rising star that was Guisborough's Mark Benton, soon to become a regular on *Early Doors* and no end of drama comedies. Defiantly non-populist, *Catterick* launched on digital channel BBC Three where it won a healthy cult before moving to BBC2.

That Reeves and Mortimer succeeded with *Catterick* where they had failed with *The Weekenders* owed much to them having formed their own production company with latterday *Shooting Stars* producer, Lisa Clark. Its name was Pett Productions and next on its agenda was a programme of altogether lighter hue, *The All Star Comedy Show*. Not since the days of Eric Sykes had a programme boasted such a cast list. A madcap stream of silly sketches, written largely by Vic and Bob, were littered with names like Steve Coogan (whose own Baby Cow company also had a hand in production), Fiona Allen, John Thomson, Alistair McGowan, Ronnie Ancona, Neil Morrissey, Mark Benton, Liz Smith, Richard Wilson, David Walliams, Matt Lucas, Reece Shearsmith, Ricky Tomlinson, Jane Horrocks, Don Warrington and Meera Syal. Many of them returned for a second series, broadcast more in hope than expectation, in 2005. Now bearing the title *Monkey Trousers*, after the outbursts made by Reeves's unintelligible noise-making lunatic Gibberish Man, only five of the six planned episodes were shown. By which time it was clear that, although a great idea in principle and not without good bits (Coogan's creepy toy shop owner being one), this particular pair of strides were a bit of a mess.

After which, and certainly until *Shooting Stars* was reborn after an anniversary special filled out into an equally entertaining sixth series in 2009, with Ulrika Jonsson still on board but with Will Self and Johnny Vegas replaced by Jack Dee and burger van owner Angelos Epithemiou (Dan Renton Skinner), Bob Mortimer took more of a back seat role as producer of such groundbreaking shows as *Tittybangbang*, an outrageous all-female sketch show which aired on BBC3 in 2005 and whose funniest regular characters were a trio of vampire slayers from Barnsley.

Vic Reeves, on the other hand, in keeping with his long-held need to both seek celebrity and send it up, appears to have adopted a policy of ubiquity in just about every entertainment field that will have him. As previously alluded to, his first volume of autobiography *Me:Moir* was published in 2006 and another book, *Vic Reeves' Vast Book of World Knowledge*, was released in 2009. Rare is the satellite channel on which he has not appeared as host or talking head - *Auction Man* (2003), *Star Sale* (2004), *My God, I'm My Dad!* (2006) and *Brainiac* (2007) among them. And along with providing voiceovers for a whole range of advertisements, in 2004 he also turned up alongside Ant and Dec - a retro Saturday night northern Variety turn owing much to Vic and Bob's trailblazing if ever there was one - in Australia's outback, via ITV's reality endurance test *I'm A Celebrity, Get Me Out Of Here*. Other reality TV show appearances since then have included *Celebrity Most Haunted, Stars In Their Eyes, Come Dine With Me* and *Hell's Kitchen*, in which latter abomination our hungry hero braved the wrath of chef Gordon Ramsay by asking for a boiled egg.

19
A Dose of Reality, My Arse

"She married a joiner; moved to Leeds.
He knocked her about a bit but... oh... her home was lovely..."
- Nana, The Royle Family.

In 1959, Roy Hudd and Max Miller were standing in the wings of the Finsbury Park Empire. According to Hudd's introduction to *Cavalcade of Variety Acts*, they were two of around thirty people watching an elderly music hall performer, G.H. Elliott, make his way through the old song, 'I Used To Sigh for the Silvery Moon'. A magic performance, according to Hudd, but seen by virtually no one. '"It's all over," said Max. I chuckled to myself, remembering that he always said in his act, "When I'm dead and gone the game's finished." Within four years he had gone, and "the game" had gone with him,' reflects the writer, wistfully.

Fast forward to the early 1990s and up and down the land, thanks largely to the Vic Reeves and Bob Mortimer experience, those same once-struggling Variety theatres were back in something like their original use. True, in an electronic era, the years when audiences would brave the elements on a weekly basis for their fix of entertainment were gone, no doubt forever. And much as the original rock 'n' roll had seen off the old ten-acts-a-night stage extravaganzas, so did comedy, the so-called 'new rock 'n' roll, bypass all conventions of middle-of-the-road 'good taste'.

582

Nonetheless, the bottom commercial line was that auditoriums were once again packed to the rafters. Following in the footsteps of Vic and Bob, youthful, trendy and openly political southern comedians like David Baddiel and Rob Newman began to sell out stadiums too. And along with the money to be made from ticket sales, the merchandising potential of videos, T-shirts and other memorabilia was rigorously exploited, by the acts and their agents-cum-managers, a disproportionately influential part of the comedy scene in their own right. Soon, the comedy industry was just that - an industry as brutal and unforgiving as any other - driven by a lust for financial profit. With the invention of DVD technology, the enterprise moved up another notch to the extent that, in these early days of the twenty-first century, the British comedy market is estimated to be worth at least half a billion pounds: on the back of comedy's very own industrial revolution, one might say. Suddenly, live gigs - well attended ones at least - were a licence to print cash. And so, to some extent, they remain. In recent years, one of the biggest has been Matt Lucas and David Walliams's nine-month long stage tour of *Little Britain,* in 2005-06.

But what of Vic and Bob's wider, culutral influence? Building on the earlier impact of *Python* and *The Young Ones,* the anarchic playfulness of Reeves and Mortimer within traditional mainstream light entertainment formats has been hugely significant in loosening up that television genre entirely. The previously rare phenomenon in UK TV of irreverent banter between presenters is now commonplace. Stuffed shirts and seriousness are distrusted. Nowadays, it is perfectly acceptable for Judy to bicker with Richard; and for Richard to retaliate with an impression of Ali G. And how long before Adrian and Christine on the BBC's *The One Show* start belting each other with frying pans? Furthermore, your average television celebrity now inhabits an ironic parallel universe, where they are as likely to be met with a bucket of cockroaches down their blouse as respectful acclaim. After the precedent set by *Families At War,* Saturday night Variety -style silliness is *de rigeur* and the more offbeat and imaginative the better, whether its B-list celebs ballroom dancing on ice or Sir Andrew Lloyd Webber enthroned like a malevolent toad prince, sitting in judgment on a desperate posse of singing nuns. And the current madcap kings of this latest Variety nirvana on the most traditionally important night of the television week? Why, only another couple of funny northerners.

In the same year that Johnny Vegas was voted the Royal Television Society's best newcomer of 2002, a couple of children's TV presenters named Anthony McPartlin and Declan Donnelly enjoyed even greater success in the ITV-sponsored National Television Awards, at London's Royal Albert Hall. Unlike, the RTS Awards and the British Academy's BAFTAs, the National Television Awards are decided annually by the Great British public. In short, to be recognised there is cast-iron proof of national popularity. So when, at the tender age of 27, the two friends won a Special Recognition Award more commonly given to mark a lifetime's achievement, their position on comedy's pedestal was already assured.

Perhaps the most remarkable aspect of that accolade was that McPartlin and Donnelly - known to all as Ant and Dec - had until then spent so much of their time in the unpromising backwaters of children's television. On the other hand, that was an environment in which their cheeky Vic and Bob-style zaniness was guaranteed to stand out; especially when it was underpinned by an obviously warm and genuine friendship grounded in shared childhood experiences in their hometown Newcastle. It was a combination that quickly made them favourites with viewers and fellow-performers alike, somewhat unusually in the now ultra-competitive business of comedy. The ecstatic response from the Albert Hall audience said it all. Budge up Alan Bennett, Michael Palin and Victoria Wood, a youthful couple of new 'national treasures' were coming through.

The Saturday morning show that confirmed the duo's household name credentials was *SM:TV Live*, which was at the end of a four-year run when Ant and Dec bounded up for their gong in 2002. The programme, also hosted by fashion model Cat Deeley, was a lively mix of costumed silliness, viewer involvement and music which, like *Do Not Adjust Your Set* and *Tiswas* before it, began to attract as many adults as children, resulting in impressive viewing figures of some two-and-a-half million per week. As usual, ITV may have limped along in second place in the arena of classic sitcoms, but it remained way out in front - in terms of edginess anyway - with the nation's kids.

Mindful of the slapping administered by *Tiswas* to Noel Edmonds's rather twee *Multi-Coloured Swap Shop* in the 1970s and early-eighties, the BBC had at least upped the irreverence quota with *Going Live* in 1987. Although hosted by clean-cut pair Phillip Schofield and Sarah Greene, that show had also featured two wackier young comics who might be seen as a prototype Vic and Bob. Trevor and Simon - real names Trevor Neal and Simon Hickson - had first met while studying drama at university in Manchester, in 1981. It was there that they formed a bizarre double act, 'The Devilfishhorn Club', which soon made a splash on the Edinburgh Fringe. In 1985, they relocated south where, a couple of years later, the call came from BBC television centre.

In both *Going Live* and its 1993 follow-up *Live And Kicking*, and some three years before *Vic Reeves Big Night Out*, the youth of Great Britain were faced with such sketches as 'The Singing Corner' (in which a couple of 1970s folk singers revelled in the catchphrase 'Swing Your Pants!') and 'The World of the Strange' (wherein two cloaked eerie types would put the most innocuous events down to supernatural intervention). Celebrity guests were welcomed into the barbers shop of 'Ken and Eddie Kennedy'. Later, in *Live And Kicking*, such stars were subjected to interrogation from both sides, while seated in the middle of a sagging settee. And in the year that Reeves and Mortimer would take such shenanigans to another level, 1990, this particular double act recorded a novelty single with the 'sixties pop star Donovan, itself following in the wake of a couple of videos and a book - *Trevor and Simon's Stupid Book*. Despite their obvious popularity, the pair were then mystifyingly dropped from the 1991-1992 series of *Going Live*, before being reinstated the following year. But by then, Vic and Bob were in full stride and despite a couple of early evening BBC shows, *The Trev And Simon Summer Special* (a one-off in 1995) and *Trev And Simon's Transmission Impossible* (which ran to two full series), like Freddie 'Parrot Face' Davies, the Chuckle Brothers and *The Goodies* before them, Trevor and Simon were finding that the stain of children's entertainment was tough to wash off.

Which makes, of course, the achievement of Ant and Dec in making that very leap and beyond all the more remarkable. For not only did they share Trevor and Simon's penchant for confusion over who exactly was who (Trev being tall, Simon short; Ant and Dec arranged alphabetically, left to right) the more chaotic ingredients of *Going Live* were in *SM:TV Live* too. There were silly puppets like Wonkey Donkey (a one-legged donkey), and unpredictable telephone calls from viewers, in which the pair first made use of an ability to take the mickey out of their public while simultaneously keeping them onside. There was 'Chums', a spoof

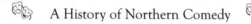

of American sitcom *Friends*, in which celebs were crawling over each other to take part. Yet behind all the childish flippancy, was unmistakable cross-generational appeal.

Its source lay in the authenticity of the central relationship itself. As with Vic and Bob, and Eric and Ernie, audiences responded lovingly. With none of Reeves and Mortimer's disconcerting weirdness to worry about, older viewers thought the boys clean-cut and wholesome in their appeal. Younger audiences could relate to their mischievous sense of fun. In true northern comedy style, Ant and Dec combined the glamour of showbiz with the normality of everyday life. Thanks to their down-to-earth nature and a natty line in self-deprecation, they came across as a throwback to traditional Variety light entertainment but with a dollop of modern-day irony mixed in. Nowhere is this more obvious than in their willingness, though heterosexual, to as good as flirt with one another for comic effect. And even when Ant and Dec not infrequently dabble in verbal cruelty, it somehow never seems cynical and is always undercut by those cheeky winning smiles and a twinkle in the eye. In an hour-long documentary narrated by John Thomson in 2006, Channel 5 could even bill the pair as *Ant And Dec: A Showbiz Marriage*. Suitably, the closing credits played out to 'Bring Me Sunshine' and their biographical detail reveals a partnership rooted very firmly in northern working-class reality.

Declan Donnelly was born of Irish Catholic stock in the poverty-riven west end of Newcastle in September 1975, the youngest of seven children. Despite that, he was by all accounts a cheerful child. About a mile up the road, meanwhile, two months later, life began in not quite so strapped circumstances for Anthony McPartlin. As youngsters, both boys showed an early interest in drama but it was Ant who first appeared on British TV screens when, in 1988, he appeared as a 12-year-old presenter on a kids' show usually broadcast in the school holidays: *Why Don't You.... (Just Switch Off Your Television Set And Go Out And Do Something Less Boring Instead)?* Then, in 1990, he landed the part that was to change his life, as wannabe disc jockey Peter 'P.J.' Jenkins, in a BBC childrens' drama serial set in the north East, *Byker Grove*.

By then, *Byker Grove* was already a series old; one of its stars being none other than Declan Donnelly, or Duncan as he was known in the show. Soon, the lads were mates, on screen and off. However, unknown to all but the scriptwriters, Ant's character was to meet with tragedy. After unwisely removing his mask during a paint-balling game, P.J. was shot in the face and blinded in a tear-jerking scene which, to paraphrase Oscar Wilde in writing about the death of Little Nell, one would have needed a heart of stone to watch without laughing. Now sightless, P.J. (and Duncan) battled on in *Byker Grove* before, equally tragically for anyone over the age of 13, opting to retain their screen names and embark upon a career as 17-year-old pop stars instead. Their first record, 'Tonight I'm Free,' only just made the charts and had nothing to do with John Inman. Their next, 'Why Me?', fared little better. So it was back to drama school they went, before a third single, an attempt to hitch a lift on the rapping bandwagon, the tongue-in-cheek 'Let's get Ready to Rumble', did a great deal better. In their baseball caps and baggy pants, P.J. and Duncan had regained the attention of teenage girls everywhere. By 1995, they had two hit albums and numerous packed-out live concerts under their belts.

More singles followed, but the pair were soon back on television as themselves when the BBC, looking for a *Byker Grove* spin-off aimed at older teenagers, settled on its two former stars as the perfect candidates. Thus was born *The Ant And Dec Show* (1995), a particularly zany affair wherein David Walliams was in the writing team and, notoriously, one unfortunate schoolgirl had her hair cut off to the great consternation of the tabloid newspapers but not much in the way of horror from the lass herself. The dear old BBC took fright at such antics and, in 1997, the duo embarked upon a fresh start with Channel 4. Though crammed with an abundance of Reevesian ideas - cut-aways to talking stuffed animals *et al* - and despite having no less a figure than Eddie Braben in and among the writing credits, the resulting *Ant And Dec Unzipped* was a little too off the wall even by Channel 4's standards. It was ditched after ten episodes.

Nevertheless, a third hit album and bookings on *Top Of The Pops* kept musical alter-egos P.J. and Duncan in the public eye, while the arrival of *SM:TV Live* in 1998 ensured that the names Ant and Dec also stayed prominent. It was increasingly obvious that a decision had to be made. Were the boys P.J. and Duncan, or Ant and Dec? Pop stars or television stars? With a more grown-up audience in their sights they decided on the latter, but did not make the most convincing of starts.

For most entertainers, a prime-time Saturday night spot on BBC1 is

an opportunity for which they spend their whole lives waiting. In 2000, Ant and Dec's chance came with *Friends Like These*, a quiz show of sorts in which, echoing Reeves and Mortimer's *Families At War*, members of the public were pitted against one another, but without the spiders. With its emphasis on testing the limits of friendship, the format of *Friends Like These* ought to have been ideal but when ITV came wooing with a transfer fee of some £2million each in 2001, the BBC failed to put up much of a fight and the duo were off to the other side, replaced by former Arsenal and England footballer Ian Wright. At first, the money apart, it looked like an ill-judged move. The pair's first Saturday night party show, *Slap Bang*, was essentially *SM:TV Live* for adults and it flopped as badly as the *Tiswas* spin-off *O.T.T.* had years before. Then came *Pop Idol*.

A sequel to ITV's hugely successful reality talent contest *Popstars*, *Pop Idol* wasn't just a hit, it was a grade 'A' phenomenon that blasted Ant, Dec and several others into superstar orbit. As hosts of this *New Faces* for a new millennium, in which they were the likeable middle men between nervy and frequently excruciatingly untalented wannabe performers and a gang of headline-grabbing hard-nosed judges, Ant and Dec might well have ended up peripheral. However, through sheer force of personality, they became a key reason for its success. To the viewers and hopefuls, these two Geordie funsters were the good guys in a harsh and unforgiving business. Sympathetic but never condescending, a clue to their charm lay in an ability to marry a consoling pat on the shoulder with a knowing glance to camera and subtle dig of their own. In effect, Ant and Dec were the viewers at home by proxy. And, in time, the duo also began to skit the judging panel, Simon Cowell and all, which took *Pop Idol* to a loftier plain still. Their public adored them for it.

The award-winning year of 2002 cemented the duo's burgeoning reputation, although one blip was the *A Tribute To The Likely Lads* special in May, alongside John Thomson and Rodney Bewes in his earlier-mentioned cameo. More durable by far was *Ant & Dec's Saturday Night Takeaway*, which launched a month later. Here McPartlin and Donnelly were back where they belonged: engaged in witty banter before a live studio audience, themselves intent on an old-fashioned knees-up. Even the show's title sequence, in which the lads crashed their way through walls in the manner of a contemporary Levi's jeans advert, might be seen as a neat metaphor for Ant and Dec's career trajectory. With its noisy crowd, broad humour, cash prizes, hidden camera stunts and celebrity hi-jinks - plus its emphasis on television advertising, of course - this was Saturday night 'seventies light entertainment reinvented for a modern, commercial age. Comfortable enough, by now, to act as a classic old-time double act, Ant and Dec's filmed inserts, too, became a staple ingredient of the show. One such was 'Ant & Dec Undercover' in which, thanks to a make-up department that buried them in a mountain of prosthetics while still leaving them relatively human, the duo hoodwinked assorted 'stars' disguised as nuns, German pop stars and other grotesques.

Already at the top of their game, in August 2002 Ant and Dec's celebrity-baiting cranked up another gear with their stewardship of *I'm A Celebrity, Get Me Out Of Here*, an ITV reality series set in the Australian outback, in which an unlikely collection of B, C and even D-listers would spend a fortnight undergoing outrageous 'Bushtrucker Trials'. Once again, Ant and Dec not only linked the events together, they included the audience at home in an apparent three-way conversation. In *I'm A Celebrity...* the interplay between the two scaled new heights, in terms of jungle walkways, comedy and knowingness. Although undeniably popular whatever the faded glory of its competitors, the show itself left much to be desired for pickier viewers. Even they, however, were surely forced to admire a level of wit and humility in its hosts that, at times, bordered on comic genius. And once again, while humiliation and cruelty was very much to the fore - fancy being buried alive in an underground pit filled with water and rats, or maybe have your arm stuck into a nest of spiders or snakes? - everyone knew that it was really the producers who were behind it. Like Morecambe and Wise and Reeves and Mortimer, Ant and Dec were just a couple of likely northern lads, having a laugh, that's all.

At the height of Vic and Bob's popularity in 1997, *Shooting Stars* and *The Fast Show* shared the same stage over thirty-two live dates at London's Hammersmith Apollo; the latest in a long line of groundbreaking Reeves and Mortimer ventures. Soon however, an original star of the latter show, Caroline Aherne, would be responsible for a revolution of her own.

Since being spotted by Paul Whitehouse and Charlie Higson on

Paramount City - shortly after winning Manchester's inaugural City Life Comedian of the Year award in 1990 - Aherne's reputation as a character comedian of great promise had blossomed. So much so that, despite the enormous success of *The Fast Show*, she was the first of its regular cast to jump ship. That leap was not entirely in the dark. It came on the back of a roster of memorable *Fast Show* characters, and a satirical chat show that made its BBC television debut in 1995. Made in Manchester, *The Mrs. Merton Show* ran over five series and three Christmas specials until 1998, with Aherne inhabiting a little old lady persona to an inspired degree.

Caroline Aherne was born on Christmas Eve, 1963, in London. The daughter of an Irish Catholic railway worker and school dinner lady, her family moved to the Manchester suburb of Wythenshawe when Caroline was just two years old. Other than being near-blind in one eye as a result of childhood cancer of the retina, a fate shared with a brother, hers was a happy upbringing. Blessed with a sharp intelligence, ready wit and gift for mimicry, she regularly entertained her clan with amusing impressions. At least partly inspired by a trip to see the Victoria Wood play *Talent*, and thereafter influenced by such playwrights as Willy Russell, Alan Bennett and Ken Loach, upon leaving convent school she chose to study drama at Liverpool Polytechnic. Later, she worked as a secretary by day in the offices of BBC Manchester, while blazing a trail on the city's stand-up comedy circuit by night. It was during this time that she also struck up a close friendship and working relationship with a fellow budding comedy writer named Craig Cash.

Aherne's TV debut as Mrs. Merton came on a Yorkshire television sitcom shown mainly in the north, *Frank Sidebottom's Fantastic Shed Show* (1992). Each week the eponymous Frank, with outlandish papier-maché head, saucer eyes, side parting and Mancunian dulcet tones, would invite viewers into his back yard for fun and frolics. The self-styled 'Timperley Superstar' - a creation of former Manchester punk rocker Chris Sievey - had risen to such heights on the back of a cult 1980s recording career, plus a variety of Piccadilly Radio and Saturday morning TV appearances in the company of his ventriloquist dummy Little Frank, or such rising northern broadcasters as Mark Radcliffe and Chris Evans. After its pilot was well received, *Frank Sidebottom's Fantastic Shed Show* lasted six inventive episodes, in which Mrs. Merton featured as Sidebottom's next-door neighbour.

A Dose of Reality, My Arse

According to the journalist Jon Ronson, in a 2006 edition of *The Guardian*, Sievey was not only responsible for the creation of Mrs. Merton but a key influence on a certain other downbeat musician too. 'Chris invented a cast of supporting characters, who would pop up between the songs on his radio show, Radio Timperley,' wrote Ronson, who claimed inside knowledge, having spent three years in the late 'eighties playing keyboards for The Frank Sidebottom Oh Blimey! Big Band, while also acting as the big-headed one's agent. 'There was the puppet, Little Frank. There was the neighbour, Mrs. Merton. Chris asked his brother-in-law's friend, the then BBC secretary Caroline Aherne, to do the voice of Mrs. Merton, which is how she came to exist. Paying close attention to Frank's burgeoning world was Graham Fellows, who went on to invent John Shuttleworth on Sidebottom principles, and eventually became more famous, a bit like Nirvana to Frank's Pixies.' Though left in their wake to some extent, Frank Sidebottom would nevertheless loiter in the margins of the Mancunian music, football and comedy scene for years to come and, most recently, has had a show on local TV station Channel M.

Whatever the character's origins, it was undoubtedly Aherne and Craig Cash who established the mischievous Mrs. Merton as a rounded personality in her own right, primarily via spots on local indie station KFM, for whom Jon Ronson also broadcasted. There, alongside a host of other Aherne characters such as Sister Mary Immaculate and the country and western singer Mitzi Goldberg, the agony aunt OAP dished out questionable advice to worried listeners. Cash had been first to arrive at KFM when the station, near Stockport, operated on a pirate basis. His partnership with Aherne began when she was taken on as a presenter after sending in her CV. Subsequently, along with Ronson, all three appear to have had the late-night run of the place and their often jointly-presented shows, with Mrs. Merton prominent, soon gained cult status. Until, that is, the station was granted a proper licence and taken over by Signal Radio. At which point, the trio were out on their ears.

All three were destined for bigger things anyway. Ronson primarily in written journalism, although he would go on to present a number of entertaining broadcast documentaries too. Caroline Aherne and Craig Cash in out-and-out comedy, where the next step up the ladder wasn't long in coming. In fact, around the time that Aherne's stand-up career

591

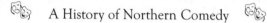

was morphing into *The Fast Show*, the Mrs. Merton character had already begun to interest the BBC, who commissioned a pilot. As a result, *The Mrs. Merton Show* became a late-night series made by Granada but shown on BBC2. From there, word-of-mouth ensured that it grew rapidly in terms of popularity and a third series, when it arrived, was broadcast on prime-time BBC1. All this attention didn't go to the old girl's head. The world of Mrs. Merton continued to be down-to-earth and homely. The show's opening credits showed women hanging out washing in cobbled streets and what followed was played out before an audience made up of the Aherne family's own friends and neighbours, specially bussed in by charabanc by the look of it. Many of them, such as Wigan trio Sylvia, Liz and Enid and cocky celebrity critic Roy, were natural comics themselves, giving a clue as to how the host's sense of humour had been formed in the first place. Yet despite its apparent cosiness, *The Mrs. Merton Show* was no fluffy northern sponge cake. Or if it was, it was a sponge cake with a razor blade hidden inside.

No longer an outspoken agony aunt, behind her prim and proper demeanour Mrs. Merton was now a fully-fledged chat show host, with a cheeky twinkle in her eye and a simultaneously subtle and cutting line in questioning. Disguised in her demure old lady's frock, 'fifties specs and matching hairdo, and backed by a disarmingly benign bear pit of genuine pensioners, the 30-year-old Caroline Aherne seemed free to ask anything, no matter how impressive (or otherwise) her guest's celebrity rating. The results were frequently as revealing as they were hilarious. Undoubtedly, her most memorable query was the one directed at Debbie McGee, the wife and one-time stage assistant of magician Paul Daniels, whom she asked: 'So, Debbie McGee, what first attracted you to the millionaire Paul Daniels?' But there were plenty more where that came from. 'What have you come as love?' she once enquired of the pop star Boy George. And along with the aforementioned puncturing of Bernard Manning, football legend George Best was asked if he would have been quite so thirsty if he hadn't done all that running around. Mostly, her guests appeared happy enough to be in on the joke even if some, like flamboyant boxer Chris Eubank, shuffled disconcertingly. 'You're going to hit me, aren't you?' said his smiling antagonist. Issue-led mid-morning talk shows were sent up too, sparked by Mrs. Merton's cheerily communal: 'Let's have a heated debate!' Altogether, it was a tasty recipe that left Aherne named Best Female Comedian at the 1996 British Comedy Awards, while the show itself earned consecutive BAFTAs for Best Entertainment Series (1996) and Best Chat Show (1997). Since when, similarly ironic chat show hosts like Rob Brydon and Sanjeev Bhaskar have proliferated. Another to reap what he and Mrs. Merton simultaneously sowed was her contemporary from Norwich, Alan Partridge, of whom more after the break.

When *The Mrs Merton Show* reached its fifth and final series in 1998, the concept was showing distinct signs of having jumped the shark. A year previously, the lady in question and her coterie of perky pensioners were sent to America, where they filmed three thirty-minute episodes of *Mrs. Merton In Las Vegas* with disappointing results. After which, her creators decided to return Mrs. Merton to the world of situation comedy. The vehicle for this was to be *Mrs. Merton And Malcolm* (1999), whose premise was based upon a series of adverts made for British Gas, in which the mother and her gormless son (played by Cash) appeared.

On the rare occasion that it is nowadays discussed at all, the first thing usually noted about *Mrs. Merton And Malcolm* is that it upset a fair amount of people, including various mental health organisations who took offence at the portrayal of Merton Jr. - a classic northern simpleton - as 'backward'. Yet although it had its problems, such a one-issue critique was too reductive. *Mrs. Merton And Malcolm* was actually rather enjoyable; a unique and, to some at the time, unsettling evocation of light and dark. Set in a Stockport terrace house in which Mrs. Merton resides with her 37-year-old mummy's boy and unseen bed-ridden husband, the pigeon hole - geographical or otherwise - did not exist that could hold it, which maybe accounts for why it was cancelled after a six-week run. In fact, the London listings magazine *Time Out* described *Mrs. Merton And Malcolm* as 'possibly the most disturbing show on television.' Its writers and stars, on the other hand, insisted that their self-contained world was actually one of innocence and old-fashioned values, in the manner of *Some Mothers Do 'Ave 'Em*. Be that as it may, Aherne and Cash were now clearly intent on marrying the northern working class culture they knew so well with a challenge to established light entertainment orthodoxy.

Meanwhile, for one of Mrs. Merton's former guests, Steve Coogan, the satirical chat show route was also a route well worth travelling, for the moment at least. And just as Mrs. Merton's torch of comedy truth not infrequently left the audience squirming on behalf of her guests, the same might also be said for Coogan's finest comedy creation, even though *every* character in the world of Alan Partridge was as fictional as his own self-delusion.

Like his friend Caroline Aherne, Coogan was another product of the Manchester stand-up circuit blessed with a revolutionary eye for comedy. In his case, though, a knack for breaking ground ran concurrent with a more mainstream career pathway that led, in time, to international film stardom on both sides of the Atlantic, like Stan Laurel, Gracie Fields and *Monty Python* before him. Yet, there was little sign of any of that to begin with. At the start of his television career, he looked to be heading for a life of impressions and funny voices. His small-screen debut in 1987, for example, saw him billed as the 'new Bobby Davro' on *Sunday Night At The London Palladium* with Jimmy Tarbuck.

Steve Coogan was one of six children born into a lower-middle-class Irish Catholic family in Middleton in 1965. And again like Aherne, impersonations played a large part in the childhood of a comedian who, forty years later, would be voted among the top twenty ever by fellow comics and industry insiders. For the young Coogan, it seems, in such a big family, doing impressions of teachers and other local personalities was a means of gaining attention. And his father, too, loved comedy. The Coogan home would rock to the laughter produced by shows like *Fawlty Towers*, *Morecambe And Wise* and *The Two Ronnies*. In conversation with Paul Jackson on BBC Radio 4 in 2001, Coogan recalled how another big parental favourite was Tony Hancock, whose pompous little Englander personality was stored away, ready to be reshaped in later decades.

Indeed, so important was comedy to the young Steve Coogan that, upon leaving school, he made a calculated and single-minded decision to make it his career. First, he enrolled at the Manchester Polytechnic School of Theatre, where he studied the dramatic arts and met a future long-time colleague and friend, John Thomson. Then, like Thomson, he embarked upon stand-up gigs around the city and earned his equity card. Soon, he was spotted by a local radio producer and began to supply voiceovers for adverts. Although still a student, it was at this juncture that he was declared Variety's next big thing on the bill of that London Palladium show with Tarby. But then, just as he was finishing drama school, there came a job offer from a much more fashionable source. He was asked to contribute voices to *Spitting Image*, beginning a five-year association with a show that did his comedy credibility no harm at all.

Coogan's continued presence on the Manchester club circuit, meanwhile, saw him meet Caroline Aherne who, in turn, introduced him to Craig Cash and Henry Normal. Impressionist spots on the Arthur Smith-hosted stand-up shows *1st Exposure* and *Paramount City* followed, as did an appearance on *Stand Up* (1989), an ITV show based, unlikely as it sounds, on Granada's *The Comedians*, in which a host of current names like Rob Newman, Frank Skinner, Mark Lamarr, Jack Dee and Patrick Marber put down their own comedy credentials. Doors were beginning to open; particularly in the south, where Coogan was busy evolving a whole new group of friends and Oxbridge-educated work colleagues to complement his working-class chums in the north. Of the London-based set, Marber and the Scots-born radio producer Armando Iannucci would prove particularly influential. For it was Iannucci who, while producing Newman, David Baddiel, Hugh Dennis and Steve Punt in *The Mary Whitehouse Experience* on Radio 1, heard the current affairs parodies of satirist Chris Morris on London station GLR and decided that there was likely to be a highly amusing show in it. The result, in September 1991, was BBC Radio 4's *On The Hour*, in which sports desk reporter Alan Partridge first unleashed his individual brand of insensitive ineptitude on an enchanted listening public.

Written by Morris, Iannucci, Steven 'Seething' Wells, Andrew Glover, David Quantick, Stewart Lee and the Yorkshire-born but Somerset-raised Richard Herring, *On The Hour* was at once like nothing heard on radio before and lots of things heard on radio before. Coogan - joined in the cast by Marber, David Schneider, Rebecca Front and Doon Mackichan - has said that when he first read the scripts he literally cried with laughter. Audiences were soon doing likewise. Although a sizeable proportion of Radio 4 listeners were confused by its clever combination of naturalism, surrealism and breathless news parody, the majority heard it for what it was: an ingenious and devastatingly funny critique of the modern day news media in all its hyperbolic idiocy. No corner of contemporary media news coverage was safe from ridicule, whether it be the urge to sensationalise unnecessarily ('...hang on, news has just come in - I'm afraid it's WAR!'); habitual shouty repetition ('THIS IS THE NEWS!') delivered in a weird rhythm of speech that is the preserve of professional broadcasters alone; the exploitation of natural tragedy ('...a musical demonstration of the effects of an earthquake'); obsequious obsession with royalty ('...a shock announcement that Prince Harry has split up'); or the patronising attitude to a public that it the media is supposedly there to serve ('...an SOS message for Mr Robert Smithson, currently being buried in Yorkshire - please return home, you're perfectly alright'). And the heartbeat of it all was the ultimate straight man Chris Morris, a by turns slick and scathing anchorman with a talent for nonsensical headline-speak: 'The Bank of England Has Lost The Pound!' or 'Penelope Keith Riots Rage On!'. On account of which, it has since become impossible to take our modern-day news purveyors anything like as seriously as they take themselves.

The two radio series of *On The Hour* were so popular that, in 1994, the programme was redeveloped for television and renamed *The Day Today*, albeit without the services of Lee and Herring (who left due to 'artistic differences' and were replaced by *Father Ted* creators Graham Linehan and Arthur Mathews). When reinforced by whizz-bang visual graphics, the sublime levels of satire became still more acute and many of the radio regulars were now to be seen in all their physical glory; among them Marber's inspired fact-lazy creation, Peter O'Hanrahanrahan ('er... that's right, Chris'). None, however, would enjoy the longevity of Alan Partridge, whose origins lay in a suggestion by Armando Iannucci that *On The Hour* would benefit from having a sports presenter. And thanks to his experience as a smooth-tongued radio voice-over man, Steve Coogan was the ideal candidate for the job. *Goal* pie!

Along with just being extremely amusing, *On The Hour* and *The Day Today* confirmed Coogan's residency at the centre of a crossroads that British comedy had been drifting towards for decades - gradually since the beginning of the 'sixties, and more forceably with the alternative boom of the late-1970s. A place where warm-hearted working-class observation might rub along quite happily with analytical middle-class satire. And the opportunity those programmes gave him to develop Partridge and a wide range of other beautifully drawn characters had not come a moment too soon. For despite performing at the Edinburgh Fringe in 1990, with Frank Skinner as his warm-up act, Coogan has since admitted that prior to *On The Hour*, he had been in real danger of sliding back into artistic complacency. Realisation dawned on holiday in Corfu the following year. While reading a newspaper, the comedian spotted a report outlining how Skinner had gone on to win the 1991 Perrier Award. Fearing he had lost his way, Coogan resolved there and then to go back to Edinburgh and win that award himself. Which is exactly what he did - in a show directed by Marber and featuring no *Spitting Image*-style celebrity impressions at all.

Though *On The Hour* was soon proving popular and the character of Alan Partridge had progressed to a radio series of his own, *Knowing Me, Knowing You... With Alan Partridge*, Coogan's public profile was at this stage still very much low key, as shown by his 1993 bit-part appearance as the lead singer of Go West on *The Smell Of Reeves And Mortimer*. The following year, however, all that changed completely when it was decided that Partridge should make the leap to television. The small-screen version followed the same structure as its radio equivalent - a half-hour chat show featuring fictional guests who reflected contemporary social figures, as played variously by Marber, Front, Schneider, Mackichan *et al.* Now, though, viewers could thrill to the contents of Alan's spectacularly unfashionable wardrobe (wherein blazers, Pringle sweaters and sports casual nylon slacks loomed large) and revel in Coogan's own well-judged gift for physical clowning. Along with verbal catchphrases - like the call-and-response: 'Knowing me, Alan Partridge, knowing you Keith Hunt, ah-ha!' Guest: 'Ah-ha!' - the show was further lit up by a ready supply of Abba cover versions and a convoluted introductory metaphor. Other treats included the Partridge hair-do, a studio set modelled on 'the lobby of an internationally famous hotel' and an array of facial expressions that would not have been out of place on a drowning man. The TV series also saw the introduction of a house band, led by the long-suffering Glen Ponder (Steve Brown) who, like his guests, was often the target of Alan's bad manners.

In short, where the deskbound radio Partridge had been a delightful if two-dimensional one-trick pony, television saw him evolve into a more complex personality with the foibles to match. We learned of Alan's conservative taste in cars (Rover or Lexus, complete with Bang & Olufsen stereo system), his favourite music ('....aah, Wings - the band the Beatles could have been'), a repressed attitude to sex and right-wing political leanings. We hooted at his spectacular shallowness and social inadequacy. And we winced at his lack of interest in anything other than his own monstrous, ambitious and fame-hungry self.

Alan Partridge would not be the only grotesque in Steve Coogan's repertoire. Hot on his heels came the student-hating, beer-swilling, fag-smoking Paul Calf (catchphrase: 'bag of shite'), a character based on the type of pub-goer Coogan tried to avoid while at drama school. Under his tatty blond-streaked mullet, Calf was a product of Coogan's live act who first came to light on *Paramount City*, before turning up on Jonathan Ross's *Saturday Zoo*. It was in the latter show that he was also given a sister, the sexually-confident Pauline Calf, as convincing a drag act as ever there was. In keeping with Coogan's enthusiasm for inventing a back story for his creations, brother and sister appeared in *The Paul Calf Video Diary*, a New Year's Day special for the BBC in 1994, in which John Thomson, Patrick Marber and Henry Normal also starred. Later that same year, the Calf family and their entourage returned for *Three Fights, Two Weddings And A Funeral*, a spoof of Richard Curtis's recent film, *Four Weddings And A Funeral*, in which Coogan's versatility was again to the fore.

Even so, it was Partridge who continued to hog the limelight until, in 1995, the men behind this true British comedy legend temporarily decided that was enough was enough. Accordingly, his days in the studio spotlight came to an end with a Christmas special, *Knowing Me, Knowing Yule... With Alan Partridge*, in which the eponymous host is sacked after hitting fictional BBC Chief Commissioning Editor Tony Hayers (David Schneider) in the face with a dead turkey, leaving a distraught Partridge to wail: 'I'll never chat again!' And so did it seem until November 1997, when Partridge returned to British television screens in a sitcom spin-off, *I'm Alan Partridge*, having in the interim plunged to the ignominious position of dawn chorus deejay on the fictional Radio Norwich.

Nowadays, for his radio show 'Up With The Partridge', Alan takes to the airwaves at the ungodly hour of 4.30am. To make matters worse, he finishes at 7.30am - exactly the time that his deadly rival Dave Clifton

(Phil Cornwell) begins his prestigious breakfast show, the cause of many an excruciating hand-over. An unglamorous local radio shift is the least of his problems however. Since we last met him, Alan has been thrown out by his wife, Carol, in favour of a fitness instructor, leaving the one-time king of chat to languish in the on-going purgatory that is the Linton Travel Tavern, equidistant between London and Norwich. Other than handyman Michael (Simon Greenall), a gung-ho former marine with a (to Alan anyway) impenetrable Geordie accent ('I'm sorry, that was just a noise'), the hotel staff treat their resident egomaniac with the respect his celebrity merits - i.e. hardly any. Partridge's sole confidante is his sad-eyed assistant Lynn, a shy and dumpy 50-year-old spinster (Felicity Montagu), whose loyalty and diligence with regard to returning her boss to his former glories, he takes entirely for granted.

In coming around to the return of Partridge, his creators had at first considered giving him another chat show. Noting that Mrs. Merton now had that genre sewn up, they opted to explore Alan's private life instead. Thanks to the tightness of its scripts, wicked eye for detail and bravura acting performances from Coogan and a terrific supporting cast, *I'm Alan Partridge* immediately became a worthy addition to Britain's situation comedy hall of fame. Where *Knowing Me, Knowing You...* had fleshed Alan out from his days as a mere sports reporter, in this latest incarnation a man who had always loved the sound of his own voice became a still more atrocious force of nature. This was no two-dimensional stereotype. In the best sitcom tradition, this was a vulnerable human being, whether physically (an apparent magnet for fungal skin infections), emotionally ('Listen, Jill, there is a romantic buffet-supper tonight at the hotel - as much as you can eat for six pounds'), or sexually (his reasons for 'accidentally' watching 'Bangkok Chickboys' on his hotel room telly are, he says, 'complicated'). Although Alan was an appalling personality who few people would willingly go within one hundred feet of, he was essentially in pain - here, as anywhere, the ideal subject for comedy. A self-deluded fool, he had long since mistaken fame for empathy and genuine human interaction and was therefore cursed to be one of life's outsiders. Not that it mattered to us. As with Basil Fawlty, Steptoe, Rigsby and their ilk, it was the monster within that rendered comedy and tragedy undistinguishable.

In 1998, Steve Coogan took Partridge and an assortment of his other

characters on the road with a two-hundred-date sell-out live national tour written in association with Henry Normal, *The Man Who Thinks He's It*. In his Radio 4 interview with Paul Jackson, Coogan declared that the aim was to 'reclaim the Variety show for our generation' and it could certainly boast a ten-week record-breaking run at London's Lyceum Theatre among its many other achievements. As a geographical aside, Coogan also noted that audiences in the north tended to laugh loudest while their southern counterparts noticed more in the way of detail. In any case, so successful was the partnership with Normal that, in 1999, and with Coogan now resident on England's south coast, the pair set up their own production company, Baby Cow (i.e. calf). And while that meant nicking Normal off Caroline Aherne and Craig Cash, there doesn't appear to have been any bitterness. As Cash himself said at the time, noting how Coogan had loyally turned down Terry Wogan 'to come on my little radio show in Stockport': 'That's fine. It makes sense for Henry because they both live in Brighton. In fact, they play lots of pitch and putt together.'

For Coogan, a major benefit of Baby Cow was the opportunity it gave him to develop shows and projects which might be inappropriate for him to do himself. One individual to benefit was Rob Brydon, a Welsh former local radio presenter for whom the darkly naturalistic *Marion and Geoff* and *Human Remains* (both 2000) provided a major stepping stone to the big time. A second was the equally gifted Julia Davis who, after appearing in the sketch show *Big Train*, accompanied Coogan on his 1998 tour before eventually appearing with Brydon in *Human Remains* and conjuring up the distinctly unnerving *Nighty Night* (2004).

Though Alan Partridge made a brief comeback as part of 1999's *Comic Relief* celebrations, Coogan increasingly began to devote more time to other characters. Some, such as the tight-trousered Portuguese 'singing sensation' Tony Ferrino and the repellent travelling salesman Gareth Cheeseman (who had first appeared in *Coogan's Run*, a series of six self-contained BBC comedy playlets first broadcast in 1995, and was in many ways a forerunner to Ricky Gervais's David Brent), were moderate hits. Others, such as the sinister Dr. Terrible, host of *Dr. Terrible's House of Horrible* (2001), played by a cross-eyed, bald-wigged Coogan, who linked a series of ghostly spoofs from an armchair at the side of a roaring open fire, were critical flops. Or as Dr. Terrible himself put it: 'That was truly diabolical.' They were better than that. Sending up TV shows like *Alfred Hitchcock Presents* (1955), *The Twilight Zone* (1959-64) and *Tales Of The Unexpected* (1979-88), together with a host of creaky old horror movies, *Dr. Terrible's House of Horrible* was a highly original concept with first rate production values. A cast that changed every week featured Mark Gatiss, Alexander Armstrong and John Thomson. The biggest problem faced by Dr. Terrible, it seems, is that he wasn't Alan Partridge. Happily, around twelve months later, in November 2002, the man himself was back.

Though some complained that it was not as good as its predecessor, the second series of *I'm Alan Partridge* was nevertheless still funnier than your average British sitcom by quite some distance. With his days on the early morning shift now behind him, Alan, as awful as ever, has wormed his way back into television, where he presents 'Skirmish', a daytime cable TV quiz show with a military theme, as well as fronting 'Crash, Bang, Wallop! What A Video!', a caught-on-camera car crash extravaganza whose sequel is 'Scum On The Run'. He is now also in possession of the 'third-best' slot on Radio Norwich, all of which leads our man to consider himself back in the big time. So much so that, some five years after we last met him, he has penned an autobiography based upon that very return to grace called 'Bouncing Back' (destined to be pulped), in which he outlines the Toblerone addiction that saw him balloon in weight and a subsequent breakdown (two years of being 'clinically fed up') which sent him scuttling off to Dundee in his car. Furthermore, with his days at the Linton Travel Tavern now a distant memory, Partridge has graduated to living in a caravan with the gauche Ukranian immigrant Sonja (Amelia Bullmore), who spends her time embarrassing her boyfriend, presenting him with tacky gifts and servicing his carnal desires ('..that was *classic* sexual intercourse'). Of the original cast, dogsbody PA Lynn and Geordie psycho Michael are still around, the former now with a male friend of her own, a former policeman named Gordon, and the latter working in a dual carriageway service station, in which Partridge appears to spend the bulk of his time. Completing the regular second series cast is northern builder John, busy with the construction of a house built to Partridge's own specifications (hence the caravan).

Apart from a brief return to the screen in a half-hour BBC special, *Anglian Lives* (2003), which purported to celebrate his remarkable career,

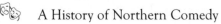

with the close of that second series of *I'm Alan Partridge* the character once again disappeared from view. However, as with any show as popular as this, talk of a comeback just will not go away. Tellingly, perhaps, Coogan himself has never completely ruled the idea out, although his Partridge collaborator-in-chief, Armando Iannucci, has traditionally been less keen. One thing is for sure, when Britain's biggest media loser does make that long-awaited return, a still-devoted audience will be ready and waiting.

Maybe, if he ever does come back, Alan Partridge will turn up in a film. For that is the medium in which Steve Coogan has been most prolific in recent years, in projects as diverse as American family movie *An Indian In The Cupboard* (1995), Terry Jones's adaptation of *Wind In The Willows* (1996), *The Parole Officer* (2001 - co-written by Coogan and Normal), and Michael Winterbottom's biopic of Mr. Manchester himself Tony Wilson, *24 Hour Party People*, in which Coogan did a sterling job in the lead role. In fact, on the big screen, a healthy mixture of mainstream and art house appears to be Coogan's preferred career option. Further projects have included Jim Jarmusch's *Coffee And Cigarettes* (2003) and a crowd-pleasing trip as Phileas Fogg in *Around The World In Eighty Days* (2004). In 2005, he also put in a remarkable performance as himself, yet not quite himself, alongside an equally post-modern Rob Brydon in *A Cock And Bull Story*, Winterbottom's take on Laurence Stern's idiosyncratic eighteenth century novel, *The Life and Opinions of Tristram Shandy, Gentleman*. Since then, Coogan's versatility has been further evident in Sofia Coppola's *Marie Antoinette* (2006), and as a Roman soldier named Gaius Octavius in two *Night at The Museum* comedies (2006 and 2009).

Silver screen success notwithstanding, Steve Coogan seems unlikely to terminate his love affair with television entirely. In America, he turned up in that medium on an episode of the Larry David comedy, *Curb Your Enthusiasm*, in 2007. By then, back in the UK, Coogan had guested in a *Little Britain Abroad* Christmas special, while Baby Cow had overseen the production of *Saxondale* (2006), of which a second series followed a year later. Here, Coogan played hirsute former roadie Tommy Saxondale, a free-thinking middle-aged philosopher with anger management issues who lives with his girlfriend Magz (Ruth Jones) and young lodger-cum-work-assistant Raymond (Rasmus Hardiker). With his days on the road behind him, Tommy is now a self-employed music-loving pest control operative in Stevenage. But more than that, he is a disillusioned world-weary fighter; a roustabout rebel sliding into a life of semi-detached suburban conformity and a walking metaphor for lost youth and the relentless march of time.

The anti-hero at the heart of *24 Hour Party People* meanwhile, Tony Wilson (1950-2007), was considered to be at least partly the inspiration behind Alan Partridge (another being the housewife's favourite gardening presenter Alan Titchmarsh). And Caroline Aherne's future career path was destined to benefit from Wilson's influence too, not least when the founder of Factory records, the Hacienda and, ultimately, the 'eighties phenomenon that became Madchester, included Sister Mary Immaculate on his Channel 4 quiz show *Remote Control* in 1991 (wherein Frank Sidebottom also appeared). The compliment was returned when Wilson was later a guest of Mrs. Merton who, as we have seen, was then put quietly to bed with the relative failure of *Mrs. Merton And Malcolm*.

The main reason why the writers of that show, Aherne, Craig Cash and Henry Normal, could react so pragmatically as they did owed much to the way in which, some six months before *Mrs. Merton And Malcolm* went to air, a certain other show penned by that trio had already begun to cause a stir in its own right. Its name was *The Royle Family* and, in so many ways, it would change British situation comedy forever.

At first sight, there didn't seem to be that much to it. Going out late at night on BBC2, *The Royle Family* was the story of a down to earth working class Manchester family whose lives revolve around their tatty living room sofa and television set. Thrifty work-shy father Jim (Ricky Tomlinson) is lord of his very own kingdom - an easy chair from which he seldom shifts and maintains exclusive rights over the remote control. On the rare occasion that he leaves that throne, it is to take up residence on another upstairs, a voyage often preceded by a regal declaration: 'I'm off for an Eartha Kitt', or some such. The true linchpin of the family, though, is his chain-smoking wife Barbara (Sue Johnston), who has her own spot in the seating hierarchy, on the end of the settee nearest Jim and closest to the kitchen. It is a place relinquished only with the arrival of her mother, Norma, otherwise known as nana (the wickedly loveable Liz Smith). When we first meet the Royles, however, the most frequent visitor is future son-in-law Dave (Cash), the pleasantly vacant boyfriend of shockingly bone idle daughter Denise (Aherne). Her less molly-coddled younger brother Antony (Ralf Little) inhabits the easy chair next to the window and door. Even allowing for the input of friends such as Jim's rotund best mate Twiggy and next-door neighbours Joe, Mary and their calorie-machine daughter Cheryl from time to time, the premise wasn't exactly promising. In fact, as they watched telly, drank tea, salivated over cheap chocolate biscuits, their level of conversation plumbed new depths of humdrum banality. Nothing ever happened. And how amusing could a bunch of unkempt Mancunian couch potatoes actually be?

Very, as it turned out. Certainly, by the time the second series came along in 1999, with Dave and Denise now married and expecting a child, and Henry Normal replaced on the writing team by former Granada press officer Carmel Morgan, enough viewers had awoken to its charms to earn the show a high-profile move to BBC1. From the opening strains of its soon-to-be iconic theme tune, the melancholy Oasis track 'Half The World Away', its growing number of fans were taken on an emotional trip to a recognisable nowhere, in which the ordinary was elevated to extraordinary along the way. Jim's wise-cracking became a particular favourite. To begin with, Antony and Denise were the most frequent butt of their father's colourful wit although, over three series and two Christmas specials, nana Norma began to emerge as a serious rival. There was the odd burst of in-house music too, again usually led by Jim, who needed little excuse to unleash his banjo or start up a sing-song.

Sometimes the underlying good humour broke down. This was no *2 point 4 Children* or *Terry and June*. Uncomfortable outbursts of anger, during which Anthony again bore the brunt of his dad's taunts, whether over small-minded accusations of homosexuality, employment prospects or his dream of starting a band. But more often the rants were less threatening, blowing over like squalls, after Jim had railed against someone leaving the emersion heater on or at slights delivered by persons absent. And in some of the show's most memorable moments there were genuinely emotional tears, as when father and daughter contemplated Dave and Denise's forthcoming wedding, or sat huddled together on the bathroom floor, while Denise's waters broke ahead of the birth of baby David (Jim: 'Are you sure it wasn't just a big piss, Denise love?'). Mostly, there was working-class love, awkward and difficult to express. The Royles were an everyday British family of the so-called lower order, huddled in an everyday British living room, transfixed by the telly and chatting about nothing, as the minutes of each day ticked by. And though northern to its core, the show's enormous popularity everywhere proved once again just how universally sympathetic the comedy of that region can be.

But in keeping with the more fluid social times, there was lots for an openly intellectual viewer to deconstruct here also. As with many great British sitcoms, *The Royle Family* might certainly be seen as existentialist in its structure and outlook. But was it really responsible for killing studio-based sitcom as we used to know and love it, as cultural observers have since led us to believe? For one thing, notwithstanding mainstream hits like *My Family* and the Lee Mack vehicle *Not Going Out*, it could be argued that traditional situation comedy was already on the slide by 1998. Certainly, that was an argument made on a Channel 4 documentary, *Who Killed The British Sitcom?* (2005), wherein *The Royle Family* was high on the list of suspects. First in the firing line, predictably, was *The Young Ones*, whose upstart antipathy towards earlier favourites like *The Good Life* had been there for all to see. Next came the birth of Channel 4 and the subsequent prominence of slick and smartly-written American examples of the genre, first with *Cheers*, then its spin-off *Frasier* (in which, incidentally, the Manchester-born John Mahoney played Dr. Crane's ex-cop father Marty, which surely leaves him culpable in Jane Leeves's dreadful Mancunian accent as Daphne), via the likes of *Roseanne*, *Friends*, *Seinfeld* and *The Larry Sanders Show* along the way. All of these, it was said, left British sitcoms looking staid and amateurish by comparison.

Which is a reasonable theory so far as it goes, until you realise that where it goes is the 1990s, when old-style favourites like *Keeping Up Appearances* and *As Time Goes By* dotted the schedules with almost the same regularity as before. And there were ballsier twists on studio-based sitcom during this era too: most notably *One Foot In The Grave*, *Absolutely Fabulous* and *Men Behaving Badly*, all of them nurtured, to some extent, from spiky alternative roots. No, what really applied the *coup de grace*, posited *Who Killed The British Sitcom?*, was the birth of reality TV, to which *The Royle Family* was at least partly a reaction.

Again, as theories go, it has its appeal. Yet can't an argument also be

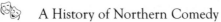

made that, rather than killing sitcom off completely as claimed, *The Royle Family* actually built upon *I'm Alan Partridge* and the under-rated police reality spoof *Operation Good Guys* (1997) in breathing new life into the format? Nor, for that matter, is there any guarantee that one-set studio-based sitcoms will not be successful again, given the right circumstances and talent. Certainly, successors to those aforementioned American hits like *Will And Grace* and *Eight Simple Rules* haven't fared too badly before 'a live studio audience' across the Pond, have they? Perhaps even more pertinently, thanks to the Royles, nuclear families were again grabbing the ratings, only in Wythenshawe rather than London. In that regard, *The Royle Family* might even be said to be less revolutionary than *The Likely Lads* and *Steptoe and Son*. And even if its creators *were* merely spotting and reacting to a reality-obsessed trend, where *The Royle Family* led, Chris Langham's *People Like Us* (1999), Ricky Gervais and Steven Merchant's *The Office* (2000) and a certain 2001 show set in a Bolton social club would follow, influencing a whole heap of other such shows in their wake. Death of the British sitcom, my arse.

Of course, where *The Royle Family* most definitely was radical was in the simplicity of its presentation. There was the lack of a studio audience and laughter track (unless we count those on the telly within the telly). It was shot in real time, usually from a fixed camera position, with lengthy gaps, pauses in conversation and an ear for a *non sequitur* that would have done Harold Pinter proud (Norma: 'She married a joiner; moved to Leeds. He knocked her about a bit but... oh... her home was lovely...'). When the camera moved in for a close-up, it was to gaze upon characters who feasted lovingly upon off-licence confectionery as if it had come from Belgium, rearranged their underwear ('I paid a quid for these underpants and I've got 50 pence-worth stuck up me arse') or made light work of a bacon sarnie. A typical plot twist might involve Jim's fly being undone: 'Ah, the cage might be open, but the beast is asleep,' or a request that his wife should rub ointment into his 'Rockford files' - horrifying prospects both, to be sure. All in all, as with *Steptoe and Son* all those years before, *The Royle Family* proved that intelligent situation comedy could indeed find a big audience. This wasn't so much revolution as evolution.

Nevertheless, in a landscape where traditional sitcom's confidence was most definitely rattled, Caroline Aherne's insistence that the show be made its creators' way or not at all was particularly courageous. After reading the first scripts, BBC executives were understandably nervous. Where was the movement? Why was the whole thing based in one room? Why not pop out into the garden or street from time to time? Or how about that pub they were always talking about, the Feathers? The men in suits had never seen anything like it. The point, of course, was that its intended audience had. Not on television admittedly, but in their own homes, surrounded by the people with whom they were most familiar.

Another huge reason why *The Royle Family* made the impression it did was a first-rate cast. True, the programme's understated scripts fairly crackled with verbal wit and visual gags (who, in their time, has not attempted to scrape wallpaper with a kitchen spatula), but it is doubtful whether the show would have struck quite the same chord without the actors who brought the Royles and their friends to life. It was certainly down to them, in large part, that *The Royle Family*'s almost forensic observance of northern working class life did not come across as patronising. Mainly, of course, that was down to the fact that just about all of them, including Caroline Aherne and Craig Cash, were of working class northern stock themselves. They knew of that which they spoke.

Top of the pile were Jim and Barbara, as played by Ricky Tomlinson and Sue Johnston. It has been said that, when casting Denise's parents, Aherne knew who she wanted from the start. Indeed, in his 2005 autobiography *Ricky* (Time Warner), Tomlinson revealed how upon bumping into Aherne at a Manchester awards ceremony in 1997, she told him mysteriously: 'You're going to be my dad'. As a man and wife double act, the two actors were already familiar to British TV audiences through a lengthy spell together as Bobby and Sheila Grant in the Liverpudlian soap *Brookside*. As Jim, the larger-than-life Tomlinson's background as a live entertainer in Liverpool clubs and more recent appearances as part of Ken Loach's cinematic entourage helped him to establish an essentially good-hearted, if occasionally cantankerous and quite bitter persona. Nor were the character's layers of personality damaged by an eventful past in which Tomlinson, born in Blackpool in 1939, had been monitored as a potential traitor by MI5, spent two years in prison as a flying picket in

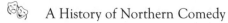

1972 and admitted to being a one time supporter of the National Front
(a right-wing political party whose odious beliefs he, happily, no longer
shares). *The Royle Family* needed its father figure to be a commanding
presence of hidden depths, not all of them pleasant, and a surface
entertainer in his own right. With his untidy beard, National Health
specs, broad scouse accent and nose like a bashed up strawberry, Ricky
Tomlinson brought all that and more. His subsequent catchphrase 'my
arse', appended to anything to which Jim has taken exception - as in:
'£98? £98? It's good to talk, my arse!' - swiftly became part of the British
vernacular.

Bringing more obvious subtlety to the circle was Sue Johnston as
long-suffering Barbara, a revelation in leggings. Born in Warrington in
1943, her understated study of a woman who worked in a confectioners
by day, put up with her smelly layabout of a husband by night, and lived
her own life vicariously through that of her children gave the show much
of its poignancy. When Denise finds a jacket in a mail order catalogue,
her mum dreams of having one too. If Antony dares to step much beyond
his family's limited horizons - a trip to London, say - his mum delights in
the thrill. And, like many working class mothers, Barbara is taken entirely
for granted. 'Get your coat on, Barb' says Jim, as he prepares to leave for
the pub. 'Why, are you taking me with you?' 'No, I'm turning the heating
off.' It's a joke and a good one, but the inference is clear. Barbara's sense
of self is defined by her family, who will probably never truly see her as
an individual with needs and hopes of her own, even when she is gone.
Another episode, wherein a menopausal Barbara storms out of the house
before returning as if nothing much has happened, renders that situation
even more transparent. A times, she gives as good as she gets. But more
often than not, her attempts at communication, usually based upon some
inconsequential event at work, are met by indifference or affectionate
derision. For better or for worse, love and responsibility dictate that
Barbara has little choice but to muddle through, taking her modest
predicament in her stride.

This wistful mood of melancholy underlying all that is best about
The Royle Family is further enhanced by Barbara's scatty and ruthlessly
acquisitive mother. Though her competitive relationship with Jim seldom
runs smooth and at times verges on the downright nasty, Norma is in

essence Barbara with several more years on the clock. As if in retaliation for being ignored (her telephone calls from her flat across town remain a source of family inconvenience) she is now deaf, or at least claims to be. As such, she talks twice as loudly as is strictly necessary and frequently repeats herself. Much to Jim's particular dismay, another of his mother-in-law's preoccupations is constipation. There are also regular references to her friend Elsie, one of a number of *Royle Family* characters never to appear (Denise's nemesis Beverley Macca being, as yet, another) and death. Nana is also blessed with a supposed antipathy to drink ('I never drink me, just a sherry at Christmas, whiskey at New Year and a bottle of stout...') and is prone to making statements of the most profound and lovely innocence: '...the specialist says he is going to remove my cataract, but he's going to leave the twinkle in my eye.'

A healthy respect for northern comedy culture is a defining feature of *The Royle Family* generally. One beautiful example of this is a song sung by neighbour Joe at the end of Antony's 18th birthday party bash, 'I'll Take You Home, Kathleen', a tune made famous by the Irish tenor Josef Locke while he and his hell-raising pal Frank Randle were tearing up the pubs of Blackpool in the 1940s. A nod to the more recent past was the famous wall-paper stripping scene in which Jim, Twiggy and Dave dance along to Lou Bega's 'Mambo No. 5'; a homage to Morecambe and Wise's classic 'Stripper' routine if ever there was one, with Barbara in equally rhythmic mood preparing the workers' sarnies in the kitchen. And when Aherne and Cash began the search for an ideal nana, they knew exactly where to find her. Born in Scunthorpe in 1921, with her sweet smile and eccentric demeanour, Liz Smith had long been a performer of formidable power and reputation. What's more, she could knit a bit too.

In fact, Smith only turned to professional acting as a 50-year-old, thanks to a phonecall from the Salfordian playwright Mike Leigh, whose 1977 play, *Abigail's Party*, is widely regarded as a template for modern-day sitcoms to come. At the time, she worked as an assistant in Hamley's toy store in London, with evening classes in acting little more than a hobby. But after starring in Leigh's film *Bleak Moments*, her career trajectory changed dramatically. A wide array of television appearances followed, among the most prominent a part as a downtrodden mother in Leigh's 1973 *Play For Today* offering *Hard Labour*. A role as Compo's date in a brand new sitcom called *Last Of The Summer Wine* hinted that there might just be a future in comedy too. When she almost stole the show as Annie Brandon in *I Didn't Know You Cared*, the suspicion was confirmed. Over the three-or-so decades to come, whether on big screen or small, Liz Smith would prove herself one of Britain's finest character actors. She appeared in films and television programmes as diverse as *Ripping Yarns, Russ Abbott's Madhouse, A Private Function* (for which she won a BAFTA), *2 Point 4 Children, Secrets & Lies, The Vicar Of Dibley* and as the voice of Mrs. Mulch in *Wallace & Gromit In The Curse Of The Were-Rabbit*, among much else. Despite advancing years, her best-selling autobiography, *Our Betty* (Simon & Schuster, 2006), revealed her as having little intention to slow down yet. But surely, the highlight of a career with many high-water marks was her moving portrayal of the dying nana in a one-off *The Royle Family* comeback, 'The Queen of Sheba', shown in October 2006 and watched by over eight million people.

In the rest of the regular supporting cast, Jim's light-fingered mate Twiggy was played by the Liverpool actor Geoffrey Hughes, who had originally come to public attention as Stan Ogden's binman pal Eddie Yates in *Coronation Street*, before going on to star as Onslow in *Keeping Up Appearances*. The Royle family's neighbours, the terminally taciturn Joe and his cheerfully batty Irish wife Mary, who wandered in through the back door unannounced whenever the mood took them, were portrayed by Peter Martin and Doreen Keogh who, like Liz Smith, had decades of experience behind them. This particular Joseph and Mary, it turned out, had a daughter, Cheryl, whose ongoing battle with the bulge was a source of cruel hilarity for her neighbours and viewers alike. Dumpy, plain Cheryl may not have been any good with diets, but she had a great line in self-delusion: 'I've lost half a stone. No. I mean half a pound.' Kathy Burke was the original choice in that role and, indeed, went so far as to attend the read-through. Committed to another project, however, she was forced to withdraw and into the breach stepped Jessica Stevenson, who bridged the gap between pathos and humour with aplomb. Making up the supporting cast were Antony's best friend Darren (the *Coronation Street*-bound Andrew Whyment), perpetual grin on the outside but little lost soul within, and Antony's girlfriend Emma (Sheridan Smith), whose revelation that she was a vegetarian prompted the immortal request from nana: '...could she have a slice of wafer thin ham, Barbara?'

A Dose of Reality, My Arse

In 1999, along with Simon Pegg, Jessica Stevenson would go on to write and co-star in *Spaced*, Channel 4's innovative pop culture sitcom which, at the beginning of one episode, paid its own tribute to *The Royle Family* by affectionately spoofing the opening credits. Sheridan Smith, meanwhile, followed her *Royle Family* appearance with a starring role in the inexplicably successful - to anyone over the age of 25 - *Two Pints Of Lager And A Packet Of Crisps...* (2001), in which her relationship with Ralf Little was reprised as the loyal if dopey Jonny and his slacker girlfriend Janet. Set in Runcorn, *Two Pints Of Lager And A Packet Of Crisps...* was a show made for teenagers about teenagers. As such, it was rude, crude and defiantly unsubtle. Along with Little and Smith (almost a good name for a double act), *Two Pints...* also featured Rawtenstall's Natalie Casey as the gobby Donna, the Stockport-born Will Mellor as her on-off (in more ways than one) boyfriend Gaz and Wigan's Kathryn Drysdale as the drippy, self-centred Louise. Donna's mum Flo was played by *Coronation Street* actor Beverley Callard. Bury-born Ralf Little, meanwhile, also went on to front his own programme - *The Ralf Little Show* (2002) - which although ultimately short-lived, does hold the distinction of including the first TV appearance of *Little Britain*'s Lou and Andy, originally intended to be Lou Reed and Andy Warhol, as played by David Walliams and Matt Lucas.

As for Caroline Aherne, before *The Royle Family* had so much as hit its stride she was adrift in the wreckage of an emotional life that might most sensitively be described as turbulent. And before the third and final full series of *The Royle Family* was broadcast in 2000, a harder-edged affair written this time by Aherne and Cash alone (and directed by the former), after making the entertaining documentary *Back Passage To India* (2000), in which she and Cash bickered their way through 'a country of amazing contradictions', psychologically bruised and battered, she announced that, after one last *Royle Family* Christmas special, her days in front of the camera would be behind her, although she intended to continue writing.

And indeed that was exactly how things did proceed initially, in the shape of Cash and Aherne's next big idea, the pub sitcom *Early Doors*. A sort of northern English *Cheers*, it was to be set amongst the regulars and staff of a down-at-heel Manchester local where, as with *The Royle Family*, nothing much happened and everybody knew your name. Alas, Caroline Aherne's involvement came to an abrupt and premature end when she and her scriptwriting partner fell out, reportedly over a second draft by Cash which the BBC preferred to an angry Aherne's own. Whatever the true cause, the Beeb's one-time golden girl walked away from the project days before filming, leaving one BBC 'insider' to tell the *London Evening Standard*: 'The show has been Craig's project from the start and we are sticking by him. He has a great deal of talent and we know he can make it work.'

Aherne, keener to escape British media attention than ever, headed as far from the spotlight as she could - 12,000 miles away to Australia where, soon, she was writing an Antipodean *Royle Family*-esque sitcom of her own. The story of a blue collar Aussie couple trying to survive the post-retirement wobbles of a long-term marriage, it was called *Dossa And Joe* (2002) and featured Anne Charleston (Madge from *Neighbours*) and Michael Caton, star of the cult Aussie-little-guy-beats-corporate-big-guy comedy film *The Castle* (1997). Although *Dossa And Joe* passed muster with the critics and was also broadcast back in the UK, it proved to be a ratings flop and was never followed up. Possibly, it was again ahead of its time, albeit in a different hemisphere. Certainly, the Australian and British public have since revealed a shared appetite for earthy Aussie humour in their mutual appreciation of *Kath And Kim*.

Nowadays, Caroline Aherne is back in England where her television appearances remain rare. More happily, she and Craig Cash appear to have patched up their differences. After that critically-acclaimed *Royle Family* comeback in 2006 - surely one of the finest examples of British situation comedy ever made - a third Christmas special was produced in 2008, self-consciously broader in tone. Missing dear-departed nana and baby-sitting Antony (under instructions from Denise to take a Christmas morning picture of her kids on his mobile phone), it was unusual in switching the action away from Jim and Barbara's living room to that of Dave's parents (a memorable couple of performances by Tom Courtenay and Helen Fraser). For some viewers, the new jauntier mood jarred. To others, it was just a knockabout piece of festive fun; another string to the northern comedy bow. Since when it has been reported that at least two more *Royle Family* Christmas specials are in the pipeline, while rumours of a new fourth series have so far not come to fruition.

Meanwhile, off to the Grapes, where Craig Cash finally opened the saloon-bar *Early Doors* in 2003, albeit now in the company of a new co-writer and long-time friend Phil Mealey, who quit his job as a mechanical engineer for the privilege after earlier joining Cash and Aherne as third writer on 'The Queen of Sheba'. And on its first showing, this latest chunk of northern reality was once again met with a response that might best be described as lukewarm. To some extent, that was inevitable. To follow a significant act like *The Royle Family* was a nigh on impossible task and the surface similarities of the two programmes simply underlined Aherne's absence. Adding to the image problem, or so it seemed at the time, was a laid back theme tune not a million miles away from the Oasis offering, Roddy Frame's 'Small World', and an equally pedestrian style of presentation. Much of the inactivity centered around one room, here a pub lounge bar although, as with the kitchen and bathroom in *The Royle Family*, there were periodic retreats to the Kitchen and men's urinals too. Unlike *The Royle Family*, though, the public house setting now allowed for a secondary major focus of attention, the upstairs living quarters of single parent landlord Ken (John Henshaw, formerly seen as Emma's 'self-made' boastful father Roger in *The Royle Family*), his adopted daughter Melanie (Christine Bottomley) and widowed mother Jean (Rita May). Cash played factory worker Joe, an incrementally less gormless version of Dave and best mate of the sexually cavalier Duffy, played by Mealey in an impressive television debut. They even thanked Caroline Aherne in the closing credits. This was just *The Royle Family* without the Royles, wasn't it?

Well, despite all the similarities, no it was not. Yes, there were rich levels of observational comedy and an all-pervasive mood of getting by. And yes this was a show about ordinary working class northerners, their limited horizons and banal conversation. From the outset, *Early Doors* was marked by cheeky good humour, melancholy and an emphasis on the social ties that bind. Here, though, the issue was one of loneliness more than anything else and, as the first series moved along, it quickly became apparent that Cash and Mealey had come up with a masterful sitcom in its own right even if, at around 1.7 million, its viewing figures were less than impressive. Soon, people weren't so much talking about how Craig Cash was trying to ape *The Royle Family*, as recognising just how great his influence on that modern day classic must have actually been.

The youngest of three brothers raised on a council estate in Heaton

Norris, Stockport, Cash, born in 1960, was clearly a highly-gifted writer in his own right. Yet after leaving school with no qualifications and then being sacked from jobs as a screen printer and a wood machinist, those gifts seemed destined to be hidden forever. 'I wanted to be a TV cameraman but I thought that was something other people did,' he told a local newspaper ahead of *The Royle Family*'s second series in 1999. 'I had no confidence. Now I'm in television I see lots of confidence but not much talent. Yet there are thousands of people out there with loads of talent and no confidence. Daft, innit?' Happily, before too much longer Cash plucked up the courage to try his hand as a pirate DJ; the road which, in time, would lead him to the side of Caroline Aherne.

Another way in which *Early Doors* echoed *The Royle Family* was in the contribution of its cast. Particularly inspiring was Henshaw's heroically embattled Ken, emotionally torn both by his unspoken love for barmaid Tanya (Susan Cookson), and the determination of daughter Melanie to find her 'real' dad. For a man still wounded by watching his wife run off with his best friend, there was also a predatory brewery to fight off, a couple of thirsty and hilariously corrupt policemen to be kept onside (Phil and Nige, brilliantly played by James Quinn and Peter Wight) and a living to be scraped from the pockets of regulars who looked as if they didn't have two pennies to rub together. High among the achievements of *Early Doors* was the way in which it portrayed Ken as a man of decency, rather than - and this really *was* revolutionary - a shifty sod or idiot, the fate usually bestowed upon middle-aged, beer-bellied working class men. Though plagued to distraction by his lazy and manipulative mother Jean - a *tour de force* from Rita May, who gave the old bat a disarming likeability - Ken was a good man who was intent on doing the right thing.

Among the rest of the Grapes' regulars, the aforementioned Joe and Duffy loomed large, dodging any hint of responsibility from marriage or the world outside. Duffy's former knee-tremble Janice (Maxine Peake) often passed through too, as did fun-seeking young mums Debbie (Lisa Millet) and Nicola (Sue McArdle), with children to shake off all. There was the grouchy OAP Tommy (Rodney Litchfield) who, despite having to force Ken's ale down with a grimace, is a fixture and fitting next to the juke box. Among several running gags, old Tommy's tight-fistedness with money and constant grumbling were a lovely counterpoint to the sunny disposition of the married couple of oddballs seated at the next table, Joan and Eddie (Lorraine Cheshire and Mark Benton), two grotesque if entirely harmless half-wits. Eddie goes on and on and on about the most mundane of matters, emphasising each point with a Oliver Hardy-esque bout of finger-twiddling. Roadworks are one such topic, as are the myriad problems of Joan's housebound (and smelly) mother. Completing the regular cast were Jean's trouble causer of a home-help Winnie (Joan Kempson) and the soon-to-be very famous indeed James McAvoy as Melanie's boyfriend Liam, whom Joe and Duffy seem perpetually intent on trying to lead astray. When viewer response improved to the extent that a second series of *Early Doors* was made in 2004, McEvoy had left to be replaced by Lee Ingleby as Melanie's new love interest Dean. Though life didn't provide much in the way of excitement for the staff and regulars of the Grapes, it did at least offer the consolation of a glass half full and the camaraderie of fellow souls on the slow, steady slide towards oblivion. And if that is the final destination anyway, Cash, Mealey and their characters seemed to agree, then why not have a laugh and another pint before we go?

After spending much of the previous decade on the bones of its backside, come the end of the 1990s old-style light Variety entertainment - albeit with a modern twist - had made the most unlikely of comebacks. What's more, thanks to the likes of Ant and Dec, *Only Fools And Horses* and *The Royle Family*, television-watching in a family environment was back on the radar, even if the burgeoning growth of internet technology and personal computers would shortly challenge such a concept all over again.

Comedians like Eddie Izzard, Jo Brand and even Vic and Bob would continue to divide generations with regard to their merits. But moving into a new millennium, in a society that was by and large settled and affluent, popularity and commercialism were no longer dirty words. Indeed, they were to be embraced. In comedy, this mood was combined with a healthier respect toward those who had dug the well from those who now drank at it.

With one or two exceptions, even for comics who remained defiantly left-field, their stage persona tended to owe more to the traditions of Variety showbiz than any austere alternative circuit. Whatever their background, comedians were on the whole 'turns' again rather than ranting agent provocateurs with a political score to settle. As a generation grew up, many of the alternative attitudes, alleviated by post-modern irony, had themselves become the norm. As such, it was again possible to judge comedy purely on the basis of whether or not it was funny.

One comedian who embodies all of that absolutely is Jenny Eclair. These days most likely to be found moaning like a middle-aged martyr in the stage and television phenomenon that is *Grumpy Old Women*, Eclair's professional comedy roots lie in her days as a punk performance poet in the 1980s. Born Jenny Hargreaves on an army base in Kuala Lumpur in 1960, but later raised and educated in Lytham St. Annes, after taking her 'A' levels she went to the same Manchester Polytechnic School of Theatre as Steve Coogan, John Thomson and Graham Fellows. After trying briefly to become 'Manchester's Toyah Wilcox' she joined a cabaret act, Cathy La Creme and the Rhumbabas where her confectionery-based stage name may well have been adopted (it is also said that she came up with 'Eclair' while pretending to be French in a Blackpool nightclub). When the Rhumbabas split so did she, to London.

It was there, after working as a waitress, that Jenny Eclair spotted an advert in the back of *The Stage* searching for novelty acts for a comedy club in Wimbledon. Taking John Cooper Clarke and her old band leader Cathy as her influence, she went along and, clad in black cocktail dress, fishnet stockings and stilettos, read out some poetry of her own. The act was seen by the owner of a local comedy club, the Finborough Arms, a venue at which she was invited to become a regular performer. Soon, the performance poet had evolved into an aggressive and foul-mouthed stand-up whose brazen persona was more than a match for any man. With her peroxide blonde hair and big doe eyes, she drank, smoked and swore like the troopers she had spent her childhood amongst, shooting her audience down with a volley of sarcasm if they so much as dared to open their mouths. No subject was off-limits, particularly so-called 'women's problems' which, in Eclair's venomous northern tones, were a badge of honour rather than some shameful secret to be packed quietly away in a ladylike world of sugar and spice and all things nice. Jenny Eclair was the prototype hard-edged female alternative comic; sexually and emotionally liberated, culturally emancipated and possessed of an urge to shock. Yet what marked Eclair out from the rest was her neurotic insecurity. For all that she might tear a heckler to shreds, verbally, merely for crossing her path, the most frequent target of her ire was Jenny Eclair herself. This combination of bitchiness and vulnerability lifted another notch when she began to incorporate it into melodramatic playlets like *Mummy's Little Girl*, which she premiered at the Edinburgh Festival in 1992.

Over the decade to come, and beginning with a television debut as one of a trio of presenters on Channel 4's late-night series *Packet Of Three* (1991), an attempt to blend stand-up with sitcom set in the Crumpsall Palladium, a beleaguered old-style Variety theatre (in which Frank Skinner and Henry Normal also appeared), like Jo Brand before her, she earned a reputation for pushing boundaries of taste that, almost imperceptibly over time, evolved into an equal reputation for giving voice to the female reality. The titles of her next three Edinburgh stage shows hint at that progress of that transformation - *Vague* (1993), *Bad Behaviour* (1994) and the Perrier Award-winning *Prozac And Tantrums* (1995). From there, acting and writing took up an increasing amount of her professional time. With the birth of Channel 5 in 1997, she fronted her own chat show, *Jenny Eclair Squats* and, in 1998, returned to Edinburgh where *The Platinum Collection* revealed that, though mellowing into middle age, she could still do abrasive when necessary.

In more recent times, this one-time firebrand has become as unthreatening and comfortable a presence on British television and radio as, well, *Grumpy Old Men* or the shipping forecast. So much so that when, in 2005, she joined Adrian Edmondson in the reality contest, *Comic Relief Does Fame Academy*, she was voted a creditable third. The former baroness of bawdiness (so described by *Time Out*) who, according to the NME, 'might literally bite your balls off' was now well and truly settled into comedy's comfy mainstream. And she was joined there by a fellow celebrity *Fame Academy* entrant to benefit from a renewed appetite for Variety, the impressionist Jon Culshaw.

Born Jonathan Peter Culshaw in Ormskirk in 1968, after launching his entertainment career in northern local radio, both as a presenter and voice-over specialist for commercials, Culshaw's big break came as a result of a tape he sent to BBC Radio 1's *Steve Wright In The Afternoon* in 1993. From there, *Spitting Image* beckoned where a producer, Bill Dare, noted his obvious talent and, several years later, recruited him for the cast of a new radio show about to launch on Radio 4. Called *Dead Ringers*, along with Culshaw, it also starred Kate Robbins, Simon Lipson, Jan Ravens (the first female president of the Cambridge Footlights and born, in 1958, on the Wirral) and Alistair McGowan. When a second series aired, of that original quintet only Culshaw and Ravens remained, to be joined by Mark Perry, Phil Cornwell and Middlesbrough's Kevin Connelly. It was that team which, henceforth, would guide the show through a ten series run and assortment of radio specials, as well as making the move to television when *Dead Ringers* was deemed worthy of a BBC2 slot in 2002.

On screen, a penchant for broadcasting in-jokes shown by the radio version (newsreader Brian Perkins, for example, being obsessively in love with colleague Charlotte Green) was toned down. Instead, pranks, spoofs and political satire were the order of the day, injecting a refreshingly surreal approach to an otherwise all-too predictable genre. Particular highlights were Culshaw as Obi-Wan Kenobi 'seeking passage to Aldershot' and Thora Hird as raised by southerners. There were also great turns as Kirsty Wark or Delia Smith from Jan Ravens, David Dickinson and Graham Norton from Mark Perry, and anything to do with sport by Kevin Connelly. Yet it was Culshaw who made the biggest name for himself, going on to launch a solo career in which his wondrous turns as language-crunching President George 'Dubbya' Bush, complete with promises to 'obliterify the bad man' or bomb Tie Rack ('that's I-raq, Mr. President'), and the former Black Sabbath and current reality TV cult hero Ozzie Osbourne, could not have been more accurate if played by the victims themselves.

Along with impressionists, another brand of Variety entertainer ripe for reinvention was the drag act. Which was just as well for Birkenhead-born Paul James O'Grady, who came to fame as the outrageous 'blonde bombsite' Lily Savage. O'Grady, born in 1955 and raised in a close-knit Irish Catholic family in Tranmere, moved down to London as an 18-year-old. Whilst making ends meet in a variety of jobs such as cleaning and social work, by night he developed the alter-ego that would make him a household name. With her big hair, tacky outfits, uncompromising views on life and withering Scouse accent, Lily was a Danny La Rue for the 'nineties. As well as looking great, she smoked, she drank, she swore, knew all about sex and wasn't afraid to talk.

O'Grady had the idea for Lily while working as a waiter in Manila in 1977. Soon, on the back of an eight-year residency at The Royal Vauxhall Tavern cabaret bar, at which O'Grady began as bartender and progressed to amateur drag night compere before having a go himself in 1985, she was a cult figure on London's gay pub and club scene. And there she seem destined to remain until, after being nominated for a Perrier on the Edinburgh Fringe and a subsequent handful of TV stand-up guest spots, O'Grady's big television break came with *Lily Savage Live: Paying The Rent*, the highlights of a 1993 gig broadcast in 1995. It was when she began to interview celebrities on what used to be Paula Yates's bed in Channel 4's *Big Breakfast*, however, that she really came to national attention.

As ever, with a new phenomenon doing the rounds, it wasn't long before the BBC came sniffing, and the upshot was an exclusive contract with the Corporation that led to two 1997 series, one prime-time, the other going out on a Sunday evening. The latter, called simply *The Lily Savage Show*, allowed O'Grady to flesh out his character's back story with a supporting cast that included family members like Borstal-boy son Jason and crooked daughter Bunty (played by 'nineties Liverpudlian pop princess Sonia). The former, in which Lily toned down her more brutal tendencies, saw her follow in the footsteps of Terry Wogan and Les Dawson as host of the revived family quiz *Blankety Blank*. Equally adept at sending up the show's wobbly sets, less than wonderful prizes and air of faded glamour, the innuendo-laden mare was an unlikely if perfect fit. Lily Savage was on her way to becoming the sort of national treasure that even Jim Royle didn't mind watching.

Also in 1997, the year in which he was voted the Variety Club of Great Britain's BBC TV Personality of the Year before being poached by ITV, *An Evening With Lily Savage* topped the Best Entertainment Programme category at the National Television Awards. Two years later, O'Grady won Best Presenter at that the very same do. Capitalising on all this attention, he took his femme fatale on the sell-out tour that would eventually turn up on television as two series of the award-winning *Lily Live*. There was also an imaginative piece of casting when Lily turned up as a character in a stage musical of the all-female cult Australian TV soap, *Prisoner Cell Block H*. Later, other live musical appearances would come in *Chitty Chitty, Bang Bang* and *Annie*.

Then, in 2002, probably as a result of overwork and heavy-smoking, O'Grady suffered a heart attack at his London flat. Upon recovery, the comedian packed in the cigs ('Lambert & Butler have had to lay off two-hundred staff,' he joked) and opted for a quieter private life on his farm in Kent. Lily too began to take things easier until, in 2004, she finally withdrew from the spotlight completely after appearing in the sell-out West End panto, *Snow White And The Seven Dwarves*. These days, she is said to be living happily in a convent.

Paul O'Grady, meanwhile, has powered onward and upward. After filling in for Des O'Connor as a guest host on the ITV daytime chat show *Today With Des And Mel*, he enjoyed himself so much that he decided to do one himself. He had already made tentative moves towards separating the drag queen from the real man through two road-documentaries *Paul O'Grady's Orient* (2000) and *Paul O'Grady's America* (2001). However, his success with *Blankety Blank* and short stint on *Today With Des And Mel* hinted that the likeable, gossipy personality and good looks beneath all that slap might be put to still more popular use. That was confirmed by ITV's *The Paul O'Grady Show* in October 2004, which became an instant daytime hit and continued to earn large ratings and a host of awards when it was later re-branded as *The New Paul O'Grady Show* on Channel 4, after ITV apparently 'forgot' to renew the presenter's contract. These days more risqué than rude, and with the emphasis on cheeky rather than vicious, O'Grady is another one-time denizen of smoke-filled alternative dens whose modern-day chat show and BBC Radio 2 showtunes persona even the most prudish of grandmas might enjoy.

As our history of northern English comedy has unfolded, time and again we have seen how if a comedian wants to establish and then maintain a national reputation, he or she must move south. Morecambe and Wise did it. Eric Sykes did it. Victoria Wood did it. Alexei Sayle did it. Vic and Bob did it. Steve Coogan did it. The League of Gentlemen did it. Paul O'Grady did it. And those are but a few.

Tellingly, perhaps, for those who stayed put - the Jimmy James, Dave Morris, Harry Korris and Al Reads of this world - posterity has been less kind. Ultimately, any entertainer with ambitions to go on to bigger and better things has needed to face the truth. London's media Establishment likes its rough-edged northern diamonds right where they can be seen.

There are exceptions to the rule. Being a homebody was fine for the comics who predominantly made a living in pubs, clubs and panto; the unglamorous north was where a large lump of the work was anyway. And if live Variety was your bread and butter, as long as you were up for spending most of your life on the road and had the talent and energy of, say, Ken Dodd, it wouldn't really matter if your base was on the moon. Even so, while Bernard Manning, Stan Boardman and Chubby Brown would seldom lack employment opportunities in time-worn and tobacco-stained concert rooms, a northern postal address did prove more of a disadvantage when it came to sustaining a presence on television, more so once the alternative crew came along. To the majority of northern comedy emigrants, work, ambition and a yearning to be in the Establishment loop were lures that most often proved irresistible.

Of course, not every comedian (or indeed northerner) who departs the land of his or her birth does so exclusively for career reasons. Some who, not unreasonably, find life more agreeable in the south cannot wait to escape. And to many a proud expat, the northern ideals are so much more agreeable when viewed safely from a distance. Anyway, thanks to the invention of railways, boats, motorways and aeroplanes, geography is no longer such an issue. Horizons have broadened since we began to opt for Benidorm over Blackpool, and take garlic in our bread. Yet lately, this also seems to have brought about a distinct wind of change. One comedian who has noticeably bucked the southbound trend first came to public attention in 1998, with a Channel 4 comedy pilot set in the unlikely environs of an M61 service station, just outside Bolton.

In Ben Thompson's 2004 tome *Sunshine On Putty*, the author, in pointing out how most sitcom directors seem to be of a rumpled and diffident upper-middle class persuasion, quotes Steve Coogan thus: 'The old social balance does tend to remain in that area... but there is a sort of natural justice at work, in that mavericks do find their way through. If you take Peter Kay, for example, he has a reputation for being difficult, but that's just because he's someone who knows exactly what he wants and has no time for lily-livered southern jessies giving him their opinion.' In his 1999 local newspaper interview, Craig Cash had earlier reflected that: 'People say it's great living in London because you can wear outrageous clothes and nobody bats an eyelid. But if I'm walking down the street in a silly hat, I want someone to say, "Cashy, you look a clown in that." Because I'm the type who might think I look great in that hat, and in London nobody would say owt.' And there you have the paradox of northern culture in a nutshell. Is it about keeping it real or knowing your place? Strength in community or fear of individuality?

For Peter Kay, reluctance to leave the north west town in which he was born in 1973 and spent the happiest of upbringings is suitably straightforward. In Johnny Dee's unauthorised biography, *That Peter Kay Book* (Andre Deutsch, 2006), he explains: 'I'm not anti-London, but I just think, "Why do we have to go to London?" I love being at home. Life is all about your family and friends. I'd rather pack it all in than go and live there.' Clearly, that is an attitude with professional dangers. On the other hand, who could deny that, without that formative Bolton upbringing, Peter Kay would be anything like as amusing as he is? There is an element in which his decision to remain in 'the second biggest town in England' is simply the repayment of a long-standing debt.

And more and more, it seems, he is not on his own. Interviewed in *The Guardian* in October 2009, *dinnerladies*, *Early Doors* and *Shameless* star Maxine Peake revealed that she, too, had decided to end a 12-year exile in London in order to move back to hometown Salford. 'I'm 20 minutes from Bolton, where I've still got family,' she explained. 'It's 10 minutes into Manchester. And the Pennines are almost on my doorstep. It's not about being proud to be northern, it's just where I'm from, where I feel comfortable. Living in Salford doesn't stop me from getting work. And, anyway, I'm in London most weeks.'

Like the comics of old, Peter Kay's enormous success is built on his accessibility to the masses. He is, it seems, one of us. It is easy to imagine him as an old Variety-style comic, maybe in a velvet jacket and dickie bow tie, securing an audience's affection through sheer force of personality. As we have seen, northern comedy has always been so much more about class than location and Kay moves in the same world as his audience, primarily the sort of people who either earn or have earned their corn in factories, supermarkets, petrol stations, cinemas and shopping precincts. His experiences are our experiences and vice versa.

A non-drinker (give or take the occasional Bailey's), neither is he the type to pepper his comedy with obscenities, thereby earning a pass for the odd 'cheeky' swear word when necessary. He has the common touch and is therefore allowed to be 'common' as the situation demands. Never one to manufacture catchphrases explicitly, he nevertheless has an ability to inspire them anyway - 'Sweet baby Jesus and the orphans' - in the way of an amusing work colleague. In a different league to the confrontational alternatives who thought that they had got rid of this sort of thing, he is a naturally funny man who can, if he wishes, elicit a chuckle with a glance of his hangdog looks. Nostalgia is grist to his mill, too, most obviously in memories of pop culture icons like *Bullseye*, *Amarillo*, the kids from *Fame* and his trusty Ferguson Videostar. In short, Peter Kay is in the business of cheering folk up, rather than colluding in their misery. Little wonder that so many of the old brigade consider him the best thing to happen to British entertainment in years, as these publicity quotes from a comeback tour of the *Original Comedians* in 2004 attest. 'He's not really interested in alternative,' says Roy Walker. 'He just thinks what's funny's funny.' Mick Miller agrees that Kay has 'brought back the old style of humour' before adding: '...there's a whole new audience for us out there.'

Others, usually of the London-centric comedy critic persuasion, have seen things differently. Ben Thompson, for example, writes in *Sunshine On Putty* that: '...if Peter Kay were really the visionary that a lot of people seem to want to claim him to be, he'd be doing this stuff at a time when the world wasn't crying out for it' - as stupid a statement as has ever been committed to print. What is Kay supposed to do, you wonder. Call up the late H.G. Wells and ask to be taken to an era where audiences find him objectionable? To be fair, it comes in an otherwise well-argued chapter in which Kay is compared not only with his closest contemporary Johnny Vegas but also Les Dawson. Vegas, Thompson decides, has more in common with Dawson as he will not pander to audience expectation. Peter Kay wants to be liked and will do anything to achieve that aim. Vegas and his drunken unpredictable alter ego are brave enough to take their chances, just as Dawson once was in the unforgiving clubs of Hull.

All of which conveniently overlooks the initial originality of Kay's act and, indeed, his eagerness to perform it in the sort of environment where routines about the melting qualities of Rich Tea biscuits and reminders of how, when you are drunk at a family wedding, those little white discs left behind by Party Poppers look like pound coins, might not have been expected to go down so well. Places like the student comedy club circuit and Edinburgh Fringe. In large part, that was the reason for Kay making the impact that he did. For all that Vic and Bob had reopened the Variety door, there was a mundanity to Kay that was defiantly untrendy, and as surprising as it was refreshing. In short, he all-but reinvented everyday observational stand-up for a modern audience, certainly from a male perspective. Stir in the modern comedy traits of irreverence and irony, and the sort of manic and almost evangelical vitality of huge American stage presences like Steve Martin and Robin Williams, and it all felt brand new. Like them, Peter Kay took his audiences on an imaginative magic carpet ride over a world they already knew and had, previously, taken for granted, albeit in a Boltonian rather than LA accent. His gift was to find the extraordinary in the ordinary; and the empathy he engendered would earn him undreamed of levels of popularity not only with northerners, but anyone who had ever had a Hylda Baker-esque nana - 'Your driving's a bit erotic' - or sparked up a George Formby grill.

But as with all northern comedy, there is an underlying darkness in Peter Kay's humour too. Sometimes it is not so much underlying, as out there on surface yammering for attention. Never is his knack for finding the essential cruelty and bleakness of day-to-day existence more evident than when he stretches his thespian muscles. And again, while Michael Pennington appears to have but one (excellent) character in his repertoire (Johnny Vegas), Peter Kay has a gallery. In that aforementioned one-off Channel 4 docusoap 'The Services' in 1998, the fresh-faced funster still had rather a long way to go before he could be spoken of in the same breath as his comedy heroes, Ronnie Barker, Peter Sellers and Leonard Rossiter. Yet, with hindsight, in this day in the life of a Bolton North motorway service station, the signs of just what a gifted character actor he would go on to become were there from the start.

If Kay's arrival on British television screens felt like a bolt from the blue, that's because it was, although he had, in fact, already established an equally meteoric reputation on the live stand-up circuit - particularly in his native north west - by the time of his big TV break. Kay's earliest routines would see him chatting away amiably about driving lessons,

624

dancing dads, the perils of mum-bought 'Rola Cola' and the (allegedly) true story of how he had once caught thrush from a bottle of Orangina, leading to a rectal examination by a female urologist. As you do.

For young Peter Kay, life's slate began to be filled during his days as a pupil and altar boy at St. Ethelbert's Roman Catholic primary school and church, before moving on to Mount St. Joseph's secondary in Deane, to whose nuns he paid tribute in the title of his autobiography, *The Sound Of Laughter* (Century, 2006). It was at Mount St. Joseph's that fledgling steps in public performance were taken, first as the school DJ and then the Cowardly Lion in *The Wizard Of Oz*, for which he wore a tatty home-made costume that is still, on occasion, brought into service - on the 2005 *Comic Relief* video for *Amarillo*, for example - and stole the show. At home, in a landscape of back-to-back terrace houses, he learned particularly to appreciate the whims and eccentricities of a mother whose strong Irish lilt was a real source of amusement, and his sister Julie's habit of taping the Radio 1 'Top 40' every Sunday teatime on a C-90 cassette. As a child and teenager, despite his stocky frame and a virtually autistic addiction to the family TV set, his wicked gift for mimicry made him popular with schoolfriends and relations alike.

Upon leaving school in 1989, a procession of what might be termed dead-end part-time jobs was his lot, frequently dull and poorly paid. Yet to Kay, always on the hunt for a laugh, they were a veritable goldmine in terms of developing a talent for people watching. To begin with, there were stints as a disc-jockey (parties and weddings a speciality). Then came a four-month period packing toilet rolls at a factory belonging to the former Manchester City footballer, Francis Lee. Following that, at various times, Kay was an attendant in an Esso petrol station, a supermarket check-out boy, a barman, bingo caller and cash and carry operative. A lifelong movie buff, he overdosed on films as a salesman in a video shop (Hollywood Nights) and was also a cinema usher. Most enjoyably, he got to strut his stuff as a steward at Manchester's Nynex arena where he was made to wear a badge bearing the name 'Mohammed' (the last one left in the box) and indulged his eclectic musical tastes when he ought to have been tracking down perpetrators of flash photography. Several of these tasks he juggled simultaneously with spells in further education - the first being a completely useless BTEC course in Performing Arts as Bolton

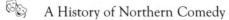

College which almost caused him to shelve his performing ambitions to completely when he left it in 1991, and the second a short-lived attempt at a combined honours degree taking in Drama and Theatre Studies, American Studies and Information Technology at Liverpool University. His third attempt at belatedly gaining a useful education, however, a two-year Media Performance HND at Salford University from September 1994, was an all together more useful and pivotal development, boasting, as it did, a course in stand-up comedy.

Finally, he had found his forte. After learning how to prepare scripts and develop his acting skills, Kay was soon marked out as a natural comic talent and invited by no less a person than Maureen Lipman to audition (unsuccessfully as it turned out) for a West End farce. He also auditioned for and won an acting job on a directors' training course at Granada Television and, in his second year, compered a student cabaret night, staged in a room above a pub in Salford. By the time of his graduation in 1996, thanks to further fledgling outings on the open-mic circuit and gigs performed as part of his official course, Kay was increasingly confident in the spotlight. Upon leaving university, and after a short and unhappy spell on the books of a local acting agency, who appear to have made the League of Gentlemen's theatre-in-education troupe Legs Akimbo look glamourous, inspired by the success of fellow Greater Mancunians Steve Coogan and John Thomson, he entered the *City Life*-sponsored North West Comedian Of The Year competition previously won by Caroline Aherne and, in 1991, a rather more mature silver fox named Dave Spikey.

The venue for his particular heat was to be the Buzz comedy club, alias another room over a pub, this time in Chorlton, where the compere and promoter bore the name Agraman, 'The Human Anagram'. After travelling there by bus and nearly choking on a good luck note hidden a little too carefully in his packed lunch, Kay blitzed it, despite being first on the bill. A notoriously tough crowd had been won over by his almost total lack of cynicism and eye for domestic detail. Fortunately, the judges were too and, a fortnight later, after this first spot in a 'real' comedy club, he found himself in the grand final at a packed Levenshulme Palace.

This time, there were ten finalists and the show's host was to be the former winner, Spikey, himself. Like Kay, Spikey, born David Bramwell in Bolton in 1950, was no two-dimensional showbiz tragic. For one thing, until October 2000, he combined his already long-established stand-up career with a highly responsible day job as Chief Biomedical Scientist in Haematology at The Royal Bolton Hospital. The pair didn't know it yet, but they were on the verge of a very important friendship.

Spikey's own comedy career had begun as part of a double act, Spikey and Sykey, with his friend Rick Sykes. Having already spent many a year writing and sending in potential sketches and routines to the likes of Russ Abbott and the Grumbleweeds, mostly without success, Spikey (named after his lively hair-do) had also, according to a rather fishy account on his official website, appeared with Sykes on *New Faces* where the duo finished '...a close third to a Todmorden whippet juggler and a Latvian plumber who played "I've got sixpence, jolly jolly sixpence" on a radiator.' Later, as a solo comic, Spikey toured the seaside talent shows (winning *Search For A Star* at Torquay's Riviera Centre) and earned his spurs in the rough, tough working men's clubs that had tormented and challenged so many of his predecessors. It was during this period that he was named 1991 North West Comedian of the Year, despite the presence of better known and hipper contestants like Dave Gorman. Most immediately, that led to a spot on Granada's Friday night arts show, *What's New?* Then, in 1993, came a call from the manager of 'eighties light entertainment superstars Cannon and Ball, asking if Spikey could get to Blackpool in half an hour (proving that a home in the north can occasionally be beneficial). Speeding to the rescue, the part-time comic duly compered Tommy and Bobby's Opera House show in front of 3,000 people and did so well that the duo employed him as a support act on two subsequent national tours.

Encouraging though that may have been, in the early 1990s gigs like those and the ones Spikey continued to struggle through in working men's clubs could not help but carry a whiff of faded glory. Fortunately, thanks to his involvement at the Buzz club, Spikey was able to maintain a simultaneous career in which he was just likely as to appear on the same bill as Eddie Izzard, Jack Dee, Lee Evans and Jo Brand. In 1994, he made his debut at London's Comedy Store. Then, in 1996, on the back of an ultimately unsuccessful turn on Jonathan Ross's *Big Big Talent Show*, he was invited to host that year's Levenshulme Palace extravaganza and had his first look at a nervous Peter Kay.

Having faced a similar situation some five years before, Dave Spikey empathised with his fellow Boltonian wannabe. If Kay was to be crowned *City Life* North West Comedian of the Year, he would not only need to be the funniest comic on view, he would have to bypass a formidable obstacle - namely runaway favourite Johnny Vegas. A potential advantage was that, this time, it was Kay who was scheduled to close the show while Vegas - currently tearing up the local circuit like the wild force of nature he is - would go sixth. In practice, Kay's delayed entrance only increased his levels of nervous tension, especially when the audience actually began to chant the St. Helens man's name. As the crowd got drunker and the turns ticked by, there seemed to be only one contender.

A major benefit of that excruciating wait, however, was the time it gave Kay to reconsider the potency or otherwise of his material. Up until now, his style of delivery was somewhat laid-back. But when Vegas then burst onto the stage like some previously long-dormant volcano, a switch flicked inside him. Following Spikey's encouraging 'don't worry folks, there's only one act to go', or a line like it, at the moment of truth, Kay ran onto the stage and slid right across it on his knees, like an excited kid on an empty dance floor. Thereafter, he let loose a barrage of tales based around his upbringing in Bolton, work experience and the idiosyncrasies of northern working class family life. The baying mob was entranced. As he later recalled in *The Sound Of Laughter*: 'Other comedians talked about sex, drugs and drink, but I didn't drink, I'd never done drugs and if I had talked about sex my mum would have battered me senseless out of embarrassment.' The upshot was victory, with Johnny Vegas beaten into second place.

There was no ill-feeling, initially at least, from Michael Pennington. Almost as soon as the contest was over, the two briefly entertained a notion of forming a double act at the Edinburgh Festival. After bombing as individuals while auditioning for a residency on Tony Wilson's Friday night ITV show, *Welcome To The Candid Café*, they performed together for the one and only time at a Round Table concert in the Midlands in 1997. A resounding flop, the idea was scuppered almost immediately.

As a solo performer, though, nothing could stop Peter Kay now.

Soon, a growing reputation in the north was supplemented by successful, if infrequent, Comedy Store appearances in the south. And his ambition to break into television was boosted when Kay was invited to devise and contribute an episode to Channel 4's pilot-strand, *Comedy Lab*. By now, Kay and Dave Spikey had begun to collaborate professionally on an array of ideas that mostly went nowhere, although one, set in the offices of northern local newspaper the Fogburrow Advertiser and News, would later be resuscitated as *Dead Man Weds* (2005), Spikey's whimsical if short-lived ITV sitcom that also found a role for Johnny Vegas. More immediately, Kay and Spikey wrote an episode for Granada's obsession-themed series *Mad For It*, entitled 'Mad For The A6', a largely improvised mock-American road trip in which they drove a Volkswagen Dormobile from Buxton to Windermere. Kay's growing stature with Granada bosses also led to a well-received acting role as a shortsighted and hungry getaway driver in 'Two Minutes', Johanne McAndrew's contribution to the writers showcase strand, *New Voices*.

By this time, Kay had taken his stage routine to the small screen too, most notably in Lee Mack's series *Gas*, followed by just about every other stand-up show going - including ITV's *Last Laugh Show*, *Live At Jongleurs* and the BBC's imaginatively-titled *The Stand-Up Show*. In 1997, he also entered another contest *So You Think You're Funny?* at Edinburgh, an event sponsored by Channel 4 and hosted by Julian Clary, which Kay won by a landslide. A now unstoppable force, he collected the BBC's New Comedy Award while he was at it. And before he had so much as stepped foot on the Royal Mile, he had also filmed his first extended television interview as part of the late-night ITV comedy programme, *Funny Business*. In it, Kay chats amiably to host Iain Coyle in a back street behind his mother's terraced house and his own less-than-palatial bedroom. It was now that Britain first became aware of Kay's dazzling and encyclopedic obsession with modern popular culture, highlighted by his collecting and cataloguing of often obscure TV shows and adverts on video. This aspect of his personality was also expressed via the segment 'Peter Kay's World of Entertainment' in the third series of BBC2's *The Sunday Show*, based at its Oxford Road studios in Manchester. Here, the self-styled 'bastard son of Alf Roberts' reminisced about old kids TV shows and span long-forgotten records. 1997 was also when Kay made a first appearance on

Coronation Street, albeit in the briefest of bit-parts as Fred Elliott's shop-fitter. Less than a decade later, in 2004, a now famous Kay would make a triumphant return to Weatherfield as Eric Gartside, would-be suitor of Rovers Return landlady Shelley Unwin (his long-time pal Sally Lindsay).

In 1998, the year in which Kay was nominated for a Perrier for a hugely-successful three-week run at the Edinburgh Festival (the judges, in a fit of tall poppy syndrome, opting for Tommy Tiernan instead), his TV activities gather paced. Although talk of a BBC sitcom called *Seaside Stories*, in which holidaying pensioners would be followed around such exotic northern resorts as Morecambe and Southport, came to nothing, he did make a half-hour special *Let's Get Quizzical*, a humourous look at the history of quiz shows as part of a themed evening's viewing. More pertinently, there was that *Comedy Lab* contribution, 'The Services', the masterful *Airport*-style reality television pastiche that launched the series, with northern street magician Paul Zenon's *Turning Tricks* going second and Dom Joly's *Trigger Happy TV* pilot number three.

The script for 'The Services' was written when Kay was in Edinburgh by night and filling in for regular presenter Johnny Vaughan on Channel 4's *The Big Breakfast* by morning. Although uncredited, Dave Spikey was peripherally involved; it was he who dreamed up Pearl, the service station manageress who, foreshadowing David Brent, has ambitions to be on the front of the *Radio Times*. A third contributor was Liverpudlian stand-up Neil Anthony (later to be known as Neil Fitzmaurice), whom Kay had beaten to the BBC's New Comedy Award and subsequently casted in 'Mad For The A6'. A former colleague of Kay's from his Salford student days, Sian Foulkes, also had a hand in the project, helping to draft a first rough script. Initially, the *Comedy Lab* producers had expected Kay just to do a straightforward stand-up act but, when he declined that invitation, it soon became obvious that they had been right to back his judgement.

Other than supporting roles from Foulkes, Fitzmaurice and two old schoolmates (Patrick McGuinness and Kay's *Wizard Of Oz* lion costume), plus a handful of real-life extras, Peter Kay played all the parts himself. Along with Pearl, there was the mullet-haired deejay Paul LeRoy ('Chorley FM - coming in your ears'), disgraced Scottish right-wing motor recovery man Alan McLarty (last seen singing Queen's 'We Will Rock You' on the hard shoulder of the M61 with his trousers round his ankles), the ponytailed Cowboy-obsessed coach driver Johnny Utah ('watch me trigger finger') and Irish drama student Matthew Kelly, a camper version of Kay himself. As a showcase for his versatility, far being mundane, a motorway service station proved to be the ideal location; a treasure trove of activity and character study. So much so that it led to a six-part series, *That Peter Kay Thing*, thus called because that is how most of its viewers would describe it the following day.

It aired in January 2000 and, though still uncredited, Dave Spikey and Neil Anthony were again drafted in as collaborators on six scripts which, like 'The Services', took the form of stand-alone fly-on-the-wall docusoaps in Bolton and the surrounding area, but now linked by recurring characters and narrated by former *Fawlty Towers* actor Andrew Sachs. Furthermore, instead of taking all the parts himself over the course of the series, this time Kay was content to play a mere fifteen, thereby allowing for the creation of his own mini northern rep company.

The six shows in question were again drawn largely from Kay's own life experiences. 'Eyes Down' (no relation to Paul O'Grady's 2003 sitcom of the same name) was based upon his exploits working in a bingo hall. 'The Arena' was set in the Manchester Nynex (or the MEN Arena as it is now known), where Kay had been a part-time employee as recently as 1998. 'Leonard' was about the oldest paper boy in Bolton, a tragicomic character based on a harmless real-life eccentric whom Kay had befriended while working at a petrol station in the early 'nineties. 'The Ice Cream Man Cometh' related the fading glories of an ice-cream-man-cum-imaginatively-titled-pornographic-video-pirate and the last in the run, 'Lonely At The Top', was the 'follow-up' story of Mark Park and Cheryl Avenue ('together - we become Park Avenue'), 'Talenttrek' winners in the opening episode, 'In The Club'. So good was that first half-hour, it would spawn one of the finest situation comedies ever made.

Since his childhood, Kay had made a habit of taping conversations - whether at the family dinner table or out in the streets of Bolton - so an ear for the nuances of working class dialogue was attuned to perfection. And as Dave Morris had also discovered nearly half a century before, in a down-at-heel northern Variety club, not only was there a ready supply of naturally amusing staff and customers, there was the intrinsic comic appeal of the turns themselves, desperate in more ways than one. It was a world that 'In

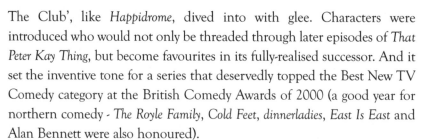
The Club', like *Happidrome*, dived into with glee. Characters were introduced who would not only be threaded through later episodes of *That Peter Kay Thing*, but become favourites in its fully-realised successor. And it set the inventive tone for a series that deservedly topped the Best New TV Comedy category at the British Comedy Awards of 2000 (a good year for northern comedy - *The Royle Family*, *Cold Feet*, *dinnerladies*, *East Is East* and Alan Bennett were also honoured).

Of all his memorable creations, few would deny that wheelchaired Brian Potter - owner of the club in question and variously referred to as 'Ironside', 'Davros' or 'Dr. Strangelove' - is Kay's best by a considerable distance. As stingy and manipulative as Rigsby and Arkwright, but with an added twist of cunning, he is a comedy monster to rival any. Having been crippled by a floating fruit machine when his original club, the Aquarius, was destroyed in a flood, here he has rebuilt it as the Neptune. And when that club too is destroyed in equally mysterious circumstances, burned down by faulty fairy lights at the end of what would turn out to be a pilot outing, the palace of delights is once more rebuilt and renamed the Phoenix. Thus did two subsequent series of beautifully observed and wickedly sharp sitcom become known as *Peter Kay's Phoenix Nights*.

Over the course of the pilot and twelve episodes of *Phoenix Nights* which followed in 2001 and 2002, Brian Potter was responsible for some of the wittiest put-downs ever heard on British television, while his philosophical asides - 'the higher a monkey climbs, the more you can see its arse' - were of a profundity matched only by President Josiah 'Jed' Bartlet in *The West Wing*, albeit with a less Biblical edge. However, as with all the great sitcom icons, Potter's appeal was far from skin deep. He was also possessed of a certain melancholy, hinting at a private well of pain never openly expressed (although his response to a student requesting a refund came close: 'I want to moonwalk, son, but life's a shithouse'). On top of that, the very fact that Potter was confined to a wheelchair was a further rebuttal to those who would see Kay's comedy as a risk-free zone. Amongst the sublime detail of *Das Boot* slot machines, tacky theme nights copied from the telly (*Robot Wars*, *Stars In Their Eyes* and the 'Talenttrek' among them), vandalised car parks and razor wire, in *Phoenix Nights* we laughed at the grim and inescapable cruelty of human existence.

Yet in attaining such heights, despite its title, *Peter Kay's Phoenix*

Nights wasn't just about Brian Potter or, indeed, Peter Kay. In this latest incarnation Dave Spikey and Neil Fitzmaurice were finally credited as co-writers. Upon auditioning for and winning the role of resident MC Jerry Dignan (aka Jerry 'The Saint' St. Clair), Spikey had already appeared as Potter's perma-tanned frontman in 'In The Club', while Fitzmaurice was largely responsible for dreaming up the sixth and final *That Peter Kay Thing* episode, 'Tough At The Top'. In *Phoenix Nights*, Fitzmaurice took on some acting duties of his own as the mobile deejay and electrical whizz Ray Von who, it is initially suspected, has literally gotten away with the murder of his girlfriend. Along with his pivotal turn as Potter, Kay this time limited himself to one other major part - that of the hard on the outside, soft on the inside doorman Maxwell 'Max' Bygraves - although, in one particularly amusing first series episode, he also reprised an earlier role as the controversial (to one person at least), fire safety officer and dog lover Keith Lard - first seen pestering Kay's bingo caller, Tom 'let's tickle those balls' Dale, in 'Eyes Down'. Alas, after complaints from a genuine Bolton fire safety inspector named Keith Laird, any chance of a return for that character was scuppered, while Channel 4 continues to apologise for any offence caused whenever that episode is repeated to this day.

Of the rest of its cast, along with walk-ons for real life celebrities like Jim Bowen, Stuart Maconie and Roy Walker, *Phoenix Nights* would give a springboard to a whole raft of northern-born stand-ups. Among them, Kay's school pal Patrick McGuinness played Max's sex-obsessed partner on the door, Paddy. The 2002 Perrier Award winner Daniel Kitson (who also appeared as St John's Ambulanceman Duncan Beech in *That Peter Kay Thing*) played the geeky deejay and barman Spencer (for which latter job his qualifications are having watched the Tom Cruise film *Cocktail* six times). Janice Connolly (aka Barbara Nice in her own act) was the cleaner and barmaid Holy Mary, and Beatrice Kelley (from 'Eyes Down') played her partner-in-grime Marion. While compering a 'War of the Roses'-style comedy contest at the Manchester Comedy Festival, Kay met a Barnsley comedian named Toby Foster and cast him as Les, one half of Jerry St. Clair's backing band Les Alanos. Its other fifty per cent, Alan, was played by Mark Jackson in 'In The Club' and Steve Edge (another *That Peter Kay Thing* regular) in the series proper. Further ongoing characters included 2000's North West Comedian of the Year Justin Moorhouse as dim handyman Young Kenny (who, thanks to a mishap at a family fun day, spends much of the second series with his face painted like a tiger), Archie Kelly as his pathological liar of a father Kenny Sr. (who along with having once slept with Bonnie Langford can, he says, blow up a bouncy castle with his mouth) and Ted Robbins as Potter's crooked nemesis Den Perry, owner of the nearby rival Banana Grove and the man responsible for again burning down the Phoenix at the end of series one.

Selecting highlights from *Phoenix Nights* is like plucking cherries from a cherry tree, but among the best were Jerry and Alan's rendition of 'Come and get your black bin bags' to the tune of Patrice Rushen's 1982 disco hit 'Forget Me Nots' in the Astley Bridge Asda; Potter's rhetorical 'What would Thora Hird do?' while stuck on his stairlift after a power cut; Max and Paddy's unwitting cross-channel smuggling of a couple of Chinese illegal immigrants - christened Ant and Dec by Potter; and those sublime closing routines wherein an array of old-style Variety auditioners are put through their paces to the hilarity of all but the turns themselves. And as a two-fingered salute to the T-shirt and trainers brigade, the penultimate episode of the first series would also take some beating. In an attempt to attract a more youthful student clientele, the Phoenix is re-branded 'The Funny Farm' for an alternative comedy club night, hosted by a stressed-out Jerry St. Clair. Whereupon, a group of middle class southern students arrive who, in a neat reversal of the usual scenario, have their accents ridiculed by Max and Paddy: 'Is this the "fanny" farm?'. Once inside, a procession of alternative comics misjudge the mood of the regular audience completely. 'Is it me,' asks one, 'or do all pensioners stink of piss?' Cue: gales of laughter from the students and a shot of an elderly lady looking bemused and unimpressed. 'You spend a lifetime waiting for Godot, and then three come along at once.' Another woman knits, nonplussed. In a bid to liven things up, compere Jerry proceeds to tell a few gags of his own but, when one of the students' sneers turn into heckling, he struggles. Soon, however, he finds some inner strength and starts to fire back an array of tried and tested put-downs - 'It's amazing! Hundred million sperm and you were the quickest' - until the humiliated heckler physically manhandles him and there comes a *Spartacus*-like moment from the OAPs led by Potter himself: 'Hey, hey, if you push him, son, you push me..'.

Sadly, if newspaper reports are to be believed (and that's a big *if*, admittedly) since the second series of *Phoenix Nights* came to a close, such levels of fellow-feeling between Spikey, Kay and other members of the cast have descended into acrimony, mainly on account of who got most credit for what. A shame given the quality of the series itself and the fact that most of those involved haven't exactly done too badly from the exposure. Daniel Kitson, for example, has carved a reputation as a quality stand-up of huge originality, as has Justin Moorhouse who, along with rising stars like Salford's Jason Manford and Liverpool's John Bishop, continues to keep the north west ahead of the game live comedy-wise. As a team captain on Channel 4's satirical panel game, *8 Out Of 10 Cats*, Dave Spikey offered a terrific counterpoint to Sean Lock. And along with turning up in an episode of *The Office*, Neil Fitzmaurice has more recently been in David Mitchell and Robert Webb's highly-innovative sitcom *Peep Show*.

As for Peter Kay himself, until his reappearance as wannabe singing star Geraldine McQueen in *Peter Kay's Britain's Got the Pop Factor... and Possibly a New Celebrity Jesus Christ Soapstar Superstar Strictly on Ice* (2008), a two-hour reality talent show spoof, he had appeared to settle into a groove of annoying his rivals and making rather a lot of money (doubtless a major reason behind that annoyance) via merchandising opportunities, rather than any sustained presence on television. Apart from developing a hit-and-miss sitcom of their own for the Max and Paddy characters, *Max and Paddy's Road to Nowhere* (2004), and helping to regurgitate 'Amarillo' for *Comic Relief*, it has mainly been a story of best-selling books and dvds, although, despite his aversion to booze, Kay did also feature in a series of very droll adverts for John Smith's bitter.

Live, the British public's hunger for anything with Peter Kay's name on it was further reinforced by his enormous and honestly-named *Mum Wants A Bungalow* national tour (2002), which was eventually watched by an astonishing 380,000 people over 180 dates in eleven months. Blessed by an attendance of 18,000, one show at Kay's former workplace, the MEN Arena, was Britain's biggest stand-up gig ever. The previous two decades' progression towards twenty-first century British Comedy plc is surely complete. Not only was every show a sell-out, the willing punters and their cash were parted by calendars, T-shirts, computer mouse mats,

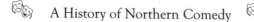

'Garlic bread?' kitchen aprons, 'Wanna brew?' mugs and plenty more besides. The DVD of that MEN gig made more than a few bob too. And such was the impact of its 'Amarillo' theme tune, its saviour even went on to belt out a rendition at Bob Geldof's *Live 8* concert in London's Hyde Park, in July 2005.

The road from George Formby senior to Peter Kay has been far longer than Wigan Pier. But having travelled it, the lad from Bolton may well be seen as squaring a circle of sorts; the return of the archetypal northern working class comic and an old-fashioned one at that. For sure, his appeal has proved to be as universal as that of, say, George Formby junior, Gracie Fields, Al Read and Morecambe and Wise, with the consequent levels of popularity. Upon the re-release of *That Peter Kay Thing* on DVD in 2003, an amazing 145,000 copies were sold in the first week, mainly to fans down south. Kay's DVD, *Live At The Bolton Albert Halls*, boasted sales of 1.3 million, far from all of them in the north. And that's without the astonishing impact of at least two mega-selling autobiographies.

As ought to be obvious by now, far from being just a vein in the body politick, northern comedy has been British comedy's very heart and soul, a fact to which the phenomenal popularity of Peter Kay further testifies. Despite what might be seen as its inward-looking nature and an emphasis on communal bonds - or more likely *because* of those things - its story has, historically, *not* been one of separation and exclusivity but one of pulling together and shared recognition. Traditionally, it has been the 'female' yin to London's masculine 'yang' and driven the British comedy industry absolutely. Along the way, Formby, Fields, Stan Laurel, Will Hay, Hylda Baker, Eric Morecambe, Ernie Wise, Les Dawson, Eric Sykes, Alan Bennett, Michael Palin, Ken Dodd, Barry Cryer, Thora Hird, Victoria Wood and, yes, Peter Kay, have been adopted as national treasures. Programmes like *ITMA*, *Bandwaggon*, *The Likely Lads*, *Vic Reeves Big Night Out* and *The Royle Family* have shifted the mediums of radio and television on their axis. And even among the revolutionary - and not quite so revolutionary - shows that appear not to have been northern at all, a peek beneath the surface will quite often reveal the input of influential Mancunians, Geordies, Scousers and Yorkshire folk there too.

In other words, although the broadcasting green lights continue to be lit by the 'Flash Harrys' down in London, it is down-to-earth, get on with it and smile *northern* comedy that has been the *real* power behind the family throne. Over the past century and a quarter or so, it has held up a subtle - and sometimes not so subtle - mirror to millions of often sad and troubled lives, while reflecting shared hope for better days. It has provided an emotional counterpoint to the wisecracking 'intellectual' dandies of the south. Such is life, northern comedians have seemed to say. We know as well as you do that its tough, so why not roll up those sleeves and try to have fun with it until the struggle is through?

The material circumstances of our existence may have improved; most of us lead warm, dry, well-fed and relatively comfortable existences these days. But we still, it seems, have an urge to belong. And for all that one part of the country is coming increasingly to resemble the rest, the comedy of Peter Kay and others like him - self-evidently 'one of us' - reminds us that, ultimately, we are all in this thing together, whether we like it or not. In the words of Graham Linehan in *That Peter Kay Book*: 'There is something about [Kay] that's touching something more than regional humour; he's touching something that's human...'.

Epilogue

'I am a Scouser, so I am supposed to be arguing that we are unique up here. We are Celtic. We are not English, we are Celtic. We have wit, we have music, we have poetry. But actually, we are no different. We are no better or worse than anyone else in this country. The danger is that if you establish that kind of cliché - we are special - then you do start getting treated in special ways; and not always for the better.'

Those were the words of Liverpudlian playwright Jimmy McGovern, when interviewed by Kay Mellor, in the BBC Radio 4 documentary *On Northern Men*, broadcast in July 2009. And of course, fundamentally speaking, McGovern was entirely correct. For when it comes down to it, people *are* intrinsically the same beasts everywhere. We all share similar psychological, spiritual and emotional responses to life's problems and so much else besides. We have the same fears, needs and dreams, go through the same life cycles and end our journeys in exactly the same way: dead. Hence northern comedy being so catholic in its appeal.

And yet, that can hardly be the full story, can it? For laid upon those basic instincts of ours is that layer of experience which we call culture.

Epilogue

The behaviour of friends, family and work colleagues, *learned* behaviour at that, also helps to shape *our* personalities and responses to the planet on which we live and the area most immediately around us. Socially, we all of us wear masks and we all of us put on a show, tailored to the type of theatre that we are in.

For those of us steeped in the culture of England's north, then, where life has traditionally been so brutal, where the social role of women has been so distinct and the notion of community so integral, it would be remarkable if such things had not influenced the ways in which we view the world and conduct ourselves within it. And over time the ebb and flow of social change must have an impact too, at which point our inheritance may primarily take shape in nostalgia. As human beings, we find it difficult - if not impossible - to let go of the past, ensuring that bygone days play a perhaps disproportionate role in shaping modern-day regional identities; as Jimmy McGovern points out, for better or worse. But there is a further complication. Despite the demolition of rows and rows of terraced housing; the political crushing of untold industrial eco-systems; the breakdown of close-knit family values; the cosmopolitan spreading of wings; the rise of information technology; and the commercial rejuvenation of once grim and sooty cities; at heart could it be that we have not actually changed all that very much at all? The past or the present - which has the strongest pull on our collective personality?

In Johnny Dee's *That Peter Kay Book*, the always quotable Graham Linehan observes that: '...a lot of [Kay's] reference points are not from the usual male references of *Star Wars* and things. His references will be *Dirty Dancing* and, for want of a better word, chick flicks. I think that comes from being close to women and understanding women a bit more. It also tends to take some of the nasty edge off your comedy when you show the female side of yourself. I think that's a real secret to him. If he had come from a household full of boys his humour would have been more edgy and defensive, because he'd be coming from a more combative direction, but he's warm and welcoming and that appeals to a lot more people.'

If nothing else, by now it can hopefully be agreed that northern comedy is about so much more than a handful of overweight blokes, clad in velvet jackets and bow ties, giving their mother-in-law a verbal kicking in the local working men's club. We have surely established, too, the all-

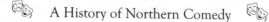

pervasive influence of northerners on the landscape of British comedy in general. And we have shown that, contrary to expectation, the northern and southern comedy mindsets have been two sides to the same coin.

From England's engine room north has come wry self-deprecation, irreverence, an emphasis on character and the escapist combination of surrealism and dark reality. In the shop window south (i.e. London), where standing out from the crowd is so much more socially acceptable, wisecracks, puns, politics and show-offs in fancy gear have been more the thing. In traditional (and quite possibly sexist!) terms, while southern comedy has been the cutting tongue of England's quick-witted father, as he casts a sardonic eye over his newspaper, then the comedy of the north has been the reassuring bosom of its hearth-based slightly batty mother. Darn sarf, comedians *do* comedy. Oop north, comedians *are* comedy.

But what about now, in these early years of the twenty-first century? As the last clanging echoes of the industrial revolution which spawned it recede ever further into history, is there now really such a thing as recognisable northern comedy? And if there is, how will it withstand the social and media revolutions still to come?

Certainly, these days, comedy of a northern bent is as likely to be as cynical and aggressive in tone as comedy elsewhere. Equally, as shown in the Jennifer Saunders sitcom that began in 2006, *Jam And Jerusalem*, a more gentle style of humour (albeit with a harder edge than, say, *Open All Hours*) is as apt to be set in Devon as Doncaster, even if Sue Johnson from *The Royle Family* is the best thing in it and the musical soundtrack is touched by the angelic Barnsley tones of folk singer Kate Rusby. As with all debates regarding a notional north-south divide, only in the minds of regional fundamentalists are matters ever absolute.

Even so, if we are looking for modern-day evidence of the 'old' ways then - leaving aside the obvious influence of Peter Kay, Victoria Wood, Craig Cash and Phil Mealey among others - it is not very hard to find. Indeed, it is right there in the second series of *Extras*, Ricky Gervais and Stephen Merchant's post-modern follow-up to *The Office*, when the BBC 'dumbs down' the fictional sitcom at the heart of the show, supposedly penned by Gervais's character, Andy Millman. The result is 'When The Whistle Blows', already mentioned here in relation to Liza Tarbuck, a clichéd factory-based panto in which even Paul Shane refuses to appear on account of it being 'too broad' (Keith Chegwin is a keen replacement). Millman, in his role-within-a-role as works manager Ray Stokes, adopts a comedy wig, outsized glasses and painful Wigan accent, with which he imparts his weekly catchphrase: 'Are you having a laugh? Is he having a laugh?' to the backing of a deliberately intrusive laugh track. Interestingly enough, away from *Extras*, when those super-smart southern funnymen Gervais and Merchant were joined by an endearingly 'simple' radio sidekick, they found him in Karl Pilkington, a former citizen of the people's republic of Manchester. A little further back in time, the reality spoofs of Gervais and Merchant, *The Office*, and Caroline Aherne and Craig Cash, *The Royle Family*, also bear useful comparison. The former Slough-based production was set fairly and squarely in the world of work, a competitive environment in which just about everybody, ultimately, is out for themselves. The latter was set in a Mancunian front room.

The use of surrealism to highlight the banal, too, remains a feature of certain northern comedians' work. Since its launch on Channel 4 in 2002, the human puppet show known as *Bo' Selecta!* (and its subsequent spin-offs) has split opinion like nothing since *Vic Reeves Big Night Out*. Its guiding light is the Leeds-born self-confessed Vic and Bob fan Leigh Francis, whose best known character is a bizarre Transylvanian 'cel-abrity' stalker-in-a-neck-brace named Avid Merrion. And in this show we see just how far the British comedy sands have shifted. Although, in keeping with established norms, there is nothing overtly political in *Bo' Selecta!* (it is silliness for silliness's sake), the emotional pull that has traditionally been at the heart of much northern comedy is here replaced by out-and-out references to sex, and the filthier and more graphic the better. Though *Bo' Selecta!* will never be everyone's cup of tea, it remains an essentially northern enterprise. For one thing, with the exceptions of Avid, his wife and sister Sacha (Barunka O'Shaughnessy) and a horny bear with the voice of Ronnie Corbett, most of its other outlandish caricatures such as one-time pop star Craig David (complete with stuffed hawk Kes), speak in cod Yorkshire accents whatever their actual nationality.

Another northern surrealist in a more traditional story-telling vein is the Cramlington-born Ross Noble, an heir apparent for a modern age to Bobby Thompson. Unlike Thompson, however, Noble's Geordie accent has reached far and wide, most notably to Australia, where his whimsy and gift for quick-witted improvisation is as readily appreciated as it is in the UK. Like Thompson, however, while Noble's self-conjured world is governed by its own surreal rules and regulations, each of them is fired by the spark of everyday observation.

Meanwhile, on the issue of mobility, although Peter Kay has achieved unimaginable fame and fortune by staying exactly where he is, in his fellow Boltonian Hovis Presley we have the perfect example of a wonderful talent for whom a preference for home meant national anonymity. To a large extent, that sad situation can also be attributed to Presley's death in 2005, when the late great 'Bard of Bolton' suffered a fatal heart attack at the tragically early age of 44. Yet even before then, the signs were there that a poet described as 'pathologically unambitious' in his *Independent* obituary was destined to remain a local dish, although the earlier reaction to Jake Thackray, Mike Harding and perhaps even Pam Ayres offers a tantalising glimpse of just what might have been.

At the start of his career, Presley, real name Richard Henry McFarlane, supported John Shuttleworth on tour, published a collection of his own poetry, *Poetic Off-Licence* (1993), and starred alongside Johnny Vegas, Kay and others in Lee Mack's Channel 4 showcase *Gas*. In time, he went on to make numerous radio appearances, locally and nationally, alongside the likes of Mark Radcliffe and Marc 'Lard' Riley. Yet Presley was a shy and unassuming man who, like Thackray, had an aversion to the glare of the spotlight. This was no better illustrated than in the way he went missing during a sell-out 1997 run on the Edinburgh Fringe. His show, *Wherever I Lay My Hat, That's My Hat*, had been described as a potential Perrier award winner, with *The Guardian* hailing the reluctant superstar a genius. Yet when the police finally located him, shaken but physically unhurt, the man of the moment declared himself unable to continue and the rest of the shows were cancelled.

Henceforth, Hovis Presley stuck to intimate settings where his act, according to *Independent* obituarist Tony Hadoke, mixed poetry and comedy with music and darts. Presley's quietly surreal world was a place where, in celebration of Manchester having attracted the Commonwealth Games, Bobby Charlton's haircut could form the five Olympic rings. A place where couples 'trip the light sarcastic', contortionists 'struggle to make ends meet' and a poem can be entitled *One For Sorrow, Yootha Joyce*.

His poetry could be self-deprecating and poignant, but with a sting in the tail. And all of it delivered in a dry, downbeat style which - in the well-chosen words of Hadoke - were performed with '...all the gusto of the cartoon character Droopy on Mogadon'. Although rooted in the firmest northern comedy traditions, Hovis Presley was a genuine original who continues to be missed, in one part of the country at least.

And sometimes, just sometimes, a southerner heads north. Witness the 'spiritual son of Frankie Howerd', Alan Carr. Born in 1976 and looking not unlike the toothy gorilla, Bingo, from the 'sixties American childrens TV series *The Banana Splits*, although raised in Northampton, Carr found his performing feet on the Mancunian comedy club scene. Disillusioned by an assortment of dead-end jobs in shampoo factories, call centres and the like, and fresh from a disappointing drama and theatre studies course in Middlesex, in 2000 he saw an advert for Manchester's *City Life* awards and decided to give it a go. Thanks to his engaging campness, offbeat looks and fruity voice, giving him the feel of a semi-ironic throwback to more traditional Variety times, Carr was voted Newcomer of the Year. It also helped that he filled his routines with an array of childhood stories, many of them featuring his football manager father, Graham. In 2001, Alan Carr followed up his *City Life* success with the BBC's New Comedy Award. Since when, the heights to which he has risen, primarily as co-host on Channel 4's *Friday Night Project* with West Country comic Justin Lee Collins, might best be described as giddy.

If any contemporary act embodies modern comedy's overlapping geographical and social boundaries, it must be that of Julian Barratt and Noel Fielding, co-founders of *The Mighty Boosh*, a wilfully obscure and surreal gang show. The pair were quite literally born either end of the M1 - former Croydon Art College student Fielding (the unusual looking one with a penchant for glam rock-style clothing) was born in London in 1973, while his urbane, deadpan, mustachioed colleague Barratt (born Julian Barratt Pettifer), is a Reading University-educated 1968 product of Leeds.

Although *The Mighty Boosh* only began life as a television sitcom in 2004, by then the concept, or something very much like it, had long been established on stage and radio. In fact, the duo first began to work together in 1996, when Fielding happened across an early Barratt stand-up gig in High Wycombe. The two swiftly became friends and, as related in a 2006 interview with Dorian Lynskey in *The Guardian*, it wasn't long before Barratt had persuaded Fielding to help him 'write the new *Goodies*.' The upshot was an absurdist cult success which saw the pair nominated for awards at three consecutive Edinburgh Festivals. It was only when *The Mighty Boosh* trod the same path as *The League Of Gentlemen* in making the move to radio in 2001, however, that their bizarre twisted logic, unconventional musical interludes and pop culture *non sequiturs* began to be appreciated by a wider audience, resulting in an avalanche of rabidly popular tours and live shows.

In considering the ways in which British comedy has evolved over the previous century or so, it is fascinating to note how, against all odds, the once unfashionable medium of radio has again come into its own in setting the national comedy agenda. Having worked for *The League Of Gentlemen*, *On The Hour* and, in later years, *Little Britain* and *That Mitchell And Webb Sound*, radio would serve *The Mighty Boosh* well too. After sporadic appearances on Radio 1, a six-episode series, *The Boosh*, aired on BBC London before then being broadcast nationally. What had been a loose collection of ideas on stage was now (ostensibly at least) set in a zoo, introducing a nominal note of structure. Now, Howard Moon (Barratt) and his childlike sidekick Vince Noir (Fielding) who, like Dr. Doolittle, can talk to the animals, were employees at Bob Fossil's Funworld (or Zoo-Niverse as it became known). Moving to television for the first of three series in 2004, Barratt and Fielding's idiosyncratic imagination was brought still further to life, aided by regular support from Rich Fulcher as the brash American Fossil, Noel's real-life brother Michael as laid-back mystical shaman Naboo and, initially, Peter Elliott as Bollo, 'the oldest ape in captivity'. All in all, *The Mighty Boosh* was a kaleidoscope of colour and darkness that was never less than extraordinary, even when it failed to score a direct hit on the funny bone.

And for all that the programme was possessed of a brand of childish slapstick and daft costumes that would have done *Hi-de-Hi* proud, and had lots to say about friendship and community, *Mighty Boosh* humour could also be quite flashily intellectual, in its arcane references to cryogenics or Howard's devotion to jazz, for example. In short, *The Mighty Boosh* is a fully-realised blend of northern and southern comedy traditions, all of it floating in an ocean of magic realism.

Epilogue

Books have seldom been good at predicting the future, but if the days of traditional northern comedy as we have come to know and love it are indeed numbered, then today's rapid escalation of technology must surely play a part in that downfall.

The story now is one of fragmentation, in popular British culture as elsewhere, rendering all predictions useless. Developments in electronic communications are bewildering, especially for those of us who once only had the wireless, or maybe two or three television channels, from which to select our evening's entertainment. Not only has the word 'closedown' long been consigned to history with *Watch With Mother*, *Mr. Pastry* and the Trade Test Transmission, the number of channels to which we can now sit glued 24 hours a day, seven days a week, has risen exponentially. By 2012, when the Government is due to switch off Britain's last analogue transmitter, goodness knows how many television channels will be on offer or, indeed, whether we will still be hooked on the box in the corner at all, given a concurrent rise - particularly among the younger generation - in internet viewing, whether on computers, mobile phones or some other upgraded item of whizz-bang must-haveness still to be invented. As ever, comedy has been and no doubt will continue to be at the forefront of those developments. The resurgence of variety indeed.

Towards the end of 2007, the BBC introduced Great Britain to its next big comedy thing, literally, in the shape of 6ft 5in Liverpool-born comic, Peter Serafinowicz. Having already enjoyed bit parts in shows like *The IT Crowd* (appropriately, the first sitcom to be launched online), *Smack the Pony*, *I'm Alan Partridge* and with co-creator Robert Popper, *Look Around You*, an immaculately observed pastiche of *Tomorrow's World* and science shows like it, *The Peter Serafinowicz Show* was a sketch show of character comedy in the traditional style. Its origins, however, lay in a 2006 working visit to Los Angeles where the comedian and friends made *O! News*, a showreel spoof of the celebrity-obsessed E! Entertainment cable channel. When posted on *YouTube*, it received over 100,000 hits in two days and became a wildfire internet phenomenon. The BBC noticed and made him an offer. Not surprisingly, Peter Serafinowicz continues to maintain a high online presence and a very entertaining one at that.

The viewing habits of yesterday, then, already appear quaint and outdated and there is no reason to expect that the trend will diminish any time soon. And of course where there are greater levels of choice, there is a consequent drop in audience numbers available to individual shows. Already, the days when millions of viewers would settle down together to watch Morecambe And Wise seem far off indeed although, interestingly, it is still those programmes with an old-style Variety feel like *Britain's Got Talent* which continue to supply such communal viewing moments as exist. A rise in niche programming might also lead to greater creativity. Either way, it is impossible to tell, at this distance, whether the concept of particularly northern comedy will be weakened, or even gain strength.

The signs, however, may be instructive. If Peter Kay is anything to go by, the north is still more than capable of churning out performers that the public adore. Warmly witty programmes like *Sunshine*, a 2008 three-part comedy drama written by Craig Cash and Phil Mealey, starring Steve Coogan and with a cameo, even, from Caroline Aherne, continue to find huge audiences too, in a world riven by cynicism and economic turmoil. More recently, Hull-born Derren Litten's *Benidorm*, which boasts a brand of broad saucy northernness to make the eyes of Frank Randle water, has been an even bigger ratings hit for that former sitcom graveyard known as ITV.

In that regard, the time may even be ripening for a comforting northern comedy comeback. In which case, expect to see Steve Delaney in the front line. For if anyone can lead the charge it is he. As Doncaster's favourite theatrical son Count Arthur Strong - a befuddled old trouper intent on turning his life story into a musical (Tourettes-style outbursts and memory lapses notwithstanding), Delaney has created an alter-ego of true genius. One-time Variety star Arthur, all nervous delusions of grandeur and jumbled speech, spends his otherwise less-than-glamourous life inflicting chaos, whether on a bus trip to Bridlington, giving lessons in acting and Egyptology, or surviving a camping expedition with the boy scouts. And usually it his unwitting victims who take the brunt of the blame. 'You'll have someone's eye out with that!' he warns them, before threatening to write a sternly-worded letter. Nor is Count Arthur averse to telling the odd outright lie if it might get him off the hook. And, in trademark Yorkshire fashion, he is also a skinflint for whom the idea of spending brass is as welcome as a female judge over the age of fifty on *Strictly Come Dancing.*

Indeed, the only disappointing thing about Count Arthur Strong is that more folk haven't picked up on his talent. Despite being in existence for well over a decade, he has spent much of his time as a cult figure on the Edinburgh Fringe, performing well-attended nationwide live shows and mainly confined to radio where, in 2009, he deservedly won a Sony GOLD Award for Best Radio Comedy, on account of BBC Radio 4's *Count Arthur Strong's Radio Show!* If there is any justice in the world, more such accolades - and perhaps even a television series - will surely follow.

As the recent flurry of biographical television dramas makes clear, it seems that we will always have a yen for bathing in nostalgia - and the lives of our comedians can tell us much if we approach their stories with an open mind. In the words of one half of the most celebrated sitcom writing double act ever, Ray Galton: 'Without a history, we are just floundering about as human beings. I think there is a newfound appreciation for how people from the past were radical and alternative.' Quite right, too. If this book has proved nothing else, it is hopefully that.

And anyway, however this nation of ours is sliced, the north west in particular shows no wish to relinquish its unofficial moniker as Britain's comedy capital. As recently as 2003, a survey by an organisation known as the Mr. Kipling Comedy Conurbation backed that up. According to research carried out in support of that year's *Comic Relief,* one in 170,000 people in the region go on to become a famous comedian, almost a third above the national average. The top city for taking a humourous view of life was Liverpool, although Manchester did run it close. When asked why it is that Manchester produces so many good comedians on the *Pride Of Manchester* website, Dave Spikey opines thus: 'I think we live in a region that has always had an optimistic outlook on life; where every cloud has a silver lining. Where at the end of a miserable, stressful or sad day a good laugh will make everything a bit brighter. I think this has always been the case and over the years of hardship and war and poverty and deprivation that the region has encountered it's always been there and has ingrained itself within the north west population. We also have the gift of being able to laugh at ourselves...'.

Whatever the reality, the gift to which Spikey refers is indisputably

one which the north in general and the north west in particular has been happy to spread around. Historically, it has been most gratefully received in times of terrible strife and trouble, much of it unimaginable to a modern sensibility. And whenever some young upstart has attempted to chart a new course, the so-called old ways have returned, reinvigorated, as buoyant as before. Northern comedy has given solace to generations, not only in raising a broad smile, but through its more subtle grace note of courage and resilience. A seemingly endless wellspring of funny men and women, stoic in the face of life's trials and tribulations, have lifted a nation just when all was at its most desperate.

No, in whatever direction British popular culture travels from here on in, the contribution from the north will surely be as profound and plentiful as ever. True, no one seems to build ships anymore. Few of us spend bleak and brutally short lives down coal mines or work for eighteen hours a day, six days a week, in dangerous cotton mills. Families no longer send their fathers and sons away to die on the Western Front, or huddle beneath the stairs during air-raids. Seldom do we even eat together at the very same table, never mind sleep in a room shared with as many as twenty filthy and diseased others. No one leaves school expecting to find a job for life or downs tools at the drop of a flat cap. Those days, it appears, are long gone. As are the pros and cons of the values which underpinned them; like community pride and loyalty; an unquestioning respect for religion and other forms authority; and an at times suffocating expectation that we will know our place and scarcely - if ever - wish to step beyond it. In their place, we have the triumph of individuality; greater social awareness; the cackle of irreverence; the get-out clause of irony; relative freedom of expression; and an all-pervasive hunger for change.

Ultimately, though, we can count on one thing. Whatever else the future holds, over the rest of this twenty-first century the British people are certain to have an otherwise pampered material existence blighted by a whole new - and as yet unforeseen - slagheap of problems and emotional woe. For one reason or another, humanity will always need a bit of cheering up. That gormless fellow with the ukulele was right all along. Hee hee - turned out nice again, 'an't it?

Curtain call

Just as this book was going to print, the author received a promotional email from the Sunderland Empire ('The West End of the North East').

It was advertising a touring production of *Grumpy Old Women Live* - 'a brand spanking new show' starring Susie Blake (*Coronation Street*, *The Victoria Wood Show*), Wendi Peters (*Coronation Street*, *Bad Girls*) and 'original Grump' Jenny Eclair (best-selling author of the first *Grumpy Old Women* book and producer of the hit TV series), with each of those fine ladies wearing a kitchen pot or pan on her head.

'Since the Grumpies were last on the road, things have gone to rack and ruin,' it began. And the name of that tour? *Chin Up Britain!* 'More fun than jumping up and down on a trampoline without a bra.'

Bibliography

The factual information contained in this history of northern comedy has been researched, compiled and cross-checked from a wide variety of primary and secondary sources, both in the written and electronic media.

Where quoted directly - in the case of books; newspaper, magazine and internet articles; television and radio documentaries for example - those sources are immediately acknowledged in the text.

However, a number of books and internet websites have been particularly helpful and enjoyable in terms of more general reading and these are listed below. Each is highly recommended to any reader seeking more detail on the personalities and eras in British comedy.

Books

Sudden Glory: Laughter as Subversive History, Barry Sanders (Beacon Press, 1995)

A Hard Act to Follow: A Music Hall Review, Peter Leslie (Paddington Press, 1978)

They Made us Laugh, Geoff J. Mellor (George Kelsall, 1982)

Hooray for Jollywood: The Life of John E. Blakeley and The Mancunian Film Corporation, Philip M. Williams, David L. Williams (History on Your Doorstep, 2001)

The Northern Music Hall, G.J. Mellor (Frank Graham, 1970)

Laurel and Hardy - Clown Princes of Comedy, Bruce Crowther (Columbus, 1987)

Blackpool's Comedy Greats, Book One, by Barry Band (C.B. Band, 1995)

Blackpool's Comedy Greats, Book Two, by Barry Band (C.B. Band, 1999)

Kindly Leave The Stage, Story of Variety 1919-1960, by Roger Wilmot (Methuen, 1989)

Writing Home, by Alan Bennett (Faber and Faber, 1994)

Untold Stories, by Alan Bennett (Faber and Faber, Profile, 2005)

Life of Python, by George Perry (Pavilion, Michael Joseph, 1983)

Live Like A Lord - The James Corrigan Story, Bob Preedy (Yorkshire & Humberside, 2003)

Windrush - The Irresistible Rise of Multiracial Britain, Mike Phillips, Trevor Phillips, Harper Collins, 1998)

Clubmen: The history of the Working Men's Club and Institute Union, George Tremlett, (Secker & Warburg, 1987)

Ha Bloody Ha - Comedians Talking, William Cook (Fourth Estate, 1994)

Dad's Army - A Celebration, Richard Webber (Virgin, 1997)

The Sound of Laughter, The Autobiography of Peter Kay, Peter Kay (Century, 2006)

Inside Little Britain, Matt Lucas, David Walliams, Boyd Hilton (Ebury Press, 2006)

That Peter Kay Book, Johnny Dee (Andre Deutsch, 2006)

Cleese Encounters, Jonathan Margolis (Chapmans, 1992)

Common As Muck!, Roy 'Chubby' Brown (Time Warner, 2006)

Life of Graham: Authorised Biography of Graham Chapman, Bob McCabe (Orion, 2005)

Sunshine On Putty, Ben Thompson (Harper Perennial, 2004)

Diaries 1969-1979, The Python Years, Michael Palin (Weidenfeld and Nicolson, 2006)
Monty Python's Tunisian Holiday, Kim 'Howard' Johnson (Thomas Dunne, 2008)
Eric Morecambe Unseen, Ed. William Cook (Harper Collins, 2005)
Spike & Co., Graham McCann (Hodder and Stoughton, 2006)
Me:Moir, Vol One, Vic Reeves (Virgin, 2006)
If I Don't Write It, Nobody Else Will, Eric Sykes (Fourth Estate, 2005)
Michael Palin: A Biography, Jonathan Margolis (Ted Smart, 1997)
Roy Hudd's Cavalcade of Variety Acts, Roy Hudd with Philip Hindin (Robson, 1997)
Radio Times Guide to TV Comedy, Mark Lewisholm (BBC, 2003 ed)
Mrs Merton's World of Television, Caroline Aherne, Craig Cash, Henry Normal, Dave Gorman (Hodder and Stoughton, 1997)
Pies and Prejudice, Stuart Maconie (Ebury Press, 2007)
Ricky, Ricky Tomlinson (Time Warner, 2003)
The Pythons Autobiography By The Pythons (Orion, 2003)
Leonard Rossiter, Robert Tanitch (Robert Royce, 1985)
Les Dawson: When You're Smiling, Mick Middles (Chameleon, 1999)
It's Behind You! The Story of Panto, Peter Lathan (New Holland, 2004)
Stan and Ollie: The Roots of Comedy, Simon Louvish (Faber and Faber, 2001)
Peter Cook: A Biography, Harry Thompson (Sceptre. 1997)
Attitude: wanna make something of it?, Tony Allen (Gothic Image Publications, 2002)
Morecambe and Wise, Graham McCann (Fourth Estate, 1998)
Reeves and Mortimer, Bruce Dessau (Orion, 1998)
The Biggest Aspidistra in the World, Peter Black (BBC, 1972)

Websites

BBC Comedy Portal (includes archive material & clips). www.bbc.co.uk/comedy
The English Music Hall. www.amaranthdesign.ca/musichall/home.htm
Theatre history online. www.peopleplayuk.org.uk/default.php
Mancunian Films nostalgia. www.itsahotun.com
Musical history. Musicals101.com.
Archive clips galore. www.youtube.com
Music Hall performers. www.rfwilmut.clara.net/musichll
An indispensable source of original Music Hall recordings. www.musichallcds.com
Centre for British Film and Television Studies. www.movinghistory.ac.uk
Everything George Formby. www.georgeformby.co.uk/index.html
History of the BBC. www.bbc.co.uk/heritage
Whirligig TV nostalgia www.whirligig-tv.co.uk/radio/itma.htm
Radio nostalgia www.radioacademy.org
The British Comedy Guide. www.britishcomedy.org.uk
Radio history. www.radiolovers.com
The Definitive Guide to Britain's Film & TV History. www.screenonline.org.uk
The Best of Yorkshire. www.ayup.co.uk
Television magazine. www.offthetelly.co.uk
UK Comedy Guide. www.chortle.co.uk
Internet Movie Database. www.imdb.com